SPEECH DISORDERS

Principles and
Practices of Therapy

SPEECH DISORDERS

Principles and

Practices of Therapy

MILDRED FREBURG BERRY

JON EISENSON

Scottish Rite Institute
for Childhood Aphasia
Palo Alto, California

APPLETON-CENTURY-CROFTS
EDUCATIONAL DIVISION
New York MEREDITH CORPORATION

ACKNOWLEDGMENTS

AMERICAN SPEECH AND HEARING ASSOCIATION for permission to adapt material from "Speech Profiles of the Preschool Child 18-54 Months" by Ruth W. Metraux, published in the *Journal of Speech and Hearing Disorders*, Vol. 15, No. 1 (1950). Used by consent of the Editor of the American Speech and Hearing Association.

HARPER & BROTHERS for a selection from "Walden" from *One Man's Meat* by E. B. White, copyright, 1939, by Harper & Brothers.

ALFRED A. KNOPF, INC. for "Mother to Son," reprinted from *The Dream Keeper* by Langston Hughes, by permission of Alfred A. Knopf, Inc. Copyright 1926, 1932 by Alfred A. Knopf, Inc.

THE MACMILLAN COMPANY for seven diagrams from *Basic Speech* by Jon Eisenson (copyright 1950); for a selection from "The Congo" from *Collected Poems* by Vachel Lindsay (copyright 1923); and for permission to adapt one illustration from *The Cerebral Cortex of Man* by W. Penfield and T. Rasmussen (copyright 1950). All the foregoing selections used by permission of The Macmillan Company.

PRENTICE-HALL, INC. for selection from *Speech Correction, Principles and Methods*, 3rd ed., by Charles Van Riper. Copyright 1954 by Prentice-Hall, Inc., New York. Reprinted by permission of the publisher.

MRS. LEW SARETT for "The Loon" from *Many, Many Moons* by Lew Sarett. Copyright, 1920, by Henry Holt and Co., Inc. Copyright, 1948, by Lew Sarett. Reprinted by permission of Mrs. Lew Sarett.

JOHN WILEY & SONS, INC. for one chart and permission to adapt some tables from "Language Development in Children" by Dorothea A. McCarthy. Reprinted with permission from L. Carmichael, ed., *Manual of Child Psychology*, 1954, John Wiley & Sons, Inc.

PREFACE

Speech disorders is a subject as old as the Hittites, but the systematic study of "cause and cure" is almost as new as Uranium 235. Only within the last two decades has our nation given any serious attention to the problems of the speech-handicapped person or to the loss to the individual and to society when speech fails as an instrument of communication. Now, however, the field is alive with researchers. Our task, in part, has been to evaluate and integrate the results of the work of these scholars who have been busy in library and laboratory. This book, then, is not a revision of our earlier textbook in this field. Too much has happened to permit us merely to "revise" the ideologies and therapies which prevailed even a decade ago. With so much research and so much creative thinking, a new rather than a revised book was in order.

Our purpose in writing this book has been to present comprehensive and systematized knowledge of the chief disorders of speech. It is knowledge which we believe the speech correctionist must possess, whether he is a member of the staff of a hospital or university clinic, public school, or a national organization serving the handicapped. We have devoted several chapters, for example, to speech retardation in children, a subject of particular interest to the public school correctionist, but we also have given very considerable attention to such problems as aphasia and organic voice disorders which are the concern more frequently of hospital and university clinicians.

For whom is the book intended? We have kept in the foreground of our thinking the student beginning his major study in this field. We believe that this book contains the essential material for a fundamental course in speech correction entailing six to eight semester hours of credit. Because of the inclusion of detailed programs of therapy, illustrative materials, historical journals, diagnostic tests, and so forth, classes in clinical methods and practices will find the book a useful text. Footnotes to current research are given throughout the book, thus affording the advanced student a bibliography for supplementary reading. We hope, of course, that doctors, nurses,

v

psychologists, and parents of speech-handicapped children will find it a valuable source-book.

To which "school of thought" does this book belong? To no school. The writers have sedulously avoided any "slant" which would ally them with a specific school. We present with equal emphasis the physiological and psychological bases of speech deviations, keeping in mind that therapy must be centered in the person, not in a symptom. We might have skipped lightly over the scientific bases of speech disorders, for scientific knowledge is not easily popularized. We have chosen not to do so because we do not believe that speech correction can be posited upon a "bag of tricks." It must be posited upon understanding, and scientific knowledge is basic to that understanding. We have tried, however, to present these scientific materials simply but accurately. They have been supplemented by numerous line drawings and illustrations.

We acknowledge gratefully our mentors, both among our colleagues and our students. We wish especially to thank Professors Andrew Weaver and John Irwin at the University of Wisconsin, Professor Atwood Hudson, Mrs. Margaret Dahlgren and Eleanor Stiegler, our faithful "collaborators" at Rockford College. We have borrowed freely, but we hope always with proper acknowledgment, from our colleagues in the field. And, finally to our respective families who have again weathered these rough times: our gratitude!

M. F. B.

J. E.

CONTENTS

SPEECH DISORDERS

Principles and
Practices of Therapy

1

The Nature of Defective Speech

Subjectively, an individual's speech is defective if more attention is paid to how he speaks than to what he says. In other words, if attention, to a significant degree, is distracted from the communication to the individual's communicative effort, then his speech may be considered defective. In our concept of defective speech, emphasis is placed on the listener and his reaction to what he hears and sees while the speaker is engaged in oral communication. The listener must, of course, be able to respond normally to what he hears. To be able to respond normally, it is presumed that the listener's auditory and visual perceptive abilities, experience with the language, intelligence, attitude, and motivation make it possible for him to understand what the speaker is attempting to express or to communicate to him as an intended listener.

From the speaker's point of view, defective speech has an additional subjective aspect. Speech may be considered defective if the speaker is excessively self-conscious or apprehensive about objectively small deviations, or assumed deviations, in his manner of speaking. In a broad sense, any speech deviation, however small, becomes a significant defect if it interferes with the speaker's social adjustment.

Objectively, speech may be considered defective if it is characterized by any of the following to a significant degree:

1. It is not easily audible.
2. It is not readily intelligible.
3. It is vocally unpleasant.
4. It deviates in respect to specific sound (consonant, vowel, or diphthong) production.
5. It is labored in production, or lacks either conventional rhythm or stress, tonal quality, or pitch change.
6. It is linguistically deficient.
7. It is inappropriate to the speaker in terms of age, sex, or physical development.
8. It is visibly unpleasant.

From the outset, it must be appreciated that speech is a developmental process. Listener expectations, therefore, must not exceed developmental norms. (See Chapter 3 for a discussion of the normal development of speech.) Articulatory proficiency, for example, is not reached by many children until they are about seven years old. Language growth begins with the child's evocation of his first word, and continues throughout his life. Little children are entitled to speak like little children without having adults consider them defective.

THE INCIDENCE OF SPEECH DEFECTS

It is difficult to obtain an accurate estimate of speech defects in the population at large. Estimates have generally been confined to the school-age population. A recent estimate of school-age children with speech defects was included in the American Speech and Hearing Association's Committee Report on the Midcentury White House Conference on Children and Youth.[1] According to this report, a minimum of 2,000,000 children, constituting 5 per cent of the school-age population (children between the ages of five and twenty-one years), have serious defects of speech or defects of hearing with which a speech defect is associated. An additional 5 per cent of the school-age population have relatively minor speech defects. These defects, though unimportant for most practical purposes, may nevertheless present significant problems for students who may otherwise wish to consider teaching or some other vocational goal that requires good speech. Also. in some instances these "relatively minor defects" may seriously affect the personal and social adjustments of the children.

TYPES OF SPEECH DEFECTS

Speech defects are frequently divided into four major categories:
1. Defects of articulation or phoneme (sound) production
2. Defects of phonation or voice production (voice disorders)
3. Defects of rhythm (stuttering and cluttering)
4. Language dysfunctions (delayed speech and aphasia)

Another approach to classification, and perhaps a more practical one, is based on categories of speech-defective individuals rather than on types of speech defects. For example, a hard-of-hearing or a cerebral-palsied child may have defects of language delay, articulation, and voice. Most cleft-palate children have defects of articulation as well as voice. Brain-damaged adults frequently suffer impairment of language function as well as of articulation. With this in mind, the following classifications are suggested:

[1] ASHA Committee on the Midcentury White House Conference, "Speech Disorders and Speech Correction," *Journal of Speech and Hearing Disorders*, Vol. 17, No. 2 (1952), pp. 129-137.

1. Defects of articulation. These include distortions, substitutions, or omissions of speech sounds.
2. Defects of voice production. These include significant deviations in quality, loudness, pitch, variety, or duration of vocalization.
3. Defects of rhythm (stuttering and cluttering)
4. Delayed speech development
5. Cleft-palate speech
6. Cerebral-palsy speech, including congenital aphasia
7. Impairment of language function (aphasia)
8. Speech defects associated with defective hearing

The percentages for types of defects among the school-age population break down as follows:

TABLE 1

Estimates of the Incidence of Speech Defects in the School-Age Population, Based on an Assumed Population of 40,000,000 [2]

TYPE OF DEFECT	PERCENTAGE	NUMBER
Functional Articulatory	3.0	1,200,000
Stuttering	.7	280,000
Voice	.2	80,000
Cleft-Palate Speech	.1	40,000
Cerebral-Palsy Speech	.2	80,000
Delayed Speech Development	.3	120,000
Impaired Hearing with Speech Defect	.5	200,000
Total	5.0	2,000,000

Functional articulatory defects, it will be observed, exceed all other categories combined. It is quite likely that among the 2,000,000 children with less serious speech involvements, an even greater proportion have articulatory defects.

SEX DISTRIBUTION OF SPEECH DEFECTS

Our speech-defective population includes a proportionately higher number of males than of females. This seems to be true for all age groups, and for most defects of speech. The ratio of differences is probably greatest among stutterers. For this group, ratios of from 2 to 10 males to 1 female are reported in the literature.[3] These sex differences, which begin to be found in significant amounts in the primary grades, continue through the

[2] This table is a modification of one prepared for the Midcentury White House Conference by the ASHA Committee (op. cit., p. 130).
[3] Hildred Schuell, "Sex Differences in Relation to Stuttering: Part I," *Journal of Speech Disorders*, Vol. 11, No. 4 (1946), pp. 277-298.

college level. Morley,[4] for example, found that at the University of Michigan, the proportion of speech-defective students was consistently higher among the males than among the females during the World War II period. Specifically, the ratios of speech-defective students ranged from 1.6 males to 1 female to as high as 3.4 males to 1 female.

What explanations can be offered for the difference between the sexes in incidence of speech defects? One possible explanation is that, in general, deviations from the norm are found in greater number among males. A second is based on our knowledge of the rate and proficiency of speech development in children. It has long been known that girls begin to speak earlier, to arrive at articulatory proficiency earlier, and to have better language control than do boys for at least the first ten years of their lives. It may well be that the cultural pressure for boys to talk as soon as girls, despite their lack of readiness for it, causes some of them to begin to talk defectively. These defects tend to persist as the boys grow older. This aspect of the cause of speech defect will be considered in some detail later when the problem of stuttering is discussed. If, however, we recognize the differences in the rate development of speech proficiency as normal sex differences, we might then conclude that males have their own norms and so are not deviant but merely different from females in their speaking abilities.

CAUSES OF DEFECTIVE SPEECH

The specific causes of speech defects will be discussed in detail later when each of the categories is considered. At the present time, we need be concerned only with general causes of defective speech.

Organic Causes

Some speech defects, at least at their outset, are clearly organic in origin. That is, a physical anomaly of the speech mechanism is the immediate cause of the defect in speech. For example, some of the articulatory and vocal difficulties of the cleft-palate child can be attributed directly to the type and extent of the cleft. Hearing impairment, if it begins early, can explain the speech difficulties of the hard-of-hearing or deaf child. Cerebral-palsy conditions involving the speech mechanism are directly responsible for some defective speech.

Imitative (Environmental) Causes

Most speech-defective children have apparently normal speech mechanisms. This is especially true of children with articulatory defects. In many instances, imitation of an older sister or brother, a playmate, or a parent or some other adult in the household, may account for the defect. Children

[4] D. E. Morley, "A Ten-Year Survey of Speech Disorders Among University Students," *Journal of Speech and Hearing Disorders,* Vol. 17, No. 1 (1952), pp. 25-31.

learn to speak—to use language, to articulate, and to vocalize—by ear. If what they are exposed to hear is faulty, and *if they have no reason to have a negative attitude toward what they hear,* they will learn to speak with the faults of their environment. This, it should be emphasized, is normal adaptive behavior. When children accept the members of their environment, they are likely to imitate the behavior of the members. Speech, as part of the behavior, will also be imitated. It is not until children grow older, and are exposed to varying influences of more than one environment, that they can perceive and evaluate differences in behavior. These differences may include those of speech. Evaluation may bring with it a desire for modification of speech patterns. For some children, this will mean the correction of established habits of speech.

Psychogenic Causes

When we say that a speech defect has a psychogenic basis, we imply that neither organic nor imitative causes can account for the defect. Moreover, we imply that there is a psychological explanation for the existence of the defect. Recent studies support the clinical impression that many defects of speech in young children can be attributed to not altogether normal psychological influences. They exist as a result of the reactions of the children to their environment and, most frequently, to their parents. In fact, some investigators believe that the primary maladjustment exists in the parents and that, by and large, the children are probably better adjusted than their parents. A typical study is one by Wood.[5] He found that a group of 50 speech-defective children showed better adjustment, on the whole, than their parents. Nevertheless, about half of the children in their reactions to a projective test (the Thematic Apperception Test) revealed dynamisms which suggested frustration, withdrawing tendencies, and a sense of a lack of affection. Other studies, which present evidence along the same lines, will be considered in our discussions of delayed speech and stuttering.

The Individual Approach

When we attempt to determine the cause of a speech defect for a given individual, we must not be hasty in coming to a conclusion. What may exist as a primary cause of a defect for one individual may have little etiological significance for another. For example, some children with relatively minor physical anomalies of the speech mechanism have definite defects. Others, with apparently greater anomalies, may have no speech defects. Some children respond adversely to the arrival of new siblings, and regress in their speech. Others, perhaps no better prepared for the new brother or sister, accept the situation without adverse effect. The speech clinician must be mindful that speech defects exist in persons. Though tendencies for reac-

[5] K. S. Wood, "Parental Maladjustment and Functional Articulatory Defects in Children," *Journal of Speech Disorders,* Vol. 11, No. 4 (1946), pp. 255-275.

tions may be anticipated, individuals vary considerably in the way they respond to comparable influences. For the child who has some need for a behavioral deviation, a minor malocclusion may be sufficient to supply the cause for the deviation. For the child without such need, even major anomalies may become just something else to overcome in the total adjustment process.

2

Correlates of Defective Speech

In this chapter we shall present a picture of the outstanding psychological and physical characteristics of persons with defective speech. In order to do so, we shall examine the results of studies that deal with the intelligence, educational achievement, motor abilities, and personality traits of persons who are defective in speech. It should be borne in mind that in this survey we shall be considering groups rather than isolated individuals. A given individual may present a picture that deviates considerably in any one or more or even in all respects from the characteristics of the group.

INTELLIGENCE AND SPEECH DEFECTS

Although persons with defective speech may be found on any level of intelligence, the incidence of defective speech is greater among the mentally subnormal than among individuals of normal and superior intelligence. Carrell [1] studied a school population of 1174 children. The type and frequency of speech defect and the intelligence of all speech-defective children were determined. The speech-defective children were found to have lower intelligence quotients than those without speech defects. In an earlier study made by Wallin [2] of an entire school system of 89,057 elementary- and high-school pupils, it was found that 26.3 per cent of the pupils in the special schools for the mentally deficient had speech defects, as compared with 2.8 per cent of the pupils in the regular grades. A further significant finding of Wallin's was that about 20 per cent of the cases referred to the school system's psychoeducational clinic because of suspected mental deficiency presented definite speech defects. Another pertinent study is that of Kennedy, [3] which was concerned with the speech of mental defectives rang-

[1] J. A. Carrell, "A Comparative Study of Speech-Defective Children," *Archives of Speech,* Vol. 1 (1936), pp. 179-203.

[2] J. E. W. Wallin, *Clinical and Abnormal Psychology* (Boston, Houghton, 1927), pp. 454-456.

[3] Lou Kennedy, *Studies in the Speech of the Feeble-minded.* Doctoral dissertation, University of Wisconsin, 1930.

ing from idiot to moron levels. Kennedy found that 42.57 per cent of her 249 morons, ranging in IQ from 50 to 69, had speech defects; that 31 of the 32 imbeciles, ranging in IQ from 21 to 47, had speech defects; and that all of the 42 idiots in the study, ranging in IQ from 20 to below test level, had speech defects.

Lewald,[4] in a study concerned with mentally deficient children, found speech defects to be present in 56 per cent of the language-speaking feeble-minded. The percentage for children under ten years old was considerably greater than for those over ten.

The general finding that speech defects occur more frequently among the mentally deficient than among the population as a whole is supported by the findings of more recent studies. Sachs,[5] for example, found that in a population of 210 mentally deficient children between the ages of ten and twenty, 57 per cent had speech defects. Gens [6] reports an even higher percentage among institutionalized mentally defective children. He found that approximately 75 per cent of these children have disorders of speech.

Any conclusions we draw in regard to the inferiority of intelligence of speech-defective persons should not be applied to stutterers. The consensus of evidence indicates that stutterers, as a group, are at least normal in intelligence. McDowell [7] found a mean IQ of 101.9 for 50 New York City elementary-school stutterers. Johnson,[8] in discussing the onset and early development of stuttering, emphasizes that stutterers are not different from other children in regard to intelligence.

The college stutterer, according to findings, seems to be superior in intelligence to the college non-stutterer. Steer [9] in his study found the average IQ of 87 college stutterers to be 116.5. Johnson,[10] in another study, found the IQ's of stutterers to range between 105 and 136. Despite this evidence, we do not think it proper to conclude that all stutterers of college age are superior in intelligence to non-stutterers. Stutterers who attend college are brighter as a group than non-stutterers because the handicap of stuttering

[4] J. Lewald, "Speech Defects as Found in a Group of 500 Mental Defectives," *Proceedings and Addresses of the American Association for the Study of the Feeble-minded,* Vol. 39 (1932), pp. 291-301.

[5] M. H. Sachs, *A Survey and Evaluation of the Existing Interrelationships Between Speech and Mental Deficiencies.* Unpublished M.A. thesis, University of Virginia, 1951.

[6] G. W. Gens, "Speech Retardation in the Normal and Subnormal Child," *The Training School Bulletin,* Vol. 47, No. 2 (1950), pp. 32-36.

[7] E. D. McDowell, *Educational and Emotional Adjustments of Stuttering Children,* Teachers College Contributions to Education No. 314 (New York, Teachers College Bureau of Publications, Columbia University, 1928), p. 9.

[8] W. Johnson, *Speech Handicapped School Children,* rev. ed. (New York, Harper, 1956), p. 245.

[9] M. D. Steer, "The General Intelligence of College Stutterers," *School and Society,* Vol. 44 (1936), pp. 862-864.

[10] W. Johnson, "Influence of Stuttering on the Attitudes and Adaptations of the Stutterer," *Journal of Social Psychology,* Vol. 5, No. 3 (1934), pp. 415-420.

probably causes many stutterers who are not of superior intelligence to drop out of school before they are ready to enter college.

Despite the very high incidence of speech defects among the definitely feeble-minded, low intelligence is probably not a direct cause of defective speech production, though it is undoubtedly directly associated with poor linguistic ability. There are many organic conditions, such as cretinism, mongolism, and brain damage, which are responsible at once for both the lowered intelligence and the deficient speech of the individual. The amount of intelligence needed for the correct production and control of speech sounds is not great. Normal articulatory efficiency, as we learned earlier, is arrived at by most children on or before seven and a half years of age. Lack of intelligence is much more likely to be the direct cause of linguistic inadequacy than of speech defect. There is a possibility, however, that linguistic deficiency may result in the development of inferiority feelings, which may manifest themselves in defective speech. This probably is more true of persons on the dull-normal and borderline intelligence levels than of those on the definitely feeble-minded levels. On the latter levels, physiological rather than psychological concomitants are likely to be the causes of defective speech.

EDUCATIONAL ACHIEVEMENT

Studies based on surveys of school children attending regular schools indicate that, in general, children with defective speech do not make as rapid progress in school as do children with normal speech. The disparity in educational achievement would be considerably greater if the speech-defective population included children in special schools and institutions for the mentally handicapped. Carrell [11] found that speech-defective children were inferior in school achievement to the general school population. Root,[12] in a survey of speech defectives in South Dakota public elementary schools, found that pupils with speech defects were retarded about six months as compared with average pupils with normal speech. The results of a study at Rockford College, conducted during the period from 1943 to 1948, indicate that lower educational achievement is also found on the college level. At Rockford, 68 per cent of the freshman students who were required to register for a speech-improvement course were found to be in the lowest fourth of their class on the entrance placement examination. In addition, they were in the lowest quarter in academic achievement as measured by their first-year grade averages.[13]

[11] *Op. cit.*
[12] H. R. Root, "A Survey of Speech Defectives in the Public Elementary Schools of South Dakota," *Elementary School Journal,* Vol. 26 (March, 1926), pp. 531-541.
[13] Unpublished study, Rockford College, Rockford, Illinois.

It should be noted that the studies we have considered were concerned with the ability of the individual to progress in school, not necessarily with his ability to learn the material taught in school. Though there is undoubtedly a very high positive correlation between capacity and class progress, there is some chance that speech defects, if they are of sufficient severity, may interfere with an individual's ability to express himself, and so prevent his revealing how much he knows. In any event, evidence based on grade progress rather than on standardized achievement tests should be considered as at least one category removed from direct proof. Fortunately, some evidence dealing directly with educational achievement is available. Moss [14] surveyed the senior second-grade pupils in the public schools of Birmingham, Alabama, in order to determine the influence of speech defects on reading achievement. The experimenter administered the Gray Standardized Oral Reading Check Test, Set I, to 36 pairs of children matched for age and intelligence, and differing in regard to the presence or absence of a speech defect. The results of this study indicated that the child with a speech defect took longer to read a given passage orally, and that he made more errors in reading, than did the child with normal speech. Hildreth [15] also found a tendency for speech and reading disabilities to be related, especially when oral reading is involved. Hildreth believes that defects of language and speech such as inaccurate articulation, stuttering, and poor auditory discrimination of speech sounds not only impair the quality of oral reading but also may interfere with the comprehension and interpretation of the written page. Artley,[16] on the basis of a review of the literature on the relationship of speech and reading disabilities, concluded that "speech and reading defects are to a substantial degree associated. Particularly is this true when oral reading is involved."

We should not, of course, expect these general findings to be true for all individual children or adults with speech defects. Certainly we can all point to children with defective speech who are accelerated rather than retarded in their educational achievement. Even so, we might well attend to one of the general findings of The American Speech and Hearing Association Committee on the Midcentury White House Conference to the effect that: "Speech defectives appear to be retarded scholastically, and to fail to take advantage of opportunities for college training, out of proportion to expectations based on intelligence test data." [17]

[14] M. A. Moss, "The Effect of Speech Defects on Second-Grade Reading Achievement," *Quarterly Journal of Speech,* Vol. 24, No. 4 (1938), pp. 642-654.

[15] G. Hildreth, "Speech Defects and Reading Disability," *Elementary School Journal,* Vol. 46, No. 6 (1946), pp. 326-332.

[16] A. S. Artley, "A Study of Certain Factors Presumed to be Associated with Reading and Speech Difficulties," *Journal of Speech and Hearing Disorders,* Vol. 13, No. 4 (1948), pp. 351-360.

[17] ASHA Committee on the Midcentury White House Conference, "Speech Disorders and Speech Correction," *Journal of Speech and Hearing Disorders,* Vol. 17, No. 2 (1952), p. 135.

PHYSICAL DEFECTS

Although most speech-defective children are physically normal, the incidence of physical deficiency and ill health is greater among persons with defective speech than among those with normal speech. In many instances, the physical defect and the speech defect are causally related. Physical anomalies such as cleft lip, cleft palate, severe malocclusion, and other mouth deformities are likely to be associated with defective speech. Pharyngeal and laryngeal deformities frequently are basic to voice disorders. Blindness and hypacuity are responsible for associated voice and speech defects. Endocrine dysfunctions, especially those showing involvements of the pituitary and thyroid glands, and neurological disturbances such as cerebral palsy, frequently present voice and articulatory concomitants. Brain lesions, inflammations, and tumors may directly affect the parts of the nervous mechanism that control the organs of phonation and articulation, and so interfere with normal speech production. Pathological conditions such as chorea and epilepsy, with their general picture of nervous irritability, may be indirectly responsible for defective speech.

An interesting study on the relationship between speech defects and physical anomalies was made by Eustis.[18] He studied a family tree covering four generations. He found that 48 per cent of individuals in the family, in addition to specific speech and reading disabilities, showed one or more of the following conditions: left-handedness, ambidexterity, or body clumsiness. Eustis believes that these conditions suggest a hereditary syndrome, which is characterized by a slow rate of neuromuscular maturation. A similar observation is made by Eames,[19] who believes that many defects of speech and reading are etiologically associated, and that both defects are essentially "neuro-physiological with psychological overtones."

Later in our discussion we shall go into greater detail in considering the relationship between some of these physical anomalies and defects in speech and voice. We do not, however, wish to leave the impression that all speech defects have a physical basis. In many cases, vocal and articulatory defects are present without any observable organic disorder. And in many instances, definite physical anomalies are present in individuals *without* significant effect on their speech.

MOTOR ABILITIES

The consensus of evidence suggests that the motor abilities of the defective in speech are probably below those of the non-speech-defective popula-

[18] R. S. Eustis, "The Primary Origin of the Specific Language Disabilities," *Journal of Pediatrics,* Vol. 31 (1947), pp. 448-455.
[19] T. H. Eames, "The Relationship of Reading and Speech Difficulties," *Journal of Educational Psychology,* Vol. 41, No. 1 (1950), pp. 51-55.

tion. The findings of individual studies are by no means unanimous. A review of several studies will help to bring out areas of agreement and disagreement in regard to the motor development and motor abilities of the defective in speech.

Bilto [20] administered a series of tests measuring large-muscle abilities to a group of 90 speech-defective children ranging in age from nine to eighteen years and a control group of children with normal speech. Elements of rhythm, co-ordination, and strength were necessary for the correct performance of the tests. The speech-defective group was composed of stutterers and those having articulatory defects without any observable organic basis. Bilto found that approximately two-thirds of the speech-defective children were inferior to the children with normal speech in the abilities tested. No one specific type of physical disability characterized the speech defectives.

In Carrell's study,[21] the sound-substitution group who were handicapped by articulatory defects were found to be inferior to the normal-speaking group in physical and psychophysical items. Karlin, Youtz, and Kennedy [22] matched a group of children with distorted speech with a control group of children with normal speech. They found that the speech-defective children were inferior to their matched controls in their ability to perform tasks requiring motor speed. Patton [23] found that articulatory defectives in the elementary grades tended to show less kinesthetic sensibility than matched control non-speech-defective children.

Albright [24] compared a group of 31 college students with good articulation with a group of 36 students with poor articulation in tests of motor and articulatory skills. He found that the students with poor articulation were inferior to the others in motor skills and in three of four tests specifically related to articulatory skills.

The studies just cited tend to support the point of view that poor speech, and especially poor articulation, is associated with reduced quality of motor performance. Several recent studies, however, permit of reservations toward this generally accepted viewpoint. Fairbanks and Bebout [25] compared a group of 30 adult students with functional articulatory defects with an equal number of students free from such defects. Among the functions compared

[20] E. W. Bilto, "A Comparative Study of Certain Physical Abilities of Children with Speech Defects and Children with Normal Speech," *Journal of Speech Disorders,* Vol. 6, No. 4 (1941), pp. 187-203.

[21] *Op. cit.*

[22] I. W. Karlin, A. C. Youtz, and Lou Kennedy, "Distorted Speech in Young Children," *American Journal of Diseases of Children,* Vol. 59 (June, 1940), pp. 1203-1218.

[23] F. E. Patton, "A Comparison of the Kinaesthetic Sensibility of Speech-Defective and Normal-Speaking Children," *Journal of Speech Disorders,* Vol. 7, No. 4 (1942), pp. 305-310.

[24] R. W. Albright, "The Motor Abilities of Speakers with Good and Poor Articulation," *Speech Monographs,* Vol. 15, No. 2 (1948), pp. 164-172.

[25] G. Fairbanks and B. Bebout, "A Study of Minor Organic Deviations in Functional Disorders, of Articulation: 3," *Journal of Speech and Hearing Disorders,* Vol. 15, No. 4 (1950), pp. 348-352.

were maximum amount of tongue force and percentage of error in duplicating a tongue position. They found the differences to be small, inconsistent, and not statistically significant. In a related study with the same students, Fairbanks and Spriestersbach [26] compared the rate of repetitive movements of the organs of articulation. They found that the male members of the group who were superior in regard to over-all articulation were significantly better than the articulatory-defective male group in control of lip movements.

Reid [27] made a study of functional articulatory defects in elementary-school children. She included a series of measurements of developmental sensory and motor factors which might be related to functional articulatory defects. Reid concluded that degree of neuromuscular control and degree of kinesthetic sensitivity are not related to articulatory ability. She observed, however, that "there are minimum levels of maturity . . . that are requisite for articulatory ability." She also found a significant positive correlation between articulatory ability and ability to discriminate between speech sounds.

Mase [28] studied matched groups of 53 fifth- and sixth-grade boys with respect to six factors commonly believed to be causally related with functional defects of articulation. The factors included rate of movement of the articulators and general muscular co-ordination. Mase found no significant differences between his experimental and control groups in regard to these factors.

It is difficult to account for the apparent differences in findings. It may be that varying populations, instruments, and types of measurements employed account for the differences. It may be that the difference lies in our definition of the terms *organic* and *functional* as they apply to articulatory problems. The writer, in reviewing the literature, noted that the higher the incidence of males in the experimental groups, the greater the likelihood that significant differences were to be found. Findings of motor differences among stutterers show considerable variation. They will be considered later in our discussion of stuttering.

[26] G. Fairbanks and D. C. Spriestersbach, "A Study of Minor Organic Deviations in 'Functional' Disorders of Articulation: 1. Rate of Movement of Oral Structures," *Journal of Speech and Hearing Disorders,* Vol. 15 (1950), pp. 60-69.

[27] Gladys Reid, "The Etiology and Nature of Functional Articulatory Defects in Elementary-School Children," *Journal of Speech Disorders,* Vol. 12, No. 2 (1947), pp. 143-150.

[28] D. J. Mase, *Etiology of Articulatory Speech Defects,* Teachers College Contributions to Education No. 921 (New York, Teachers College Bureau of Publications, Columbia University, 1946).

PERSONALITY TRAITS OF SPEECH DEFECTIVES

Speech-Defective Children

In considering the personality traits of speech defectives, we should bear in mind the relationships we have indicated between speech defects and intelligence, physical conditions, and motor abilities. When an individual is defective both in speech and in mentality, or in speech and in physical health, or in speech and in motor ability, it is difficult to determine readily whether the speech handicap or the correlated deficiency, or a combination of both, is responsible for any peculiarity of personality which may be manifest. Properly, in order to determine the influence of speech defects on the personality of an individual, we should deal with persons whose defects are purely and wholly functional in origin, defects which, as far as we can discern, have no organic basis and no organic correlates. Unfortunately, there is little experimental evidence of any sort that touches on the possible influence of speech defects on personality, and the experimental evidence that is available has not always taken cognizance of the possible concomitants we have mentioned. For the most part, mature persons, usually students at college, have been the subjects of experimentation. Such subjects constitute a highly select group, and should not be considered representative of the speech-defective population as a whole. Fortunately, several recent studies deal with the problem of evaluating the personality and behavioral tendencies of the speech-defective child. Some of the investigations were concerned with the personalities of the parents of speech-defective children, and others were concerned with both parents and children.

Perrin [29] used a questionnaire approach designed to determine the social status of a group of speech-defective children as compared with their non-speech-defective classmates. She questioned a group of 445 children in grades one through six in a small midwestern community. The group included 37 children with speech defects. The majority had defective articulation, a few were stutterers, and two had voice problems. Perrin found that 37 speech-defective children included a third more "isolates" as compared with the total number of children. She concluded that "the assumption that many speech-defective children are not readily accepted members of their classroom group is probably correct."

Wood, after studying the behavioral traits of 50 speech-defective children and their parents, concluded that "functional articulatory defects of children are definitely and significantly associated with maladjustment and undesirable traits on the parts of the parents, and that such factors are usually maternally centered." [30]

[29] Elinor H. Perrin, "The Social Position of the Speech-Defective Child," *Journal of Speech and Hearing Disorders*, Vol. 19, No. 2 (1954), pp. 250-252.
[30] K. S. Wood, "Parental Maladjustment and Functional Articulatory Defects in Children," *Journal of Speech Disorders*, Vol. 11, No. 4 (1946), pp. 255-275.

Moncur [31] used a questionnaire approach to compare attitudes of mothers of young stutterers and non-stutterers. He found that the mothers of the stutterers were inclined to hold their children to excessively high standards, and to be overprotective and oversupervising. These tendencies were used as devices for maintaining dominance over their children. Glasner,[32] in an earlier study, found that on the whole, stuttering children had a background significant for overprotection and pampering. Their parents were inclined to be overanxious and excessively perfectionistic.

Later, when specific groups of speech defectives are discussed, other studies will be considered in some detail. For the present, the likely effect of a speech defect on the young, developing personality may be summarized by the following excerpt from the Midcentury White House Conference Report: [33]

Generally speaking, so far as the individual's self evaluation and intimate personal adjustments are concerned, a speech defect tends to be primarily frustrating and demoralizing. . . . Aggression, hostility, and resentment are among our most common reactions to significant frustration, and they are to be found accordingly, among children and adults frustrated in speech.

Speech-Defective Adolescents and Post-adolescents

Templin [34] studied the single trait of aggressiveness, using the revised Moore-Gilliland test as a measuring instrument. A group of 71 students enrolled in the Speech Clinic at Purdue University and 49 students with normal speech were the subjects. The members of the speech-defective group were classified according to their major symptoms into subgroups of rhythmic defectives (stutterers), voice defectives, and articulatory defectives. The results, though not statistically significant because of small differences and too few subjects, tended to show that the normal speakers were more aggressive than the speech defectives. Of the speech defectives, the stutterers were somewhat more aggressive than the voice defectives, who were in turn a bit more aggressive than the students with articulatory defects.

A study by Moore [35] dealt exclusively with individuals who presented voice quality deficiencies. The subjects were a group of 119 students at Colorado State College and Kent State University. On the basis of ratings

[31] J. P. Moncur, "Parental Domination in Stuttering," *Journal of Speech and Hearing Disorders,* Vol. 17, No. 2 (1952), pp. 155-164.

[32] P. J. Glasner, "Personality Characteristics and Emotional Problems in Stutterers under the Age of Five," *Journal of Speech and Hearing Disorders,* Vol. 14, No. 2 (1949), pp. 135-138.

[33] ASHA Committee on the Midcentury White House Conference, *op. cit.*

[34] M. A. Templin, "A Study of Aggressiveness in Normal- and Defective-Speaking College Students," *Journal of Speech Disorders,* Vol. 3, No. 1 (1938), pp. 43-49.

[35] W. E. Moore, "Personality Traits and Voice Quality Deficiencies," *Journal of Speech Disorders,* Vol. 4, No. 1 (1939), pp. 33-36.

on the Bernreuter Personality Inventory, it was found that students with breathy voices were likely to be high in neurotic tendencies and introversion; that those with a whine were probably emotionally unstable and lower in dominance; and that those with harsh and metallic voices were inclined to be dominant and more emotionally stable. Moore's experiment is interesting in that it indicates a possible relationship between types of voice-quality deficiencies and personality traits. We should hesitate, however, to generalize too broadly from the limited data of this study.

In the spring of 1940, Eisenson directed a preliminary study at Brooklyn College that sought answers to the following questions: (1) Do the personality traits of college speech defectives as measured by a standardized personality inventory differ from those of normal college students? (2) Do the personality traits of the speech-defective student attending the college speech clinic differ appreciably from those of the college classroom speech defective? The Bernreuter Personality Inventory, 1935 edition, was used as the measuring instrument. Three groups of students were used. One, the clinic group, was composed of 13 men and 2 women with defects such as stuttering, lisping, and serious voice problems. The second was a group of 17 freshmen students with substandard speech, who presented such defects as vowel distortions, sound substitutions, foreignisms, and minor voice disturbances. The third was a control group of 6 men and 8 women students with normal speech, who were attending an elective speech class. These were mainly speech majors and upperclassmen.

On the basis of the scores for the six traits measured by the Bernreuter Inventory, it was found: (1) The clinic group was slightly more *neurotic* than the class speech-defective group, and both of these were more neurotic than the normal-speech group. (2) There was no difference in degree of *self-sufficiency* between the two defective groups, but both were slightly less self-sufficient than the normal-speech group. (3) The clinic group was more *introverted* than the class speech-defective group, which was in turn appreciably more introverted than the normal-speech group. (4) The clinic group was lower in *dominance* (more submissive) than the class speech-defective group. The normal speakers were more dominant than either the clinic or class speech defectives. (5) The clinic group was less *self-confident* than the class speech-defective group, and the latter group was more self-conscious (less self-confident) than the normal-speech group. (6) There were no appreciable differences in degree of *sociability* among the groups considered.

Now, going back to the original questions which this preliminary study sought to answer, the following conclusions seem to be indicated by the results: (1) The personality traits of college speech defectives are different, slightly and undesirably so, from those of college students with normal speech. (2) The differences in personality traits which appear between mild speech defectives and normal speakers become increased in seriousness when clinic students with more severe speech defects are compared with normal speakers. We might summarize these results with the observation that there is a positive relationship between the seriousness of a speech deficiency and the tendency for the defective individual to possess undesirable personality traits. Though the differences between the groups were not large enough to be statistically significant, the results of this study fall in line generally with those of the other studies mentioned.

There have been a fairly large number of significant studies dealing with the personality traits of stutterers. These will be discussed later when the question of stuttering is considered in some detail.

What conclusions can we draw from the results of the several studies presented? There seems to be a tendency for speech-defective individuals to present a personality picture which includes traits considered to be socially undesirable. Tendencies towards maladjustments seem to increase as the speech defectives grow older. It is possible that in very young children the speech defects are a response to parental personality traits and attitudes. The tendency for speech defectives to have other limitations such as poor motor control, lesser intellectual capacity, and somewhat lower educational achievement makes it difficult to determine the direct relationship between the personality maladjustments and the defective speech. It may be that together, the speech defect *and* the other limitations constitute a constellation which is conducive to maladjustment. We should not, however, overlook the likelihood that many speech-defective children and adults are thoroughly wholesome individuals who come from well-adjusted families. Our studies and our discussions dealt with groups and with tendencies found in groups with defective speech. The differences, where they were found, differed in degree and not in kind from what is generally found in the population at large.

3

The Normal Development of Speech

When does a child begin to speak? Most of us, recalling the first word uttered by baby brother or sister, are likely to fix the time somewhere between twelve and eighteen months of age. But the beginnings of speech go back to a much earlier period. The beginnings of speech go back to the moment of birth and the cry with which the infant hailed his own arrival. From the birth cry to the utterance of the first conventional, adultlike word, the infant progresses through a series of essential developmental stages as he learns to speak. Each child will pass from stage to stage according to a rate in general keeping with his physical and mental development. Ill health may retard the progress, but unless the illness brings with it permanent physical or mental injury directly related to the functioning of the speech mechanism, the retardation is likely to be only temporary. Though we shall have occasion to speak of the "average child" and "his" rate of development, it might be well to remember that "he" is only a convenient fiction, created to make discussion and writing easier.

STAGES IN SPEECH DEVELOPMENT

Reflexive Vocalization

The newborn infant, on his arrival into a world of buzzing confusion, lacks both the experience and physiological maturation to make order out of chaos. In fact, without in the least knowing what it is all about, the infant adds his own voice to the chaos. Yet, in his own way, the infant has begun to speak. Because he is unable to make head or tail out of the environmental stimuli, and because he is not yet able to respond differently to different situations, he cries alike in response to all stimuli, regardless of their particular characteristics. Because the infant does not know that he possesses hands and feet, fingers and toes, and a mechanism peculiarly well adapted for making noise, the entire mass of him participates in his crying. The birth

18

cry, and all the infant's vocalizations during the first two or three weeks of his life, are reflexive, total bodily expressions in response to stimuli within and without him. As such, the expression is innate, and takes place without intent or awareness on the part of the infant. Vocalization itself arises as a result of a column of air reflexively expelled from the lungs passing between vocal folds tense enough to produce sound. Though the infant's early sounds are produced without purpose and lack specific meaning, they constitute a response to a world in regard to which the infant has formulated no intentions and from which he has received no meaning.

At the end of the first two or three weeks, the interested observer should be able to detect differences in the infant's cries. The crying is still an expression reflexive to a situation, but the manner of crying indicates that the world has begun to assume form and shape, that there is a bit more of order and somewhat less of chaos. The infant has matured enough, physically and mentally, to react with greater differentiation to varying stimuli. His vocal responses, though still on a reflexive level, are more directly related to the nature of the stimulating situation than heretofore. The sensation of hunger, for example, which is caused in part by a contraction of the muscles of the stomach walls, is accompanied in the infant by changes in the tonus of many muscles of the body, including those of the speech mechanism. When vocalization occurs, the result is a cry which becomes characteristic of the hunger state. Thus, also, thirst, cold, heat, skin irritation, pain, and external or internal pressures give rise, because of special muscle-pattern sets, to characteristically different cries according to the nature of the stimulating situation. The mother is now able to recognize the vocalizations of her child. The different cries, though they are still produced reflexively and without intent on the part of the infant, may in a sense be considered a crude vocabulary. The cries tell persons in the child's environment not only that he is responding to a situation, but in a rough way, something about the kind of situation. Without being aware of it, the infant is announcing in his reactions to internal stimulation what his physical needs are. Though he is not initially aware of the differences in his new manner of crying, he is a dull child indeed who does not soon know that crying makes a difference.

Babbling

At about six or seven weeks of age the infant begins to show by his reactions that he is aware of the sounds he is making. He indicates definitely that he enjoys producing sounds, and that he produces sounds when he is enjoying himself. The coos and gurgles and general vocal play, which delight the parents as well as the infant, bring the child to a new developmental speech level called babbling. If we listen to an infant's babbling we may note that he is producing a number and variety of sounds that are greater than those contained in any given language or combination of languages. Moreover, the particular racial or linguistic ancestry of the child will in no way determine the sounds he babbles. Linguistically, the Aryan and the non-Aryan, babblers from the Occident and babblers from the Orient, are all related. Babbled sounds are uttered completely at random. By chance some of the sounds may be repeated; most sounds are not repeated. As the child matures, the sounds produced resemble words spoken by older members of the environment. In this respect the babbling stage constitutes a definite advancement in the progression towards the use of a real spoken language.

Although there is no predetermined order of appearance of the various sounds heard in babbling, the likelihood is that the child will produce vowels before consonants. Of the vowels, a variety of [ɑ] repeated at length with variations in pitch and loudness will probably be among the first to be heard. Labial consonants such as [p] and [b] are likely to follow, and then the probable order is gutturals [g], dentals [ð] and [θ], and finally nasals [n]. It may be of some interest to note in passing that though the infant's crying is nasalized, and though displeasure states in general are accompanied by nasalized vocalization, the production of nasal consonants, which is apparently an enjoyable activity, appears in pleasure states.

The babbling stage may be considered a training and preparatory period for later articulate utterance. The infant, unconsciously of course, is practicing articulation; he is learning to produce sounds which he will soon need in the more advanced stages of his speech development.

Lalling

Up through the babbling stages of speech development, the progress of the normally hearing and that of the congenitally deaf child are about the same. After this stage, there is a distinct difference in speech development between the deaf and the hearing. As far as we know, a child does not need to hear in order to babble. Because babbling is essentially reflexive and is largely a response to internal stimulation, the deaf child babbles as well as the hearing child. Beginning with the lalling stage, however, hearing plays an important role. Lalling, which usually begins during the second six months of the child's life, may be defined as the repetition of *heard* sounds or sound combinations. The deaf child may be heard to repeat selected sounds or combinations of sounds, but these are repeated because of the pleasure derived from oral activity and not as the child's response to his environment. The great significance of lalling is that hearing and sound production have become associated. The seemingly endless repetition of "ba-ba" or "ma-ma" or "gub-gub" affords the child, if not all listeners, considerable satisfaction. Successful imitation becomes an incentive for repetition, and repetition for further attempts at imitation. Auditory as well as tactual and kinesthetic impressions are becoming associated with feelings of pleasure and satisfaction. The hearing child, having learned to imitate his own sounds, is readying himself for the imitation of sounds he will hear other persons produce, sounds which are basic to the language he will be expected to speak.

During the lalling period, the child may be observed to be making practical use of his vocalizations. He may cry, and it will be a special kind of cry, to attract attention. Particular kinds of sounds will accompany the motor responses with which he accepts or refuses favors, or makes demands on his environment. In a way limited by his mental and physical maturation, the child is expressing himself, and in doing so he is controlling the activities and expression of those about him. When the child becomes aware of the potency of his vocalizations, he is well on the way toward true speech.

Echolalia

At about nine or ten months of age, the child may be heard imitating sounds which *others* have made, and which are prevalent in his environment. Sounds which the child recognizes, such as those he has himself made during the lalling stage, are likely to be imitated first. Thus fortified, the child is now ready to imitate any and all sounds, though he seems to reserve the right to select those which please or amuse him. In the echolalic stage, which the child has now reached, there is no actual comprehension of the sounds imitated. It is a distinct advance over lalling, however, in that the child reveals a definite acoustic awareness of *other* persons. Furthermore, the repertoire of sounds and sound combinations the child is building up is one confined to the sounds of the language of his environment, a repertoire that he will have to be able to produce at will before speaking, in the adult sense, has been learned.

Some infants demonstrate a remarkable ability to echo sound combinations of extreme intricacy and complexity. The fond parent should not, however, be overhasty in concluding that the infant is showing early signs of genius. Though it is not our intent to deflate proud parents, it may be pointed out that the Mongolian idiot, who is an all-round good mimic, possesses an amazing ability to echo long, tongue-twisting sound combinations without experiencing the slightest intellectual reaction to what he is echoing.

True Speech

Somewhere between twelve and eighteen months of age, the "average child" really begins to talk. Some "real" children may begin to talk somewhat earlier; others seem content to wait awhile longer before they begin. By "talking" we mean that the child *intentionally* uses conventionalized sound patterns (words) and that his observable behavior indicates that he anticipates a response appropriate to the situation and the words he is uttering. Obviously, before the child can truly speak, he must himself be able to understand speech. By "understanding speech" we mean that the child responds with appropriate mental or motor (mostly motor) behavior to the spoken words of other persons. It is highly probable that the child will have considerable verbal understanding before he begins to speak, and that as he matures his verbal understanding will continue to be appreciably in excess of his own verbal utterance.

THE LEARNING PROCESS IN SPEECH

Before we enter upon our discussion of the nature of the child's first words, we will do well to pause for an analysis of the underlying learning process by which the first words are acquired. We have spoken of the feeling of pleasure and satisfaction that evidently accompanies and stimulates the child's sound utterances in the lalling and echolalic stages. This point should be kept in mind as we observe how the child learns to utter and use words in the manner of adults.

In all likelihood, the first conventional word the child speaks is an accidental product. That is, the child produces a sound or combination of sounds without intellectual intention or appreciation of the significance of what he is saying. The sound combination "ma-ma" is a convenient and typical example. We know that "ma-ma," because it is an easy combination of sounds to produce, is likely to be uttered many times in the child's vocal play during the first six or eight months of his life. But relatively few mothers, proud as they are, permit themselves to believe that "ma-ma," at this age, means "mother." When children are about a year old, however, their mothers are ready to believe many things about them. Fortunately, many children are sufficiently mature mentally and physically to make credible their mothers' beliefs. Now, should the child playfully utter the sounds "ma-ma," mother may come a-running and imitate "ma-ma." Mother, we know, has long been a source of great satisfaction and pleasure to the child, and so he may repeat "ma-ma," and mother may imitate the repetition. Something of great importance has just taken place! The child's utterance of the sound combination "ma-ma" has caused something to happen in his child's environment that he finds desirable, and there is a glimmer of realization on the part of the child that producing special kinds of sounds *makes* desirable things happen. Thus, the sounds "ma-ma" become transformed into the word *mama*. Whenever hereafter the child says "mama" in order to call his mother to him, or to indicate that he knows she is present, the child is truly speaking. He is using a conventionalized combination of speech sounds to bring something about, and he is using the sounds with intent and awareness.

Speech-learning, from its very inception, is a process of stimulus and response and strengthening of responses, a process in which associations are formed that are at first unintentional, random, and meaningless, but that later become selective, intentional, and meaningful.

In the early developmental stages, the child is his own greatest source of stimulation. For the most part, as we have pointed out, his responses are of a reflexive nature. Nevertheless, in these early stages, he learns to produce and control sounds which are basic for his later speech. At this point we might represent the learning process graphically thus:

Reflexive sound activity (stimulus)→Hearing (response)→Repetitive sound production→Pleasure of production.

Unless there is some satisfaction or pleasure in sound production, repetition and learning cease. In the later developmental stages, much of the stimulation for sound production is supplied from without. The child imitates and echoes other persons, and so learns to produce sounds which are prevalent in his environment. Now, a graphic representation of the process would go somewhat thus:

External sound stimulus → Imitative response → Satisfaction of imitation → Continued repetition.

When meaningful words are learned the graphic representation becomes:

Imitative repetition→Pleasurable response from environment→Intentional repetition→Continued repetition with glimmer of meaning.

We can further indicate the importance of outside forces in speech-learning by an examination of the illustrations presented by the psychologist Allport (Fig. 3-1).

We note that the chance sound "da" causes an adult person to say "doll," in imitation of the child's "da." The adult also presents the object "doll" while repeating the word. Finally, the child associates the sound "da" both with the object "doll" and with the adult word *doll*. Once this association has been formed and strengthened on repetition, the object "doll" or any other desired object should not be presented to the child unless he produces some articulated approximation of the original word. Unless this rule is observed, the child will lack motivation for the learning of true speech. Children are likely to continue getting what they want in earlier and easier ways, if adults permit it. A child who has no need to talk will not bother to learn how. As soon as a child indicates that he has reached speech maturity, he should be provided with occasion to speak, and should derive through his speech more immediate satisfaction of his wants than would otherwise be the case. Parents should be warned, however, that progress is slow, and that new words can be learned only as the child has new experiences and acquires new ideas.

As we review the process just described, these points become apparent. The first "word" was an accidental product of vocal play. The product was imitated by a member of the child's environment, and the imitation brought about an echolalic repetition on the part of the child. What perhaps is not so apparent is that much else besides mere vocalized utterance has taken place in the learning of the first word. Although the mother's imitation was confined to the child's vocalized articulation, the child's initial utterance was accompanied by considerable overt bodily activity, which was not imitated. For a long time, overt bodily activity will accompany the use of words.

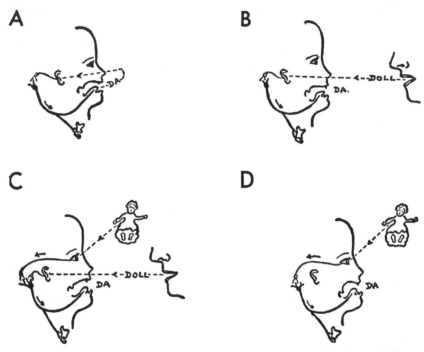

FIGURE 3-1. (From F. H. Allport, *Social Psychology* [Boston, Houghton, 1924], pp. 181-183.)

A. *Stage 1.* — *Random articulation of syllables with fixation of circular responses.* Chance articulation of the syllable *da* causes the baby to hear himself say it. The auditory impulse is conveyed to the brain centers where it discharges into the efferent neurons to muscle groups used in pronouncing the same syllable. An ear-vocal habit for *da* is thus established.

B. *Stage 2.* — *Evoking of the same articulate elements by the speech sounds of others.* An adult speaking the word *doll*, which is closely similar to *da*, causes the auditory excitation again to discharge into the response *da*.

C. and D. *Stage 3.* — *Conditioning of the articulate elements (evoked by others) by objects.* In C the process shown in B is repeated. A doll shown at the same time stimulates the baby's eye, and forms a visual connection with the motor neurons being used in pronouncing the syllable. There is thus established a conditioned response between the sight of the doll and the speaking of *da.* The sight of the doll alone (D) is now sufficient to evoke its name (*da* being as close as the baby can come to the pronunciation of *doll*).

As the child grows older, the amount of motor activity becomes reduced until finally it becomes almost completely suppressed.

After the child has acquired his first few words, there is generally a marked interval before other words are learned. This is a trying period for parents who unwittingly expect the acquisition of verbal utterance to be a speedy and continuous process once it has begun. The child, however, seems to be content to rest on his laurels, perhaps for a long month or two. But the child is actually doing much more than resting. He is spending his time learning the meanings of many new words. The typical mother's complaint, "He seems to know what we're talking about but he doesn't say anything new himself," represents the normal picture. There is, of course, no cause for complaint unless the "no-new-words" period becomes abnormally long.

We are now almost ready to consider briefly the nature and special significance of the child's early true utterances. Before beginning, however, we wish to caution the reader that though we have spoken of different stages of speech development, it should not be thought that the several stages are discrete. Overlapping is the rule between all stages. Echolalia and even babbling continue as speech characteristics long, long after the child has acquired an appreciable vocabulary of real words.

LANGUAGE DEVELOPMENT

The First Words

The first words spoken by the child are either monosyllables or duplicated disyllables such as *ma, mama, pa, papa*. The tendency toward sound duplication may possibly be a carry-over from earlier developmental speech stages. It is characteristic, we recall, of lalling, and continues in echolalia. We have said that the first word spoken is an echoic repetition of another person's imitation. Actually, of course, the first word is more an approximation than a direct echo, because the child is lacking both in articulatory skill to echo exactly, and in acoustic discernment to realize the quality of his own imitation. At most, we have the right to expect a "reasonable facsimile" from the child's first words. Thus, "da" stands for "doll," and "wa" for "water." As the child matures, the approximations should more closely resemble the conventional adult speech product. We must bear in mind, however, that our expectations should be in accord with the child's mental and physical capacities rather than with our own or our neighbors' criteria for correctness. On the other hand, it is quite wrong to accept a rough approximation of a word when the child is patently capable of a better performance.

The first words, even though spoken as isolated words, are really sentences, in that they express complete thoughts. For example, "da" may mean "Give me my doll," or "Take my doll away," or "Look at the doll," or any one of many other possible contexts. The particular meaning is indicated by the setting in which the child speaks and by his gestures, vocal expression, and inflection.

Because more can be expressed by nouns than by any other parts of speech, and because the child hears more nouns than he does other parts of speech, his first words are likely to be nouns. These noun word-sentences are usually spoken with wish-fulfilling import. The small child is much more interested in letting persons around him know how he feels or what he wishes of them, or of objects near him or them, than in indicating merely that he has mastered a name for a person or an object. The several sentences presented in the preceding paragraph for the word "da" (*doll*) are of this nature. It might also be pointed out that not only does the small child use isolated words as sentences, but what he understands of adult sentences is determined by his ability to recognize an isolated word he knows. If the sentence is so constructed that a known word stands out boldly and clearly in relation to the other words, comprehension is likely to take place. If, however, the word is lost because of the total word context, comprehension may not occur. Initial or final position within a sentence or emphatic position within a phrase makes for ready recognition and comprehension. A medial position, or the appearance of the known isolated word late in a long sentence, interferes with recognition. An eleven-months-old child had learned to respond to the word *ear* by placing her hand to her ear. She was also able to perform appropriately when she heard the sentence "Baby puts her hand to her *ear*." The child, however, completely ignored a typically poorly-trained aunt who said, "I'll bet the baby can't put her hand to her ear when I ask her." Even if the baby could, she didn't. The known word *ear* was so obscured in the lengthy sentence that the child was unable to pick it out and to react to it. If a small child does not perform verbally for company, it is usually because the company does not call forth a proper verbal performance. Skill in questioning needs to be developed by the person stimulating a small child to speak, as well as by the teacher of older children.

Vocabulary Growth and Development

Following the first few noun-words, verbs are next likely to appear in a child's vocabulary, followed then by adjectives and adverbs. Pronouns are acquired rather late in the child's language development. Articles, prepositions, and conjunctions make their appearance last, and are often omitted in speech after they have been learned. This is so because they constitute comparatively less essential parts of speech, parts that adults find it economical to omit when paying for written speech by the word, as in sending a telegram or a cable. Interjections, from the very beginning, form a large part of the vocabulary of younger children. As the child grows older, his vocabulary contains a decreasing proportion of nouns and interjections accompanied by an increasing proportion of adjectives, adverbs, pronouns, conjunctions, and prepositions. An examination of Table 2 will help to keep the matter of parts of speech in mind.

TABLE 2

Mean Per Cent of Each Part of Speech by Age and Sex,
Based on Total Number of Words Used [1]

AGE IN MONTHS	SEX	NOUNS	VERBS	ADJEC.	ADV.	PRO-NOUNS	CON-JUNC.	PREP.	INTERJ.	MISC.
18	B	43.6	16.7	5.1	5.1	12.8	.0	.0	16.7	.0
	G	51.5	13.1	10.7	8.5	9.8	.6	.0	5.5	.3
	All	50.0	13.9	9.6	7.9	10.3	.5	.0	7.6	.3
24	B	49.3	15.3	5.8	3.7	15.0	.0	2.0	3.4	5.4
	G	35.5	22.6	11.6	8.0	14.5	.7	4.1	2.2	.8
	All	38.6	21.0	10.3	7.1	14.6	.5	3.6	2.4	1.8
30	B	25.4	24.9	14.4	6.3	21.0	.5	4.3	1.5	1.8
	G	26.0	22.3	14.3	6.9	17.6	2.5	4.9	3.8	1.7
	All	25.8	23.4	14.3	6.7	19.0	1.7	4.6	2.8	1.8
36	B	23.6	23.5	15.4	7.8	21.3	1.1	5.4	1.5	.6
	G	23.2	22.5	16.7	6.3	17.3	3.7	8.4	1.5	.5
	All	23.4	23.0	16.1	7.0	19.2	2.4	6.9	1.5	.5
42	B	18.5	25.3	15.1	8.4	19.7	3.0	6.7	2.4	1.0
	G	18.5	27.0	16.6	7.0	21.8	1.3	5.8	1.6	.5
	All	18.5	26.0	15.7	7.8	20.3	2.3	6.3	2.0	.8
48	B	19.7	26.8	13.7	6.7	20.5	3.3	7.3	.9	1.0
	G	20.4	25.3	15.4	5.2	22.5	3.8	6.2	.6	.6
	All	20.1	26.0	14.6	5.9	21.6	3.6	6.7	.8	.8
54	B	19.4	25.0	14.4	7.7	21.1	4.0	6.7	.9	.9
	G	19.3	25.3	16.1	6.3	19.9	3.5	7.6	1.4	.6
	All	19.3	25.1	15.2	7.0	20.5	3.8	7.1	1.2	.8

In regard to vocabulary size, it might be well to make it clear that we have in mind the *oral* vocabulary, the number of words used in conversation. There are other kinds of vocabulary which differ in function and size from that used orally. For example, our *auditory* vocabulary consists of the words we understand in the oral speech of other persons and our *reading* vocabulary is the number of written words we understand. There are certain words we understand in the speech of others, but which we do not ourselves use, and there are many more words we seldom hear spoken, but which we understand when we meet them in contextual written material. Sometimes we find ourselves surprised to learn that a word of our *reading* vocabulary, with unusual spelling, and a word of our *hearing* or even *speaking* vocabulary are one and the same.

At the age of one, our mythical average child has an oral vocabulary of two or three words; by the age of two, his number of words is close to 300, and by the age of three it is almost 900. Vocabulary continues to grow

[1] From Dorothea A. McCarthy, *Language Development of the Pre-School Child*, p. 114, by permission of the publisher, The University of Minnesota Press, Minneapolis, Minnesota, 1930.

very rapidly until the age of six, and somewhat less rapidly after this age. Less is known about the vocabulary of older children than of younger children because of the increased difficulty in making well-controlled studies of speaking (oral) vocabularies. For the most part, studies have been concerned with measuring the number of *words comprehended,* which is always far in excess of the number of words actually spoken by an individual.

NON-LINGUISTIC DEVELOPMENTAL PROFILE OF THE EIGHTEEN-MONTH-OLD CHILD

Because many children have begun to use words—to speak—by eighteen months, it should be of interest to study the non-linguistic patterns of behavior which are displayed at that age.[2]

Motor Development

The eighteen-month-old child reveals a strong motor drive which includes both repetitive movement and variation of movement. He walks on a broad base, with his feet wide apart. He likes to close an open door, flush the toilet, and hand over objects with which he plays. He can build a two-block tower, and usually a three- or four-block tower. In playing with blocks he demonstrates that he can release them as well as hold them.

Release activity and developed finger dexterity enable the child to hold a tiny pellet between thumb and finger and to drop the pellet into a bottle. He can throw a ball in a crude, casting fashion and can fit a round block into a round hole.

In painting or in drawing, the eighteen-month-old child uses his arm as a whole to make arc-like lines on a paper. He usually makes a few strokes to a page, and is likely to shift his brush or crayon from one hand to the other.

Social Behavior

The eighteen-month-old child shows definite awareness of relationships between possessions and their owners—including himself. He may be able to take a hat, pocketbook, or pipe to the proper owner. He is likely to have formed an attachment to a favorite toy or object and may be unable to fall asleep without a specific toy or blanket.

He knows where things are kept in the house and goes to the appropriate places to procure them. If the desired objects are out of reach, he may use gestures or words to enlist help in obtaining them. He is likely to be able

[2] The highlights of behavior are based on the findings of Dr. Arnold Gesell and his associates at the Yale University Clinic of Child Development. The findings are discussed in detail in the books by A. Gesell and F. L. Ilg, *Infant and Child in the Culture of Today* (New York, Harper, 1943), and A. Gesell and H. Thompson, *Infant Behavior: Its Genesis and Growth* (New York, McGraw, 1934). See Appendix 2, Composite Table of Developmental Characters.

to mimic household activities such as sweeping or dusting, and may be able to turn on the radio.

The child begins to be able to handle books, and turns pages a few at a time in a rough, crude manner. While turning pages, he usually pauses to attend to pictures of familiar objects.

Adaptive Behavior

When being dressed, the eighteen-month-old child may show awareness of a sequence of actions and "co-operate" in the process. He may try to put on his own shoes, but usually has more success in removing them than in putting them on. He responds to definite words and gestures, as well as to broad visual and auditory cues.

Auditory Responses

The eighteen-month-old child shows awareness of sounds other than those of speech. He may sway his body or hum as he listens to music. He recognizes different mechanically produced sounds such as a bell, a whistle, or a ticking clock. He seems to enjoy the noises of his environment, including those of persons, animals, and moving mechanisms.

The child's own voice shows a wide range in pitch, intensity, and tonal quality. In general, the voice is not well controlled and readily reflects changes in feeling and activity. He imitates the sounds of words as well as non-linguistic sounds in his surroundings. Although he may have begun to talk, he still plays with sounds much as he did when he was only nine months old. His repertoire of sounds is more selective than it was before he began to use words. There is considerably more sound repetition and less randomly produced sound.

He responds to the speech of persons around him. He may obey a few simple spoken directions, especially if they are reinforced by appropriate gestures. His most accurate responses will be made to single words or short phrases such as "Ball" or "Get the doll!"

If the child is not yet using words, by eighteen months he should be using gestures to indicate his wants or to reveal his state of being. Such gestures might include calling attention to soiled pants, or pointing to the sink for water.

FACTORS INFLUENCING LANGUAGE DEVELOPMENT IN THE CHILD

Physiological Condition and Motor Ability

The greater the number of the child's experiences and the broader the child's environment, the richer his vocabulary should be. A child in good health, one whose physiological condition permits him to be vigorous, active, and energetic, is likely to have richer and more varied experiences than the child whose general health and physiological condition cause him to live in a limited and circumscribed environment.

In the earlier speech stages the development of a new motor skill seems to interfere temporarily with vocal activity. Shirley [3] observed that infants tended to decrease their vocalization during the period of time a new motor act was being established. For example, the response of reaching for objects develops in most children between the fourteenth and twenty-third weeks. During this period infants vocalize less than between the fifth and thirteenth weeks. After this time, vocalization increases from about the twenty-fifth to the thirty-first week, when it again shows a sharp decrease. The thirty-first week is the median age at which a child may be expected to sit alone. Vocalization decreases while the child is learning to walk; after walking is established, vocalization increases very rapidly and far beyond the amount heard in the pre-walking period. Beyond this point, observations indicate that there is a positive relationship between motor control and skill in speech-sound production. [4]

Intelligence

Because language plays so important a part in most tests of intelligence, the exact relationship between language development and intelligence is not known. There seems, however, no cause to doubt that the more intelligent children have richer vocabularies and in general a control of language which is superior to that of dull and normal children. One way to determine whether this is true would be to compare bright and normal children in a series of non-language as well as language tests of intelligence. This was done by Hildreth, [5] who found that children who scored well on verbal intelligence tests were also superior to average-scoring children in non-language tasks involving drawing and motor skills.

Further evidence of the important relationship between intelligence and language development comes to us through the studies of observers who have noted the ages at which children began to talk and their intelligence as later measured by objective tests. Mead [6] found that mentally deficient children began to talk about a year later than mentally normal children. Boys, whether normal or feeble-minded, learned to talk later than girls of

[3] M. M. Shirley, *The First Two Years,* Vol. 2 (Minneapolis, University of Minnesota Press, 1933), pp. 69-71.

[4] B. L. Wellman, I. M. Case, I. G. Mengert and D. E. Bradbury in their study of "Speech Sounds of Young Children" (*University of Iowa Studies in Child Welfare,* Vol. 5, No. 2 [1931]) found correlations of .67 and .65 between a tracing-path test of motor control and the total number of speech sounds and consonant blends produced correctly by children between the ages of two and six years.

[5] G. Hildreth, "Mental Ability Measured by Verbal and Non-Verbal Tests," *Teachers College Record* (November, 1932), pp. 134-143.

[6] C. D. Mead, "Age of Walking and Talking in Relation to General Intelligence," *Pedagogical Seminary,* Vol. 20 (1913), pp. 460-484.

equal intelligence. Children of superior intelligence, other studies revealed, began to talk earlier than did those who were of average intelligence.[7] It should not be concluded, however, that a child who begins to talk late is necessarily retarded or at best "just normal" in intelligence. It would be much safer to conclude that feeble-minded children as a group begin to talk at a later age than do those who are normal or bright, but that some normal or bright children may begin to talk as late as many dull children.

Irwin,[8] in reviewing some of the literature and the results of his own research on the relationship between intelligence and speech development in the infant and young child, concludes that: "It is apparent then that after the twentieth month the factor of intelligence is a definite, although not an exclusive one in the development of infant speech."

Irwin's own research was based on the type and frequency of vowel and consonant sounds produced during the first two and a half years of the infant's life. It may be generalized, then, that intelligence as a factor in speech development is important for speech-sound control as well as for actual language usage.

Economic Status

In a study by McCarthy, to which we have already referred, it was found that children of parents who were lawyers, doctors, teachers, and so forth were superior in language development to children of parents in the semi-skilled and unskilled labor groups. The possibility presents itself that the difference in language ability can be explained by a difference in intelligence between the two groups. To determine this, statistical comparisons between the groups were made with the mental ages of the children in the higher and lower occupational groups held constant. The results continued to reveal that the children of the higher occupational group were superior in language development to those of the lower group. A likely explanation of this is that children whose parents are in the professional and managerial classes (upper group) are exposed to a better language influence at home and in their general environment and reflect this influence in their vocabularies.

Irwin[9] studied the relationships between age, parental occupational status, and the use by the infant of speech-sound types. He found that during the first eighteen months, there was little difference in sound produc-

[7] C. H. Town, "Language Development in 285 Idiots and Imbeciles," *Psychological Clinic,* Vol. 6, pp. 229-235.

Dorothea A. McCarthy, *The Language Development of the Pre-School Child,* pp. 59, 92, and 121.

[8] O. C. Irwin, "Speech Development in the Young Child: 2. Some Factors Related to the Speech Development of the Infant and Young Child," *Journal of Speech and Hearing Disorders,* Vol. 17, No. 3 (1952), pp. 269-279.

[9] O. C. Irwin, "Infant Speech: The Effect of Family Occupational Status and of Age on Sound Frequency," *Journal of Speech and Hearing Disorders,* Vol. 13, No. 4 (1948), pp. 320-323.

tion of infants whose parents were professional, business, or clerical workers as compared with infants reared in homes where the fathers were laboring men. After eighteen months, however, clear-cut differences begin to appear in favor of the children from the professional, business, and clerical group. Irwin attributes the difference to the greater amount of parental stimulation for speech the infants receive in the non-laboring group.

From the studies of Irwin and his associates it becomes apparent that the advantages of living in a home where better speech and more stimulation for speech is present begin to show their favorable effects even before the habit of the use of language becomes established.

Sex

Girls begin talking at an earlier age than do boys, and the extent of the vocabulary of girls is greater than that of boys. McCarthy [10] found other factors which indicate the general superiority of girls over boys in regard to language development. Girls' utterances are comprehensible at an earlier age than are boys', and girls precede boys in the use of short sentences. Although these differences decrease as the children grow older, girls are evidently reluctant to surrender their advantage, even after they enter and while they progress through school. On the average, girls continue to excel boys in linguistic functions; they are superior in rote memory, in word-building, and in sentence-completion tests; they write more lengthy compositions and use longer sentences in them than do boys, and with all that, girls receive higher average school marks in language work.

It is difficult to determine the extent to which these differences in language function are inherently connected with sex or with factors related to differences in the social environment of boys and girls. The earlier physiological development of girls may be a factor explaining, at least in part, their initial linguistic superiority and attainments. On the other hand, the maintenance of their advantage may possibly be accounted for in the play life of girls, a play life in which dolls and talk-in-imitation-of-mother assume very essential roles. Small boys, despite inclinations, very soon learn that it is not "manly" to play with dolls and to imitate mother's way of talking. Their toys make mechanical sounds which are not identifiable as words. And the language usage of boys which is in-imitation-of-father may possibly explain why they use more emotionally intoned words and not altogether classifiable words than do girls.

Some of McCarthy's observations [11] tend to support the present authors'. She believes that the girl can identify more readily with the mother than

---

[10] Dorothea A. McCarthy, *The Language Development of the Pre-School Child.* Also, "Language Development in Children," in L. Carmichael, ed., *Manual of Child Psychology* (New York, Wiley, 1954), pp. 492-630.

[11] Dorothea A. McCarthy, "Some Possible Explanations of Sex Differences in Language Development and Disorders," *Journal of Psychology,* Vol. 35 (1953), pp. 155-160.

can the boy. The mother is at home more and talks more than the father. The girl can more closely approximate the vocal pitches of the mother than the boy can those of the father. "Echo-reaction" is more possible and more satisfactory for the girl who identifies with the mother than it can be for the boy who attempts to identify with the father. Although the girl is also exposed to the father and his voice, McCarthy points out that:

It may be argued that the girls also experience the father's voice about as much as do boys, but they probably feel less need to imitate and to identify with him than do boys, for they are already making good progress in echoing the speech of the mother, and are finding considerable security and satisfaction in so doing.

McCarthy implies that one of the reasons why boys have more speech disturbances as they grow older than do girls is that the attempts of boys to identify with their fathers is apt to be disturbing, confusing, and unsuccessful. She also believes that parental attitudes in general are more favorable for girls than they are for boys. As a group, boys

. . . are the objects of more disciplinary measures, and are usually handled more harshly than are girls. This would seem to indicate that they are more often frustrated by parental treatment, and must therefore experience a greater degree of emotional insecurity, which could lay the ground work for later language disabilities as well as other behavior disorders.

Whatever the reasons may be for difference in linguistic proficiency along sex lines in our culture, we cannot help but recognize that they exist, and begin to become apparent at an early age. Irwin and Chen,[12] for example, found that the variety of speech sounds are practically identical for boys and girls during the first year of life, but that differences in speech-sound control in favor of girls begin to appear during the second year of life when true speech begins to be established. During the period from twenty-four to thirty months a definite tendency appears for girls to exceed boys in regard to variety of sound control.[13]

Home Influences

McCarthy,[14] in reviewing home influences as factors that influence language growth, gives a prominent place to mother-child relationships. The results of studies suggest that the amount of contact the child has with the mother is related to the rate at which language develops. Even the early vocalizations of children are affected by the amount of individual attention and "mothering" received. It has been found, for example, that babies who

[12] O. C. Irwin and H. Chen, "Development of Speech During Infancy: Curve of Phonemic Types," *Journal of Experimental Psychology*, Vol. 36, No. 5 (1946), pp. 431-436.

[13] O. C. Irwin, "Speech Development in the Young Child: 2. Some Factors Related to the Speech Development of the Infant and Young Child," *Journal of Speech and Hearing Disorders*, Vol. 17, No. 3 (1952), pp. 269-279.

[14] Dorothea A. McCarthy, "Home Influences," in National Council of Teachers of English, *Factors That Influence Language Growth* (Chicago, 1953), pp. 8-16.

are brought up in a normal family environment vocalize more and show greater maturation in their vocalization than do children brought up in an institutional environment.[15] In general, children who receive adequate attention from well-adjusted parents are definitely at an advantage over other children in regard to language development. The negative side of the picture with respect to undesirable parental attitudes will be considered in some detail in the discussion of delayed speech in Chapter 5.

Bilingualism

It was once rather widely assumed that the bilingual child, who may be characterized as the child who is subjected to the influence of two or more languages before he has arrived at a fair degree of proficiency in one, was generally inferior in language accomplishment to the monolingual child. Early and even more recent experimental evidence tends to substantiate this point of view. Thus, in a study of the effects of bilingualism on classroom examinations in the third through the eighth grades, scores made by bilingual (Spanish American) children were compared with scores made by monolingual (Anglo-American). The results indicated that the Spanish American children earned lower scores than did the Anglo-American children on both objective- and essay-type tests, with a greater difference between the essay- than the objective-type test.[16]

Is it proper to conclude from the rather typical results of Caldwell and Mowry that bilingualism is a cause of deficiency in every aspect of language? We believe not. In the first place, studies of bilingual children concerned themselves usually with measuring the subject's ability to use the second language, the one spoken outside of the home environment. If a test could be devised to measure proficiency based upon ability to use a combination of two or more languages, what would the results then be? A child with a vocabulary deficient in English words might still be able to express himself in many situations using the terms of another language. Is such a child linguistically handicapped, or is he merely deficient in the use of the English language?

Another important point to be considered is the intelligence of the groups studied in bilingual experiments. We would expect, and we find, that bilingual children score lower on tests of verbal intelligence than do monolingual children.[17] But have we the right to assume that the representatives

---

[15] A. J. Brodbeck and O. C. Irwin, "The Speech Behavior of Infants Without Families," *Child Development,* Vol. 17, No. 3 (1946), pp. 145-156.

[16] F. D. Caldwell and M. D. Mowry, "The Essay Versus the Objective Examination as Measures of the Achievement of Bilingual Children," *Journal of Educational Psychology,* Vol. 24, No. 9 (1933), pp. 695-702.

[17] R. Pintner and R. Keller, "Intelligence Tests of Foreign Children," *Journal of Educational Psychology,* Vol. 13 (1922), pp. 214-222. Also

R. Pintner, "The Influence of Language Background on Intelligence Tests," *Journal of Social Psychology,* Vol. 3 (1932), pp. 235-240.

of various national groups studied are of equal mental capacity? The various groups have migrated from Europe to the United States for different reasons. Some groups have come here because the members were unequal to the keen economic competition in their homeland. It is likely that these members do not represent the best intellectual stock of their country. Of late, migrations have been forced on persons who were economically too successful, and who were probably intellectually superior to the majority of their ejectors. Still other groups were forced to come to the United States because of their liberal or radical political philosophies, or to escape religious persecution. Only if it can be proved that all of these groups are of equal intelligence, and their children (who will be bilingual) comparable in intelligence, will we have an answer to the effect of bilingualism on general language proficiency.

SPEECH ERRORS OF YOUNG CHILDREN

Errors in Sound Production

If we examine the speech of young children with a view towards comparing their accuracy of sound production with that of older children, we become aware of a large number of errors and faults. For example, a two-year-old child who has begun to speak is very likely to lisp. His sibilant sounds may be produced with a lingual protrusion, or perhaps a *t, d,* or *th* sound substituted for them. Guttural sounds are inaccurately produced, with dental substitutions common and frequent. For example, "a good girl" may be produced as "a dood dirl." In the speech of a young child, one sound in context frequently and unduly influences others, causing sound substitutions, distortion, or repetition. A twenty-one-month-old girl, for example, insisted that her naughty doll "kucked her bumb." Here the *k* in "sucked" resulted in a *k* for *s* substitution, and the bilabial *m* in "thumb" changed the *th* of "thumb" to a bilabial *b*.

Transposition of letter sounds within a word is another common characteristic of the speech of small children. The word "ask," for example, is frequently pronounced "aks," and "lets" may readily become "lest." Frequently the elements of two words may be combined and pronounced as one word. Thus "good girl" may become "googirl," and "baby-doll" be changed to "badoll."

Are these rather typical errors in the speech of young children to be considered defects? The answer should depend largely upon the degree of control a child might be expected to have in regard to the various speech sounds. Though the infant produces all the speech sounds of any language in his vocal play, the mastery and voluntary control of sounds is another matter. Some sounds are easy to control; others are more difficult. Some require fine small-muscle co-ordination, others call for more gross-muscle movements. The manner of production of some speech sounds can readily be observed; others are so produced that their articulatory movements are partly or entirely concealed. In general, the fewer and grosser the speech organs involved in sound production, and the more readily discernible the manner of sound production, the earlier should the sounds be mastered and voluntarily controlled by the child.

It is obvious that the typical errors presented above should not properly be considered defects. A speech error becomes a defect when the voluntary sound production of a child falls significantly below our proper expectations. Some idea of what we may expect in regard to accuracy of sound production may be obtained by a consideration of Poole's [18] research. Poole studied the ability of 140 preschool children to articulate 23 consonant sounds in words. According to her data, children who are physically and mentally normal may certainly be expected to reach maturity of articulation by the age of eight. Girls arrive at articulatory efficiency at about six and a half years of age, and boys approximately a year later. In regard to the individual sounds studied, the following table summarizes Poole's data.

AGE OF ARTICULATORY EFFICIENCY OF 23 CONSONANT SOUNDS

Age	Sounds Mastered
By 3½	[b], [p], [m], [w], [h]
4½	[d], [t], [n], [g], [k], [ŋ] (*ng*), [j] (*y*)
5½	[f]
6½	[v], [ð] (*th* in *that*), [ʒ] (*z* in *azure*), [ʃ] (*sh*), [l]
7½	[s], [z], [r], [θ] (*th* in *thin*), [hw] (*wh*)

In another study [19] along this line, 204 preschool children were examined at the Iowa Child Welfare Research Station. Both consonant and vowel sounds were tested. The findings indicate that there is a wide variation in the difficulty of the different sounds, as determined by the percentages of children giving correct responses. The girls tended to be superior to boys on consonant elements; the differences between girls and boys in regard to vowels were too small to permit of definite conclusions. The study also showed a high positive relationship between the ages of the children and their ability to produce speech sounds correctly, and a substantial positive relationship between motor ability and sound production.

In a more recent study Templin [20] found that girls tended to be ac-

[18] Irene Poole, "Genetic Development of Articulation of Consonant Sounds in Speech," *Elementary English Review*, Vol. 2 (1934), pp. 159-161.

[19] B. L. Wellman, I. M. Case, I. G. Mengert, and D. E. Bradbury, "Speech Sounds of Young Children," *University of Iowa Studies in Child Welfare*, Vol. 5, No. 2 (1931).

[20] Mildred C. Templin, "Norms on a Screening Test of Articulation for Ages Three Through Eight," *Journal of Speech and Hearing Disorders*, Vol. 18, No. 4 (1953), pp. 323-331.

celerated in articulation development as compared with boys from about four and a half years on. By age seven, the girls approximate mature articulation, while boys take another year to reach the same degree of proficiency. Templin's findings substantiate the results of the Poole study.

Repetition

The tendency to repeat sounds, syllables, words, or entire phrases or sentences is a normal aspect of speech development for all young children. The severity, as manifested by the amount of tension and number of overt mannerisms which accompany repetitions, and the frequency of repetition vary considerably from child to child and for the individual child from time to time. In the speech profiles which will be presented later, we will be able to note that repetition and blocking are common characteristics of children between the ages of eighteen and fifty-four months. Repetition, of course, begins at birth and is heard in infants' crying. Although the general tendency is for repetition to decrease with age, Davis [21] found that the average child between the ages of twenty-four and sixty-two months repeats forty-five times per thousand words spoken in free play speech. Repetitions, in order of occurrence, were greater for phrases than for words and syllables. Boys tended to repeat syllables more often than girls.

SPEECH PROFILES

Metraux [22] studied the speech of 207 children at seven preschool age levels (18, 24, 30, 36, 42, 48, and 54 months). She observed that "vowel production in the child's speech appears to be more than 90 per cent correct by 30 months and consonant production appears to be 90 per cent or more correct by 54 months." The children, all average or above in intelligence, attended the Guidance Nursery at Yale University.

Metraux was only incidentally interested in specific sounds and age levels at which sounds are produced with approximate adult proficiency. Primarily, she was interested in arriving at a synthesis of "some of the things known about the speech of the child at various ages." Condensations of the Metraux speech profiles are presented below.[23] They should serve as guides to the student, teacher, or parent of the child and are definitely not to be interpreted as norms. It is also important to remember that the children included in the Metraux study were a select group in regard to intelligence, none of them being dull or below average. In view of our knowledge of factors which correlate with speech development, it is likely that somewhat

[21] Dorothy M. Davis, "The Relation of Repetition in the Speech of Young Children to Certain Measures of Language Maturity and Situational Factors," *Journal of Speech Disorders*, Vol. 4, No. 2 (1939), pp. 303-318 and Vol. 5 (1940), pp. 235-241.
[22] Ruth W. Metraux, "Speech Profiles of the Pre-School Child 18-54 Months," *Journal of Speech and Hearing Disorders*, Vol. 15, No. 1 (1950), pp. 37-53.
[23] *Ibid.*

lower percentages of correct sound production would have been found if several below-average children had been included in the Metraux study.

18 Months

The child typically leaves off the beginning and the end of phrases. He makes himself understood through the use of a proper vowel, a medial consonant, and proper vocal inflection. He is uncertain and inconsistent in the production of almost any word.

The child's voice is not well controlled and tends to become high-pitched and strained. "He experiments a great deal with voice and pitch, and there is a variety of vocal overflow with little or no phonetic value, such as a laugh, sigh, or whisper."

The child repeats syllables or words "more frequently than not" in an easy, unconscious manner.

24 Months

The child telescopes phrases in his pronunciations; there is usually a beginning consonant, though not necessarily an appropriate one; a final consonant is often present, while medial consonants tend to be slighted.

The voice shows better pitch control than at 18 months. In general, the pitch is lower. There is still some straining, and squeaking is common.

Repetition of a word or phrase is almost of a compulsive nature. Syllable repetition is also present. The sound "uh" [ʌ] is frequently used before the child finds the correct response to a question.

30 Months

Pronunciations of words continue to show telescoping, with the medial consonant frequently slighted. Specific word pronunciations are unstable, so that the same word may be pronounced with different vowels and consonants within a few minutes. For example, the word *cross* may be pronounced as "kwoss," or "kwaw," or "koss" in succeeding evocations.

The voice continues to show wide variability in pitch, although a firm base is generally established. Under stress, the voice may change quickly from a low-pitched tone to a high, thin, nasalized squeak.

Repetition, especially for phrases, is even more marked than at twenty-four months. The repetitions appear to arise out of an inner compulsive drive.

36 Months

Pronunciation continues to be characterized by a shortening of words and phrases; medial consonants may be omitted or substituted. Final consonants appear more regularly than at 30 months. Substitutions for the sound "th" are frequently made.

The voice is usually well controlled and is in general "of an even, normal loudness." The child begins to use a whispered voice to gain attention.

Repetition is still characteristic, but without the suggestion of compulsion which was present at the two earlier age levels. The repetition is easy, not self-conscious, and only infrequently is a tonic block evidenced.

42 Months

Pronunciation continues to be characterized by omission or substitution of the medial consonant of a word or phrase.

"A high, full-volumed yell seems to be the normal speaking tone." Whispering, though still a strong characteristic, readily gives way to the yell if a response is not immediately made to the child's request.

Repetitions are frequent, and suggest the inner compulsive drive of the 30-month-old child. Blocking on initial syllables suggestive of "developmental stuttering" is prominent. Sometimes the blocks are accompanied by grimacing, cocking of the head, and other overt manifestations of "tension overflow." In general, the repetitions and blocks appear to be related to demands for attention, information, or encouragement. The general rate of speech seems to be more rapid than at earlier levels. This may be related to the child's efforts to keep up with his group.

48 Months

Medial sounds, especially t, d, and th, continue to be omitted. Pronunciations and mispronunciations of specific words, except for those containing th, r, and l, are generally stabilized.

The voice is somewhat subdued compared with that of the 42-month-old child. Many children, especially boys, persist in the use of the loud, raucous voice. Vocal inflections tend to be marked and dramatic.

Repetition is in general sharply reduced. When repetition of a word or a phrase occurs, it is without the characteristic compulsive quality suggested at earlier age levels. Blocking and associated overt mannerisms such as grimacing and head movements continue for some children.

54 Months

Pronunciations are generally stabilized, except for sounds such as th, t, and s with which the child has difficulty. Reversals of the order of sounds within a word, such as lats for last, are occasionally present. Words are sometimes shortened to enable the child to communicate his needs rapidly.

The voice has become well modulated. Girls' voices may become imitative of those of their mothers or of other women with whom they are in frequent contact.

Repetition is seldom present, except for purposes of emphasis. Many children may use "um" or "uh" at the beginning of sentences. Children who have formerly blocked may on occasion continue to do so.

4

The Pathways to Speech

Propositional or meaningful speech may be considered man's supreme achievement. Speech is perhaps the most important means by which man has sought to intervene in his environment to produce the kind of world he wanted; it has been the means by which he has arrived at mutual understanding with his fellow men. And if speech is dependent upon thought, it also must be true that the development and refinement of ideas are dependent upon speech! Certainly in childhood it is talk which, more than any other aspect of behavior, organizes thought into socially vital and acceptable patterns. Through speech and language development, the average child conventionalizes his social behavior and thus becomes, in a sense, a conformist. The contrast is marked in the unconventional and unpredictable behavior of the deafened child whose verbalizations are extremely limited. Equally remarkable is the transformation of the behavior and personality of the cerebral-palsied child as he acquires mastery of speech. Speech structures our thinking and our behavior.

But if speech is man's crowning achievement, it also is his most capricious and mutable acquisition. "I was so frightened, I was dumb; I could not speak." Who has not had this frustrating experience? Indeed one's voice, one's speech, shows daily changes reflecting both the physical and emotional states of the individual. It is a highly unstable mechanism, subject to all the tides of life, to every good and ill wind that blows. Its instability may be explained on a dual basis: (a) the complexity of the neural integration necessary to effect speech, and (b) the anatomical imposition of speech on organs primarily designed for the basic life processes of breathing, chewing, and swallowing.

NEURAL INTEGRATION FOR SPEECH

We speak with the entire body—nerves, muscles, glands, and blood. All must enter into superb integrations, which are in turn correlated with past learning. No human activity, perhaps, requires greater co-ordination than speech. It is a superior nervous system which has made possible the complex synergy and hence must receive the credit—or blame—for our linguistic achievement.

There are no neat charts which we can draw for you to show exactly what happens in the nervous system to produce speech. We might like to reduce speech processes to reflexes or chains of reflexes, but this would present an incomplete and distorted picture. On the other hand, we might wish to limit our description of speech to clearly defined pathways and "centers" in the cerebral cortex. Investigators have not been able to elicit speech by electrical stimulation of cortical "centers" and pathways. They could interrupt speech by electrical stimulation; they could produce phonated sounds and movements of the lips, tongue, and jaws; but the sounds and movements bore little resemblance to speech.[1] Present knowledge may be incomplete, even fragmentary, yet we believe that it is essential for the student to understand present views on the operation of the nervous system in producing speech. If this is the student's introduction to neurological discussion, he will not get lost (we hope!) if he keeps in mind these subheads of the discussion: (1) Basic concepts of neural functions associated with speech; (2) Anatomical units of the central nervous system important in speech; (3) The role of the central nervous system in speech; (4) The role of the peripheral nervous system (cranial and spinal nerves) in speech; (5) The sensory-correlating-motor systems: their contribution to speech; (6) The autonomic system: its contribution to speech; and (7) The summing up: neural integration for speech.

Basic Concepts of Neural Functions Associated with Speech

Before we can examine either the structure or the function of the nervous system as it relates to speech, we must understand certain fundamental concepts pertaining to nervous activity. We need to know about the processes that go on in the nervous system, the characteristics of these processes, and the modifications that take place when various parts of the system work together.

The Character of the Nerve Impulse. First, the nervous system is composed of specialized cellular units called neurons, which are linked together by synaptic junction to form conduction pathways for nerve impulses. When such an impulse sweeps along a nerve fiber, there is a burst of electrical activity called the action potential. These action potentials or waves of the brain may be visualized by the use of the cathode-ray oscillograph; the resulting record is called an electroencephalogram (EEG). The EEG is sometimes used to determine the cause of severe speech handicaps. A comparison of the EEG records of children possessing normal

[1] W. Penfield and T. Rasmussen, *The Cerebral Cortex of Man* (New York, Macmillan, 1950), pp. 106-107.

speech with those of children handicapped by severe dyslalia, for example, has revealed startling differences indicative of brain damage in the latter group.

Second, neurons transmit impulses at different speeds and at different intensities, and possess varying thresholds of response. The neurons making up the hypoglossal nerve innervating the front tongue, for example, have five times the speed of conduction which the nerve to the soft palate has. Moreover, the tongue nerve will respond at one-fourth the threshold of the palatal nerve, which is to say that the palatal nerve requires a stimulus four times as great to "trip it off." Children in the third or fourth grades in school who have not mastered articulation of speech sounds frequently reflect a familial pattern of neuromuscular in-co-ordination. The supposition is that the threshold of excitation of the nerves controlling the speech organs is high and the rate of conduction slow.

Third, neurons are fatigable. After an impulse has been transmitted, the neuron cannot be stimulated again immediately. Although the argument has been advanced that some nerves maintaining postural tone, for example, continue to be stimulated indefinitely, it is more probable that postural tone is maintained by the alternate stimulation of different groups of neurons.

Fourth, neurons often must summate their strength or action potentials if they are to cross the synapse. So one's response to a touch on the shoulder may not be evoked until several neurons carrying the sensation have a combined power sufficient to "jump" the synapse between sensory and motor neurons. Whether the electrical potential at the synapse must be higher than in the nerve fiber, or whether a greater potential is necessary in order to liberate a chemical substance, acetyl-choline, which is highly concentrated at the synapse, is not known.

Fifth, nerve networks exhibit the phenomena of recruitment. In recruitment, repeated stimuli appearing at the moment when a nerve is somewhat excitable may "recruit fibers" and thus produce a response when a single stimulus was unsuccessful. These stimuli may come from widely separated areas, from ears or eyes, to play upon the efferent arc, which conducts the motor impulse outward from the central nervous system. So a touch on the shoulder may not evoke any response unless other sensory end-organs contribute to the stimulus. A loud "Hi!" assaults your ears, a familiar figure appears; the result: you jump and respond with an even louder "Hi!"

The Reflex Arc. (Fig. 4-1) Some of these phenomena pertaining to neural behavior can be demonstrated more clearly if we consider a network of neurons utilized in a single response. A reflex usually is defined as a "relatively fixed pattern of response or behavior which is similar for any given stimulus." [2] It must be remembered, however, that in man these patterns

[2] E. Gardner, *Fundamentals of Neurology* (Philadelphia, Saunders, 1952), p. 107.

are highly differentiated, modifiable, and variable, so that one should not conceive of the nervous system as "a mass of such stereotyped patterns." [3] The simplest type of *unlearned reflex* may be demonstrated by a two-neuron chain which involves a receptor, an afferent limb (which conducts the sensory impulse from the periphery toward the central nervous system), a synapse (a functional connection in the central nervous system), and an

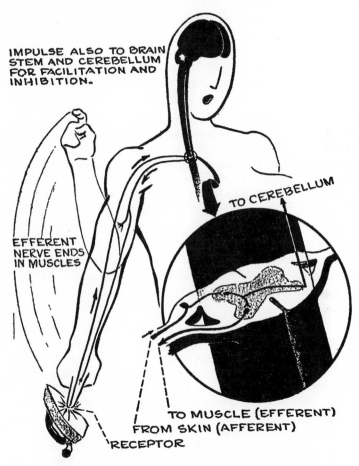

FIGURE 4-1. Diagram of reflex arcs indicating higher controls.

effector organ (a muscle or gland). The *stretch reflex* is such an unlearned two-neuron chain response in which a stretched muscle responds by contracting and thus opposing the stretching force. Anyone who has worked with the cerebral-palsied is familiar with the characteristic exaggerated tone and activity indicative of the fact that the stretch reflex in the cerebral-

[3] *Ibid.*, p. 115.

palsied has been freed from "higher controls." This reflex has been called an unlearned behavior response, yet it is clear that pathways from higher brain centers impinge upon the reflex arc.

These relatively unlearned reflexes can be inhibited, reinforced, or facilitated, demonstrating the same behavior as neurons. The sneeze reflex may be inhibited by pulling or biting the upper lip. The reflex response in such an activity as walking normally inhibits the tensor reflex in the knees. The disturbance of this phenomenon of reciprocal inhibition is apparent in all who suffer from stage fright in speaking situations.

Learned or Conditioned Reflexes. Learned or conditioned reflexes are more complex, usually involving several reflex arcs. Langley and Cheraskin give the following illustration of the operation of conditioned reflexes: [4]

In driving a car, man steers in large measure by [conditioned] reflex movements. If he is on a straight highway and the car begins to drift subtly to one or the other side, reflexly he turns the wheel in the opposite direction. . . . When the neophyte drives he pays constant attention to the road and to his steering, and even with all that the car swings from side to side. But with practice reflexes are brought into play which employ not only vision but the tactile apparatus as well as the equilibratory mechanisms. They represent the afferent limbs of this complex pattern. The arms and hands constitute the effector organs.

Another phenomenon of conditioned reflexes implicit in this illustration is *reciprocal innervation.* Black and Moore call this principle "feedback" and apply it aptly to the speech process. [5]

Essentially this is a process of automatic self-regulation. . . . After one has learned to say "top" he does not need to think, "Now my tongue has touched the tooth ridge. It is time to drop it, open my jaw, and say *ah.* Now I have said *ah.* It is time to close my lips quickly to get the *p* sound." The rapid sequence of movements is partly regulated by the reciprocal innervation from muscles in action. . . . You will observe how impulses arising from movements of the tongue feed back to the nerve center (nucleus of the hypoglossal nerve) which activates the motor nerve of the tongue. You will also observe that other nerve centers, which activate other speech muscles, also receive the feedback. Actually, this feedback mechanism is repeated in all the other nerves that serve the speech muscles. By this mechanism, centers about to be brought into action as well as those already in action receive messages that indicate the moment-to-moment state of muscular contraction in all speech structures. These feedback mechanisms as well as the coordinating processes of the cerebellum and extrapyramidal pathways are below consciousness. Much of speech, therefore, both in respect to the meaning and the manner of production, tends to become routinized, stereotyped, automatic.

[4] L. L. Langley and E. Cheraskin, *The Physiology of Man* (New York, McGraw, 1954), p. 76.

[5] J. W. Black and W. E. Moore, *Speech* (New York, McGraw, 1955), p. 28.

Other phenomena of reflex physiology are demonstrable in the speech process. Man modifies the breathing reflex so that exhalation is longer than inhalation. He modifies the ear-vocal reflexes to acquire meaningful sounds. He may counter or inhibit the unlearned autonomic responses of fear, for example, by the assumption of the posture and muscular tonus of poise or "non-fear." Often an individual facilitates his articulatory responses by calling into play generally the bodily reflex patterns of heightened mobility. Or, he may find that stimuli in the "chain-reflex" of talking summate to his disadvantage. One "bumble" provokes a second mistake! He may stimulate pleasurable autonomic reflexes by calling on memory arcs of pleasant speech experiences from the cerebral centers.

In sum, in speech-learning man utilizes these learned and unlearned reflexes, co-ordinating some into complex patterns, inhibiting others which are not useful, facilitating some by emotional reinforcement, subjecting all to modification from memory arcs of earlier learning through the control of cerebral and subcerebral "centers." Is it any wonder that speech is highly susceptible to arrest or breakdown? The nature of these arrests and breakdowns will be discussed in subsequent chapters.

Functional Arcs. (Fig. 4-2) Traditionally, the cerebral cortex is considered the highest station along the neural route to speech. This concept has been questioned seriously in recent years by investigators who do not accept this picture of neural hierarchies with the cortex as king imposing its inhibitions over all "lower levels" of the nervous system. They see the nervous system as a network of functional arcs in which subcortical centers are in a reciprocal relationship with cortical areas. The result is a kind of circular phenomenon in which nuclei in the subcortex (the striate bodies, thalamus, and midbrain) contribute to activity in the cortical areas just as the cortical areas play upon these "lower centers." The arc to which we have just referred might be conceived as the cortico-strio-thalamic unit. Another arc might involve the cerebellum, pons, and cortex; hence it would be known as the cortico-ponto-cerebellar unit. The concept of functional arcs is useful because it supports the observation that oral expression is dependent on many areas and on multiple routes which are circular in function. And it is possible that in some of these circular routes the highest point of potential may not be in the cerebral cortex but in certain subcortical areas. At any rate the concept of functional arcs impresses one with the fact that speech is a result of a total response of the central nervous system, and that its complex integrations do not "reside" exclusively in the cerebral cortex.

Localization of Functions in the Cerebral Cortex. (Fig. 4-3) For over a century the debate has been waged over cerebral localization. The traditional view is that definitive areas can be assigned to sensory, motor, and associative (memory) functions in the cerebral cortex. In the case of the primary motor areas, a point-to-point relationship has been described, so that stimulation of a specific point on the cortex produces, for example, a movement of the fingers. The establishment of "centers" has been achieved largely through electrical stimulation of the cortex and the study of the effects of behavior through destruction of specific areas. By these means, areas for general sensory reception, for the control of primary motor responses, and for such associative functions as interpretation of visual and auditory symbols, speech elaboration and organization, and memory have been postulated. The methods of investigation have been questioned by many. The results of the study of lesions are inconclusive, partly because

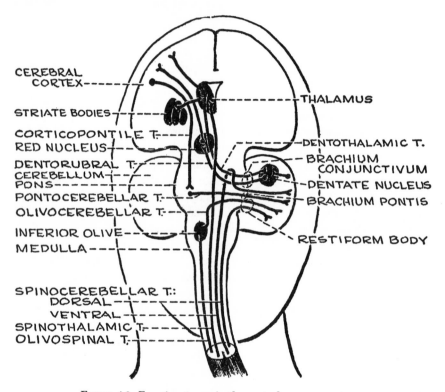

FIGURE 4-2. Functional arcs in the central nervous system.

"the occurrence of a defect following a cortical lesion does not necessarily indicate that the opposite of the defect is a function of the removed area. Furthermore, if no defect follows a cortical lesion, one cannot conclude that this area has no function. A brick can be removed from the foundation of a column; but if the column does not fall, one does not conclude that the brick served no purpose." [6] Moreover, lesions in specific areas have not produced uniform behavioral deficits; their effects vary from person to person. And although a single behavioral deficit is often assigned to a specific

[6] Gardner, *op. cit.*, p. 310.

area, it is found that when the total behavior of the individual is studied the lesion has produced not one but a complex of behavioral alterations.

Every student of speech is familiar with *Broca's area,* the area rather sharply delimited and assigned to the elaboration and organization of speech patterns before they reach the motor projection areas. Penfield and Rasmussen, among others, have demonstrated the presence of other speech-organizing areas. Some areas which have been very carefully delimited now are having their borders extended. The primary motor area, formerly confined to a narrow strip in the frontal lobe, now has been widened considerably, and some neurologists have outlined primary motor areas in other lobes.[7] (See also Fig. 4-11.)

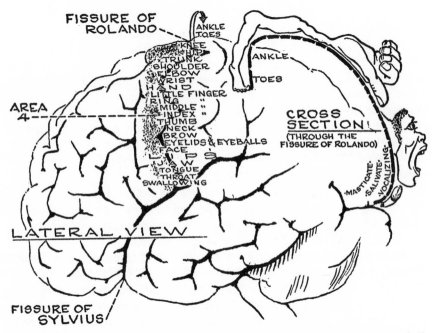

FIGURE 4-3. Motor homunculus (lateral view). (Adapted from W. Penfield and T. Rasmussen, *The Cerebral Cortex of Man* [New York, Macmillan, 1950], p. 57.)

Any discussion of cerebral localization of function must also take into account the position of those who see the cerebral cortex as part of functional arcs embracing areas below the cortex. Interruption or damage may occur in a subcortical structure and so produce an effect upon cortical areas which apparently have suffered no damage. In support of this view, Morgan and Stellar conclude that the interpretation of sound is not wholly or even largely a function of the cerebral cortex; "the lower centers of the brain

[7] *Op. cit.,* pp. 106-107.

stem in the medulla are the most important contributors to auditory sensitivity." [8] Other investigators are convinced that it is the amount of neural tissue lost which determines the behavioral impairment, not the specific site of the damage. In their view, the brain functions as a whole and cannot be analyzed in terms of specific areas.

In the light of our present knowledge, it is probably reasonable to assume that there are areas where great groups of fibers having to do with a specific function converge and thus establish a "center," that there may be other "centers" in other parts of the cerebral cortex and in the brain stem, but that the ones now designated as primary areas for sensory, motor, and associative or memory activities are those on which man has shown his greatest dependence.

Hemispherical Dominance. Many activities may be represented in both cerebral hemispheres, but in motor and expressive behavior a dominant hemisphere is predicated. In right-sided individuals this is the left hemisphere. The question has been raised frequently: Is speech dependent upon the integral activity of the two hemispheres? The midline organs which subserve speech—such as the jaw, lips, tongue, and larynx—have bilateral representation. In other words, both sides of these organs are represented in both hemispheres. It has been found, however, that when the giant "trunk line"—the band of white fibers—connecting the two hemispheres is completely severed, only a temporary fleeting awkwardness (anarthria) in speech results.[9] One must conclude that only the neurons in the primary motor projection area in one hemisphere are needed for speech. But it must be remembered that although the *mechanism* of vocalization and articulation has bilateral representation, the *skill* or organization and elaboration necessary for speech is found only in the dominant hemisphere. These organizing and elaborating areas in the dominant hemisphere apparently depend upon "separate projected connections between the diencephalon (thalamus) and the elaborative areas rather than *across* the cortex." [10] Hearing also is represented in both cerebral hemispheres in the sense that the cochlear nerves in both ears send impulses to both temporal lobes. Speech sounds, however, are recognized only in one hemisphere: the left in right-sided individuals, the right in those who are dominantly left-sided.[11]

[8] C. T. Morgan and E. Stellar, *Physiological Psychology* (New York, McGraw, 1950), p. 226.

[9] Penfield and Rasmussen, *op. cit.,* p. 218.

[10] *Ibid.,* p. 219.

[11] Bauer and Wepman have presented recently the interesting hypothesis that "while right-handedness tends to be comparatively consistent (and probably means left-hemisphere dominance) left-handedness and ambidexterity are so similar and so inconsistent that no dominance can be determined from the behavior noted. This would imply that no right-hemisphere dominance exists, but rather some failure or difference of cerebral lateralization develops with maturity." R. W. Bauer and J. M. Wepman, "Lateralization of Cerebral Functions," *Journal of Speech and Hearing Disorders,* Vol. 20, No. 2 (1955), pp. 171-172.

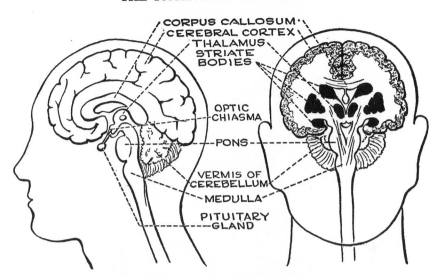

FIGURE 4-4. The cerebral cortex and brain stem.

Anatomical Units of the Central Nervous System Important in Speech

The Cerebral Cortex. If you will look at Figure 4-4, you will note that the outer covering of the two cerebral hemispheres is called the cortex. Cortex literally means "bark," the outer covering of a tree; the cortex, then, is the outer covering of the cerebrum. The covering is soft, spongy, and rolled up into many folds or convolutions. In these convolutions (*gyri*) are found roughly 14 billion gray cells and their underlying fibers (white substance). For ease in locating points in the cerebral cortex, it has been divided into five topographical units much as any geographical area is mapped. In Figure 4-5 you will note four units or lobes which are visible on the surface: frontal, parietal, temporal, and occipital. The *frontal lobe,* the foremost section of the cerebral cortex, is separated from the *parietal lobe* by a deep sulcus called the *fissure of Rolando* or central sulcus. The *temporal lobe,* which is the lateral section of the cortex, is separated from the frontal and parietal lobes by another deep sulcus, called the *lateral fissure* or *fissure of Sylvius.* The *occipital lobe* is the most caudal point of the cerebrum and is separated from the parietal by the parieto-occipital fissure. The *insula* (*island of Reil*) is the fifth topographical division and is not visible on the surface of the cortex. It is a triangular elevation lying buried in the lateral fissure.

Later we shall consider the chief functions of each unit in detail. At this point the student should remember only that the cerebral cortex is responsible, in large part, for the highest mental activity which distinguishes man from the rest of the animal kingdom. Man's ability to remember and to adapt to new situations through using past experience, his expert integration of perceptive and responsive powers to effect speech, for example, are the result, in large part, of the development of the cerebral cortex.

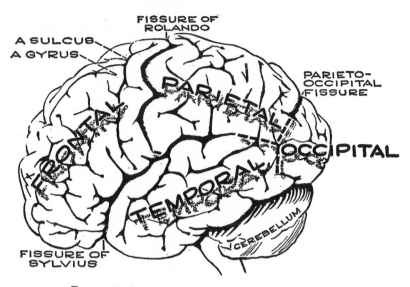

FIGURE 4-5. Lateral view of the brain, showing lobes.

The Cerebral Ventricles. In Figure 4-6A, a mid-frontal section of the brain, sketched to show the subcortical structure, also exposes the cavities or ventricles in the interior of the brain. In the interior of each cerebral hemisphere is a *lateral ventricle* which communicates with another space in the midline called the *third ventricle.* This ventricle is continuous posteriorly with a very narrow channel through the midbrain, known as the *aqueduct of Sylvius.* The fourth is the last ventricle of the brain, the floor of which is formed by the pons and medulla; the roof is formed by the cerebellum. A special kind of tissue, the *choroid plexus,* which lines the ventricles is responsible for the manufacture of the cerebrospinal fluid which circulates through the brain and cord and also through the spaces between the immediate covering of the brain and the dura mater. If viri or bacteria invade the ventricles, serious brain injury usually results. In the chapter on cerebral palsy you will find further discussion of the brain damage resulting from such abnormal conditions.

The Striate Bodies (Basal Ganglia). Buried in the forepart of the medullary substance of each cerebral hemisphere below the cerebral cortex are three gray nuclear masses individually designated as the *caudate, lenticular,* and *amygdaloid nuclei.* In Figure 4-6B you will note that the caudate ends in a *cauda* or "tail"; the lenticular suggests a lenticle or "bean"; and the amygdaloid resembles an almond in shape.[12] Two of these nuclei, the caudate and the lenticular (made up of the *putamen* and *globus pallidus* or "pale body"), are separated by a portion of the white substance known as the *internal capsule*. In the internal capsule are crowded the great pathways going to and from the cerebral cortex. The great importance of these nuclei in achieving the precise motor components of speech will be discussed in a subsequent section.

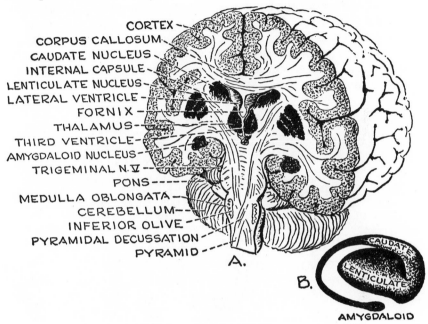

CORTEX
CORPUS CALLOSUM
CAUDATE NUCLEUS
INTERNAL CAPSULE
LENTICULATE NUCLEUS
LATERAL VENTRICLE
FORNIX
THALAMUS
THIRD VENTRICLE
AMYGDALOID NUCLEUS
TRIGEMINAL N. Ⅴ
PONS
MEDULLA OBLONGATA
CEREBELLUM
INFERIOR OLIVE
PYRAMIDAL DECUSSATION
PYRAMID

A.

B.

CAUDATE
LENTICULATE
AMYGDALOID

FIGURE 4-6. Diagrammatic frontal section through the brain.

The Thalamus. The nuclear mass which makes up the thalamus proper lies medial to the striate bodies and, in part, below them on either side of the third ventricle (Fig. 4-4). In the wings of the thalamus which extend lateralward are two nuclear masses, the *geniculate bodies,* of great importance in reflex vision and audition. The section immediately below the main mass of nuclei is called the *hypothalamus.* Its outline can be distinguished easily by the optic chiasma and the stock of the pituitary gland. A good landmark for the posterior limit of the thalamus is the *pineal body,* which projects in the midline from its dorsal surface. The thalamus is known as the great sensory "relay station," since all visual, auditory, somatic, and visceral impulses end or synapse here before continuing to the cerebral cortex. Hence, it is sometimes called the affective or "feeling" center of the brain.

[12] Fulton includes other brain-stem nuclei found at lower levels in the substantia nigra and reticular formation in the term, "basal ganglia." See J. F. Fulton, ed., *Textbook of Physiology,* 16th ed. (Philadelphia, Saunders, 1949), p. 275.

The Midbrain. Immediately below the thalamus is the midbrain. In Figure 4-7 you will recognize this anatomical unit by the two great feet or peduncles which form its ventral section. These peduncles are a continuation of the internal capsule and contain the great motor pathways originating in "higher centers." Just above these feet is a strip which has a black appearance and is called the *substantia nigra;* its importance in fine motor co-ordination will be discussed later. In the middle you can see a pair of nuclear masses called the *red nuclei,* which are a part of the motor co-ordinating system. The midbrain is further distinguished by the presence of four eminences or "hills" on the dorsal surface known as the *superior* and *inferior colliculi.* These nuclear bodies are reflex stations for sight and hearing. The midbrain also has "arms" which connect it with the cerebellum; they are called the *brachia conjunctiva.*

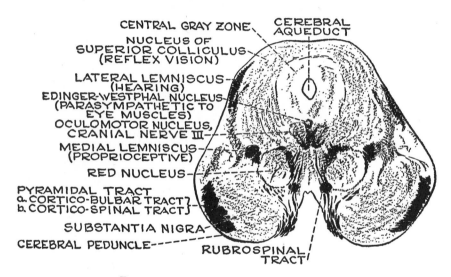

FIGURE 4-7. The midbrain in cross-section.

The Pons. (Fig. 4-8) The main bridge between the brain stem, cerebellum, and cerebral cortex is the pons, which lies just below the midbrain. It is what its name implies, a bridge for "merging traffic." Pathways going to and from the cerebellum and the cerebrum meet on this bridge, the pons. The "arms" of the bridge which extend to the cerebellum are known as the *brachia pontis.* In the ventral section are great bundles of fibers which can be detected in cross section by the striations. They are a part of the motor system. Within the pons there are also great nuclear centers which act as reflex stations for functions such as breathing and circulation.

The Medulla. The *medulla* or bulb, which is continuous at its lower end with the spinal cord, really is an enlargement of it. The great descending (motor) pathways which you saw in the midbrain now will form two pyra-

mids on the ventral surface of the medulla, and the pathways will be called
the *pyramidal tracts*. (Fig. 4-6A) At the caudal section of the medulla, these
tracts will cross to the opposite side. The rostral part of the medulla will fan
out to form the third connection with the cerebellum, known as the *restiform
body*. In the medulla will be found many sensory tracts going toward the
cortex. There also are important nuclei at this level which control respiration and circulation. Eight of the twelve cranial nerves will have their nuclei
of origin or termination in the medulla.

The Cerebellum. (Fig. 4-8) You already have been made aware that the
cerebellum is not a part of the brain stem but is closely connected with the
"mainland" by three bridges: the brachium conjunctivum, the brachium

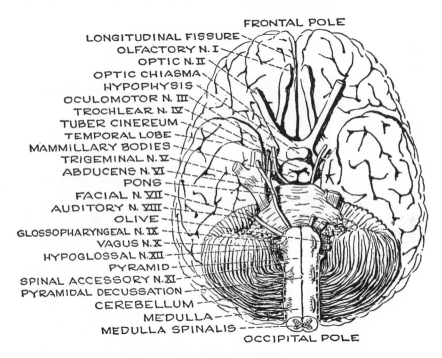

FIGURE 4-8. Basal view of the brain.

pontis, and the restiform body. It is strange that they are called collectively
the *cerebellar peduncles* (feet), not cerebellar brachia (arms). The cerebellum, lying beneath the occipital lobes of the cerebrum and above the
pons-medulla, is divided into two hemispheres and a midportion called the
vermis (Fig. 4-4). The cover of the cerebellum is composed of gray matter
or nuclei, one group of which is known as the *dentate nuclei*. The white-
fiber tracts of the interior of the cerebellum are continuous with the tracts
in the cerebellar peduncles. The cerebellum is in a strategic position to receive information from all parts of the body and so to influence the move-

ment of all parts of the body. Its great importance to speech is through its contribution to the elaborate control of voluntary muscle movement.

The Spinal Cord. Continuous with the medulla is the spinal cord, which runs in the spinal canal, decreasing in diameter as it proceeds downward. There are four anatomic divisions: cervical, thoracic, lumbar, and sacral, which also give their names to the nerves leaving from the respective divisions. A transverse section at any level (Fig. 4-9) reveals the same structure: the gray matter arranged in the shape of the letter H, with dorsal and ventral horns extending into each half of the cord and with a connecting bar of gray matter through the middle. The central canal in the middle of the bar is continuous with the fourth ventricle. At each level the afferent or incoming sensory neurons are found in the dorsal and dorsomedial posi-

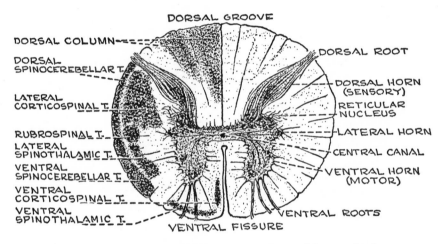

FIGURE 4-9. Cross-section of the spinal cord at mid-thoracic level.

tions, the efferent or outgoing motor neurons in the lateral and ventral sections of the cord. Here is a schematic representation of the cord showing the major ascending and descending tracts and their cell bodies (Fig. 4-10). The spinal cord and spinal nerves must receive and transmit sensory impulses coming from the body wall to the brain. They must assist in transmitting the outgoing impulses from the brain to the muscles of the body. Through other fibers, they assist in the sympathetic control of smooth muscle, circulation, and glands, which have a distinct part to play in speech.

So far, we have considered the structure of the brain and spinal cord, describing general function only as it was necessary to make clear the structural relation of the several units. Now with this view of the "building" clearly in mind, we are ready to furnish it, to describe in detail the functions present at each level which contribute to neural integration for speech.

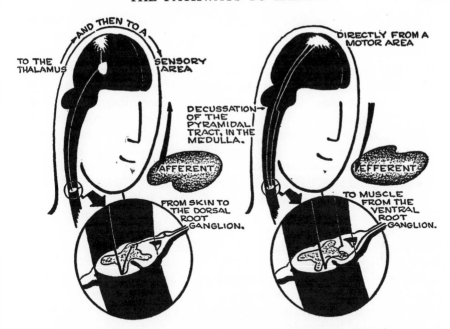

FIGURE 4-10. Schematic representation of ascending and descending tracts.

The Role of the Central Nervous System in Speech

The Cerebral Cortex. All the lobes of the cerebral cortex are important to speech if we remember that any sensory or incoming stimulus—providing it reaches the cortex—may make connections with the speech association areas, and thus may be a part of the S-I-R (stimulation-integration-response) arc of speech. Earlier in this chapter we discussed the theory of localization of function in the cortex. Figure 4-11 is a "relief map" of the cortex showing the traditional areas of localization. Let us begin with auditory perception in the temporal lobe and point out current concepts of the significance of each area to speech. Auditory perception, of course, is very important, since we are so largely dependent upon it for learning and maintaining our patterns of speech. Phases of hearing reception will be found at several levels, but its cortical representation is limited largely to the temporoparietal area. Along the fissure of Sylvius in the superior temporal gyrus is one primary *auditory receptive area* (*Area 22;* Fig. 4-11). The receptive fields for hearing encircle this area and extend into the parietal lobe. If these receptive areas are intact the individual may perceive the sounds of the words but he may not understand the meaning of the words. This ability to understand or interpret the significance of the sound units has been allocated loosely to another area (*Area 41-42;* Fig. 4-11) at the far end of the fissure of Sylvius in the region of the supramarginal gyrus and the posterior part of the first temporal gyrus. It is called *Wernicke's apperceptive area.* These are some areas in the cerebral cortex which are associated with the reception and perception of speech by the auditory route. There is considerable evidence that other areas exist in the parietal lobe and in the insula (island of Reil). If the nuclei in these areas are absent or damaged, or if the fibers from subcortical areas, or the association and intercalary (connecting) neurons between these areas, are damaged or congenitally absent, then failure to comprehend spoken language (auditory aphasia) results. In an area posterior to the auditory apperceptive zone is a field for the interpretation of *visual symbols* (Fig. 4-11). Damage here may result in dyslexia, a failure to comprehend the meaning of the written word.

In the parietal lobe, immediately behind the fissure of Rolando, are fields (*Areas 1, 2, 3;* Fig. 4-11) which make possible a sense of awareness of touch, pressure, temperature, and muscle movement. These sensory impulses, providing they are sharp and integral, may be projected to association areas concerned with speech. A keen awareness of tongue movements in articulation, for example, may be one of the chief stimuli in provoking or continuing speech. Every person has had the experience of attempting to formulate the proper verbal response by "internal speech" or subvocalization. So we try to recall a name by repeating similar names. Through the proprioceptive awareness of similar muscle movements we hope to "run up" on the appropriate response.

Immediately in front of the fissure of Rolando are specialized cells, pyramidal in shape, which make up one of the *motor projection areas* for voluntary movement (*Area 4;* Fig. 4-11). You will note in Figure 4-3 that a considerable portion of this area is devoted to phonatory and articulatory movement. Other nuclear areas which mediate voluntary movement have been located both in the parietal and in other sections of the frontal lobe.[13] The fibers from all these primary motor projection areas make up the *pyramidal tract* or pathway. Hence the areas are known as the *pyramidal areas.* Over this route, for example, are sent the impulses to the striated muscles of pharynx, larynx, tongue, lips, and jaw, which produce contraction.

Spreading out in front of *Area 4* is another field even larger than the voluntary motor areas. This nuclear field is called the *extrapyramidal area* (*Area 6;* Fig. 4-11). It should be noted that there are other extrapyramidal areas in the striate bodies, thalamus, midbrain, pons, and cerebellum, all of which contribute fibers to the extrapyramidal system. These fields in the cortex, brain stem, and cerebellum give rise to pathways which once were thought to be a part of an ancestral motor system; a more accurate description might be a neo-motor system. It has a part, for example, in producing those refinements in motor expression which are peculiar to man's highest development. The interplay of antagonist and protagonist

[13] T. C. Ruch, "Motor Systems," in S. S. Stevens, ed., *Handbook of Experimental Psychology* (New York, Wiley, 1951), p. 177.

muscle-sets; the delicate synergies of facial expression and gesture which underwrite verbalization; the modal sequence in vocal-fold adduction, resonance, and articulation; the qualities of intonation and rhythm: all these activities subserving expression are dependent on the extrapyramidal system. We become particularly aware of the damage to this system in the athetoid spasms of the cerebral-palsied.

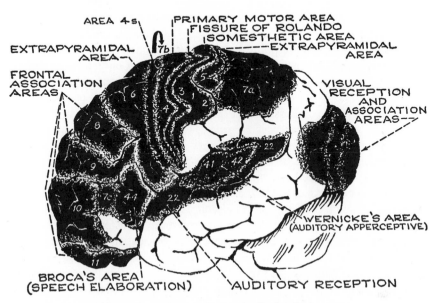

FIGURE 4-11. Localization areas in the cerebral cortex.

Find next in Figure 4-11 *Area 44* in the lower section of the frontal lobe. This area was first defined by Paul Broca, a French brain surgeon, as a formulative and elaborating area for speech. Although such functions cannot be ascribed exclusively or even largely to this area, certainly it is one zone where many fibers from other areas concerned in the speech process converge and synapse around nuclei from which connecting fibers will go to the motor projection areas subserving the muscles of speech. Other researchers in this field claim that there are other "Broca's areas" in the frontal and parietal lobes.[14] Two such areas, *7B* and *7A,* have been located respectively in the frontal lobe along the longitudinal fissure and in the parietal lobe behind and below the major sensory areas. It is claimed that another area, *7C,* in the frontal-orbital cortex is concerned with the final formulation of speech but in a very special way. Having established that the thalamus, the "emotion center," is connected directly with this area, these investigators assume that Area *7C* is concerned with the integration of the emotional concomi-

---

[14] Penfield and Rasmussen, *op. cit.,* pp. 106-107.

tants of expression. It is significant, in other words, in the production of the emotional overlay of speech.

Then there are fields (*Areas 8, 9, 10,* and *11;* Fig. 4-11) that might be called ideational association areas. Speech must also call upon past experience, upon memory of ideas, the loci of which we cannot state with certainty. We know that the greater the number of intercalary neurons or correlating pathways, the more variable and less stereotyped is man's response through speech. Some neurologists locate these highest constellations of memories which form the basis of abstract thinking and of the higher creative activities in the area anterior to the premotor area in the frontal lobe. "Large lesions in the prefrontal lobe of the dominant hemisphere not only cause defects in complex association, but produce disturbances of judgment, of the will, and of emotional behavior with resulting regressive changes in character. All these belong to the expressive part of the personality and may be regarded as motor defects of a high psychic order." [15] About this problem of localization of ideational areas, Ranson and Clark raise the question: "Is it possible that memory is dependent upon nerve impulses originating out of external stimuli that are stored, as it were, in perpetually reverberating currents awaiting a time at which some facilitating impulse might lower the threshold of a side chain to the appropriate circuit and allow the 'stored memory' to enter a conscious realm?" [16] We must conclude that nuclei and tracts mediating abstract thinking, reasoning, and memories of learned patterns have potential connections with, or are a part of, the speech arcs which play upon the final motor pathways to expression.

The Striate Bodies (Caudate, Lenticular, and Amygdaloid Nuclei). We already have said that the cortex, striate bodies, and thalamus are nodal points in the speech arc and probably act as one unit. This unitary concept is supported by Penfield and Rasmussen, who were not able to elicit speech in man by stimulating *Areas 44, 7A, 7B,* or *7C,* the speech organization and elaboration areas. By such stimulation they sometimes arrested speech, or produced cries and sounds, but they could not produce verbalization.[17] One may infer that the stimulation did not involve sufficient nodal points in the arc to produce meaningful speech. Apparently some of these "critical nodes" in the speech arc are contained in the striate bodies (*basal nuclei*) (Fig. 4-6). Two of these bodies, the caudate and lenticular nuclei, are of especial importance to us because they belong to the extrapyramidal system, and some of their axonal fibers end around the motor nuclei of the brain stem concerned with speech, the neurons innervating the muscles of the face, larynx, pharynx, and tongue. One finds a close association between the basal

[15] O. S. Strong and A. Elwyn, *Human Neuro-Anatomy* (Baltimore, Williams & Wilkins, 1948), p. 393.

[16] S. W. Ranson and S. L. Clark, *The Anatomy of the Nervous System,* 8th ed. (Philadelphia, Saunders, 1947), p. 313.

[17] Penfield and Rasmussen, *op. cit.,* pp. 106-107.

nuclei and *Area 6* in the cortex. It is possible that the two areas act as a unit in such synergic movements as expression, postural adjustment, and locomotion. Damage to any sector in this unit may produce the slow, writhing spasms in voluntary and emotional activities evident in the articulatory in-co-ordination, gesticulation, and facial grimaces of the athetoid. It is believed by some investigators that these involuntary movements do not originate in the basal nuclei but in the *release* of the precentral motor cortex (*Area 4* and others) from the normal inhibitory control which the basal nuclei and the extrapyramidal areas in the cortex (*Area 6*) exercise over the pyramidal nuclei and tract and other brain-stem "centers" in the pyramidal system. In other words, the normal restraint upon excitation exercised by the basal nuclei and the extrapyramidal system has been destroyed.

The Thalamus. The thalamus is generally regarded as a distinct anatomic division; but sometimes it is referred to as one of the basal nuclei.[18] Certainly it belongs to a functional unit embracing the cortex, striate bodies, thalamus, and perhaps the reticular formation in the midbrain and pons. So direct are the projection pathways from the thalamus to the cortex and, more important, *from* the cortex to the thalamus, that some neurologists have suggested that the "centrally placed mechanism," the highest integrative mechanism for speech, "may be situated in some cerebral area, such as the thalamus, and not in either cerebral cortex."[19]

The contributions of the thalamus to our sensory awareness and to the extrapyramidal system are fairly well established. All sensory tracts, both from special organs such as sight, sound, and smell, and from the general sensory end-organs mediating touch, pressure, and proprioception, have their great relay station in the thalamus. Is it not reasonable to assume, then, that the affective or feeling components which must be mediated through the autonomic system are here organized as entities, or to put it in another way, become integral parts of a unified response from this point in the cortico-strio-thalamic arc? These sensory-emotional components may be modified by the cortex (extrapyramidal area) or by the striate bodies, but the spark plug giving impetus and form to the emotional response probably is the thalamus. The quality of the voice, the expression of the face, the subtle bodily gestures, must be dependent, then, upon the innate potential and the multiplicity of connections of this nodal point in the speech arc. Because the thalamus is the receptor for all incoming sensations, it is also believed that the conceptual entities of form, size, quality, intensity, and texture are here organized and presented to the cortex. Insofar as these discriminative patterns are a part of ideation for speech, the thalamus is making still another contribution to the speech circuit.

The Midbrain. Next we come to a consideration of the function of the midbrain, which, you will remember, lies directly below the thalamus. The

[18] See Gardner, *op. cit.,* p. 20.
[19] Penfield and Rasmussen, *op. cit.,* p. 219.

pyramidal tracts which you have traced from the cortex through the internal capsule here form the feet (cerebral peduncles) of the midbrain. The midbrain also is a part of the extrapyramidal system through its great nuclear masses, the *substantia nigra* (black substance) and the *red nuclei*. These nuclei have two-way connections with the striate bodies (basal nuclei), the thalamus, and the premotor cortex. Lesions in the substantia nigra have resulted in muscular rigidity and tremor interfering with the ease and rapidity of volitional activities. The emotional play of the muscles of expression likewise is reduced or absent, the face appearing immobile or masklike.[20] The red nuclei are associated closely with the cerebellum in the grading and timing of muscular contraction.

In addition to its functions as a part of the pyramidal and extrapyramidal systems, the midbrain has nuclei in the inferior colliculi which act as relay stations for hearing. Whether perception of the loudness of sound is a function of these nuclei is still the subject of experiment.[21]

The Pons. The pons (bridge), like the midbrain, "allows passage" to the great sensory and motor pathways. Among its special contributions to the speech synergy are the nuclei in the reticular formation which are linked closely with the cerebellum and the basal nuclei; they therefore may be considered a part of the extrapyramidal system. Another group of nuclei in the pons of importance to the speech synergy make up the pneumotaxic center; this center, which has a direct connection with the hypothalamus, is important in stimulating exhalation and maintaining respiratory rhythm.

The Medulla. Those who have observed the paralyzing effects of bulbar poliomyelitis know the many functions which are dependent on the bulb or medulla. Here are the great centers which control the respiratory and circulatory systems, centers which regulate the rate and rhythm of breathing and which control vasomotor activities. The center for breathing responds not only to the incoming sensory impulses from the end-organs in the diaphragm and from cortical and subcortical areas, but also to the impulses from the chemoreceptors in the carotid and aortic capillaries. The breathing center in the medulla is also sensitive to any change in its own immediate chemical environment. A change in the acidity, or the pressure of carbon dioxide, in the blood produces an immediate response in this center. It must be remembered that other parts of the brain stem and the cortex may modify both the force and the rhythm of the individual respiratory movements for speech. The dominant phase in the breathing rhythm to sustain life is inspiration;[22] expiration in quiet breathing is passive. During speech this balance is partially reversed; the expiratory phases become more dominant. Certainly such a modification must be made by the inter-

[20] Strong and Elwyn, *op. cit.*, p. 259.
[21] Morgan and Stellar, *op. cit.*, p. 225.
[22] R. F. Pitts, in J. F. Fulton, ed., *Textbook of Physiology,* 16th ed. (Philadelphia, Saunders, 1949), p. 824.

ruption of the rhythm of the medullary center by impulses from higher areas in the brain. The arhythmic nature of breathing in stutterers, for example, may be associated with the conflict between higher controls subserving speech and those basic controls residing in the pons and medulla. Similarly the speech sequelae in bulbar poliomyelitis emphasize the importance of the pons-medulla area of the brain stem in any study of speech disorders.

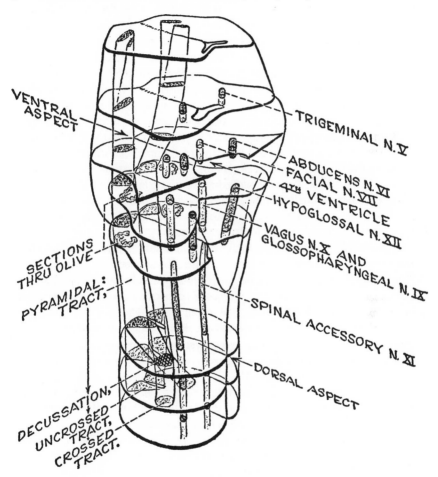

FIGURE 4-12. The brain stem, showing nuclei of cranial nerves.

The pyramidal pathways, as in the pons, occupy the ventral section of the medulla, and shortly before they enter the spinal cord the majority of fibers will cross the midline and descend on the opposite side in the cord (Fig. 4-12). A lesion involving the pyramidal nuclei or pathway above this crossing will impair the muscles of the body on the side opposite that of the lesion. Here in the medulla are also the motor nuclei (lower motor neurons) of several nerves (cranial nerves VII and IX through XII) which will send fibers to innervate muscles of the mouth, pharynx, and larynx engaged in speech production (Fig. 4-12). If there is a lesion in one half of the medulla, the contralateral side of the tongue, for example, will be paralyzed and atrophied. Under such conditions the tongue-tip will deviate toward the healthy side if the tongue is held inside the mouth.[23]

The Cerebellum. (See Fig. 4-2.) It will be remembered that the cerebellum is not a part of the brain stem, yet it is connected with it by large fiber tracts which make up the *cerebellar peduncles.* The cerebellum is of great importance to speech because it is the area in which we find elaborate control of voluntary muscle movement. If it is damaged, the smooth, sweeping, continuous movements of the normal individual are dissociated into their constituent parts. The alternation of control in muscular movement essential to modulation in phonation, for example, is done so slowly and clumsily that the speech seems to be jerky, slurred, and thick. The rhythmic disturbance in speech is so pronounced that one can "hear" the change as muscle groups take over from their antagonists; rapid alternation of muscle contraction is impossible. A person suffering from ataxia presents the symptoms of cluttered speech and an unmodulated voice most clearly, but minor evidences of these symptoms may be found in the so-called normal individual suffering from arhythmic and indistinct speech.

The cerebellum is connected with "the mainland" by great fiber tracts at several points: midbrain, pons, and medulla. Its connections with nuclei in the midbrain (red nuclei) and pons (pontine nuclei), and with nuclei in the thalamus, striate bodies, and premotor cortex, are proof of its membership in the extrapyramidal system. Without the cerebellum the integrative synergy in voluntary motor movement would be seriously impaired.

The Spinal Cord. Conduction is the first important function of the cord. (See Fig. 4-13.) All the sensory impulses (proprioceptive, interoceptive, and exteroceptive) from the extremities, body wall, viscera, and so on will be transmitted in fiber bundles or tracts in the dorsal and lateral sections of the cord. Some of these fibers will end in the cerebellum and thalamus and thus may play upon the speech response either directly or indirectly. Likewise the control of many motor activities of the body (except the face and neck) which accompany speech are mediated finally through the lower motor neurons (anterior horn cells of the cord) which send fibers to the muscles controlling posture, movement, and gesture. The cord also acts as an integrating center of its own for many reflex patterns, including the stretch reflex discussed in an earlier section of this chapter.

---

[23] Outside the mouth, the tip will deviate toward the affected side "because the genioglossus muscle pushes the base forward and the unopposed action of one side pushes the tip out toward the paralyzed side."

R. R. Grinker and P. C. Bucy, *Neurology* (Springfield, Illinois, Thomas Publishing Company, 1949), p. 266.

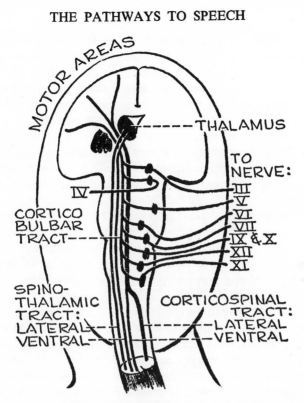

FIGURE 4-13. The spinothalamic (proprioceptive) and corticobulbar and corticospinal (motor) tracts.

The Role of the Peripheral Nervous System in Speech

The Cranial Nerves Associated with Speech. In the sense that speech is a total bodily function, all cranial nerves might be considered to be associated with speech. We shall include here, however, only those nerves most directly associated with the speech mechanism. These nerves are the *trigeminal* (triplet) (V), *facial* (VII), *glossopharyngeal* (tongue-pharynx) (IX), *vagus* (wandering) (X), *accessory* (XI), and *hypoglossal* (tongue) (XII).

The *trigeminal nerve* (V) emerges from the side of the pons at midpoint (Fig. 4-8) and contains both sensory and motor fibers of importance mainly to the articulatory movements of speech. This nerve transmits (1) sensations of movement (proprioception) from the muscles of mastication, (2) sensations of touch, pressure, pain, and temperature from the face, and (3) voluntary motor impulses to the jaw muscles. The motor nucleus of this nerve in the pons is called the lower motor neuron, since there are nuclei in the cerebral cortex and in subcortical areas which exercise inhibition and direction upon these pontine nuclei; their fibers go to control the muscles of the jaw.

The five remaining cranial nerves, VII and IX through XII, possessing motor components, will leave the medulla to innervate muscles engaged in speech production. Emerging at the junction of the medulla and pons (Fig. 4-8) are the roots of the *facial nerve,* cranial nerve VII, which supplies the striated muscles of the face, the expressive muscles, and the stylohyoid and stapedius muscles. Its nuclei constitute the lower motor neurons, normally under the control of its sisters in the cerebral cortex and the subcortex. Lesions of the facial nerve produce a paralysis, both reflex and voluntary, of the face on the same or ipsolateral side. Smiling and emotional responses are gone, as is the ability to wrinkle the forehead or to show the teeth or to pucker the lips.

The *glossopharyngeal nerve,* cranial nerve IX, performs many of its functions in connection with the tenth or vagus nerve, but it also acts independently. One function of importance to us is the innervation of the stylopharyngeus muscle, which forms a part of the sphincter in velar closure. The nerve also mediates proprioception or sense of movement of the posterior third of the tongue.

The *vagus nerve,* cranial nerve X (Fig. 4-8), has so many components that it is difficult to select those most important in speech. In conjunction with the ninth and eleventh cranial nerves, it innervates all the striated or voluntary muscles of the pharynx and larynx involved in speech. Their cells of origin (nucleus ambiguus) in the medulla are known as the lower motor neurons, since they are subject to control from higher brain levels. Some of the fibers from the upper motor neurons have crossed the midline before they reach the nucleus ambiguus; other fibers from the nucleus ambiguus cross before they leave the medulla, so a lesion on one side *within* the medulla will not produce complete paralysis of the muscles of phonation. The result is that these terminal branches of the vagus which make up the superior and recurrent laryngeal nerves going to the larynx contain both crossed and uncrossed fibers.

Sensory impulses relaying muscle position and movement (proprioception) also come into the medulla through these nerves and make a functional connection with the cerebellum and other stations along the extrapyramidal route which, you will remember, effects the fine co-ordination, graded contraction, and tonic control necessary for such a complex process as speech.

The independent functions of the *accessory nerve,* cranial nerve XI, subserving speech are few. In addition to its assistance to the vagus in the voluntary motor control of the pharynx and larynx, it provides specific innervation to two muscles of breathing, the trapezius and sternomastoid muscles.

The *hypoglossal nerve,* cranial nerve XII (Fig. 4-8), has one great function: to innervate the striated muscles of the tongue. The hypoglossal nuclei, like the other lower motor neurons providing voluntary control, are clustered around the ventricle in the medulla. The major part of the axones of the upper motor neurons originating in the cortex cross the midline to synapse with lower motor neurons on the opposite side, although some fibers remain uncrossed.

The Spinal Nerves Associated with Speech. We may repeat here a statement made in connection with the cranial nerves. Insofar as speech is a total bodily process, all spinal nerves are concerned with speech. There are thirty-one pairs of spinal nerves, each carrying both sensory and motor bundles. All incoming sensory impulses (interoceptive, exteroceptive, and proprioceptive) from the extremities, the trunk, and the viscera must be transmitted mainly by the spinal nerves. The somatic trunk line mediating voluntary impulses to the great muscles of the body emerges from the anterior horn of the cord and terminates in the motor end-plates of the muscles, thus producing contraction. Through their autonomic fibers they also assist in the sympathetic control of smooth muscle, circulation, and glands which have a general part to play in speech.

In one sense, the most important speech role of the spinal nerves is the transmission of motor or efferent impulses which have been carried down in the pyramidal pathway from the brain to synapse with the anterior horn cells in the cord, from which they go to activate the muscles of breathing for speech. In another sense, the peripheral spinal nerves are important in speech because they carry the impulses providing for general integration through the autonomic system.

So far, we have considered the divisions of the brain and the spinal cord and their peripheral nerves as if they were independent wholes. Obviously, such is not the case. We have taken this approach in order to facilitate understanding of each unit. Now it is time to integrate this knowledge in terms of the great functional or operational pathways which make speech possible.

The Sensory-Correlating-Motor Systems: Their Contribution to Speech

There are three major highways in the central nervous system: sensory, correlating, and motor, which are involved in every activity from the reflex or spinal level to the highest cerebration.

The Sensory Tracts. Man depends upon perception for protection, for knowledge, and for the integration of such a function as speech. Perception, in turn, is derived largely through our senses: through our general sense of touch and pressure, of pain and temperature, and of proprioception (muscle position, tension, and movement), and through our special senses of sight, hearing, smell, and taste. By our faculty of perception we receive and integrate these sensory clues with past experience. The receptors for our senses are specialized nervous tissue and are grouped according to their position and to the type of stimulus to which they respond. The receptors may be in the skin or body wall, receptors which are sensitive to touch, pressure, pain, and temperature: they are *exteroceptive*. Or the sensation may come from receptor end-organs in muscles, tendons, and joints which pick up stimuli of position, movement, and tension: they are *proprioceptive*. And finally, there are those receptors in smooth muscle, in the blood vessels, and in the glands of the viscera: they are *interoceptive*. You touch a hot iron; you encounter one more step than you expected on a dark stairway; it is long past your dinner hour and your stomach reminds you noisily of its state: each of these stimuli, exteroceptive, proprioceptive, and interoceptive, will be translated into impulses which may reach the central nervous system.

In the uncomplicated reflex arc the sensory impulse is not carried far. In touching the hot iron, for example, the impulse comes into the spinal cord; its central, short axon synapses with the dendrites of a connecting (intercalary) neuron at the same level in the gray matter of the cord; its terminal arborization, in turn, connects with the cell body of a motor neuron which carries the impulse directly to the muscle. But other sensations will be carried as impulses in great trunk lines through the cord and as far as the medulla, by which time they will have crossed to the opposite side, and then will ascend in the dorsal section of the brain stem. In *proprioception,* these tracts make up the *dorsal columns* in the back part of the cord which synapse in the medulla and then cross over to ascend as the medial lemniscus as far as the thalamus [24] (Fig. 4-13). In this great sensory relay station the impulse may end or it may be relayed further to the cerebral cortex. Since proprioception is responsible for the direction, rate, force, and extent of voluntary movement, it is clear that impairment of this tract or its terminal connections will be evidenced by movement lacking in smoothness, precision, and grace. These proprioceptive tracts can also initiate impulses which participate in such "chain reflexes" as walking, dancing, or driving a car. We have described the course of one of the great sensory tracts mediating proprioception. The *ventral and lateral spinothalamic tracts* (from the spinal cord to the thalamus) convey impulses of touch, pressure, and temperature.

Now let us turn to a *special sensory tract* also of great importance to speech: the tract for hearing. Let us suppose that you are at a meeting. Some one whispers in your ear, "Make your motion now." What happens in the nervous system? (See Fig. 4-14.) In the cochlea of the ear there is a mechanism by which the mechanical energy of the air pulsation of the whisper is transformed into electrical impulses. So the stimulus is transformed into a nervous impulse by the receptors in the cochlea. Following the course in Figure 4-14 you will see that the auditory impulses from the cochlea are transmitted to the medulla where the fibers may synapse with cochlear nuclei, then cross the midline and ascend in the *lateral lemniscus* through the pons to the midbrain. There they will encounter another relay

[24] Recently the presence of proprioceptive fibers in the pyramidal tract has been established.

station (in the inferior colliculi), then continue to yet another station in the thalamus (medial geniculate body). Finally they will reach auditory receptive areas in the temporal and parietal lobes in the cerebral cortex. The representation and awareness of certain qualities of sound may be in the thalamus and the midbrain. It is believed, for example, that quality, loudness, and pitch are synthesized and "recognized" in these subcortical areas, not in the auditory areas of the temporoparietal lobes of the cortex.[25]

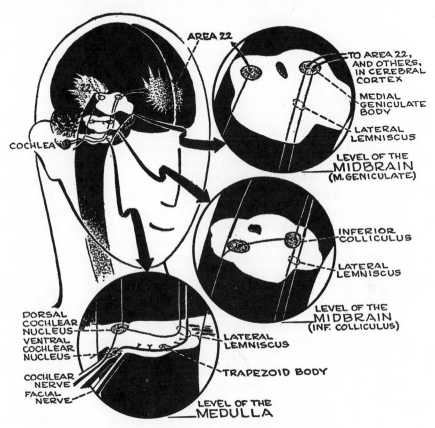

FIGURE 4-14. Diagram of the auditory pathway.

Simultaneously, other stimuli are playing upon the central nervous system. You are practicing subvocally how to "get your tongue around" the terms you must use in phrasing the motion. Proprioceptive impulses from end-organs embedded in the muscles of the tongue, lips, and jaw are reporting lightninglike shifts in position and tension which must be undertaken. As you stand and walk forward, you are vaguely aware of a quickened heartbeat, moist hands, and "butterflies." The interoceptors, the specialized

[25] Fulton, *op. cit.,* pp. 405-406.

nervous tissue in the muscles of the heart, respiratory organs, and stomach, send impulses which will play upon autonomic centers and so affect the speech response. Many functions of the sensory system have been utilized in the total summation of sensory impulses upon the speech response.

The role of the sensory arm of the speech arc may be clearer if you consider what happens when some of these sensory routes are damaged as in cerebral palsy. The exteroceptors for hearing may be impaired so that the individual is not able to pick up the necessary auditory stimulation to learn the speech sounds as easily as you have learned them. Many of the proprioceptive clues which the cerebral-palsied receives from his muscles and tendons are false, producing exaggerated and un-co-ordinated muscle movements. The impulses from the interoceptive end-organs (in smooth muscle, glands, and so on) often are so numerous as to "flood" the sympathetic branch of the autonomic system which mediates the responses. Having lost the central control to inhibit these sensations, the cerebral-palsied individual reacts maximally to every stimulus.

The Great Correlating Systems. In the normal individual all these sensory impulses *may* reach the brain stem and the cerebral cortex where they are perceived. From these final receiving stations, impulses proceed to other areas in the cortex, areas concerned with organization, elaboration, association, or inhibition of components of the response. Just as there are sensory tracts, so there are correlating or association pathways. These fibers are so numerous that it is safe to say that every neuron has a potential connection with every other neuron. There are short association fibers, some of which dip into the white substance beneath the cortex; others connect different portions of the same gyrus in the cortex. There also are long association fibers connecting widely separated parts of the cerebrum (Fig. 4-15). Some of these fibers are collected in compact bundles known as the *superior longitudinal fasciculus, cingulum,* and so on. Those which cross the midline, the *anterior* and *posterior commissures* and the *corpus callosum* (Fig. 4-4), connect the two hemispheres, although the nature of the connection is not understood. Severing the corpus callosum, for example, has produced no detectable difference in behavior.

Let us return to the person about to make a motion in a public meeting. What correlating pathways must be operating to organize and elaborate certain components and to inhibit other components of the response? We may assume that the auditory impulse has been received and its meaning understood through the utilization of areas in the perceptive and apperceptive areas in the temporoparietal areas and subcortical areas. (See Fig. 4-11.) But they must be integrated further with "memory" arcs of past experience in the frontal and possibly parietal lobes. They must be elaborated through association with other ideational areas. There is an awareness of other impulses associated with proprioception and touch and pressure which have been received in the parietal cortex and the subcortex; these must be associated with the speech-organizing areas in the frontal lobe and in the subcortical areas. At the same time, impulses from the cerebellum, the striate bodies, and the reticular nuclei in the midbrain may play upon the speech-organizing and motor projection areas in the frontal and parietal lobes and in the subcortical centers. In all, propositional speech requires so many intricate correlations that one should not be amazed when it goes "out of kilter."

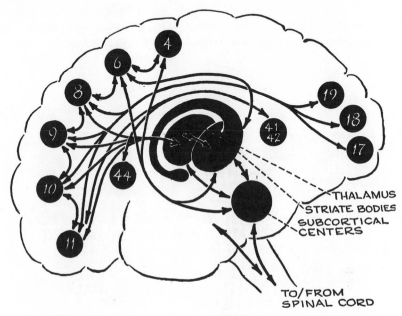

FIGURE 4-15. Diagrammatic sketch of integration of neural areas for speech.

The Motor Systems. The Pyramidal System: Corticospinal and Corticobulbar Tracts: At last, the response in speech is organized and sent to the motor projection areas in the frontal lobe (*Areas 4* and *6* among others) and possibly to nuclei in the subcortex. The fibers from these nuclei carry impulses destined for control of the muscles and glands engaged in the response. Some of the fibers comprising the *corticospinal tract* undoubtedly go directly from their origin in the motor and premotor areas through the brain stem to the spinal cord. Others will synapse in the medulla with the lower motor neurons, which will send their fibers through the cranial nerves to muscles. This route, called the *corticobulbar tract,* is of great importance to speech, since it will activate the muscles of the tongue, lips, jaw, pharynx, and larynx for the precise and purposive movements involved in speech. If the cortical and subcortical nuclei for this pathway are in-

jured, as in severe cerebral palsy, the nuclei of the brain stem, having lost
the control of "higher centers," will initiate their characteristic activity of
nonpurposive disorganized movements indicative of primitive or reflex behavior. If the injury is slight, it may be noticeable only in a clumsiness of
the tongue or in a tense, uninflected vocal quality. (See Chapter 15 for
a discussion of cerebral palsy.)

The position of the pyramidal system has been pointed out at each level
of the brain stem (Fig. 4-12). You will remember that it leaves the frontal
lobe through the internal capsule, then courses through the ventral section of
the midbrain, pons, and medulla. Now with this general picture in mind, and
attending to Figures 4-13 and 4-16, follow the detailed summary of its

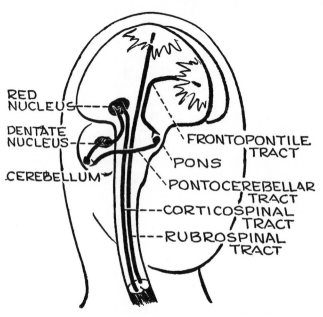

FIGURE 4-16. Correlation and projection tracts in the central nervous system (fronto-
pontile, pontocerebellar, corticospinal, and rubrospinal).

course. The corticospinal tract with its first cells of origin in the precentral
gyrus and associated gyri of the frontal lobe of the cerebral cortex, and possibly in subcortical centers, leaves the cerebral hemispheres by way of the
internal capsule, forms two eminences on the ventral section of the midbrain
(the cerebral peduncles), and continues in the same ventral position in the
pons and medulla until its major bundles of fibers cross the midline (decus-
sate) in the lower medulla. The bundle then will pass into the lateral column
of the spinal cord where its fibers will synapse with the motor cells in the
anterior horns of the cord, from which fibers will run in the spinal nerves

to effect voluntary muscle contraction. The corticobulbar tract will follow the same course until it reaches the pons and medulla where its fibers will synapse with nuclei (lower motor neurons) of the cranial nerves V and VII through XII, from which fibers will go through the peripheral tracts of these cranial nerves to effect voluntary movement of the muscles of breathing and of the lips, tongue, jaw, pharynx, and larynx (Fig. 4-13).

The pyramidal system is the most important of those concerned with movement, and in particular, with fine, discrete movement. Its control is predominantly contralateral, although some fibers descend without crossing. Some neurologists believe that this double innervation, crossed and uncrossed, is limited to muscles requiring simultaneous bilateral action for functioning, as for example, the larynx, pharynx, palate, tongue, and mandible muscles. In tracing the course of these tracts making up the pyramidal system, we have oversimplified greatly the process, since such a single and unmodified route probably does not occur. The corticospinal tract, for example, may not end primarily upon anterior horn cells, but will be connected with them through an elaborate system of internuncial neurons.[26] Both corticospinal and corticobulbar tracts, moreover, are influenced strongly by the activity of the extrapyramidal system which we shall now discuss.

The Extrapyramidal System (Fig. 4-17). This system of nuclei and fibers in the cortex, brain stem, and cerebellum is also of vital importance to the co-ordinated motor activity necessary for speech. This extrapyramidal pathway is made up of neurons which have their origin in nuclei in the precentral motor cortex, basal nuclei (striate bodies), thalamus, midbrain, pons, and cerebellum. Grinker and Bucy's description of its organization most nearly fits present concepts of the system. "All of these subcortical structures," they state, "which are the recipients of impulses from the precentral cortex have two principal projection systems. 1) They project to the lateral nucleus of the thalamus and thence back to the precentral region (cortex) and 2) they have a descending pathway down the spinal cord to the anterior horn cells." [27] So the cortico-ponto-cerebellar tracts, the cortico-strial-reticular-cerebellar tracts, and the cerebellar-thalamic tracts are in a two-way circuit, both sending fibers to and receiving fibers from the precentral cortex. The great importance to speech of this system becomes apparent when we consider that it "controls, activates, and inhibits the associated musculature or protagonistic muscles which must be appropriately contracted. . . . It controls the reflex innervation of the skeletal muscles to produce what is commonly known as tone. It deals with refinements of motor expression peculiar to man's highest development. It controls, at least in some measure and certainly incompletely, the activity

26 Ruch, *op. cit.,* p. 154.
27 Grinker and Bucy, *op. cit.,* p. 274.

of the vasomotor and visceral portions of the body through the sympathetic and parasympathetic nervous system." [28] The damage to the extrapyramidal system is best seen in the slow, sinuous movements of the athetoid whose reflex tone and postures have been "freed" from control by the extrapyramidal system.

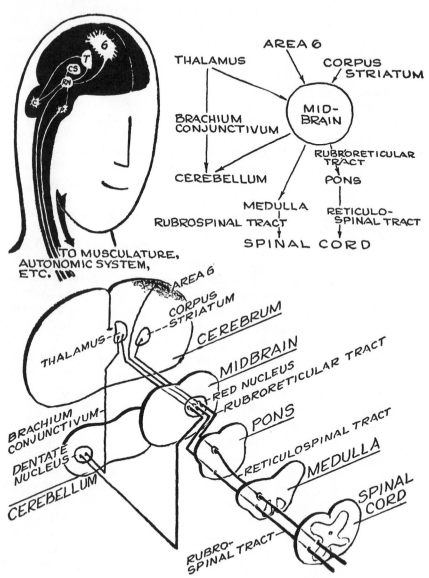

FIGURE 4-17. Diagram of some extrapyramidal pathways.

[28] *Ibid.*, p. 274.

The Autonomic System: Its Contribution to Speech

The autonomic nervous system controls the internal environment of the organism. Both divisions, the *sympathetic* and the *parasympathetic,* innervate smooth muscle, cardiac muscle, and glands and thus are responsible for the "milieu interne" of the individual. The internal organs such as the lungs, heart, and viscera (stomach, intestines, spleen, pancreas) are served by both divisions of the autonomic system; the peripheral organs are served chiefly by the sympathetic. Both systems are, by traditional definition, motor systems, yet there must be sensory fibers coming from the organs activated by the autonomic system.[29] Our awareness, for example, of a "lump in the throat" while speaking is dependent upon such afferent connections.

The effects of the two divisions are, in general, antagonistic. The sympathetic division, man's ancestral co-ordinator, is characterized by generalized, highly diffuse, and excitatory effects. Unlike the cranial nerves, its response to a stimulus may affect not only one muscle or one organ, but a series of muscles or organs. Its response, moreover, may exceed the time and energy requisites of the situation; its effect may continue as a kind of reverberation for several hours after the event. It acts as an emergency mechanism, but any one who has experienced shock in a physical or mental crisis knows that the sympathetic excitation continues long after the emergency is over. The body exhibits the "fight, flight, or fright reactions" of one's ancestors. Speech also is a response to a crisis and hence calls heavily upon the sympathetic system in meeting the response. The "great speech" may be over, but the increased heart rate, the flow of blood to skeletal muscles, and the dilation of the bronchi continue long after the conclusion.

In many respects, the parasympathetic division acts as an antagonist to the sympathetic division. In general, the former serves to inhibit, conserve, and protect the organism. In contrast to the excitatory function of the sympathetic division, it will attempt to resist change in order to maintain a constant internal environment. Its chief purpose is to insure the normal operation of the processes of respiration, circulation, and digestion, but normal operation may demand inhibition of one organ, acceleration of another. On occasion it will increase stomach activity, for example, but will slow down heart action.

In a "crisis," which may occur in any speech situation, it would appear that in the initial stage, the sympathetic system may dominate only momentarily; the parasympathetic assumes a later and more lasting control. The mouth and throat, for example, suddenly may become very dry as a result of the sympathetic constriction of the submaxillary and sublingual glands. This state may be followed by a period of excessive salivation as a

[29] Fulton regards the autonomic as a sensory-motor system (*op. cit.,* p. 232).

result of the dilatory action by the parasympathetic system on these glands.

For both systems a "neurohumeral mediator" is posited. It is thought that a chemical substance, acetyl-choline, is liberated at the synapses and terminals of the parasympathetic system and an adrenalin-like substance (sympathin) at the sympathetic junction.

The Sympathetic Division. This division originates in the thoracic and upper three lumbar segments of the spinal cord, and hence is known as the thoracicolumbar section of the autonomic system. The fibers from its cell bodies, located in the lateral columns of the cord, leave the cord ventrally and are called preganglionic fibers until they synapse with nuclei which make up the sympathetic ganglion chain and the three cervical ganglia above the chain (Fig. 4-18). This chain extends on each side of the vertebral column from the base of the skull to the coccyx. There are ten to twelve collections of cell bodies (ganglia) in the chain. It should be noted that preganglionic fibers may synapse directly with nuclei in the ganglia at the same level or they may pass to other levels in the chain or to the cervical ganglia. The fibers from the nuclei in the sympathetic chain are postganglionic and join the spinal nerves to terminate in blood vessels, sweat glands, and smooth muscle.

The Parasympathetic (Craniosacral) Division. The cranial section has its origin in special nuclei in the brain stem associated with these cranial nerves: oculomotor (III); facial (VII); glossopharyngeal (IX); vagus (X); and accessory (XI). Their preganglionic fibers terminate in ganglia close to the organs to be innervated: III, to the ciliary and constrictor muscles of the eye; VII, to the lacrimal, salivary, and sublingual glands in nose, mouth, and throat; IX, to the salivary glands; X and XI, to the muscle and glands of heart, lungs, and abdominal viscera (Fig. 4-18).

The nuclei of the sacral portion are in the second and third sacral segments; their preganglionic fibers exit ventrally to end in the ganglia within the walls of the pelvic viscera.

A chart summarizing the course and function of both divisions of the autonomic system will be found in Appendix 2.

Central Control. The autonomic system has its co-ordinators at many levels in the brain: medulla, pons, thalamus, and hypothalamus; and although the precise areas are not delineated, it also is represented in the cerebral cortex. Emotional expression, for example, is one of the concomitants of speech which must depend upon the integrity of these higher areas of control. Not only does the hypothalamus exercise control over such visceral activities as metabolism, elimination, and sleep, but it also has effector centers of emotional expression which, when released from cerebral inhibition, may reveal intense states of hyperexcitability.

Apparently certain areas in the cerebral cortex act as excitants to the autonomic system; other "depressor areas" inhibit or hold in line the effectors of the autonomic system. It is now thought that both respiration

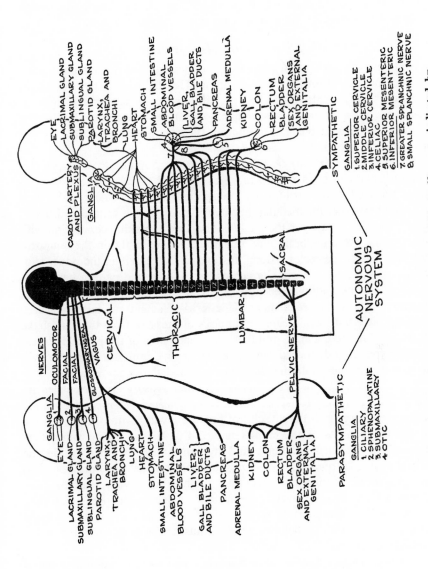

FIGURE 4-18. The autonomic nervous system. (Preganglionic fibers are indicated by heavy lines, postganglionic fibers by light lines.)

and circulation may be subject to cortical control. The role of the autonomic system as excitant is visible in the moist forehead and palms of the stutterer as he anticipates a block in his speech. Any student who has produced a dry, rough throat through worry over the "big speech" knows the power of central inhibition of the submaxillary and sublingual glands.

The Summing Up: Neural Integration for Speech

And now you ask that these "pieces" of knowledge of the nervous system be assembled in an orderly configuration. The difficulty is that no single, discrete, inflexible pattern can be drawn for speech. The neural integration may involve few or many areas at spinal, brain stem, or cortical levels. The S-I-R Gestalt is variable. Let us sum up by reviewing one possible pattern or Gestalt for speech.

The Stimulus Arcs of One Speech Pattern. Suppose that the primary stimulus comes through your *hearing* as a friend greets you. Sensory impulses received in the cochlea are transmitted by the cochlear nerve, and as these fibers enter the medulla they may synapse in the ventral and dorsal cochlear nuclei, then cross the medulla and ascend making connection with nuclei in the pons, midbrain, and thalamus, ending finally in the temporoparietal areas of the cortex. Along this line in the centers in the pons, midbrain, and thalamus, certain characteristics of the sound pattern have been perceived. In the auditory receptive areas of the temporoparietal lobes of the cortex, the further refinement of patterns of sound has taken place.

At the same time, *exteroceptive* impulses of pressure from the handshake are received in the thalamus and the somesthetic area of the parietal cortex. You see your friend; special sensory exteroceptive impulses from the eyes are received in the midbrain, the thalamus, and the occipital cortex.

In preparation for the act of speaking, other sensory arcs are called in. The breathing synergy for speech must be established. *Interoceptive stimuli* from the end-organs in the muscles of breathing will be transmitted via the sensory components of the cranial nerves IX, X, and XI to subcortical "centers" in the medulla, pons, and hypothalamus, and perhaps in the parietal cortex. *Proprioceptive impulses* (mediating tension, position, and direction sense in muscles) from the diaphragm, larynx, pharynx, and articulatory organs will travel in the posterior columns, the pyramidal tract, and the medial lemniscus to terminate or make connection in the great sensory areas of the cerebellum, the thalamus, and the parietal area in the cerebral cortex.

The Integration Arcs of One Speech Pattern. Integration and elaboration do not proceed in the cerebral cortex alone; many subcortical areas undoubtedly take part in this process. Association of meaning with the speech sounds (the greeting) takes place in the auditory apperceptive area (Wernicke's area) in the cortex and possibly in other areas. The cerebellum, midbrain, thalamus, and striate bodies in co-operation with the cerebral cortex must interpret the proprioceptive and interoceptive impulses so that they may present organized patterns of gradation, force, and direction to the primary motor areas governing the speech muscles (muscles of breathing and of the pharynx, larynx, tongue, jaw, and lips). These patterns will determine the vibrancy and modulation in voice, the modal sequence in vocalization, the speech rhythm, the precision of articulation, the facial expression—all the highly expressive components of speech. They will be mediated largely through the extrapyramidal system. The memory patterns of previous experiences with this person are aroused (Fig. 4-11, *Areas 8, 9,* and *10*). At last all these arcs converge on the final organizing and elaboration areas for speech (*Broca's area* and other areas in the cerebral cortex [Fig. 4-11, *Areas 44, 7A, 7B,* and *7C*] and possibly the thalamus). From these elaboration and organizing areas fibers are projected to the primary motor areas (*Area 4* among others). The richness of the connection of all these areas by cortico-cortical and cortico-subcortical fibers will determine, in large part, the complexity, speed, and excellence of the response.

The Response Arcs of One Speech Pattern. The final common pathway to words must include the projection pathways from all the areas mediating pyramidal, extrapyramidal, and autonomic activity. The subcortical and spinal nuclei of the autonomic system will project their responses so as to produce the homeostasis necessary for the stress of speech. Salivation, blood pressure, and glandular secretions of thyroxin and adrenalin will reflect the activity of this system. The pyramidal and extrapyramidal fibers will play upon the lower motor neurons of the cranial nerves V and VII and IX through XII to produce the rapid, finely graded and co-ordinated muscular contractions in the speech organs which permit you to respond to the greeting: "I haven't seen you in years!" Speech is, we repeat, man's most complex neural response to his environment. The reader, we daresay, agrees.

THE ENDOCRINE CO-ORDINATING SYSTEM AND SPEECH

> A voys he hadde as smal as hath a goat.
> No berda hadda he, ne never sholde have,
> As smothe it was as it were late y-shave;
> I trowe he were a gelding or a mare.

So Chaucer, in his description of one of the travelers to Canterbury, records (quite unwittingly, one suspects) knowledge of glandular insufficiency in the Middle Ages. And although our knowledge has been vastly expanded, the total sum at present represents only a meager beginning in the study of an ancient co-ordinating system: the endocrine glands. Indeed, had we followed developmental order, discussion of the endocrine system would have preceded that of the nervous system, for the endocrine is the older, the more primitive co-ordinator. It is linked with the nervous system in a kind of co-operative enterprise, the purpose of which is to "adjust internal processes to changing conditions in the external world." [30] The linkage with the sympathetic system is so close that a substance, called sympathin, liberated through the stimulation of sympathetic nerves, appears to be very similar to, if not identical with, the adrenalin secreted by the medulla of the adrenal gland. It may be that the adrenomedullary function is only an emergency source, a "helper" for the sympathetic system, "extending and perhaps co-ordinating its activities." [31] In addition to this close linkage with sympathetic nervous activity, the endocrines also serve as growth and maturation agents and as internal metabolic regulators affecting the disposition of foodstuffs, water, and electrolytes in the body.

As the word "endocrine" implies, the glands which make up this system are ductless, pouring their secretions (hormones) directly into the blood stream. It is a system embracing reciprocal influence and balance among the glands. The anterior pituitary gland affects, and, in turn, is affected by the thyroid. The thyroid affects the adrenals; the adrenals influence thyroid activity. Stimulus to glandular activity may come not from other glands but from the biochemical state of blood and body tissues. Elevation of the glucose level of the blood, for example, is an immediate stimulus to the secretion of insulin, which acts to remove sugar from the blood; if the converse is true, that is, if a low glucose level obtains, adrenalin is secreted, which enhances the release of sugar from the liver. In such states of "excitement" as speaking, adrenalin probably becomes the assisting agent mobilizing and releasing the sugar stores for utilization by the body. It is well known that speaking for prolonged periods under conditions of tension produces complete depletion of the blood sugar. The body is exhausted.

Unlike other glands of the body, the endocrines may have more than one functional unit contained within each gland. The adrenals, for example, have two distinct anatomic and functional divisions: the inner core or medulla, and the "cover" or cortex. The medulla secretes adrenalin (epinephrin); the cortex secretes cortin.

Since interactivity between glands and with the nervous system is characteristic of these chemical co-ordinators, it is not possible to delimit all the functions of each gland. There are, however, general areas of operation presented, in outline form, in Appendix 2.

The Pituitary Gland

The *hypophysis* or pituitary gland is an unpaired gland attached to the floor of the brain at the level of the hypothalamus (Fig. 4-19). Its anterior and intermediate lobes are derived from the oral cavity, its posterior lobe from the forebrain. Great significance is attached to the anterior lobe inas-

[30] C. D. Turner, *General Endocrinology* (Philadelphia, Saunders, 1948), p. 48.
[31] Fulton, *op. cit.*, p. 1136.

much as it secretes hormones promoting growth and also provides hormones which act as stimulators to other ductless glands, notably the thyroid, adrenal cortex, and gonads. These trophic hormones, known as gonadotrophin, adrenotrophin, and thyrotrophin, mediate their effects on their respective "target glands" by promoting the maturation of the glands and the formation and secretion of their hormones.

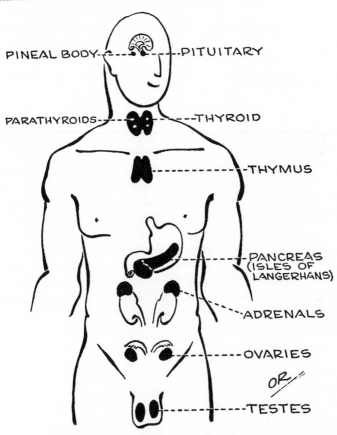

FIGURE 4-19. Chart of the endocrine organs.

The significance of the growth hormone of the anterior pituitary is clearly seen when an excess of this protein substance produces the adult disease of acromegaly or its juvenile corollary, gigantism. The growth of the jaw, thickening of the skull, and enlargement of the bones of the extremities are familiar clinical signs of acromegaly. In the acromegalic, the hoarse quality of voice and indistinct articulation are corroborating evidence, respectively, of the abnormal growth of the larynx and of the hyoid bone and jaw, which destroys the delicate balance of muscular synergies associated with these organs in the production of speech.

The Thyroid Gland

The thyroid gland develops as an invagination from the pharynx and lies in the form of a double vesicular pouch just below the cricoid cartilage with the band or isthmus connecting the two pouches stretched across the anterior surface of the trachea. It is one of the largest endocrine organs, averaging 20 grams in weight. The clear, colloidal substance which it secretes, called thyroxine, increases the rate of all metabolic processes and of oxygen consumption. Qualitative and quantitative *deficiencies* in thyroxine produce cretinism in the child, and myxedema in the adult, with the familiar clinical syndrome of dry, coarse skin; slow, clumsy speech; husky, unmodulated voice; thick tongue and lips; coarse hair; reduction in sensitivity to stimuli of the peripheral nervous system; and general weakness and lethargy. Dwarfism is also characteristic of cretinism.

The results of *hyperthyroidism,* in which an excess of thyroxine is thrown into the bloodstream, are manifold, but the most obvious are muscular tremor, weight loss and fatigue, nervous tension, accelerated breathing, and palmar sweating. In the extreme state of hyperthyroidism, thyrotoxicosis, such nervous disorders as psychasthenia, neurasthenia, and manic-depressive psychoses are common. So sensitive is the voice to an excess of thyroxine that one very quickly detects a fine tremor, an inconsistency of pitch, and a breathy quality. All these symptoms reflect the excessive tension and inability of the muscles to maintain steady contraction and synergic relationship. It should be remembered, however, that certain types of hyperthyroidism may be produced experimentally, not by the administration of thyroxine, but by the injection of anterior pituitary extracts containing thyrotrophin.

The Parathyroid Glands

The parathyroid glands are small bodies lying within the thyroid lobes or in close proximity to them. The effects of their secretion, parathormone, are two: (1) the maintenance of a stability of threshold at synapses and end-plates of motor nerves, and (2) the regulation of the calcium-phosphorus metabolism. The lowering of the level of diffusible calcium in the bloodstream, or the disturbance of the normal calcium-phosphorus ratio (0.8—2), for example, acts to increase the excitability of motor nerves by decreasing their resistance at synaptic junctions and end-plates. In extreme states of calcium depletion, synaptic resistance is erased, resulting in tetany and convulsions. Whether there is a relation between subclinical states of hypoparathyroidism and stuttering has not been substantiated. Certainly some of the spasms of the stutterer resemble subtetanic convulsions produced by an increased irritability of the motor nerves, subserving speech. Kopp's report of the calcium-phosphorus imbalance of the stutterer supports the postulate that some types of stuttering may be produced by a reversal in the calcium-phosphorus ratio, or by a deficiency in the mediator of calcium, vitamin D.[32]

The Adrenal Glands

The adrenal glands sit like cocked hats over the rostral border of the kidneys. They are a combination of two glands, distinct in origin, anatomy, and function. The inner core, or medulla, secretes *adrenalin* (epinephrin); the outer covering, or cortex, provides the hormone *cortin*. So closely do the effects of adrenalin resemble those of the sympathetic nervous system that the two are conjoined as the sympatho-adrenal circuit described earlier in this section. Like the sympathetic nervous system, the adrenals act as an emergency mechanism in times of stress, producing a speedy and generalized adaptation of the organism. Blood pressure and pulse rate are heightened; oxygen consumption is increased; the carbohydrate stores of the body are mobilized for release. The body is alerted for stress. Recently a new substance, nor-adrenaline, has been added to the secretions of the adrenal medulla; apparently it acts as an "excitor" and may be identical with sympathin E alluded to earlier in this discussion.

The relation of cortin, the secretion of the adrenal cortex, to speech functions is entirely conjectural. The secretion from the cortex is controlled almost entirely by the adrenotrophic hormone from the anterior pituitary gland. Cortin is of great importance in the normal metabolic processes and in the protection of the body from external insults: shock, cold, and infections. Cortical deficiency results in grave metabolic disturbances, muscular weakness and lethargy, and a change in pigmentation of the skin. Hyperfunction of the adrenal cortex, on the other hand, produces nervous tension, sexual precocity, and muscular exhaustion.

The Isles of Langerhans

Scattered through the pancreas are islet cells to which has been ascribed endocrine function. These isles of Langerhans are responsible for the manufacture and release of a secretion known as insulin. Since insulin's chief role is to act upon glucose storage and release, and to make glucose useful to body tissues, it becomes the chief governor of the sugar level of the blood. In diabetes, the result of insulin deficiency, both carbohydrate and fat metabolism are upset because fat depots are called upon to provide the energy when carbohydrate stores have been depleted. The central nervous system is as sensitive to glucose deficit as it is to oxygen deficit. Many individuals are aware of heightened sympathetic activity in a marginal state of hypoglycemia or low blood sugar. Some people believe that this condition is beneficial in meeting speech or "stress" situations of short duration. The logic of such an argument is questionable.

[32] G. Kopp, "Metabolic Studies of Stutterers," *Speech Monographs,* Vol. 1, No. 1 (1934).

The Gonads

The gonads have a double function of proliferating germ cells and manufacturing hormones. Sex, it must be recognized, is not a 100 per cent phenomenon. In each individual reside secondary sex characters, both of male and female. It is the ratio of strength of these traits which determines differentiation. As *hormonal agents,* the gonads are concerned with the establishment of secondary sex characters and the regulation of the accessory ducts and glands of the gonads. The voice of pubescence, distribution of fat and hair patterns characteristic of the sex, and other external features which distinguish the sexes are the end results of this endocrine activity. The increase in the secretion of the male hormones, androgens, or the increase in the sensitivity of the tissue to the androgens, at puberty accounts for the alteration in the voice. Apparently androgens stimulate the growth of the laryngeal cartilages and muscles; the vocal folds are elongated and the anterior-posterior dimensions of the larynx in relation to the pharynx are increased suddenly and markedly. This latter change means that the adolescent must learn quickly how to adjust the laryngeal vibrations to a new and changing resonator.

How the hormonal co-ordinators co-operate with the nervous co-ordinators in such a process as speech is partly conjectural. Certainly if speech is to be considered a response of intervention, of "action in crisis," the emergency mechanism of neuro-endocrine organization must operate quickly and expertly. Anyone who has held the "damp hand of frustration," heard the tremorous tones, and noted the broken respiratory rhythm of a speaker under tension has been witness to endocrine activity. Thyroxine has speeded the heart rate, breathing, and pulse. Parathormone may have shifted the calcium-phosphorus balance, thus rendering motor nerves more excitable. The adrenals in conjunction with the isles of Langerhans undoubtedly have mobilized the body's sugar and released it into the blood stream. In conjunction with the sympathetic nervous system, adrenalin has acted to relax the smooth muscle of the bronchi increasing oxygen intake, has heightened muscle tone and, to a certain point, has facilitated motor coordination. The pituitary, through the secretion of many stimulator hormones, has acted as excitant to other glands in the ring.

* * * * *

This road of neural and endocrine organization for speech has been long, with many a turning. It is, however, one road which should be followed if the student is to understand the problems of the speech-handicapped. At every junction we have tried to suggest that there may be other equally good subsidiary highways and perhaps some main routes which we did not or, in the light of our present knowledge, could not take. We have presented *one* way which we believe to be based upon neural and endocrine concepts widely held at this time.

5

Retarded Onset and
Development of Speech

"Oh, dear, what can the matter be? Johnnie's so late—in talking. Yes, he babbles a little, but there are no words which we can understand. Can you tell me what is wrong?" The mother's voice is filled with apprehension. It is not "the known, but the fear of the unknown which doth confound us."

And even more frequent is this clinical introduction: "Andy began to talk late, very late. Now he is five and he talks, but only I can understand him. Some sounds he can't say at all, and sometimes he mixes up the syllables or leaves them out altogether. Do you think he will ever talk right?"

To answer Johnnie's mother and Andy's mother and the many anxious parents who inquire, "What can the matter be?" requires something more than a brief inquiry into family history and a quick test of tongue and lip mobility. It is quite possible to assess all the "knowns"; study every aspect of the child's inheritance, familial backgrounds, prenatal and postnatal history, and developmental schedule; administer all the tests in the battery; and still be forced to answer: "I do not know what is wrong." The boundaries of our knowledge are limiting even in this century of scientific progress. There are a few principles of which we are certain, but even these principles are often negated by contrary advice. "My doctor said I shouldn't worry. Johnnie will 'outgrow it.'" The question is the antecedent. What is *it* which he will "outgrow?" *When* will he outgrow it? At fifteen? At eighteen? Or will he admit even at twenty: "It's still hard for me to say many words."

Often an alternative to this "do-nothing policy" has been the proposal to remove the tonsils and adenoids, with some assurance that the operation will solve the speech problem. There may be a modicum of truth in this advice. If the posterior portion of the tongue and the pharynx are chronically inflamed and swollen, it is logical to conclude that the child may find it more comfortable to speak with a minimum of tongue and pharyngeal movement. Such an operation also may result in great improvement of the health of the child and thus give the necessary impetus to speech development. Unfortunately, our experience cannot support these claims. The advice, more often, would seem to stem from evasion of the facts, wishful thinking, or lack of knowledge. Even the mother suspects that something more than time or surgery will be necessary if her son is to develop intelligible, "normal" speech.

But what is "normal" speech development? In an earlier discussion we considered several factors which influenced the child's progress toward true speech and language. Included among the factors were physical condition, motor ability, intelligence, sex, and bilingual influences. It was pointed out that with these factors normal, and with a proper degree of motivation, most children begin to talk between the twelfth and eighteenth months of their lives. Irwin concludes that the average baby under two months old is equipped with about seven phonemes, seven front-vowel "families." At one and a half years, he has mastered the front vowels and the back consonants. Having mastered 27 phonemes at two and a half years, he decelerates in the acquisition of further sounds but accelerates in the frequency of uttering his sound-vocabulary. Although he begins with vowel families, after the first year his acquisition of consonants exceeds that of vowels.[1]

Between the twelfth and eighteenth months, the average baby has said his first words; by the time he is two years old, he has advanced to phrases; by the age of three, he is using simple sentences. By three and a half years, practically all his responses should be comprehensible.[2] To the extent to which the child does not maintain this time schedule, we may say that his language development is not normal. But speech also is retarded if there are deviations from the norm in sound patterns, syllable patterns, and word patterns. If we accept the norms established by Metraux,[3] Templin,[4] and others, we should expect the child to articulate correctly more than 90 per cent of the vowels and diphthongs by the age of two and a half and 90 per cent of the consonants by the time he is four and a half years old. The deviations may consist in the omission, addition, substitution, or distortion of sounds. The five-year-old boy who asks the grocer for gʌgə, ʔʌŋ, kæ̃ŋɪ, aɪkɪ (bubble gum, candy, ice cream) is omitting or making substitutions for all consonant sounds articulated by the lips or tongue-tip and

---

[1] O. C. Irwin, "Speech Development in the Young Child: 2. Some Factors Related to the Speech Development of the Infant and Young Child," *Journal of Speech and Hearing Disorders,* Vol. 17, No. 3 (1952), pp. 269-279.

[2] Dorothea A. McCarthy, "Language Development in Children," in L. Carmichael, ed., *Manual of Child Psychology,* 2nd ed. (New York, Wiley, 1954), pp. 492-631.

[3] Ruth W. Metraux, "Speech Profiles of the Pre-School Child, 18-54 Months," *Journal of Speech and Hearing Disorders,* Vol. 15, No. 1 (1950), pp. 37-53.

[4] Mildred C. Templin, "Speech Development in the Young Child: The Development of Certain Language Skills in Children," *Journal of Speech and Hearing Disorders,* Vol. 17, No. 3 (1952), p. 284.

TABLE 3

Language Development of the Child

(AGE IN YEARS)

(AGE IN MONTHS)

MEASURE OF DEVELOPMENT	1 / 12	1½ / 18	2 / 24	2½ / 30	3 / 36	3½ / 42	4 / 48	4½ / 54	5 / 60	5½ / 66	6 / 72	6½ / 78	7 / 84	7½ / 90	8 / 96
APPEARANCE OF INDIVIDUAL SOUNDS		(The indicated age of appearance of the individual sounds represents the upper limit of normality. Any sound may—and frequently does—appear before the age indicated.)				[m], [b], [p], [h], [w]. All Vowels of English		[k], [g], [t], [d], [n], [ŋ] (ng), [j] (y)		[f]		[v], [ʃ] (sh), [ʒ] (zh), [l], [ð] (th)		[s], [z], [r], [hw] (wh), [θ] (th), [tʃ] (ch), [dʒ] (j)	
NUMERICAL SIZE OF VOCABULARY	First Word	20 to 100 Words	200 to 300 Words		900 Words		1500 Words								
WORD TYPE (EACH TYPE APPEARS WITH THE MOST COMMON AT THE TOP.)	Nouns	Nouns and some Verbs and Other Parts	Nouns, Verbs, and Other Parts		Verbs, Nouns, Pronouns, and Adjectives		Verbs, Pronouns, Nouns								
SENTENCE LENGTH IN WORDS		Single Word Sentences	Two Word Sentences		Three Word Sentences										
PERCENTAGE OF INTELLIGIBILITY OF CHILD'S SPEECH		25%	66%		90%				100%						

1 Adapted from J. K. Duffy and J. V. Irwin, *Speech and Hearing Hurdles* (Columbus, Ohio, School and College Service, 1951), p. 11.

blade. If the speech of the child of four years shows such deviations that it is unintelligible to one outside of the immediate family, his speech development is retarded.

Finally, the speech growth of the child may be considered atypical if the *quantity* of his speech—his vocabulary of sounds, words, phrases, and sentences—is below the norm for his chronological age. "He talks—but so little; he tries all the substitutes for speech," one mother complained. At three years his vocabulary should contain 900 to 1200 words. He should speak in well-formed sentences using plurals. He should refer to himself by pronoun. At four years he should use conjunctions, understand prepositions, and possess a vocabulary of 1500 words.[5] At five, his speech should be clear and relatively free from infantile articulation.[6] Table 3 presents the profile of normal language development.[7]

Now we are ready to take up the negative aspects of the problem of speech development, to consider factors which retard the child in arriving at that stage of speech proficiency which we have called *verbal utterance*. Before we go much further in our discussion, it might be well for us to understand what the term *delayed speech* signifies. Just when is a child delayed in his speech? How late must a child be in starting to speak and how poorly must he speak to be *delayed* in speech? When and under what conditions should parents show concern, and at what time and in what circumstances ought something to be done? We should like to be able to set forth conditions and criteria against which each child could be measured for an answer to these questions. Unfortunately, the data at our disposal will not permit us to do as we should like. A rule of thumb may perhaps evolve out of our discussion, but the exceptions to the rule will be numerous.

CHARACTERISTICS OF DELAYED SPEECH

A child may be said to be delayed in speech when the manner or content of his language usage is significantly below the norm for children of his age. The child who continues to rely almost entirely upon gestures when he should be using oral words is delayed in speech. So also is the physically normal child who uses oral words, but in so mutilated and distorted a fashion that few people can understand him. We also consider that a child is delayed in speech whose vocabulary and sentence length and complexity vary significantly, and undesirably, from the quantitative norms for his age and sex (see p. 85). In all, we may consider that the speech of the child is delayed when (*a*) it fails to appear or is late in appearance; (*b*) there are deviations in the sound, syllable, and word patterns so marked as to

[5] A. Gesell, *The First Five Years of Life* (New York, Harper, 1940), p. 202.

[6] A. Gesell and Catherine S. Amatruda, *Developmental Diagnosis* (New York, Paul B. Hoeber, 1948), p. 13.

[7] J. K. Duffy and J. V. Irwin, *Speech and Hearing Hurdles* (Columbus, Ohio, School and College Service, 1951), p. 11.

disturb the intelligibility; or (c) the vocabulary and language patterns are below the norm for one of his chronological age and sex. Delayed speech, then, is a matter of manner, quality, and quantity of performance. We shall not discuss delay in the appearance of speech as distinct from delay in the development of speech, because both are the result of an interruption in the developmental or normal learning process. We hold with Milisen that "conditions which precipitate and maintain articulation defects after the child has begun to speak are only an extension of the conditions which limited the production and differentiation of sounds and which interfered with the development of a communication attitude before he began to speak." [8]

Speech Readiness

The "average" child, we said, begins to talk somewhere between the twelfth and eighteenth months of his life; some children begin a bit earlier, and others seem content to wait until they are about two years old before they start to speak. What is there about this period which extends roughly from the last quarter of the first year to the close of the second year that is of such fundamental importance for speech? Stinchfield [9] holds that this is the period of *speech readiness,* a period of development most favorable for the acquisition of speech. Stinchfield argues that the ability to speak depends upon the functional maturity of both the motor and sensory tracts of the nervous mechanism. Failure to capitalize upon the physiologically favorable conditions found during this period of readiness may very seriously retard the later acquisition and development of speech by the child. There is then, according to Stinchfield's view—and it is shared by others—an optimum period for the child to learn to talk, and she recommends that active speech training be initiated at this time. Later (see Chapter 7) we shall discuss the recommended method. It is well to bear in mind that the special period of speech readiness, if it exists, must be variable and flexible, and should be timed neither by clock nor calendar, but be predicted in terms of behavior on the part of the child which indicates that he is physiologically and neurologically mature. The rate of maturation of the nervous system varies greatly from individual to individual, and varies significantly for members of the same family. Little brother need not necessarily be expected to talk by twelve months because his sister and older brother did. Little brother may have a nervous system with a mind of its own as to when it will mature.

Although observers are in general agreement as to when most children begin to speak, there is no such accord as to how late a child may begin to

[8] R. Milisen, "A Rationale for Articulatory Disorders," *Journal of Speech and Hearing Disorders,* Monograph Supplement 4 (December, 1954), p. 8.

[9] Sara M. Stinchfield and Edna H. Young, *Children with Delayed or Defective Speech* (Stanford, California, Stanford University Press, 1938), p. 17.

speak and still be considered normal as to the time of speech onset. In a study of the speech development of 500 children, Berry established twenty-four months as the mean age of the development of speech intelligible to members outside the immediate family.[10] Van Riper agrees that "by the time a child reaches his second birthday he should be talking." [11] West [12] allows a full year and a half beyond the twenty-four months permitted by Van Riper and Berry before recommending concern and positive action. Our own recommendation is that in the absence of any evident cause for delay, no special training beyond speech stimulation through play therapy need be instituted for a child who has not begun to speak recognizable words by thirty months. If a child is not speaking by the age of three years, however, appropriate action is definitely indicated.

CAUSES OF RETARDED ONSET
AND DEVELOPMENT OF SPEECH

Now we return to the question posed by Johnnie's mother, "What is wrong?" The possible answers are many. They include intellectual factors such as mental deficiency and short auditory memory span; organic and physiological factors such as neuromotor disorders, defective hearing, slow maturation, and debilitating illnesses; psychological factors such as inadequate or improper stimulation and motivation for speech; and special environmental influences that make for unconventional characteristics in speech. These factors are by no means independent in their effect upon speech development. An organic condition such as deafness or blindness has a direct influence in making it difficult for a child to perceive speech and so to learn to speak. An indirect influence may also be exerted by an organic defect in that it may cause the child to be associated with atypical persons in an atypical speech world (other deaf or blind persons) and so retard his speech development. Furthermore, one factor alone may not have the power to retard speech, but may help to cause retardation when it becomes one of a constellation of deleterious factors. Fred, five years old, enrolled in the Rockford College Speech Center, is a fair example. He did not begin to talk until he was almost four years old; now at five years he talks, but his speech is almost unintelligible. One is impressed immediately by his clumsy speech mechanism. Movement of the articulatory organs is slow and poorly coordinated. There may have been some neurological impairment present at birth, because the mother reports that the velar-

[10] Mildred F. Berry, "The Developmental History of Stuttering Children," *The Journal of Pediatrics*, Vol. 12, No. 2 (1938), p. 215.

[11] C. Van Riper, *Speech Correction*, 3rd ed. (New York, Prentice-Hall, 1954), p. 111.

[12] R. West, L. Kennedy, and A. Carr, *The Rehabilitation of Speech*, rev. ed. (New York, Harper, 1947).

pharyngeal sphincter did not operate properly in feeding. Because he suffers from asthma his general health has not been good. The mother admits that she has been overprotective, partly because of the asthmatic attacks and partly because Fred is the youngest child in the family. Fred, moreover, evinces poor motivation in speech. He is often unwilling to leave his mother for the therapy sessions and resorts to very infantile behavior. There may be an undetermined familial influence, since two first cousins of Fred's also have been very retarded in developing speech. His intelligence is above average. It is possible that no one of these factors alone produced the retardation, but that an unhappy combination of events at a critical juncture in the child's life conspired against him.

We shall consider, therefore, the several factors which are causally related to retarded speech, recognizing that the list is not exhaustive and that the inter-relationships among the factors have not yet been fully explained.

Organic Deficiencies and Disorders

Whether Fred inherited a defect in the central nervous system (incomplete maturation of the proprioceptive fibers, for example), or whether he received an injury to the central nervous system before, during, or after birth, we do not know. Both the defect and the disorder may have been etiological factors. In discussing organic defects and disorders we shall make three rather arbitrary subdivisions of the subject: (1) neuromotor impairment involving the central nervous system; (2) physiological disorders not directly related to the central nervous system; and (3) special sensory defects: defects in auditory acuity, discrimination, and memory.

Neuromotor Impairment Involving the Central Nervous System. Retarded speech is more than a chance occurrence in many families. The comment, "His father could not talk plain until he was in the upper grades," appears in case records with such regularity that *inheritance of a defective central nervous system* must be given as one cause of retarded speech. Specifically what is inherited is conjectural. It may be a delay in maturation or a disorganization in the neuromuscular synergy subserving speech. We do not know precisely what section of the neuromotor pattern is missing or "behind schedule" which would account for the asynergy. We can present several possibilities. The delay may be in the maturation of the proprioceptive fibers which provide the stimuli for synergic muscle action. The proprioceptive impulses are the cues to motor co-ordination. If they are slow in arriving or fail to arrive with sufficient intensity to play effectively upon the efferent pathways, the motor impulses to the speech organs will be slow and nonrhythmic. Other investigators would localize the delay in the slow myelinization of cranial motor nerves which would retard the conduction of the impulse to the muscles. Karlin and Kennedy, who support the theory of delayed myelinization, state that sensory fibers are myelinated before motor association fibers and that the process occurs earlier in females than in males.[13] It is also possible that the difficulty may lie in the absence or delay in the development of the requisite sensory, motor, and speech "elaboration areas" in the cerebral cortex, basal nuclei, thalamus, or cerebellum. Finally, the theory has been advanced that the focus of trouble is in the lack of power at the synapses of connecting and projecting neurons. The areas themselves may be intact, but the connections among the areas are retarded possibly because of a low electrochemical potential at the synapse. Such a delay at the synapses (or in myelinization) in the extrapyramidal path from cortex to basal nuclei to cerebellum, for example, could produce the defect in timing of fine muscular co-ordination which is evident in many speech-retarded children. The impulses are "too little and too late." Patrick's measurement of the speed of movement of articulators in the production of consonant sounds in a study of speech-retarded children supports the general conclusion of a basic defect in the neuromuscular pattern.[14] In a study of the motor skills of a similar group, Schiefelbusch found a mean retardation of two and a half months in skills not subject to training (balance, for example) and a direct relationship between the degree of speech retardation and lack of motor skill.[15]

Retardation or disorganization of the neuromotor system also may be linked with the condition of mixed or unestablished laterality in "one-sided activities." It is caused apparently by a failure to establish dominance in either cerebral hemisphere or by the development of nearly equal power in both hemispheres. The relation of ambilaterality or non-laterality to speech is not entirely clear, but we know that hand preference usually begins to be manifested about the same time as the onset of true speech. We also know that there is a greater incidence of mixed laterality among speech-retarded children than in the normal population. Of course, a person does not use one hand exclusively. He may shift from left to right hand in the course of a single operation such as dealing cards or picking up objects. But in the majority of situations of the same orientation involving "unlearned or undirected" unilateral activities, most people show a hand preference. We are not suggesting that confusion in laterality or the presence of ambilaterality is the cause of the speech retardation. Both problems, however, may have a common neurological denominator, and, therefore, their appearance together may be a clue to one cause of defective speech. The fact that mixed laterality also is found frequently in children who have reading disabilities suggests that all three—speech retardation, reading disability, and mixed or unestablished laterality—might be placed on a common neurological denominator.

[13] I. W. Karlin, A. C. Youtz, and L. Kennedy, "Distorted Speech in Young Children," *American Journal of Diseases of Children,* Vol. 59 (June, 1940), pp. 1203-1218.

[14] May Patrick, *Common Denominators in School Children with Articulatory Defects.* Master's thesis, Rockford College, 1953.

[15] R. L. Schiefelbusch, *A Study of the Development of Speech-Retarded Children.* Doctoral dissertation, Northwestern University, 1951, p. 89.

Parents should realize that in most children there will be marked shifts of handedness during the first year of life, followed by a period of ambilaterality. By the age of two, just as speech is emerging, the use of a dominant hand generally is emerging. Ambilaterality may be fairly common even when children reach elementary school. For the child with normal speech and intelligence it may be tolerated, but in the speech-retarded child, ambilaterality in such unimanual activities as writing, throwing, eating, and cutting certainly should be discouraged. Indiscriminate shifting from left to right may lead only to further neural disorganization.

Another answer that we are prone to give all too quickly in accounting for neuromotor retardation is *defective mentality*. A speech clinician should come cautiously to the conclusion that the child's deficiency is cortical, that he does not have the requisite number of neurons and neural connections in the cerebrum. "He must be stupid; listen to his speech," may be a simple but also a very inaccurate diagnosis. It is true that feeble-minded children as a group begin to talk at a later age than those who are intellectually normal or bright. Mead,[16] for example, found that feeble-minded boys began to talk at approximately thirty-nine months and feeble-minded girls at about thirty-seven months, compared with approximately sixteen and fifteen months respectively for normal boys and girls. The child who is so feeble-minded that he is classified as a severe ament may never learn to speak because he may never develop the learning capacity needed for speech. Low intelligence undoubtedly is responsible for many cases of delay in speech, but speech delay also is the cause for much apparent low intelligence. Many of the better standardized and widely used intelligence tests are heavily weighted with items which require linguistic competence to be answered correctly. When performance tests (non-language) are given to children with delayed speech, they frequently do better than in standardized verbal tests. This was found to be the case in the studies of Stinchfield and Young[17] and Karlin, Youtz, and Kennedy.[18] Furthermore, there is some evidence to the effect that when children are taught to speak there is a concomitant increase in their intelligence quotients. Whether this increase results directly from the ability of the child to use language in a conventional manner, or whether the child who speaks makes a generally more adequate adjustment to his environment, and to the taking of intelligence tests, is not certain. In any event, Stinchfield and Young report that all of the fifteen delayed-speech children who were taught to speak at the Hill-Young School of Speech showed improvement in personality, in general adjustment, in increased comprehension and power of communication, and in intelligence as measured by the Stanford-Binet and Kuhlmann-Binet Tests

[16] C. D. Mead, "Age of Walking and Talking in Relation to General Intelligence," *Pedagogical Seminary,* Vol. 20 (1913), pp. 460-484.

[17] *Op. cit.,* p. 35.

[18] *Op. cit.,* pp. 1203-1218.

of Intelligence.[19] These observations are consistent with the findings of one of the authors based on studies of delayed-speech children trained at the Queens College Speech and Hearing Clinic.

The possibility that apparent mental deficiency occasionally may be a symptom of an emotional disorder deserves consideration. Recent studies employing play therapy with children whose initial psychometric results would classify them as mentally deficient suggest that significant changes in functional mental ability may in some instances be expected. Ricciuti, for example, found that two of seven children improved so much in psychological test scores that the diagnosis of mental deficiency could no longer be made. One child who scored IQ 76 on the Kuhlmann Intelligence Test scored 84 after twenty-four play-therapy sessions; another increased his score from 60 to 96 on the Merrill-Palmer after twenty-four play-therapy sessions.[20] These increases are higher than we ordinarily find in test-retest studies. According to Freeman: "Data accumulated over approximately the last thirty years have rather consistently shown the probable error of prediction of an IQ is about 5 points. . . ."[21]

Peter is a typical "slow learner." He is four and a half years old and has a vocabulary of 75 to 100 words but no phrases or sentences. His articulation of his limited vocabulary is characterized by omissions and substitutions; s, z, l, sh [ʃ], ch [tʃ], th [θ], th [ð], k, g, and r are missing. "Pussy-cat" becomes [puʔ]; "cake" is [tej]; "ball," [bɔ]; "shoe," [u]; "baby," [bej]; "car," [tɑ]; "milk," [mɛə]; "thank you," [æŋə]; "coat," [tow]. When the examiner asked him a few questions, such as "Are you a little boy or a little girl"?, he merely "echoed" the last word in each sentence. His voice is husky and unmodulated; his face expressionless. Hearing for speech apparently is satisfactory. He was quite content to play with the blocks but attempted no construction beyond lining them up in a row, and if the therapist destroyed the line and suggested that he build a house, he merely began a new line. His mother reported that at home he would line up chairs in the same way. Echolalia and perseveration are present both in language and in non-verbal activities. His inadequacy in the matching of colors of objects, of numbers and simple designs, is further proof of his lack of perception of his environment. From the observation of his social, motor, and learning adjustments over a period of several weeks, from his score on the Leiter Intelligence Scale, and from an evaluation of his speech and language development, one concludes that his general learning status is

[19] Stinchfield and Young, op. cit., pp. 38-40.

[20] F. B. Ricciuti, "A Study of Differential Diagnosis Using a Modified Play Technique," The Training School Bulletin, Vol. 51, No. 6 (1954), pp. 135-145.

See also V. Axline, "Mental Deficiency; Symptom or Disease?" Journal of Consulting Psychology, Vol. 13 (1949), pp. 313-328, and S. B. Sarason, Psychological Problems in Mental Deficiency (New York, Harper, 1949).

[21] F. S. Freeman, Theory and Practice of Psychological Testing (New York, Holt, 1950), p. 502.

most like that of a child two years, nine months old. The disparity between Peter's chronological and mental ages is apparent when one compares this report with the Binet measure for the four-year-old child. At this age, a child should be able to: identify pictures of sixteen common objects by name, complete the outline-drawing of a man, discriminate eight of ten forms by matching (circle, square, triangle, and so on), comprehend simple questions, repeat four numbers, find essential differences by pointing to the one that is not the same as the others, and execute three simple commissions (put the pencil on the chair, open the door, and bring the box). Peter will progress in speech and language as he progresses in general mental maturation—very slowly.

We have discussed so far the inheritance of a familial pattern of general neuromotor retardation, of which speech retardation is a part. We also must recognize that it is possible to inherit neuromotor retardation limited to specific parts of the central nervous system. It is thought, for example, that some children are delayed in speech because myelinization of the eighth nerve alone is behind schedule. Since the child cannot learn speech until the ear-vocal reflexes have been established, a delay in the maturation of the acoustic circuit could account for delayed speech. We also have reports of "lazy tongues" which right themselves apparently as the neuromuscular co-ordination of the tongue catches up with general maturation.

Injuries to the Central Nervous System. But inheritance does not tell the whole story. The central nervous system may be subjected to a widespread injury or to injuries so minute and discrete that they are detected only by the defect in speech. The most common injury to the central nervous system occurs in connection with the "hurdle of birth." The physician-poet, Oliver Wendell Holmes, scarcely thought of it as a hurdle when he wrote,

> So the stout fetus, kicking and alive,
> Leaps from the fundus for his final dive.
> Tired of the prison where his legs were curled
> He pants, like Rasselas, for a wider world.
> No more to him their wonted joys afford
> The fringed placenta and the knotted cord.

Holmes' optimism seems ill-founded in the light of what we know now about the physiological demands upon the newborn. The child must achieve homeostasis—a steady internal environment—within a short period of time and against great odds. As Gesell says, "Never again will the body have to acquire so much wisdom in so short a time. . . . Even in the adult the nervous system suffers when the limiting concentrations of hydrogen, oxygen, glucose, water, sodium, and calcium are transgressed." [22] The newborn infant is much more susceptible to these transgressions and much less

[22] Gesell and Amatruda, *op. cit.,* p. 218.

able to counter them. How many escape completely without injury is any-one's guess. Strauss and Lehtinen report that "in the spinal fluid obtained from newborn infants who appeared entirely normal, traces of blood could be found, indicating the existence of a brain trauma. In first-born infants the incidence of those serological findings has been reported in some in-vestigations to be as high as 60 per cent to 80 per cent." [23] We can only assume that in spite of the almost universal occurrence of such slight in-juries, the ability of the newborn to overcome the effects of damage is remarkable.

The injuries to the neonate may be caused directly by the circumstances of his birth. Premature babies (birth weight less than five and a half pounds) are particularly susceptible to anoxia and intracranial hemorrhage. Damage to the brain also may be caused by such external factors as the pressures of delivery or the use of forceps. Unfavorable conditions in em-bryonic life are responsible for some cases of neural damage. Rh incom-patibility in the blood of mother and child producing anoxia and intracranial hemorrhage, and such infectious diseases as measles and influenza suffered by the mother during the first trimester of pregnancy have had demonstrable deleterious effects on the central nervous system of the child.

Although the great incidence of brain damage is before, during, or imme-diately after birth, we must recognize the possibility of such an occurrence at any time in the developmental period. Influenza, pneumonia, measles, or scarlet fever may invade the nervous system, producing encephalitis (in-flammation of the brain) and damaging irreparably the nervous system. The viri in whooping cough and bulbar poliomyelitis attack with special virulence the ninth, tenth, and eleventh cranial nerves. In these cases the speech retardation may be very mild or so pronounced as to be recognized as dysarthria. Parents report frequently that the child was progressing nor-mally in speech learning until he was stricken by one of these diseases. All speech learning may be "erased," and in some instances a year elapses be-fore the child attempts speech again.

Schiefelbusch corroborates our study of the developmental problems as-sociated with speech retardation when he concludes that "the more seriously speech-retarded group . . . presents a background of developmental prob-lems which seem to be of an organic and medical nature. . . . The back-ground of serious illnesses and high incidence of medical treatment imply that these children more often experienced the debilitating effects of poor health. . . . Discrete and subtle motor impairments, then, as well as gross indications of motor disturbances or motor retardation may be associated with unsatisfactory speech and language maturation." [24]

One is faced, then, with the possibility that neural damage may be exten-

[23] A. A. Strauss and L. E. Lehtinen, *Psychopathology and Education of the Brain-Injured Child* (New York, Grune and Stratton, 1951), p. 113.

[24] Schiefelbusch, *op. cit.,* p. 89.

sive or localized in area, minimal or maximal in severity. If the lesions are widespread and maximal in their intensity, they will impair all developmental processes: intellectual, emotional, motor, and so on. Speech delay and retardation are inevitable results. Indeed, speech may never develop. Or the neural lesions may cover wide areas and be minimal in their intensity. Carol, four years old, enrolled in a clinic because of the late appearance of speech, presents evidence of minimal damage to all developmental processes. There is still some retardation in postural, locomotor, and prehensory behavior, although she is compensating well for the injury. Strabismus and a scarcely perceptible facial asymmetry are present. Carol now is saying single words, such as *mamma, daddy, baby,* and *bow-wow,* and will imitate single vowel sounds made by the therapist: *ä* [ɑ], *ē* [i], and *ō* [o]. It is hopeful to note in this connection that Gesell believes that "more commonly minimal injuries show a tendency toward resolution and even complete recovery." [25]

In other cases, multiple pinpoint lesions may be so subtle in their effect on the child's behavior that the parents are unaware of any defect except in speech. Although the results are inconclusive because of the small number tested, atypical brain waves similar to those of *petit mal* epilepsy were found in the encephalograms of a group of children with severely retarded speech. The deduction is that both *petit mal* epilepsy and speech retardation are present as a result of pinpoint lesions.

When the damage is restricted to the motor areas and pathways, it is called cerebral palsy. The speech of the cerebral-palsied may not be delayed in appearance, but the motor involvement certainly will make language learning and the acquisition of speech very difficult. (Chapter 15 is devoted to the speech of the cerebral-palsied.) In other instances the injury is confined to certain perception, elaboration, and projection areas in the brain. The resulting language impairments are known as aphasia and will be treated in Chapters 16, 17, and 18.

We indicated earlier the possibility of highly selected areas of injury affecting only the cranial motor nerves involved in speech (V [motor section], VII, IX, X, XI, XII). In Hans, five years old and retarded in speech, the injury was restricted and minimal. The mother reported that there was initial difficulty in feeding; the child's sucking and swallowing movements were weak and non-co-ordinated, but at two months of age he presented no further problem with feeding. The chief diagnostic sign was a general minimal dysarthria involving the tongue, larynx, and facial muscles. At five years his connected speech was limited in quantity and still was generally unintelligible, although single words and short phrases were quite clear.

Physiological Disorders not Related Directly to the Central Nervous System. Undoubtedly any physical disorder of considerable duration or in-

---

[25] Gesell and Amatruda, *op. cit.,* p. 247.

tensity that occurs during the developmental period in speech affects it adversely. We shall discuss here the general influence upon speech of any prolonged illness, and then consider briefly two groups of disorders which have been associated most frequently with speech retardation: virus diseases and endocrine disorders. Structural deviations of the speech mechanism that may cause speech retardation will then be discussed.

Ill Health. In our earlier discussion of the development of speech we noted that the infant progresses from stage to stage of speech maturity, crying, babbling, and echoing sounds of others before he begins to use words meaningfully. The onset of illness during the time when the child normally passes through these stages is likely to result in speech retardation. Babbling and lalling arise out of vocal play. Ill children lack the energy for such play and so in a very real sense miss the preliminary articulatory practice upon which verbal utterance is founded. The convalescent child usually continues from about where he left off in his speech progress, and before very long he will probably make up for lost time. The usual effect of a small child's illness is to impede, but not permanently to retard, speech development. Occasionally, if the illness is prolonged, there may be greater difficulty. The child who had already begun to use words before becoming sick, and who has had small use for words while sick because his every will was anticipated and satisfied, may still refuse to speak. Such a child will require careful motivation if his inertia in regard to the matter of speech is readily to be overcome. Another type of problem is presented by the child who normally would be using words but who was disturbed in his progress by illness. Such a child should not be expected to speak merely because he is of an age when most children speak. The vocal articulatory preliminaries should be encouraged and the need for speech established. When the child demonstrates that he is again capable of making and combining speech sounds, and is given experiences which will stimulate expression, the use of meaningful words should be expected and may be taught. Though parents may be temporarily embarrassed by having their three- or even four-year-old child indulge in babbling and lalling, they are apt to be even more embarrassed if they insist on the use of words for which the child is not prepared.

Virus Diseases. Children who suffer frequently from upper respiratory infections such as the common cold are more likely to be retarded in speech than children who are resistant to such infections.[26] It seems logical to suppose that the obstacles imposed by swollen membranes, disturbed respiration, and blocked nasal and pharyngeal resonators would deter any child from trying out his speech instrument. The second reason is that the system is so weakened by frequent virus attacks that the body does not have suffi-

---

[26] R. E. Beckey, "A Study of Certain Factors Related to Retardation of Speech," *Journal of Speech Disorders,* Vol. 7, No. 3 (1942), pp. 223-249.

Mildred F. Berry, "A Study of the Medical History of Stuttering Children," *Speech Monographs,* Vol. 5, No. 1 (1938).

cient energy to give to speech development. The third link between virus diseases and speech retardation relates to the possibility, mentioned earlier in this chapter, of their invasion of the central nervous system. It is thought that such virus diseases as measles (rubella), whooping cough, chicken pox, mumps, and pneumonia frequently enter and damage the nervous system. Some investigators limit the damage to the cerebrum; others believe that the destruction is limited to the peripheral nerves. In either case the injury would affect the neural circuits subserving the speech instrument. The fact that parents report frequently a cessation of all speech activity or a "change in speech development" after the child has had influenza, measles, or whooping cough suggests more than a coincidental link between speech retardation and virus diseases.

Endocrine Disorders. As you will remember from an earlier discussion (Chapter 4), the glands of internal secretion have three main functions: to stimulate growth, to influence metabolic activities, and to regulate the physical metamorphoses of children. Any disturbance of the processes of metabolism and growth will affect speech development as it affects all learning processes. Because the glands interact in the endocrine "ring," it is difficult to define metabolic dysfunction in terms of one gland. Because they also interact with the autonomic nervous system, it is difficult to restrict the action even to the endocrine system. Cretinism (endocrine dwarfism) has been associated primarily with severe thyroid deficiency, but it must be remembered that the thyroid is acted upon by the hypophysis, adrenal, gonadal, and other glands.

Although the glands have independent functions, they also work together. Deficiencies of thyroid, anterior pituitary (hypophysis), and adrenal hormones will produce some specific behavioral responses, but they also will yield effects in common, namely, a slow developmental rate; hypotonic, flaccid muscles; a low metabolic rate; subnormal levels of nervous irritability; and sluggish mentality.

The specific effect of hypothyroidism on speech development is seen in its extreme form in the infantile language, meager ideation and "thick-tongued," arhythmic speech of the cretin. Such cases are rare today because of the efficacy of thyroid medication, but mild hypothyroidism is not uncommon and may be detected by behavioral symptoms suggestive of cretinism.

Adrenalin (from the medulla or core of the adrenals) mimics the action of the autonomic nervous system; its secretion may well be identical with the secretion from autonomic nerves, the presence of which was demonstrated by Cannon and co-workers.[27] Since adrenalin speeds the heart, raises the blood-sugar level thereby providing energy for brain and muscles, and increases oxidation through its action on the thyroid gland, one sus-

[27] W. B. Cannon, "The Argument for Chemical Mediation of Nerve Impulses," *Science,* Vol. 90 (1939), pp. 521-527.

pects that the slow, poorly timed, and hypotonic muscular contractions of the speech muscles in some cases of retardation may be caused by latent adrenal deficiency.

The hypophysis or pituitary body is the spark plug of the endocrine system and thus will set the metabolic coefficient for the body by exercising a master control over all other glands. Among its many functions is that of stimulation of growth. A failure in speech maturation may be one manifestation of a failure in general maturation, for which the hypophysis is largely responsible.

If calcium metabolism, which is regulated by the parathyroid hormones, is subnormal, the irritability of the nervous system and particularly of its sympathetic division is increased. There is a special type of speech retardation in which articulation is unclear because muscular responses are so hurried as to be incomplete and non-co-ordinated. It is thought that parathyroid deficiency may account for this type of retardation.

More research is needed before positive statements can be made about the specific influence of endocrine deficiency on speech development. At present, research is confined largely to experiments on animals; extrapolations to man from such research are hazardous. It is safe to say only that dysfunction of the endocrine system will be reflected in aberrant speech development.

Structural Deviations of the Speech Mechanism. Whenever one ascribes articulation problems to a structural defect of the tongue or palate or jaw, some one will observe that the atypical organ is exactly like another child's who "has no defect in speech." It is well to repeat here that retarded speech is distinguished not by simplicity of causation but by its complexity. In the absence of other contributing causes, Joe may be able to compensate for the "tight tongue" or "undeveloped jaw" or "open bite." He also may have greater motivation, greater motor skill, and better intelligence with which to overcome the structural handicap than John who suffers from retarded speech. In John's case the structural deviation is the most important single handicapping factor.

We look, first of all, to the tongue. John does not have a tongue-tie (inability to extend the tongue beyond the lips), but the vertical fold of mucous membrane under the tongue, the frenulum, is so short as to make it impossible to point the tongue or raise the tip to the alveolar ridge. As a consequence, John is unable to produce any of the alveolar sounds: *t, d, n,* and *l.* Even more handicapping was Donald's tongue which was bound securely to the floor of the mouth, not by the frenulum alone but by other fascia which almost completely immobilized the body of the tongue. He was six years old when he entered the Rockford College Speech Center, and his speech was almost unintelligible. Surgery to mobilize the tongue was successful, and he now is able to make most alveolar sounds.

Another child, Cynthia, who has a repaired cleft palate, also has what might be called a cleft or bifid tongue. Brown and others have described the occurrence of this type of tongue in cleft-palate cases.[28] Cynthia's speech is peppered with distortions and substitutions which must be charged not against the cleft palate but against the tongue.

A second structural deviation is the undeveloped mandible also frequently associated with facial clefts.[29] Within one year the Rockford Center has had three cleft-palate children in whom the mandible was so underdeveloped at birth that the tongue had to be sutured to the cheek to prevent suffocation. One of these cases, Joan, has been reported in medical journals.[30] Joan's tongue, now normal in size, cannot be contained easily within the lower jaw and, as a consequence, all the front lingual consonants are distorted.

A third structural anomaly is an extremely high, narrow palatal vault. In many lingua-alveolar and lingua-palatal consonants the front tongue must obstruct the breath stream partially or completely by occlusion with the palate. If the palatal arch is very high and narrow, occlusion may be weak or absent. Gross structural deviations, cleft lip and palate, are discussed in a separate chapter (see Chapter 14).

Other structural deviations which probably play a part in speech retardation are dental malformations and "open bite" malocclusions.[31] The role of these anomalies in the speech development of the young child has not been established, but it seems reasonable to assume that the fricative sounds, *f, v, th* [θ], *th* [ð], *s,* and *z,* which are dependent for their acoustic properties on regular dental formation and occlusion would be affected by these deviations.

Finally, one might consider the presence of hypertrophied tonsils and adenoids to be structural deviations of a temporary nature. The writer had been skeptical of the influence of hypertrophied tonsils and adenoids on speech development until Robert, five years old, came to the Rockford Speech Center. Although he had not suffered from diseased tonsils according to his mother's report, his tonsils were so greatly enlarged as to press upon the posterior tongue and practically close the oropharyngeal aperture. Having ruled out other possible causes of the very poor speech, we are now con-

[28] G. V. I. Brown, *The Surgery of Oral and Facial Diseases and Malformation* (Philadelphia, Lea and Febiger, 1938), p. 482.

Mildred F. Berry, "Lingual Anomalies Associated with Palatal Clefts," *Journal of Speech and Hearing Disorders,* Vol. 14, No. 3 (1949), pp. 359-362.

[29] R. B. Stark, "The Pathogenesis of Hare Lip and Cleft Palate," *Plastic and Reconstructive Surgery,* Vol. 13, No. 1 (1954), pp. 20-39.

[30] S. Pruzansky and J. B. Richmond, "Growth of Mandible in Infants with Micrognathia," *American Journal of Diseases of Children,* Vol. 88 (July, 1954), pp. 29-42.

[31] G. Fairbanks and M. Lintner, "A Study of Minor Organic Deviations in 'Functional' Disorders of Articulation: 4. The Teeth and Hard Palate," *Journal of Speech and Hearing Disorders,* Vol. 16, No. 3 (1951), p. 278.

vinced that hypertrophied tonsils and adenoids can be a cause of serious retardation in speech.

Special Sensory Defects: Defects in Auditory Acuity, Discrimination, and Memory.[32] Good speech is dependent upon a sound hearing mechanism, but the full import of this statement is still to be explored. Speech is learned through hearing and imitating the speech of others. The peripheral mechanism of hearing, the cochlea, and the auditory section of the eighth cranial nerve must be intact for the reception of sound.[33] What parts of the central mechanism of hearing are essential to speech learning? Auditory nuclei in the medulla (ventral and dorsal cochlear nuclei), the midbrain (inferior colliculi), the medial geniculate body, the thalamus, and the auditory receptive areas in the temporal lobe of the cortex all have a role in the reception of the sound impulse. Apperceptive areas in the temporo-parietal lobes give meaning to the speech sounds received by the cochlea. But we cannot explain satisfactorily the neural basis for all the modalities of speech or sound reception and perception. What neural routes and areas, for example, are essential for the sense of discrimination between sounds? Is the recognition of pitch a cochlear function? How are differences in intensity perceived? Is perception of intensity a result, in part, of muscular tensions in the middle ear? These are questions for which we do not have the answers.

Loss in General Acuity. A general reduction in auditory power may be caused by an interruption at any one of these points along the hearing route: (1) The stimuli for sounds may not be transmitted adequately by the tympanum-ossicular chain mechanism to the oval window of the cochlea. (2) The cochlear section of the auditory nerve (cranial nerve VIII) which carries the auditory sensations from the cochlea to the cerebral cortex may be undeveloped or impaired so that either the vibrations in the cochlea do not stimulate the hair cells, the end organs of the cochlear nerve; or the sensations are not transmitted properly to the cerebrum. (3) The receptive areas in the temporal cortex of the cerebrum which receive the auditory sensations may be impaired or undeveloped. The determination of the type and degree of loss will be considered later in this chapter. A separate chapter is devoted to a discussion of the child severely handicapped in hearing (see Chapter 19). Here we are pointing out only marginal losses in acuity, sufficient to retard speech but not to characterize the child as deaf.

---

[32] H. Myklebust, who has done extensive work with delayed-speech children and with children with hearing disorders, categorizes their auditory disorders into four types: peripheral deafness, aphasia (cortical deafness), psychic deafness, and mental deficiency. In his manual, *Auditory Disorders in Children* (New York, Grune and Stratton, 1954), Myklebust describes each of the categories and presents case history, behavioral, and clinical test characteristics for evaluating the individual child and arriving at a differential diagnosis.

[33] Apparently hearing has bilateral representation in the cortex, and, therefore, one ear and one hemisphere only need be intact.

Auditory Imperception. Some children who appear to be able to hear and who respond appropriately to non-speech sounds, nevertheless fail to develop speech. In studying the early prelingual sound development of this kind of child where reliable parental recollections were available, the child is described as having babbled and repeated sounds he made as an infant. He may even have repeated a few words such as *mamma* and *papa* and *baby*. His vocal tones seem normal, so that hearing loss is not suspected. Pure tone testing, if the child is co-operative and permits testing, or psychogalvanic testing may well show a normal audiogram. Yet the child does not learn to speak. He seems able to understand very little of what he hears, and in many respects appears to behave like a child with severe hearing loss. One important difference can be discerned between this type of child and the child with severe peripheral hearing loss. The difference is in the child's own voice characteristics. His voice is like that of the child who can hear, and who normally learns to speak, rather than like that of the severely hard-of-hearing or deaf child whose voice is characteristically non-melodious and poorly modulated.

Several explanations may be offered for the child who seems to hear but does not normally learn to speak. One is that the child may have an island or islands of hearing loss in the middle and upper parts of the speech frequency range. The child can hear voices, and hear and recognize some of the sounds of speech, but does not hear or cannot discriminate many other sounds. Consonants generally have a higher frequency than vowels and are the components which make speech meaningful and intelligible. Afflicted with a loss of 30 to 40 decibels in the middle and upper frequency range, the child has little chance of imitating successfully the speech of others. Speech sounds vary in frequency from 1000 to 8000 double vibrations per second; those of greatest importance fall in the area from 1000 to 3000 double vibrations. *s* and *sh* [ʃ], for example, have frequencies ranging up to 8000 or 10,000 d.v. The measurement of speech reception is complicated, moreover, by the fact that one does not hear speech sounds—vowels, consonants, and glides—as independent units. Cues to perception reside, in part, in the transitional changes which consonants produce upon adjacent vowels. In the continuous flow of speech it may be these kinematic or transitional changes which provide the strongest cues to perception. Other changes may be associated with duration, phonetic power, inflection, and fundamental frequency of the sounds which cannot be measured in absolute units but will vary with the context. One cannot say, therefore, that the ability to hear isolated sounds is always an accurate measure of one's ability to hear these sounds in the connected flow of speech.[34] At any rate, this child afflicted by islands of loss in hearing can at best achieve only a partial understanding of speech, and the amount of understanding is not sufficient for the child to

[34] J. F. Curtis and G. E. Peterson, "Systematic Research in Experimental Phonetics," *Journal of Speech and Hearing Disorders,* Vol. 19, No. 2 (1954), pp. 147-169.

learn to imitate and produce oral speech. He may learn gestures, and he may develop a fairly good gesture language. Without special instruction, however, he may be indefinitely delayed in learning oral speech.

Another possibility is that there is a delay in maturation of the acoustic nerve (cranial nerve VIII) which subserves hearing. Normally, the period of its most rapid myelinization is the latter part of the first and the early part of the second year of life,[35] but some investigators report that myelinization of the cochlear branch may be delayed until the third or fourth year.

Closely allied to the problem of general acoustic reception is that of discriminating between consonant sounds. Unlike other sensory modalities—taste, pressure, or pain—which permit great individual variability, acoustic sensation must be sufficiently acute to enable one to distinguish between closely related sounds. The child who is not able to perceive the difference between the consonants *t* and *th* [θ], for example, will continue to say "tumb" for "thumb" unless he is trained in some approach other than auditory discrimination. A disability in sound discrimination is most noticeable in the high-frequency or consonant sounds. Since consonants rather than vowels are the determinants of word intelligibility, a serious defect in consonant-sound discrimination is a deterrent to speech learning.

Another explanation for some children with auditory imperception is that much of what they hear is heard only on the level of sensation. That is, the child hears sounds physically but, possibly because of incomplete or atypical cortical development, *cannot interpret what he hears.* These children may be said to have cortical or sensory aphasia. It is likely that in time, perception and evaluation of what is heard becomes complete. If the child does not become negatively inclined toward speech while "waiting for cortical maturation," hearing for speech and speech itself may become normal. If, however, the child is pressured into learning to speak before he is neurologically and psychologically ready for it, negative attitudes may develop and delay may become prolonged.

A third and related possibility is that a child may not be able to identify himself with the adult members of his environment, and may become psychologically deaf to their speech. Auditory imperception is then functional rather than organic. Such a child may continue to be resistant to speech learning unless his environment is changed, or unless the personalities of the adults are modified so that identification becomes possible. We have treated such children who had previously been variously diagnosed as being deaf, aphasic, and schizophrenic. One such child spoke no words, but was able to repeat melodies and vocalize like a hearing child. He was also able to reproduce, through a succession of vowel sounds, the melody pattern (inflections and intonation) of American speech. This was of special significance because both of the child's parents spoke English with a marked German

[35] B. M. Patten, *Human Embryology* (Philadelphia, Blakiston, 1946), p. 399.

accent. Because the child did imitate American rather than German speech melody, we thought that it was possible that the child was negating German as a dynamism for rejecting his parents. Ultimately, the child was placed in an American nursery school, and the parents, after considerable resistance, accepted the need for psychotherapy. Within a few months, the child learned to speak.

It is entirely possible that this child had an organic imperception for speech sounds when early attempts were made to teach him to speak. His inability to learn, and his parents' inability to accept failure to speak when the child was past two years old, may have created an attitude which made normal speech development difficult. The frustration of not being able to do what was expected may have produced a continued psychological deafness when imperception per se was no longer present. In a large measure, improper teaching methods on the part of the parents were responsible for continued speech delay. This cause of delayed speech will be considered in somewhat greater detail later.

Short Auditory Memory Span. Not infrequently, a child is brought to a speech clinic because of retarded speech and upon examination is found to have an abnormally short auditory memory span. The child may be able to repeat one or two speech sounds with a fair degree of accuracy, but be unable to repeat several successively presented speech sounds, or he may be able to repeat several sounds immediately upon hearing them, but fail to do so if delay is introduced before he is permitted to respond. His attempts to reproduce connected speech that he has heard results only in "verbal hash." A ten-year-old child, despite a year of re-training, still says "tapetoes and gavery" for "potatoes and gravy," "pip it uk" for "pick it up," and "my dloy" for "my dolly." Such a child may have a vocabulary consisting almost entirely of monosyllabic and disyllabic words, not all of them necessarily conventional or readily recognizable words, but they will be in general keeping with the child's memory span.

A short auditory memory span is likely to be associated with reading and spelling as well as speech disability. As a result, the child all too frequently presents a picture which is mistaken for mental retardation. This faulty impression is strengthened if a verbal intelligence test is administered. Experimental evidence does not support the supposition that there is a significant positive relationship between auditory memory span and intelligence. Anderson [36] found that "correlation values, when memory span is compared with measures of intelligence, are inclined to run low." Metraux [37] found no significant correlation between mental age and auditory memory span for vowels and consonants at any age for children between the ages of four

[36] V. A. Anderson, "Auditory Memory Span as Tested by Speech Sounds," *American Journal of Psychology,* Vol. 52 (1939), pp. 95-99.

[37] Ruth W. Metraux, "Auditory Memory Span for Speech Sounds: Norms for Children," *Journal of Speech Disorders,* Vol. 9 (1944), pp. 31-38.

years, six months and twelve years, five months. Most such children can be trained to increase their auditory memory span and to retain auditory memories long enough to learn to speak, though they may perhaps be slow in using polysyllabic words or long sentences. Association of auditory impressions with the visual or kinesthetic may help the child to learn to speak, even if it does not directly remedy the basic cause for initial retardation.

Unfavorable Speech Environment

Lack of Motivation. A child cannot be expected to speak unless there is some reason for him to want to speak. There must be some motivation for him to change from his infantile, prelingual way of getting responses from and responding to his environment to the more conventionalized and mature way of accomplishing his ends. Obviously, if the use of pantomime and an assortment of grunts and groans constitute an adequate medium of expression for the child, and enable him to get along satisfactorily in his environment, he has no need for any other type of speech. A child may even develop a complex system of pantomime and unconsciously train those persons who are more frequently around him in the use of his visible language. Because he has got along quite well so far, there is no particular reason for trying anything new. One boy of six had not only not begun to use words, but had not even bothered to develop much pantomime. He was the only child of intelligent and well-educated parents. But in his home also lived a maiden aunt and his grandparents. It was quickly admitted by the mother that the relatives vied with one another in finding out what the child might want, and in doing it for him before the want was expressed. The boy had almost no use for speech, except as a way of removing the hovering anticipators from his presence, and for this a few violent cries and gestures sufficed. There are occasions, of course, when a child's wishes and needs should be anticipated. One cannot always wait for a sick child to make verbal announcements. But anticipation should stop when the child is well, and at no time should a child be permitted to feel that there is more value in not talking than in talking.

Caution should be exercised in motivation, and expectations should not exceed the child's capabilities. Vocabulary growth is not a continuous process. The small child, we recall, learns to say a few words, and then stops for a time. If the anxious parents urge too hard and expect too much, if they refuse to recognize all grunts and pantomime because a few words have been spoken, and if they compel verbal imitation, the child may acquire an attitude toward speaking which is neither pleasant nor mentally healthy. It is not easy to learn to speak. The new motor and mental skills are acquired with difficulty by the mature adult learning a foreign language. For the small child, oral speech is foreign both in manner and content.

The use and extension of verbal speech should be nurtured by appropriate rewards and encouragement. The child should be made to feel that oral speech is worth while because it has greater value for him. Thus, the child will be motivated to use it as much as he can. However, a child should not be suddenly and completely ignored in his attempts to convey his wants by his early speech means if his oral speech is still inadequate.

Some children, according to parents' reports, begin to speak and then "just stop." Not infrequently it will be found that the children who made a start at speech and then stopped were expected to speak with adult proficiency, and were not afforded the attention they previously were given before they used their first words. Such children may very well have decided that adult standards of speech were too much for them. Rather than subject themselves to criticism for not speaking well, they may give up the business of speaking as not quite worth the effort involved. Aspiration levels of adults should not be imposed on children, for whom speech and speaking is an experimental endeavor to be continued or dropped, for a time at least, if ready *over-all satisfaction is not obtained*. It should, however, be realized that maturation in general frequently progresses in steps and plateaus. During the plateau periods a considerable amount of integration of specific skills and habits into total behavior patterns takes place. The steps and plateaus may resemble "starts" and "stops." It is likely, however, that each "stop" is a period of incorporation of gains to make the next "start" possible.

Silent Environment. Some parents do not realize that a "talking environment" is necessary if the child is to learn to talk. Every child needs to hear his own trial sounds reproduced and refined, but he also needs to hear the normal speech patterns of adults. If the only speech that he hears is "baby talk," one may expect him to establish infantile patterns, and once they are established, to use them far beyond the normal period, since he has not been made aware in the speech-learning period of adult patterns. An even more undesirable situation is for the child to hear little or no speech. Although it seems incredible, one mother reported that she rarely talked to her child. "Both her father and I are the silent type," she admitted. "We rarely talk to her or to each other!" In investigating the home environment of a large group of speech-retarded children, Schiefelbusch found that these children had "little or no stimulation to talk," that the methods used in teaching them to talk were less adequate, and that parental absenteeism was much more common than in the control group.[38]

Poor Teaching Techniques. Early in the text it was pointed out (see Chapter 3) that in the child's initial speech stages, he imitates his own sound (lalling) and then begins to imitate sounds of the members of his environment (echolalia). The first real word that the child uses is one which is a direct imitation or a reasonable facsimile of a single- or double-syllable word which he hears in his environment. At this stage, direct parental teaching effort should take the form of reinforcing the word the child has used.

[38] Schiefelbusch, *op. cit.*

That means that a quick, pleasurable response in keeping with the word used by the child is in order. If the child has said "da" and looks toward his doll, then the doll should be given to him. This is not a time for the parent to explain to the child that "daddy" is "da," and the toy is "doll." Neither is it the time to begin to establish new words, and to announce an indefinite series of names about pictures, objects, people, places, and things. *After the child has demonstrated that he has learned a few words of his own choosing,* the parent may introduce a new word, made up of sounds that the child has used, and naming an object or person or action the child needs or enjoys. Thus, words such as *up* and *down* may be introduced in association with appropriate action. Specifically, if the child reaches from his crib or play pen to be picked up, the parent should then say "up" while the child is being picked up.

It is of great importance for parents to remember that children, in vocal play, produce many sounds and combinations which resemble words. That does not mean that the child is speaking, and that the parents have a right to expect repetition of such "word-resembling sounds." Children, even very bright ones, rarely begin to use real words before a year of age, and *most* not before fifteen to eighteen months. The child who senses that his parents are displeased with his failure to speak is much more likely to stop talking than he is to continue speech efforts.

Finally, parents should remember that children do not learn a few new words each day, in the manner of the well-regulated adult who undertakes to enrich his vocabulary. The small child learns in spurts. He takes time to secure what he has learned before trying to acquire new words. If, in the meantime, he undertakes a new skill such as walking or feeding himself with a spoon, speech learning may seem to mark time. The child seems to work on the principle that one skill at a time is enough. During these apparent plateaus of learning, the parents must learn to exercise patience, and be grateful for what speech the child continues to use.

Failure of Identification. For a child to wish to speak, he must first be able to identify himself with a speaking person who loves (accepts) him. The speaking person with whom identification is most frequently made is usually a parent. If parents are otherwise too occupied, or for some reason unable to attend to their children, and engage a nurse to do the job for them, the child may make the identification with the nurse if she loves (accepts) the child and attends to him beyond merely satisfying his basic biological needs. Many children demand attention, and will disturb the environment if attention is not given them. Some children make no such demands, or stop making them when their demands are not satisfied. Some nurses find these "good children" easy to care for, and some parents are content to keep a nurse engaged for their "good children." The result for some of these children is verbal isolation. They do not hear speech, they are bathed only in tepid water but not with warm words, and they do not associate sound-making with pleasure. Their own pleasure in making sounds diminishes at the beginning of the second year. They require adult acceptance and approval to continue sound-making and to progress from lalling to echolalia and from echolalia to true speech.

Occasionally children present histories which indicate that their speech development was normal up to a given time and then came to a rather sudden halt. Cases are reported in speech clinics of children who stopped talking after their fathers left home for military service, or for extended business trips. It may well be that in such cases the child identified himself with the father. With the father away, identification and speech are disturbed. Children sometimes stop talking when their parents are divorced. Here both the emotional turbulence in a home in which a divorce is imminent, as well as the separation from a parent with whom the child has identified himself, may contribute to the child's disturbance in speech development.

Unfavorable Parental Attitudes and Personality Traits. For the young child, undesirable relationships of persons in his home, and the manner in which these relationships are expressed, may be directly responsible for speech delay. If speech is used as an expression of anger, if the older members of a home are constantly angry, or sound as if they are angry, or irritable, or annoyed with one another, speech may become associated with these unpleasant attitudes. For the young child, avoidance of speech may be his device for avoiding unpleasantness. His attitude might be verbalized as "These people talk, and are constantly unhappy. If I don't bother to talk, at least not the way the grownups do, then maybe I will keep out of trouble." The authors have interviewed several mothers who reported that their children stopped talking when the parents were overtly quarrelling.

There are other sources of family tension produced by the child's speech retardation which increase his speech problems. In an investigation at the community speech clinic affiliated with Queens College, it was found that the parents of children with retarded speech tended to be *unrealistic, rigid, and overprotective.* The mothers tended to be so to a greater degree than the fathers. Similar findings were made by Pekarsky [39] who compared a group of twenty-six mothers of children with delayed speech and a control group of mothers of children with normal speech. Taken as a group, the mothers of the delayed-speech children were found to be "overprotective, rigid individuals who are restrictive in their demands upon their children." The home environment was reported to be characterized by "confusion, tension, and a lack of organization in the performing of routine tasks." Although these traits and attitudes were not absent in the homes of the mothers with normal-speaking children, they were generally found to be present in more moderate degrees.

Rejection is another attitude which parents sometimes exhibit toward a

[39] A. Pekarsky, *Maternal Attitudes Toward Children with Psychogenically Delayed Speech.* Ph.D. Thesis, New York University, School of Education, 1952.

speech-retarded child. It is unlikely that many parents have conscious wishes to reject their children. But children have no insight into what is disturbing parents who are highly critical of them, who demand a degree of perfection of performance for which the children have no need and capacity. Children are likely to respond to such parental attitudes as rejection. They are not able to understand, as some adults rationalize, that not they but their efforts are being rejected. If parental rejection is conscious, the child is quick to become aware of it. If his speech efforts are ignored, or criticized when not ignored, the child is likely to stop talking, or to continue to talk in an infantile manner.

Rejection on a level which is conscious or close to conscious is not infrequently found in cases where children have physical abnormalities. It is understandable if not entirely excusable that the parents of a child born with a crippling condition or a facial disfigurement should wonder, "Why did this have to happen to us?" The effect of this attitude on the child is likely to be drastic. The child cannot escape from himself, or from the unfavorable reactions of persons in his environment. Withdrawal, and with it a cessation of speech, may be a direct result.

Unrealistic Aspiration Levels. Occasionally we find that parents of children with deformities set about to compensate to the children in the form of continuous instruction and training in the hope of establishing superior ability. This may explain the hypercritical behavior of the parent. Unfortunately, these educational efforts may begin too early for some children, and constitute but one more obstacle for the child to overcome. In a very important sense, the overcritical parents are ones whose aspiration levels are unrealistic. They expect more than their children can achieve. They refuse or are reluctant to accept what their children can produce, and dissatisfaction is general. Frequently, these parents manifest unrealistic aspiration levels for aspects of behavior other than speech. For example, the parents of the delayed-speech children in the Queens College study revealed disappointment that their children were not toilet trained, or did not begin to walk or feed themselves as early as they thought proper. The parental expectations exceeded those of the established norms of the Vineland Social Maturity Scale. Occasionally, parents (mothers) succeed in establishing early bladder or bowel control. An associated result of this control may be speech delay. Speech is one activity over which a child has his own control. He may produce or not produce. Unfortunately, because speech is a skill which requires practice for improvement, the child who chooses for a time not to produce speech may be delayed in speech when he becomes motivated and ready to speak.

These attitudes of rigidity, rejection, and unrealistic aspirations will produce emotional tension and maladjustment in the child just as surely as will open strife and turmoil in the home. Our observations have been reinforced by McCarthy, who concludes after commenting on emotional insecurity produced by disturbed family relationships: "The home atmosphere as determined by the personalities of the parents seems to be the most important single factor influencing the child's acquisition of language." [40]

Influence of Siblings. Retarded speech has also been ascribed to the presence of substandard speech among siblings and close associates in the home. A younger child in a family where an older sibling has distorted speech is likely to be handicapped, but it is difficult to determine in such a case whether imitation of a poor model or developmental factors common to both siblings is the true cause. Irwin reports that the presence of older siblings does not affect materially the speech development of the younger siblings in the family. [41]

Another type of sibling influence which Irwin does not consider is the psychological effect of the advent of a younger sibling. The birth of a baby, for whom the older child may or may not have been prepared, is sometimes associated with delay, and occasionally with regression, in speech development. The new baby naturally becomes the center of attention and effort in the home. The new baby, a crying, non-talking child, literally "steals the show" from the older child. The latter, in the hope of winning back some of the lost attention and what he believes to be lost affection, may emulate and imitate the ways of the "usurper." Not infrequently we find that immediately older children who have not become too firmly established in speech proficiency regress to infantile talk, and sometimes refuse to talk. Other manifestations of regression may accompany the resumption of baby ways. Children who have been toilet trained may have accidents. Children who have learned how to handle their spoons and forks and to feed themselves may insist on being fed. It helps mothers not at all to tell such children that "only babies are fed; big children feed themselves." This unwitting remark merely emphasizes what the older children are trying to point out to their parents. Life was happier when there were no babies, no rivals who are successful because of their very helplessness.

Twins. Closely allied to the question of sibling influence is the influence of twinning upon speech development. Twinning creates a special environmental influence which seems to be disadvantageous for speech-learning and language development. Twins begin to speak later than do single children and are significantly retarded, at least until the age of six, in their ability to produce sounds correctly. [42] The speech of twins is characterized by substitutions and distortions of sounds for a much longer period than that of single siblings. Consonants are often omitted so that speech may be difficult to comprehend. Consonant substitutions such as *w* for *r*, *d* for *th* [ð] and *t*

[40] Dorothea A. McCarthy, "Language Disorders and Parent-Child Relationships," *Journal of Speech and Hearing Disorders,* Vol. 19, No. 4 (1954), pp. 514-523.

[41] Irwin, *op. cit.,* p. 272.

[42] E. A. Davis, *The Development of Linguistic Skill in Twins, Singletons with Siblings, and Only Children from Age 5-10 Years* (Minneapolis, University of Minnesota Press, 1937).

or *th* [θ] for *s* are frequent. It is not clear whether the speech retardation of twins can be accounted for entirely or even largely on an environmental basis. From an environmental point of view, one can conclude that because twins are so much more in one another's company than single children, they are constantly being exposed to a mutually poor linguistic environment. Furthermore, twins understand each other's speech however defective it may be. Frequently they develop special words (idioglossia) or gestures which serve adequately as instruments for their own communication, but which are unlike those used by other persons around them. Because twins understand each other fairly well, their need for being understood by others is not as great as that of single children. With a decreased need for conventional speech, there is a smaller chance of getting twins to speak well. However, although "social isolation" among twins may account for some language retardation, the deleterious effect on language development attributed to twins' preferential use of a "secret language" appears to be overstressed.

There is considerable research, however, to support the view that physiological factors may account for the speech retardation of twins. These investigators believe that atypical neural organization or neural impairment makes the control of the function of speech a later and more difficult acquisition than it is with single siblings.[43] Karn states that multiple births are distinguished by an excessive incidence of prematurity and birth traumas.[44] This report is substantiated by Zazzo, who ascribes a part of the over-all difference in the IQ's of twins and singletons to biological factors such as the increased prematurity rate in twins, their lower weight at birth, and the higher maternal age.[45] Although the exact cause of the IQ deficit in twins is not readily apparent at this time, Lorimer suggests in a longitudinal psychometric study of British school children that adverse conditions of gestation and birth might frequently result in relatively inconspicuous impairments of cerebral structures and intellectual function.[46] Both physiological and environmental causes probably should be considered for a complete explanation of the retarded speech development of twins.

Bilingualism. The influence of a bilingual environment is a possible cause of retarded speech. The effect of bilingualism is not always directly measurable because of its association and inter-relationship with other fac-

[43] Mildred F. Berry, "Twinning in Stuttering Families," *Human Biology*, Vol. 9, No. 3 (1937), pp. 329-347.

[44] R. Luchsinger, "Die Sprachentwicklung von ein- und zweieiigen Zwillingen und die Vererbung von Sprachstörungen," *Acta Geneticae Medicae et Gemellologiae*, Vol. 2 (1953), pp. 31-48.

[45] R. Zazzo, "Situation gémellaire et développmentale," *Journal de Psychologie Normale et Pathologique*, Vol. 45 (1952), pp. 208-227.

[46] F. Lorimer, "Trends in Capacity for Intelligence," *Eugenics News*, Vol. 37 (1952), pp. 17-24.

tors. Many bilingual children come from homes with limited economic and educational advantages. For such children, it is possible that the languages to which they are exposed are not as well spoken as in monolingual homes. Even in homes where the economic and occupational level are average or above, bilingual influence seems to have an adverse effect on speech development. Smith,[47] for example, studied Honolulu children who ranged in age from thirty-seven to seventy-seven months. The children spoke both Chinese and English. Smith found that the children had below-average-sized vocabularies in either Chinese or English. Even when the vocabularies of the two languages were added together, only two-fifths of the children exceeded the norms for monolingual children. Smith suggests that "only the superior bilingual child is capable of attaining the vocabulary norms of monoglots and that a name for a large number of concepts is more desirable than two names for many of a smaller number of concepts."

Bilingual influences, except possibly for the superior child, necessitate constant adjustments which make the learning of one language a difficult task. The child must exert special effort to maintain himself in a given linguistic groove. If the effort becomes excessive, emotionality may result which is likely to interfere with further language learning. Wherever possible, therefore, it is advised that the young child be exposed only to the influence of the language which will become his educational tool. The young superior child may not be adversely affected by bilingual influence. The judgment of superiority, however, is usually difficult to make unless the child has made considerable progress in a language. As a general procedure, therefore, we recommend that a preschool child be exposed only to one language.

Emotional Disturbances in the Child

Excessive Emotionality. Without an adequate and commonly accepted means of adjustment, children with delayed speech are likely to develop into frustrated, overemotional individuals. The writers have observed that such children frequently resort to temper displays when their efforts to communicate are not understood. Their excessive and continued dependence on a few persons, usually members of their family, for the satisfaction of their needs, prevents children with delayed speech from gaining a proper degree of independence as they mature. These children cling to their parents in the clinic, so that there is frequently great difficulty in initiating speech therapy. Even when speech begins to be established, the habits of overdependence so long maintained are not readily broken. Their behavior is characterized by undue emotionality, temper tantrums, and excessive motor activity.

[47] M. E. Smith, "Measurement of Vocabularies of Young Bilingual Children in Both of the Languages Used," *Journal of Genetic Psychology*, Vol. 74 (1949), pp. 305-310.

Emotional Immaturity. Occasionally, the child's history reveals that the speech retardation is one aspect of a picture of general emotional immaturity. One seven-and-a-half-year-old boy of better than average intelligence was from early infancy a definite feeding problem; negativistic tendencies and a constant demanding of attention were noted in his examination. In addition, he demonstrated a sibling-rivalry pattern in regard to his younger brother. In fact, during his examination he betrayed considerable anxiety lest his younger brother, who had also been examined, might have achieved a better score on the intelligence test than he. The child's speech displayed the same immaturity as his general behavior. He elided and substituted sounds, his sentences were crudely constructed along infantile lines, and he resorted frequently to the use of gesture.

Emotional Disturbance Following Physical Trauma. Sometimes children stop talking or retrogress in speech following specific incidents of physical trauma. We have seen several children whose parents reported normal development of speech up to the time when they were involved in accidents. One five-year-old child, for example, who had begun to speak at the age of two, stopped speaking after his mouth was injured when a playmate struck the toy horn which he was blowing.

Accidental injuries do not always have to involve the speech mechanism to disturb speech. One child whom we saw in the clinic was struck by an automobile when he was seven years old. He stopped oral talking when he was hospitalized, and did not resume talking, except for brief periods immediately before holidays associated with gifts. During the two years of non-oral speech, the boy developed a detailed system of gestures by which he made all his wants known.

The dynamics which result in speech cessation following trauma cannot always be discovered. It is possible that in some instances the accidents and injuries are associated with feelings of guilt on the part of the child. Where the organs of articulation are injured, the direct association with speech can be understood. If the child was playing with a prohibited toy, or putting a toy into his mouth despite parental warnings to the contrary, the child may stop talking in order not to have to confess his guilt. Sometimes the displays of attention and affection given the child are unsagaciously associated in a cause-and-effect relationship with not talking. The child may not wish to risk resumption of speech for fear that he will lose attention, be expected to "confess," or both. In some instances the disturbance of speech in the young child is comparable to hysterical disturbances, in speech or in other functions, in the adult.

Negativism. An attitude of extreme negativism may be responsible for interference in normal speech development. This attitude may be a general characteristic of the behavior of the child or may be directed toward particular persons responsible for his speech training. If negativism is a general characteristic, it will be manifest in other aspects of behavior besides speech.

A thorough analysis of the child's emotional life and his relationships with persons in his environment will help to make this clear. If the negativism is directed toward particular persons, it is probably a product of conflict or unhappiness associated with these persons. A child who has had an unhappy school experience may refuse to talk, just as he may resist learning to read, to write, or to do arithmetic. A scolding by a teacher, or any unfair treatment, real or imagined, suffered by the child and associated with the teacher, may set off an attitude of negativism which interferes with further learning. Because instruction in the early school grades is largely in the language field, difficulty with speech is not an unlikely result.

It is not always possible, however, to trace or attribute the emotional disturbances of the child to the parents, or to some other members of the family or household. Frequently, on the basis of what the clinician is able to learn, the parents seem to be well adjusted and the home a well-ordered one, parental expectations are reasonable and proper, and the child is both wanted and loved. Despite this home background, some children reach and go beyond the age of speech expectancy and still do not speak.

Autism. In some instances, the emotional disturbances of children become manifest in a withdrawal or a detachment from their environment. In its most extreme form, the detachment may be so complete that the child seems not to be able to hear and may be diagnosed as having peripheral deafness.[48] What seems to have happened, however, is that the child, in his need to withdraw from a threatening world, has ceased to listen, so that hearing nothing, he will have nothing to fear. Myklebust designates this type of child as one who has psychic deafness. Psychologists and psychiatrists are likely to diagnose the child as suffering from *primary* (infantile) *autism* or from childhood schizophrenia.

The child with primary or infantile autism is one who shows atypical emotional development from infancy. The autistic child may reach the age of five or six without ever speaking, and with apparently a very limited comprehension of the language of his environment. He seems also to show little need for a substitute for oral language, and so is not likely to develop a gesture system in the manner of a deaf child. His wants are likely to be met by direct action. If he cannot take what he wants, he uses an adult to extend his reach. So, the child may take an adult's hand and walk with him to the desired object rather than attempt to communicate his wish through gestures.

The autistic child, unlike many other emotionally disturbed children, shows little affection or dependency on any adults. A clinician can separate such a child from his parents without fear of havoc in the clinic. He will accept anybody's hand because he seems to require no particular hand.

The autistic child is not likely to respond to sound, especially to human

[48] See H. Myklebust, *Auditory Disorders in Children* (New York, Grune and Stratton, 1954), Ch. 7.

sounds. Sometimes, however, he will make a more or less appropriate response, except that it will be delayed. For example, such a child may do nothing, and show no awareness of having heard a direction such as "Pick up the ball." He may continue to seem not to hear subsequent directions to do other things after his failure to "pick up the ball." But after a lapse of time in which the clinician may no longer remember that anything was said about a ball, the child may walk over to it, and pick it up and possibly even say "ball." This may be done in a manner completely impassive, as if the child were an automaton carrying out a direction about which he had no feeling and which had no meaning for him. Sometimes a child will echo sounds or words he hears without doing anything ordinarily associated with such sounds or words. At other times the sounds seem to be "stored" for future production. Kanner characterizes this tendency as "delayed echolalia." [49]

Although autistic children do not use words, they may occasionally use voice. Except that pitch and volume may show greater extremes than for other children of their age, their voices are not characteristically different from those of normal children. Vocalizations, however, may be produced as if the children had no part in the production. The vocalizations will also be apparently unrelated to what the children may be doing, or to what other children around them may be doing. Observing them, we would have to conclude that the verbalizations of autistic children are related to their private, inner worlds rather than to the external world which surrounds them but does not seem to affect them.

Occasionally an autistic child may use a particular object in an atypical way. For example, he may use a wood block as a doll, even though a doll may be available. One delayed-speech child diagnosed as having primary autism insisted on using the steps of the Queens College Speech Clinic as his place for a nap. His clinician was instructed not to argue the wisdom of his choice with him, but to provide him with a small pillow and cover him with a blanket whenever the child decided it was time for a nap. By doing this, we hoped that the clinician might get a toe into the child's private world, even if the child refused to enter the more commonly populated world of the clinician.

Kanner, in his *Child Psychiatry*,[50] describes the early history of a group of 39 children who were diagnosed as having *early infantile autism*. Most of the children were first believed either to be feeble-minded or to have a severe hearing loss. The "common denominator in all these patients is a disability to relate themselves in the ordinary way to people and situations from the beginning of life." Their parents describe them as being "self-

[49] L. Kanner, *Child Psychiatry*, 2nd ed. (Springfield, Thomas Publishing Company, 1946), p. 717.
[50] *Ibid.*, pp. 716-721.

sufficient," or behaving as if "in a shell" or as if "other people weren't there."

A second common denominator, according to Kanner, is that "there is a great deal of obsessiveness in the family background." Further, says Kanner, "In the whole group there are very few really warmhearted fathers and mothers. For the most part the antecedents and collaterals are persons strongly pre-occupied with abstractions of a scientific, literary or artistic nature and limited in a genuine interest in people." [51]

Most children with primary autism acquire speech. Sometimes, however, linguistic structure is bizarre, and is used more for self-expression than for conventional communication. Many autistic children have apparently better than normal ability for rote and serial language content and for echolalic reproductions of word forms. They may be able to hum or even sing songs, recite the alphabet, or memorize verse. They may, frequently in a delayed-response fashion, echo long words, phrases, or sentences. They are not likely, however, to show any affect appropriate to the language they are evoking. Communicative language, when employed, is likely to consist of single-word utterances to identify objects or actions.

About half of the children diagnosed as having primary autism and who had no communicative language began to speak after a period of from one to two years as members of a delayed-speech group at the Queens College Speech Clinic. From our experience, these children differed from those who failed to develop speech mostly in regard to their parents' willingness to accept the diagnosis of emotional disturbance and to receive guidance for themselves as well as for their children. The following closing note on one of the children who attended the Queens College Speech Clinic suggests the nature of the improvement as well as the continued needs of the child:

R. is now substantially less withdrawn. He is using speech to communicate his needs and to establish non-physical contacts with other children. He calls the clinician by name, in contrast with his earlier use of the same name for all clinicians. He stays with the group for the entire period and no longer separates himself by asserting "good-night" after a few minutes in the play room. He now rests on a floor rug rather than on the steps leading to the Clinic. He still repeats phrases, and responds to verbal commands with delayed behavior, but the time between the command and the response has become sharply reduced. R. now plays with other children. He will catch and return a ball and will allow himself to be pulled in a cart. He will ask for help when unable to complete a task. This represents a marked improvement over his earlier need to be by himself and to leave or destroy the results of an unfinished effort. He is no longer preoccupied with bathroom activities. He apparently enjoys finger paints, presently preferring green or red rather than black which was for months the only acceptable paint.

[51] *Ibid.,* p. 720.

SUMMARY

In this chapter we have presented a profile which distinguishes the child whose speech is retarded in onset or development. After reviewing the normal development of speech, we defined the characteristics of retarded speech. Many specific etiological factors have been discussed at length under the general classifications of (a) organic deficiencies and disorders; (b) an unfavorable speech environment; and (c) emotional disturbances in the child. The list of causes is long, yet it is not exhaustive. Clinicians undoubtedly will meet cases of retarded speech for which no cause or group of causes listed here seems to be the right one. We still have much to learn about the child with retarded speech.

6

Testing the Child Retarded in Speech

In the preceding chapter we have presented many causes of retarded speech, recognizing that in general a complex of factors rather than a single cause will account for the retardation. Careful observation and testing are necessary if one is to evaluate correctly all the factors and their relative importance in the etiological complex.

STUDYING THE SPEECH PROFILE

Before we can answer the mother's question about Johnnie, we must ask her many questions about the child and his environment, observe his behavior and responses over a period of time, and secure an accurate record of his speech and language. We also will need complete data on his physical health; his intellectual status; his emotional maturity; his social adjustment; his neuromotor development as reflected in motor proficiency and laterality; and his auditory speech acuity, discrimination, and memory.

Good bookkeeping is necessary in careful observation. The Historical and Diagnostic Journal for Retarded Speech which has been reproduced completely in Appendix 4 is an outline of the data which we have found to be most valuable in studying cases of speech retardation. The outline also will serve as a review of the discussion of the preceding chapter.

EVALUATION OF SPEECH

Development of Speech Sounds

In this text will be found three useful tables for the determination of the child's normality with respect to his early development of speech. They are the Developmental Sequences of Language Behavior by Gesell, a Composite Schedule of the Emergence of Speech Sounds based on the work of several investigators, and the Table of the Genetic Development of Articulation of Consonant Sounds by Poole. The first two are included in Appendix 3; the last appears in Chapter 3, page 36.

Articulation and Language Proficiency

In testing the articulation of speech sounds, pictures, objects, and words are used most frequently to secure responses which will be indicative of the child's ability to produce each sound in all positions in the word. The therapist can construct satisfactory picture or object tests, providing the stimuli are classified so that they call forth verbal responses appropriate to the chronological age of the child. The word-responses also must be chosen on the basis of frequency of use and on frequency of error of sounds. The test must be organized so that each sound is presented in the initial, medial, and final position in the word. There are many published tests of articulation, but they often are too difficult to administer or they have not been standardized. Among those which have enjoyed wide use are the Blanton-Stinchfield Articulation Test,[1] the Bryngelson-Glaspey Picture Test,[2] the Templin Articulation Test,[3] and the Clark Picture Phonetic Inventory.[4] The Blanton-Stinchfield test presents 100 sounds with 100 test words and standardized pictures. Although widely used, the Bryngelson-Glaspey test presents some pictures calling for word responses not in the vocabulary of a young child. The Clark Picture Phonetic Inventory, like the preceding test, provides for the recording of sound substitutions, distortions, and omissions. Unlike other tests, the Clark Inventory presents for testing not only the consonants, but also vowels, diphthongs, and consonant combinations. The scoring is simple; it is based directly on the number of "critical sounds and sound-combinations" the child can produce correctly. A copy of the Clark Picture Phonetic Inventory test sheet and scoring directions is included in Appendix 3.

In any study of speech production, the best measure is probably a tape recording of the child's spontaneous and continuous speech from which a record of sound omissions, substitutions, and distortions can be made. A recording is also valuable in determining the degree of distortion of sounds. In any articulation test the examiner should indicate not only the presence of articulation errors but also the degree of misarticulation. Sounds mildly distorted are graded plus 1; clearly distorted, plus 2; and severely distorted, plus 3. Further information is provided in a tape recording of the frequency of occurrence of the distorted sounds in the child's speech. Finally, a recording permits one to study other characteristics—such as voice, rhythm, and rate—which are important in understanding the complete speech profile.

A projective device to determine the order of correction of sounds in a

---

[1] Published by the C. H. Stoelting Company, Chicago.
[2] Published by Scott, Foresman and Company, Chicago.
[3] From the *Journal of Speech Disorders*, Vol. 12 (1947), pp. 392-396.
[4] Published by the Communication Foundation, Ltd., Box 8865, University Park Station, Denver.

given case is the Stimulability Test.[5] In this test, multiple stimulation (seeing, hearing, feeling) of the sound is presented to the child, following which he is asked to imitate the sound. The examiner notes the sounds to which the child responds easily and well and which are therefore most amenable to correction, those which are only modified by multiple stimulation, and those which are not changed at all.

The chief indices of language development are two: vocabulary and sentence length. The vocabulary of children has been studied extensively from both a quantitative and a qualitative point of view. Because vocabulary is an index of intelligence, all verbal tests of intelligence include vocabulary lists, but they are predicated on the ability of the child to comprehend the meaning of the word, not to use it. The Children's Wechsler and the Stanford-Binet (Forms L and M) Intelligence Tests contain usable word lists. The Ammons Full-Range Picture Vocabulary Test, a nonverbal test of intelligence, is particularly useful to the speech clinician who wishes to measure the "understood vocabulary" of a child who does not talk. (See Appendix 3.) Another well-known and standardized measure is the Smith-Williams Vocabulary Test for Pre-School Children.[6] Research to establish the length of sentences used by preschool children has produced reliable indices. The average child of two years, for example, will use 1.8 words in a sentence; the three-year-old, 3.4 words; the four-year-old, 4.4 words; and the five-year-old, 5.1 words. In addition to Gesell's Developmental Sequence of Language Behavior, we include in Appendix 3 a composite table of mean sentence length based upon McCarthy's summary.[7]

DETERMINATION OF THE DEVELOPMENTAL QUOTIENT

In the preceding chapter we referred frequently to the relation between speech development and general maturation. Gesell and Amatruda have established developmental sequences for the first five years of life in four modalities: motor behavior, adaptive behavior, language behavior, and personal-social behavior. In Appendix 3 is a summary chart of these four aspects of maturation. We suggest, however, that the student have a thorough understanding of the philosophy upon which this chart is based before he attempts to compute the developmental quotient.[8]

[5] R. Milisen, "A Rationale for Articulation Disorders," *Journal of Speech and Hearing Disorders,* Monograph Supplement No. 4 (December, 1954).

[6] M. E. Smith and H. Williams, *Smith-Williams Vocabulary Test,* University of Iowa Studies in Child Welfare, Vol. 13, No. 2 (1937).

[7] Dorothea A. McCarthy, *Language Development in Children,* in L. Carmichael, ed., *Manual of Child Psychology,* 2nd ed. (New York, Wiley, 1954), pp. 546-549.

[8] A. Gesell and Catherine S. Amatruda, *Developmental Diagnosis* (New York, Paul B. Hoeber, 1948).

A. Gesell, *The First Five Years of Life* (New York, Harper, 1940).

A. Gesell, *Infant Development: The Embryology of Early Human Behavior* (New York, Harper, 1952).

DETERMINATION OF THE INTELLECTUAL QUOTIENT

Psychometric Evaluation Scales

There are many measures available to the clinician trained in the theory and skills of psychological testing. Among the standard tests for children, the most useful for our purposes are the Wechsler Intelligence Scale for Children (WISC),[9] the Stanford-Binet Test of Intelligence (Merrill-Terman Adaptation),[10] the Ammons Word-Picture Test,[11] the Arthur Adaptation of the Leiter International Performance Scale,[12] and the Columbia Mental Maturity Scale.[13] Since the Stanford-Binet test depends largely upon verbal responses, it is less valuable than others in testing very young children. In the majority of cases the Arthur Adaptation of the Leiter Scale and the performance items of the Children's Wechsler Test give a fair estimate of the child's learning potential when these results are corroborated by laboratory observation and study and by the Gesell measures of general development (DQ).

The Wechsler Intelligence Scale for Children may be used for the testing of children from five to fifteen years old. In the ten-test scale there are five verbal and five performance tests. Included in the verbal battery are measures of general information, general comprehension, arithmetic, similarities, and vocabulary. In the performance section are tests of picture completion and arrangement, block design, object assembly, and coding or mazes.

The Ammons Full-Range Picture Vocabulary Test consists of sixteen plates, each with four cartoonlike drawings. Common objects, human activities, and familiar scenes are pictured. The test words and norms are printed on the answer sheet. (See Appendix 3.) The child is told that he will be asked to point to some pictures and the first plate is shown with the question, "Where is the pie?" If he seems not to understand the procedure, further questions may be asked, using words other than those in the scale and creating a gamelike atmosphere until he clearly sees what to do. Testing starts with the easiest item on each card, and proceeds until

[9] D. Wechsler, *Wechsler Intelligence Scale for Children* (New York, Psychological Corporation, 1949), pp. 1-6.

[10] L. M. Terman and M. A. Merrill, *Measuring Intelligence* (Boston, Houghton, 1937).

[11] R. B. Ammons and Helen S. Ammons, *The Full-Range Picture Vocabulary Test* (New Orleans, R. B. Ammons, 1948).

[12] G. Arthur, *The Arthur Adaptation of the Leiter International Performance Scale* (Washington, D. C., The Psychological Service Center Press, 1952).

[13] B. B. Burgemeister, L. H. Blum and I. Lorge, *Columbia Mental Maturity Scale* (New York, The Psychological Corporation, 1954).

all items have been failed at three successive mental-age levels. Questions may be varied to avoid monotony, the examiner saying "Put your finger on the ————," "Where is the ————," or "Show me the ————." There is a close correlation between the scores on this test and the Stanford-Binet.

The Arthur Adaptation of the Leiter Scale is designed to measure the ability of children from three to eight years old and is particularly valuable in testing the child with delayed speech. The pattern strips are held in place in a wooden frame into which one-inch cubes with patterns bearing *some* relationship or analogy in color, shade, form, design, genus, or number to the pattern strip must be fitted by the child. In year IV, the child should be able to (*a*) select properly, according to color and form, blocks bearing triangles, squares, and circles which match the pattern strip; (*b*) match eight geometric forms; (*c*) demonstrate knowledge of the number concept of 4 by matching lines, balloons, and flowers with blocks bearing black dots from one to four in number; and (*d*) match form, color, and number, all three concepts being represented on one block. In year V he should (*a*) demonstrate his understanding of genus by matching, for example, cow with horse, hen with rooster, man with woman; (*b*) match two-color circles; (*c*) match clothing (glove with hand, shoe with foot, girl's hat with girl, etc.); and (*d*) copy a block design involving perception of colors and diagonals.

The Columbia Mental Maturity Scale is a test which requires no verbal responses and a minimum of motor responses. It is, therefore, especially suitable for cerebral-palsied children and for others with serious physical impairments or limited language ability. The test consists of one hundred items each on a separate card. The basic task is for the subject to indicate which among a series of drawings is different from the rest.

EXAMINATION OF THE PERIPHERAL SPEECH MECHANISM

The evaluation of the adequacy of the peripheral speech mechanism (lips, teeth, mandible, tongue, and palate) is difficult because we have no norms for size and *relative dimensions* or for mobility of the articulatory organs. The estimate of normality in structure must be based on previous observations of the articulatory organs of children with defective and with normal speech. Through repeated observation and practice the student will be able to make subjective but fairly reliable estimates of normalcy. The Sylrater test may be a future means of establishing norms for the speed of articulatory movements in speech; at present its use is largely experimental. In the Historical and Diagnostic Journal for Retarded Speech (Appendix 4), we have outlined specific structural deviations for which the student should look, and have suggested exercises to test mobility of the structures.

TESTS OF AUDITORY ACUITY, SOUND
DISCRIMINATION, AND AUDITORY MEMORY

Whisper and watch tests of hearing are unreliable indices because there is insufficient control over intensity or over the frequencies which are variable and of unknown modality. As yet, there is no reliable measure of the hearing of very young children. The psychogalvanic skin-reflex test may prove to be of value in testing infants and small children who cannot cooperate in audiometer tests. The supposition is that a measurable change in the electrical potential of the skin follows the administration of a sound stimulus, if the hearing mechanism is intact. The test, however, may not measure the integrity of the entire hearing mechanism; the change in potential may indicate only that reflex hearing (midbrain level) is intact.

For children of school age and adults, two types of tests of hearing may be employed: (1) the audiometric evaluation of hearing acuity which measures one's standard threshold perception of pure tones, and (2) the tests for speech hearing or tests of speech articulation and intelligibility. In the first type of test, the hearing threshold of the individual is measured in dimensions that are relative to the threshold for a standard observer. The hearing-loss attenuator in a pure-tone audiometer subtracts a constant number of decibels from voltages that vary with the frequency of the tone and the assumed normal threshold. The amount of hearing loss, or threshold, denoted in decibels is plotted on an audiogram. An all-frequency loss of 10 to 15 decibels may not be significant and, likewise, a loss above 20 decibels in a single frequency is not generally considered to be a serious deterrent to communication. There is considerable support for the belief, however, that if the impairment in the better ear reaches 25 decibels or more at 512, 1024, and 2048 cycles, the child's speech will show serious defects.[14]

In an effort to evalute the over-all hearing function, and not simply one's sensory capacity to perceive sounds of various frequencies and intensities, tests of speech hearing have been constructed. There are two principal types. One measures the threshold or the lowest level at which a subject can hear the test material; it is called the Speech Reception Threshold Test. In this test, the intelligibility of speech is based on a threshold which is defined "as the intensity of speech at which an observer can repeat 50 per cent of the speech that is presented." [15] Digits or sentences of equal difficulty are generally used. The second type of test, The Articulation and Speech Intelligibility Test, measures, generally at an easily audible level, the ability of the subject to hear the speech sounds correctly. A speech audiometer is employed in this test which is made up of phonographic or

[14] W. G. Wolfe, "Comprehensive Evaluation of Fifty Cases of Cerebral Palsy," *Journal of Speech and Hearing Disorders*, Vol. 15, No. 3 (1950), p. 241.
[15] I. J. Hirsch, *The Measurement of Hearing* (New York, McGraw, 1952), p. 128.

magnetic tape recordings of phonetically balanced one-syllable words (P B Lists), or of lists of two-syllable spondee words.[16] (The lists are included in Appendix 5.) Each group of fifty monosyllabic words in the P B Lists contains a distribution of speech sounds as they occur in conversational American English. The Spondee test also is made up of words, but they are two-syllable words with equal stress on each syllable. A score is obtained by measuring the difference in decibels between the intensity of speech required by a subject in order to hear 50 per cent of the words spoken and the intensity required by a normal listener to hear the same percentage. In this type of speech audiometer, the phonographically recorded lists of the Psycho-Acoustic Laboratory, Harvard University, or of the Central Institute for the Deaf are used most frequently.[17] It also is necessary to know how fine a discrimination an individual can make among speech sounds when the intensity of the speech sounds is no longer an important factor. The discrimination loss is not measured in decibels but by the difference between the percentage of words heard correctly and 100 per cent, a presumed maximum score for normal listeners. If the subject gets 90 per cent or more correct, his discrimination is normal. Again, the most common materials are phonographic recordings of the P B Lists. Other tests of speech reception specifically designed for children are discussed in Chapter 19, The Handicapped in Hearing.

Pronovost, Mansur, and others have devised a Speech Sound Discrimination Test for children which we have found to be a helpful diagnostic tool.[18] Word pairs, which are phonetically balanced so that only one phoneme varies in each word of a pair, and picture designations of the words form the basis of the test. For each pair of words there are three combinations represented on the test page: one "unlike" pairing and two "like" pairings. For example, for the word pair, *cat-bat,* there are pictures of two cats, one above the other; a cat and a bat; and two bats. The position of the pictures of the word pairs was selected at random in order to eliminate the factor of patterned responses. Simple line drawings are used for the pictures. If the child is able to make 65 correct responses out of a total of 72, his speech sound discrimination is considered to be average. A score below 59

[16] Hirsch demonstrated that when an articulation test of speech hearing is constructed using spondee-word lists, and presented at controlled intensities, the listener is able to repeat more words than if the phonetically balanced lists are used. In other words, the intelligibility of speech, measured by articulation gain, is greater for spondee than for phonetically balanced monosyllables.

[17] Auditory Tests Nos. 9, 12, 14 of Psycho-Acoustic Laboratory, Harvard University.

Auditory Tests No. W-1, No. W-2, No. W-22, Central Institute for the Deaf, obtained from the Technisonic Laboratories, 1201 South Brentwood Boulevard, Brentwood, Missouri.

[18] W. Pronovost and C. Dumbleton, "A Picture-Type Speech Sound Discrimination Test," *Journal of Speech and Hearing Disorders,* Vol. 18, No. 3 (1953), p. 266.

Boston University Speech Sound Discrimination Picture Test (Boston, Boston University, 1955).

indicates poor ability in speech sound discrimination. The word-pair lists and the instructions for administering and scoring the test are included in Appendix 3.

As we indicated in the preceding chapter, there is no test which measures adequately auditory memory for the kind of connected speech which the child must imitate in establishing his own patterns. The Metraux adaptation of Anderson's Test for Auditory Memory Span for Speech Sounds is contained in Appendix 3.[19] In this test the vowel, diphthong, and consonant units are non-meaningful, progress in number in the series, and are arranged so that the sounds are evenly distributed throughout the test. Unfortunately the test does not take into account memory for sound combinations or perceptive cues by which we recall speech patterns.

TESTS OF MOTOR PROFICIENCY

Among the various tests of motor skill which have been evolved are three particularly suitable for the testing of children: the Heath Rail-Walking Test,[20] the Oseretsky Test of Motor Proficiency,[21] and the Sylrater Test of Repetitive Movement.[22] The Heath Rail-Walking Test, which involves walking heel-to-toe on three rails of varying width and length, is an index of gross motor control and general locomotor co-ordination. A more valuable diagnostic tool is the Oseretsky Test which measures finer motor skills. "It is a year scale of motor proficiency and is comparable in structure to the Binet-Simon scale for measuring intelligence and the Vineland Social Maturity Scale for measuring social competence. And, like them, it affords a standard means for the clinical evaluation of a distinctive aspect of behavioral development."[23] The tests, which may be demonstrated by the examiner, consist of six groups for each age: (1) general static co-ordination; (2) dynamic co-ordination of the hands; (3) general dynamic co-ordination; (4) motor speech; (5) simultaneous voluntary movements; and (6) asynkinesia (ability to perform without superfluous movements). The test is relatively free from intellectual components, aside from the fact that the child must be able to comprehend the commands and be able to respond. A copy of The Oseretsky Test of Motor Proficiency is included in Appendix 3. The Sylrater, an electric-acoustic instrument constructed by

[19] Ruth W. Metraux, "Auditory Memory Span for Speech Sounds: Norms for Children," *Journal of Speech and Hearing Disorders,* Vol. 9 (1944), pp. 31-38.

[20] S. R. Heath, "Relation of Rail-Walking and Other Motor Performances of Mental Defectives to Mental Age and Etiologic Type," *Training School Bulletin,* Vol. 50 (October, 1953), pp. 119-127.

[21] E. A. Doll, ed., *The Oseretsky Tests of Motor Proficiency* (Minneapolis, Educational Publishers, Inc., 1947).

[22] J. V. Irwin and O. Becklund, "Norms for Maximum Repetitive Rates for Certain Sounds Established with the Sylrater," *Journal of Speech and Hearing Disorders,* Vol. 18 (1953), pp. 149-160.

[23] E. A. Doll, ed., *The Oseretsky Tests of Motor Proficiency* (Minneapolis, Educational Publishers, Inc., 1947), p. 1.

Irwin and Becklund, measures the speed of repetitive movement of lips and tongue by recording the maximum number of speech sounds produced in five seconds. Norms for three syllables only, [pə], [tə], and [kə], have been established. The sound-pulse meter also measures the rate of production of such non-speech sounds as unilateral and bilateral finger-tapping.

Other tests of the speed and accuracy of movement of the tongue, lips, and mandible are indicated in the Historical and Diagnostic Journal for Retarded Speech (Appendix 4). Although there are no norms available, the examiner can secure a fair estimate of the motor proficiency of the articulatory organs by these informal means.

TESTS OF LATERALITY

If we had the proper tests we might find the *relation* of eye, foot, and hand dominance much more important than tests of handedness alone. Social and environmental influences weigh heavily upon the development of handedness, but they do not affect the establishment of eye or foot dominance. Fifty per cent of the adult population is left-eyed whereas only 5.2 per cent (6.6 per cent male, 3.8 per cent female) is left-handed. It is possible that these influences have operated to make our society largely right-handed.

The establishment of laterality is not easily determined because it involves repeated observations and tests. Parents can assist the therapist by keeping a daily record over a month's period of hand-preference and superior performance in such activities as ball-throwing, or in use of the spoon in feeding, or in such fine co-ordinations as "taking" and "putting" objects and completing motion. In offering objects to the child in these tests, one must be sure that the object is in the center position before him. The number of trials will depend, in part, on the surety of the response. Certainly nothing can be concluded by one trial or ten trials of a single activity. A sampling of 75 trials in many activities scattered over a month may be indicative of the child's laterality. In Appendix 3 will be found three batteries of laterality tests which, taken together, should provide a fairly reliable index of the sidedness of a child. The Iowa Performance Test of Selected Manual Activities by Johnson and Duke is reproduced in its entirety.[24] Modifications of Abram Blau's Objective Tests of Laterality [25] and the Harris Tests of Lateral Dominance are presented.[26] (See Appendix 3.)

[24] W. Johnson and D. Duke, "Iowa Performance Test of Selected Manual Activities," in W. Johnson, F. L. Darley, and D. C. Spriestersbach, eds., *Diagnostic Manual in Speech Correction* (New York, Harper, 1952).

[25] A. Blau, "Objective Tests of Laterality," in H. Bakwin and R. M. Bakwin, *Clinical Management of Behavior Disorders in Children* (Philadelphia, Saunders, 1953), p. 297.

[26] A. J. Harris, *Harris Tests of Lateral Dominance* (New York, The Psychological Corporation, 1955).

TESTS OF EMOTIONAL AND SOCIAL MATURITY

There are so many valid tests of emotional and social adjustment that it is difficult to name the ones most suitable for use with children handicapped in speech. Although the Goodenough Draw-A-Man Test was designed as an intelligence test, it provides considerable insight into the emotional life of a young child. As Bakwin and Bakwin state, "the figure which the child draws is, to a considerable extent, an index of his feelings about himself, a mirror which can be viewed by the examiner. The child's body image concept varies according to the developmental level and is constantly modified by experience. In the drawing of the human figure are reflected perceptual and personality problems, problems in the control of motility, compensatory efforts and efforts at control of impulses with rigidity, fears, withdrawal, or aggression." [27]

Another projective test, much more complex and exhaustive, is the Children's Apperception Test (CAT).[28] Like its "parent," the Thematic Apperception Test (TAT), it makes possible inferences about themata of import in the subject's life and, in turn, further inferences about the needs and pressures affecting the underlying dynamics of his personality. Because children identify more readily with animals than adults, the test, which is designed for children three to ten years old, consists of ten pictures of animals engaged in activities and situations similar to those peculiar to young children. The subject is to make up a story about each picture telling the events leading up to the present situation, the outcome of the present situation, and a description of the feelings and thoughts of the characters. The subject's stories are analyzed in terms of (1) the types of individual with whom the subject identifies himself: a hero, happy, defeated, or rejected; (2) the needs the hero manifests; (3) the environmental forces with which the hero must contend; (4) the interaction between the hero's needs and external pressures; and (5) the success or failure of the outcome. "The frequency of positive and negative outcomes, and the factors that occasion them, such as the presence of the father, for example, whenever things go wrong; the consistency of any special needs, as for example, the need for power, for love, for punishment; the nature of the environmental forces with which the hero contends, namely, authority, economic deprivation, and others, are all calculated and correlated with one another." [29]

The California Personality Scale is also a projective test, designed for use with groups of children of school age. Its purpose is to identify and reveal the status of certain highly important factors in personality and social

---

[27] H. Bakwin and R. M. Bakwin, *Clinical Management of Behavior Disorders in Children* (Philadelphia, Saunders, 1953), p. 227.

[28] L. Bellak and S. Bellak, "Introductory Note on Children's Apperception Test (CAT)," *Journal of Projective Techniques,* Vol. 14 (1950), p. 173.

[29] Bakwin and Bakwin, *op. cit.,* p. 233.

adjustment usually designated as intangibles. It is a means of learning about people in order to guide them to better personal and social development. The test consists of two sections, self-adjustment and social adjustment, answered by "yes-no" responses to *situations*. It also provides for a record of interests and activities which may be used in group therapy to good advantage.

The Vineland Social Maturity Scale is an outline of detailed performance in which children show a progressive capacity for looking after themselves and participating in those activities which lead ultimately to independence as adults. The age range of the scale extends from a few months to twenty-five years. Such aspects of social ability as self-sufficiency, occupational activities, communication, self-direction, social participation, and a progressive freedom from need of assistance in direction or supervision on the part of others are explored. The needed information must be obtained from someone intimately familiar with the person being scored although the examiner, not the informant, makes the scoring judgment.[30] Each item is a measure *only* of general social maturation, and does not measure IQ, personality adjustment, skills, or other specific characteristics.

The tests and measurements described in this chapter are representative of the general types with which a speech diagnostician should be thoroughly familiar. They should serve as a guide in evaluating and planning therapy for the speech-retarded child.

[30] E. A. Doll, *Vineland Social Maturity Scale, Manual of Directions* (Minneapolis, Educational Test Bureau, 1947).

7

Training the Child Retarded in Speech

Speech development is best described as a dynamic learning process, not as a "still life" picture. It demands from the learner the energetic and cooperative use of many sensory, ideational, and motor faculties. It demands from the teacher the same kind of dynamism, expressed in his motivation, ingenuity, and intelligent guidance and reflected in a pervading atmosphere of good humor and encouragement. Genevieve Arnold has expressed well this belief in the dynamics of speech in the title of an excellent manual, *Speech Is Fun*.[1] It is your business as a teacher to make it so. The dull drillmaster has no place in this scheme of things.

SPEECH STIMULATION FOR THE CHILD WHO DOES NOT TALK

The first step in a therapeutic program for the child who does not talk is to determine the cause and, if possible, to deal with it. We cannot always find the cause or remove it when we do find it. There are, however, general principles underlying therapy which should be observed without respect to cause.

1. The child must be made to feel that the performance of speaking is an achievement worth the effort. Using oral language must be worth while, if the child is to give up grunts and gestures. Attention to the child's early efforts at speech must be quickly given. If the child finds that he gets less rather than more attention because he has begun to speak, he would be an unwise child to persist in speaking.

2. The child must feel accepted and loved by an older speaking person so that he can identify himself with that person and emulate his speech.

3. Children have individual rates of development into which speech acquisition must be fitted. Tom's development should not be judged by Mary's accomplishments. Each child is a law unto himself.

[1] Genevieve Arnold, *Speech Is Fun* (Houston, Texas, Speech Clinic, University of Houston, 1953).

4. To stimulate the child to imitate speech sounds, the therapist should first imitate the child's babbling. Changes in the sound pattern should be introduced subtly. The first words are the child's. New words should be presented to the child for his approval, but they should not be imposed on him. The child will not learn words, or remember them for long, unless he has use for them. If the words are not likely to be useful, there is no point in teaching them to him. A single word for him often stands for a sentence. His first one-word and two-word sentences should be praised.

5. Periods of speech stimulation should occur at the optimum time when a child is well, happy, and not absorbed in another activity.

6. Grammar and sentence usage are skills a child learns by imitation.

7. Children do not progress steadily and methodically in learning to talk. There are periods of acceleration broken by fairly long plateaus of learning. Articulatory proficiency for physically and mentally normal children is not reached by many children until they are past seven years old. Girls acquire articulatory proficiency somewhat earlier than boys, and first children somewhat earlier than second children. A child is not consistent in his early sound acquisition. He should not be expected either to be more consistent or more proficient than the other members of his environment.

8. It is probably more harmful to do too much too soon than to wait. If the child seems to be delayed in speech, appropriate diagnosis and treatment should be made and planned by professional speech clinicians, and not by friends, neighbors, or well-meaning relatives.

Stimulation Through Sounds in the Environment

Both the mother and the clinician will capitalize on sounds in the child's environment by copying them and motivating the child to imitate the copy. Such possibilities are innumerable. The familiar sounds in the house—a food mixer, a telephone bell, door chimes, a ticking clock, a singing tea kettle—all can be "copied" by the mother, and the child in turn will imitate, or should imitate, the mother's copy. Animal sounds likewise may be imitated. The barking dog (wuf-wuf), the hungry kitty (mee-ow), the angry kitty (f-f-f), the buzzing fly (z-z-z) are familiar examples. The child's noise-making toys—truck, mouse, or doll—also are sources of imitation. There are "distant" sounds outside the home which should provide stimuli: the chug (choo-choo) of a train engine, the putting (p-p-p) of a motor boat, the hum (m-m-m) of an airplane, and the shriek of a siren (u-u-e-e-e).

Nursery Rhymes and Finger Plays

Nursery rhymes and finger plays are excellent speech stimuli because they generally are associated with pleasurable activity. Even if the child attempts only the opening or final phrase of the rhyme or finger play, it is a successful motivator of speech. Here are opening lines of some nursery rhymes which have simple images and language:

a. Tee-diddle dumpling
   My son John —
b. Pat-a-cake, pat-a-cake, baker's man
   Make me a cake as fast as you can.
c. Baa-baa, black sheep
   Have you any wool?
d. Little Bo-Peep
   Has lost her sheep —
e. Little Boy Blue
   Come blow your horn.
f. Humpty-Dumpty sat on a wall
   Humpty-Dumpty had a great fall.
g. Hey, diddle-diddle,
   The cat and the fiddle—

Children generally will not try any part of the speech accompanying the finger play in first trials. They should not be expected to verbalize until they have mastered the action. Among the many jingles with accompanying finger plays are the following:

a. Pit-a-pat,
   What was that?
   Eight fat raindrops
   On my hat!
b. Here's a cup
   And here's a cup
   And here's a pot of tea.
   Pour a cup, and pour a cup
   And drink a cup with me.
c. Here's a ball
   And here's a ball
   A great big ball I see.
   Shall we count them?
   Are you ready?
   One, two, three.
d. Knock at the door,
   Peep in;
   Lift up the latch,
   Walk in.
e. Bozo, the little clown, goes hopping,
   Hopping along;
   Here is his song: Hop-hop;
   Hop, hop; hop down!
f. Here are mother's knives and forks
   And this is father's table
   This is sister's looking glass
   And here's the baby's cradle.

g. Two little dickybirds, sitting on a wall
One named Peter, one named Paul
Fly away, Peter; fly away, Paul
Come back, Peter; come back, Paul.

h. Two tall telephone poles
Between them a wire is strung,
On hopped two little birds,
And swung and swung and swung.

i. Two little houses shut up tight
Open the windows and let in the light
Ten little finger people standing up straight
Ready for the kindergarten, half past eight
March, march, march, march, march.

j. Fee, fie, foe, fum
See the little brownie run.
Fee, fie, foe, fum,
Four fingers having fun.
Fee, fie, foe, fum,
My brownie is a Thumb.

k. Eency weency spider
Climbed up the water spout,
Down came the rain
And washed the spider out.
Out came the sun
And dried up all the rain,
So the eency weency spider
Climbed up the spout again.

Toys

Always popular in a children's clinic are building blocks, balls, toy postal stations, tracks, trains, cars, dolls, doll furniture and doll house, and toy animals, which may be used in a variety of ways to motivate speech.

Books

There are excellent books for speech stimulation which employ both sounds in the environment and speech sounds. These attractively illustrated and printed books have been worn thin and shabby in our clinics:

a. *The Indoor Noisy Book* and the *Country Noisy Book* (all about the noises which that remarkable puppy, Muffin, does and does not hear)

b. *Listening for Speech Sounds* (stories and line drawings to illustrate sounds in context; phonic approach emphasized)

c. *The Noisy Clock Shop* (about all kinds of clocks which never tick or strike the same way)

d. *Picture Sounding Rhymes* (full-page pictures illustrating such original but simple rhymes as "The cow in the pasture/ Has nothing to do/ But eat green grass/ And say Moo-moo-moo") *e. See It, Say It, Do It* (word-stimulating pictures of flag, fire, fan, fish, etc. to identify and reproduce)

   f. See It (brightly colored action pictures involving objects and situations within a young child's experience)

   g. What We Do Day By Day (pictured activities of children)

   (Complete references to these books will be found in Appendix 3.)

Phonograph Records

Among the many available phonograph records we have found the following to be especially good for speech stimulation:

   a. Genie, The Magic Record
   b. What's Its Name, An Auditory Training Album
   c. I'm Dressing Myself
   d. The Circus Comes to Town
   e. The Little Fireman
   f. I Wish I Were—
   g. The Chugging Freight Engine
   h. Let's Help Mommy
   i. Old MacDonald Had a Farm
   j. The Owl and the Pussy Cat
   k. The Choo Choo Train
   l. Tootle

   (Complete references are included in Appendix 3.)

Group Games and Motion Songs

   a. The "whisper game." The therapist whispers the "secret" (a single sound or word) directly into the child's ear. The child then whispers the "secret" to the next child in the circle. The game is to receive and transmit the "secret" without error.

   b. Playing train. The children line up with hands on the hips of the child ahead. As they move forward, one represents the "chug" of the engine, another the whistle, a third the sound of wheels over rails, (t-k-t-k), a fourth the bell, etc.

   c. Picture charades. Cardboard cutouts of animals (dog, cat, cow, sheep, etc.) parade behind a stage screen (a cheesecloth-covered frame with a strong light behind it). The first child who says the sound the animal makes receives the picture.

   d. Animal sounds. The children appear, one at a time, "on the stage" behind the screen. Each makes a sound of an animal. The children guess the name of the animal.

   e. Playing "drop the handkerchief." The child running around the circle, drops the handkerchief behind the child who says the loudest "me."

   f. Motion songs:

     (1) "A-Hunting We Will Go"

       O! A-hunting we will go; A-hunting we will go;
       We'll catch a fox and put him in a box, and then we'll let him go.

(2) "Looby Loo"

    (a) Here we go looby loo,
        Here we go looby light,
        Here we go looby loo,
        All on a Saturday night.
        Put your right hand in,
        Put your right hand out,
        Give your right hand a shake, shake, shake
        And turn yourself about.

    (b) Put your left hand in, etc.

    (c) Put your right foot in, etc.

    (d) Put your left foot in, etc.

    (e) Put your head way in, etc.

    (f) Put your whole self in, etc.

(3) "Hickory, Dickory, Dock"

    Hickory, dickory, dock; tick tock,
    The mouse ran up the clock; tick tock,
    The clock struck one,
    The mouse ran down;
    Hickory, dickory, dock; tick tock.

TRAINING THE CHILD WHOSE SPEECH IS RETARDED IN DEVELOPMENT (ARTICULATORY PROBLEMS)

Now the child is speaking—the initiation of speech may have been "on time" or late—but the quality of his speech is not up to standard. It is marked by omissions, substitutions, distortions, and sometimes, by additions of sounds.[2] The worried parents have brought the child to the speech clinic. After the orientation period is over, and the historical data and results of diagnostic study have been assembled, the clinician must consider several questions before beginning therapy.

1. What is to be the program of habilitation? The answer depends upon many things. Therapy, first of all, must fit this particular child. It must take into consideration the findings as reported in the historical and diagnostic journal (see Appendix 4). One must take into account, for example, the child's mental age, developmental quotient, motor proficiency, and sensory abilities and disabilities (hearing, auditory discrimination, memory span, kinesthesia). Therapy must be planned in terms of his interests, his motivation, and his personality. As a consequence, any outline of therapy will have to be modified to meet the individual child's need. Recognizing this need

[2] Roe and Milisen state that sounds are likely to be first omitted, then substituted, finally distorted. (V. Roe and R. Milisen, "The Effect of Maturation Upon Defective Articulation in Elementary Grades," *Journal of Speech Disorders,* Vol. 7, No. 1 [1942], p. 44.)

for adaptation, we present an outline of the steps which we generally follow in planning therapy:

a. Development of an awareness of environment and of himself in relation to his environment.
b. Increasing acoustic perception through training in auditory stimulation and discrimination.
c. Increasing perception of articulatory positions by strengthening visual-kinesthetic cues.
d. Developing articulatory flexibility.
e. Setting the new pattern in isolation, in structured speech in the clinical situation, and in free conversational speech.

2. The clinician will also have questions about procedure. Which sound or sounds should be attacked first? Probably it should be the sound easiest to correct on the basis of his score in the stimulability test (see Appendix 3). One also must consider whether it is a sound which occurs frequently in his speech and which, if development had been normal, should be in his speech at this time. Remember that many children as late as the second grade make substitutions for r and s. Certainly if the child is four years old, one should not attack the w for r substitution.

In what position in the word should the sound first be taught? This is difficult to determine except through trial and error. Usually one begins with the isolated sound in the initial position, but with some sounds it is easier to achieve success by establishing it in a blend or in the final position. We have a child in the clinic at present who can say "best" but cannot say "sake" or "stake" without distorting the s. When w is substituted for r, for example, a child often can produce r in a tr blend, probably because the lips must be everted for t so there is less opportunity to round them for w.

3. What *materials and equipment* are needed in training the child with retarded speech? An individual speech notebook or journal, we believe, is essential in teaching children. It constitutes a daily "log of operations" which is helpful to the parent, teacher, and child, all of whom should share in its construction. The materials will be adapted to the child's motivation, age, and interests. For the five-year-old it may include colored pictures cut from magazines or inexpensive color and story books which call for the new sound patterns.

One child's notebook begins with the labial sounds, p, b, m, in large colored symbols. The introductory units are entitled: (1) "Can You Hear the Sound?" (pictures and exercises for auditory stimulation); (2) "Working the Speech Machine" (picture exercises of tongue and lips to increase kinesthetic sensitivity); and (3) "Can You Make the Sound?" (clown pictures for visual stimulation of the position of tongue and lips). (4) Then there are pictures designating a single object or person, calling for the sound in the initial position in the word: *baby, mamma, papa, ball, boat, bike.* (5) Other pictures follow to elicit the sound in medial and final positions. (6) As the therapy progresses to the final steps there are such picture units as the following: Myself (parts of the body; dressing myself, etc.); My family; Playtime at home (pets and toys); Time to eat! (food, table-setting, manners); Excursions for fun (going to the farm, zoo, circus, park); Special events (my birthday party, Thanksgiving, and Christmas). (7) At the close are songs and stories which the child has dictated and descriptions of speech-centered projects outside the clinic. It may be argued that such training is too highly organized and routinized. However, even very small children enjoy organized activity and take pride in tangible evidence of their effort. The notebook also provides motivation and organization for homework. It is a valuable piece of equipment in the clinic.

Other indispensable aids in teaching the speech-retarded child are a tape recorder, a phonograph, a collection of records particularly useful in sound stimulation and discrimination, and an individual portable amplifier of sound. There are innumerable books, games, and educational toys which can be adapted easily to speech learning. Such a list, appropriate for young children, is contained in Appendix 3.

Much of the best material in our clinics has been constructed by the clinician to meet particular needs and interests. In the several therapy rooms at this time are two groceries, a miniature zoo, a farm, dolls and a doll-house, puppets and a puppet stage.

These preliminary questions settled, let us return to the outline of therapy. In expanding this outline we shall include chiefly illustrative materials intended only to suggest to the teacher the various procedures which may be employed.

Outline of Therapy

A. **Development in The Child of an Awareness of Environment and of Himself in Relation to His Environment.** How can one make this child aware of himself as a person? How can one motivate him, not only to want to speak but to speak intelligibly? These are some concepts which may aid in attaining the goal.

1. The child must feel, first of all, that he is a very important person in the clinic, that this is "his school." The therapist must show her acceptance of and interest in him as a person. He must feel that the clinic is a friendly place.

2. The child must find basic interests which draw him back to the clinic day after day. For Jack the present interest is an animal farm which he has been making; for Steve it is boats in which he has taken "trips" to lands both real and imaginary; for Linda it is a suitcase filled with dolls;

for Shirley (a little girl who has not attended school) it is traveling across town alone with a notebook under her arm, "like other children"; for Krissie it is furnishing the play house and carrying on the housekeeping.

3. Even very small children like sociability. In their group class they carry on speech-centered activities with other children. They learn how to greet one another, to thank others for favors, to plan a game, to buy at the store, to ask directions from the policeman, and to say good-bye.

4. The cerebral-palsied child or the child with a cleft palate knows very early in life what his speech problems are, but the child with retarded speech generally hears only vague references to himself as the "child who can't talk plain" or the "child with queer speech." When we heard a child in the clinic tell another youngster, "my tongue doesn't work just right," we felt that the therapist had given the child a reasonable if not a complete explanation of his difficulty. At least it had helped the child to objectify his attitude. In another instance, a small group of children were discussing why they must make the lips move when they talked. One child showed the group how he could teach Bozo, the puppet, to say the words for him; Bozo also had occasional trouble in pressing his lips together for *p* and *b,* and his tongue, too, did not always strike the roof of the mouth hard enough for *t* and *d.* In a sense, the child had projected his differences to Bozo, but at the same time he had become more aware of these differences in his own speech.

B. *Training in Auditory Stimulation and Discrimination of Speech Sounds.* The materials included in the preceding section devoted to general auditory stimulation may also be used to stimulate an awareness in the child of specific speech sounds. He may link the "new sound," *s* or *th* or *f* or *p,* with familiar sounds in his own environment, or with recordings of the sound in nature and in the speech of others. The teacher can bombard the child with the "new sound" by simple repetition. She may vary the manner of repetition by using an amplifier, concealing the visual image of the sound, or using a tape recording of repetitions.

The child must also learn how the new sound pattern differs from other sounds. To this end, the teacher will present widely contrasted sounds and similar sounds and, if the child distorts the sound, she may contrast his pattern with the correct pattern. The following exercises are for auditory discrimination of the *th* [θ] sound but may be used for any sound. They should be suggestive of ways to make training in speech discrimination enjoyable for young children.

1. Picture games. There are four pictures on a large card. All pictures will denote words which sound nearly alike. Only one picture contains the *th* [θ] sound. Tell the child: "Find the picture with the 'snake sound,' the 'angry kitty sound,' or the 'bottle sound'."
2. "Flag the Sound." Oral presentation of series of similar sounds, or series of phonetically similar words, or recordings of stories emphasizing par-

ticular sounds.[3] Each child holds a small flag; when he hears the sound, he is to wave it.

3. Employing the materials in 2 (above), the teacher may use the following methods of identification of the new sound pattern:

   a. The child puts a block through the proper slot in the Play-School Postal Station when he hears the *th* [θ] sound.

   b. The child places toy money in a bank when he hears the sound.

   c. The child places a piece of "coal" in the first, middle, or last car of a train according to the position of *th* [θ], initial, medial, or final, in a word.

   d. The child places colored paper balloons in his notebook when he hears the sound.

   e. Colored counters are placed in the center of the table. If the child identifies the sound correctly, he takes a counter; if he makes a mistake, he gives up a counter.

   f. Pick Up Sticks. When the child hears the sound, he may pick up a colored stick.

   g. "Stars in my Crown." The child may put a star in his good-speech crown when he hears the *th* [θ] sound.

4. Picture Sound Game. A series of line drawings of common objects, animals, etc., represented by phonetically similar words are placed on the left half of a card. These pictures and one additional picture represented by a phonetically dissimilar word are on the right half. Strings with magnetic ends are attached to pictures on the left side. The child places the string on the matching picture at the right when the teacher says, "Find the ———." (These pictures are reproduced in full in Appendix 3.)

5. Sound chairs: Chairs are lined up as in the game of "Musical Chairs." The children walk around the chairs as long as they hear a certain sound. When the teacher stops making the sound, the children sit down in the nearest chair. The child left without a chair is out of the game.

6. Who Am I?: The child represents an animal, machine, or object which makes the "critical sound." The first one making the proper identification jumps up and repeats the sound.

7. Surprise Box: The teacher gives the child a catalogue or magazine and scissors. If he finds three pictures beginning with the *th* [θ] sound, he may open a box with a surprise in it.

8. The teacher hides pictures of objects in the room, some of which denote words containing the *th* [θ] sound. He is corrected if he brings a "wrong" picture or object to the teacher.

9. The teacher reads a short story containing many *th* [θ] sounds. When the sound is produced incorrectly, the child taps a bell.

[3] Records designed specifically for speech discrimination are as follows:
Laila L. Larsen, *Consonant Sound Discrimination* (Bloomington, Ind., Indiana University Audio-Visual Center, 1950).
E. Mikalson, *Speech Development Records for Children* (Pasadena, California, Pacific Records Company, AC-120).
C. Van Riper, *Fun with Speech* (Wilmette, Ill., Encyclopaedia Britannica Films, 1952).

10. Present pictures, or better, objects represented by the key words in this jingle, *I Hear It.* Have the child hold up the appropriate object or picture as the key word is said.[4]

> "I hear it in *thumb,* but not in *arm,*
> I hear it in *thimble,* but not in *farm,*
> I hear it in *bathtub,* but not in *door,*
> I hear it in *three,* but not in *four,*
> I hear it in *thread,* but not in *bat,*
> I hear it in *toothbrush,* but not in *cat,*
> I open my teeth
> Let my tongue peek through.
> I heard it again
> In *through* ——— did you?"

11. Cards are dealt with various pictured sounds on them. The teacher says, "I would like the angry goose sound." If the child has the card bearing the sound, he says quickly *th-th* [θ-θ] and puts the cards in the dummy. The first one to give up all his cards wins. If he improperly identifies the sound, he must take a card from the dummy. The cards bear such pictures as motor boat, *p-p;* child pouring water from bottle, *b-b;* angry kitty, *f-f;* airplane, *v-v;* snake, *s-s;* bee, *z-z;* angry goose, *th-th* [θ-θ]; engine, *ch-ch* [tʃ-tʃ]; etc.

12. The Parson's Goat. One child is the leader. He thinks of a word to describe the goat containing *th* [θ] sounds. For example, "The parson's goat is a *th*in goat." He says only the first sound of the word. The other children must guess what the word is. The one who guesses it correctly becomes the leader.

13. Sound Hop-Scotch. The children advance a step when they hear the new sound. If a child makes a mistake in identification he must go back two steps.

14. Listen-Act Game. The child is instructed to do what the word tells him— *if* it has the new sound in it. For example: listen for *s;* skip, hop, sweep, run, stand, lie down, rest, sit.

C. *Strengthening the Visual-kinesthetic Cues.* To heighten kinesthetic perception is difficult because we do not know the best way to teach it. It is certain that many children with retarded speech are not aware of the muscle tension necessary to reach the palate with the tongue-tip. Or they may not be aware of the position or the movement of the muscles; their sense of making contact with the palate in *t* and *d,* for example, is weak. How can these valuable cues to sound production be strengthened? The following exercises are designed to increase the child's awareness of visual-

---

[4] L. B. Scott and J. J. Thompson, *Talking Time* (St. Louis, Missouri, Webster Publishing Company, 1951), pp. 71-72.

kinesthetic cues. He should be seated before a mirror so that he receives visual and kinesthetic cues simultaneously. Direct him as follows:

1. Push the tongue against a tongue depressor or strengthener 5 times, relaxing and contracting the tongue rhythmically. This should increase awareness of pressure against resistance.
2. With the tongue-tip, remove peanut butter from the alveolar section of the palate (where the tongue must make firm contact for *t, d, n*). Be sure that the mouth is open as for the *t, d, n* sounds.
3. Remove strip of adhesive tape placed on the lower lip by pressure and movement of the lips. Do not use the tongue as helper!
4. Retract the lips as for *ē* [i]; as the therapist holds them back, force the lips into protrusion.
5. Curl the tongue around the orange stick placed along the median raphé.
6. Learn to make quick shifts in movement by:
   a. Practicing the "rocking chair" tongue: *t-k; t-k; t-k.* Begin slowly, then increase the speed.
   b. Trill with the tongue, *l-l-l*, then with lips and tongue, *b-l-l-l; b-b-l-l-l*, etc.
7. Chew gum, rolling it to the side, "plaster" it against the palate, slowly move the gum back over the palate, etc. Attempt to feel the tongue position with each movement.
8. The child is to concentrate now only on the visual cues in the teacher's speech. The teacher will say the consonant sounds in which the focal point of articulation is visible: *p, b, t, d, l, n, j*, etc. The child is to imitate the tongue and lip movements of the teacher, for each sound, but he is not asked to produce the sound. He answers the question of the teacher, "Where does my tongue go when I say 'l', by imitating her tongue placement. He is trying to create a new image of the way the sound *looks*.

   D. *Increasing the Flexibility of the Articulators.* Practice in intensifying the visual and kinesthetic cues will affect articulatory flexibility to a degree, but special practice in co-ordinating the skills involving speed, pressure, and accuracy of movement usually is necessary. These skills, moreover, must be directed to the front mouth: the focus of activity should be shifted from the glottis to the front tongue, lips, and jaw.

   1. *The Lips.* Sharpening the action of the lips is valuable not only because labial mobility is necessary in itself, but also because it has a salutary effect on other muscles—tongue, palate, and mandible—which are a part of the synergy. Labial agility has a tendency to produce lingual agility.

   a. Imitate the faces of clowns by retracting the lips, protruding the lips, and by dropping the jaw as far down as possible while producing the vowel sounds of *ä* [ɑ], *o͞o* [u], and *ē* [i].
   b. Imitate the sound of a squeaky see-saw: *ē-o͞o; ē-o͞o; ē-o͞o* [i-u; i-u; i-u].
   c. Imitate the sound of popping corn by pressing the lips firmly together and then releasing them suddenly.

d. Whistle with an exaggerated pucker of the lips; then retract the lips in a broad smile.

e. Blow plastic boats across the table, directing them carefully in lanes by blowing through a glass straw.

f. Blow ping-pong balls up an inclined plane.

g. Imitate the wind blowing first softly, then very hard: *hoo-oo-oo* [hu-u-u].

h. Imitate the owl's call: *to-whit; to-whoo.*

i. Exaggerate the explosion of the breath stream in the consonants:

> *pa-pa-pa; ba-ba-ba.*
> *pa-pa-pa; ba-ba-ba.*

2. *The Tongue*

a. Babble *lah-lah-lah,* first with the tongue-tip on the lips, then on the teeth, next against the alveolar ridges, and finally against the hard palate. Turn the tongue-tip over as you go back. Gradually increase the speed and intensity of the action.

b. Wipe candy lipstick or "fudge frosting" from the lips, carefully removing it from the corners of the mouth. Now wipe vinegar from the lips (retract and hump the tongue in the mouth).

c. Imitate a kitty lapping milk from a dish.

d. The tongue cleans house: dust off the roof (palate); sweep the floor, wash the walls, shake out the mop, walk around the block (around the lips), rest behind the teeth, etc.

e. Using only the tip of the tongue, "call" on each tooth from side to side, beginning with the molars.

f. Place the tip of the tongue behind the lower teeth; bulge the blade and dorsum; alternate retracting and pushing the tongue forward against the lower incisors.

g. A train is running very fast over the rails. Imitate as rapidly as you can the sound of the wheels: *k-t, k-t, k-t,* etc. The train slows down, pulls into the station with a *hwuh, hwuh, hwuh.* Now the steam escapes with a sharp *s-s-s-s.* The conductor calls "All Aboard!"

h. Imitate the sounds in a farm in the morning. First the cock crows: *cockle-doodle-dooo!* Then the cow bawls as she waits for the farmer to come for the milk: *moo-moo-moo.* The little lamb cries *baa-a-a-a* as he frisks about in the sun. The fat pig grunts *guh-guh-guh,* as he hurries to the trough for his breakfast of mash. The hen clucks *k-k-k-k* as she flies off the nest. Morning is here!

i. Imitate the barker selling lemonade and peanuts at a circus.

3. *The Jaw*

a. Drop the jaw as far as you can in imitating the church bell, *dong, dong, dong;* a crow's call, *caw-caw-caw;* a dog barking, *bow-wow-wow.*

b. Exaggerate the movement of the jaws as you prolong the vowels in *Wee-ee-ee-ee; why-y-y-y-y; wo-o-o-o; wah-ah-ah-ah-ah.*

c. Say *ouch-ouch!* dropping the jaw as far as you can on *ou* [au].

d. Laugh heartily: *hee-hee-hee; hoh-hoh-hoh; haw-haw-haw.*

4. *The Velar-pharyngeal Sphincter*. It is difficult to isolate the control of the velar-pharyngeal muscles which close the nasal port because the action is not visible and not very precise. One must rely chiefly on kinesthetic stimulation, on the feeling of velar action. These memory patterns of muscular action generally are checked against the acoustic result in sound production. In other words, auditory evaluation corroborates the kinesthetic sensation. It is our experience that when the focal point of tension in articulation has been shifted from the pharynx to the front mouth, and lip, tongue, and jaw mobility has been increased, then velar control improves. It is understandable if we think of the articulatory mechanism as being "all of one piece." If the front tongue, lips, and jaw are agile, the velar-pharyngeal muscles also are likely to be agile. To increase awareness of this action to close the nasal port we suggest the following exercises. For additional materials consult Chapter 14 on cleft palate, pages 305-351.

a. Begin a deep yawn with the jaw in the "ah" position. Look into the mirror and note how the back of the tongue lowers, the velum rises and the pillars of the fauces widen as you yawn. Repeat until you have a fairly intense feeling of the rising velum and open pharynx.

b. Before you complete the yawn, say *ä* [ɑ:] with the mouth as widely open as possible.

c. Go from a prolonged *ä* [ɑ:] to *p*, holding the air in the mouth under pressure before exploding the consonant, *p*. As the pressure increases in the mouth, can you feel the velar action?

d. Open the mouth wide and pant like a dog, [hɑ-hɑ-hɑ].

e. Check the velar control by placing a hand mirror horizontally below the nose as you say *ä, ō, ô, ē, ōō* [ɑ, o, ɔ, i, u]. If the mirror clouds, repeat the vowel until there is no evidence of nasal emission of the breath stream.

f. Change swiftly from velar relaxation to contraction in *m-pah, m-pah, m-pah*, puffing out the cheeks between *m* and *pah*. Now try *m-bay, m-bay; m-bou, m-bou; ng-kah, ng-kah*, etc.

g. Since the sphincter closes most precisely for *ē* [i] and *ōō* [u], there should be a noticeable difference in tension between *ē* [i] and *ä* [ɑ] and *ōō* [u] and *ä* [ɑ], for example. Can the child feel this difference?

h. Have the child pinch the nostrils, then release them as he hums *m-m-m-m*. As he closes the nose, can he feel the mounting constriction in the pharynx? Increase this feeling by trying to swallow as the pressure mounts.

i. Negative practice. Talk with the tongue retracted and bunched in the back of the mouth. Does it sound like "Donald Duck speech"? Quickly move the tongue forward to the front mouth. Try to sense the changing focal point of tension and contrast the acoustic result.

5.   Exaggerate all articulatory movements in

a. Tut-tut-tie!
Never tell a lie.
Tit-tat-too!
It will hurt you if you do.

b. Pease-pudding hot,
Pease-pudding cold,
Pease-pudding in the pot,
Nine days old!

c. Little Tommy Tittlemouse
   Lives in a little house,
   Someone is knocking,
   Guess who! Guess who!
d. See the shoemaker
   Mending a shoe
   Rap tap a tap

Tap a tap,
Tap, too.
e. "No-ah; no-ah
   We won't go-wa,"
   Cried Mama Boa
   and Papa Boa.

E. *Establishing the New Sound Pattern in Isolation.* Following training to reinforce acoustic-visual-kinesthetic cues and to increase articulatory skill, the child is ready to produce the sound in isolation. After the sound has been presented again by the teacher several times, the child is ready to try the sound. After each trial he checks the way the sound looks, feels, and sounds when he produces it with the instructor's observation. The instructor and the child take turns recording the sound pattern on tape; in the playback the two compare the production. When the child can produce the sound successfully and easily in isolation, he is ready to transfer the new pattern to carefully structured speech situations in which his response is limited to a word or phrase. Many such situations were discussed in connection with the speech notebook. Here are other opportunities to try out structured speech:

1. *The Treasure Chest.* Objects or pictures of objects calling for words containing the new sound patterns are placed in a brightly colored box. As the child takes an object or picture from the box which is held above his head, the instructor asks, "What did you find?" The child replies ———— (*l*amp, ba*ll*oon, be*ll*, pai*l*, etc.).

2. *The Speech Tree.* Brightly pictured objects are pasted on cards. If the child names correctly the object which includes the new sound pattern he hangs the card on the tree.

3. *Fishing for Words.* Pictured words containing the new sound patterns are printed on cardboard fish and put in the "pool." With the aid of a magnet, the child pulls out a card. If he says the word correctly, he gets to keep the "fish."

4. *Roulette.* Simple words are printed in large letters on a wheel drawn on the floor. The children walk around the wheel with their eyes closed. As they walk they say, "Fee-diddle-dee, what word will it be?" When the instructor calls "stop," each child must say the word before him.

5. *Ring Toss.* There are several poles placed at varying distances from the player. Each pole bears a flag on which is printed a phrase of a story. The most distant flag bears the end of the story. As the child rings each pole, he says the phrase on the flag. The one who progresses the farthest wins the game.

6. *Spin-It Game.* A milk bottle is filled with slips of paper with words and pictures printed on them. The children spin the bottle, and the one to whom it points must draw a slip of paper from the bottle. If he does not say the word correctly, he must step out of the game.

7. *The Postman.* The child delivers envelopes containing pictures which will elicit the new sound pattern in words or phrases.
8. *Telling Time with Timmy Time Clock.* Each number on the face of "Timmy Time Clock" is a separate block which is removable. The clock also has movable hands. The children sit in a circle with the clock in the center. The teacher moves the hands to one o'clock and asks a child, "What time is it?" The child says, "It is one o'clock." If he says it correctly, he may take the block.
9. Conversation games:
    a. A room is chosen which the children will furnish. The teacher asks the questions: (1) Where should the lamp go?; (2) Is there a stove in the bedroom?; (3) Does it belong *under* the table or *over* the table? etc.
    b. The instructor says, "I'm thinking of ———" and describes a toy, an animal, or food, the name of which includes the new sound pattern. The children guess the name.

F. *Setting the Pattern in Structured Speech.* By this time the child should be ready to build the new pattern into the total speech synergy. Correction rarely is made by the teacher except in general terms of the total effect of the communication. The child makes spontaneous corrections and criticizes his own efforts. Here are some suggestions for making this part of the program good fun:

1. Wearing speech badges.
    a. The therapist bandages the child's thumb. When he meets his friends and the staff during the day, each one asks, "Now what has happened to you?" The child replies, "I hurt my *th*umb."
    b. The child wears a badge with a picture of a famous animal character. He shows the picture to five people and says, "Bet you can't guess what I am." "I am ——— (Pooh-Bear, Lassie or Lady, Stuart Little, Flopsy or Mopsy, etc.)"
    c. Other badges: "Ask me my name." "How old am I?" etc.
2. *Let's telephone.* One play telephone is needed with many "extensions." The receivers are cardboard megaphones attached to the main play telephone. One child at the main telephone calls another child: "Hello, who is this?" "This is ———." "How are you?" "I am fine, thank you."
3. *Let's broadcast!* A group of children make up a program for the Radio Hour which they tape-record. It is presented at some special occasion.
4. *Fill-In Stories.* As the story is told the child says only the one line which he has rehearsed several times. The following stories are examples:
    a. *The Three Little Pigs.* ("I'll huff and I'll puff and I'll blow your house down.")
    b. *The Little Red Hen.* ("Not I," says the duck, goose, etc.)
    c. *Billy Goats Gruff.* ("Who's walking over my bridge?")
    d. *Chicken Little.* ("The sky is falling. We must go to tell the King.")

5. Creative dramatics, simplified version. The children select well-known characters from stories, movies or television. They make up their own lines and also make their costumes. These are some popular stories with small children: *Chicken Little, Lady and the Tramp, Little Black Sambo, Goldilocks and the Three Bears, Jack and the Bean Stalk, Lassie, Snow White and the Seven Dwarfs.*

G. Checking the Establishment of the Pattern in Free Conversational Speech. In a resident center there is ample opportunity to check transfer of the new patterns to conversational speech outside the clinical situation, particularly if "indirect therapists" are employed who associate closely with the children in crafts, recreation, preschool, the dining room, and the dormitory. Parties and excursions to the movies, zoo, circus, and parks provide further opportunity to test results. The indirect therapist offers only gentle reminders, such as: "I guess you've lost your Sunday speech," "There must be a Mr. Lazy Lips in the room," or "Where is your Good Speech Cap?"

It is more difficult to check on the reinforcement of the patterns at home. The notebook is an aid in securing the continuous co-operation of the parent. Visits to the child's home are the best way to gain reassurance—or to increase one's doubts!

If the child is in school, the classroom teacher generally is co-operative in planning opportunities for the speech-handicapped child to try out his new patterns. It is the therapist's responsibility to inform the teacher regularly about the sound patterns on which the child is working. Speech correctionists in the public schools may prepare speech bulletins for the school staff which describe the therapy and progress of each child receiving speech help.

Speech training is a co-operative project utilizing resources of the teacher, the child, and the clinic, but it also makes demands on the family and the community who must share the responsibility.

Special Aids for Common Substitutions and Distortions of Sounds

The S-sound: Lisping. This sound deserves special consideration for two reasons. It is a difficult sound to make and consequently is frequently distorted. The sound demands great precision in movement, balance, and pressure of the articulators. Although there are variants, this is the way one acceptable kind of s-sound is made. The lips are retracted and slightly tensed. The teeth should be in fairly close approximation, a position sometimes difficult to achieve because it depends upon the ability of the mandible (lower jaw) to make the necessary adjustments to meet the upper jaw. The teeth also must be sufficiently regular in outline so that they can obstruct the breath stream at all points. The incisors present a sharp, cutting, partial obstruction for the narrow channel of air sliding along the tongue. This channel is made by elevating the tongue, and cupping it so as to produce a groove or trough along the median raphé (the longitudinal line of union in the tongue). The sides of the tongue are pressed against the inner edges of the gum as far forward as the central incisors, but the tongue-tip is free. It either is raised toward the alveolar ridges or is dropped behind the lower teeth. (See Fig. 7-1.) The muscles of the pharynx and velum contract, closing the opening into the nose. Admittedly, the production of a clear, sibilant *s* is a difficult operation.

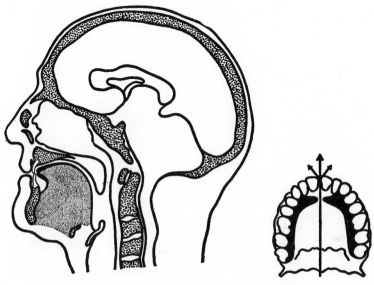

FIGURE 7-1. Articulatory picture of a normal *s* (*z*) and palatogram of normal *s* (*z*). Note that tongue-tip may be raised or lowered in production of sound.

The second reason for special consideration of the *s*-sound is that it has the highest frequency of all speech sounds and any distortion consequently produces an acoustic effect which is noticeable. One can hear a "lateral *s*," for example, above the hubbub of conversation in a great hall. No other sound calls quite so much attention to itself when made incorrectly.

Types of Defective S-sounds. Strictly speaking, any distorted sibilant sound, *s-z, sh* [ʃ]-*zh* [ʒ], *ch* [tʃ]-*j* [dʒ], is a lisped sound, but because of the frequency of distortion of the *s*-sound, the term "lisping" has been restricted to deviate productions of the *s-z* sounds. Among the several types of defective *s*-sounds described by phoneticians, we shall consider four major deviations: the central *s*-lisp, the lateral *s*-lisp, the whistling or prolonged sibilant *s*-lisp, and the recessive *s*-lisp.

The *central* s-*lisp* is made by obstructing the narrow channel of air by placing the tongue-tip too far forward either against the teeth or between the teeth; or by pressing the tongue-tip against the alveolar ridges instead of allowing it to be free. If the mandible is small and the tongue of normal size, the child may not be able to retract the tongue far enough to pull the tip away from the central incisors. If the frenulum is short, so that the tip and blade are not free, it may be impossible to form a central groove in the tongue or to arch the tongue upward and away from the central incisors. Sometimes the whole body of the tongue is immobile and flabby; the tongue cannot be cupped or grooved but lies flat in the mouth. A protruding or recessive mandible or maxilla (upper or lower jaw) can produce severe malocclusion, and the tongue in a compensatory effort is flattened

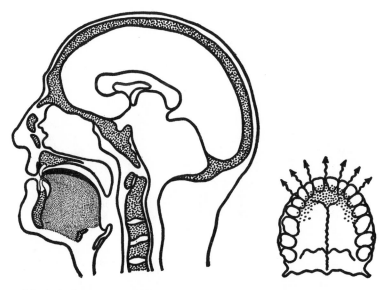

FIGURE 7-2. Articulatory picture of two types of central s-lisp (interdental and dental) and palatogram showing weak emission of breath stream through broad, partially occluded channel.

in an attempt to block the wide opening. In some cases the fault does not lie in the articulatory mechanism but in the failure to initiate a sufficiently strong air stream to bring the required energy to the sound. A central s-lisp on a strictly habitual basis is not uncommon among children who in the interim between first and second dentition thrust the tongue into the space left by the central incisors and so form an undesirable lingual habit for speech. Figure 7-2 presents two positions of the articulatory organs which will produce a central s-lisp. The linguagram and palatogram show, respectively, the portion of the tongue which is juxtaposed against the palatal borders and the portion of the palate and gum-ridge with which the tongue makes contact.

In the *lateral* s-*lisp* the air escapes over the sides of the tongue, producing a sound similar to *sh* [ʃ] or a voiceless *l* (Fig. 7-3). Frequently excessive saliva seems to be present, so that there is a bubbling or thick quality to the sound (the "inebriate's sound"). The excessive salivation may be one cause, but more frequently the tongue action is faulty. The tip touches the center of the alveolar section of the palate or the upper front teeth, so that the air is forced over one or both sides of the tongue. The acoustic effect is a voiceless *l*. In other cases the tongue is flabby and non-co-ordinated so that no channel or central groove is formed; the air literally slides in all directions, producing a sound approaching the *sh* [ʃ] sound. In other cases, dental malformation and malocclusion make it impossible for the tongue to block completely the space as far forward as the central incisors.

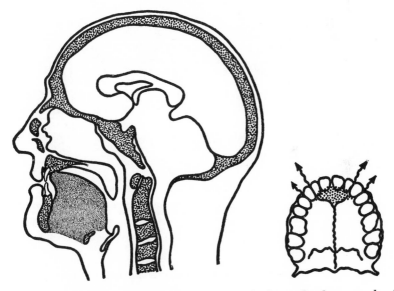

FIGURE 7-3. Articulatory picture of one type of lateral s-lisp and palatogram showing lateral emission of breath stream.

The *prolonged sibilant* or *whistling* s-*lisp* is more common in adults than children. This "pedantic *s*-sound" may be made in a variety of ways, but usually it is produced by too great tension in all the articulators: mandible, lips, and tongue. The tongue blade may be held with too great tension against the alveolar ridge so that the opening for the emission of the breath stream is too small. Or the tongue may be retracted rather than arched forward in the mouth so that the blade makes contact with the prepalate rather than the alveolar ridge.

In the *recessive* s-*lisp,* the tongue generally is sluggish, assuming a position as for the retroflex *l,* the lips are lax, and the air is deflected backward, escaping through the nose. Figure 7-4 makes clear the position of the tongue and palate in the production of a recessive *s*-lisp.

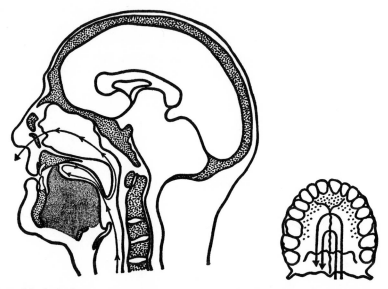

FIGURE 7-4. Articulatory picture of one type of recessive *s*-lisp (nasal emission of breath stream) and palatogram of retroflex *s*-lisp.

Special Techniques to Correct the S-lisp. The steps outlined in the preceding section on the development of all speech sounds should be followed. In the case of the *s*-sound, visual stimulation is particularly valuable because much of the articulatory movement is visible. Additional specific suggestions follow:

1. To aid in the establishment of a narrow channel along the tongue for the breath stream:
    a. Groove the tongue along the median raphé with a slender orange stick, and ask the child to curl his tongue around the stick.
    b. Test the central emission of the breath stream by means of paper flags or feathers placed just in front of the lower lip.
2. To aid in the establishment of lateral occlusion of the tongue and a free tongue-tip:
    a. Direct the child to "suck" the tongue up against the palate, then release it. Alternate this movement. The same result may be obtained by asking the child to raise the whole tongue and "paste" the sides against the molar and premolar teeth, leaving only the tip of the tongue free.

    b. If the child persists in placing the tongue-tip against the teeth, push the tongue back with a tongue depressor. Direct the child to make a hissing sound while you hold the applicator in place.

    c. Direct the child to swallow with energy and midway in the process, release the tongue-tip from the palate. A hissing *s*-sound may be attempted as the tip is dropped.

3. In case of a recessive *s*-lisp, employ the exercises for front focal placement of the articulators and for velar control outlined in the preceding section, pp. 138-140.

4. In case of a lateral *s*-lisp have the child retract the lips sharply and push the body of the tongue forward.

5. Try to shift from related sounds which the child possesses in this manner:

    a. Begin with the position for *th* [θ]; as the breath stream is continued, draw the tongue sharply backward and up, being sure that the sides of the tongue are touching the inner edges of the upper teeth as far forward as the central incisors.

    b. Begin with the position for *sh* [ʃ]; then retract the lips and push the tongue slightly forward.

    c. Begin with the sound *t,* holding the period of plosion for some little time; retract the lips, then drop the jaw slightly. If the grooving has been maintained, a sharp *ts* should be heard. Continue the *s*-sound.

6. *Animal Lotto.* As each child draws a picture card, the teacher asks a question about the animal pictured on the card which the child must answer. For example, "Is the pu*s*sy cat a*s*leep?" "Ye*s*, the pu*s*sy cat i*s* a*s*leep." "Does the *s*nake *s*lide and hi*ss*?" "Can thi*s* fly buzz?" "Can thi*s* pig *s*queal?"

7. *I See Something You May See Game.* The teacher says, "I *s*ee something you may see. Guess what it is." The child says, "Do you see a ———?" and names some object or picture in the room whose designation contains the *s*-sound.

8. *What Is Missing?* A series of line drawings of objects; in each object one essential part is missing. The teacher says, "What is missing?" The child replies, "The doll's slipper is missing," "The seat is missing on the tricycle," "Bunny's nose is missing," etc.

9. *Socks Game.* Colored paper socks with words containing the *s*-sound printed on them are put in a "laundry bag." The child is told that whenever he says the word on the sock correctly he may "hang the sock on the line to dry."

10. *S-blend Exercise.* Have the child name all the things that he can do, such as smile, sniff, sneeze, slide, skate, sweep, stand, stoop, scream, etc.

11. Rhymes and songs containing many *s*-sounds.

    a. Sammy Snake is a good little snake,
       He lies on a rock all day.
       He sleeps, and sleeps, and sleeps in the sun
       And then he awakes and he'll say
           s-s-s-s-s-s!

    b. Did you ever see a lassie, a lassie, a lassie;
       Did you ever see a lassie do this way and that?
       Do this way and that way, and this way and that way,
       Did you ever see a lassie do this way and that?

    c. Here we go round the Christmas tree,
            Christmas tree, Christmas tree,
       Here we go round the Christmas tree,
            So early Christmas morning.
       (Tune: Here We Go Round the Mulberry Bush)

    d. Pussy cat, pussy cat, where have you been?
       I've been to London to visit the queen.
       Pussy cat, pussy cat, what did you there?
       I frightened a little mouse under the chair.

    e. I have a little pussy;
       Her coat is silver grey.
       She lives down in our meadow
       And never runs away.
       She'll always be a pussy,
       She'll never be a cat.
       Her name is pussy willow;
       Now what do you think of that?

    f. Skip along and sing your song,
       Swing your arms all day long.

    g. Skipping is fun, skipping is fun,
       Skipping is fun for everyone.
       The longer you skip, the better you skip.
       So skip, **skip**, skip, skip.

    h. Cut, **cut; sew**, sew!
       Press, **press**, press.
       That's **how** Mother makes a dress!

12. Stories containing many *s-z* sounds:

    a. The Sailboat That Ran Away, by Madge L. Chastain.[5]

    b. The Wizard of Oz, by F. L. Baum; animated by Julian Wehr.[6]

13. *Talking-Tracing Games.* Duplicated sets of mazes with accompanying pictures of the setting and characters in a well-known story. The child is instructed, for example, to "help Lassie find her way home to her mistress"; "look for the mittens lost by the naughty kittens"; "trace Goldilocks' way in the house of the Three Bears."

14. Excursion: Going to the zoo. One child is the leader in recounting a recent experience; members of the group contribute to the story. The leader: "Yesterday all of us went to the zoo in a big bus. The sun was hot so we each spent seventeen cents for straw hats. What did you see, Sally, that you liked?" Sally: "I saw the monkeys in the monkey house." Sam: "I saw the polar bears swimming in a cement pool." Sue: "I saw two baby elephants with long trunks." Steve: "The giraffes were silly-

[5] Racine, Wisconsin, Whitman Publishing Company, 1950.
[6] Akron, Ohio, The Saalfield Publishing Company, 1944.

looking animal*s*; they have long neck*s*." Leader: "We were tired and thir*s*ty *s*o we ate our *s*upper before we got on the bu*s* to come home. We drank milk from pla*s*tic cup*s* and had cookie*s* and i*c*e cream. We all went to *s*leep on the bu*s* coming home—all ex*c*ept the driver."

Special Aids in Correcting Other Common Substitutions and Distortions

1. Common substitutions for [l]:   [w] and [j]

   "I want a lolly-pop" [aɪ wɑ̃ ə wɑwɪ pɑp]

   "I saw a yellow balloon" [aɪ sɔ: ə jɛjo bɔjun]

   a. Retract the lips sharply, holding them back with the fingers if necessary and ask the child to sing "la-la-la."

   b. If the child has an open bite (upper and lower incisors do not occlude) and a high palatal arch, the tongue may not reach the alveolar ridge easily. Ask the child to put the tip behind the lower teeth and make palatal contact with the dorsum of the tongue.

   c. If the child substitutes [j] for [l] have him prolong the [j] sound and while doing it, force the tip and blade of the tongue forward against the alveolar ridges. Generally this action will force the mid-section of the tongue down which has been raised for [j].

   d. Show the child a picture of the placement of the tongue as it makes an [l] with the tip of the tongue raised touching the alveolar ridge. Then show him another picture of the placement of the tongue as it makes [j] with the blade and middle of the tongue touching the palate.

   e. Lick a Lollipop. The teacher "marks" the place on the alveolar ridge with a lollipop where the child is to place his tongue to make a correct [l]. If the child puts his tongue in the right place he tastes the flavor of the lollipop. This also can be done with peanut butter or honey.

   f. Lightning Bugs on the Lawn. When the child says a word containing an *l*-sound correctly, he is allowed to take a "lightning bug" from the lawn and put it in a box. The one with the most "lightning bugs" wins. (The "lightning bugs" are bent paper clips with a piece of yellow yarn tied onto them; the lawn is a grass mat.)

   g. Loo, lee, lah,
      Loo, lee, lah.
      My tongue can do things, if it tries.
      Loo, lee, lah,
      Loo, lee, lah,
      It takes its morning exercise.[7]

   h. *Doggie's Tongue*

      Lap, lap, lap, lap, lap
         Goes my doggie's tongue
         When he takes a drink.

---

[7] Scott and Thompson, *op. cit.*, p. 105.

Lap, lap, lap, lap, lap
   The water is gone
   Quicker than a wink.[8]

i. Picture Rhymes.[9] Line drawings of six pictures, three in a series. The child is to identify the pictures and make up a rhyme about them. [l] pictures are:

a lamb, a pillow, a wall
a leaf, a dolly, a stall.

j. Stories: *Lu-Lu the Duck* by S. Porter.[10]

2. Substitutions for [k]: [t];   for [g]: [d].
   "Give me my cap" [dɪv mi maɪ tæp]
   (These sounds are treated together since [d] and [g] are the voiced analogues respectively of [t] and [k.])

a. Show the child a picture of the placement of the tongue as it makes a [k] or [g] with the dorsum of the tongue humped up and touching the soft palate. Then show him another picture of the placement of the tongue as it makes [t] or [d] with the dorsum down and the tip of the tongue up touching the alveolar ridge.

b. Put peanut butter on the soft palate. If the child articulates [k] or [g] correctly, there will be peanut butter on the dorsum of the tongue.

c. Anchor the tongue-tip behind the lower teeth, holding it down if necessary with a tongue depressor. Buckle the back of the tongue and build up oral pressure. Release the tongue quickly, exploding the breath stream.

d. Alternate the raising of the back and front tongue in a rocking movement: [k-t]; [k-t]; etc. A cut-out picture of a rocking chair may be used to show the child how the tongue is supposed to go.

e. Let's Play Telephone. On a toy phone the child calls the teacher. The teacher asks such questions as, "How did you come to the clinic?" (In a *c*ar.) "It is cold today. What are you wearing?" (A *c*oat and *c*ap.) "What do you have in your po*c*ket?" (I put a ba*g* of *c*andy in my po*c*ket.) "What else did you bring?" (My boo*k* and my lunch.) "What will you have for lunch?" (Coo*k*ies and mil*k*.)

f. Songs and Rhymes.

(1) Old MacDonald Had A Farm. (On the farm he had a *c*ow, a du*ck,* a do*g, g*oose, etc.)

(2) *G*ood morning, *g*ood morning,
*G*ood morning to you.
*G*ood morning, *g*ood morning,
We're *g*lad to see you.

---

[8] *Ibid.,* p. 105.

[9] *Speech in the Elementary School,* Los Angeles City School Districts, Curriculum Division, Publication No. 479 (1949), p. 28.

[10] New York, Capital Publishing Company, 1948.

(3) To mar*k*et, to mar*k*et
To buy a fine pi*g*.
Home a*g*ain, home a*g*ain
Ri*g*-a-ji*g*-ji*g*.

(4) Listen to the *k*itchen *cl*o*ck*
Ti*ck*-to*ck;* ti*ck*-to*ck!*

(5) Patty *C*at and Tabby Ann
To *c*atch a rat a race began.
But that fat rat bit Patty *C*at
And Tabby Ann just ran, and ran, and ran.

g. Stories:

   (1) CARRIE KANGAROO [k]

Carrie was a big mother Kangaroo. The farmer bought her from a circus and took her home to another animal neighborhood. A kangaroo, you know, is a big, kind animal with small front legs and large back legs on which it runs very fast. And in front, the mother kangaroo has a pocket in her skin where she can carry her baby kangaroo in case of danger. So the kangaroo's name was Carrie because she could carry her baby kangaroo in her pocket.

But all the animals on the farm had never seen a kangaroo before. They thought Carrie was a funny-looking animal. They wouldn't be nice to her or to her baby kangaroo. This made her feel very sad.

"I kill mice," said Mrs. Cat in a cross voice. "What can you do?"

"I can carry my baby in my pocket, and run fast,'calumph, calumph,'" said Carrie Kangaroo sadly.

"Oh, pooh," said Mrs. Cat. "That isn't much. *I* can carry my kittens in my mouth."

"Moo, I give milk. What can you do?" asked the cow.

"I can carry my baby in my pocket and run fast, 'calumph, calumph,'" said Carrie Kangaroo sadly.

"Pooh," said the cow, "I can run 'calumph, calumph' if I wish."

Just then a cuckoo bird in a cuckoo clock who heard what the animals were saying, came out of his little door. "Cuckoo!" he cried.

All the animals laughed. "Yes, Carrie Kangaroo is cuckoo!" they cried. And poor Carrie Kangaroo put Baby Kangaroo in her pocket and went home on her long back legs, "calumph, calumph, calumph."

A few days later, Carrie Kangaroo, leaving her baby at home, was going "calumph" down the road. Of course she was alone because all the animals were so cross to her that she did not like to talk to them. Then she noticed Mrs. Cat's three kittens playing in the middle of the road. Mrs. Cat had told them not to play in the road for a big car might hit them. Carrie Kangaroo saw Mrs. Cat coming to get them, so she went on her way. But all of a sudden Carrie heard Mrs. Cat go "Mew, Mew" very loud. She looked back. Mrs. Cat was trying to pick up her kittens in her mouth to carry them out of the road. The three kittens were too frightened to move. And no wonder! Down the road came a great big car! Surely it would run over the three little kittens who were too frightened to move. And Mrs. Cat would have time to carry only one kitten in her mouth to safety.

"Calumph! Calumph!" went Carrie Kangaroo. She ran back to the kittens as fast as she could go. And while Mrs. Cat carried one kitten in her mouth, Carrie Kangaroo put the others in her pocket and carried them off the road before the car could hit them!

Mrs. Cat was so happy that she couldn't stop thanking Carrie. She was sorry for the cross things she had said to Carrie. She told the other animals how brave Carrie Kangaroo had been to save the kittens. The other animals knew they had been wrong. They made Carrie Kangaroo their friend. And the cuckoo clock never called Carrie "cuckoo" any more.

(2) GERRY GOOSE [g]

This is the story of Gerry, the Goose who wanted to get fat. But every time she went near the corn field, Gobo, the Goat chased her away. "Go away, Gerry Goose," he cried and would not let her eat although there was enough for both of them. Then Gobo would butt Gerry Goose with his horns. Gerry could not get enough to eat to make her fat. What should she do? Gerry Goose walked along the road. Soon she met a black crow. "Oh, Crow, what shall I do? Gobo Goat chases me away from the corn and I cannot get fat." "Caw! Caw!" said Black Crow. "Ask the girl coming down the road."

"Oh, Girl, what shall I do?" asked Gerry. "Gobo Goat chases me away from the corn and I cannot find food to make me fat." But the girl did not know what to do. "Come with me, Gerry," she said. They went to the farmer. "Farmer," said the girl, "what shall Gerry Goose do? Gobo Goat chases her away from the corn and she cannot find food to make her fat."

"We'll see about that," said the farmer. He took Gerry Goose to the corn field. Gobo came rushing out of the field to butt Gerry Goose. And what do you think? At that very minute the farmer closed a big gate in the fence so that Gobo Goat could not go back in the field. Gerry Goose was small enough to go through the bars.

"There," said the farmer, "they who will not let others eat shall have no food for themselves." And he went away, leaving Gobo outside the field, looking very, very hungry. As for Gerry Goose, she became very fat indeed.

(3) Other stories:

(a) *Can Can* by Fritz Willis [11]
(b) *Crybaby Calf* by H. and A. Evers [12]
(c) *Gidappy* by E. Church [13]

3. Common substitution for *th* [θ]: [f];   for *th* [ð]: [v].
   "I think that's right" [aɪ fɪŋk væts raɪt]

   a. Evert the lips slightly and let the tip of the tongue show between the upper and lower teeth. The contact of teeth against tongue should be *very light*. Direct the breath stream in a continuous flow over the center of your tongue and between your teeth.

[11] Hollywood, The Marcel Redd Company, Mistletoe Press, 1945.
[12] New York, Rand, 1941.
[13] Garden City, New York, Garden City Publishing Co., Inc., 1950.

b. Pant as a dog does, with the mouth open and tongue extended beyond the teeth.

c. Hold the lower lip down and away from the teeth. Slowly protrude the tongue between the teeth.

d. Pretend that you are cooling the tongue after tasting hot soup by putting it "outside the door" (teeth).

e. Hold a lollipop close to the child's lips. When he says the *th* [θ] sound correctly, his tongue will touch the lollipop.

f. Hide the Thimble Game. The teacher hides the thimble somewhere in the room. The child guesses the place, saying, "Did you hide the *th*imble in the ———?" A variation of the game would be to mount pictures of the rooms of a house on a poster board. Then the teacher hides an imaginary thimble in one of the rooms of the house. (This also affords practice on words such as ba*th*room, ba*th*tub, ba*th*towel, mo*th*er's room, fa*th*er's room, etc.)

g. The leader says, "I'm thinking of an animal wi*th* (or without) ———;" (a long trunk, a fan for tail feathers, etc.). "Guess what?" A child replies, "You are *th*inking of an elephant wi*th* a long trunk," etc.

h. Stories:

(1) THE MOUSE AND THE THUNDER (*th*) [θ]

Once there was a little mouse who was afraid of thunder. When she saw thick dark clouds in the sky she would run and hide.

"Thunder! Thunder scares you!", the other mice would cry. They would chase her and say, "Thunder! Thunder! Run!" And it scared the little mouse so she ran and hid.

One day she went for a long walk. She was far, far away. It was hot. "I'm thirsty," said the mouse. "Oh, I want a drink. I am so thirsty!" Just then it began to thunder but the little mouse was so thirsty that for a moment she didn't hear the thunder. Then a great thunder rolled out of the sky. It scared her and she cried and began to run. Then she saw a frog.

"Thunder!" he said. "I'm glad. Now my pool won't dry up." The frog liked thunder.

Then she saw a duck. "Thunder! Hurrah!" he said. "Mud is nice." The duck liked thunder.

"Why, they are glad it thunders," said the mouse. She thought and thought. "I know! When it thunders we have rain," she thought, "and rain is good. If it rains, I can have some water. And I'm so thirsty!"

The mouse was right. Soon it rained. She got her drink of water and thunder didn't scare her after that.

4. Common substitution for [t], [d], [l] in medial and final positions: the glottal stop, [ʔ].

"Little Robin Redbreast:" [lɪʔə rɑbʔ rɛʔ brɛʔ]

"Niddle noddle went his head:" [nɪʔə nɑʔə wɛnʔ hɪ hɛʔ]

a. Relax the muscles of the throat. Open the mouth for [ɑ] as in *father* and making sure that the back-tongue is down, slowly raise the front-tongue to the alveolar ridges. If the contact is light, an [l] should result;

if hard, the tongue should be in a position for the *t*-sound. In making [l], the child should feel the lateral emission of the breath stream.

b. Change the focal point of articulation to the front mouth. Stress the lip and tongue-tip exercises (pp. 139-140). In producing the glottal stop, the tongue generally is retracted in the mouth and the front tongue is immobile. Move the center of tension forward! Make the tongue-tip flexible.

c. A bulletin board shows Santa's sleigh overturned and Santa and his toys flying through the air. Each child picks up a toy: do*ll*y, ba*ll*, ba*t*, scoo*t*er, etc. which he would like from Santa.

d. Rhymes and songs:

(1) Pe*t*er, Pe*t*er Pumpkin Ea*t*er

(2) "I'm a li*tt*le teapo*t*, shor*t* and s*t*ou*t*,
Here is my li*tt*le handle, here is my spou*t*.
When I ge*t* all s*t*eamed up, then I shou*t*,
Jus*t* *t*ip me over and pour me ou*t*."

e. Stories: *Trouble, the Careless Kitten,* by D. and S. Stearns [14]

5. Common substitution for [f]: [p];   for [v]: [b].

a. While the child is saying *a* as in *father,* place his lower lip under the edge of the upper teeth and direct him to blow the breath stream between lip and teeth so that the friction is audible.

b. If the lips are retracted as in smiling, it will be difficult for the child to say [b] for [v].

c. Say slowly, "fee-fie-foe-fum," placing the lip under the teeth before beginning each syllable. The contact of lip and teeth must be sufficiently light to allow the air to escape.

d. If all other methods fail to keep the lower lip under the upper teeth when saying [f] or [v], put a piece of masking tape tightly over the lower lip to increase awareness of position of lower lip.

e. Trace the outline of the child's hand in his notebook. How many fingers? Count them: one, two, three, *f*our, *f*ive *f*ingers.

f. Fishing Game. The child finds toy fish around the room. Every time he finds one, he says, "I *f*ound a *f*ish."

g. Valentine Game. The child is allowed to "mail" one valentine every time he says a word containing [v] correctly. Then the child says, "I am mailing a *v*alentine to ———," etc.

h. A *V*isit to the *F*arm. The child tells all the people, animals, and places he visits on the farm. For example, "I *v*isit my grandmother on the *f*arm;" "I *v*isit the cows on the *f*arm;" "I *v*isit the barn on the *f*arm."

i. Guess What Game. Many mounted pictures which should call forth the key sound are arranged on the walls around the room. The teacher reads the incomplete sentence: one picture on the board will give the right answer. The child presents the picture to the class and says the "*f*" word:

[14] Kenosha, Wisconsin, John Martin's House, Inc., 1945.

(1) Tommy caught a big ——— on his line.

(2) John must wash his ———.

(3) On the Fourth of July we put up the ———.

(4) Airplanes ——— in the air.

(5) If you play with matches you may start a ———.

(6) My bunny has a coat of ———; but Chicken Little's coat is made of ———.

(7) Mary hurt her knee when she ——— down.

(8) Around this picture is a wooden ———.

(9) He is a little animal that lives in a pond and is called a ———.

(10) My dog's name is Flink; he was hurt in a ———.

(11) By my plate are a ——— and a ———.

(12) I can see a tiny green ——— on that tree.

(13) In my garden are some pretty ———.

j. Stories:

(1) Beads of two colors are given to a child who acts as judge. Another child tells the story of Flink, his dog. Each time he says the [f] sound correctly, a red bead is dropped into the box; when an error is made, a green bead is dropped. "Flag is our neighbor's cat. She washes her face with her paws and most of the time she gets along fine with Flink, our dog. They only fight when Flink tries to eat Flag's food. When Flink comes near Flag's bowl, she humps her back and says, 'f-f-f.' But why should Flink like to eat Flag's food? It smells like fish and dogs shouldn't like fish. It's hard to figure out dogs—sometimes, I think."

(2) *Forgetful Bear* by N. Raymond [15]

(3) *The Story of Ferdinand,* by Munro Leaf [16]

6. Common substitution for [r]: [w].

"She has a red rose:" [ʃi hæz ə wɛd woʊz]

a. The *r*-sound is difficult to master and should be attempted only after easier sounds have been learned.

b. Unround the lips forcibly; exaggerate the retraction.

c. Intone [ɑ] as in *father;* raise the tongue-tip and blade, cupping the tongue toward the palate but not touching the palate.

d. While saying [l] pull the lower jaw down slowly until you reach the [r] position.

e. *Purr-r-r-r-r* like a kitten; imitate the rooster waking people up in the morning, *r-r-r-r;* growl like a tiger, *gr-r-r-r-r.*

f. Right or Wrong Game. The child says in response to statement made by the teacher, "That is right" or "That is wrong."

g. Feel the position of the tongue as it makes [i] and then work toward [r] by lowering the tongue slightly.

[15] Grand Rapids, Michigan, Fideler Company, 1943.

[16] New York, Viking Press, Inc., 1949.

7. Common substitutions for *ch* [tʃ]: [t];   for *j* [dʒ]: [d].

    a. Place the tongue for [t]; quickly pucker the lips and explode the [t].

    b. Sneeze forcibly: [kɝtʃuː].

    c. Imitate a train picking up speed: [tʃuː tʃuː]; the croaking of a frog: [kɝtʃɔg; gɝtʃɔg].

    d. If the child is having difficulty in making these sounds, *ch* [tʃ] and *j* [dʒ], tell him to make *t* and then *sh* [ʃ] separately. First slowly, and then increasing the speed until the two sounds become *ch* [tʃ].

    e. Johnny the *Ch*icken says, "*Ch*eep, *ch*eep, *ch*eep." (Use a toy chicken or a picture of a chicken for motivation.)

    f. *J*immy the *J*abberwockey Bird says, "*J*abber, *j*abber, *j*ibber, *j*ibber, *j*abber." (Use a picture of an odd-looking bird for motivation.)

    g. Stories:

      (1) THE TWO CHICKS (*ch*) [tʃ]

Once there were two baby chicks who wanted to see the world. One was as black as charcoal. One was as white as chalk.

"Cheep, cheep," said the black one. "Let us see the world."

"Chirp, chirp," said the white one. "Let us see the world." So they set out upon their way.

Soon they met Gray Squirrel. "Chatter, chatter," said Gray Squirrel; "where are you going, chicks?"

"Cheep," said the black one, "to see the world."

"Chirp," said the white one, "to see the world." Gray Squirrel laughed.

The baby chicks went on their way. Soon they met old Dobbin, the horse. He was eating hay, "champ, champ." "Where are you going, chicks?" he asked.

"Cheep," said the black one, "to see the world."

"Chirp," said the white one, "to see the world." But Dobbin, the horse, went on eating, "champ, champ," and smiled a bit at the silly chicks.

The two chicks were tired. They thought they had traveled so far that they must be nearly to the end of the earth.

"Oh, chirp, we are lost;" "Oh, cheep, we are lost," they cried.

But a robin heard them. "Cheerup, cheerup," he cried, and gave them a cherry to eat. "You'll find your way home," he said, "cheerup, cheerup," and he laughed.

"We are so far from home. Why do they laugh?" asked the chicks. Then they went around a bush, and what do you think they saw? Their own chicken coop, with Mother Chicken calling them. They rushed up to her.

"Oh, Mother, cheep, cheep, we have been around the world," said the black chick.

"Oh, Mother, chirp, chirp, we have been around the world," said the white chick. Mother Chicken laughed.

"Why, you haven't been out of the farmyard," she said. The chicks looked around. And sure enough, they hadn't!

8

Correction of Articulation in Older Children and Adults

The procedures, techniques, and materials in the previous chapter were based on the assumption that the young child needs to be enticed and to find pleasure in the ways of correct speech. Though this assumption may in some instances also hold for older children and adults, we believe that in general a different premise may be assumed for them. The different premise is that faulty articulation has been sufficiently penalizing to make the individual want to correct his defects. For the most part, therefore, the speech therapist need not spend much time in wooing the speech defective, or in playing sound games as an inducement for correction. Games, if they are on a level of interest for the adolescent, may be used for variety or as reward. Usually, we think, a direct approach in which the individual is made aware of his defect or defects, a statement of objectives, and an outline of a program and approach should be sufficient for most older children. It certainly should be sufficient for most adults.

Of course, all the suggestions for creating awareness of sounds discussed in Chapter 7, Training the Child Retarded in Speech may be applied, when appropriate, to the older child and to the adult. We may take it for granted that an individual who comes to a speech clinic on his own initiative has some idea of what is wrong with his speech. In school and college situations, however, some adolescents and young adults with articulatory defects may occasionally be found who have somehow escaped knowing that they produce some sounds defectively. Creating awareness that there is a problem may be a necessary first step after referral to the clinic.

BASIC PRINCIPLES FOR CORRECTION OF ARTICULATORY DEFECTS

The principles to be outlined are actually only formalizations of procedures and approaches which were relevant for the younger child. The statement of working principles is based on the assumption that we will be dealing with the normal adolescent or adult who does not have a neurotic need for his defective articulation. Further, we will assume that the individual has no significant organic anomaly of the articulatory apparatus which must be treated before acceptable articulation can be achieved. With these assumptions in mind, the following principles should generally pertain:

1. The individual must be made aware of his specific sound defect or defects.

2. The specific defect must be analyzed to determine what makes it unacceptable. The individual must learn to recognize the acoustic and the kinesthetic differences between the desired sound and the sound which he is producing.

3. With whatever individual adjustment is found necessary, the articulatory-defective person needs to be trained to produce the desired sound at will, in isolation, and in context.

4. Through the use of practice, in formal exercises or in "normal" speech situations, the desired sound must be established and reinforced so that it will be habitually and unconsciously retained.

5. Full use should be made of the intelligence, curiosity, and learning ability of the individual. He should be given as much information about his sound-production mechanism as he can relate or apply in his training. A vocabulary about speech production will be helpful to him.

CREATING AWARENESS OF DEFECTIVE SOUND PRODUCTION

If the adolescent or adult is not aware, or is only vaguely aware, of his defective articulation, active awareness must be created. If a recorder is available, the individual should have a recording made of some material especially constructed or selected for its above-average incidence of the specific sound to be corrected. Some conversation oriented to the incorporation of key words should also be included in the tape recording. The written material should also be recorded by the therapist so that the individual may be able to contrast his sound production with that of a non-defective articulator.

When the individual has become aware that his articulation is defective, training to recognize the defective and the correct sound is in order. Approaches toward this end include the following:

1. The therapist informs the case (person undergoing therapy) that he will read a list of words and intentionally imitate the case's articulatory error one or more times. The case is to check each word on which an error is made from his own list. The accuracy of the checking is itself to be checked by the therapist.

2. The therapist may read a list or a paragraph and intentionally make

one or more errors in the reading. The case is to signal each time he hears the error.

3. The therapist and the case engage in conversation. The case is informed that an intentional error will occasionally be made. The case is to signal each time he hears an articulatory error.

4. The therapist directs the case to read a list of selected words and to exaggerate his error in the production of the key sound. Through exaggeration, conscious awareness of both articulatory activity and acoustic product is created.

ANALYSIS OF DEFECTIVE SOUND AND CORRECT SOUND

The last suggestion for creating awareness of the defective sound may become the first step in analyzing why the sound is defective. Through a slow and exaggerated articulation of the defective sound, its voluntary production may be established and so controlled. The therapist, through observation of what the case does, should be able to demonstrate to him how the defective sound is produced. In turn, the case is directed to imitate the defective effort.

The next step is to establish auditory recognition of the correct sound. Among the techniques which may be used are the following:

1. The therapist may read a list of nonsense syllables including the key sound. Most of the key sounds will be articulated correctly, a few will intentionally be produced defectively. The case is directed to signal according to arrangement for the correct and for the defective sound—for example, "thumbs up" when the sound is correct and "thumbs down" when it is defective.

2. The same approach may be used with a list of words or a paragraph. Signals may be varied for variety.

3. A diagram or a palatogram may be made of the essential articulatory position or contact for the defectively produced sound and for the correct sound. The case may be directed to point to the appropriate diagram as the approach in (1) or (2) above is used. The therapist must be certain, whenever a diagram or other illustrative material is used, that (a) the material clearly serves the purpose for which it has been selected or constructed, and (b) that it is readily and completely understood by the person with whom the therapist is working. A diagram which is clear and meaningful for one person may not have the same significance for another. If at all possible, the illustrative material should be made by or with the help of the individual who will be using it.

4. A visual symbol may be used to denote the defective sound. For example, if the patient produces an s with a left lateral emission, the symbol s may be used, with an arrow heading indicating the direction of the emis-

sion; the correct sound may be represented by the phonetic symbol or some other agreed-upon symbol.

5. The sounds may be given names to suggest the undesirable characteristic and the aspired-for characteristic. Encourage the case to use his ingenuity in finding a name for the sounds. If an *s* sounds "slurpy," then it may well be called the "slurpy *s*."

ESTABLISHING THE DESIRED SOUND

In establishing the correct sound, the therapist should make use of multiple avenues of stimulation. Usually visual and auditory stimulation are most easily combined. For some individuals, however, kinesthetic stimulation may be more important than either the visual or the auditory. If experience with an individual indicates that his sound (auditory) discriminative ability is weak, and his visual or kinesthetic responses relatively strong, emphasis should be placed in training through the sensory avenue or avenues which are most potent for him.

Sound Stimulation

Training up to this point has been devoted to recognition of what is wrong with the way a sound is produced and with the acoustic result. When this has been established, emphasis is shifted to the recognition and production of the correct sound. In general, the following steps are involved for correct sound stimulation:

1. The therapist articulates the correct sound in isolation so that the case hears it and sees the activity involved in the production.
2. The isolated sound is imitated by the case.
3. The product is evaluated by the therapist and the case.

If the correct result is obtained, the case should be instructed to repeat the effort so that it becomes as clearly identified as was the incorrect sound. If the produced sound continues to be defective, the therapist should instruct the case to modify his effort in whatever respect seems indicated.

In individual cases this general procedure may need to be modified. We have found that sometimes it is better for the individual to pantomime the sound so that it is seen but not heard before attempting to produce it so that it is both seen and heard. Some persons do better by closing their eyes after they have been shown what is wanted and then making their effort with thinking directed to the feeling and the movement of the sound. After this is established, the visible element is again introduced.

The procedure just outlined follows the "natural" or unconscious manner in which most of us learn to speak acceptably. As infants, we hear and see speech, and somehow manage to learn to do whatever is necessary to speak like the persons in our environment. Few of us have to be told what to do with our articulators to produce acceptable speech. Somehow, while playing with sounds even before we are able to say words, we learn to associate sounds and articulatory movements and to produce and reproduce them at will. Later we learn to combine sounds into what ultimately become words, phrases, and sentences.

Most of us, surprisingly enough, produce individual sounds in much the same manner. Sometimes, however, we produce a sound in a somewhat deviant manner. For example, though most of us produce an *s* with a high tongue position, a few of us, speech therapists included, may produce the *s* with the tongue-tip close to the lower gum rather than the upper gum ridge. There is, of course, no objection to this manner of articulation unless either the acoustic end result is faulty or the visible movements are distracting. If this is true, corrective procedures are in order. For those persons for whom the *sound stimulation procedures* are not sufficient to establish the correct sounds, other methods need to be tried. One which is time-honored is the phonetic placement technique.

Phonetic Placement

The student who has studied phonetics is likely to have learned descriptions and directives for the "proper" placement of the articulators for the production of the sounds of his language. These phonetic descriptions are based on observations of what most persons do to articulate the sounds they speak. Thus, for example, the student is likely to have learned that the *s* in American English speech is a voiceless, lingua-alveolar fricative. Translated into more common parlance, this means that the *s* is usually produced with the tongue elevated and the tip partly in contact with the upper gum ridge as in the diagram below. Though this may be sufficient for the student of phonetics, the person with a defective *s* who cannot learn the correct position "by ear" may be helped with the following information as to necessary articulatory adjustments:

1. The entire tongue is raised so that the sides of the tongue are firmly in contact with the inner surface of the upper back teeth.

2. The tongue is slightly grooved along the midline.

3. The tip of the tongue is placed about a quarter of an inch behind the upper teeth.

4. The teeth are brought in line (or as much in line as the individual's dental formation permits) so that there is a narrow, barely perceptible space between the rows of teeth.

5. Breath is directed along the groove of the tongue toward the cutting edges of the lower teeth.

6. The soft palate is raised to prevent nasal emission of the sound.

Experience has shown that many good speakers vary from this described articulatory position. Some have their tongues close to the lower gum ridge and others produce an acceptable sound with a fairly flat tongue. In the final analysis, the phonetic descriptions are suggestive and not prescriptive.

In working with a person with a defective sound, adjustments will need to be made according to the individual and the limitations of his mechanism.

If phonetic placement is used as a procedure, diagrams, mirrors, and direct imitation of the therapist are useful. The therapist must, however, be certain that his own manner of producing the problem sound is in keeping with the description he is presenting to his case. Sometimes it is helpful to use a tongue depressor or a rounded stick to bring the tongue into the desired position. Occasionally it is necessary only for the therapist to touch the articulatory organs at the point of contact. For example, awareness of the position for the *k* may be created by touching the back of the tongue and the soft palate with a tongue depressor and then directing the case to make contact between the touched parts.

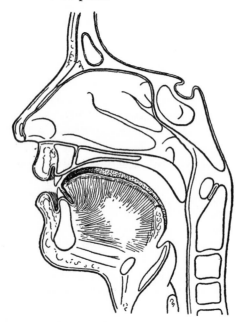

FIGURE 8-1. Representative tongue position for [s] and [z]. (From J. Eisenson, *Basic Speech* [New York, Macmillan, 1950], p. 102.)

Moving from One Sound to Another

We have found that in working with adults, correct sound placement can be taught by using another acceptable sound as a point of departure. For example, an individual with a defective *s* who produces his *t*-sounds correctly can have the *t*-position become the basis for the modification of his *s*. He may be directed to place his tongue in position of the *t* as in *too,* and then to drop the point of his tongue while maintaining the rest of his tongue in the initial position. Frequently it helps to direct the individual to follow a *t* immediately by an *s* as in the words *its* and *hats.*

Analysis of Sound Combinations

The therapist who uses phonetic placement devices should be careful not to overgeneralize his instructions. He should know, for instance, that there are a variety of *t*-sounds in American English speech, and that he is not to instruct his case to produce the *t* of *two* in the same manner as the *t* of *lets, its,* or *cats.* He should also be aware that there is more than one way to produce an *r*-sound, and that sound context is important. With this in mind, he will appreciate that there are differences for the articulators' position for the *r* in *rose, three,* and *crack.* In his corrective efforts, he must help his patient to correct only those sounds, or sound contexts, which are defective and not to permit his case to try to modify sounds in combinations which are being correctly produced.

Practicing Sounds in Context

When the sound has been correctly established in isolation, practice of the sound in context is in order. We recommend the use of nonsense syllables with the key sound in initial, medial, and final position and in more than one position. When this is established, words, phrases, sentences, and paragraphs may be used. We strongly recommend that "tongue twisters" be avoided until the individual is doing so well that he would like to demonstrate his superior skill. The initiative to practice "tongue twisters" should come from the case. Their use is not recommended as regular practice materials.

The therapist should note and bring to the attention of his case words which are correctly pronounced as far as the key sound is concerned. It is encouraging to be told that some words, even though they contain the demon sound, are correctly pronounced and need no longer be of concern. Attention can thus be concentrated on the problem words and contexts in which they are included.

We recommend that at the outset some unfamiliar but useful words be included for practice. The unfamiliar words will give the case an opportunity to establish initially correct pronunciation with the difficult sound rather than calling for a correction of pronunciation of the more familiar words. This device is of help in encouraging the case to feel that despite his articulatory defect or defects, there is much about his articulation that is entirely acceptable.

Conversation

Correction and control of a sound is put to the final test in conversational situations. If the individual can engage in talking and think more of the subject than of the manner of his speaking, and yet have the manner correct, he has established control. Practice toward this end should be part of the training program and should be started as soon as possible. At first, the therapist and his trainee might agree that the conversation will be brief and will center about a few key words with the problem sound. If the key words are correctly pronounced, then the conversation will be considered a success. Later, the therapist may increase the number of key words. Finally, all words containing the sound, whether or not they were anticipated, must be correctly pronounced for a "successful conversation." Ultimately, of course, spontaneous conversation with persons other than the therapist must be included in the individual's self-tests of speech sound control.

PRACTICE MATERIALS

Older children and adults are themselves the best sources for practice materials. Their interests and needs and their motivated resourcefulness should enable the speech therapist to have a constant flow of material for each of the persons with whom he is working. With instruction from the therapist, each case may be expected to make up word lists, phrases, and sentences for practice purposes. Reading materials may come from newspapers, from magazines, and from books that are readily available. This, of course, does not excuse the therapist from having his own supply of practice materials. Even well-motivated persons forget assignments, or lose them, or occasionally find themselves unable to prepare them. With this among other things in mind, we are including materials for articulatory training in this chapter.

The materials are based on words selected from the Thorndike-Lorge *Word List*.[1] Other recommended sources include the Buckingham and Dolch *Combined Word List* [2] and the list contained in Durrell's *Improvement of Basic Reading Abilities*.[3]

The materials are divided into two sections. The Intermediate Exercises, intended for older children, are based on the first 5000 of the Thorndike-Lorge list. The Adult Exercises, intended for educated adults and college students, are based on words chosen from those found above the first 5000 according to the Thorndike-Lorge list.

An explanation is in order for our not using known selections of poetry and prose to supplement the words for articulatory drill. Known material, whether on the intermediate or adult levels, would most likely be uttered in habitual ways. Because these ways are defective from the point of view of articulation, we hoped that new material might help to reduce the likelihood of error once the isolated sounds and words have been learned and correctly produced. If, by some chance, the reader or the individual whose speech is

[1] E. L. Thorndike and I. Lorge, *Teacher's Word Book of 30,000 Words* (New York, Teachers College, Bureau of Publications, Columbia University, 1944).

[2] B. R. Buckingham and E. W. Dolch, *A Combined Word List* (Boston, Ginn, 1936).

[3] D. C. Durrell, *Improvement of Basic Reading Abilities* (Yonkers, N. Y., World Book, 1940).

being corrected enjoys the verses and occasional "stories," that will be considered added and unsought good fortune. One of the authors at least will be especially grateful for this.

Because of our desire to conserve space, we have not felt it necessary to include lists of nonsense syllables with the articulatory drill material. This omission of nonsense syllables should not be taken to mean that the authors do not recommend their use. On the contrary, we insist that the nonsense syllable should be mastered before real words are used for drills. The reader will recall that we recommend that the isolated sound be taught first, then the sound in primary, medial, and final positions in nonsense syllables, and then real words, phrases, sentences, and selections containing the sound. The therapist can build up his own nonsense syllables according to principles indicated earlier.

The materials of this section are intended to be suggestive rather than all-inclusive. It is expected that each therapist will be resourceful and build up his own sets of material for general use as well as particular materials "custom-made" for his individual case.

Intermediate Level

The exercises in this section are built about the consonant sounds which some children in the grammar grades continue to produce defectively.

The brief phonetic descriptions are so worded as to be of help to the bright older child and to the adult who is able to follow verbal directions. The descriptions need not be used if the *sound stimulation procedures* have been sufficient to establish the correct articulatory result.

t

Phonetic description: The sound *t* when followed by a vowel or in final position is produced by contact and quick release between the upper gum ridge and the tip of the tongue in the following manner:

1. The tongue is elevated so that the sides near the tip are in contact with the upper gum ridge, while farther back the sides of the tongue are in contact with the molars.
2. The tongue, extended and tense, is held in the initial position for a fraction of a second. Then, quickly and completely, the tongue is pulled back to produce and release a slight puff of air.
3. The soft palate is elevated to prevent nasal emission of the sound.

Initial		Final		Medial	
tell	tomorrow	against	left	afternoon	later
ten	took	boat	least	between	letter
till	tip	front	light	better	litter
time	ton	late	quite	contain	return
told	twenty	last	waste	continue	water

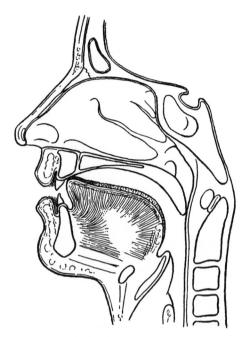

FIGURE 8-2. Contact tongue position for [t] and [d] and [l]. Essentially the same tongue-tip and gum-ridge contact is made for the [n]. The [n], however, is produced with a relaxed and lowered soft palate. (From J. Eisenson, *Basic Speech* [New York, Macmillan, 1950], p. 94.)

SENTENCES

Ten and ten are twenty.

Can you tell time?

It took a long time to come.

Try to join us on our trip.

We were told to wait till tomorrow.

Drink a little water between meals.

We will continue after a rest in the afternoon.

Earlier is better than later.

The envelope contained a letter.

The light was out in front.

It was late when we left.

The last is not always least.

"Waste not, want not" is a good motto.

We thought to travel by boat.

d

Phonetic description: The sound *d* is produced in the same manner as the sound *t*, except that it is accompanied by vocal-band vibration.

Initial		Final		Medial	
dance	desire	add	field	admire	needing
dare	dew	bread	glad	admit	shadow
dark	die	child	hard	garden	today
day	door	crowd	old	hidden	under
delight	dozen	fade	would	maiden	window

SENTENCES

It is a delight to feel the dew at daybreak.
The dress was made of dark cloth.
Few persons desire to die.
The sign on the door read "Only those with courage dare to enter."
Girls usually enjoy dancing more than boys.
The child had been taught to add.
The hungry are glad to eat bread.
The old man enjoyed being in a crowd.
We saw the sun fade over the edge of the field.
He who would learn must be ready to work hard.
We admired the flowers in the garden.
The maiden put the wedding cake under her window.
The shadows are growing long today.
We had to admit that we needed more help.

SELECTION—*t* AND *d*

Tender is the dew in the early morning light,
Tender are the blossoms when the sun shines bright,
Tender is the breeze as it strokes each gentle flower,
Tender is the Maytime each delightful hour.

s [4]

Initial		Final		Medial	
center	sing	grace	once	ask	hasten
city	smile	helps	peace	asleep	instead
sail	south	hoarse	puts	basket	most
salt	summer	loss	race	beast	past
sea	sweet	miss	trips	glasses	receive

SENTENCES

The sea is salt.
We set sail for the South.
Sugar is sweet, but a smile may be sweeter.
Peace is sometimes won with a sword.
We will miss you once you are gone.
Trips on horseback are pleasant.

Help us to win peace.
Grace won the girl's race.
The beast was asleep.
We received a basket of fruit.
We were lost on the coast.
The things that are passed are mostly good.

---

[4] For phonetic description see page 163.

z

Phonetic description: The sound *z* is produced in the same manner as the sound *s,* except that it is accompanied by vocal-band vibration.

Initial		Final		Medial	
zeal	zinc	as	his	busy	pleasant
zealous	Zion	because	moves	closing	reason
zebra	zone	choose	nose	easy	rising
zenith	zoo	days	these	lazy	season
zero	Zurich	does	was	music	used

SENTENCES

The wild zebra was kept in the African zone of the zoo.
The zinc statue came from Zurich.
The student from Zion City worked with zeal.
Zealous students seldom are given a zero.

These Spring days are pleasant.
Pinocchio's nose grew long because he told lies.
His nose was as long as an elephant's trunk.
Choose your moves with care when playing chess.

The shopkeeper was busy at closing time.
The music made us feel pleasantly lazy.
During the summer season one must get up early to see the sun rising.
To be able to reason is a sign of being civilized.

SELECTIONS

Are you sleeping, baby sister,
The wind is singing soft and low;
Are you dreaming, baby sister,
Dreams of things that fairies know?

Look to the West when the sun sets,
See the birds against the sky,
Watch as the day turns drowsy
And the moon rides up on high.

Hush, winds that sing of sorrow,
Hold back your lonesome song;
Your sighs must wait the morrow
To which your tunes belong.

sh [ʃ]

Phonetic description: The sound *sh* [ʃ] is a voiceless, blade-tongue, fricative sound. It is produced in the following manner:

1. The tongue is raised as in the position for *s,* except that the entire tongue is drawn back slightly and broadened.

2. The stream of breath is forced over a broad surface rather than through a narrow groove as for the *s*.
3. The lips are usually slightly rounded (pursed).
4. The soft palate is elevated to prevent nasal emission of the sound.

Initial		*Final*		*Medial*	
shade	shop	bush	finish	ashamed	motion
shall	shore	dash	punish	dishes	nation
sheep	should	dish	push	finishing	ocean
ship	shout	flash	wash	fished	washing
shoe	sure	flesh	wish	machine	wishing

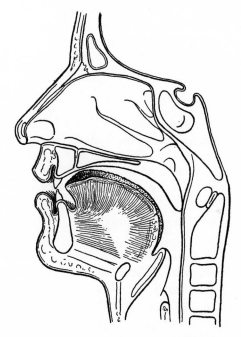

FIGURE 8-3. Tongue position for [ʃ] and [ʒ]. (From J. Eisenson, *Basic Speech* [New York, Macmillan, 1950], p. 106.)

SENTENCES

We should shop for shoes.
The sheep are in the shade.
The ship is near the shore.
Should we shout for help?
We wish we could catch some fish.
In a flash the runner completed his dash.

The child was punished for not washing behind his ears.
Most boys prefer that girls wash the dishes.
The new washing machine works well.
Our nation stretches from ocean to ocean.

zh [ʒ] [5]

Phonetic description: The sound *zh* [ʒ] is produced in the same manner as the *sh* [ʃ], except that it is accompanied by vocal-band vibration.

azure	measure
confusion	seizure
conclusion	usual
division	treasure
explosion	garage
erosion	mirage

SENTENCES

An azure sky is one of nature's treasures.
There was much confusion following the explosion.
Children of ten can usually do long division.
The garage was measured for its size.
A division of soldiers accomplished the seizure of the town.

ch [tʃ]

Phonetic description: The sound *ch* [tʃ] is a voiceless affricate. It combines some of the characteristics of the stop plosive *t* and the fricative *sh* [ʃ]. The *ch* [tʃ] is produced by first placing the tongue in position for the *t* and, immediately upon its production, moving the tongue back for the *sh* [ʃ]. The result is a blend of the two sounds to produce the different sound *ch* [tʃ].

Initial		*Final*		*Medial*	
chain	cheer	catch	rich	catching	reaching
chair	chief	church	teach	marching	richest
chance	child	each	touch	picture	teacher
change	chill	march	watch	matches	touching
charge	choose	much	which	question	watches

SENTENCES

What charge did the chief make?
Let the child choose his chair.
Give us a chance to choose.
The children went to church.

The teacher explained the picture.
Ask your teacher who is the richest man.
We set our watches before we began marching.
We reached for the fruit but touched only the cherry leaves.

[5] No English words contain the initial sound *zh* [ʒ]. For the most part, words containing the pure consonant *zh* [ʒ] are found among those less frequently used (above the fifth thousand) on the Thorndike-Lorge Word List.

Each may choose which way to go.
Teach him how to catch a ball.
Each may choose his church.
The watch had to be changed for each time zone.

j [dʒ]

Phonetic description: The sound *j* [dʒ] is a voiced affricate. Except for the element of voice, it is produced like the sound *ch* [tʃ].

Initial		*Final*		*Medial*	
general	journey	age	language	agent	imagine
gentle	joy	bridge	large	changed	magic
jaw	July	carriage	oblige	charged	pages
job	jump	edge	manage	danger	soldier
join	just	engage	orange	engine	stranger

SENTENCES

Justice should be gentle.
Joe just found a job.
Join those gentlemen who are just.

Keep the edges of the pages clean.
Judge not lest you be judged.
The soldier became an engineer.

ng [ŋ]

Phonetic description: The sound *ng* [ŋ] is a velar nasal continuant. It is produced by raising the back of the tongue to make contact with a lowered soft palate. The articulatory contact is maintained while the vocal bands are in vibration. The sound is emitted nasally.

Final		*Medial*	
belong	evening	bank	sings
bring	ring	belongs	single
calling	running	bringing	stronger
crying	song	longing	thank
doing	strong	longer	think

SENTENCES

He could not think of a single thing to say.
We were singing a merry song.
Were you taking the money to the bank?
We were thinking whether to walk the shorter or the longer way.
Hang your hat where it belongs.
Sing a song we like to hear.
The ring of gold was strong.
We were thinking of calling you.
What are you doing this evening?
Running and jumping are good fun.

"Ding, dong, hear my song,"
Says the clock in the steeple.
"Ding, dong, hear my song,
Listen to me, all you people.
"Ring, rong, goes my song
As I sing it from the steeple;
Ring, rong, ding, a-long,
Can you hear it, all you people?"

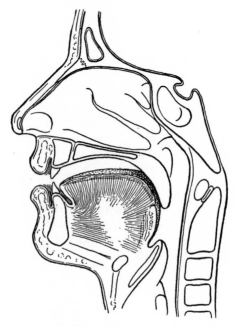

FIGURE 8-4. Tongue position for [ŋ]. (From J. Eisenson, *Basic Speech* [New York, Macmillan, 1950], p. 118.)

l

Phonetic description: The sound *l* is a lingua-alveolar, voiced lateral. It is produced in the following manner:

1. The tongue is raised as in the *t*-position so that the tongue-tip is in contact with the upper gum ridge.[6]
2. The part of the tongue just behind the tip is relaxed so as to permit the air to escape over the sides of the tongue.

[6] See diagram, page 168 for the illustration of the position.

3. The middle part of the tongue is elevated and spread so that the sides are in contact with the molars.
4. The soft palate is raised to prevent nasal emission of the sound.

Initial		*Final*		*Medial*	
lake	lesson	all	general	allow	clean
land	like	ball	girl	alone	clock
laugh	list	bell	mile	already	close
learn	love	cool	mill	always	gentlemen
left	lower	coal	small	class	gold

SENTENCES

We went to the land of lakes.
Learn your lessons daily.
We like to laugh.
Lower the flag to the left.
List the things you love.

We come to class at nine o'clock.
Gentlemen try to please ladies.
Drink milk daily.
We do not like always to be alone.
Gentlemen keep clean.

We will walk a mile.
Ring the bell of gold.
We are glad the day is cool.
The girl held the golden ball.
The mill is a mile down the way.

SELECTION

I know where the lilies grow,
I know where the swift streams go,
I know where the daffodils
Play on fields and distant hills.
I know flowers whose colors bright
Sparkle in the morning's light,
I know these things, and many
    more,—
And so does she whom I adore.

r

There are several ways of producing the sound *r*, according to context. The *r* before a vowel is usually described as a voiced fricative. It may be produced in the following manner:

1. The tongue-tip is raised toward the gum ridge, but actual contact with the gum ridge is avoided.
2. The vocal bands are set into vibration.

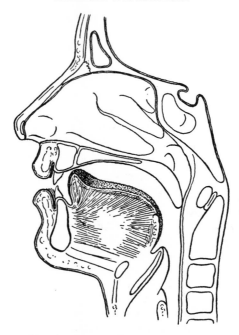

FIGURE 8-5. Tongue position for fricative [r]. (From J. Eisenson, *Basic Speech* [New York, Macmillan, 1950], p. 114.)

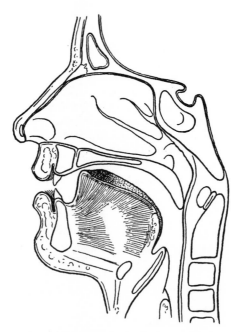

FIGURE 8-6. Tongue position for retroflex [r]. (From J. Eisenson, *Basic Speech* [New York, Macmillan, 1950], p. 111.)

3. The soft palate is elevated so as to prevent nasal emission of the sound.

Initial		*Final*		*Medial*	
race	river	car	our	front	dress
ran	rock	ever	shore	crown	trip
rapid	roll	far	there	free	prove
remember	roof	fire	where	broken	pretty
rest	rose	nor	were	grass	grew

SENTENCES

We ran a rapid race.
Remember to rest each day.
Did you read the report?
The river rose above its banks.
The rock rolled off the roof.

The king's crown was broken.
We grew weary on our trip.
The Miss wore a pretty dress.
France must be set free.
The Prince was proud and great.

Where is the car?
Were all of you there?
The fire is our light.
The shore is far away.

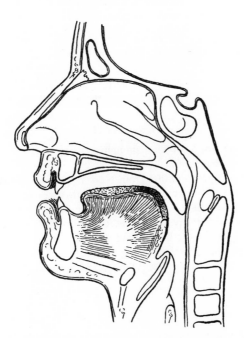

FIGURE 8-7. Tongue position for velar [r]. (From J. Eisenson, *Basic Speech* [New York, Macmillan, 1950], p. 112.)

SELECTIONS

Proud trees bend their branches,
The summer is done,
Now winter is ready
For his kind of fun.

Winter is a sober fellow.
In the fall the leaves are yellow,
Red and yellow, gay and bright;—
Winter's color is snow white.

In the Spring,
When the air is fresh and free,
My thoughts go wandering
To the rolling sea.

th [θ]

Phonetic description: The sound *th* [θ] is a voiceless lingua-dental fricative. It is produced in the following manner:

1. The tongue-tip is placed either against the back of the upper front teeth, against the cutting edge of the upper teeth, or between the upper and lower front teeth.
2. Air is forced between the tongue-tip and the place of contact to produce the characteristic fricative quality.
3. The soft palate is raised to prevent nasal emission of sound.

Initial		*Final*		*Medial*	
thank	thought	both	length	anything	nothing
thick	thousand	cloth	mouth	author	something
thin	three	death	north	bathtub	birthday
think	through	earth	path	faithful	everything
third	throw	fourth	strength	lengthen	strengthen

SENTENCES

Thank you for your kind thoughts.
Throw the ball to third base.
It is three thousand miles from New York to England.
At great length he regained his strength.
Independence Day is on the fourth day of the month of July.
In the north the leaves fall to earth earlier than in the south.
Anything is usually better than nothing.
Everything at a birthday party is fun.
The faithful believe in everything and ask for nothing.

th [ð]

Phonetic description: The sound *th* [ð] is a voiced lingua-dental fricative. It is produced like the *th* [θ], except for the element of voice.

Initial		Final		Medial	
than	these	bathe	scythe	although	gather
that	they	breathe	teethe	another	mother
their	those	clothe	unclothe	brother	neither
themselves	though	smooth	with	either	other
therefor	thus	soothe	wreathe	father	without

SENTENCES

These clothes belong to them.
There is nothing to that story.
I like that though it is cold.
They wanted nothing for themselves.
I'd rather wear old clothes than new ones.
Brother and father went for a walk.
In the Spring we do without heavy clothing.
Neither father nor mother nor brother likes hot weather.

SELECTION—*th* [θ] AND *th* [ð]

When the breath of winter is in the trees
Leaves fall to earth,
Their dance of mirth
Is final. Winter sees
That life must rest—
Thus is it best.

Adult Level [7]

The exercises included in this section are concerned with those consonant sounds which we have found to be most troublesome for adults. The *th* sounds are included particularly for the foreign-born adult.

t

Initial		Final		Medial	
tab	tidings	aft	gut	atone	huntsman
taciturn	toll	asphalt	incite	brittle	inter
tangle	trend	comet	lout	cruelty	patent
taunt	twain	deliberate	palliate	dialectic	rotary
terse	twit	emit	suite	fateful	unity

The Westerner was terse when not taciturn.
Did the tidings indicate a trend?
The tangled rope did not permit the bell to be tolled.
He who indulges in the twit and the taunt makes few friends.

---

[7] Sound descriptions are not included. For descriptions refer to discussions in previous section.

The astronomers of the asphalt each identified the comet differently.
Many can incite, only the wise few know how and when to palliate.
Those who will not atone for their cruelty often resort to dialectic.
A patent has been defined as that which gives one the right to sue and be sued.

The candle lit at both ends
Still burned a bit too slow;
It's lit now at the middle—
I've no time to watch it go.

d

Initial		Final		Medial	
dab	drape	amid	pallid	adapt	foundry
debit	dross	elude	raid	ado	girder
diet	dune	greed	shod	bedlam	hardship
doleful	dupe	hoard	stolid	candor	prudent
dolt	dyke	mermaid	trend	eddy	sunder

Ladies who diet are frequently doleful.
A dab of paint may make the dross shine.
The pursuers were eluded in a race across the sand dunes.
Bedlam is wherever there is always much ado about nothing.
The prudent save against hardship; the greedy hoard to create it.
Candor is the oft given excuse for unkindness.
Those who live amid and make a trend seldom see it.

s

Initial		Final		Medial	
sanctuary	scruple	deafness	replace	aspect	mystic
satire	senior	emergence	tense	consideration	professor
savory	serene	flouts	terse	explanation	realist
scandal	silvery	hoarse	waywardness	intensive	unceasing
scoff	stroll	mace	yachts	jurist	wistful

There is no sanctuary from satire.
To lack scruples is to court scandal.
The moon-lighted sea appeared silvery and serene.
The savory dish was prepared in a saucepan.
It is waywardness not to replace divots when playing golf.
With a few terse remarks the thesis was refuted.
Typical old-age deafness results in a loss of high-frequency sounds.
The mystic spoke with a wistful air.

The jurist insisted on a full explanation of the matter under consideration.
"Genius," defined the professor, "is an ability to work unceasingly and intensively."

Sere leaves are a token
Of a spirit that's broken
And a life that is spent,
That weeps for the living,
Spent life that is giving
Its final lament.

His strength was as the strength of ten
Because his heart was pure;
Her strength was also as of ten
Because she seemed demure.

In the consonant combinations *sks* and *sts,* the production of the *s* may be somewhat more difficult than *s* in combination with other sounds. The difficulty may arise from the precise and quick tongue movements required for the articulation of the *s* when followed as well as preceded by a *k* or *t.* The following materials are for the practice of *s* in "troublesome" contexts.

asks	pastes	lisps
asps	pasts	crisps
frisks	posts	lapst
ghosts	rasps	snakes
hasps	tracks	whisps
rests	speaks	toasts

Ghosts make no tracks.
Words such as frisks and asps are tricks for one who lisps.
A man who asks many questions should not have a voice that rasps.
Have you ever found sea snakes along the sea coasts?
Toasts frequently are made with the juice of grapes.

z

Initial		*Final*		*Medial*	
zany	zest	avows	symbolize	Beelzebub	materialism
zealous	Zeus	daubs	synthesize	blizzard	nozzle
zebra	zinc	eaves	systematize	frenzy	rosin
zenith	zodiac	goads	transpose	laziness	visitation
zephyr	zoo	snores	yearns	stanza	vizor

One need not be a zany to live a life of zest.
The sign of Zeus may be found in the zodiac.
The zebra is an interesting zoölogical specimen.
Star-eyed poets reach their zenith when they find words to rhyme with zephyr.
Man yearns for pleasing surroundings.
The young painter's canvas won first prize.
Persons who systematize life seldom sympathize with those who do the living.
Clever designing can transpose eaves into things of beauty.
The travellers were dazed by the intensity of the blizzard.

Satan is supposed frequently to visit with Beelzebub
Materialism is Satan's strongest argument.
Rosin is used by violinists.

> Red and yellow leaves all wind-kissed,
> Dancing leaves and whispering trees
> Holding parleys now with nature,
> Whispering softly with the breeze:
> What's the story of your whinings
> What's the promise of the breeze?
> Does he tell you that tomorrow
> There will be surcease of sorrow,
> Does he tell you that your pinings
> Can at last be put to rest?
> Red and yellow leaves now wind-kissed,
> Falling leaves and bowing trees,
> Are you now at peace with nature,
> Have you yielded to the breeze?

> Is there a season
> When man cannot reason?
> Does woman choose
> When man's sure to lose?

th [θ]

Initial		Final		Medial	
thaw	thirteen	broth	myth	atheist	lethargy
theme	thoughtful	dearth	thirteenth	athlete	orthodox
theory	thrall	hundredth	troth	deathbed	python
thesis	threat	monolith	uncouth	enthusiasm	ruthless
therapeutic	thyroid	moth	zenith	lengthy	slothful

The thermometer indicated that the snow was about to thaw.
The theme of the story held us in thrall.
He showed thought in the presentation of his theory.
Threats seldom have therapeutic value.
The lengthy theme induced universal lethargy.
The orthodox feel wrathful about atheists.
The ruthless wait for their deathbeds to regret their deeds.
The slothful should avoid the company of a python.
The troth was kept on the thirteenth.
There is seldom a dearth of the uncouth.
The hundredth burnt moth sets no example for the hundredth and first.
The myth of the magic broth was exposed.

To distinguish between *th* [θ] and *t*

thank	tank	troth	trot
thin	tin	oath	oat
thought	taught	quoth	quote
bath	bat	ruthless	rootless

The tank was made of a thin sheet of tin.
It is now thought that emotions can best be taught by example.
Most boys would rather bat a ball than take a bath.
It would do a horse little good to take an oath not to eat an oat.

Poor thing of earth,
Hath a lady you in thrall?
Your former mirth
Is gone. Hath she all
Your heart and mind?
Yes, love is unkind.

th [ð]

Initial		*Final*		*Medial*	
theirs	therein	blithe	seethe	brotherly	lather
thenceforth	thereunto	lathe	soothe	fatherland	logarithm
thereabout	therewithal	loathe	tithe	fathom	northerner
thereat	they'll	scathe	wherewith	feathery	smother
therefrom	they've	scythe	wreathe	heather	wherewithal

Thenceforth it was hoped there would be peace.
Theirs was the first choice.
Despite their having the wherewithal, they've accomplished nothing.
Brotherly love and love for the fatherland sometimes conflict.
The Northerner was expert in the use of logarithms.
The absent-minded barber almost smothered his client in lather.
Ripe heather is feathery.
Those who pay a tithe are seldom blithe.
A face wreathed in smiles can soothe when another can't.
Those who are truly American hate despotism.

To distinguish between *th* [ð] and *d*

then	den	lather	ladder
there	dare	loathe	load
thy	dye	tithe	tide
there	dare	wreathe	read

Do you dare to go there?
The cake was a failure though the cook prepared the proper dough.
Even a mule may loathe too large a load.

l

Initial		*Final*		*Medial*	
laborer	liberate	ale	eel	album	dilute
lamentable	lieu	artful	guile	alert	elicit
languish	loan	bail	revel	ballad	eliminate
lapse	lucid	cabal	vigil	blunder	eloquent
lenient	lyric	cannibal	yawl	clan	pallid

The rise in wages of labor generally lags behind prices.
A loan seldom liberates the borrower.
A lyric, to be pleasing, must be lucid.
It is lamentable for adults to have defective *l*'s.
The electric eel need not use guile.
We will revel as we sail on our yawl.
The artfully told tale held us in thrall.
The villain left jail on bail.
It is not filial even for a cannibal to kill his parent.
Eloquence precedes elections.
Ale seldom contains a high percentage of alcohol.
Artillery fire turns ladies pallid.
Ballads are narrative lyrics.

A tale is told of a New England farmer who owned a large apple orchard. In the Fall he would pick the apples and place them in large barrels in the cellar of his house. Frequently he would go to the cellar to get some apples for his family. He would look the apples over carefully and select a few speckled ones. His principle was to have his family eat the speckled apples before those that were clean and completely unspoiled. Somehow, and this is the sorry part of the tale, there were always some speckled apples left and the family, despite complaints, never ate one that was completely unspoiled.

> Please to listen, my fair lady,
> There's a lyric in my soul;
> There's a lilting, lovely lyric
> That I'd like to tell you whole.
> But the lady will not listen,
> Someone has her heart in thrall;
> So I must keep a vigil
> Till I can tell her all.

Words in which the *l* is preceded by a *p* or *b* may be somewhat more difficult than *l* preceded by some other consonant or by a vowel. Lip movement, appropriate for the *p* or *b,* is to be avoided in the production of the *l.* Practice material follows:

blame	plush	obliterate
blast	pleura	stable
bleed	plot	apple
blow	plough	displace
placard	plunder	displease
plant	able	replete
plead	ablate	replica
pleasant	oblong	reply
plume	oblige	unpleasant

r

Initial		Final		Medial	
rabies	realist	aspire	insure	apprehend	criminal
racial	recant	char	leer	aroma	fraud
rally	roundelay	dire	loiter	brandy	frugal
ramble	rotate	drear	pier	brig	irascible
random	routine	financier	sere	bromine	nitrogen

Even realists may have random thoughts.
François Villon was a writer of roundelays.
Strict adherence to routine gets one in a rut.
Some holders of racial theories are better able to induce than contract rabies.
Sere leaves are a drear sight.
Most financiers insure their interests.
The irascible criminal was placed in the brig.
Women who wear ermine are rarely frugal.
Nitrogen and bromine are chemical elements.
By ruse and fraud, the widow's property was appropriated.

> Darling, are you growing cold?
> Tell me, is our love grown old?
> Shall we hold it—bated breath,
> Or slowly chant its song of death?
> Darling, has our love grown stale,
> Or was your color always pale?

Words in which the *r* is immediately preceded by a *p* or *b* may be more troublesome than other words with *r*-sounds. If lip movement, appropriate for the *p* and *b* is carried over to the *r,* an infantile sound resembling a *w* may be produced. The following material is for practice purposes:

brand	abbreviate
bright	abridge
broil	debris
brown	umbrella

pray	apprise
press	disprove
prig	repress
proud	supreme
prune	surprise

The combinations *gr* and *kr* are also rather difficult for some speakers. Practice material follows:

grace	crag
grip	crawl
groan	cream
growth	crime
grub	cruel

The pauper may dream of riches.

Coffee and cream is a favorite drink for many Americans.

The pretty young girl carried a brightly colored umbrella under her arm.

Three members of the ship's crew were thrown into the brig because of their poor behavior.

Green apple cores bore witness to why one uncomfortable boy was crying and groaning.

9

Voice Disorders: I

The "Voice of America" abroad is judged too often by the voices of Americans abroad. The general effect is not such as to impress the world either with our culture or with our maturity. The raucous, rasping, or nasal overtones of the American tourist confound people who have been prepared to treat him and his opinions with respect. And even in top-level international conferences, American voices all too often belie the true meaning and intent of a people invested with the mantle of leadership. At home one need only recall the strident, hysteric tones emanating from our convention halls to realize the indifference of our leaders to acceptable voice standards. We are still quite unconscious of the importance of the voice in communication.

NORMAL AND DEFECTIVE VOICES

The Normal Voice: A Definition

When one attempts to answer the question, "What is the normal speaking voice?" one's troubles multiply at a rate defying even statistical expectation. Colleagues quite regularly question the speech teacher's decision when she suggests that a student's voice is substandard and in need of special training. "Her voice sounds all right to me; she gets her ideas across, doesn't she?" is the challenge. Awareness of voice and vocal standards vary greatly even among educators. They vary also from section to section. The southern teacher, long "exiled" in the North, exclaimed about a stranger's voice, "That's sweet music from South Carolina," and apparently was unaware of the nasality which accompanied that "musical" speech from the Deep South. We are "wonted" to the patterns of voice and diction to which our ears were attuned in our youth. Voice also is a highly personal attribute. Like the crooked nose, it somehow belongs to the person; one does not tamper with a "work of nature."

Finally, the characteristics of tone which make up the normal voice are not readily measurable in the laboratory. We cannot put into the scientific hopper so much of pitch or loudness or quality and come out with the normal voice. How much nasal resonance, for example, do you put in to secure normality? You recall that Chaucer's Nonne traveling to Canterbury "entuned in hir nose ful semely," a mark of refinement at least in that age. In their laboratory study of voice normality, Dreher and Bragg [1] conclude that "although it seems reasonable to assume that 'normality' in time, pitch, and quality can be accurately determined, the evidence on hand indicates that, as a group, listeners cannot agree when a voice is normal or time/pitch distorted if they are not acquainted with this voice. . . . it may be the case that in respect to pitch-time-quality variations no physical norm actually exists to vary from, our evaluation of them being in terms of very different criteria (e.g., socially conceived standards)." Absolute standards cannot be established because voice is dependent upon too many variables: upon the size and structure of vocal organs, upon physical and emotional status, and upon environmental influences, or as Dreher and Bragg have said, "upon socially conceived standards."

If we should use a familiar criterion of vocal normality—a voice which does not call attention to itself—we would have to reckon with the "famous" voices of the world which have produced an unusual effect on the auditor, in part, because the voice was attention-getting. The sonorous thunder of John L. Lewis, the guttural emphasis of Sir Winston Churchill, the "gravelly" voice of Tallulah Bankhead: each has won favor because of the unusual qualities on which he or she might ring the changes. A voice may not meet the norm in the sense that it varies from the typical or average voice, yet it may not be defective. A defective voice calls adverse attention to itself because one or more of its characteristics—pitch/time, quality, or loudness —fails to meet the socially conceived standard of pleasantness.

Voice may be defined as the laryngeal tone which is heard or measured. The normal voice should possess certain minimal characteristics of pitch, loudness, and quality, which make meaning clear, arouse the proper emotional response, and ensure a pleasant tonal effect upon the hearer. On this basis, 75 per cent of our population could profit by training in voice improvement. Our concern at this juncture is not for this population but rather for a smaller segment, about 15 per cent, who have voice problems so marked that the average hearer would conclude "there is something wrong with that voice." Generally we would say that a voice is defective in these circumstances: (a) when a defective structure or organic disorder of the vocal organs produces patterns of pitch, loudness, or quality which are sufficiently atypical to interfere with communication; (b) when voice production *results* in organic disorders of the vocal organs; or (c) when the habitual manner of voice production results in atypical patterns of pitch, loudness,

[1] J. J. Dreher and V. C. Bragg, "Evaluation of Voice Normality," *Speech Monographs*, Vol. 20, No. 1 (March, 1953), pp. 73-78.

or quality which are not appropriate to the sex and chronological age of the speaker or which detract markedly from the meaning or feeling that he wishes to communicate.

Interlocking Causes of Voice Disorders

The cause of a vocal disorder may be structural, physiological, or psychological. And—this is a far more common occurrence—several interlocking causes can produce the voice defect. The weak voice, for example, may be the result largely of a structurally poor mechanism, but general physical and psychological factors also may be true contributors to the disorder. Lettie, a college freshman, has small vocal folds and a tiny mouth and pharynx, but one is reluctant to attribute her weak voice to these structural limitations alone. More significant, it would seem, are her low margins of vitality and motivation. She is psychologically one of the submerged tenth—submerged by a complex of factors: four dominant older brothers, unhappy parents, and a mediocre mind. Multiple attack may not appeal to our desire for discrete analysis, but it is often a more realistic and rewarding approach to the problem. It is the skilled clinician who will find the several causes and assess their relative importance in the total complex.

Interrelated Voice Defects

Defective attributes are not easily isolated because they do not appear alone. It is difficult to single out one characteristic of a voice—loudness, for example—and say that it alone is defective. The voice is made up of a complex of tonal factors which interact upon each other. So loudness affects pitch, pitch affects quality, and so on. Listen to the voices of students at a college "mixer." Mary is talking above the din and her voice is very loud. You also are aware of a high pitch and twangy quality which you had not noticed in class. Why? Fletcher partially answers the question when he points out that "the essential effects of marked increase in vocal intensity upon the tonal complex are the increased amplitude of most partials and the extension of the measurable frequency range . . . the fundamental frequency is much less prominent at high intensity than at low intensity." [2] To put it in another way, the higher partials have much greater vitality than the lower ones. The low partials in Mary's normal voice were drowned in the welter of the stronger high partials. Then why did loudness also affect the quality? One possible answer is that in order to produce the loud voice, Mary developed tensions in the voice instrument resulting in the discordant overtones, which we identified as a twang. The phoniatrist must decide which factor initiated the undesirable chain of events if therapy is to be effective.

[2] W. W. Fletcher, *A Study of Internal Laryngeal Activity in Relation to Vocal Intensity.* Unpublished doctoral dissertation, Northwestern University, 1950.

DETERMINANTS OF VOICE

Physical Determinants

Voices have family histories. The size and shape of the costal cage; the length, thickness, and density of the vocal folds; the size, shape, and texture of the resonators: these are obvious structural determinants which are passed down the family line. In the case of the constitutionally small larynx, for example, the speech therapist may find that the resultant small voice cannot be changed without damage to other parts of the speech mechanism.

We do not know the precise effects of the resulting space relationships upon voice. If the oral aperture is small in relation to the cross-sectional area of the pharyngeal orifice, one may expect a kind of resonance which muffles the tone. Or if the anterior nares are narrow in relation to the area of the nasopharyngeal orifice where the breath stream enters the nose, a nasal twang may result. The physical tone and density of the resonating surfaces of the pharyngeal and oral cavities and the absorbent index of the resonators, both subglottal and supraglottal, also may alter the tonal character, although their precise influence is still debatable. The traditional concept of the resonators as amplifiers of sound has been questioned by some voice scientists. They claim that only 20 to 30 per cent of the energy produced at the larynx is found in the oral cavity.

Voices, too, are dependent upon the speed with which muscles can cooperate in the synergy, and this ability frequently is a familial pattern. The drawl of the Mississippi mule-driver is not exclusively a phonetic problem; the voice also reflects the hypotonic and slow muscular co-ordination. Although it is not possible to measure the neural excitation to the muscles of phonation, we may infer from the studies of the response of the cranial nerves serving the articulators that there is a dynamic or neural gradient which is fairly constant among family groups.

Voice is also dependent upon our central powers of discrimination of pitch, loudness, and quality—powers of perception which are basically inheritable. The college student with monotonal speech and no training in auditory discrimination finds it difficult to copy the pitch pattern of the instructor. He may admit that he hears no pitch change in the voice, or he may detect the change but insist he cannot remember it long enough to copy it. Auditory discriminatory powers residing in the central nervous system play an important role in the final character of the voice.

The physical determinants which we have discussed so far have been established from birth. They are largely the product of inheritance. There are other physical conditions resulting from trauma or disease which affect the voice. These physiological dysfunctions may be limited to the voice instrument, or they may be sequelae of such general systemic disorders as pneumonia, influenza, hyper- or hypothyroidism, allergic diseases, sinusitis and chronic colds, or lesions in the central nervous system (poliomyelitis, cerebral palsy, and so forth). Examples of special physiological problems which are limited generally, but not entirely, to the voice mechanism are hypertrophied and diseased tonsils and adenoids, structural deviations or growths in the nose, and laryngeal ulcers, nodules, and carcinomas. Injuries to the nerves or muscles employed in phonation may be the result of surgical or other accidents. Such injuries have been observed following operations on the thyroid gland, mastoid process, and lingual tonsils.

Psycho-emotional Determinants

A voice reflects the intellectual and emotional dynamism of the person. Frequently when a listener concludes "there is something wrong with that voice," he is reporting an unpleasant effect produced by a sameness in all the vocal attributes: pitch, loudness, and quality. Such a dull mono-voice could be indicative of a dull mind and personality. Equally unacceptable is the voice which reflects prolonged emotional states of tension: fright, anxiety, exhilaration, or insecurity. The possible manifestations are many. Sometimes the voice is too loud or high-pitched or strident in quality. In other cases the emotional instability produces hoarseness and functional aphonia (voicelessness).

Cultural Determinants

Voice will reflect the cultural standards of a social group often as clearly as will dress, diet, or decorum. The chief agent of cultural transmission is language—"mankind's fundamental institution"—and of oral language, voice is a major component. So certain cultural groups are repelled by loud or nasal or high-pitched voices which are quite acceptable in other groups. In some business or cultural groups an established pattern of rigid jaw muscles or a buckled tongue produces a very unpleasant metallic or harsh vocal quality. Zerffi found that these abnormal tensions often restricted laryngeal action so markedly as to produce vocal nodules and aphonia.[3] A child takes on the voice pattern of those around him, and often is unaware of its unpleasant characteristics until he enters adulthood and shifts to other social groups. The influence of mass media of communication—radio and television—may result either in greater flexibility of voice patterns or in the production of the "universal voice." The immediate environment of home and family also affects vocal patterns. Children quite unconsciously copy the vocal patterns of parents. Tim, a college freshman with an over-loud voice, ascribes his difficulty to competition for attention in a family of seven sisters and brothers. On the other hand, a very soft voice may reflect the domination by a parent; the breathy voice, an insecurity in the im-

[3] W. A. C. Zerffi, "Laryngology and Voice Production," *Annals of Otology, Rhinology, and Laryngology,* Vol. 61, No. 3 (September, 1952), pp. 643-647.

mediate environment; the strident voice, an overcompensation for or defiance of one's environment.

One must realize, however, that only rarely may a voice problem be traced to a single cause. Often the psychological substratum has coalesced with the physical and cultural so firmly that the components contributing to vocal dysfunction cannot be identified. Here is a dull, denasal, monotonous voice. Is it the product of a dull, uninteresting personality? Or is a structural deviation, hypertrophied adenoids perhaps, the major factor to be reckoned with? What role does the low general tonus of the body play in the etiology? Or is this voice like many others in the cultural group to which the person belongs? The great problem is to assess the relative contribution of each of these factors to the etiological complex.

ATTRIBUTES OF VOICE: PITCH, LOUDNESS, AND QUALITY

The student of voice may notice at once that *time* has not been included in the list of vocal attributes. We have made this omission for two reasons. Time or duration of sound is more closely associated with articulation than with voice. We are interested in the duration not of the tone but of the sound, syllable, or word, and in the articulated speech intervals between sounds and words which are marked by the absence of tone. Secondly, we believe that time might be considered a factor of pitch. Time is dependent completely and pitch partially upon the wave of compression from the breathing muscles. The glottic cycles which determine pitch are, in turn, dependent upon the timing of the breathing mechanism. Time, then, scarcely could be considered independently of pitch.

Pitch

Pitch, as we have just stated, is partly dependent upon the intercostal-abdominal-diaphragmatic synergy of muscles. It is also dependent upon the muscular action of the larynx which serves as a kind of oscillator to act upon the wave of compression initiated by the breath pulse. By the time the sound wave leaves the larynx, the pitch has been established. What we perceive as pitch is a subjective auditory impression of the frequency, or the number of vibrations per second, of these oscillating waves of compression and rarefaction. We describe the pitch as high or low on the musical scale, and we can measure it very easily in the physics laboratory. We can determine the number of cycles per second from the oscillogram. But we cannot measure so easily the physiological determinants of pitch: the cross-sectional area of the laryngopharynx; the length, elasticity, and thickness of the vocal folds; the tensions of the breathing and laryngeal muscles; the supraglottic and subglottic pressures, and so on; yet they all must be evaluated when one attempts, for example, to find the cause of a very high-pitched voice.

The narrow limit of the pitch range in many voices raises the question: How high and how low can the voice go? The limits apparently are within three octaves, but generally one's speaking voice is about one and one-half octaves.[4] Women's voices are approximately two-thirds of an octave higher than the pitch levels of men's voices and exhibit a narrower functional range than is characteristic of men's voices, if we can generalize from a study of superior speakers.[5] The normal pitch level for men is one octave below middle C (256 double vibrations) on the musical scale or approximately 141 cycles. The increase for women of two-thirds of an octave would place the female voice two tones below middle C or 233 double vibrations. One's natural pitch level cannot be ascertained with certainty. The usual practice of finding an optimum pitch level by a resonance reinforcement in a fixed region was not supported by Thurman's study. In an experimental study in which his subjects hummed or intoned the scale, he was unable to locate an "intensity swell corresponding to an individual's 'natural pitch level.' In only 11 per cent of the total 150 performances did the intensity peaks fall within a frequency range for an optimum pitch level." [6] It would seem reasonable to assume, however, that there is a level at which the larynx produces tone most efficiently and that this level probably falls in the lower one-fourth or one-third of the total singing range.

Loudness

This is a psychological term describing the magnitude of the effect of the sound upon the ear, both peripheral and central. A voice is loud or soft depending upon its effect upon the auditory reception and perception of the hearer. But hearing is subject to wide individual differences, both fixed and fluctuating. The loudness level for reception is fairly stable in the individual; it is a fixed factor. The physiological and psychological conditions of the hearer will vary from day to day and hence are fluctuating factors. The individual's interpretation of loudness depends not only upon the sensitivity of peripheral hearing and upon the total number of nerve impulses per second which are received in the temporal lobe in the cerebrum, but also upon such factors as fatigue, nervous tension, and physical illness. One's sensation of loudness will vary, too, as the physical composition of the sound wave changes. The loudness of a complex tone is not the algebraic sum of the "loudnesses" of the simple tones which went into its make-up.

[4] V. A. Anderson, *Training the Speaking Voice* (New York, Oxford, 1942), p. 173.
E. Hahn, C. W. Lomas, D. E. Hargis, and P. Nadraegen, *Basic Voice Training for Speech* (New York, McGraw, 1952), p. 76.
[5] J. C. Snidecor, "The Pitch and Duration Characteristics of Superior Female Speakers during Oral Reading," *Journal of Speech and Hearing Disorders,* Vol. 16, No. 1 (March, 1951), pp. 44-52.
[6] W. L. Thurman, *An Experimental Investigation of Certain Vocal Frequency-Intensity Relationships Concerning Natural Pitch Level.* M.A. Thesis, University of Iowa, August, 1949.

Certain tones, in fact, may have their loudness contribution diminished by conflicting with other tones in the tonal complex.

Intensity, a second factor in the physical composition of the sound wave, is most directly related to loudness. Intensity should be measured in terms of the physical energy of the vibrating column of air. Actually, however, the energy of the sound emitted orally constitutes only about a fifth of the total energy initiated by the breath pulse. Its force is steadily dissipated "in parasitic vibrations and in the sound pulse in the trachea and bronchi." [7] Although we formerly have calculated intensity from the product of the squares of the frequency and amplitude ($I = F^2A^2$), recent researchers [8] now maintain that there is no consistent relationship between the amplitude of vocal-fold movement and intensity. Voelker concludes that intensity is dependent directly upon the duration of closure of the vocal folds.[9] Fletcher finds this factor only one of several variables.

There are probably three major determinants of intensity: (1) the strength and duration of the breath pulse, (2) the duration and force of the closure of the glottis, and (3) the coupling factors in the resonators. Tracheal air pressure, dependent on the muscles of expiration and the resistance which this moving air column meets in the vocal folds, will decide primal or laryngeal intensity. If we could measure the length of the closed cycle of vocal-fold vibration and the force with which the folds are pressed together, we would have a fairly accurate index of laryngeal intensity. The third determinant may change markedly the auditor's impression of vocal loudness. Here we must deal with the modification of laryngeal intensity by the resonance system through the principle of coupling. The human resonators, varying greatly in texture, shape, density, and rigidity, cannot approach the requisite of an ideal resonating system with frequencies closely synchronized. Curry maintains that theoretically the maximum resonance and, therefore, the strongest intensity should occur "when the lowest natural resonating frequency of the cavities is the same as the fundamental of the larynx," [10] yet in practice, the strength of the high partials increases beyond that of the fundamental tone as the intensity becomes greater.

Frequency (pitch) is a third component of the sound wave which affects loudness. If a pure tone lies near the middle of the frequency range (1000 to 2000 d.v.), a given intensity will sound much louder than if it is at either extreme of frequency (200 or 10,000 d.v.). On the other hand, if the

[7] R. Curry, *The Mechanism of the Human Voice* (New York, Longmans, 1940), p. 50.

[8] W. W. Fletcher, *op. cit.*

Bell Telephone Laboratories, *High Speed Motion Pictures of the Human Vocal Cords.* Mimeographed lecture, Bureau of Publications, 463 W. 81st Street, New York, 1940.

[9] C. H. Voelker, "Education of the Speaking Voice," in E. D. Froeschels, *Twentieth Century Speech and Voice Correction* (New York, Philosophical Library, 1948), p. 280.

[10] Curry, *op. cit.*, p. 55.

intensity is very great, the sound will seem to be equally loud at all frequencies.

Loudness may be related also to volume, but they are not synonymous terms. Volume probably is dependent upon the *extent* of stimulation of the cochlea of the ear. If a relatively large strip of the basilar membrane of the cochlea is stimulated, the sensation of volume is perceived centrally as large or "extensive." [11] Volume, then, is a measure of the "size" of the sound.

We judge loudness of tone chiefly by the audibility of speech, but it probably is also the determiner of that dynamic factor of communication known as vocal projection. "Loudness," say Black and Moore, "not only differentiates the inaudible from the audible but distinguishes animated from lifeless talking." [12]

Quality

Voice teachers have consistently referred to the resonators as the chief, if not the sole, determinants of voice quality. Recent investigations, however, suggest that quality may be determined by and in the larynx, not by the articulator-resonator adjustments. The articulatory movements act only as accessories to the laryngeal action. The high soprano has a small larynx and thin, short vocal folds in contrast to the baritone's large "voice box" and long, heavy vocal cords. The vocal quality of the two voices differs as the anatomy of their larynges differs. Despite the prevailing opinion that quality is that characteristic which distinguishes one voice from another, some scientists claim that quality does not vary greatly among individuals, that the truly significant differences by which we identify one voice from another are in tempo, phrasing, inflection, and articulation. Fletcher, among others, holds the opposite view that it is "largely the type of voice (quality aspect) . . . [which] helps to identify the person who is speaking;" quality "is dependent on the vibration characteristic of the vocal cords." [13] Other investigators hold that the larynx and the resonators together are determiners of vocal quality.

Much of our uncertainty about this attribute of voice arises quite naturally from its many-sided character and from the subjective descriptions we give to vocal quality. It is difficult to separate factors of quality from factors of pitch and loudness. Sue, a college freshman, has a shrill, strident voice. Should the defect be called one of quality? Only in part, for when the pitch is lowered and the loudness decreased, the stridency is noticeably diminished. Children's voices have a clear, oral quality, but again, articulatory habits may contribute much to the impression of oral quality. During

[11] H. Fletcher, *Speech and Hearing in Communication* (New York, Van Nostrand, 1953), p. 176.

[12] J. W. Black and W. E. Moore, *Speech* (New York, McGraw, 1955), p. 48.

[13] H. Fletcher, *op. cit.*, p. 5.

residence in a foreign country, the writer noticed that it was much easier to understand the speech of the children than of their parents, not solely because of the oral quality of the children's voices, but, perhaps more significantly, because of the openness of the mouth, the precise lip and tongue action, the absence of elision, and the slower rate in speaking.

The confusion in terminology is another indication of our inability to distill the fraction called quality from the complex of vocal attributes. Unpleasant voice qualities are variously described as throaty, harsh, pectoral, breathy, nasal, denasal, muffled, guttural, shrill, whangy, thin, or heavy. Pleasing voice quality is called rich, orotund, or vibrant. If we could pluck out all the intermingled characteristics of voice, we might adopt a psycho-acoustic definition of quality, namely: the hearer's impression of the complex sound wave, its harmonic and inharmonic partials, and the relative intensity, number, and duration of these components. Such an impression he judges in terms of pleasantness or unpleasantness. Or, if we accepted the physiologist's definition, we would say that quality depends upon (1) the power and control of respiration; (2) the size, elasticity, length, and surface condition of the vocal folds; (3) the size, shape, tension, and flexibility of the resonator-articulator mechanism; and (4) the rigidity, density, and surface conditions of the walls of the resonators. Special note should be made of the fact that gross size or area of the resonators may not be so important as the cross-sectional area at two points: the vocal conduits at the faucial arches and at the oral aperture. Some phonologists hold that the opening of the faucial isthmus should be as large as the cross-section area of the buccopharynx and the opening at the oral aperture should be at least one and one-half times the area of the faucial isthmus.

To simplify the classification of deviations in voice quality is a necessity although we may incur further pitfalls in accuracy and completeness. Employing descriptive terminology, we would mark the following deviations: hoarse, guttural-strident, metallic, falsetto, and nasal qualities. If, on the other hand, we should classify the deviations according to cause, the following divisions might be drawn:

1. Deviations arising from structural anomalies or inadequacies, namely, very short, thin vocal folds, short soft palate, a submucous cleft of the palate, nodules on the vocal folds, asynchronic resonators producing ineffective coupling, etc.

2. Deviations arising from the physiological state of the organism, e.g., chronic rhinitis or sinusitis resulting in inflammation of the mucosa of the pharynx and larynx; constant, chronic irritation of the larynx through excessive smoking, vocal abuse, etc.; a lower energy-index reflected in shallow breathing, slumped chest; simple hyperthyroidism, exophthalmic goiter, etc.

3. Deviations neurological in origin, viz., lack of perception of the tonal character (sound discrimination, tonal memory, etc.); a low neuro-

logical gradient affecting all muscular co-ordination; and paralysis, peripheral or central, involving, for example, the recurrent laryngeal nerve, the superior laryngeal nerve or the cranial facial nerve.

4. Deviations psychogenic in character, as for example, the denasal quality found occasionally in hypochondriacs, the conscious imitation of the throaty voice of a movie star, or the breathy quality of the hypertense, emotionally maladjusted individual.

5. Deviations which may be called environmental, reflecting a vocal pattern acceptable, perhaps, in one cultural group but which does not meet the standard of the dominant cultural group of the area.

Studying the Voice Profile

The principal of your school has referred to you a high-school senior with this note: "Ellen's parents are concerned about her unpleasant voice. Apparently it always has been 'different' but it is much more disagreeable now than formerly. They hope you will give her the necessary correction."

It is obvious that neither the principal nor the parents appreciate the magnitude of their order, and you will, of course, spend some time in giving them an insight into the complexities of voice problems. Your next step is to make an analysis of Ellen's voice. What questions will you ask? What observations will you make? What tests can you give? What can you learn by direct examination of Ellen's voice mechanism? The outline contained in the Historical and Diagnostic Journal for Voice Disorders (Appendix 4) will serve as a guide in your study and as a summing up of etiological factors which you must consider. If you will turn to the outline, you will note the need for information about her medico-physical background and her observance of the rules of vocal hygiene. You will determine her auditory sensitivity and perception through a series of tests and will study the psycho-emotional factors which may have a bearing on her voice problem. You will record the phonemes which reflect the voice deviation more than other sounds. It will be necessary to observe carefully the operation and control of each part of the voice instrument: breathing, phonation, and resonation-articulation. The examination of the peripheral structures of mouth, nose, and throat may reveal structural or organic conditions about which you may need a physician's advice before making an assessment of their significance. If the voice is husky or hoarse, referral to a laryngologist probably should be made before any therapy is instituted. When all these data have been collected—information, observations, medical reports and tests— you probably will have gained a fair insight into the many angles from which you must view not only Ellen's problem but all voice problems.

THE TREATMENT OF VOICE PROBLEMS

I. Deviations in Pitch

Pitch, as has been suggested previously, may be atypical in three or four respects: it may be too high or too low; it may approach a monotone; or the intonation pattern may be repetitious or so peculiar that it acts as a barrier to communication.

The correction of pitch, moreover, is complicated by its relationship to other voice characteristics such as quality and loudness. Janet, a college senior, succeeded in lowering her pitch after considerable training, but in so doing she resorted to a monotone; her voice quality became hoarse, and one was scarcely able to hear her. In her case, the high pitch was appropriate to the vocal structure. In order to speak on a lower pitch level, it was necessary for her to keep the laryngeal mechanism in an inflexible state with the resulting untoward effects, not only on pitch but also on quality, on loudness, and on the physiological state of the larynx itself. We shall discuss the treatment, however, of each deviation without reference to the several concomitant problems which may be present.

The High-Pitched Voice. Causes. An excessively high pitch may be the result of *a small larynx "in a small frame";* the vocal folds may be short, thin, and light; the subglottic pressure may be weak because the breathing structure is weak. This description fits Janet, the girl to whom we referred in the preceding paragraph. The cause is structural and, hence, irremediable. Nature's handiwork, even if it is not done well, cannot be altered by the speech therapist. Janet is going to be known as the girl with the squeaky, tiny voice.

Then there are general *physical factors* which may affect vocal pitch. A delay in maturation of the secondary sex glands, in either sex, will have its effect upon the larynx. In the male, if the larynx does not show the normal pattern of accelerated growth at pubescence, the voice is characterized as "eunuchoid," high-pitched and oral. In the female, it remains a "baby voice." Another physical condition which may produce a high, unstable pitch in women's voices is hyperthyroidism. Obviously the vocal pitch reflects the general neural and muscular hypertension of the body. Reference is made to it here only because the voice change often is the initial sign of a physiological disturbance.

A larger group of high-pitched voices has its etiology in a fundamental *lack of perceptive power,* particularly in the areas of pitch discrimination and tonal memory. This lack resides in the central nervous system, but it is difficult to define its precise nature. Neither the specific neural areas nor the tonal characteristics contributing to a decrement in one's power of tonal discrimination and memory can be described accurately. Such a power may depend, in part, on the number and sensitivity of the neural receptors in the cochlea, the gradient or "power" of the auditory fibers, and the integrity and multiplicity of their synapses in the subcortical and cortical areas of the brain. The tonal constituents of discrimination and memory, likewise, have not been defined. Does one distinguish between sounds, for instance, by detecting an *absolute* difference in one of the tonal attributes— pitch, quality and loudness—or through the perception of a *relative* difference in the total pitch-quality-loudness pattern? The evidence on the "quality component" of this pattern is inconclusive, but there is considerable support for the belief that the perception of the pitch-loudness pattern is one determinant of tonal discrimination and memory.[14]

The *psycho-emotional causes* are more prevalent and numerous. In our American society many folk live perpetually in a state of emotional excitement and tension. The fast tempo of our lives, the common occurrence of maladjustment within the family, the environment of national crisis: all have wrought their effect on personalities. The writer once escorted a venerable Chinese philosopher past a large club room where three hundred women were gathered for a bridge-luncheon. In "mid-passage," the philosopher stopped and looked wildly about for an exit. "What are they all quarrelling about?" he asked. It was difficult to explain to him that these women were reacting vocally in strict accordance with scientific observation, namely, that side tone increases loudness.[15] This observation that one reflexively increases the loudness of his voice in the presence of noise is the basis of the Lombard test to detect malingerers in hearing. A hearing person will raise his voice above the level of the masking noise introduced into the headphones of the audiometer, whereas a person who suffers from a valid hearing loss will not exhibit this reflex unless the masking noise becomes so loud that it affects even his impaired hearing.[16] Mrs. Albee, penned up in a house with three preschool sons, also does not understand this principle very clearly. She admits that she has taken to "out-shrieking the small fry" in order to attract their attention. Her high-pitched, tense voice is a good barometer of the state of perpetual frustration in which she lives. There are others who adopt the high-pitched voice more or less consciously. Imitation or simulation of the dependent woman, some women believe, may be best carried off by the cultivation of a high, oral voice. As long as women's journals continue their premiums on "femininity" and complete dependence on "the man in your life," a certain part of the female population will hold to the baby voice as a mark of the "womanly woman."

Therapy. No single regimen can be recommended to correct all cases of high vocal pitch. If the cause is rooted in an anatomical anomaly or in

[14] J. C. R. Licklider and G. A. Miller, "The Perception of Speech," in S. S. Stevens, ed., *Handbook of Experimental Psychology* (New York, Wiley, 1951), pp. 1068-1069.

[15] C. Lightfoot and S. Morrell, *Loudness of Speaking: The Effect of the Intensity upon the Intensity of the Speaker,* U. S. Naval School of Aviation Medicine, Joint Report No. 4, Bulletin Medical Research Project No. MN001053 (1949).

[16] L. A. Watson and T. L. Tolan, *Hearing Tests and Hearing Instruments* (Baltimore, Williams & Wilkins, 1949), pp. 173-174.

general physiological dysfunction, the clinician's recommendations may or may not include vocal retraining. If the voice problem, however, is largely functional in nature, the student may follow this program of re-education:

1. FINDING YOUR OPTIMUM PITCH. This is difficult because we have no proven methodology for accurate determination. The belief that one can locate a point where amplification is greatest and production easiest has not been borne out by recent investigations.[17] Judgment based on the study of expert speakers would indicate that the optimum pitch level should be in the lowest third or fourth of the pitch range. Common practice is to stop the ears by pressing the tragus over the opening and then to intone *ah* at various points on the scale until you locate the tone which appears to you to reverberate loudest in your head. This may be your optimum pitch. Another check which, in many ways, is preferable is to experiment on intonation until you locate the point of maximum ease in phonation. We have used both methods—with varying results.

2. LOCATION OF YOUR HABITUAL PITCH. Read a descriptive prose passage aloud several times to your instructor until he is able to select the pitches which you use most frequently. With the aid of the piano or pitch pipe he will attempt to locate this habitual pitch on the musical scale. Next, in conversational speech, retell or discuss what you have read. Again, the instructor will select what appears to be the most frequently used pitch and determine its frequency.

3. DETERMINATION OF YOUR PITCH RANGE. With the aid of a piano, intone *ah*, noting the number of tones you can sing, both below and above middle C. The range probably will not exceed twenty tones. This is your singing range, but your speaking range probably will be in the lowest third or fourth of your singing range. Now read a prose selection to your instructor who will attempt to match your highest and lowest speaking tones with the piano tones. Check it as before with a sample of conversational speech. By repeated trials you and your instructor should arrive at a fair calculation of your speaking range. It should be remembered that the functional pitch range of men is greater than that of women.

4. PERCEPTIVE TRAINING. Although ability in pitch discrimination and tonal memory does not always improve markedly with training, you must use the power in perception which you have to good advantage. Many a college student will report that he has not been aware of the vocal pitch of his own voice or of others. Listening attentively and repeatedly to your own recorded voice, comparing it with the tape recording of the voices of your classmates, and imitating the "good tones" will activate the sensitivity which you do possess. Increasing the intensity of the speech in the playback will emphasize further the high frequencies, thus calling attention to their unpleasantness and facilitating your identification of them.

[17] Snidecor, *op. cit.*

5. CHANGING COUPLING OF RESONATORS THROUGH A CHANGE IN THE MUSCULAR TENSIONS IN THE FACE AND NECK. Because of its visibility and its connections with the musculature of lips, tongue, palate, fauces, and extrinsic muscles of the larynx and pharynx, the mandible is a good initial point of attack. Teaching conscious relaxation of the jaw, speaking with a widened oral aperture, and increasing flexibility by exaggerated easy activity of the mandible will do much to release the tensions within the mouth and throat. (See Chapter 10 for specific exercises on articulatory flexibility.) As the conduits increase in area at the faucial isthmus and the lips, the lower frequencies in the pitch range should become more dominant. Detailed exercises conclude this section on pitch defects.

6. SOCIAL AND EMOTIONAL READJUSTMENT. The tests of social and emotional adjustment are many. Among the most useful are the Minnesota Multiphasic Inventory, Rorshach Psychodiagnostic Test, Vineland Scale of Social Maturity, Bell Adjustment Inventory, Rogers Test of Personality Adjustment, Haggerty-Olson-Wickham Behavior Rating Schedules, and California Test of Personality. (See Appendix 3.) In the hands of those who are trained in clinical psychology, they can be very valuable. Other instructors will use the interview, conference, autobiography, or free and controlled association tests to locate the source of tension. The removal of these tensions is a far more difficult task, often involving family, friends, and colleagues. The outlook is most hopeful when you recognize the sources and are able to readjust yourself to your environment, or to intervene in your environment and so change it.

Monopitch and Repeated Pitch Pattern. These two problems will be considered together because the causes are essentially the same, and whether the individual repeats a single pitch or the same series of pitches the effect is the same: monotony and reduced comprehension on the part of the auditor.[18]

Causes. The most frequent cause of monopitch and repeated pitch pattern among college students is the *lack of sense perception of the characteristics of tone.* Terry, whose voice approached a perfect monotone, was one of the most popular girls in her class. No small part of her popularity came from her willingness to "solo" in "America the Beautiful" and other old favorites using a melody that was uniquely Terry's! Her scores on tests of tonal discrimination and tonal memory were sub-zero. Through signs, gestures, and sketching of pitch in speech samples, the instructor attempted to visualize changes in pitch inflection for Terry. The results were not very rewarding despite the student's genuine motivation and persistence.

A second cause is a *stiff, unresponsive vocal mechanism.* The inflexibility

---

[18] Glasgow demonstrates that audience comprehension is reduced by 10 per cent in the case of monopitch.

G. Glasgow, "A Semantic Index of Vocal Pitch," *Speech Monographs,* Vol. 19, No. 1 (March, 1952), p. 68 ff.

of muscles may be the consequence of a general neuromuscular impairment caused by cerebral palsy, of traumatic infections (such as whooping cough, measles, or scarlet fever), or of damage to peripheral nerves controlling phonation. In such cases, the speed of synchronous action and of shift in action is so slow as to make monopitch the only manageable speech for the subject. In other cases, the basically poor neuromuscular co-ordination is a constitutional pattern which may have appeared in several generations.

Sometimes monopitch and repeated pitch pattern are found in individuals exhibiting *general hypotension,* which, in turn, is the product of low physical and/or neural vitality. How common this etiology is cannot be determined. We have encountered such cases, and although there were several persons with the same monopitch in one family in two instances, which would make one suspect imitation or other environmental factors, the most reasonable explanation was one of physique and vitality. Although normal in frame, all members of the family were thin, undernourished, and slow in all movement. When the clinician suggested to one of them, a boy nearly sixteen years old, that he learn to walk faster or go out for some form of athletics, he protested: "Pop says we would get all wore out if we had to move as fast as you do!" And to another person, a girl with a dreary pitch pattern who lived in a colony of a religious sect, we suggested that she learn to dance. Although she was twenty years old, she refused to try such an exercise because she had seen people dance at a university party and it made her "tired just to watch them." There are others whose low vitality is a product of prolonged debilitating illness. The muscles of phonation, like the general bodily musculature, respond at the lowest point of the energy index. Probably such cases would profit more by medical than by psychological therapy.

Often linked with a constitutional lack of physical energy is *low intellectual vitality.* The requisite sensitivity is absent; the capacity for response is limited. The therapist may or may not choose to deal with what, after all, is only a symptom: a dull voice, the product of a dull mind. As Glasgow has said, "level monopitch may thus be conceived to have a unique function of symbolizing thoughts which are low in the intellectual values generally attached to ideas and concepts. Hence, level monopitch expresses the ideas of a mentally subnormal person very well." [19]

Environmental determinants may account for the monopitch. The conscious cultivation of an abnormally low pitch on the part of some women results in lack of variety and expressiveness. Movie, television, and radio "stars" undoubtedly have influenced certain social groups to adopt this type of voice as a mark of sophistication. The harmful effects of this practice on vocal quality are discussed in a subsequent section. In other instances, the monopitch may be indicative of a maladjustment to one's environment.

[19] Glasgow, *op. cit.,* p. 68.

The feelings of rejection and negation may be recently acquired or they may be long established patterns of reaction, the result of inferiorities, self-consciousness, or regression to infantile behavior. In Elsa's case it was a familial pattern. The family faced multiple problems: they belonged to a racial minority, suffered from perennial economic insecurity, and on the whole, possessed physically unattractive features. Elsa, a truly brilliant girl, offered her own analysis: "I think I felt the rejection of my classmates almost from the first day in public school. I remember still that I was painfully conscious of my poor clothing, my homely face, and near-sighted vision. Yet I also know that I was eager and fairly aggressive until I reached the sixth grade. I had learned to read before I entered school, and my teachers tried to help me by praising me before my classmates. But the one thing I wanted most of all I could not have: social acceptance and companionship. And although others might have found adequate compensation in an A record, I did not. By the seventh grade I know that I had withdrawn completely from the group. I had given up the struggle. Perhaps if I had been less sensitive, I would not have allowed life to pass me by." From a visit with the family the clinician found that Elsa's reactions were fairly typical of the whole family. Despite their good minds, they felt unequal to the struggle and had accepted the philosophy of negation of life. The repeated pitch pattern of their voices was only a mirror of this philosophy.

There are other cases of emotional maladjustment which the writers might discuss, but the story grows long. Others have undoubtedly encountered families who have been schooled in repression in speech and manner. Emotions, even the most laudable, are not to be expressed. Life is a stern and sober reality against which one must not rebel. To give vent to one's feelings is positively unhealthy and must not be tolerated. The re-educative process in those families involves a complete reversal in outlook. The way is not easy.

Loss in hearing acuity in the speech range also may account for the monopitch and repeated pitch pattern, but it is generally associated with more radical alterations in loudness. They will be discussed in greater detail in a subsequent section on acoustic handicaps.

Therapy. The therapist will select from the following suggestions those which will be most helpful in light of the causal factors. In many cases, the therapy might well include the total regimen:

1. Locate (by the method described in the preceding section) the habitual pitch and also the pitch of maximum ease in production. Are they the same? At what level of his pitch range does the subject speak habitually: low, middle, or upper?

2. Raise the habitual pitch. This should increase the range. Imitation of the instructor's voice, tone-copying from records, tape recorder, and radio, and matching tones on the piano or other musical instruments will

be helpful in realizing this end. Henrikson and Irwin warn the clinician against depending entirely upon the subject's recognition of his vocal pitch in recordings of his voice. The subject does not hear his voice as you, the therapist, hears it, for he hears himself "with the same lack of critical judgment with which he hears others." They point out that 20 per cent of 189 students whom they tested "actually agreed less with the advisor's rating of pitch of their voices, after hearing the recording than they did before." [20] And even trained teachers of speech agreed in only 20 per cent of the cases in their judgment of the pitch of the voices when they were asked to classify them as high, medium, or low.

3. Increase the flexibility of the total speech mechanism.

    a. Vocal drill

        (1) Glide up and down the scale on a single vowel, *ah* or *oh.* Begin on a higher pitch than is your habit and attempt to expand the range.

        (2) "Step off" into speech from a mid-pitch level and modulate the voice upward and downward from the mid-pitch.

        (3) Using dramatic poetry, prose, and speech, convey the emotional changes by great vocal shifts. Do not be afraid to exaggerate.

    b. Strive for (1) strength in the muscles of breathing, (2) relaxation in the neck and (3) release of tension, and increase of flexibility in the articulators: jaw, lips, tongue.

    c. In the gross movements of the body while walking, working, gesturing, etc., strive for ease, strength, and flexibility. Situational pantomime, impersonations, dramatizations, and mimicry of others will help to attain the objective. Active sports—fencing, tennis, bowling— also should be recommended for general flexibility to those suffering from hypotension, monotension, or hypertension.

4. Utilization of the subject's abilities in pitch discrimination after they have been determined by the Seashore tests of pitch discrimination and tonal memory [21] or by these less exact methods of measurement which also may be used as training devices:

    a. Select 15 pairs of notes at various levels with a difference of two semitones. With the aid of a pitch pipe hum these pairs of notes. Hold a card before your face so the subject has no visible clue to the difference in pitch. Ask the subject in each instance to tell you whether the second note is higher or lower than the first. Successful administration of this test depends, in large part, on the ability of the examiner to produce the stimulus tones accurately.

[20] E. H. Henrikson, and J. S. Irwin, "Voice Recording: Some Findings and Some Problems," *Journal of Speech and Hearing Disorders,* Vol. 14, No. 3 (September, 1949), pp. 227-233.

[21] C. Seashore, *Measures of Musical Talent* (New York, The Psychological Corporation, 1955).

b. To gain a rough estimate of the subject's memory of pitch change, ask him to sing "America" or some popular song. Follow this with playing a series of 2, 3, 4, 5, and 6 notes on the piano, all within the range of three octaves, from C^1 (128 d.v.) to C^3 (512 d.v.). Ask him to reproduce or copy the "tune" after each playing.

c. Visualize the possible inflections for single words, *yes* or *no,* by pencil drawing:

and ask the subject (1) to intone the inflection pattern with you, then (2) without your help, to follow the pattern.

d. Next, ask the subject to take the indicated vocal steps between words or phrases:

(1) oh ——
          no ——

(2) *what*
      a
        pi
          ty!

      can't
        and I
          won't
            believe

(3) *I*   *it!*

(Check carefully lest the subject substitute a change of loudness for pitch. This is a very common response.)

      UP!
(4) STEP
    STEP
      DOWN!

(5) BE
    QUI
      ET!   (Be quiet!)

e. Read the following selections over and over, introducing as many pitch changes as you can. Do not be afraid to exaggerate.

(1) The dog came along
    And found his bone,
    Ha! Ha! Ha!
    He laughed all the way home.

(2) The piper came along
    With a merry song.
    Chee! Chee! Chee!
    See how well the world treats me!

(3) "Bimeby big Frog holler: 'Dis deep nuff? Dis deep nuff?'
"Mr. Rabbit 'low: 'Kin you jump out?'
"Big Frog say: 'Yes, I kin! Yes, I kin!'
"Mr. Rabbit say: 'Den't ain't deep nuff!'
"Den de Frogs they dig and dey dig, tell, bimeby, big Frog say:
'Dis deep nuff? Dis deep nuff?'
"Mr. Rabbit 'low: 'Kin you jump out?'
"Big Frog say: 'I des kin! I des kin!'
"Mr. Rabbit say: 'Dig it deeper!'
"De Frogs keep on diggin' tell, bimeby, big Frog holler out:
'Dis deep nuff? Dis deep nuff?'
"Mr. Rabbit 'low: 'Kin you jump out?'
"Big Frog say: 'No, I can't! No, I can't! Come he'p me!
Come he'p me!'
"Mr. Rabbit bust out laughin', and holler out: 'RISE UP,
SANDY, AN' GIT YO' MEAT!' and Mr. Coon riz."
—JOEL CHANDLER HARRIS, *Daddy Jake, The Runaway* (1889)

(4) *Mother to Son*

Well, son, I'll tell you:
Life for me ain't been no crystal stair.
It's had tacks in it,
And splinters,
And boards torn up,
And places with no carpet on the floor—
Bare.
But all the time
I'se been a-climbin' on,
And reachin' landins,
And turnin' corners,
And sometimes goin' in the dark,
Where there ain't been no light.
So, boy, don't you turn back.
Don't you set down on the steps
'Cause you finds it kinder hard.
Don't you fall now—
For I'se still goin', honey,
I'se still climbin',
And life for me ain't been no crystal stair.
—LANGSTON HUGHES [22]

5. Emotional rehabilitation.

The therapy may be direct or indirect. In direct therapy one seeks by standardized tests,[23] structured interviews with the subject and family,

[22] From *The Dream Keeper* (New York, Knopf, 1926).
[23] Among such tests are the following: (a) Bell Adjustment Inventory, (b) California Test of Personality, Adult Form A, (c) Minnesota Multiphasic Inventory, (d) Thurstone Personality Test, (e) Rorschach Psychodiagnostic Test, (f) Vineland Social Maturity Scale, (g) Rogers Test of Personality Adjustment, (h) Haggerty-Olson-Wickham Behavior Rating Schedule.

autobiography, and so forth, to get an insight into the contributing causes, and to encourage the subject to gain the same understanding. Bryngelson would go farther and ask the subject, once having attained insight, "to admit, verbalize, and advertise it." [24] How quickly one may move to this final step will depend upon the subject's response to the therapist, motivation, and response to the treatment. The clinician should check the progress by considering these questions at periodic intervals:

a. Is the subject truly desirous of change? Is he purposive, motivated, willing to work on assignments, desirous of more frequent rather than fewer conferences, always punctual and faithful?

b. What is his true attitude toward the therapist: resentful, belligerent, indifferent, friendly, co-operative, enthusiastic? Does he profess acceptance of therapy, yet really resist and counteract all suggestions?

c. Has he gained a genuine insight into his problems or does he reflect changeable concepts and highly subjective responses?

Another approach to emotional rehabilitation is through non-directive or "client-centered" therapy.[25] In following this method, the subject has permissiveness to talk, and by talking he comes to an acknowledgment and acceptance of his basic attitudes. The subject, not the therapist, does the questioning, probing, and telling. The therapist's role is to assist the subject in the clarification of his feeling, to accept his statements and, in some instances, to restate their content. At no time does the therapist give information, or engage in persuasion, disapproval, or criticism. By his own "oral thinking," the subject becomes aware of the choices he must make and thus gains insight into his behavior. Only after the subject has gained a measure of insight does the therapist offer encouragement or interpretation. The clinic provides the "counselling atmosphere . . . for the client's emotional catharsis and re-evaluation." [26]

II. Deviations in Loudness

Causes. The weak or "soft" voice may result from one of several causes: loss in auditory acuity; physiological and pathological states in the laryngeal or breathing musculature; and psychoneurotic conditions of which the loudness is but one manifestation. The soft voice of the person afflicted with conduction losses in hearing need not be considered here, except to remind the student that its presence sometimes leads to the detection of hearing loss.

A weak voice which has its origin in laryngeal or costal pathology rarely

[24] B. Bryngelson, "Personnel Counselling and the Speech Clinic," *Journal of Speech Disorders*, Vol. 13, No. 2 (1948), pp. 107-113.

[25] C. R. Rogers, *Counseling and Psychotherapy* (Boston, Houghton, 1942).

W. U. Snyder, *Casebook of Non-Directive Counseling* (Boston, Houghton, 1947).

[26] Katherine Thorn, "Client-Centered Therapy for Voice and Personality Cases," *Journal of Speech Disorders*, Vol. 12, No. 3 (September, 1947), pp. 314-318.

appears as a simple manifestation. A hoarse, breathy quality and distorted pitch generally are concurrent symptoms. Chronic laryngitis, laryngeal new-growths, paralysis of the vocal folds, respiratory diseases and anomalies are considerations with which the medical specialist must deal. The speech therapist will make prompt referral to the medical clinic of such cases before undertaking voice therapy.

A weak voice may be symptomatic of general systemic frailty. *M. S.* is such a person. She is slight in build, pale in complexion, and easily fatigable. Her breathing is exceedingly shallow, at times clavicular. When she makes an effort to increase vocal loudness, she clears her throat or coughs slightly before and after phonation.

Psychoneurotic origins are commonly associated with weak voices. Repression, insecurity, excessive tension, fears, and anxieties may be main or contributing causes. Here the problem generally has triple concomitants: a high pitch, breathy quality, *and* poor carrying power. The discussion of the environmental milieu in cases of pitch deviations (p. 202) applies with equal force here.

Excessive loudness occurs less frequently. Sometimes it is associated with cases of reception deafness with which we are not now concerned. The loud voice may be characteristic, too, of the over-expressive and arrogant, although the writer recalls several instances in which the stentorian tones were a "cover" for a very insecure, over-defensive personality. Again, loudness per se might not be so objectionable were it not for the accompanying increase in the number of inharmonics; the result is a disagreeable pitch and quality in addition to excessive loudness. Sometimes the over-strong voice is a product of environment. Constant association with loud voices, or work in a factory where noise must be surmounted if one is to be heard, can establish deeply ingrained patterns of excessive loudness.

Therapy. For *the weak voice in a weak body,* medical therapy and general physical habilitation must precede speech therapy. Once systemic strength has reached its maximum, exercises for breath power and control and for sustained glottal attack may proceed with profit.

1. Exercises for breath power and control:

   a. Demonstrate the essentials of breathing for speech: (1) shoulders relaxed and level; (2) steady expansion of the thorax through action of the thoracic muscles; (3) control of the muscles of exhalation chiefly by resisting the pull of the abdominal muscles and thus holding the diaphragm and the costal cage muscles to a slow, steady return to a position of rest; (4) relaxed jaw and wide oral aperture.

   b. Vocalize *yä-yō-yô-yoō* [jɑ-jo-jɔ-ju]. Can you detect escaping breath before you begin or between the syllables? Lengthen the vowels in each series until your total vocalization occupies at least 18 seconds. Repeat, using a megaphone as an additional resonator. Is the difference marked?

c. Count from one to five, increasing the loudness with each step but keeping the pitch constant. Then reverse with decreasing loudness, 5—4—3—2—1.

d. Begin the following jingle with a loud, steady tone; in the second verse gradually reduce the loudness:

(1) DONG DONG DONG!
    Bonged the great big gong.
    The Hong Kong gong
    Had a long sad song
    Of woe and wrong,
    Of woe and wrong!
    BONG BONG BONG
    DONG DONG DONG

(2) Bong Bong Bong Bong!
    Dong Dong Dong!
    You can hear the gong
    In old Cantong.
    The Hong Kong gong
    In old Cantong.
    You can scarcely hear the gong
    The Bong-Dong gong.

e. Vary the volume, following the clues in size of type in the following jingle. Listen for unvocalized breath, and watch for signs of excessive tension in the larynx.

(1) OOOOOOO NOOOOOOO!
    OOOOOOO NOOOOOOO!
    Yelled the frightened soul,
    Perched up high on the telephone pole.
    OOOOOOO NOOOOOOO!
    OOOOOOO NOOOOOOO!
    Don't chew, dear mole,
    The wood off the bottom of the telephone pole.
    Yo Ho, MOLE!
    Spare a lone, lost soul
    Way up here
    On a telephone pole.

(2) Only an echo reached the mole in his hole,
    Ooooooo noooooo from the lone lost soul.
    Ooooooo noooooo from the telephone pole.
    The mole didn't care about an echo from a soul.

f. Carry on a conversation with your instructor against a background of noise. Note your loudness carefully as the instructor cuts off the masking noise. Can you maintain the same level of loudness, despite absence of the side tone?

g. Consciously widen the oral aperture as you describe an exciting incident which you observed or in which you participated. Check the results by mirror observation.

In dealing with *the neurotic and emotional substratum of a voice too strong or too weak,* one of the regimens outlined in the preceding section (see p. 206) should be followed. We cite a summary of a college freshman's report of an emotional conflict which accounts, in part at least, for her very inadequate voice. Gretchen was a thin, slight, shy student for whom her parents and kinfolk had but one aim in life: the concert stage.

Gretchen was, indeed, a musical genius. She practiced six hours every day and prepared her academic subjects late at night. During the day she flitted from her room to classes and to the music hall, always alone, scarcely speaking to fellow classmates. Her speech in class was particularly ineffective; although she prepared conscientiously, she was never able to make herself heard beyond the front row. In conference she said that it seemed to her as if she were shouting in class. To decrease general fatigue we suggested that she spend less time in music practice. She became greatly upset, wept, and declared the suggestion impossible to carry out because she had promised her parents to spend six hours in daily practice. The day of her recital came and with it the family: parents, grandparents, and three spinster aunts! In their hands, she was a first-grader without a chance of growing up. The conduct of her family became corridor conversation and Gretchen, perhaps for the first time in her life, showed some signs of irritation at the weight of the parental shackles. Irritation led to resentment, at which point she told the speech therapist she had cut her music practice periods in half. Conferences with the psychologist produced miracles. Gretchen found she enjoyed the companionship of other girls; she practiced less but played more for pleasure; she improved her physical appearance markedly; she learned to swim and to dance. True, she continued clinical practice in voice, but it must be admitted that her transformation in personality and in physique had a far greater effect on her voice than clinical drill.

For the overloud voice, the product of an environment of loudness, the best offense is probably defense. Building a defense through heightened sensitivity and awareness of voice, constant checking by instructors, learning inhibition through practice, and conscious development of ease of manner and utterance are aids in finding a more nearly normal voice despite a noisy world.

III. Deviations in Quality

The nomenclature of voice qualities is picturesque, confusing, and generally misleading. What is a "rain-barrel quality" or a "sheet-metal tone" or a "hen's cackle"? We might exclude such metaphorical descriptions and still be confounded by the sheer number of classifications: husky, hollow, coarse, harsh, hard, breathy, strident, metallic, brilliant, rich, thin, heavy, oral, orotund, guttural, pectoral, nasal, denasal. And this list of adjectives is not exhaustive. In a few instances they are synonyms, but they cannot be reduced to four or five categories. The quality of one's voice is complex. Even the physicist who can determine the number of overtones of your voice by the oscillogram knows that he also must reckon with the shape, repetitive consistency, and extent of each formant or overtone.

In this discussion of variants in voice quality we shall select those which occur most frequently, are the least debatable, and most clearly defined.

We shall consider voices characterized by: (a) hoarseness, (b) gutturality, (c) metallic quality, (d) nasality and nasal twang, (e) denasality, and (f) falsetto quality.

The Hoarse Voice. Descriptive (though imperfect) analogies are throaty-husky, hollow, coarse, and harsh-breathy. The clinician is not interested in the voice with a transient hoarseness accompanying a cold, or following a football game, but rather in the hoarseness which is becoming progressively worse, recurs with increasing severity and duration, or is always present and is known as the characteristic vocal quality of the person.

Hoarseness Produced by Pharyngeal and Laryngeal Pathologies. The laryngologist, who generally examines the person suffering from hoarseness before he is referred to the speech clinician, will have taken account of the possibility of laryngeal tumors, benign and malignant; of tuberculosis of the larynx; and of partial paralysis of one or both vocal folds through peripheral damage to the recurrent or superior laryngeal branches of the vagus nerve. Such a paralysis may be the sequela of bulbar poliomyelitis, diphtheria, or scarlet fever. Peripheral neural lesions affecting the larynx also may result from enlargement of the thyroid gland, aneurysms of the internal carotid artery, or growths upon the cervical glands. Because of the tortuous course particularly of the recurrent laryngeal nerve, it may be severed or damaged in thyroidectomy, thus resulting in unilateral paralysis of the vocal fold. The affected vocal fold will lie intermediately between abduction and adduction. In phonation the normal fold will move to the midline and perhaps in a compensatory movement beyond the midline. The chief result of this type of paralysis is marked hoarseness.[27]

The superior laryngeal nerve, likewise, may be damaged by pressure of the enlarged thyroid or by thyroidectomy; the lesion results in a lack of fixation of the thyroid cartilage on the cricoid cartilage. The lack of tension in the vocal edges produces a hoarse-breathy quality. Spontaneous recovery may occur up to 18 months after the injury.

If the paralysis has been caused by damage to the recurrent laryngeal nerve and is bilateral and permanent, excision of the attachment of the muscles to the arytenoids which normally widen the glottis permits the folds to approximate at the midline for phonation.[28] The voice will be hoarse, however, and lacking in modulation.

Other organic causes of the hoarse voice are myasthenia laryngis (pathological weakness of the intrinsic phonatory musculature, especially the thyroarytenoid muscle) and chronic infection of the pharynx, larynx,

[27] L. H. Clerf, "Unilateral Vocal Cord Paralysis," *Journal of the American Medical Association,* Vol. 151 (1953), pp. 900-903.
[28] J. A. Harpman, "On the Management of Bilateral Paralysis of the Vocal Cords Following Operations on or Diseases of the Thyroid Gland," *Journal of Laryngology and Otology,* Vol. 66, No. 12 (December, 1952), pp. 599-603.

nose, and sinuses by bacteria, or by subjection of the laryngeal mucosa to hot, dry, dust-filled air, or air containing irritating vapor from chemical substances. Such general organic conditions as a low physical gradient in children, the result of extreme hypothyroidism, or a very low intellectual gradient, as in amentia, will produce a hoarse vocal quality. In the case of myasthenia laryngis, which is a true muscular disability, the speech clinician can do little beyond recommending complete rest of the laryngeal muscles which have suffered from strain and undue muscular exertion, and instituting a plan of vocal re-education outlined below for contact ulcer. In chronic infection of the mucosa, avoidance of the provocative agents should be advised.

Hoarseness Produced by Misuse of the Larynx and Pharynx. We grow hoarse for other reasons, easier to understand but more difficult to resolve because the resolution is not centered in the larynx but in all the bodily tensions and anxieties to which "the flesh is heir." And in the complex, determined, highly competitive American culture, these tensions are legion. Watch the people on any New York subway train at five o'clock; note the rigidity of facial muscles, the stiff jaw, tongue, and lips; listen to their speech produced with too great breath pressure, with tense pharynx and elevated larynx. Compare their speech with the easy, lilting voice of the Scandinavian also homeward bound, or even your compatriot, the friendly Englishman catching the five o'clock express. You will be struck by the contrast in people who have a common ancestry and, for the most part, common ideals, but who live at a slower tempo.

SINGERS' NODULES. Misuse of the voice may cause the formation of granuloma on the vocal folds, variously described as *singers' nodules* or *chorditis nodosa*. Since vocal abuse probably accounts for the development of the granuloma in 90 per cent of the cases, it must be considered a functional and not a pathological anomaly. Speaking with too great intensity and with lowered pitch pulls the vocal folds to the midline with such force that they impinge upon each other exactly as a tight shoe may impinge upon a toe and produce a thickening of the epithelium. Zerffi believes that much of the tension producing nodules arises in the tongue and in the extrinsic laryngeal muscles which also act in deglutition. These muscles assist in the sphincteric action to close the glottis by pulling back upon the partially closed larynx, as they would do in swallowing, at the same time that the powerful abdominal muscles are attempting to drive air through the larynx. Such a conflict of forces reacts unfavorably upon the vocal organ.[29] The effect of the tension, whether external or internal in origin, is to restrict the freedom of movement, particularly of the anterior one-third section of the vocal folds. As a result of tension and contact, the area becomes degraded, and increased layers of epithelium are built up forming the nodule. In

[29] Zerffi, *op. cit.*

addition to the low pitch, hoarse quality, and glottal plosive attack, one is aware of a type of explosive speech in which there is far too much intensity and breath pressure, a narrow pitch range, and a stress pattern in which accentuation occurs too frequently. Susceptibility varies widely among individuals, but incidence is high among those who speak in an internal environment of excessive tension or an external environment of smoke, noise, or extreme changes in temperature. Secondary causes of the disability are focal infections arising from a cold or influenza, excessive smoking, and pertussis (whooping cough).

Formerly, vocal retraining was begun after the nodules had been removed surgically. Now vocal re-education generally is the first step; surgery is undertaken only when it is clear that reduction of the nodules cannot be effected by vocal retraining. In planning the program of re-education, the therapist will include these practices:

1. Observing the rules of vocal hygiene: avoidance of smoking and smoke-filled rooms, avoidance of excessive fatigue, development of serenity and quiet living.

2. Changing the habitual pitch, thus changing the area of vocal fold contact.

3. Learning a new pattern of controlled, easy breathing for speech.

4. Developing a sense of general bodily relaxation, a freedom from tension.

5. Developing a new melody pattern to take the place of the staccato emphasis and narrow range.

6. Changing the focus of energy from the chest, larynx, and neck to the front tongue, lips, and jaw. In this last process even the blade and dorsum of the tongue should assume a forward position.

Whispering should not be permitted these subjects as was demonstrated by Griesman in his planigraphic studies of the larynx. Not only were the vocal folds in vibration in whispering, but the ventricular folds were approximated, the aryepiglottic area was compressed, and the whole larynx was elevated.[30]

CONTACT ULCER. Another manifestation of vocal abuse resulting in hoarseness is the contact ulcer which appears generally in the posterior one-third section of the vocal folds. Before Peacher's detailed study of this subject, contact ulcer was thought to be caused by a pathological condition. Peacher established clearly that this is a disorder of function, the effect of misuse of the speaking voice.[31] The disorder principally affects adult males and is subject to wide individual variability. In other words, what constitutes vocal abuse for one individual may be within the limits

[30] B. L. Griesman, "Mechanism of Phonation, Demonstrated by Planigraphy of the Larynx," *Archives of Otolaryngology,* Vol. 38 (1943), p. 25.

[31] Georgiana Peacher, "Contact Ulcer of the Larynx, A Clinical Study of Vocal Re-education," *Journal of Speech Disorders,* Vol. 12, No. 2 (June, 1947), pp. 179-190.

of tolerance for others. The resulting vocal quality also varies from a light huskiness to an intense hoarseness. Formerly, surgical removal of the damaged tissue, preceded and followed by periods of non-vocalization, was standard procedure. Peacher and Halinger have demonstrated, however, that better results are obtained through vocal re-education than by surgical excision and/or a period of silence.[32] The plan of re-education, essentially the same as that outlined for the individual suffering from vocal nodules, is presented in detail on page 213.

Other Types of Hoarseness. The functionally hoarse voice reflecting patterned responses of tension may be the result of a single factor or a complex of factors. In some cases one notes that the pitch of the voice is abnormally low, the intensity pronounced, the tone unmodulated. In others, the production is forced, the breath pressure is spasmodic and intense; there is a basic asynchrony among the various systems: breathing, phonation, and resonation; and within the resonators, an asynchrony in coupling between mouth, pharynx, and nose. It is possible that this conflict in "coupling" between the resonators and the source of the vibration reacts unfavorably upon the larynx. One would surmise that the resurgence of energy frays the edges of the vocal folds, fatigues the vocal muscles, and generally puts them "out of joint" so that adduction is poorly timed and executed. Still others, who exhibit rigidity of face and neck and speak with jaws clenched, place an equal strain on the larynx because they inhibit free laryngeal movement.

Therapy. We cannot change the environment which has produced the hoarse voice, but we can give both general and specific directions to change the individual's response to his environment. *MM* came to the speech clinic on the recommendation of a laryngologist whom he had consulted about a vocal hoarseness which had been present for six months. The vocal folds appeared inflamed and frayed, but no pathology could be found. *MM* was a successful operator of a foundry. He was proud of his financial success which he had achieved against stiff competition and after periods of great risk and uncertainty. When he arrived for his first appointment he literally "blew in," shook hands too vigorously, and rasped out: "Well, Doc says you people can help me get back my voice. How much do I pay you?" During the visit he volunteered information about his humble beginning, his lack of formal education, his determination to show the community that he could succeed, concluding with, "And by God, I did!" On the second visit he was accompanied by his wife, attractive and soft-spoken. She volunteered the information that her husband not only encountered frustrations in his business, but that he also was frustrated by his daughter's lack of ambition, her desire for pleasure, and satisfaction with mediocre achievement in high school. Apparently *MM* constantly chided this girl, his only child, hoping

[32] Georgiana Peacher and P. Halinger, "Contact Ulcer of the Larynx: The Role of Vocal Re-education," *Archives of Otolaryngology,* Vol. 46 (1947), p. 623.

that she might excel in the high-school education which had been denied to him.

Psychotherapy was carried on indirectly through his wife, who brought him to understand his projection of his own ambitions to his daughter, and encouraged him to reduce the vigor of his reactions to problems in the foundry, and to bear the inevitable frustrations of his business with serenity and poise. He, himself, decided to spend one afternoon in midweek away from the foundry; he took up golf, and at the end of the summer took his first vacation in twenty years, a two-weeks' fishing expedition with his family.

Direct voice training followed the general regimen prescribed for all disorders of quality (see p. 213), with these modifications which should be made in practically all cases of hoarseness:

1. A considerable time was spent on the removal of spasmodic, arhythmic breathing patterns and on the reduction of breath pressure.
2. The pitch was raised with a somewhat spectacular improvement in quality.

The subject listened to a tape recording of the voice with raised pitch, and concluded immediately that not only did it "sound better," but that its production also "felt better." Once having hit upon his optimum pitch, he was able to hold this pitch level and to use it in the clinic. He also made the transfer to conversational speech more rapidly than might be expected. The reduction of muscular tensions in the neck and chest, and the transference of this energy to lips, tongue, and jaw followed the general prescription in vocal re-education (p. 204). Speaking with a wider oral aperture also contributed materially to an improvement in the quality of the "new voice."

The Guttural-strident Voice. This voice quality resembles the hoarse voice in its manner of production but, in terms of the acoustic effect, the production reacts on the supralaryngeal mechanism in a different manner, producing a dysphonia, which if the pitch is high, we call strident; if low, it is described as guttural. You may recognize extreme forms of stridency in public speakers who have been trained in an era of public speaking without the advantage of a public-address system. The voices of Adolph Hitler and Wendell Willkie which have been recorded in *I Can Hear It Now* [33] are clear examples of this strident quality.

Causes. The cause may be either functional or organic. In some cases, it is clearly the reflection of the individual's hostile reactions to his environment, or of a personality dominated by absolutism and a corresponding lack of sensitivity and sympathetic understanding. Common organic causes are (1) a congenital, pathological weakness of one or more parts of the phona-

[33] Edward R. Murrow and F. W. Friendly (narrators), *I Can Hear It Now* (1933-45), Vol. I, Columbia Masterworks Set, MM 800.

tory system, or myasthenia; (2) damage to the faucial arch in tonsillectomy producing cicatrices and a small faucial opening; and (3) muscular weakness resulting from partial paralysis, sequelae of poliomyelitis, or of infection of the respiratory system.

In functional cases particularly, one will note an atypical muscle-set of the laryngeal and supralaryngeal structures. As the jaw is pulled forward, the geniohyoid muscle acts to draw the hyoid bone forward and fix it at the wrong point, thus raising the larynx into the hyoid notch. Russell observed that when this action occurred, "the red-surfaced muscles which lie above the vocal cords begin to form a tense channel and press upon the vocal cords themselves. . . . Consequently, but a very small strip of the glottal lip is left free to vibrate." [34] The vibrations, or "friction noises," which are superimposed upon the laryngeal tone (defective in itself because of the restriction of free movement of the folds) may come from several tensed membranes: the ventricular folds, the membranous covering of the palatoglossus or palatopharyngeus muscles; even the soft palate may have a hand in the "caterwauling" noises produced. The retraction and elevation of the dorsum of the tongue may be attributed to the geniohyoid and the digastric muscles which raise the floor of the mouth when they contract. The pressures, both infra- and supraglottal, are excessive, thus producing an accompaniment of glottal stops, clicks, and other sounds as the subglottal pressures blast the vocal folds apart. The increased tension in the vocal folds may be induced, partly, by the subject's attempt to counteract the waste resulting from spasmodic exhalation. Not only are the intrinsic muscles of the larynx affected, but many extrinsic muscles are held in contraction, thus restricting vocal-fold vibration. Thus, failures in timing, co-ordination, and coupling are part of a chain reaction producing a strident-guttural quality.

Therapy. Retraining to improve the strident voice should follow the general regimen outlined in the succeeding chapter (pp. 239-243), with these particular emphases and modifications:

1. To establish the optimum muscle-set in breathing, phonation, resonation, and articulation, develop in the subject a feeling of ease and strength. Note the posture of the subject; if necessary, change the basic posture in order to relieve the tensions in the costal cage. Cultivate an easy rhythm in walking, gesturing, and other motions. Avoid all abrupt movement, both of the large and small muscles. The following exercises will serve as a beginning in relaxing the pharynx, larynx, and mouth:

    a. To relax the throat and neck, drop the head forward, chin toward the chest, the muscles of the neck thoroughly relaxed. Gradually lift the head to its original position. Repeat a number of times.

[34] G. O. Russell, "Physiological Causes of Guttural and Piercing Deaf Voices," *Oralism and Auralism,* Vol. 8, No. 2 (1929), p. 102.

b. Drop the head forward as before, rotating the head from the shoulders from right to left. Note that when the jaw is fully relaxed, the mouth falls open as the head is rotated backward.

c. Relax the jaw by letting it fall as the head is held upright. Don't pull the jaw down but let it drop of its own accord. Close the mouth and repeat.

d. Repeat the syllable *suh*. Keep the tongue relaxed and let the jaw fall open after the consonant sound. Repeat several times.

e. Take a deep breath. Relax as much as possible. Let out a deep sigh. When you do so, try to let the throat and muscles "go." Then try vocalizing *ah* as you sigh. Try for pure tone without tension.[35]

f. In developing freedom and flexibility of the lips, tongue, and jaw, make sure that the jaw is retracted and the tongue forward in the mouth. Test the flexibility of other facial muscles in smiling, laughing, etc.

2. Establish the proper timing in phonation.

   a. Produce a prolonged, unvocalized sigh; follow with a vocalized sigh. Slowly! Easily!

   b. Intone the vowels: *ä* [ɑ], *o* [o], *ô* [ɔ], *ōō* [u] in vocalizing the expiratory phase of a yawn.

   c. Combine the vowels with *h: hä* [hɑ], *hō* [ho], *hô* [hɔ], *hōō* [hu]; ask the subject to sense the change in tension at the glottis between *h* and each vowel.

   d. Demonstrate failures in valve timing by negative practice: (1) When the folds are blown open suddenly, a glottal click precedes the vowel: [wʔɑ, wʔɔ, wʔo, wʔu]. (2) When the folds open too gradually, an aspirate *h* precedes the vowel: *hä* [hɑ], *hô* [hɔ], *hō* [ho], *hōō* [hu].

3. Determine the optimum pitch level. In most cases, the habitual pitch level will have to be raised. Test the subject's ability to perceive the change in quality as pitch changes. By repeated ear-vocal stimulation, develop an acoustic and kinesthetic awareness of the new pitch level.

4. A program of psychotherapy, if needed, may accompany, or precede, or take the place of formal vocal re-education. In most cases, it would be well to provide both psychotherapy and direct vocal re-training. Certainly any voice will be improved through the cultivation of a basic sense of freedom, poise, and relaxation.

The Metallic Voice. In our clinical experience, the metallic voice quality has been limited almost entirely to women, and is characterized by an absence of recognizable overtones. The oscilloscope bears out this observation. Richness and color are lacking. Van Dusen agrees with our conclusions with respect to the metallic voice in women. He finds, however, the converse

---

[35] Anderson, *op. cit.*, pp. 77-79.

to be true in the male metallic voice: there is a spread of energy in the very high overtones, producing noisy, discordant elements.[36]

This quality in women is marked in certain cultural groups. There are sections in New York and Chicago, for example, where the metallic quality is pronounced in the female voice. In these cases, one notices a striking, atypical manner of speech production in which the facial and laryngeal structures are fixed with the exception of the mandible. Both laryngeal and articulatory movements are highly inflexible. Possibly a vibration of the ventricular (false) bands also is a concomitant. Imitation or deep psycho-physical disturbances may be the cause. Curry suggests that the pharynx is distended and that the ventricular bands press down upon the upper surfaces of the vocal cords so that "probably only the extreme edges of the cords are free to vibrate." [37] In addition to the general program of vocal and psychological rehabilitation outlined in the succeeding chapter (pp. 239-247), the clinician should pay especial attention to relaxation in the neck and face, to the development of subtle, graded energy in the fine muscles of phonation, resonation, and articulation, and particularly, to fuller and more flexible use of the mouth and pharynx.

The Nasal Voice (Excessive Nasality and Nasal Twang). Much of what we shall say about the nasal voice does not apply to the nose, but to what the layman and sometimes the clinician have associated with nasality. If the faucial isthmus is large and the oral aperture small, apparently a *cul-de-sac* resonance results which strikes our ears as excessive nasal reverberation (hyper-rhinolalia). If the tongue is large in relation to the oral cavity, and is buckled in the back of the mouth, again the quality seems to be hypernasal. A nasal twang, by definition, should be a vocal quality produced by partial nasal occlusion and resulting in inharmonic vibration. Yet it has been demonstrated that tensions at any point in the supraglottal region can produce what we, heretofore, have called a nasal twang. The vibration of tense aryepiglottic folds or of the epiglottis itself, or the violent contraction of the larynx with a narrowing of the laryngeal aperture may superimpose vibrations of a high frequency which our ear interprets as nasal twang. Likewise, excessive tension of the pharyngeal constrictors or the pillars of the fauces, or of the levator palati muscles, can produce the discordant twang. None of these vocal effects can be attributed to the nose, yet we associate them either with excessive nasality or with nasal twang.

We encounter a second difficulty if we say that freedom from nasality is dependent entirely upon the effectiveness of the velar-pharyngeal sphincter. There are wide individual differences in requirements for the velar-pharyngeal seal. Apparently the shape of the palate, the width of the oropharynx at the faucial pillars, the position of the tongue, and its relation

[36] C. R. Van Dusen, *Training the Voice for Speech* (New York, McGraw, 1953), p. 140.
[37] Curry, *op. cit.,* p. 82.

to the size of the mouth opening are important determinants of nasal resonance. In 1952, a three-year-old boy was admitted to the Rockford College Speech Clinic with an unrepaired cleft of the velum. He received daily therapy in speech development, in articulation, in flexible tongue and lip action, in speaking with an open mouth, and in easy production of tone. The final evaluation by the Speech staff and by the members of the staff of a nearby medical center was that the voice quality was remarkably normal, and that this child would not be known as a boy handicapped by cleft-palate speech. In 1954, the child returned to the clinic. The cleft had been repaired surgically. The speech was marked by extreme hypernasality, by glottal stops and clicks. The child had lost free front-tongue action. He scarcely opened his mouth in talking. What had happened to produce this unfortunate turn? The repaired velum was very taut; the faucial arch had been narrowed; there was no observable velar action. In attempting to close the nasal port, the child apparently had learned to use the muscular synergy of swallowing which retracted and raised the dorsum of the tongue. No one would mistake the problem. He now *is* a boy handicapped by cleft-palate speech. It is possible that the configuration of the nasopharyngeal area may have been changed by the downward growth of the floor of the nose from the base of the skull, thus changing the relation of the posterior border of the palate to the posterior pharyngeal wall. The involution of adenoids may have had some contributory influence.[38] Whether surgery, new articulatory patterns, or developmental configurations were the prime mover we do not know.

Are there measurable differences in "nasal tolerance" among voices? This is a third variable about which we cannot be positive. Certainly the high-pitched, thin soprano voice cannot tolerate without disastrous effect the same measure of nasal resonance which appears unnoticed in a full bass voice. This observation is supported by spectograph studies of vocal quality. It was found that the addition of nasal resonance weakened the formant in the area of 2500 cps (or double vibrations) and accentuated higher partials in the area of 3300 cps. These experimental investigations by Smith and Joos also lend support to a widely held view that the high vowels, $\bar{e}$ [i] and $\bar{oo}$ [u] take on nasal resonance more easily than other vowels.[39] That these high vowels are most seriously affected by any release in the velar-pharyngeal sphincter is supported indirectly by the research of Hagerty, Hixon, and others [40] who found that the high vowels demand the closest velar-pharyngeal seal of all English vowels. The opposite view is held by several

[38] R. M. Ricketts, "The Cranial Base and Soft Structures in Cleft-Palate Speech and Breathing," *Plastic and Reconstructive Surgery*, Vol. 14, No. 1 (July, 1954), pp. 46-56.

[39] S. Smith (Copenhagen), "Vocalization and Added Nasal Resonance," *Folia Phoniatrica*, Vol. 3, No. 3 (1951), pp. 165-169.

[40] R. Hagerty and F. S. Hoffmeister, "Velo-pharyngeal Closure an Index of Speech," *Plastic and Reconstructive Surgery*, Vol. 13, No. 4 (April, 1954), pp. 290-298.

investigators including McIntosh [41] who observes that the high vowels ē [i] and ōō [u] are less frequently nasalized than other vowels. It is our observation that one finds nasality in these sounds more unpleasant than in other vowels. A definite answer to the question of "nasal tolerance" cannot be given.

Structural and Physiological Anomalies Producing Hypernasality. Velar insufficiency, or the congenitally short palate, has been recognized for a long time, but until surgical means of lengthening the palate were devised, vocal re-education was the only remedy. There is another type of velar insufficiency, less well known, which produces a marked hypernasality. The epithelium of the velum is intact, but apparently the muscle is deficient or lacking. Stark, who studied palatal clefts in human embryos, concludes that the lack of mesodermal penetration, present in the clefts, also would account for "the individuals who have perfect palates apparently, but who indicate a defective mesoderm by speech which exhibits rhinolalia aperta." [42]

The velar-pharyngeal seal also may be inadequate because of the *peculiar structural configuration of the pharyngeal wall.* If the occipital bone (to which the pharyngeal muscles are attached) is unusually high, the angle becomes so obtuse as to make closure of the nasal port impossible.

Damage to the velum, or to the muscles which make up the velar-pharyngeal sphincter, should be investigated when the subject reports, for example, that his voice was normal until he had a tonsillectomy. The clinician should remember, however, that the hyper-rhinolalia may be caused, not by damage, but by the absence of the adenoidal block and by a velum made functionally weak or "paralyzed" through lack of use.

Bulbar poliomyelitis may produce *partial or complete paralysis* by damaging the cranial nuclei in the medulla which are responsible for innervation of the velar-pharyngeal muscles controlling the nasal port. The sphenopalatine nerve, a branch of the ninth cranial nerve is the chief innervator, but branches of the tenth and eleventh cranial nerves also may contribute to the innervation. In cases of irreversible damage to the cranial nuclei, there is no possibility of restoration of velar-pharyngeal function. The voice will remain hypernasal. When there is evidence of incomplete loss of function, the clinician should establish the degree of impairment. This can be done by observing velar movement in the gag reflex and in yawning, and through testing its efficiency by having the subject drink fluid through a straw, by spirometric readings of breath pressure with the anterior nares open and closed, and so forth. Morley suggests that restoration or improvement of velar-pharyngeal control demands stimulation in kinesthesia for the

---

[41] C. W. McIntosh, *An Auditory Study of Nasality.* Unpublished Master's thesis, State University of Iowa, 1937.

[42] R. B. Stark, "The Pathogenesis of Harelip and Cleft Palate," *Plastic and Reconstructive Surgery,* Vol. 13, No. 1 (January, 1954), pp. 20-39.

muscle movement with supplementary visual and auditory stimulation to re-inforce muscle training.[43]

Note also should be made of the fact that such *structural anomalies* as narrow faucial pillars, hypertrophied lingual tonsils, and a tongue too large for the oral cavity may contribute to the production of hypernasality.

Hypernasality Resulting from Improper Function. No section of the country can claim freedom from hypernasality. It was as characteristic of the lip-lazy, palate-lazy grocer at a crossroad in Alabama where we stopped to inquire about direction, as it was of the maid in the hotel in Shawegan, Maine, or of the airport manager in Wenatchee, Washington. Imitation, undoubtedly, is one cause; a low energy index, another. The low energy index, or general bodily hypotonicity, may be an acquired response, a familial pattern, or a result of an enfeebled mind, or it may be indicative of a basic lack of interest in life.

Therapy

1. *Auditory training.* In all cases of hypernasality, the subject should be taught *to distinguish by ear the effect of the right way and the wrong way.* With children, the clinician may use the following speech games for this auditory training:

   a. An ordinary pasteboard box is divided into two compartments. One-half is painted red, one-half black. A small chute leads into each compartment. The child is given large red and black marbles. The instructor, with her face hidden, presents nasal and non-nasal sounds. If the sound is "good," a red marble is rolled into the red compartment, if "bad," a black marble into the black compartment.

   b. Crossing the goal line. The children stand on a chalk line with their backs to the clinician. Each time the instructor makes a "good" tone the child advances to the next station. If the tone is "bad," (hypernasal) he stands still. If he advances when the tone is "bad," he must go back two "stations."

   c. The story book. There are three pictures on each page, two of which indicate objects, the names of which include the sound *m* or *n*. The third contains no nasal sound. The preceding page contains the beginning of the sentence: "Paul went to the store. He wanted to buy something to play with. He bought a ————." On the following page are pictures of a mop, a top, a knob. Read the sentence and then turning the page, ask, "Did Paul buy a mop, a top, or a knob? Point to the right one." The proper answer will contain the word without a nasal sound.

[43] D. E. Morley, "Speech Disorders Resulting From Bulbar Poliomyelitis," *Journal of Speech and Hearing Disorders,* Vol. 20, No. 2 (June, 1955), pp. 156-163.

d. With a portable hearing aid amplifying the clinician's speech, ask the child to raise his hand when the "right" word comes up. Pointing to the toe, say, "This is my *n*oe, my *b*oe, my *t*oe." Pointing to the nose, say, "This is my *d*ose, my *n*ose, my *f*ose." "I put my hand on: my *h*ead, my *n*ead, my *b*ed." "The chicken's name in the story was hɛdɪ pɛdɪ, hɛbɪ pɛbɪ, hɛnɪ-pɛnɪ (henny-penny)," etc.

2. In some cases retraining should consist in the *direct stimulation of stronger velar action,* for which we suggest the following exercises:

   a. Swallow forcibly and at the height of the action, hold the position until you have a definite kinesthesis of the action of the velar-pharyngeal sphincter. Hold the hand at the angle of the jaw to sense the pharyngeal action.

   b. Place a tongue blade against the hard palate and move it back until it presses the velum with sufficient force to set off the reflex action. Note in the mirror the extent to which the velum rises, the action of the levator palati and tensor palati muscles. Does the uvula remain close to the dorsum of the tongue, or does the entire velum rise? If the subject is a child, ask him to watch the "back door" close, and notice how the voice now comes out the "front door."

   c. Yawn, and on the exhalation phase, intone the vowel *ä* [ɑ]. If it is free from excessive nasality, repeat the action until you are sure that you have a clear motor-kinesthetic memory of the velar action.

   d. Blow out the cheeks and explode the air forcefully, then gently, through puckered lips.

   e. Blow up a soft balloon and allow the air to leak back in the mouth until the mouth is filled with air.

   f. Demonstrate nasal and non-nasal emission in these ways:

      (1) Place a mirror in a horizontal position immediately below the nose. Intone *ä* [ɑ], *ô* [ɔ], *ō* [o]. If the mirror is clouded, excessive nasal emission is present.

      (2) Retain the feather on the second step of the two-step speech ladder while producing the plosive: *p, k, t.* (On each crossbar is a feather. One crossbar is at the nasal outlet, the other at the oral outlet.)

      (3) Alternately pinch and release the nostrils while intoning *ä* [ɑ], *ô* [ɔ], *ō* [o]. Is there a difference in the quality of the sound when you constrict the nares?

      (4) Produce hypernasal, then non-nasal vowels: *ä* [ɑ], *ô* [ɔ], *ō* [o], *oō* [u], *ē* [i]. Can you open and close the velar-pharyngeal sphincter at will?

      (5) Hold the *p*-sound which demands firm closure of the nasal port for a second before "exploding" it into the vowels *ä* [ɑ], *ô* [ɔ]; repeat with *t;* with *k.*

      (6) Prolong the implosive phase of each stop consonant in the following sentences:

         (*a*) The big dog grabbed a bite of biscuit.

(*b*) Bo-Bo, the goat, scares the pigs, ducks, and geese.

(*c*) The wolf said, "I'll huff, I'll puff, I'll blow your house down."

(*d*) The dairy maid said, "He would like a little bit of butter on his bread."

3. *The development of oral pressure and breath direction* can be aided by such gentle blowing exercises as the following:

a. Blow through a large straw inserted into a plastic box partially filled with feathers, or confetti, or colored tissue strips; direct the breath stream gently forcing the "pieces" into some kind of pattern.

b. Retain paper butterflies on a mirror by blowing gently against them.

c. Through a large plastic straw, direct the breath stream against a ping-pong ball. Blow the ball to points in the "Market Place" designated by the instructor.

d. Blow ping-pong balls up an inclined plane, increasing the angle of the plane as proficiency increases.

e. Make the ping-pong ball hop from notch to notch on a "knitting bar." (A heavy piece of wood 1½ inches wide, with 12-15 notches of equal size. The subject can judge both the force and duration of the breath stream.)

4. *The development of a new pattern of oral resonance.* Some subjects with hypernasality will not profit as much by velar exercises as by establishment of a new pattern of oral resonance involving a larger mouth opening, a relaxed jaw, and mobile front tongue and lips.

a. A larger oral aperture and relaxed jaw. It is generally believed that if the mouth opening is much larger than the faucial opening, the tendency to *cul-de-sac* resonance will be reduced. The vowels are used in these exercises because they do not require great changes of the articulators. The chief need is to attend to "volumetric expansions and contractions of the speech cavities," and to develop awareness of the acoustic result.

(1) Before the mirror with the jaw relaxed, mouth open wide, intone *ĕ* [ɛ], *ä* [ɑ], *ŭ* [ʌ], *ô* [ɔ], *ō* [o]. The instructor will note "the best" vowel, i.e., the one with least nasality and clearest vibrant tone. Practice producing the vowel again and again. Note the mouth formation in the mirror.

(2) When you are sure that you can produce this vowel at will, intone the vowel, gradually increasing the mouth opening until you reach the "key" position. Note the results; tape-record it and listen to the playback.

(3) Move from the "key vowel" to other vowels, attempting to copy the muscular set of the key vowel.

(4) Note on the oscilloscope the difference in the number of partial vibrations when *ô* [ɔ] is intoned with open mouth and with a narrow oral aperture.

(5) Intone the vowels in combination with labial sounds: *w, m, b*.

   (*a*)   wä, wē, wô, wō, wōō [wɑ, wi, wɔ, wo, wu] etc.

   (*b*)   Prolong the *m* and make a clear break between it and the vowel:

        m—ē [i]; m—ä [ɑ]; m—ō [o]; m—ô [ɔ]; m—ōō [u].

   (*c*)   [ɑmɑ   ɑwɑ   ɑbɑ]
        [imi   iwi   ibi]
        [ɔmɔ   ɔwɔ   ɔbɔ]
        [omo   owo   obo]

(6) Watch the mouth opening on all vowel sounds. Drop the jaw consciously.

   (*a*)   — ah, bitter chill it was!
        The owl, for all his feathers, was a-cold;
                      —JOHN KEATS, "The Eve of St. Agnes"

   (*b*)   See my bee!
        Hmmmmmmmmmmmmm, he sings
        Fly to me!
        Ai-ee! He stings!

   (*c*)   Down in the valley, the valley so low,
        Hang your head over, hear the wind blow.
        Hear the wind blow, dear, hear the wind blow;
        Hang your head over, hear the wind blow.
               —from *Down in the Valley* (mountaineer song)

   (*d*)   Sweet month of May,
        We must away!
        To-day! to-day!
            —SAMUEL TAYLOR COLERIDGE, "Song," from *Zapolya*

   (*e*)   And all should cry, Beware! Beware!
        His flashing eyes, his floating hair!
        Weave a circle round him thrice,
        And close your eyes with holy dread,
        For he on honey-dew hath fed,
        And drunk the milk of Paradise.
               —SAMUEL TAYLOR COLERIDGE, "Kubla Khan"

   (*f*)   "Over the Mountains
          Of the Moon,
          Down the Valley of the Shadow,
          Ride, boldly ride,"
          The shade replied,—
        "If you seek for Eldorado."
               —EDGAR ALLAN POE, "Eldorado"

   (*g*)   Tell me where is fancy bred,
        Or in the heart or in the head?
        How begot, how nourished?
        Reply, reply.

It is engender'd in the eyes,
With gazing fed; and fancy dies
In the cradle where it lies.
Let us all ring fancy's knell:
I'll begin it,—Ding, dong, bell.
                    —WILLIAM SHAKESPEARE, *Merchant of Venice*

(7) Exercising conscious control to maintain an adequate oral aperture, tell your clinician

    (*a*) How to reach the shopping district by bus;

    (*b*) About the last concert you attended;

    (*c*) Your reaction to the statements: 1) "The American college girl has banked the fires of her brain." 2) "Conversation has sunk to the 4-D's: dress, diet, disease and domestics."

b. *Increased lip flexibility.*

(1) Pucker the lips as for whistling and send the breath stream in small puffs through this narrow orifice.

(2) Using the same lip formation, intone *ōo* [u] at different pitches, noting any differences in nasality with each pitch. Can you find the tone level at which there is the least noticeable nasality?

(3) Compress and release the lips rapidly as you say:

> b-b-b-b-b-b—ee
> p-p-p-p-p-p—ah
> m-m-m-m-m-m—oh
> f-f-f-f-f-f—oh

(4) As you sing the "dwarfs' song," check with the mirror to see if the lips are clearly rounded for *ō* [o] and everted for [ai] in "Hi."
"Hi-ho, hi-ho! It's off to work we go; Hi-ho; hi-ho; hi-ho!"

(5) Make the lip action in the final plosives as strong as in the initial plosives:

> HEP HEP HEP!
> Better keep in step!
> Bawled the sergeant to the ranks.
> HEP HEP HEP!
> Better keep in step
> When you march in flanks.
>
> To the private in the rear
> The command was faint
> The hep hep hep was faint.
> h e p   h e p   h e p   h e p!
> Then the sergeant made him hear
> HEP HEP HEP HEP HEP HEP HEP!

(6) Read these sentences with relaxed jaw, open vowel production and *precise lip action:*

(*a*) Fat black bucks in a wine barrel room
Barrel-house kings with feet unstable,
Sagged and reeled and pounded on the table.
Pounded on the table
Beat an empty barrel with the handle of a broom
Hard as they were able
Boom! Boom! Boom!

—VACHEL LINDSAY, "The Congo" [44]

(*b*) "Penny wise and pound foolish" is an old aphorism.

(*c*) Who wah wah; who wah wah,
Iowa, Iowa;
Who wah wah.

(*d*) BOM BOM BOM BOM!
POM POM POM POM!
Black men beat the Tom-tom.
BOM BOM loud.
POM POM hard.
Black men beat the Tom-tom.
BOM BOM BOM BOM!
POM POM POM POM!
BOM BOM BOM BOM!
POM!

Black men in a far-off town
Heard the sound nearly drown.
Bom Bom soft.
Pom Pom faint.
Bom Bom Bom Bom!
Pom Pom Pom Pom!
Bom Bom Bom Bom!
Pom!

c. *Increased flexibility of the front tongue.*

(1) Watch the action in the mirror. With mouth wide open, rest the tip of the tongue on the teeth. Now raise the tip only toward the palate; now the blade and tip.

(2) Sing a familiar tune with *La-La-La*. Be sure that only the tongue tip is touching the alveolar ridge. Do not raise the whole tongue or any part of the dorsum if you can avoid it.

(3) Trill *l-l-l* with the tongue blade touching the alveoli, the tip free.

(4) Keep the tongue forward in the mouth, making the occlusion at mid-palate for the *k-g* sounds. Keep the occlusion approximately the same whether the plosive is followed by a front or a back vowel:

[44] From *Collected Poems* (New York, Macmillan, 1923).

key-kaw; key-ko; key-koo.
hickory, dickory, dock.
tick-tock; tick-tock.
clickety-clack; clickety-clack.

(5) Curl the tip of the tongue behind the lower front teeth and force the blade and dorsum forward. Now return the tongue to a position of rest with the tip resting on the lower incisors. Repeat until you have a kinesthetic awareness of a forward tongue position.

(6) With tongue forward and low in the mouth, practice the nasalized, then the un-nasalized vowel:
[ɑ], [ɑ̃], [ɑ], [ɑ̃].

(7) With a conscious effort to keep the body of the tongue forward and the tip up for *l, t, d* sounds, read the following:

THE LOON

A lonely lake, a lonely shore,
A lone pine leaning on the moon;
All night the water beating wings
Of a solitary loon.

With mournful wail from dusk to dawn
He gibbered at the taunting stars—
A hermit-soul gone raving mad,
And beating at his bars.

—LEW SARETT [45]

The Nasal Twang. We referred earlier in this section to a pseudo-nasal twang, the product of violent contraction or tension of muscles in the supraglottal areas (p. 218). Although the majority of cases probably fall in this classification, there also is a true nasal twang caused by structural deviations in the nose: a deflected septum which closes off the nares at mid-point, or nasal polypi (a thickening of the membranous covering of the turbinates), or a very high palate which becomes a convex floor of the nose, so arched that it obstructs the flow of air in the nose. Or the nose may be so narrow and thin that the breath stream is impeded at some point in its egress. Chronic inflammation of the nasal mucosa, as in allergic rhinitis and sinusitis, produces a swollen and irregular lining. The breath stream enters the posterior nares only to meet obstruction. The force of the breath induces the tissues in the constricted area to vibrate. These discordant vibrations, dominant because they have a relatively high frequency, are superimposed upon the laryngeal tones. The result: a "caterwauling" in the nose, a truly unpleasant acoustic effect.

[45] From *Many, Many Moons* (New York, Henry Holt, 1920; Lew Sarett, 1948).

In some instances a functional nasal twang also occurs when the upper lip is pulled down or when the nasal alae are contracted. The elimination of the twang, whether it is produced by discordant nasal reverberation, or by tensions and constrictions in the oropharynx, is achieved by the same general methods: (1) development of acoustic awareness of the twang; (2) relaxation of the chest, neck, and facial muscles; (3) increase of the size of the oral opening in all speech; (4) increase in the flexibility of front tongue, jaw, and lips; (5) development of the maximum potential of all the resonators (particularly mouth and throat) by the practice of vowels combined with nasal consonants.

This regimen has been described in detail in a preceding section (see p. 220). In many cases there is a need for psychological counselling and retraining. Whether the twang is nasal, or oral, or pharyngeal, it can be a deeply ingrained part of a personality that is rigid and unbending; or quite the contrary, it may reflect the personality of a dependent, helpless wallflower who "twangs"and whines her way through life. Of course, the person also could be one who has been surrounded by a family of twangers—and has succumbed. Each will need counselling if the subject is to gain an understanding of her problem.

The Denasal Voice. All voices need a measure of nasal resonance for richness and brilliance. The absence of this resonance in the nose is called denasality or negative nasality. The voice is lifeless; "he talks as if he has a cold in the nose." The cause may be either organic or functional. Obstructions in the nasopharynx such as enlarged adenoids blocking the posterior entrance to the nose and polypi on the superior turbinates are a cause. Congestion in the nasal mucosa as in allergic sensitivity can be so severe as to occlude the nares completely, thus producing a denasal voice.

After the obstruction has been removed by surgery, or after the nasal congestion has been relieved, the denasal voice often becomes hypernasal. Prior to surgery, there was no need to use the velar-pharyngeal sphincter, and the muscles became functionless with disuse. Direct training of velar closure is necessary in such cases in order to correct the hyper-rhinolalia.

Williamson [46] and others find that *functional* denasality is the more common occurrence. It arises from a failure to develop a full resonance both in the nose and the mouth. Some subjects are not aware of their nonresonant voices. Others have acquired a denasal voice through unconscious imitation. And there are some people in whom it is a cultivated response—a mark of sophistication. In others it is a reaction to an environment in which they meet defeat, or in which they have little interest. Life has passed them by, and they now, in return, reject life. There is no simple code of directions to the last two groups, both of which are probably in need of psychological readjustment. Indirect voice therapy based largely on psychological coun-

[46] A. B. Williamson, "Diagnosis and Treatment of Eighty-four Cases of Nasality," *Quarterly Journal of Speech,* Vol. 30 (1944), pp. 471-479.

selling is discussed in a later section in this chapter (see pp. 243-247). Unless the clinician has been trained in this field of psychology, however, he should not undertake psychological counselling. The interests of the subject will best be served by direct referral to a clinical psychologist. Whether indirect voice therapy is or is not prescribed, it is our belief that all cases of functional denasality, without respect to cause, will profit by direct training in voice production emphasizing the development of full resonance and variety in pitch and loudness. Such a course of training has been outlined in detail in the next chapter (see pp. 239-247).

The Falsetto Voice. The voice scientist should be able to recognize a falsetto voice easily although he may find it difficult to correct. The exact mode of production of the falsetto quality has not been definitely established. Perhaps there are several ways. Phoniatrists are agreed that only the upper edges of a small portion of the vocal folds are vibrating, that the vibration is very rapid but limited in extent. Curry agrees that the extent of the movement of the folds is reduced but he maintains that upward displacement of the folds is increased.[47] Frequently there is an elliptical opening at mid-point. The pitch range is high, and, in the female, is sometimes called the head register. The specific muscles which are involved in this action are also debatable. According to Tarneaud,[48] the thyro-arytenoid muscle is relaxed, but the external laryngeal muscles are tense so that the whole larynx is elevated. The edges of the vocal folds are thin and stretched. As the extrinsic contraction increases, the ventricular bands press upon the upper surface of the vocal folds, thus permitting only the free edge of the fold to vibrate. Baisler[49] did not observe any actual impingement upon the true folds, but he adds that "some narrowing of the entrance to the ventricles may occur," and there is a "marked 'crowding in' of these (supraglottal) structures." Infraglottal pressure is greater than that in normal voice production.

In treating this disorder, relaxation of the muscles of breathing and of the extrinsic muscles in the laryngeal and oral pharynx is of first importance. A conscious effort to lower the pitch and to develop full use and freedom of the resonators should be made. Freud emphasizes "long, regular, audible exhalation to obtain the optimal physiologic tension of the vocal folds, and thus the normally pitched voice."[50] The goal, as in all vocal retraining, should be the relaxed, easy, controlled operation of the voice instrument (see pp. 239-247).

[47] Curry, *op. cit.,* p. 46.
[48] J. Tarneaud, "Semeiologie Stroboscopique des Maladies du Larynx a de la Voix," *Revue Franc. de Phoniatrie,* Vol. 6 (1938), pp. 19-22.
[49] P. E. Baisler, *A Study of Intra-Laryngeal Activity During Production of Voice in Normal and Falsetto Registers.* Doctoral dissertation, Northwestern University, 1950. Pp. 87, 90.
[50] Esti D. Freud, "Clinical Language Rehabilitation of the Veteran, Methods and Results," *American Journal of Psychiatry,* Vol. 107 (1951), p. 884.

10

Voice Disorders: II

VOICE PROBLEMS IN DELAYED PUBERTY

Adolescent Voice Changes

The voice of the adolescent generally undergoes basic changes in pitch and quality between the thirteenth and the sixteenth years. In girls the change is much less profound and occurs earlier than in boys. The female vocal folds lengthen, however, and the lining of the pharynx becomes thicker and softer. This modification of the pharyngeal wall increases the absorptive coefficient and diminishes the reflective power which formerly gave a metallic brilliance to tone. The voice of the female, as a result, becomes more mellow and rich in quality as pubescence advances.

In the male, the angle of the thyroid becomes pronounced. The vocal folds increase greatly in mass and length (by one-third) and the pitch becomes lower by about one octave. The rapid growth of cartilage and muscle in the male sometimes results in an unmanageable voice instrument. Without provocation, it shifts from high to low; the quality is hoarse, then mellow, then lapses into a childish treble as if two sets of vocal folds were vibrating instead of one. The "break" may be a whole octave. It is understandable why some boys do not know how to manage the instrument which neither feels right nor sounds right. In the process of physiological change, it is difficult for the boy to decide whether to cling to his old voice or to try to adjust to a mechanism in which the vibrator is changing in length and thickness, often from day to day. The hoarse quality apparently is caused by the increase in size of the laryngeal muscles which prevents the posterior section of the vocal fold from approximating the midline. As a result of the strain imposed upon the folds, they become inflamed and swollen, thus producing hoarseness. This hoarseness may be noted in adolescent girls as well as boys. In an examination of 80 boys, 40 of whom were fourteen years old, it was found that 80 per cent of the fourteen-year-old subjects were "hoarse-husky" in voice.[1] It should be noted, too, that the voice is particu-

[1] E. T. Curry, "Hoarseness and Voice Change in Male Adolescents," *Journal of Speech and Hearing Disorders,* Vol. 14, No. 1 (March, 1949), p. 25.

larly susceptible to any slight change in physical or mental state in this period of endocrine adjustment. When the phonatory muscles have adapted themselves to the physiological changes in the larynx, the pitch is no longer uncontrolled and the quality no longer falsetto. The higher notes in the male have disappeared and the lower notes have improved in quality. Maturation normally is completed in a six-months' period, but it may be prolonged from eighteen months to two years.

The Juvenile Male Voice

How should the clinician advise the boy whose voice is still juvenile at seventeen years? Anderson suggests that one can make this differential diagnosis (1) by observing whether his voice has a clear, true quality; (2) by observing his laughter; and (3) by having the boy "sing down the musical scale, beginning with Middle C or whatever tone is easiest for him." [2] A clear, true quality is indicative of the fact that the voice probably has reached maturity, despite the high pitch and thin quality. If the boy laughs in a low, normal voice, he should be able to develop a low, normal speaking voice. If he can sing in the lower range, he should be taught how also to speak in the lower range.

On the other hand, if the parent or boy reports that other secondary sex characters also are delayed in development, the boy should be referred to an endocrinologist before voice therapy is begun. The clinician also must rule out emotional maladjustments or psychic traumas which can cause serious delays in development of the mature voice. If the therapist finds such behavioral symptoms as excessive shyness, negation or introversion, or other atypical social behavior, he should enlist the co-operation of a clinical psychologist.

In the largest group of boys troubled by juvenile voices, the difficulty probably is rooted neither in an endocrine disorder nor deeply seated emotional maladjustment but in a lack of awareness and understanding of what needs to be done to establish the new voice. Generally they will profit by therapy along these lines:

1. Auditory training (heightened sensitivity to his voice and the voice of others)
2. Laryngeal and pharyngeal relaxation followed by vowel intonation
3. Vocalized sighing
4. Determination of the basic pitch and practice in its establishment
5. The development of flexible, free resonance and articulation.

All these techniques have been discussed in detail in the preceding chapter.

[2] V. A. Anderson, *Improving the Child's Speech* (New York, Oxford, 1953), pp. 242-243.

APHONIA

"In the presence of the great realities of life we are dumb, we cannot speak." Some people find that every crisis, minor or major, is a "great reality;" they are without voice. Others—and this group is the substantial majority—face situations of anxiety and security, too, but they have learned to "roll with the punch," to adjust, not succumb, to the emotional assault. It is the first small group with which we are now concerned; in these people the response of voicelessness becomes a stereotyped reaction called functional or hysterical aphonia.

Hysterical aphonia, or voicelessness, occurs much more frequently in girls (the ratio is 7:1), and may appear as early as puberty. Although the highest incidence is between 18 and 34 years, Bangs and Freidinger [3] report a case of a thirteen-year-old girl who had suffered from hysterical aphonia from the age of six. Functional aphonia has been precipitated in innumerable ways. Physicians who met the problem frequently in World War I attributed the disorder to hysterical conditions resulting from mental and physical strain, prolonged fear and anxiety, or physical trauma. In some instances it was reported to be the aftermath of colds and throat infections or exhausting illnesses.[4] In our experience an upper respiratory infection may be the immediate precipitating factor of aphonia but deeply seated emotional problems have been established as the true etiological agents.

The descriptions of the symptoms of aphonia are as varied as explanations of cause. Generally the onset is sudden. In the typical picture the vocal folds do not adduct to the midline. They either may be completely abducted or a partial approach to the midline is made forming an elliptically shaped glottis. In some cases a spasmodic contraction has been observed in which both the true and the false vocal folds are pressed tightly together.

The treatment of cases of functional aphonia involves one or more of the following courses: (a) mechanical or electrical stimulation (faradic current) of the larynx; (b) psychotherapy; and (c) voice exercises.

We present summaries of two cases, one by Bangs and Freidinger,[5] and the other from our files. In the first instance, the case of a thirteen-year-old girl who had suffered from hysterical aphonia from the age of six, psychotherapy including hypnosis was tried without success. On the assumption that the psychic trauma had been resolved, the clinicians proceeded with a program of speech rehabilitation. The outline of therapy is presented in detail since it offers one plan of attack.

[3] J. L. Bangs and A. Freidinger, "Diagnosis and Treatment of a Case of Hysterical Aphonia in a Thirteen-Year-Old Girl," *Journal of Speech and Hearing Disorders,* Vol. 14, No. 4 (December, 1949), pp. 312-317.

[4] H. Bloomer and H. Shohara, "Speech Disorders Among European Military Personnel in World War I: Part I," *Journal of Speech and Hearing Disorders,* Vol. 16, No. 4 (December, 1951), pp. 352-364.

[5] *Op. cit.*

1. Breathing and laryngeal exercises to restore the tonus of the laryngeal musculature. The patient was instructed to inhale deeply, exhale vigorously, and stop the exhalation by closing the glottis, while at the same time closing the fist. Coughing exercises were also used. Both exercises developed adductor action of the vocal folds and the extrinsic laryngeal muscles. Force, speed of movement, and *maintenance* of the closure of the glottis were the goals.

2. Development of sound combinations
    a. Humming in a soft monotone followed by production of *m, n, z,* and *v.*
    b. Combining of consonants and vowels *na, ni, mo, ma,* etc.

3. Progression from sounds to words.

4. Reading
    a. At first, subject was forced to take a breath after each word.
    b. Training in interpretative reading.
    c. Negative practice: conscious lapse into whispered reading on command, followed by vocal reading.

5. Transfer to speech for conversation
    a. Talking outside of clinical situation.
    b. Given commissions to read to younger, bed-ridden children.
    c. Given interviews, shopping tours, etc.

The approach in the second case of functional aphonia emphasized psychotherapeutic techniques ranging from directive counselling based upon personality inventories, autobiography, and suggestion to non-directive or client-centered counselling. Voice exercises were included because the subject was eager to try them, but they were not the core of the remedial program.

A. M. is a teacher of vocal music, twenty-two years of age, who lost her voice ten months ago. After consulting several laryngologists who found no pathology, she finally came to the speech clinic. Her parents accompanied her and gave considerable information about their daughter's problem. The onset of voicelessness had been sudden. One day in the early spring she had come home from the public school where she was employed, very tired and visibly upset. She helped with the preparation of the evening meal and retired immediately after the meal. The next morning she tried to greet her mother in the kitchen but was unable to vocalize. The frightened parents called a physician at once who diagnosed the illness as acute laryngitis and prescribed medication and rest. After three weeks of rest the voice had not returned; the search for further help began. One of the laryngologists reported that the vocal folds were partially adducted in an elliptoid shape and indicative of a functional paralysis of the thyroarytenoid muscles.

At the beginning of the therapy sessions in the speech clinic, *A.M.* was highly resistant to any kind of psychological therapy, direct or indirect. In permissive writing sessions she generally scribbled illegibly. If a musical record were played on the phonograph she would run from the room. She listened to records of speech without protest. She appeared on time for each appointment and gradually evinced interest and pleasure in coming. Her first real achievement was an autobiography which she left in a sealed envelope on a side table in the therapy room without calling it to the attention of the therapist. The emotionally fraught situations slowly came to light. Her brother, to whom she had been too deeply attached, married a woman who quite promptly decided that the association of the brother and sister was not healthy and forbade *A.M.* to come to the new home. Shortly after this unpleasant situation developed, her only intimate girl friend was killed in a car accident. *A.M.* also had had a leading position in a small church choir, but a month prior to the onset of aphonia a newcomer to the city had joined the choir. *A.M.* felt that the new member was trying consciously to "out-sing" her. She was sure that she had strained her voice in an effort to be heard above the newcomer; this could indeed have been one of the precipitating causes. There also were discipline problems with the boys in her music classes in the public school, problems which she had met so unsuccessfully that the principal had asked for a conference with her. Apparently this conference preceded immediately the loss of voice. The therapy sessions gradually shifted to client-centered counselling in the form of long writing sessions. In one session she expressed a desire to go back to college to complete the theoretical part of her music education. When the subject was raised in a succeeding session, she only shook her head and wrote, "Impossible!" but when it was repeated several weeks later she nodded approval and evinced genuine interest in our exposition of the advantages of such a plan. In the meantime, we had devoted a part of each therapy session to "progressive relaxation" (Jacobsen's method) and to exercises for controlled respiration, including the production of prolonged sighs, but no tone. We then proceeded to interruptions of exhalation as in coughing until *A.M.* was able to produce a good "Ha!" She then tried other combinations of the vowels with the aspirate sound: *ha; hi; ho; hu;* etc. Slowly she proceeded to words and connected speech. *A.M.* is now in college, and up to this moment has had no recurrence of aphonia.

ESOPHAGEAL SPEECH

On a very cold morning in a town in Minnesota, the location of a renowned medical center, a policeman noticed a man on the opposite corner, standing motionless, apparently interested in nothing more than surveying the frozen landscape and catching the feeble light of a December sun. The officer watched the man intently, then crossed the street for a closer view. Again he stared incredulously at the figure with his chin thrust into his coat collar. There was no frost on the collar, no cloud of vapor as his breath met the frigid air. It was time, the officer allowed, for the law to step in. "Say, fellow," he blurted out, "Do you know you are dead? I've been watching you, and you haven't breathed in fifteen minutes!" The "ghost" turned and walked away. The laryngectomized patient, breathing through a fistula in the neck rather than through the nose or mouth, would meet on his road back to "normal" life even more baffling situations than a policeman.

So great is the psychic trauma attendant upon laryngectomy that the physician who finds that the laryngeal tumor is malignant, and must recommend removal of the "voice box," prepares the patient with considerable care. He assures him that he will learn to speak again, and that the hole in his neck, the new respiratory tract, need not be obvious. A laryngectomized subject who has mastered esophageal or pharyngeal speech visits the patient and demonstrates his new speech. With the aid of a speech clinician, he may give him a preview of the lessons by teaching him how to "gulp" air into the oropharynx and perhaps the esophagus. He shows him how pressure of the abdomen on the costal cage will act to return this air bubble, and if the pharyngeal area, or the esophageal lips, are constricted, the air will be vibrated just as it was by the vocal folds before the operation. The patient also may be shown a film, *New Voices,*[6] a record of the experiences of other laryngectomized patients in surgery and in speech rehabilitation. It is hoped that by these means the patient's fear of the future is reduced.

After the larynx is removed from a point below the cricoid cartilage to the hyoid bone, an opening in the neck is made to which is sewn the severed end of the trachea. The opening in the neck is protected by a tubular valve. The portions of the inferior constrictor muscle which were freed from their laryngeal attachments are sutured together, and the pharynx now acts only as the passageway into the esophagus. Air reaches the lungs through the tubular valve in the neck.

Speech habilitation generally begins within two to four weeks after surgery and consists essentially of three parts: (1) the intake of air into the posterior oropharynx or esophagus; (2) the smooth ejection of that air to produce phonation; and (3) the synchronization of the articulators with the vibrating air stream (see Fig. 10-1). There are two possibilities for a pseudoglottis. In the so-called "pharyngeal voice," the air is locked in the throat by the occlusion of the dorsum of the tongue against the palate in a forward motion. When the occlusion has been made, "a slight thump will be felt in the throat." [7] When this occurs, phonation of ä [ɑ] should be attempted immediately. Apparently the constriction of the narrowed pharyngeal wall, or of the scarred remnants of the inferior constrictor muscle, or of the tongue edges will substitute for the "lost cords." The system operates independently of respiration. Anderson [8] finds that because of its great mobility the tongue contributes to good volume, but since the tongue is engaged in phonation, "it is not free to serve at optimum efficiency as an articulator, and therefore articulation and clarity of speech suffer."

The formation of the pseudoglottis at a lower point, immediately above

[6] R. W. Chapin (Author and Director), *New Voices* (film), Cleveland Hearing and Speech Center, 11206 Euclid Avenue, Cleveland, Ohio.

[7] C. R. Nelson, *Post-Laryngectomy Speech* (New York, Funk and Wagnalls, 1949), p. 44.

[8] J. O'D. Anderson, *A Descriptive Study of Elements of Oesophageal Speech*. Doctoral dissertation, Ohio State University, 1950, p. 18.

or at the mouth of the esophagus, is a more common practice, and considered superior by many clinicians. In this method, the chief vibrating agent is the cricopharyngeus muscle at the mouth of the esophagus. It is a stringlike striated muscle, consisting of the transverse fibers of the inferior constrictor, which surrounds posterior and lateral aspects of the cricoid cartilage and the mouth of the esophagus. The innervation is from the

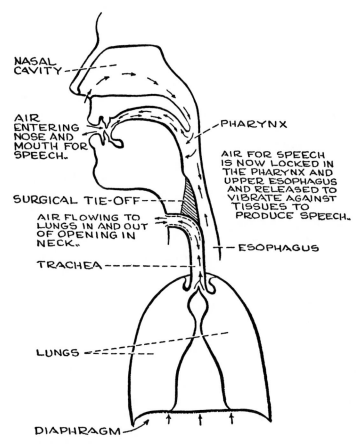

NASAL CAVITY

AIR ENTERING NOSE AND MOUTH FOR SPEECH.

PHARYNX

AIR FOR SPEECH IS NOW LOCKED IN THE PHARYNX AND UPPER ESOPHAGUS AND RELEASED TO VIBRATE AGAINST TISSUES TO PRODUCE SPEECH.

SURGICAL TIE-OFF

AIR FLOWING TO LUNGS IN AND OUT OF OPENING IN NECK.

ESOPHAGUS

TRACHEA

LUNGS

DIAPHRAGM

FIGURE 10-1. Diagrammatic sketch of production of esophageal speech. (Adapted from C. R. Nelson, *Post-Laryngectomy Speech* [New York, Funk, 1949], p. 57.)

pharyngeal plexus to which the ninth, tenth, and eleventh cranial nerves contribute fibers, and is subject to voluntary control. The esophagus acts as a good air reservoir since it can store 18 to 25 cubic centimeters of air, is capable of voluntary "inhalation" of the air, and can expel the air with some control of rate and amount.

The first step in inhalation is the *voluntary relaxation of the esophageal sphincter*. To do this, Morrison states, the geniohyoid, mylohyoid, and anterior belly of the digastric muscles raise and pull forward the hyoid bone, at the same time exerting a strong pull on the cricopharyngeus muscle, causing it to relax.[9] During this action, negative intrathoracic pressure is created by fixing the chest and performing short, jerking contractions of the diaphragm, thus aiding in sucking in the air into the esophagus. When filling has been accomplished, the patient closes completely, or partially, the sphincter and raises the intrathoracic pressure. (The positive pressure may be as high as 30 to 40 mm-Hg.)

The articulators assist in this operation: The velar-pharyngeal sphincter is closed, the air is drawn in through slightly open lips; then the lips are closed, the tongue dorsum rises (but is not retracted), forcing the air through the relaxed cricopharyngeal sphincter. The ejection of the air is effected through the sharp expiratory effort of muscles ordinarily associated with respiration. The esophagus itself behaves as a passive tube.

Whether the pseudoglottis is formed in the posterior oropharynx or in the esophagus, the problems in learning to gulp air and to produce vibratory tone on expulsion are about the same.

1. *The subject must dissociate vital respiration from speech,* interrupting fundamental muscular and nervous synergies. He must learn to hold his breath, while ejecting the air by sharp expiratory movements. If he exhales through the trachea at this moment, he decreases the chest cavity thus lessening the pressure on the oropharynx and esophagus. Moreover, tracheal exhalation can be so noisy as to dampen the oropharyngeal or esophageal sound. To assist the subject in this dissociation of the two processes, have him practice as follows:

  a. Check suddenly the inspiration while air is insufflated into the posterior oropharynx or upper portion of the esophagus.
  b. Inspire, expire, then hold the breath and insufflate the air quickly.
  c. Hold the hands over the chest, thus aiding in the resistance to motion during insufflating and expelling of air.
  d. Stop the cannula with the finger and then expel the insufflated air.

2. A second problem is the *reversal of peristalsis.* Air in considerable amounts should not enter the stomach. If the esophageal lips are to be the vibrators, the esophagus should be filled only from the pharynx to the diaphragmatic opening. Air in the stomach is wasted for there is no evidence that stomach air is belched out to form the speech sound. The normal peristaltic wave which would send the air into the stomach must be inhibited and reversed.

3. *The subject must learn to control the degree of contraction in the oropharynx and esophagus* so that the air will be used most economically in the production of speech sounds. In the beginning, the clinician may expect

9 W. Morrison, "The Production of Voice and Speech Following Total Laryngectomy," *Archives of Otolaryngology,* Vol. 34 (1941), pp. 413-431.

the patient to produce no more than a single sound of short duration on one air-fill, but within two months he should be able to utter eight or nine syllables on a single "fill."

4. *The subject must develop intrathoracic pressure without excessive tension* of the whole body. The arms, head, and abdominal muscles should be relaxed. Nelson [10] says on this point, "By putting very little pressure on the diaphragm and breathing naturally and easily you are able to control the speaking air and avoid any unpleasant sound caused by escaping air." Fatigue should be avoided at all costs.

5. If the vibration of the esophageal lips is the aim, *the subject should be discouraged in his tendency to use a buccal whisper.* As Stetson [11] says, in buccal speech the sphincter of the esophagus must be closed in order to maintain the necessary high pressure in the mouth. This action is directly opposite to the sphincteric relaxation necessary for esophageal speech.

Once the subject has learned to air-fill the esophagus and to expel the air slowly, he can proceed to learn how to articulate the movements of jaw, tongue, and lips with the air-expulsion. Moolenaar-Bijl [12] contends that the voiceless plosives, *p, t, k,* should be used as starters, since the articulatory movement in the aspiration of air through partially closed lips resembles the articulation of these sounds, and since there is a demonstrable expansion with each production of "pah," "tah," or "kah." He proceeds directly from these syllables to monosyllabic words such as "put," "cap," or "tick." Other clinicians prescribe work at first only on vowel sounds, to be followed by work on the laterals *l* and *r;* the glides, nasals, voiced continuant consonants, plosives, voiceless consonants, and finally the fricatives. Still others go directly from voiced tone to monosyllabic words as in counting, or to such useful words as "Hi," "Yes," "No," and "Bye." So they build disyllabic words, sentences, and meaningful speech. In this process, articulation is extremely important, since intelligibility depends not so much upon the volume of air as upon the economical and clear molding of this air stream into meaningful sound.

As in all cases of speech rehabilitation, individual differences make it impossible to predict final results. Age; motivation; health; freedom from fear, guilt, and shame; learning ability; self-confidence; and faithfulness in practice are considerations which must be reckoned with in rehabilitation. There may be some who will not be able to master esophageal speech. After an extended course Gardner [13] found that "14 per cent are unable to speak a

---

[10] *Op. cit.,* p. 56.

[11] R. H. Stetson, "Esophageal Speech for Laryngectomized Patients," *Archives of Otology,* Vol. 26 (1937), pp. 132-134.

[12] A. Moolenaar-Bijl (Groningen), "Connection Between Consonant Articulation and the Intake of Air in Oesophageal Speech," *Folia Phoniatrica,* Vol. 5, No. 4 (1953), pp. 212-216.

[13] W. H. Gardner, "Rehabilitation after Laryngectomy," *Public Health Nursing,* Vol. 43 (1951), pp. 612-615, 647.

continuous series of words. . . ." This criterion of good speech is that one can talk over the telephone and be understood. The great majority, however, will learn to speak so that they can make themselves understood. They will speak more slowly; the pitch modulations will be few; the rhythm will be measured, but the goal for them has been realized. They may join the "Lost Cord League" because they have learned to talk without a larynx.

GENERAL PRINCIPLES OF VOCAL RE-EDUCATION

Some defects in voice quality resulting from pathological or organic states are not remediable. In other organic problems affecting quality, the therapy depends upon the alleviation of the physical condition by medication or surgery, and is specific for the particular disorder. Vocal retraining to remove functional defects of voice quality, on the other hand, may follow a general regimen. We present these general principles as a summary and a guide, but the student will remember that modification and supplement of this regimen to fit particular needs have already been made in the discussion of each atypical quality.

Direct Voice Training

1. *Recognition of the Acoustic Effect of One's Voice.* The subject must be trained to recognize the true quality of his present voice and to distinguish between its basic tone and that of the "new voice." It is well to begin with the vowels because the modification of the phonatory sound wave takes place in the larynx and, hence, the student need not attend to articulation; the vowels require only expansions and contractions of the speech cavities. The instructor intones *ô* [ɔ] using both good and faulty tones repeatedly. Then, without example by the instructor, the student attempts to reproduce both good and faulty qualities. He listens to his own production on the tape recorder. In some cases, amplification of his own tones by a portable hearing aid aids him in perceiving the good and the poor tones.

From a tape recording by the instructor of all gradations of acceptable and unacceptable vocal qualities in the production of the vowel *ô* [ɔ], the student records by number the least and the most desirable. Then he attempts to match these qualities orally as each sample is played.

2. *Development of a Kinesthesia of the Proper Muscle Synergy, the Proper Tensions and Timing in the Larynx and Pharynx.*

   a. With thumb and index finger outlining the mandible and the remainder of the hand over the pharynx, the subject feels the difference in tensions in larynx, pharynx, and jaw between the old and "new" voice.

   b. Placing the hand over the larynx, he should intone *ô* [ɔ], *ä*[ɑ], *ō* [o] without excessive tension, checking the result each time to make sure that the glottal stop does not precede the vowel.

c. Have the subject check further his own aural perception by projecting single vowels on the oscilloscope. The oscilloscope will present a visual record of the presence or absence of the glottal click.

d. The subject intones ô, ä, ō [ɔ, a, o] at various pitches until he has found the best quality at an optimum pitch. In hoarse, guttural, and metallic voices, the optimum pitch generally should be much higher than the habitual pitch the subject is using.

e. In order to cultivate flexibility in the vocal folds, have the subject slide up and down the scale on the word, "No," or "Yes." In this way he may sense the difference between a rigid, restricted melody pattern and expressive, free, modulation.

3. *Development of Breath Control.*

a. Yawn slowly, and on exhalation intone ô [ɔ].

b. In a reclining position (without pillow) inhale slowly, easily, and as easily intone ô [ɔ].

c. Clasp your hands over diaphragm and, as you intone ô [ɔ], resist the tendency of the abdominal muscles to relax and the costal cage to collapse quickly.

d. Place two or three books on the abdomen. As you intone ô [ɔ] watch the descent of the books. With each succeeding trial increase the number of books and attempt to make the descent a slow and smooth process.

e. Repeat these exercises increasing the number of vowels until you can produce the series: ē [i], ä [a], ō [o], ô [ɔ], ōō [u], ā [e].

f. Now combine the vowels with a single plosive: bē, bā, bä, bō, bô, bōō [bi, be, ba, bo, bɔ, bu]; and with the same steady, easy, controlled exhalation, intone each syllable on a single inhalation. Then combine two and three syllables.

g. Practice humming, beginning with the optimum (easy) pitch, proceeding from small to great changes in pitch.

h. Standing with easy, controlled posture, chant the following:

(1) Ahoy-oy. Ahoy; Ahoy, (prolonging "oy" in each syllable.) A ship A-hoy! Ahoy!

(2) The soul is doomed who sounds his own knell.

(3) Cold! Cold! How cold it was!

(4) Boom! Boom! Boom!

(5) Send it all around the room!

(6) do-do-do-do-do
no-no-no-no-no
Go low! Go low.

(7) "They are all gone away;
There is nothing more to say."

(8) Home comes the sailor
No more to roam;
Blow long, O heaven,
Blow him soon home.

(9) The mole has only a hole in the ground for a home.
But the mole knows the hole is a good home for a mole.
A mole, a mole, finds it cool and cozy in a hole.

(10) Hoo! Hoo! Hoo
                oo
                        oo!
The hoot of the owl fills the night
With moods cold and bleak
With thoughts dark and deep.

(11) Le Tour Eiffel: A tall black spire caught by the evening
                        sun is turned into sparkling fire.
But below, its four wide-spread feet are planted
                        solidly in cold concrete.

(12) Dreams like golden keys
Unlock the treasure-trove
Of unremembered hopes and deeds
Cornered from life's seven seas.

4. Shift in the Focus of Energy from Larynx to Lips, Front Tongue, and Jaw.

a. Before the mirror watch the action of the lips, tongue and jaw in saying rapidly the following exercises:

(1) b-b-b-b-bah

(2) p-p-p-p-pah

(3) pt-pt-pt-pt-pt

(4) pa-la-pa-la-pa-la

(5) pa-ta pa-ta pa-ta

(6) pa-ka pa-ka pa-ka

(7) Woe, woe, woe for
Joe, Joe, Joe.
Who couldn't call
Whoa, whoa, whoa
To the horse named Zoe.

(8) Lulu, the loony loon
Went whoop, whoop, whoop
With the whooping croup
Poor Lulu, the loony loon.

(9) Weary the weevil
Began to weep
When he saw only weeds to eat
And not a sheaf of wheat.

b. Intone *ä* [ɑ] with open mouth, then slowly close the aperture while continuing the sound and note the change in vocal quality.

c. With clenched teeth say *ä* [ɑ]; then slowly relax and lower the mandible, noting the change in quality as you do so.

d. Read the following excerpts with conscious attention to flexible jaw, energetic lip action, and accurate, quick front-tongue movement:

(1) "I confess that there are several parts of this Constitution which I do not at present approve but I am not sure I shall never approve them: for having lived long, I have experienced many instances of being obliged by better information, or fuller consideration, to change opinions even on important subjects, which I once thought right, but found to be otherwise." —BENJAMIN FRANKLIN

(2) "This same people have wisely given their public servants but little power for mischief; and have, with equal wisdom, provided for the return of that little to their own hands at very short intervals."

—ABRAHAM LINCOLN

(3) "Do you not understand now that which the nation is dying of is the darkness in which there is such an obstinate determination to leave her?" —EMILE ZOLA

(4) "If we fail, then the whole world, including the United States, including all that we have known and cared for, will sink into the abyss of a new Dark Age, made more sinister, and perhaps more protracted by the lights of perverted science."

—WINSTON CHURCHILL [14]

(5) "Miss Nims, take a letter to Henry David Thoreau.

Dear Henry: I thought of you the other afternoon as I was approaching Concord doing fifty on Route 62. That is a high speed at which to hold a philosopher in one's mind, but in this century we are a nimble bunch.

On one of the lawns in the outskirts of the village a woman was cutting the grass with a motorized lawn mower. What made me think of you was that the machine had rather got away from her, although she was game enough, and in the brief glimpse I had of the scene it appeared to me that the lawn was mowing the lady. She kept a tight grip on the handles, which throbbed violently with every explosion of the one-cylinder motor, and as she sheered around bushes and lurched along at a reluctant trot behind her impetuous servant, she looked like a puppy who had grabbed something that was too much for him. Concord hasn't changed much, Henry; the farm implements and the animals still have the upper hand." —E. B. WHITE [15]

(6) "As for the surface car or *trikk,* as it is called in Norway, it too has an appreciation of human nature which is quite unique. In the first place, its crew regard the traveling public and themselves as belonging to the same race of people. Not only do conductors help old folks and women with baby-carriages on and off the trolley car, but if the motorman observes someone running to catch the car, he does not fiendishly pull away from the hapless mortal but actu-

[14] From *Their Finest Hour* (Boston, Houghton, 1949), p. 226.
[15] From "Walden," in *One Man's Meat* (New York, Harper, 1939).

ally waits the ten or fifteen seconds necessary for him to make contact with the *trikk*. Besides such practices, frowned upon in other cities as incompatible with urban transportation, the Oslo streetcars have humanized traffic in yet another way.

Instead of employing New York's heartless door-slamming or restaurant-bouncer technique to get away from rush-hour crowds, the *trikk* solves the situation both effectively and tactfully. When the motorman thinks enough human beings have piled aboard, he merely eases his chariot through the crowd and away from the carstop. Those persons still on the ground act as a kind of scraper which removes most of the loosely attached passengers. Watching the situation carefully through his rear vision mirror, the driver waits until any remaining doubtful cases have made up their minds whether to cling aboard or return to terra firma and then puts on full speed to the next stop where the performance is repeated."

—PHILIP BOARDMAN [16]

5. *Setting the New Pattern in Connected Speech in the Clinical Situation.*

a. Recall an interview, conversation, or conference in which you engaged recently. Set down ten or more sentences from the talk and then practice them before the mirror checking yourself carefully on controlled breathing, relaxation in the pharynx and larynx, flexibility in the front mouth, lips, jaw. Be sure that the oral aperture is adequate.

b. Prepare an interview with your employer. Record it and, in the playback, signal to your instructor when you lapse into the old pattern.

6. *Transfer of the New Pattern to Conversational Speech Outside the Clinic.*

a. Try your new voice at a specific time and place outside the clinic. Let the first trial be limited to a greeting, a question about direction, or the weather.

b. Increase the number of times and situations in which you use the new voice outside the clinic.

c. Converse with a friend and make mental note of the number of "lapses" in your voice quality.

d. Try out the new voice in a variety of situations: with your employer, with members of the family, with strangers, with friends, in noisy surroundings, under great excitement, in a relaxed quiet atmosphere. Can you maintain the new voice in all situations?

Indirect Voice Therapy

It will be apparent in the discussion that follows that the approach to the voice problem, in some cases, may be largely a psychotherapeutic approach, that no direct vocal retraining may be indicated. It is our experience, how-

[16] From *How to Feel at Home in Norway* (Oslo, H. Aschehough and Company, 1950).

ever, that even if the course is dominantly one of psychotherapy, some direct vocal re-education has a salutary effect on the clinic subject.

Myfanwy Chapman makes use of psychotherapy in a program of indirect training designed particularly for boys and girls in the upper grades of the secondary schools.[17] It is a course which public-school clinicians might follow with profit and, hence, is presented in detail:

Several personality tests . . . are often useful as a sort of springboard for getting at adjustment problems.[18] These tests should be interpreted only by individuals who have had extensive training in clinical psychology. The speech therapist without such training can often make use of interpretations provided by a school psychologist. In any event, the speech therapist is interested in those specific adjustments which have a direct relationship to the speech problem. A speech therapist coming into the picture must first establish rapport with the students. . . . Following conferences where the therapist and student discuss the problem, the student determines whether he wishes some help in the management of it, or prefers to ignore it. . . .

In working with the student who has a speech problem, it is not enough to give thought to the speech mechanism alone; it is necessary to consider the individual who is doing the speaking and to help him gain insight into his way of speaking and acting. For instance, we frequently use the term "objective," meaning that we try to make the student "conscious of self" instead of "self-conscious."

Self study is approached in various ways; i.e., the student may examine himself in the light of studies on child growth and development. He thus finds that he shares many characteristics with his age-mates and has diverse characteristics peculiar to himself alone. He finds that growth takes place at different rates not only in speech but also in other aspects of the developmental pattern. Such differences are normal and cannot be avoided. It probably means being only temporarily out of step. This knowledge often helps the student face his own differences and avoid being seriously disturbed.

Mental mechanisms are studied in a general sort of way. The student learns the meaning of compensations, rationalizations, projections, introjections, identification, and the like. As he understands these mechanisms and finds that everyone about him is resorting to such behavior, he is able to verbalize his own insecurities and analyze his own use of psychological mechanisms. The fact that he does not stand alone is important to him. The student in the secondary school hates to be different from his age group. He is extremely sensitive to what those of his own age think of him.

How do some of these mechanisms relate to speech problems? The student having a speech problem finds that he is likely to project his evaluation of the disorder onto those in his environment. He evaluates his speech difficulty as something of which to be ashamed. He eventually thinks that nearly everyone has the same idea about it as he has. As he projects in this fashion, he resorts

[17] Myfanwy E. Chapman, "Improving Specific Adjustments," *Speech and Hearing Problems in the Secondary School.* The Bulletin of the National Association of Secondary-School Principals, Vol. 34, No. 173 (November, 1950), pp. 89-94.

[18] For a detailed description of personality tests, see Appendix 3.

more and more to withdrawal from speech situations or to compensations of an undesirable nature. He becomes more and more fearful of any situations which involve speaking. . . . Compensations are varied and range from complete withdrawal—seeking solace in books, day dreams, and aloneness—to extremely boisterous, over-bearing ways of behaving. Through the understanding of how these mechanisms operate in others, the student is able to analyze his own reactions and to do something constructive about them.

Another means of guided self-analysis is through mirror study. Here the person studies himself in a large mirror. The mirror reveals many exterior things about the individual, but it also gives clues—through behavior, gestures, and the like—to the thinking of the person. The student analyzes his reactions to his physical appearance as revealed in the mirror. . . . Clues to the unhealthy evaluation of self are revealed. . . . With these clues as a guide, the student seeks insight into his behavior, and, through devices such as autobiographies, he is able to reveal the cause of such undesirable evaluation. By bringing fears, insecurities, and worries into the open, by discussing them with the speech therapist and associates, the individual is often able to get a new point of view and to gain a feeling of security.

Group therapy is particularly helpful for certain types of adjustment problems. In working with others of his own age range, the student has the benefit of group suggestions. Where group dynamics are well established, the give and take, the evaluation of one another can be very effective. Having others of his age point out what they consider healthy and unhealthy attitudes and behavior patterns gives the student clues which will help him in better group relationships. The group approval and acceptance is that which he seeks constantly. . . . It is well for the student who feels particularly frustrated because of inadequacy in verbal self-expression to have a safety-valve. The speech therapist often becomes the good listener and so-called safety-valve. . . .

Socio-drama, in which the group acts out a solution to a behavior problem, is sometimes used to help the self-conscious student. The criticism of the performance and the evaluation of things presented often give further clues to individual problems and aid the students in the solutions of their own difficulties.

It is not enough for the student to be able to carry out assignments within the sheltered walls of the speech room. He must put himself to test and meet the world outside his laboratory. The person who has avoided the telephone is asked to make numerous telephone calls. The timid, weak-voiced girl is asked to invite the principal to a demonstration and report back to the group whether she was asked to repeat because she was not heard the first time. . . .

During adolescent years, the parent-child relationship changes. The students grow independent of parents as helpers and guides and at the same time depend on parents. This is confusing both to the student and parent. The parent-education phase . . . is, therefore, extremely important. The speech therapist needs office hours for consultation with parents. . . . He discusses some of the speech problems with them and points out ways in which the parent can aid in the adjustment program. In turn, the parents give valuable clues to insecurities which they observe in the home and elsewhere. . . . Individual conferences as well as group meetings are necessary . . . with the classroom teachers.

Indirect Voice Therapy for Adults. In all voice problems largely or even partially functional in nature, psychotherapy may be the sole route or the companion route with direct vocal retraining to the goal of improvement. The metallic voice of a middle-aged woman in the writer's acquaintance reflects her aggression, frustration, and disappointment which have been her lot. The self-made factory manager with the nasal twang comes to the speech clinic for a few lessons "to help the voice," now that he has become the president of a local luncheon club. The case to be presented here in detail was treated surgically in the first instance, yet it was evident from the beginning that the psychological maladjustment was the underlying cause of the vocal disorder. Either direct or indirect means can be used in bringing the subject to analyze the psychological mechanisms of negation, compensation, rationalization, and projection in his own behavior, to evaluate them objectively, and to find a healthy and socially acceptable mode of adjustment to life. Non-directive counselling has been described in Chapter 9 (see p. 207). The therapy employed in the case of *ML* is a "hybrid variety," a cross between directive and non-directive counselling with a "recessive factor," speech exercises, introduced chiefly to increase *ML*'s assurance that something was being done for her.

ML was referred to the Speech Clinic by a laryngologist following removal of vocal nodules. The voice continues to be hoarse in quality and unsustained in pitch six months after surgery, despite the physician's assurance that the vocal folds appear to be quite normal. *ML* is an attractive woman, 41 years of age. She is groomed with impeccable taste and holds high standards for herself in other respects as well. On the basis of interviews, biographical study, and permissive writing conducted by the voice therapist and reports on the Sachs Sentence Completion test and the Rorschach Psychodiagnostic test by the psychologist, one concludes that *ML* is confused, insecure, and unhappy despite the warm, happy facade she presents in the clinic. The voice is symptomatic of inner tensions and anxieties. Apparently the fundamental anxiety centers in the state of her marriage. The aunt who reared *ML* discontinued all associations when *ML* married a man of whom the aunt strongly disapproved because of a difference in religion. A year prior to the onset of her voice disorder *ML* reported, "My husband and I weren't getting along at all." She believes now that her difficulties have been "straightened out." She has three children, 20, 15, and 7 years of age, but neither the children nor the husband ever refer to her voice. Apparently she has little interest in the children. ("They drive me nuts, you know!") She does not attend P.T.A. meetings and refused to help with a Brownie troop to which her daughter belonged. When she discussed her relation to her children, she repeatedly asked the question, "Do you think this is bad?" Her reaction to insignificant problems is apparent in this instance: She came to the clinic recently, speaking only in a whisper and reported that she had not slept the night before because she had discovered a bald spot on her head!

ML always appears at the clinic at least 30 minutes ahead of schedule; apparently she likes the attention she is getting. She has pretty largely heaped her problems on the counsellor's shoulders. Her responses are those of a very immature person: she pouts, exhibits childish anger on occasion, and on other occasions dresses and responds as a romantic girl of twenty years. It is our belief that *ML* feels that she can keep the attention of her husband and the concern of her children only by reverting to girlish behavior and illness. Consequently she will keep the "sick voice" as long as it brings her attention. The fact that she has no social outlets and no kinfolk to whom to turn beyond her immediate family, makes her live in perpetual fear of losing the status she has. In the Sachs Completion Test she finished the sentence, "I feel that a real friend ———," "turns out to be your enemy." Although she avows hatred of married life, and says her secret ambition is "to speak well so I can get a fine position," actually she holds onto her "sick voice" so she will not be able to seek a position.

By accepting *ML*'s statements without criticism or disapproval, the therapist has encouraged her to talk freely and thus reveal her feelings. Through restatement and limited assistance in interpretation, she has brought recognition of the true feelings and some insight into the total problem. At the end of a six months' period in the clinic, *ML* is about to "take action" to solve her problems. Perhaps the most valuable portion of the therapy was truly non-directive counselling, but *ML* felt that she benefited also by direct suggestions from the therapist and by exercises which she maintained helped her control her voice. The mixing of directive and non-directive techniques is supposed to nullify the beneficial effects of both. Perhaps this is the exception to the rule.

Whether direct vocal retraining or psychotherapy should receive the chief emphasis in functional voice problems depends entirely upon the diagnosis. Suffice it to say that both roads may be followed with profit in the majority of cases.

11

Stuttering

In the introductory statement to his chapter on stuttering in his *Speech Therapy, A Book of Readings*,[1] Van Riper says in part:

Students preparing themselves to do speech therapy find the disorder of stuttering very hard to understand. There seem to be so many theories and therapies conflicting with one another that in the confusion nothing seems certain. Then, too, the literature is so vast that few individuals have ever read more than a part of it.

The present authors have done research and experimentation in the field of stuttering. They have worked with stutterers and with parents of stutterers. They have read widely, but do not pretend to have achieved the impossible task of having read all that has been written on stuttering or stutterers. They will attempt, in this chapter, to present several current points of view about the nature of stuttering and its causes. In the two following chapters, points of view about therapy for stutterers will be presented. It is hoped that these three chapters will not confuse the student, but will help him to understand the problem of stuttering and motivate him to do a considerable amount of independent reading and thinking on the subject.

THE NATURE OF STUTTERING [2]

Although most of us are fairly certain that we can recognize a stutterer when we observe one speaking, we are not in complete agreement as to which aspect of a speaker's behavior makes us respond to him with the evaluation of *stutterer*. Moreover, occasionally we may be surprised to learn that the person we considered to be a stutterer does not think of himself as such, and that other listeners may not evaluate his non-fluent speech as stuttering. They may, perhaps, use a term such as *hesitant, slow, labored,* or *dysrhythmic* to characterize the type of speech which we have decided is

[1] C. Van Riper (New York, Prentice-Hall, 1953), p. 43.
[2] In our discussion no distinction will be made between stuttering and stammering.

stuttering. One rather pertinent study on the evaluation of stuttering in children indicated that "parents of stutterers significantly exceeded parents of non-stutterers in the extent to which they diagnosed both the stuttering and non-stuttering children as stutterers." [3]

Most speech clinicians will at some time in their careers meet an individual who thinks of himself as a stutterer, but who shows few overt manifestations of stuttering behavior. There is little non-fluency, with only occasional repetition or blocking. There are no apparent tics or grimacings. What the clinician hears and sees appears to be normal and acceptable speech. And yet the speaker himself insists that he is a stutterer and wants to be helped. Stuttering, we might conclude tentatively, has both external and internal aspects. It may not be quite the same pattern of behavior for all listeners or for all speakers. Subjective evaluations as well as the evaluations of other persons become involved in our concepts of stuttering, and in our decisions as to who is to be considered a stutterer and when.

Individual traits and behavioral manifestations associated with stuttering are as variable as the individuals who stutter. There are, however, some characteristics which are common to stutterers as a group and which pertain to the direct speech effort. Stuttering is usually characterized by repetitions, blockings, or prolongations of sounds, syllables, or words which disturb the rhythm of speech. These speech non-fluencies are usually associated with tics, grimaces, facial spasms, or spasmic movements of other parts of the body. These overt non-lingual elements apparently develop as the stutterer becomes aware of his dysrhythmic, non-fluent speech, and may be interpreted as efforts or devices to delay or avoid the act of speech, or to help the stutterer initiate or release the flow of speech.

Primary Stuttering

Primary stuttering consists of repetitions, hesitations, and prolongations in speech which occur without apparent awareness and anxiety and without evidence of struggle on the part of the speaker. These non-fluent aspects of speech, however, must occur so often that the incidence exceeds the amount normal for most persons in terms of age, sex, and the speaking situation. Van Riper reserves the term "primary stuttering" for the non-fluencies which appear under conditions when most of us would expect little non-fluency to occur.

If a child repeats, hesitates or is non-fluent so frequently that his speech calls attention to itself and markedly interferes with communication, then our society tends to call him a stutterer and so do we. However, if these symptoms comprise the total of his abnormality and occur automatically and without evidence of self-awareness, avoidance or struggle, and they appear in situations where

[3] O. Bloodstein, W. Jaeger, and J. Tureen, "A Study of the Diagnosis of Stuttering by Parents of Stutterers and Non-Stutterers," *Journal of Speech and Hearing Disorders*, Vol. 17, No. 3 (1952), pp. 308-315.

most children are fluent, then we would insist that he be diagnosed as a *primary stutterer* and treated as such.[4]

The authors of this text accept Van Riper's distinction between normal non-fluency and primary stuttering.

Secondary Stuttering

Stuttering becomes secondary when the speaker becomes aware of his non-fluencies, and attempts to modify or avoid them. The overt accessory movements cited earlier then become associates of the speech act. As part of the characteristics of secondary stuttering we may include the reactions of the individual to himself as a person, and to the act of communication in general. It should be emphasized, however, that the amount and severity of stuttering varies considerably for the individual from time to time and according to the situation. Some stutterers can predict when they will experience difficulty, and know their stuttering to be limited to situations involving specific persons, specific speaking tasks, or even specific sounds. Many, however, appear to be oblivious to overtly comparable stuttering in other situations. Almost all stutterers are relatively free from difficulty in some situations, of which they may or may not be aware. Even the most severe stutterers have many moments of fluency, and some may be fluent for days on end. The question of stuttering as a possible situational difficulty will be considered later in our discussion.

The Incidence of Stuttering

If we accept early childhood non-fluencies as stuttering—and we do not —then almost all children would be considered stutterers. If early non-fluent speech is not to be included under the category of stuttering—which we recommend—then only about *one per cent* of the population would be classified as stutterers. According to the Midcentury White House Conference Report (see p. 3) approximately .7 per cent, or 280,000 school-age children (up to twenty-one years of age), are stutterers. This means that, at a minimum, seven children out of every thousand suffer from and react unfavorably to their speech characterized by irregular interruptions of the rhythmic pattern of evocation with associated spasms, tonic or clonic in form. The spasms may involve any part of the speech mechanism—breathing, phonation, resonance, and articulation—as well as parts of the body not directly involved in the normal speech effort.

There are more males than females in the stuttering population. Though specific figures vary according to definitions of stuttering and the selected groups studied, ratios of from two to ten males to one female are reported

[4] C. Van Riper, *Speech Correction*, 3rd ed. (New York, Prentice-Hall, 1954), p. 351.

in the literature.[5] The higher incidence of stuttering among males is consistent with other findings that maleness as a genic factor has its peculiar liabilities. The mortality ratio at every stage of life is higher for males than for females. Males outnumber females in the incidence of such disorders as chorea, rickets, asthma, tetany, convulsions, and epilepsy. Male infants have more birth injuries than female infants, and males are born with more structural anomalies such as severe cleft palate than are females.

In regard to language development, it has already been pointed out (see p. 32) that little girls soon exceed little boys. The difference in linguistic proficiency, which begins to appear at the beginning of the second year continues up to the high-school period.

Schuell, among others, believes that the liabilities of maleness may become directly translated into an increased tendency to stutter. She holds that: [6]

A tenable hypothesis would seem to be that the male child, whose physical, social, and language development proceeds at a slower rate than that of the female, encounters more unequal competition, and consequently more frustration, particularly in relation to language situations, than the female child, and that as a result he exhibits more insecurity, more hesitancy, and more inhibitions in speech. If the frustrating situations are too many, if his speech behavior is compared unfavorably with that of other children, or if he becomes aware of unfavorable reactions toward it on the part of other people, it is conceivable that anxieties and tensions and the overt behavior regarded as stuttering might develop.

Age of Onset

Stuttering may appear at any age, although it rarely begins in adult life. The sharp peaks of incidence occur between five and seven years and between twelve and fourteen years. If we were to include early non-fluencies, then the first peak would occur between two and three and a half years.

IS THERE A STUTTERER'S PROFILE?

Many students of stuttering, who have done a considerable amount of observation and research on stutterers and their manifestations, are quite certain that despite individual differences, there are undeniable common physical and psychological traits which distinguish stutterers as a group from the population at large. Some of the students believe that stutterers have a biologically inherited background which predisposes them towards

[5] See Hildred Schuell, "Sex Differences in Relation to Stuttering: Part I," *Journal of Speech Disorders,* Vol. 11 (1946), pp. 277-298.

[6] Hildred Schuell, "Sex Differences in Relation to Stuttering: Part II," *Journal of Speech Disorders,* Vol. 12 (1946), p. 295.

their speech difficulty. Other students, such as Johnson, deny that there are any native differences which characterize stutterers. On this point, Johnson says: "The reason why stuttering tends to run in families seems to be rather definitely a matter of tradition rather than genes." [7] Further, Johnson holds: [8]

So-called stuttering children are not different from children not so diagnosed, with respect to birth injuries, other injuries, diseases, and general development as indicated by such indexes as age of beginning of speech, sitting and standing without support, and teething. They are not different with regard to intelligence. In general they are normal children.

We shall observe later that despite Johnson, there are many workers in the field of stuttering who do believe that stutterers may be different in almost every respect but intelligence from other children. The differences, to be sure, are usually believed to be quantitative rather than qualitative.

We shall not, at this point, attempt a definitive answer to the question: "Is there a stutterer's profile?" Later, varying points of view, and answers to that question, will be presented in our discussion of theories of causation. For the present, however, we will describe some of the speech characteristics which both the present authors believe to be common to many stutterers.

Speech

Over and above the repetitions, blocks, prolongations, and hesitations of the stutterer, there are other characteristics which distinguish his speech. The voice of the stutterer tends to be rigid; there is present a vocal inflexibility suggestive of the spastic type of cerebral palsy. Even during relatively fluent speech, the voice tends to be limited in pitch range and somewhat lacking in expressive coloring.

The stutterer's breathing while speaking may show marked irregularities. The normal respiratory ratio, characterized by a short period of inspiration and a longer period of exhalation, may be reversed, or changed to relatively equal inspiration-expiration periods. The breath may be held, or may be almost completely expired before the stutterer begins to speak. These modifications of breathing are probably manifestations of the stutterer's attempts to break through his blocks, or part of the anticipatory behavior of dealing with a block.

In many instances, articulation as well as voice is defective. Lisping, lalling, and sound substitutions are present more frequently in the speech of stutterers than in that of other children. Many stutterers' histories reveal that they were retarded in the onset of speech, and maintained infantile patterns of articulation for longer periods than do most children.

---

[7] W. Johnson, ed., *Speech-Handicapped School Children,* rev. ed. (New York, Harper, 1956), p. 233.
[8] *Ibid.,* p 245.

It may be of interest to note at this point that recent studies have revealed marked similarities in environmental background for stuttering children and for those with delayed speech or defective articulation. For all three groups, the parental attitudes are apparently characterized by unrealistically high standards of expectation for speech performance in particular and social performance in general.[9]

Intelligence

As a group, stutterers are normal in intelligence and are superior to other speech defectives. Berry [10] found the mean intelligence quotient of 166 stutterers to be slightly above 99. Other studies have shown comparable results. It is likely that stutterers who attend college may test higher on entrance than other freshmen. This difference may be attributed to selection rather than to the superiority of stutterers as a group. The handicap of stuttering may discourage students of average intelligence from trying to enter college. The brighter stutterers may, however, attend college despite the handicap of their speech.

Psychological Traits

There are several psychological and emotional traits which appear to be more characteristic of the mature stutterer than of the prepubescent stutterer. Among these traits are anxiety, undue sensitivity and embarrassment, fears, and depression. The findings do not make it clear, however, whether the undesirable traits are the causes of stuttering or evolve as consequents. We know that normal speakers may stutter on occasions when they are momentarily embarrassed or afraid; we recognize also that "chronic" stuttering, with its many uncomfortable visible as well as audible elements, may give an individual cause for fear and anxiety about himself in social, educational, and vocational situations. This, of course, is much more likely to be true of adolescents or adults than of stuttering children who have not yet become aware of the effect of their speech upon other persons in their environment. It is undoubtedly true that part of the difficulty in adjustment experienced by the adult stutterer is directly related to the stutterer's own reaction to his defective speech.

Home Influences

Emphasis on the early home influences of stutterers has been made by research workers and therapists with widely different points of view. Johnson, who considers the stutterer an essentially normal person except for

[9] See K. S. Wood, "Parental Maladjustments and Functional Articulatory Defects in Children," *Journal of Speech Disorders*, Vol. 11, No. 4 (1946), pp. 255-275, and J. P. Moncur, "Parental Domination in Stuttering," *Journal of Speech and Hearing Disorders*, Vol. 17, No. 2 (1952), pp. 155-164.

[10] Mildred F. Berry, *The Medical History of Stuttering Children*. Doctoral dissertation, University of Wisconsin, 1937.

(or despite) his stuttering, nevertheless believes that the important differ-ence between the child who stutters and the one who does not may be found in the reaction of the parents to the way he speaks. The parents of the child who becomes a stutterer are anxious about the speech of their child. The parents, because of their own anxieties, begin to think of their child as nervous, unstable, or somehow defective. The parents are specifically anx-ious about the child's speech and may be anxious about his behavior in general.

Unreasonable expectations in regard to speech proficiency, and faulty evaluation of early non-fluencies, were found by Bloodstein and his associ-ates.[11] They found that the parents of stuttering children "diagnosed" spon-taneous recorded speech of young children as that of stutterers more often than did the parents of non-stuttering children. Half of the twelve children recorded were stutterers; the others were not. Glasner,[12] believes that many young stutterers are initially different in personality type from children who do not stutter. He believes that on the whole the stuttering children he has studied have a background significant for overprotection and pampering. Their parents are described as overanxious and excessively perfectionist.

Some students of older stutterers also emphasize early home influences on the development both of the speech defect and of the over-all personality picture. Glauber[13] looks upon the male stutterer as an inadequate individual who identifies himself almost completely but defectively with the mother, the father being a passive person dominated by his wife. The basic fault and the underlying cause of the stuttering is to be found in the personality of the mother, in her ambivalent attitudes toward all the members of family and particularly toward the stutterer.

On the basis of case histories and clinical studies, Douglass and Quar-rington[14] found that a group of stutterers who manage to control or "in-teriorize" their symptoms, but who continue to think of themselves as stutterers, appear to come from homes and families which are upwardly oriented and employ practices of child-rearing and discipline ". . . particu-larly suited to the development of a child who will strive to maintain and enhance the social status of the family. Moral training in such a family is by means of anxiety-producing threats to withhold affection or actually withholding affection until the child conforms with the expectations of the parent."

---

[11] Bloodstein, Jaeger, and Tureen, *op. cit.*

[12] P. J. Glasner, "Personality Characteristics and Emotional Problems of Stutterers Under the Age of Five," *Journal of Speech and Hearing Disorders,* Vol. 14, No. 2 (1949), pp. 135-138.

[13] I. P. Glauber, "The Mother in the Etiology of Stuttering." Abstract of a report in the *Psychoanalytic Quarterly,* Vol. 20 (1951), pp. 160-161.

[14] E. Douglass and B. Quarrington, "The Differentiation of Interiorized and Ex-teriorized Secondary Stuttering," *Journal of Speech and Hearing Disorders,* Vol. 17, No. 4 (1952), pp. 377-385.

An interesting study by Moore, Soderberg, and Powell [15] directs attention to how the stutterer feels and reacts in his speech to his parents. A group of sixteen adolescent stutterers were asked to speak on the topics of parents, future hopes, misdeeds, fears, associates, and good times. Moore and his associates found that the stutterers had greatest difficulty in talking about their parents.

Social Adjustment

There is considerable disagreement on the part of workers as to the over-all social adjustment of stutterers. Perhaps the most extreme point of view comes from the psychoanalytic group. Coriat,[16] for example, characterizes stutterers as "narcissistic infants who have compulsively retained the original equivalents of nursing and biting." It may be, of course, that stutterers who come to the attention of psychoanalysts are sufficiently maladjusted to warrant such a characterization. Psychologists and speech clinicians tend to be more moderate in their clinical judgments and in the interpretation of their personality-test findings.

Richardson,[17] using a combination of psychological instruments, found that stutterers tended not to recognize their inner promptings, and tended to be more socially introvertive and more depressed than non-stutterers. Spriestersbach [18] compared the verbal evaluations of a group of male stutterers enrolled at the State University of Iowa with a group of normal-speaking students and with 20 male psychotic patients. Evaluations were made of a series of pictures which were rated as to the degree to which they fitted such words as *fun, worthwhile,* and *undesirable.* Spriestersbach concluded that the stutterers' evaluations were markedly different from the psychotics. When compared with the normal speakers, the stutterers had evaluated reactions which were interpreted as suggesting relatively mild degrees of maladjustment.

Many more evaluations, some based on subjective observations and others based on objective studies, could be added to the few which have been cited. The results should be an array of points of view, not always consistent with one another, which might be summarized as follows:

1. Stutterers, as a group, are perfectly normal persons who happen to have speech handicaps. If they have maladjustments, it is because stutterers are human beings, and as such may have maladjustments.

15 W. Moore, G. Soderberg, and D. Powell, "Relations of Stuttering in Spontaneous Speech to Content and Verbal Output, *Journal of Speech and Hearing Disorders,* Vol. 17, No. 4 (1952), pp. 371-376.
16 I. H. Coriat, "The Psychoanalytic Conception of Stuttering," *The Nervous Child,* Vol. 2 (1943), pp. 167-171.
17 L. H. Richardson, "A Personality Study of Stutterers and Non-Stutterers," *Journal of Speech Disorders,* Vol. 9, No. 1 (1944), pp. 152-160.
18 D. C. Spriestersbach, "An Objective Approach to the Investigation of Social Adjustment of Male Stutterers," *Journal of Speech and Hearing Disorders,* Vol. 16, No. 3 (1951), pp. 250-257.

2. Stutterers are maladjusted persons for whom stuttering is a manifestation of maladjustment.

3. Stutterers, because of their stuttering, tend to become maladjusted.

4. Stutterers are anxiety-ridden persons who concretize their anxieties and insecurities in their speech.

5. Stutterers are infantile persons who revert to infantile oral behavior because of their anxieties and insecurities.

6. Stutterers are severely maladjusted, passive, schizoid persons who require psychoanalytic therapy if they are to recover.

It is entirely possible, of course, that each of these generalizations is true for some stutterers, and none for all stutterers. The authors know many stutterers who are apparently well-adjusted persons making a contribution to their homes and to their communities. They also are acquainted with stutterers who are mentally sick persons in need of considerable help. Stutterers as individuals range from the well-adjusted to the extremely maladjusted. Perhaps more of them whose speech symptoms continue to be relatively severe as adults fall among the not-too-well-adjusted part of the population. It is certainly not too difficult to appreciate that a communicative handicap, whether or not it might initially be the cause or effect of a personality problem, might be conducive to maladjustment, or to additional problems of adjustment, as the individual grows older.

Cultural Factors

Are there any factors peculiar to a culture which may be conducive to increased incidence of stuttering? Conversely, are there any cultural characteristics which may be correlated with an absence of stuttering? Although factual data for an answer to these questions are still meager, some trends seem to be indicated. Snidecor,[19] after a two-year study of the Bannock and Shoshone tribes of Southeastern Idaho, observed that few if any pure-blooded Indians stutter. If we limit Snidecor's observation to the groups observed, the following factors may have some causal relevance. Among the Bannock and Shoshone tribes there were: (1) little effort to change native handedness; (2) standards and methods of child care and training which were easygoing and permissive compared with white American standards; (3) specifically, in regard to speech, acceptance of deviations without penalty or apparent criticism. No matter how a child spoke, it seemed to be accepted as the way he should speak, so that no child was made aware of differences in his speaking ability.

In contrast with the Snidecor observations, we have those of Lemert [20] based upon a study of a number of Indian groups on the Northwest Pacific

[19] J. C. Snidecor, "Why the Indian Does Not Stutter," *Quarterly Journal of Speech,* Vol. 33 (1947), pp. 493-495.

[20] E. M. Lemert, "Some Indians Who Stutter," *Journal of Speech and Hearing Disorders,* Vol. 18, No. 2 (1953), pp. 168-174.

Coast. Lemert found both stuttering and persons regarded as stutterers among contemporary coastal Indians, as well as well-defined concepts of stuttering and stutterers in the language and culture of all the Indian groups studied. Lemert believes that the cultural inclination among the Pacific Coast Indians to penalize deviants for their deviations, physical or behavioral, is associated with the presence of stuttering. "In this culture, fat persons, very small persons, . . . left-handed people and those with speech disorders became the objects of pity, mockery, satirization, humor and patronage of the sort shown small children." The culture, in general, was rejecting rather than permissive. Its training for children was stringent, with severe penalties or threats of penalties inflicted on children to make them conform to tribal standards and customs. Lemert believes that ". . . it is plain that the cultural and socio-psychological prerequisites for the development of stuttering were strongly operative in the Northwest Coast." These factors included: (1) cultural recognition and symbolizing of stuttering; (2) social penalties for stuttering; (3) specific anxieties on the part of parents about the speech development of children; and (4) internalization of sensitivity about speech in both the child and the adult.

In brief, and tentatively, we might conclude from the Snidecor and Lemert studies that the more an American Indian culture approximates white American culture, the greater the tendency for stuttering.

Conditions Associated with Increased Stuttering

We have noted that there appear to be general cultural influences as well as more immediate environmental home influences which are associated with stuttering. Are there specific situations or types of situations with which stuttering is associated? The answer seems to be "yes." A review of some recent studies would lead us to conclude that to a considerable extent, the incidence of stuttering is predictable. For individual stutterers as well as for stutterers as a group, there are specific factors associated with the speech situation, as well as with what the stutterer has to say, which are related to an increase or decrease of stuttering.

Linguistic Factors. Several studies by Brown [21] indicate that the stutterer tends to have verbal cues which are related to increased stuttering. These cues include (1) initial words in sentences, (2) longer words in sentences, (3) accented syllables within words, and (4) nouns, verbs, adjectives, and adverbs compared with other parts of speech. Brown concludes from these findings that the stutterer interprets these verbal cues as threatening and anxiety-producing, and so conducive to increased stuttering.

Eisenson and Horowitz [22] found that stutterers increased their stuttering

[21] S. F. Brown, "The Loci of Stutterings in the Speech Sequence," *Journal of Speech Disorders,* Vol. 10, No. 3 (1945), pp. 181-192.

[22] J. Eisenson and E. Horowitz, "The Influence of Propositionality on Stuttering," *Journal of Speech Disorders,* Vol. 10, No. 3 (1945), pp. 193-197.

as the intellectual significance or meaningfulness (propositionality) of read material was increased. The materials which the stutterers were required to read ranged from nonsense words to significant prose paragraphs. It is possible to interpret the Brown findings along the same line. All the factors found by Brown to be associated with increased stuttering are ones which may be related to meaningfulness in linguistic content.

Is it possible for a stutterer to decrease his stuttering with the "same" linguistic content? Johnson and Knott [23] found that when stutterers read the same passage several times in succession, there is a reduction in the average amount of stuttering from reading to reading. More recently, Newman [24] found that a reduction in the severity of stuttering takes place in recurring, self-formulated communicative speech. Newman compared the severity of stuttering of a group of twenty stutterers in an oral-reading and a communicative-speaking situation. The subjects read prepared descriptions of a set of picture sketches and formulated their own oral descriptions of the sketches. Stuttering was measured by the Iowa Scale of Severity of Stuttering. In the self-formulated speaking situation, the greatest decline in stuttering took place on the third trial; in the oral-reading situation, the sharpest decline took place on the second trial. The reduction in the severity of stuttering was always less in the self-formulated speaking situations than in the oral reading.

Successive readings of a passage, or successive evocations of any linguistic content, modify the intellectual significance of the content. What may have meaning when first uttered becomes semi-automatic and nonmeaningful when uttered a third or fourth time. With a reduction in the intellectual significance or propositional value of speech content, there tends to be a reduction in the incidence of stuttering. This is not at all surprising when we recall and appreciate that most stutterers have less difficulty with memorized content than with meaningful conversational speech. Memorization is usually established through repeated evocation. In the process, the intellectual significance or meaningfulness of the content is likely to be reduced or to disappear. In recurring self-formulated speech, exact repetition of content is not likely to take place, so that intellectual level is likely to continue on a higher plane than in repeated readings of a set passage.

Communicative Responsibility. Students of stuttering have long known that stutterers have varying difficulty according to the nature and size of their audience. Almost all stutterers are completely fluent when talking aloud to themselves in the privacy of their own rooms. They can talk with normal or almost normal fluency when addressing animal pets. Adult stut-

---

[23] W. Johnson and J. R. Knott, "The Distribution of Moments of Stuttering in Successive Readings of the Same Material," *Journal of Speech Disorders,* Vol. 2, No. 1 (1937), pp. 17-19.

[24] P. W. Newman, "A Study of Adaptation and Recovery of the Stuttering Response in Self-Formulated Speech," *Journal of Speech and Hearing Disorders,* Vol. 19, No. 4 (1954), pp. 450-458.

terers usually have little difficulty in talking to small children. When we analyze the relatively easy situations for most stutterers, we find that a "common denominator" of the speaking situations is a relative *absence of communicative responsibility.* On this basis we can also understand why stutterers rarely have difficulty in singing, either alone or in a group, as well as why stutterers can usually do well when reciting aloud in a chorus. It also helps us to understand why a change in manner of speaking, such as speaking in a sing-song fashion, or changing the pitch or rate of speaking, or speaking without voice, helps temporarily to reduce the incidence and severity of stuttering. When the speaker concentrates his attention on the manner of his speaking rather than on the communication of content, he stutters less. He is less concerned with presenting thoughts to listeners. In his modified manner of speaking, he has been temporarily relieved of true communicative responsibility. In effect, he is saying words aloud rather than speaking. A study by Bloodstein [25] tends to support these observations. Bloodstein found that adolescent and adult stutterers as a group reported reduction or absence of stuttering under conditions which included (1) a reduced need to make a favorable impression or (2) changes in speech pattern, and under conditions in which the stutterer was not individually responsible for his utterances.

THE ETIOLOGY OF STUTTERING: POINTS OF VIEW

Why do people stutter? Although it is conceivable that there may some day be discovered a single underlying cause for stuttering, no attempt will be made to persuade the student about any one theory or explanation of stuttering in this text. Instead, several contemporary points of view will be presented.[26]

It will be noted that some theorists support their viewpoints by some parts of the clinical and research data presented earlier and tend to ignore or even to refute other data inconsistent with or not directly confirming their theories. Data not previously considered will be presented in relation to particular etiological theories of stuttering.

Stuttering as an Inherited Disorder

The possibility that stuttering—or at least stuttering in some instances—occurs on an inherited basis is suggested by some research findings. The

[25] O. Bloodstein, "A Rating Scale Study of Conditions Under Which Stuttering Is Reduced or Absent," *Journal of Speech and Hearing Disorders,* Vol. 15, No. 1 (1950), pp. 29-36.

[26] The limits of this text do not permit the discussion, even in brief form, of the numerous theories and explanations of stuttering. The interested reader may refer to E. H. Hahn's *Stuttering: Significant Theories and Therapies* (Stanford, California, Stanford University Press, 1943) for a review of some modern theories.

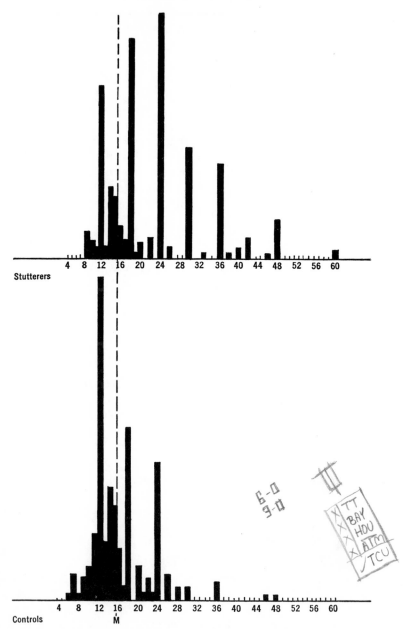

FIGURE 11-1. Age of onset of speech (in months). (From Mildred F. Berry, "The Developmental History of Stuttering Children," *The Journal of Pediatrics*, Vol. 12, No. 2 [1938].

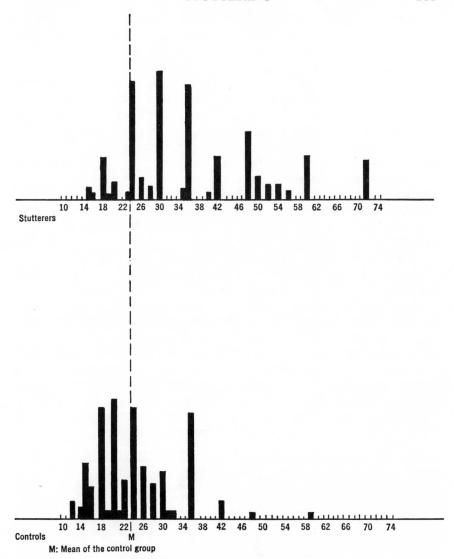

FIGURE 11-2. Age of development of intelligible speech (in months). (From Mildred F. Berry, "The Developmental History of Stuttering Children," *The Journal of Pediatrics*, Vol. 12, No. 2 [1938].

results of Nelson's [27] study of 204 stuttering families in which more than 50 per cent showed stuttering in the family strain for several generations are in keeping with observations of other workers relative to stuttering as a biologically inherited tendency.[28]

There is a strong likelihood, too, that in the stutterer's family there will be found one or more left-handed members. Sinistrality is far more common in these families than in families free from stuttering, as has been shown by the research of Wallin, Milisen, Quinan, and Nelson.[29] There is a greater number of twins in the family background than in non-stuttering families, a fact which may be linked with the greater incidence of left-handedness both in stuttering and in twinning families.[30]

Additional evidence which suggests that stuttering may be inherited is found in the developmental history of stutterers. Berry [31] found that stuttering children began to speak later and became intelligible in their speech later than non-stuttering children.

The early motor co-ordination of stutterers as evidenced by their record in learning to walk is not up to par when compared with a similar number in a control group. The stutterer takes his first steps approximately two months later than the non-stutterer.[32] That he continues to be less skillful is suggested by the results of a number of experiments performed to investigate voluntary muscular movements and motor abilities among stutterers. West found that stutterers were slower than non-stutterers in their rate of repetitive muscular movements. The experimental task involved control of the muscles of the jaw and eyebrow.[33] Hunsley required a group of twenty mature stutterers to follow a pattern of clicks according to a presented auditory pattern. The muscles of the jaw, lips, and tongue were involved. The stutterers were found to be inferior to a control group of normal

[27] R. West, S. Nelson, and Mildred F. Berry, "The Heredity of Stuttering," *Quarterly Journal of Speech,* Vol. 25, No. 1 (1939), pp. 23-30.

[28] See J. M. Wepman, *Is Stuttering Inherited?* Unpublished M.A. thesis, University of Wisconsin, 1934.

[29] J. E. W. Wallin, *Studies of Mental Defects and Handicaps,* Miami University Bulletin, Series 22, No. 5, 1925.

R. Milisen, *A Comparative Study of Stutterers, Former Stutterers and Normal Speakers whose Handedness Has Been Changed.* Thesis, University of Iowa, 1933. 82 per cent of 23 stutterers recorded left-handedness in their hereditary background, and of 28 former stutterers, 84 per cent reported a similar history.

C. Quinan, "Sinistrality in Relation to High Blood Pressure and Defects of Speech," *Archives of Internal Medicine,* Vol. 27 (February, 1921), pp. 255-261.

West, Nelson, and Berry, *op. cit.,* pp. 23-30.

[30] Mildred F. Berry, "Twinning in Stuttering Families," *Human Biology,* Vol. 9, No. 3 (September, 1937), pp. 329-346.

[31] Mildred F. Berry, "The Developmental History of Stuttering Children," *Journal of Pediatrics,* Vol. 12, No. 2 (1938), pp. 209-218.

[32] *Ibid.,* pp. 211-212, Table IX. The Gesell and Amatruda norms may also be found in Appendix 3.

[33] R. West, "A Neurological Test for Stutterers," *Journal of Neurology and Psychopathology,* Vol. 38, No. 10 (London, 1929), p. 14.

speakers in their ability to follow the presented pattern.[34] In another experiment, the voluntary movements of the diaphragm, tongue, lips, and jaw of a group of stutterers and a control group of normal speakers were studied by Blackburn. The findings indicated that the stutterers differed from normal speakers in the regularity and rate of their muscular movements.[35] The results of these experiments are consistent in their findings. Stutterers are generally found to be inferior to non-stutterers in their ability to control voluntary movements of muscles of the eyebrow, tongue, lips, jaw, and diaphragm even when these muscles are not being used for speech. In such motor tasks as running, jumping, balancing, and climbing, the stutterers, likewise, are inferior to children without speech defects.[36] When measured by standardized motor tests they also compete unsuccessfully with non-stutterers. In all but one of the five standard tests used by Westphal the non-stutterers were superior to the stutterers.[37] Cross, who tested a group of 42 college stutterers and matched them with a group of 31 right-handed and 11 left-handed normal speakers, found the stutterers inferior to the normal speakers in bimanual activity and in the rate of movement of the right hand and the left hand, although the differences between the right and left hands of stutterers were less than for normal speakers.[38] According to these studies, the stutterer compares unfavorably in motor ability with people who have fluent speech.

Other studies on the motor performances of stutterers have produced results which are not consistent with those just cited. Strother and Kriegman,[39] for example, found no significant differences between stutterers and non-stutterers in regard to rate of repetitive movement (diadochokinesis). In a more recent study employing the Oseretsky Tests of Motor Proficiency, Finkelstein and Weisberger [40] found that a group of 15 stuttering children performed at least as well as a matched group of non-stutterers and were essentially normal as a group on the basis of the test norms. Lightfoot [41]

[34] Y. L. Hunsley, "Disintegration in the Speech Musculature of Stutterers During the Production of a Non-Vocal Pattern," *Psychological Monographs*, Vol. 49 (1937), pp. 32-49.

[35] W. B. Blackburn, "A Study of Voluntary Movements of Diaphragm, Tongue, Lips, and Jaw in Stutterers and Normal Speakers," *Psychological Monographs*, Vol. 51 (1931), pp. 1-13.

[36] W. Arps, "Motor Efficiency of Elementary Grade Pupils in Speech Corrective Schools, in the Common School, and in Schools for Handicapped Children," *Hamberger Lehrzeitung*, Vol. 13 (1934), pp. 597, 599.

[37] G. Westphal, "An Experimental Study of Certain Motor Abilities of Stutterers," *University of Iowa Studies in Child Development*, Vol. 4 (1933), pp. 214-221.

[38] H. M. Cross, "Motor Capacities of Stutterers," *Archives of Speech* (1936), pp. 112-132.

[39] C. R. Strother and L. S. Kriegman, "Diadochokinesis in Stutterers and Non-Stutterers," *Journal of Speech Disorders*, Vol. 8 (1943), pp. 323-335.

[40] P. Finkelstein and S. E. Weisberger, "The Motor Proficiency of Stutterers," *Journal of Speech and Hearing Disorders*, Vol. 19, No. 1 (1954), pp. 52-58.

[41] C. Lightfoot, "Serial Identification of Colors by Stutterers," *Journal of Speech and Hearing Disorders*, Vol. 13, No. 3 (1948), pp. 193-208.

found that his experimental group of stutterers was not significantly different from a group of non-stutterers in a task requiring rapid serial identification of colors.

It is difficult to account for variability in the findings about the motor abilities of stutterers. It may be that different groups and different procedures may account for some of the variation. In any event, the present evidence does not permit of a confident generalization that stutterers as a group are essentially different from non-stutterers in their over-all motor abilities.

Neurological Theory

If some or many stutterers, by reason of heredity, are different from more fluent speakers, the results of the differences may be manifest in atypical neurological control over the speech function. This essentially was the point of view of Orton [42] and Travis, and still is the point of view of Bryngelson.[43]

The neurological theory, in its broad aspects, explains stuttering as arising from a failure of the paired musculature employed in speech to receive properly timed innervating impulses from the integrating centers of the central nervous system. This defect may be caused either by a lack of clear cerebral dominance because initially such dominance was not established, or by interference with established dominance associated with a change of handedness. It is also possible that other integrating centers, specifically either the thalamus or cerebellum, may not send properly timed impulses to the paired speech musculature or may compete with the cerebral cortex for control of the speech musculature.

Bryngelson believes that in approximately 45 per cent of cases, stuttering is a symptom of an atavistic state in which the individuals have an ambilateral rather than unilateral neurological control over speech. This, according to Bryngelson, is probably due to an "arrested" development of the neural system. Other causes which modify neurological control include interference with native laterality, and illnesses accompanied by prolonged fevers which somehow affect the nervous system.

Some support for the possibility that high-fever illnesses may be etiologically associated with stuttering may be found in reviewing the early histories of stutterers. Two great groups of diseases: (1) specific infectious disorders involving the respiratory system and accompanied by a high fever; and (2) nervous disorders (encephalitis, epilepsy, convulsions) which are the ac-

[42] S. Orton, *Reading, Writing, and Speech Problem in Children* (New York, Norton, 1937).

[43] B. Bryngelson, "Sidedness as an Etiological Factor in Stuttering," *Journal of Genetic Psychology,* Vol. 47 (1935), pp. 204-217.

In a letter to one of the authors (Eisenson), dated February, 1955, Bryngelson stated that this is still his position.

cepted sequelae of the first group, appear far more frequently and with greater severity among stutterers than among normal speakers.[44] For the first group—severe respiratory infections, rheumatic fever, scarlet fever, whooping cough, bronchitis, and pneumonia—there has been demonstrated in individuals a constitutional predisposition or "residual diathesis." Whether the specific inheritance resides in an inability of the body to build up resistance to these invasions, or in a specific gene providing a favorable chemical subsoil for the disease, remains to be determined.

The theory that these illnesses may be causally related to the speech dysfunction is strengthened by the report that from 16 to 20 per cent of the stutterers began to stutter immediately upon recovery from one of these diseases.[45] Whether the illness merely served to excite a latent stutter or is truly the cause of the stuttering is still unknown. If one can conclude that any diseases are "typical" of the stutterer, these are nervous and respiratory disorders accompanied by a high temperature, which attack him more frequently and disastrously than the non-stutterer.[46]

Karlin, though aware that he cannot present anatomic proof, hypothesizes that the basic factor in stuttering "is a delay in myelinization of the cortical speech areas."[47] Karlin, in keeping with his theory, also suggests that the lower incidence of stuttering among girls may be explained by the greater degree of myelinization at age three or four than is the case with boys. "Stuttering occurs more often in boys because myelinization begin earlier in girls."

The process of myelinization—the covering of the nerve fibers with a protective sheath—is recognized as being correlated with physiological maturation and the development of control of function. Myelinated nerve fibers transmit impulses more precisely than those which are not completely myelinated. Conversely, nerve fibers which have not been completely myelinated may transmit impulses, but the effect may be one of a movement, or sequence of movements, lacking in precision and fine co-ordination. In reference to speech, impulses which are initiated or controlled by a brain cortex not well co-ordinated may, according to Karlin, result in the production of a dysrhythmic, repetitive, interrupted flow of speech.[48]

[44] Mildred F. Berry, "The Medical History of Stuttering Children," *Speech Monographs*, Vol. 5, No. 1 (1938).

[45] West, Nelson, and Berry, *op. cit.*

[46] Many workers believe that allergies should be included in the group of "typical" diseases. It must be remembered, however, that many more males than females suffer from allergic disorders; hence, since more stutterers are males, there is likelihood that allergies would appear more frequently among stutterers than in the normal population.

[47] I. W. Karlin, "Stuttering—the Problem Today," *Journal of the American Medical Association*, Vol. 143 (1950), pp. 732-736.

[48] Karlin believes that at age three or four emotional stress may serve as a "catalytic agent" in producing stuttering in a child who has delayed cortical myelinization.

Psychosomatic Viewpoints

The underlying point of view of psychosomatic medicine is that in some persons a somatic (bodily) variation is present which may be causally related to personality maladjustment. Travis [49] in applying this viewpoint to stuttering, says that "in certain individuals there exists a somatic variation producing a certain imbalance within the constitution which may lead through personality disturbances to stuttering." Travis believes that the specific somatic variant for stutterers is the tendency for both brain hemispheres to be more nearly equal in potential and control of speech function than is true of non-stutterers. Travis supports this part of his thesis by studies which indicate that during speech as well as during periods of silence differences are found between recorded electrical brain impulses of stutterers and non-stutterers. [50]

Travis does not argue that the brain potential differences alone account for stuttering. If this were so, it would not be possible to explain the occasional fluent speech of stutterers. Instead, Travis believes that the biologically determined somatic variant exists "only as the pathophysiological subsoil of stuttering." Stuttering itself develops because our (Western) culture demands

... an early, harsh, complete and uncushioned renunciation of infantile and childish behavior, works in conjunction with the somatic variant possessed by a few infants and children to produce stuttering. Stuttering may be considered then as a failure of the child to deal successfully with a given life demand, a failure to find socially acceptable gratification for subjective needs under given circumstances. (Travis, "My Present Thinking on Stuttering," *loc. cit.*)

In essence, then, Travis believes that the child who becomes a stutterer starts life with a deviant cerebral mechanism which prolongs infantile behavior patterns and so makes for difficulty in adjustment. As the stutterer grows older, he does not mature emotionally but continues to employ infantile adjustment patterns. Early dynamic forces—childish wishes, hates, and fears—force their way into the stutterer's expression and become part of the symptomatology of stuttering. The stutterer, in his attempt at speech, does not successfully inhibit infantile impulses. The stutterer wants to express his thoughts and feelings; he would like to "express himself." At the same time, unfortunately, he fears doing precisely what he wants to do. Stuttering itself then becomes a compromise between expression and inhibition, between "revealing one's self and concealing one's self."

Aside from the basic pathophysiological factor, Travis' viewpoint has

[49] L. E. Travis, "My Present Thinking on Stuttering," *Western Speech*, Vol. 10 (1946), pp. 3-5.

[50] See L. E. Travis and J. R. Knott, "Brain Potentials from Normal Speakers and Stutterers," *Journal of Psychology*, Vol. 2 (1936), pp. 137-150, and L. C. Douglass, "A Study of Bilaterally Recorded Electroencephalograms of Adult Stutterers," *Journal of Experimental Psychology*, Vol. 32 (1943), pp. 247-265.

much in common with some of the psychoanalytic theories. According to Travis: [51]

Stuttering may be conceived as an advertisement of strong unconscious motives of which the stutterer is deeply ashamed. Repression falls on the verbal expression of these motives and may fall on all words and sentences for fear they might lead to these motives. When any person stutters, he is blocking something else besides what you and he may think he is trying to say; something else that is pressing for verbal expression but which will be intolerable to you and to him alike should it be uttered.

*   *   *

Stuttering may be conceptualized then as a final defense or block against the threatening revelation through spoken words of unspeakable thoughts and feelings. It may be visualized as a sieve through which some materials and force can pass, emerging in reduced amount and altered form. Both the repressed feelings and the restraining force (sieve or stuttering) derive some satisfaction. The former does get out albeit in reduced amount and altered form and the latter does hold even if it has to give a little. Certainly it held to the extent that few if any of the listeners really knew what the stutterer said when he stuttered.

In our earlier discussion of possible neurological factors related to stuttering, Karlin's theoretic assumption of delayed myelinization was briefly considered (see p. 265). Karlin considers delayed myelinization as the primary somatic factor which becomes the basis for stuttering. The secondary (psychological) factor which may produce stuttering is the exposure and reaction of the young child to undue emotional stress and strain during the negativistic period. This period ordinarily comes between the ages of three and four. "The emotional stress will act like a catalytic agent in bringing forth stuttering. If judiciously managed, and if the emotional stress is lessened, his speech will improve, while time is allowed for myelinization to develop so that ability to perform the fine co-ordinated movements for speech is fully established." [52]

Karlin and others who believe, along with Travis, that some somatic deviation may be a primary factor in stuttering, do not come to the same conclusions as to the psychological impact of this factor. The therapeutic approaches vary considerably according to the second (psychological) factor.

West places stuttering in the "twilight zone of psychogenic disorders." He believes that stutterers have an inherent or constitutional predisposition to stuttering but that the speech difficulty need not appear unless some condition brings it out. According to West, there is some point in consider-

[51] L. E. Travis, "The Unspeakable Feeling of People with Special Reference to Stuttering," in L. E. Travis, ed., *Handbook of Speech Pathology* (New York, Appleton-Century-Crofts). In press.

[52] I. W. Karlin, "A Psychosomatic Theory of Stuttering," *Journal of Speech Disorders*, Vol. 12, No. 3 (1947), pp. 319-322.

ing stuttering or spasmophemia "as the psychophysical complex of which stuttering is the outward manifestation. . . . Spasmophemia is the condition; stuttering is the manifestation of that condition. . . . Stuttering is a phenomenon; spasmophemia is an inner condition." [53] Social, psychological, and physiological factors may all be causally related to stuttering. Among the social and psychological factors associated with stuttering are those which induce anxiety, embarrassment, or self-consciousness.

Chief among the possible physiological factors which West thinks differentiate stutterers from non-stutterers, aside from the spasms which occur during speech, are (1) slowness of repetitive movements (diadochokinesis) and (2) lack of vocal inflection. West believes that the slower rate of diadochokinesis is readily manifest in the rate of articulatory activity. The lack of vocal inflection may be an additional manifestation of a spasticity of musculature which characterizes the movements of the stutterer.

Stuttering as a Perseverative Phenomenon

Somewhat akin to West's stand is Eisenson's view that stuttering is a manifestation of perseveration. This is a tendency for a mental or motor process to continue in activity after the situation which called it forth ceases to be present. To test his point of view, Eisenson administered a series of tests [54] in non-speech activities in which a response was elicited for an original situation, and immediately thereafter a second situation was presented calling for a new and different response. The results of these experiments revealed that the stutterers showed a greater tendency to resist change, a greater tendency for a response, once made, to be made again although the situation called for something different. More recently King [55] administered a series of motor and sensory tests to measure specific manifestations of perseveration as well as tests to measure dispositional rigidity. King found that stutterers showed significantly more perseverative tendencies in general than non-stutterers and were significantly more perseverative on specific tests which required a continuous change of set. If this type of behavior is carried over into speech, as Eisenson believes the case to be with stutterers, an articulatory act which is once initiated would tend to be repeated. If the tendency is inhibited, blocking rather than articulatory repetition would result.

To determine the cause of stuttering, one would first have to know the cause or causes of perseveration. The perseverative phenomenon is univer-

[53] R. West, *Rehabilitation of Speech* (New York, Harper, 1947), p. 85.

[54] J. Eisenson and E. Pastel, "A Study of the Persevering Tendency in Stutterers," *Quarterly Journal of Speech,* Vol. 22 (1936), pp. 626-631. Also J. Eisenson and C. Winslow, "The Perseverating Tendency in Stutterers in a Perceptual Function," *Journal of Speech Disorders* (1938), pp. 195-198.

[55] P. T. King, *Perseverative Factors in a Stuttering and Non-stuttering Population.* Doctoral dissertation, Pennsylvania State University, 1953.

sal, and makes its appearance under special conditions. All of us find it difficult to make ready and rapid adjustments to quickly changing situations when we are tired. The landlubber needs time to adjust to sea legs, and the seagoer, some time to learn to walk comfortably on land. Epileptics perseverate after attacks, and manic-depressives perseverate in the depressive phase of their psychosis. Persons who have suffered injury to their nervous mechanisms, aphasics for example, perseverate to a marked degree both in their speech and in their general behavior. Perseveration may be indicative of a lack of adaptability due to a temporarily or permanently lowered vitality following mental or physical trauma. It may be the way a weary and protesting nervous system defends itself against complete exhaustion.[56] Possibly it may constitute an organism's response when some immediate reaction is called for, but when the complete and adequate reaction has not yet been determined, or cannot be given because of the possible harmful effects on the organism.

Eisenson considers stuttering to be a transient disturbance in *communicative, propositional language usage*. Speech, the medium for oral language usage, is involved because the basic tool of speech, language, is temporarily disturbed. The linguistic disturbance becomes most apparent in situations which require the speaker to formulate the language symbols (the propositional unit), to evoke the proposition orally, audibly, and individually, and to anticipate a specific response appropriate to the situation and the evocation.

The tendency to stutter becomes least apparent in situations in which: (1) The speaker has a reduced responsibility for the language formulation. (2) The language formulation is non-propositional (emotive, nonsense, or memorized content). (3) There is a shared responsibility for the evocation (choral situations). (4) A general rather than a specific response is appropriate to the situation and the evocation, for example, "Hello" or "How are you?" as a response to an acknowledgment of greeting. (5) The speaker is addressing himself to no one in particular (speaking aloud alone) or to a person or animal not considered fully capable of understanding him. Essentially, all of these situations tend to reduce the intellectual significance and individual responsibility for the linguistic content. Whenever mere *sounds which resemble words are to be evoked*, speaking becomes comparatively fluent for the stutterer.

It is important to distinguish linguistic content in terms of word forms from intellectual linguistic content. What we say changes in significance with

[56] In a study by A. G. Bills ("The Relation of Stuttering to Mental Fatigue," *Journal of Experimental Psychology*, Vol. 17 [1934], pp. 574-584) in which stutterers and non-stutterers were required to continue at a sensori-motor task until the fatigue point was reached, it was found that the stutterer's record bore a striking resemblance to those of normal subjects who were extremely fatigued.

the situation, the listener or listeners, and the number of times and manner in which we evoke the content. To say "Today is Monday" as an answer to the question on "What day is today?" has a different significance than to utter alone "Today is Monday." When we repeat such an utterance five or six times, its significance continues to change. The last utterance is likely to be spoken with different effect from the first, and in a manner which is devoid of intellectual or communicative import.

Stuttering as a perseverative manifestation takes place whenever the speaker finds himself unequal to the demands of the speaking situation. The perseverative manifestation may have either an organic or psychological origin, or a combination of both. Where it is predominantly organic, as Eisenson believes it to be in about half of the stuttering population, it probably represents a mild amnesic (word-finding) disturbance for high-level propositional language usage. This may arise because of peculiarities of cortical development, competition between cortical and subcortical centers for control of language function, or actual damage to cortical tissue.

The degree of neurological difference may be slight, so that the potential stutterer may function well under optimal conditions. These conditions were briefly outlined above, and considered earlier in our discussion of the Bloodstein study.[57] Under unfavorable conditions, where the needs for intellectual language usage are on a high level, and the situation is quickly changing, as in serious conversation, stuttered speech may be produced. In general, it may be observed that the stutterer speaks with least fluency under conditions which cause the normal speaker to exercise most control to maintain relative fluency.

Nonorganic Stuttering. About half of the adolescent and adult population do not belong to this "organic group." In the nonorganic group we may find some persons who began to stutter on an imitative basis, and who continued to stutter because of the psychological value or "secondary gain" associated with stuttering. This subgroup is likely to be helped considerably through therapy which re-evaluates the present need and significance of the stuttering for the individual and which modifies the habit pattern of stuttering behavior.

A larger and more seriously involved subgroup consists of persons for whom stuttering is a manifestation of a basic emotional disturbance having its origin in early childhood. The "psychogenic stutterer" has his speech most disturbed in situations in which he is required to give of himself and "speak himself." Superficially, these appear to be the same situations which cause difficulty for the organic stutterer. The dynamics, however, are quite different. The probable basic psychodynamic problem of the psychogenic stutterer is his inability to give of himself, and so he cannot readily evoke words. His need to speak and his difficulty in giving of words produce am-

---

[57] See Bloodstein, *op. cit.*

bivalent situations which are characterized by perseverative—blocked and repetitive—speaking.

The seriously disturbed psychogenic stutterer may have considerably more difficulty with non-propositional speech than the organic stutter. Even counting and other automatic or semi-automatic (non-propositional) content may trouble the psychogenic stutterer if he becomes aware that he is responsible for the mere act of evocation. He seems unwilling or unable to separate even meaningless words from himself. Frequently, and perhaps not altogether just incidentally, he succeeds in holding the attention and concern of the listener for a longer time than would be possible if he were to speak with ease and fluency.

No attempt has been made in the presentation of this point of view to account for the possible individual causes for all stuttering. The author's (Eisenson's) emphasis is that many causes may give rise to the psychological phenomenon of perseveration. These causes may include constitutional organic differences, neuropathologies, as well as varying degrees of psychosomatic disturbances and psychopathologies. It may well include speakers for whom specific situations are anxiety-producing and so conducive to stuttering, as well as persons who suffer from more generalized anxieties about the act of speaking. It may also include persons who, somewhat unsagaciously, generalized their reactions which included acute non-fluency for a specific situation to other situations which have incidental but objectively not significant similarities. Thus, a child who is frightened by a dog, or by an ominous-looking man, may generalize his fear and his stuttering to situations involving other dogs or other men, to places which resemble the one in which the original fear reaction took place, to persons who resemble ones involved in the original fear-producing situations, and so on and so on. Here a learned, perhaps even an appropriate response, becomes generalized and reproduced in other situations for which the response is in no objective or logical way appropriate. If such a response becomes reinforced through attention a child might otherwise not be able to obtain, the normal laws of learning can explain a not altogether normal reaction. It may, of course, still be necessary to explain why very few children who are frightened by dogs, or by people, or who get attention from people by stuttering for a brief time, continue to stutter when they grow older. Perhaps we will be in a better position to offer adequate explanations when we begin to evaluate stuttering as a disturbance with many facets which may be brought about by a multiplicity of causes.

Stuttering as Learned Behavior

The exponents of the point of view that stuttering is a form of learned behavior would in general accept the thesis that stuttering is a *speech disturbance which can happen to anyone*. Earlier Johnson (see p. 252), one of the leading exponents of this point of view, was cited as insisting that so-called stuttering children are essentially normal children. Johnson, to be sure, does not accept the research data of some other students who have found what they consider to be important differences in respect to early physical development, age of beginning of speech, diseases, and personality traits.[58]

Johnson defines stuttering as *an anticipatory, apprehensive, hypertonic avoidance reaction.* ". . . stuttering is what a speaker does when (1) he expects stuttering to occur, (2) dreads it, and (3) becomes tense in anticipation of it and in (4) trying to avoid doing it. What he does in trying to avoid stuttering amounts to a complete or partial stopping of speech." [59]

The *onset of stuttering in children* is explained by Johnson as arising out of a faulty evaluation of normal non-fluency. Almost all children are non-fluent on occasion. Parents who mistakenly interpret normal non-fluencies as stuttering, and who become concerned and anxious about the speech of their children, are likely to transmit their anxieties to their children. When a child becomes aware of parental anxiety in regard to his speech, he may himself begin to experience anxiety in anticipation of speaking, or during the speaking act. "It is the stutterer's anxiety and strain, the fear and the effort with which he pauses or says *uh*, repeats sounds or prolongs them, that serve to distinguish him from the so-called normal speaker." [60] Although parents are the persons most likely to mis-evaluate the non-fluencies of children as stuttering, and so to produce apprehension and anxiety in association with speaking, other adults may have the same influence. To have such influence, the adults must be in a position to affect the behavior of the child. Included among such persons would be teachers and older relatives who live in the same home as the child.

How does the specific-anxiety reaction become associated with non-fluent speech to become a chronic attitude and habit pattern? Stuttering and its consequences are apparently unpleasant, and tend to be more punishing than rewarding for the individual. To understand the persistence of stuttering we have to be able to understand the persistence of other forms of behavior with consequences which are apparently more punishing than rewarding. Such behavior would include habit tics, compulsive acts, and other types of anxiety manifestations. To begin with, a child may actually enjoy the attention and the intensity of reaction created by his stuttering. He may be excused from class recitations or derive other material benefits from his speech impediment. For a time, stuttering may actually be more rewarding than punishing. When the initial rewards or gains wear off, and the stuttering behavior is essentially more punishing than rewarding, another explana-

[58] See W. Johnson on "Stuttering," in W. Johnson, ed., *Speech Handicapped School Children,* rev. ed. (New York, Harper, 1956), Ch. 5. See also W. Johnson, ed., *Stuttering in Children and Adults* (Minneapolis, University of Minnesota Press, 1955).
[59] *Ibid.,* p. 217.
[60] W. Johnson, *People in Quandaries* (New York, Harper, 1946), p. 457.

tion is required. One explanation of this intricate phenomenon is offered by Wischner,[61] who proposes that

... the act of stuttering may be specifically reinforced by virtue of its relatively close association with anxiety-tension reduction accompanying the removal of a feared word. It is assumed that a feared word arouses a state of expectancy (anxiety) and that the act of stuttering on the word is reinforced by the tension reduction accompanying the completion of the word on which difficulty is experienced.

In brief, the stutterer fears he will stutter on a certain word. He becomes tense and anxious in anticipation of the feared word. When because of or despite great effort, he evokes the feared word, there is a momentary reduction in anxiety-tension. This moment of pleasurable relief reinforces an entire act, and so tends to perpetuate stuttering behavior.

Another point of view in regard to stuttering as a learned form of behavior is held by Sheehan.[62] He looks upon stuttering as arising from opposed and conflicting urges to speak and to hold back from speaking. The "holding-back" or wish not to speak may be due either to learned avoidance or to unconscious motives. According to Sheehan, the stutterer blocks in his speech when the opposing approach and avoidance tendencies reach an equilibrium. The stutterer is enabled to continue talking because the occurrence of stuttering reduces the fear which elicited it. During the period of the block there is a sufficient reduction in the fear-motivated avoidance so that the specific conflict is resolved. This permits release of the blocked word. Unfortunately, subsequent words or situations continue to be dominated by the opposing wishes to talk and to hold back from talking, so that stuttering behavior tends to be recurrent.

An Eclectic View of Stuttering

Van Riper believes that stuttering may have multiple origins. The difficulty usually begins between two and four years of age, a developmental period when the child is normally having some trouble in mastering his fluency skills. Most children, we have observed, show some non-fluency during this period. Most, also, are exposed to influences which Van Riper characterizes as fluency disruptors. In their attempts to talk and to verbalize their feelings and thoughts, children are likely to meet with considerable competition from adults who are superior in their abilities as well as in their authorities. Despite this negative influence, most children survive this period

[61] G. J. Wischner, "Stuttering Behavior and Learning: A Preliminary Theoretical Formulation," *Journal of Speech and Hearing Disorders*, Vol. 12, No. 4 (1950), pp. 324-335.
    See also W. Johnson, ed., *Stuttering in Children and Adults* (Minneapolis, University of Minnesota Press, 1955), p. 23.
[62] J. G. Sheehan, "Theory and Treatment of Stuttering as an Approach-Avoidance Conflict," *Journal of Psychology*, Vol. 36 (1953), pp. 27-49.

with little or no damage to their speech. A few, however, are not equal to the pressures and demands upon them and so are likely to be among those who become the stutterers. These children may be distinguished from those who do not become stutterers in one of the following ways:

1. They may have low frustration tolerance.
2. They may have speech environments with an excess of fluency disruption.
3. They may have a constitutional predisposition (dysphemia) to prolonged non-fluency or to stuttering.
4. They may have parents who misevaluate their speech or for some other reason react to their non-fluencies with anxiety, or penalty, or both.
5. They may be ones for whom dysrhythmic, non-fluent speech may be a manifestation of an underlying emotional conflict.
6. They may be victims of some combination of the above.[63]

Although stuttering may have a multiple origin, Van Riper believes that the disturbance is most likely to arise as a result of the stress felt by children if "driven by their parents, they try too swiftly to master the art of talking in phrases and sentences. . . . Our culture stresses the acquisition of adult forms of speech at too early an age and at the same time it provides no adequate methods of teaching the child to be fluent." [64]

Stuttering usually has a slow and gradual development, so that its specific date of onset cannot be determined. Occasionally, however, stuttering may be precipitated by a sudden, dramatic, and traumatic incident.

Van Riper, we have noted, is careful to distinguish between normal non-fluency and primary stuttering. He also stresses the distinction between primary and secondary stuttering. When the stutterer begins to objectify his difficulty, to become apprehensive about approaching situations requiring speech, to scrutinize words with anxiety, he has become a secondary stutterer. The favorable prognosis possible for many primary stutterers is no longer in order. Secondary stuttering tends to be self-perpetuating.

Van Riper explains that stuttering symptoms may become reinforced in a number of ways. One of these is by an error in judgment on the part of the stutterer. The error is in confusing two sequential bits of behavior as cause and effect acts. ". . . the contortions, tremors, and other unpleasant abnormalities which cause the stutterer so much distress are terminated by the utterance of the word. No matter what silly gyrations his mouth goes through, finally the word comes out. When it does, the panicky fear belonging to that word subsides." [65] Because of the reduction in fear and anxiety,

---

[63] C. Van Riper, *Speech Correction*, 3rd ed. (New York, Prentice-Hall, 1954), p. 344.
[64] *Ibid.*, p. 349.
[65] *Ibid.*, p. 373.

and probably because of the emotional state preceding and accompanying the block, the stutterer unsagaciously concludes that his struggle behavior was directly responsible for his release from anxiety. Henceforth, the stutterer apparently decides he must repeat this behavior to break through the spasm and gain release from anxiety. Van Riper compares the stutterer with a cat in a puzzle box "who happens to look under its left leg at the moment its tail hits the lever that opens the cage. The cat will attempt to assume the same head position when it is put back in the cage." [66]

Essentially, what Van Riper is saying is that the stutterer responds neurotically to his own efforts at speech. When, for some reason, the stutterer is caught in a spasm, he reproduces a complicated act of behavior which previously occurred when release from spasm, and associated anxiety, was obtained. According to Van Riper, the actual release from blocking is better explained as resulting from the fact that the stutterer has experienced sufficient abnormality to satisfy his morbid expectation.

Other aspects of Van Riper's theoretic position will be considered later in our discussion of therapeutic approaches to stuttering.

SUMMARY

An attempt was made in this chapter to survey some of the current significant theoretic points of view about stuttering. No attempt was made to include all points of view deserving of consideration. The theories selected were limited by the basic objective of this text as an introduction to speech correction.

The representative points of view on the etiology of stuttering emphasized (1) the essential organic or constitutional nature of stuttering, (2) the essential psychogenic nature of stuttering, (3) the essential psychosomatic nature of stuttering, and (4) the relatively normal environmental influences which may nevertheless produce stuttering.

The therapeutic implications of these viewpoints, and some common approaches to the treatment of stutterers regardless of specific theory, will be considered in the next two chapters.

[66] *Ibid.*

12

Therapeutic Approaches for the Primary and Young Stutterer

In the previous chapter several theories of stuttering were presented in some detail, and others were more briefly described. It must have become apparent to the reader that there were wide differences in thinking about the cause of the speech abnormality called stuttering, and about the kind of a person the stutterer is. A reader might logically conclude that therapeutic approaches might be as diverse as the theories about stuttering. Though such a conclusion would be logical, it would not be entirely consistent with the facts. Although theorists and therapists are by no means in complete accord as to what to do for the stutterer, they are considerably closer together than they are as to the cause or causes of stuttering. In this chapter, although some of the diversities as to therapy will be considered, the emphasis will be on the numerous common approaches and procedures for the stutterer and his speech.

TREATMENT OF PRIMARY STUTTERING

The first step in the treatment of the young child suspected of being a stutterer is to determine whether the label of *stutterer* is justified. The clinician must be convinced that the child is not merely normally non-fluent. By way of review, we should recall that almost all young children engage in some hesitations and repetitions when speaking. Occasional blocking may also be expected. If the child is normally non-fluent, these take place without awareness and without evidence of struggle. If, however, non-fluencies are in excess of what is normal for a child and occur in situations in which most children are relatively fluent, we have primary stuttering. Further, we have observed, the child who is merely non-fluent has most of his repetitions taking place on whole words and phrases; the primary stutterer is likely to repeat many syllables and sounds as well as words and phrases.

It is possible that the difference in non-fluencies may be attributed to differences in speech motivation and thinking. The child who repeats whole words and phrases may have more desire for speech and for "verbal contact" than he has thought and linguistic content to accompany the desire. If he succeeds in making contact with a listener, and is not criticized for his failure to "say something," his speech effort may be satisfying. The primary stutterer, on the other hand, may be revealing concern about his thinking, or about the nature of his initiated verbal contact. Perhaps that is why he is more likely to interrupt his words than he is to repeat whole words or sentences.

Emphasis in the treatment of primary stuttering is on the prevention of awareness. Awareness of non-fluent speech results from the child's observation of reactions of members of his environment when the non-fluencies occur. It follows, therefore, that the *prevention of awareness* can be accomplished only through establishing control of the reactions of persons who may create awareness. Basically, therefore, the primary stutterer is best treated through his parents and, directly or indirectly, through dealing with persons who are in contact with the child and whose reactions may influence the child. The approach to treatment is succinctly stated by Van Riper: "It can truthfully be said that the way to treat a young stutterer in the primary stage is to let him alone and treat his parents and teachers." [1] Some aspects of the treatment of the parents, teachers, and other "critical" members in the environment of the child thought to be a stutterer will now be considered.

The Indirect Approach

We recommend that therapy for the child believed to be a primary stutterer be carried on through indirect approaches. That is, the child is not to be informed that he is receiving treatment for his speech and the parents are to be informed that therapy, as far as the child is concerned, will be directed to trying to determine what is disturbing the child which results in disturbed speech. Active therapy may involve the parents. They are the ones who can supply information about the child, who can reveal their attitudes toward the child. If necessary, parents may have to assume active roles in modifying their attitudes. This may require education, information, and possibly psychological counselling. The areas of information and the types of counselling will be considered later in the chapter.

If a child who is believed to be a primary stutterer is not to be treated directly, it follows that attendance at any class or clinic where speech per se is treated is not recommended. Attendance in permissive play groups is approved. In such groups, the child through his activities may unconsciously give the therapist information about his relationships and his responses to pressure. The therapist may be able to observe conditions which are con-

[1] C. Van Riper, *Speech Correction,* 3rd ed. (New York, Prentice-Hall, 1954), p. 353.

ducive to the child's increased non-fluencies. These observations may become the basis for discussions with the parents, and for the application of other techniques by the parents, by other adults in the child's environment, and by the therapist.

There are a few things that can be done with the child which will help him indirectly with his speech, and directly with his over-all attitudes and behavior. The primary stutterer who can be helped to feel that he "belongs," that he has friends, and that he has some abilities which his peers and the adults in his environment respect, will be helped to a feeling of self-worth. With this feeling, he may be able to put up with his speech non-fluencies, and perhaps live with them until he can get over them. If it is possible, a child should be helped toward some new skill which may command respect. A new skill is best built upon some old one. If the child has shown some ability with tools, then a tool-using skill should be encouraged. If, however, a child is awkward with tools, then it is better to look in some other direction for the establishment of a new skill. Certainly, the parent should not impose any requirement for the use of any kind of material or toy which the child rejects.

Maintaining Health

During periods of illness, or periods immediately preceding or following illness, speech fluency is likely to be somewhat disturbed in most children. Non-fluency may become intensified in the child who is inclined along this line. This should be recognized by the parents so that it does not constitute an additional cause for anxiety. Parents may also be somewhat relieved if they are helped to recall that in the child's very early stages of language learning, periods of illness were frequently accompanied by actual though temporary setbacks in functional linguistic ability. Moreover, adults when ill are also likely to suffer somewhat in their fluency and general linguistic ability.

It is important that the child believed to be a stutterer be maintained in good health because of the general as well as the specific influences of illness upon speech proficiency. Adequate rest and sleep are essential. The parents must, however, not become obsessed with the child's need for rest and sleep. Few children can be forced to fall asleep, or to rest when their bodies and their inclinations are to be awake and active. If the parents will provide opportunity for resting and sleeping according to the child's needs, both the child and the parents will be the better for it.

Determining Conditions Associated with Non-fluencies

To determine the conditions and situations associated with more than normal non-fluency we must interview the persons who are in frequent contact with the child. We are most likely to begin with the parents. We ask them to describe the child's speech, to imitate it if possible, so that we have some idea of what the parents have in mind which makes them entertain the fear of stuttering. The questioning takes place while the child is busy at play in a room away from the parents. We also engage the child in speech away from his parents as well as in their presence to determine what influence they have on the frequency and nature of the child's non-fluencies, if and when they occur. If it becomes apparent that the child, despite the fears of the parents, is still "normally non-fluent," an effort is made to have the parents understand the nature of repetition as an aspect of the total behavior of the child, and as a necessary and normal aspect of growth and development. We ask the parents to think about and tell us in what activities aside from speaking the child is likely to be repetitious. Parents, through such a procedure, are likely to become consciously impressed that their child, in common with most normal children, can beat a drum *ad nauseam,* can ride a tricycle *around and around and around,* can listen to the same records *over and over again,* and can enjoy listening to the same story told or read to them without alteration of word or syllable, time after time and day after day. Parents must be helped to realize the normality of repetition—that its presence in speech is not in and of itself to be evaluated as an abnormal phenomenon.

It is also of considerable help to the child, though it may be of some discomfort to the parents, to have them turn a mirror and reflect on their own speech. Are they completely fluent, or even as fluent as they would like their children to be? How about their friends and neighbors, or their critical relatives? We instruct parents to listen to radio and television interview and discussion programs which are conducted without benefit of prepared scripts. Are the speakers completely fluent? If these assignments are carried out by the parents, they can be guided to a conclusion that a considerable amount of non-fluency in speech is normal.

We do not take parents to task because they are concerned about their child's speech. Nor do we belittle their concern. We do, however, talk frankly about the possibility that any excessive concern may be transmitted to the child who may then become anxious and insecure about his speech efforts. Anxiety plus insecurity plus non-fluency, we point out, is the formula for primary stuttering. Non-fluency without awareness or anxiety is normal speech behavior.

Information as to Expected Speech Proficiency

There are several aspects of speech and language development about which parents should be informed so that they might know what to expect from their own children. Such information might help the parents toward reasonable goals and aspirations. For the most part, this area was considered in our earlier discussion of the normal development of speech (see pp. 25-37). Some of the highlights, and suggested emphases for parents, may be briefly reviewed.

1. Speech proficiency is related to the position of the child in the family. Parents should know that an only child and a first child is usually a more proficient speaker than a second or a third child. Exceptions occur when there is a wide space of years between the first and second child or later child.

2. Girls are usually more proficient speakers than boys. In a family when a girl is the first child, a boy born two or three years later may by comparison seem abnormally slow in his speech development. It may help the parents considerably to know that their observations may be accurate, and yet that the situation may be wholly normal.

3. A child who has the advantage of attentive but non-anxious adults is likely to be more proficient in his speech development than one who has only other children for speech models.

4. Children use speech for purposes of pleasure even after they have learned to use words in more or less conventional adult fashion. They may use words, or parts of words, for the pleasure of utterance or for expression of feelings, regardless of how repetitious such utterance may be. Adults should not confuse all sound-making, even when the sounds resemble words, with communicative speech. Communication, as an objective of speech, is only one of the several purposes speech has for children. Proficiency in communication cannot be imposed on the child. He must first feel the need to communicate. Even after this need is felt, the child should not be denied the earlier pleasures he has obtained through sound-making.

Analysis of Situations Associated with Increased Non-fluency

If a young child shows marked increase in intensity and frequency of non-fluencies, note should be made of the situation or situations associated with the disturbed speech. Questions such as the following need to be raised: Do the marked non-fluencies occur at a particular time of the day? Do they occur with particular persons or with animal pets? Do they occur in situations which recall a previously experienced fear reaction? Do they occur when the child is unduly fatigued? Do they occur when the child believes that he has misbehaved, or that an adult will consider that he has misbehaved? Do the non-fluencies increase markedly when the child is asked direct questions which call for specific language in his answers? Do they occur when certain persons, places, or experiences are named or implied? Do they occur on some words more frequently than on others? Do they occur when a child is merely trying to make contact through words or merely to express himself, and he is required instead to "say something"? Do they occur when the child is hurried because he is not "saying something" quickly enough for an adult listener? Do they occur when the child is trying to seek attention? Or after, in a fluent but vain attempt to gain attention, he succeeded when he became non-fluent? Do the non-fluencies increase in the presence of a critical listener, or with one who is inclined to correct the child "for his own sake"?

Answers to these questions will help the parents or other adults concerned about the child's welfare to determine whether the child's non-fluent speech is a response to a form of pressure which is excessive for him. Such pressure may be exerted directly, though not necessarily consciously, by a member of the child's environment, or may exist as part of a total situation for which no one person is directly responsible. If, for example, a child is in a home where children are considered as persons to be seen but not heard, or at least not attended to when heard, non-fluent speech may be used as a mechanism for compelling active attention. If it is not recognized that many children enjoy making sounds-which-resemble-words as they did as infants, and demands are exerted that a child "make sense" each time he speaks, increased non-fluencies may result. Incidentally, adults who insist that children regularly "make sense" when they talk might well examine their own speech for significant content. If adult speech is always significant in content, the speakers are losing a good deal of enjoyment which may be derived from speaking for the sake of speaking.

If a child tends to be non-fluent at a particular time of day, the events which usually occur at that time, or immediately preceding that time, should be examined and evaluated. If it is a time when the child is likely to be normally fatigued, and so have relatively poor control over his speech production, then communicative, significant speech should not be required. Instead, the situation should be modified so that the child may be a passive participant in a play situation. He may be permitted to listen to the radio or the phonograph, or to watch television, or to look at books, or in some other way to engage in an activity in which speech is not required. Parents should avoid asking a tired child to relate the day's events, or to answer questions which, however important they may be to the adult, are better delayed for a period of the day when the child is not likely to be fatigued. The child who may be unaware of his non-fluencies may become aware of them if they occur frequently. It is far better not to encourage speech, or not to require it when the child is apt to be non-fluent, than to hope that the child will continue to be unaware of his manner of speech. It should be emphasized, however, that the adult is not to tell the child, "Don't talk now. You're tired and you don't talk well." Instead, the adult is to arrange a situation in which neither he nor the child expects speech because the situation does not normally require speech. In short, if the need for speech ˙s obviated in situations in which a tired child is likely to be non-fluent, the child will not have occasion to practice non-fluencies, and so will not have opportunity to become aware of and become concerned about them. Incidentally, neither will the adult!

If a child shows signs of primary stuttering on given words, the significance of these words should be determined. If the words stand for ideas or situations which are associated with pressures, the pressures should be removed from the child or the child from the pressures. If they cannot be entirely removed, then every possible attempt should be made to reduce the extent of the pressure, or to help the child to understand and accept them within the limits of his capacity.

Adults are frequently unaware of how often a child is interrupted or ignored in his speech attempts. Parents, concerned with their own thoughts and problems, may interrupt a child who is trying to tell them something in order to engage in their own conversation. The child may attempt to compete with them. If he is successful, he may be told to keep quiet. If he fails, he may feel frustrated. In either event, a child may experience interruption imposed on him, or self-imposed, so that he "keeps quiet" until it is a proper time for him to speak. Unfortunately, he may never know when the proper time arrives, and further speech attempts may be stopped. If this type of experience becomes frequent, the child may begin to inhibit his own speech or his urge to speak, and self-interruption, hesitation, and blocking may result.

Controlling Reactions to Child's Non-fluencies

In some homes, a child's non-fluencies, normal or otherwise, become the core of a family phobia. In the non-fluencies of the child, parents and other relatives may concentrate and project their own anxieties. It is as if they have decided "Now, at last, we have found something deserving of our worry." Relatives, friends, and neighbors, more or less well intentioned and considerably less than more informed, may discuss, justify, and reinforce the anxiety. Certainly, each relative, friend, or neighbor can recall at least one child who began with exactly such non-fluencies as their child and who has never stopped stuttering.

If the family of a child who is showing signs of primary stuttering is an anxiety-ridden one, then training must be directed and concentrated on the members of the family. Psychotherapy is definitely indicated. Glauber, with this type of family in mind, recommends psychotherapeutic treatment. The aim of such an approach is not to cure the child's stuttering per se. Glauber holds that: "Rather the aim is to normalize the psychological constellation of the family so as to free each member toward further ego maturation. Under these circumstances, the stutter ceases to be a family phobia. It then loses the excessive charge of anxiety with which it is invested by each member of the family." [2]

Although Glauber considers this type of constellation typical for the stutterer's family, we have found it to be only occasionally rather than generally characteristic. Most parents are justifiably concerned about their children's speech. Many can be relieved of their anxieties and reassured

[2] I. P. Glauber, "The Treatment of Stuttering," *Social Casework,* Vol. 34, No. 1 (1953), pp. 162-167.

through information such as has been outlined in the previous pages. Most parents, without entering into a psychoanalytic relationship, are even able to learn not to react with overt emotion to their children's non-fluencies or actual stuttering blocks. Parents are motivated and usually able to learn this when they are helped to appreciate that, consciously or unconsciously, their child will respond to their display of feelings with feelings and displays of his own. The parents who look concerned, who look wide-eyed and open-mouthed when their child begins to speak, fearful of an emergent non-fluency, will induce apprehension and fear in their child, and with these feelings non-fluencies and blocks are almost inevitable. The parents who show impatience may cause the child to hurry in his speech, and so induce non-fluency. The parents who heave sighs of relief when the child's words are fluently evoked, may lead him to decide that there must be something wrong with his speech most of the time, if his parents seem especially pleased with his speech some of the time. Parents and other adults must learn to listen without overt reaction to the manner in which the young primary stutterer does his speaking. Non-fluencies should be accepted with patience and with nondiscernible fortitude. The child should not be interrupted, or commanded to slow down, or to hurry, or in any other conscious way to modify his manner of speech. The child should be permitted to have his say in whatever way he is able to say it. Moreover, he should not in any way be able to detect that any of his listeners is disturbed by his manner of speaking. If such control can be established by members of the family, teachers, and other grown-ups in the primary stutterer's environment, there will be no increase in his non-fluencies as a result of his responses to older persons' responses to his speech.

The home life of a primary stutterer should be as calm and as well controlled as the adults can accomplish. Evidence of hustle and bustle should be eliminated, at least as far as the child can observe. If adult members act and talk quickly and with a show of impatience for one another, it will not be possible for a sensitive child to behave otherwise. If possible, and where necessary, relatives who are not members of the immediate family and who are living in the stutterer's home may need special help to attain the desired attitude of calm. If the attainment is not possible, then a different living arrangement should be considered.

Providing Opportunity for Relatively Fluent Speech

Earlier we recommended that it is advisable not to require or encourage a child to speak in situations where he is frequently non-fluent. The corollary to this negative recommendation is the positive one that the child should be encouraged to speak in situations when he is usually relatively fluent. These will usually be found in situations free of tensions or pressures of the types previously considered. The child will then have opportunities to practice speaking in a manner considered good by adults. He will, through such practice, reinforce fluent speaking. If, for example, the child speaks well when he retells a story, or a moving picture, or a radio or television play, he should be provided with a ready and attentive audience. This is especially important if, before the indirect therapy program for the child was begun, the adults were more attentive to the child's non-fluent speech than to his relatively normal speech. The primary stutterer must be able to appreciate that he will be listened to with interest and attention however he speaks. Some young children, as we implied earlier, may use markedly non-fluent speech as an attention-getting device. The child who observes that he can gain and hold attention when he is fluent as well as when he is non-fluent, will not have his non-fluencies reinforced. In psychological terms, non-fluency will be weakened rather than strengthened because no special value will be associated with it.

The teacher of the primary stutterer can also provide him with opportunities to speak in situations where he is usually fluent. This may be in reciting memorized verse, or in acting out roles in plays, or in reading aloud. The particular situation or situations, however, will be selected by the teacher based upon her knowledge of the child involved.

Caution should be observed by all adults who are concerned with the primary stutterer's welfare, that he is not made aware of why he is encouraged to speak in some situations and not in others. This is a matter best kept secret by the adults. The primary stutterer should not be told, "Do recite this poem, you speak well when you recite." A child who hears such a remark will begin to wonder about himself and become aware of tendencies which are better kept from him.

Cancellation of Reactions to Non-fluencies

Van Riper strongly recommends that "the parents and teachers should seek to cancel all the child's unpleasant memories or experiences of stuttering." [3] We heartily agree with this recommendation as we do with the others in Van Riper's therapeutic program for primary stutterers. If the child experiences a block or shows any other evidence of difficulty in evoking a word, it is a good idea to do something soon thereafter which the child finds pleasant. Doing something may consist of distracting the child's attention to something else he enjoys. The purpose of this is to have the final memory a pleasant rather than an unpleasant one, so that the child will not avoid talking for fear of being non-fluent. A child's reactions to his own non-fluencies may also be reduced, if not eradicated, if the adult listening to him pretends or fakes a block on the same word, or on other words, while talking to him. In this way, the experience of an occasional block may be considered as not too serious because respected adults also

[3] *Op. cit.,* pp. 356-357.

have them. If the child observes and remarks about the adult's blocking, he may be told, "Oh yes, I do this sometimes. But it doesn't really matter."

Care should be exercised by the adult that there is some relevancy and reasonableness in what is done in the attempt to eradicate unpleasant memories of blocked speech. If the adult tries to cancel the child's unfavorable reactions by giving him things or by doing things that are ordinarily not done, the bright primary stutterer is likely to realize that there is too much of a fuss, and decide that the reason for the fuss is his non-fluent speech. If he enjoys the fuss a great deal, he may, consciously or unconsciously, engage in non-fluent speech in order to bring about the pleasurable but not initially intended result.

We are aware that in many homes it is not possible to produce the calm and unemotional attitude necessary for the welfare of the child. It is not always possible for parents to accept the need for psychotherapy, or to find it available if the need is accepted. Sometimes the problem is one of not being able to afford psychotherapy even when the need is felt and treatment is available. If a single member of a family unit is the cause of the tension at home, it is frequently necessary for the primary stutterer to learn to accept this member rather than to hope for an adult, with years of practice in maladjustment, to achieve the necessary changes. Removal of the "offending" member from the household is not always a feasible solution. Grandparents or other relatives who live in the home of the primary stutterer sometimes cannot be sent elsewhere. Even if they could, the resultant feelings of guilt and anxiety on the part of parents of the stutterer might be just as unwholesome an influence as the continued presence of the original cause of environmental tension. This type of reality situation calls for a realistic approach. Such an approach requires that the child involved— the primary stutterer—be helped to learn "to take" the pressures in his home if the pressures cannot be appreciably reduced. A significant advantage to this approach is that it does not overprotect the child and leave him defenseless against pressures and forces outside of his home over which the family has no control. Instead, it helps the child to become hardened and "desensitized" against hurts from playmates, from adults within and without his home, and from school situations which cannot always make allowances for the child's feelings or weaknesses. Van Riper calls the approach *desensitization therapy*.[4]

Adjustment to Environmental Pressures

Although the child is actively involved in desensitization therapy, if at all possible, he is still kept from becoming aware that he is receiving therapy for his speech. The therapist works to establish a social relationship with

[4] *Ibid.*, pp. 359-361.

the child. Together they may be working on a block house, or a model of a car, or laying out materials on a sand table, or doing something else appropriate to the age and abilities of the child. The therapist finds it necessary to comment aloud as if to himself as he works. This is done to encourage the child to do the same. The therapist also addresses simple questions, or makes short, readily understood observations about their activity. If all goes as planned, the child soon begins to do the same kind of talking. Because he is not conscious or aware of the purpose of the talking, it is likely to be relatively or completely fluent.

"Then, once the basal fluency level has been *felt* by the child, the therapist begins gradually to inject into the situation increasing amounts of those factors which tend to precipitate repetitions and non-fluency in that particular child. He may, for instance, begin gradually to hurry him, faster and faster. *But,* and this is vitally important, the therapist stops putting on the pressure and returns to the basal fluency level as soon as he sees the first signs of *impending* non-fluency. How can he tell? Experience and training will help, but we have found usually, that just before the non-fluencies appear, the child's mobility begins to decrease—he freezes, or his general body movements become jerkier, or the tempo of his speech changes. There are other signs peculiar to each child, and a little experimentation will help the therapist to know when to stop putting on the pressure just before the stuttering appears." [5]

The therapist, by learning when and to what extent to apply pressure, helps the child to become toughened, and to increase the amount of pressure he can take before his speech becomes disturbed. Pressure devices may include speaking at an increased rate of speed to the child so that he will feel hurried, urging the child to speed up, pretending not to be attentive to the child as he speaks, or in some other way reproducing, in token if not in complete form, the type of behavior in the child's home or school environment to which he reacts unfavorably. Each time the child shows signs of oncoming stuttering, the therapist diminishes his pressure so that the child is able to return to his basal fluency level. According to Van Riper, the first increment of pressure the child is able to take is likely to be quite large. Subsequent tolerance gains are likely to be smaller, so that it becomes inadvisable to expose the child to more than three or four pressure experiences per session. If the therapist is skillful, the child is never pushed to the point of stuttering. Instead, he feels that "he is being fluent-under-pressure." The realization that he can be fluent despite pressure is of extreme importance. Van Riper, who has used this approach, observes that: "The effects of toughening to stress are not confined to the speech therapist; the child seems to be able to stay fluent even when his father keeps interrupting him."

Any approach which accepts the recommendation that "What can't be

[5] *Ibid.,* pp. 360-361.

cured must be endured" is worthy of consideration. Desensitization therapy is not, however, a technique for amateurs, or for the hurried or harried therapist who must work with groups of children. It is rather an approach for the professional speech therapist who has the ability, inclination, and time to establish a social relationship with a child, to study the child in such a relationship, and to try out techniques which might endanger the relationship but improve the child. In psychotherapeutic terms, what takes place is probably something along this order: After a good relationship is established between the therapist and the primary stutterer, the child transfers some of the feelings he has for other adults to the therapist. Eventually, the gains of the relationship, including the specific one of being able to maintain fluency under pressure, are transferred from situations including the therapist to situations involving other adults.

Handedness Training

There are comparatively few therapists or theorists today who believe as once many did that stuttering is caused by a change or interference with a child's native handedness. Nevertheless, therapists will often be asked a practical question by parents of small children who may be either normally non-fluent or primary stutterers. The question is: "Shall I encourage my child to be right-handed?" This question deserves a practical answer.

If a child shows no hand preference, and does not resist encouragement to use his right hand, this should probably be the hand of choice. Our culture and environment are, for the most part, right-handed. Table settings, the placement of door knobs, and many physical arrangements are made on the assumption that the users are likely to be right-handed. Except in the world of sports, there are few if any possible physical advantages in being left-handed. There are some doubtful psychological advantages, mostly in the form of added notice or attention, for the left-handed person. If there is some question as to the child's handedness tendency, then handedness should, if possible, be related to other sidedness activities. These may include his footedness, eyedness, and even "earedness." Tests inventories such as the Harris Laterality Tests and other tests described elsewhere in this text (Appendix 3) may be administered. The results may be used to determine training for hand preference.

Once the decision as to preferred handedness is made, it is strongly advisable to encourage if not to insist on unilaterality in the child's motor activities. We are not so much concerned with any possible direct effects of using the "wrong hand," or both hands, on brain control as we are with avoiding ambivalent behavior in regard to a motor activity. We prefer that the child know with what hand he will lead if the activity is bimanual, or what hand he will use if it is a single-handed activity. We want the child to have no doubt about which hand will hold the block for placement on another block, or throw the ball, or move the paint brush. Moving an object from hand to hand before an act is executed means that the child is entertaining doubt. He is called upon to make decisions in behavior which should be automatic. The child who is inclined to talk as he acts, as many small children do, is likely to interrupt his speaking while he makes up his mind about his hand. Some of the hesitation may then be carried over into his speech, and become habitual. During the period when handedness is becoming established it is advisable for the child to avoid bimanual activities such as piano-playing, or typing. Instead, he should be encouraged to engage in other activities appropriate to his age and interests which call for the dominant use of one hand.

TREATMENT OF THE YOUNG STUTTERER

Many children in the primary grades, because of or despite the efforts of their parents or other adults to correct their non-fluencies, think of themselves as stutterers. They have become aware of their non-fluencies, and have "beneath-the-skin" as well as overt responses to their speech. They reveal in their blockings, repetitions, prolongations, or occasional struggle responses that they have communicative problems. They look at their listeners, or avoid looking at them, in a manner which suggests that they anticipate disapproval of their speech efforts. Van Riper calls this stage *transitional stuttering*. From the point of view of the child, its features are: "the growing awareness that his speech has something socially unpleasant about it, an increasing feeling of communicative frustration, the changing of the automatic easy repetitions into slower but highly tensed prolongations, the growth of stuttering tremors and the development of fixed interrupter movements amid the random strugglings." [6]

Van Riper recommends that the transitional stutterers be treated essentially along the same lines as the primary stutterer. If their own reactions, or the reactions of members of their family, are not too severe, struggle reactions may be reduced or eliminated, and only the symptoms of primary stuttering will remain. If struggle reactions persist, we feel that there is little point in hoping that the child will not become aware of them. Therapy which involves the child as well as the parents must then be undertaken.

Parent-directed therapy has as its objective the acceptance of the child and his stuttering as well as the elimination of unhealthy attitudes about either the child or his stuttering. Child-directed therapy has as its immediate objective the child's acceptance of himself as somebody worthy of love despite his stuttering. Further, the child must be hardened to take name-calling, and to use name-calling as a device of his own. Desensitization therapy may be used in an individual relationship situation.

In addition to these approaches, group therapy is recommended. The

[6] *Ibid.*, p. 367.

group may be made up of from three to six children who are transitional stutterers. The atmosphere of the group must be completely permissive. No penalties of any sort are to be attached to non-fluency. Instead, each child must learn through actual participation that no matter how he talks he will be listened to with attention and interest. Through this group experience, the child will appreciate that he is not alone in his speech difficulty. He need not be told that other children as well as adults are sometimes non-fluent. He will hear their non-fluencies. The speech therapist and any other adults who participate in the group therapy may help the cause along by faking non-fluencies if they do not come of their own accord. Our observations have been that children in such groups forget their self-consciousness and that this results in a marked reduction in blockings, in prolongations, and especially in struggle behavior. Many children, we have been told by their parents, stopped stuttering after participating in permissive groups where games, singing, finger painting, and building were the activities of record. Incidentally, the time while the children are at play may be well employed as group mental-hygiene sessions for their parents.

13

Therapeutic Approaches
for the Secondary Stutterer

With the secondary stutterer, emphasis in therapy is directed toward having the stutterer learn to accept his environment and modify his own reactions to it. Similarly, the stutterer is helped to accept himself, and to modify his reactions to his stuttering. The secondary stutterer is aware of his speech disturbance and of the reactions he assumes other persons have to his speech. The secondary stutterer's maladaptive behavior to his speech, to his environment, and to his listeners all require modification. His apprehensions and anxieties in regard to his speech, or those which may exist and which may not be directly related to speech, call for treatment. Speech habits which characterize stutterers as a group as well as those which are peculiar to the individual stutterer need modification. Attitudes and adjustment techniques which may not always be directly related to the stuttering may also need to be modified.

Some of the therapeutic objectives for stutterers can be attained in group relationships; others can probably be attained more surely and more quickly in an individual patient-to-therapist relationship. The program for the secondary stutterer will have to be determined on an individual basis. Practical considerations such as the number of stutterers in treatment by the clinician, the age of the stutterer, the duration and severity of his difficulty, the assets and liabilities of the stutterer, as well as the training and abilities of the therapist all will serve to determine the nature and direction of emphasis of the program for the stutterer. We hope that under no circumstances will a stutterer be exposed to treatment by any person, no matter how well intended, who is not trained for such work. This recommendation is made in the interests of both the would-be therapist and the stutterer.

PSYCHOTHERAPY

The need for psychotherapy for stutterers should be determined by what the clinician finds in his analysis of the individual patient. Some of the traits which have been found in studies of many stutterers were discussed earlier (see pp. 251-256). These may be looked for by the clinician, but he should not assume that they must be present in his patient because they have been found to be present in many others. Some therapists assume, *a priori*, that stutterers, by virtue of their stuttering, have underlying personality disorders which require treatment along very specific lines. Glauber,[1] for example, believes that stuttering is a character distortion, and holds that therapy for stuttering can be effective only if it is psychotherapeutically oriented. For Glauber, and for others who incline toward the psychoanalytic for theory as well as therapy, the basic principles of psychoanalytic therapy must underlie the treatment of the stutterer. As an explanation of the improvement which apparently takes place in therapeutic programs which emphasize the control of speech symptoms, Glauber argues "it is due to the therapeutic relationship and it is not the result of a particular exercise or regimen." A recommended program of treatment along psychoanalytic lines, according to Glauber, should include:

1. Modification of the defective self-image of the stutterer.
2. Treatment to overcome schizoid and self-punishing defenses which are assumed to characterize the stutterer.
3. Treatment of special problems such as the stutterer's conflicts about speaking and being silent.

Glauber believes, along with Travis and others who are psychoanalytically oriented, that the amount of work to be done directly with the stutterer will depend on the age of the patient. With preschool stutterers, the parents may be the only ones requiring direct treatment. With older stutterers, a more direct therapeutic relationship with the stutterer needs to be established. Parents, however, are not to be neglected. Regardless of the age of the stutterer, if he is living with his parents, better understanding and acceptance must be established. According to Travis: [2]

The core of the cure is for the stutterer to experience the troublesome conflicts emotionally with the therapist (parental image) and then correct them in a new relationship. The new relationship has a chronologically older person (patient) with the infant still within him and an acceptant, tolerant, empathetic parental image (therapist) who can accept anything and everything the patient has to release. This relationship will expose the patient, under favorable conditions, to emotional situations which he could not handle in the past. . . . Because the therapist's attitude is strikingly different from that of the authoritative and frustrating persons of the past, he gives the patient an opportunity to face again and again, under practically perfect circumstances, those emotional experiences

---

[1] I. P. Glauber, "The Treatment of Stuttering," *Social Casework,* Vol. 34 (1953), pp. 162-167.

[2] L. E. Travis, "My Present Thinking on Stuttering," *Western Speech,* Vol. 10, No. 4 (1946), pp. 3-5.

which were formerly unbearable and to deal with them in manner different from the old.

Travis, Glauber, Coriat, and others who are identified with psychoanalytic viewpoints recommend specific, though by no means identical, procedures for the appropriate relationship to be established between therapist and patient. There is little question, however, that whether or not the therapist is inclined to any form of psychotherapy, considerable value is derived by the patient from a good relationship with his speech clinician. The amount of value is not readily measurable. Whatever it is, it may account in large part for the relief many stutterers get from a treatment regimen, regardless of what the apparent emphasis is in the course of treatment. From the point of view of the patient, psychotherapy, whether it is a conscious objective or an incidental gain of treatment, is of help to the stutterer. Anything which can improve the mental hygiene of the patient helps to make his stuttering more bearable, reduces the negative value and possible need for the speech symptoms, and so may serve to improve speech fluency.

Regardless of whether the clinician feels that there is a need for psychotherapy for the stutterer, one basic understanding must be established with the patient. The stutterer must accept himself as a person who stutters. Once speech therapy has begun, and for as long a period thereafter as necessary, the stutterer must cease trying to pose as a normally fluent person. This does not mean that even without the conscious exercise of controls which will later be recommended the stutterer will not frequently be quite fluent. The point is that for a while he must *stop trying to be what, by virtue of his coming for treatment, he is not*. Too often, when stutterers find themselves fluent, "they grit their teeth" in an effort to continue to be fluent. The result, almost inevitably, is disappointment and renewed non-fluency. We believe that this is the necessary starting point in the treatment of the secondary stutterer. This is so whether the clinician is psychotherapeutically inclined, or plans to work only toward modifying and controlling the overt speech manifestations of his patient's stuttering.

Regardless of whether the therapist believes that stuttering has essentially a physical, psychological, or psychosomatic basis, the nonverbal mannerisms and the over-all evidences of struggle behavior may be assumed to be superimposed on the original repetitions and prolongations. This aspect of stuttering is the essence of its abnormality. It arises almost always out of the stutterer's conscious or unconsciously learned attempts to avoid or conceal, and so somehow to release himself from, the blocks he anticipates or feels. If the stutterer begins by admitting that he is a stutterer, and will give up trying to pose as a normal speaker, he will be saved the anxiety that comes with the fear that he will be found out.

In our initial interviews with stutterers, we have frequently been able to point out the dramatic reduction of stuttering manifestation which accompanies an attitude of willingness for the patients to talk about their difficulties rather than to conceal them. Many stutterers are surprised, and some occasionally annoyed, by finding themselves quite fluent when they come to talk about how much they stutter. When this observation is made, we point out that it is probably the result of the stutterer's lack of attempt to conceal stuttering. With attempts at concealment and associated anxiety absent, there is a feeling of relative ease in talking. This attitude of no concealment, we emphasize, is one which will be helpful in carrying out a therapeutic program.

If the stutterer can openly admit that he is a stutterer and adopt the attitude that his stuttering is a temporary problem to be accepted, evaluated, and controlled, he will become a patient with a hopeful prognosis. The techniques for accomplishing the control, and in many instances the eventual conquest of stuttering, will be discussed later. At this point, however, it may be pointed out that if the stutterer is to be helped to accept himself as a worthwhile person, despite his stuttering, such help should begin with the therapist who must reveal in his attitude that his capacity for tolerating stuttering is limitless. The therapist must be careful not to complete words or phrases, must be able to wait out repetitions and blocks, no matter how intense their severity or how long their duration.

Another essential area of mental hygiene which must be taken up with the stutterer is the matter of gains and values which may be an outgrowth of the stuttering. Many young stutterers are excused from oral recitations in school either because the teacher is impatient and cannot wait for the stutterer's replies or is oversympathetic and does not wish to embarrass the stutterer. It does not take very long for some stutterers to decide that there are exemptions and immunities associated with stuttering which might be worth maintaining. Stutterers deprived of attention may enjoy what they are able to get through their speech abnormality. Some may enjoy the punishment they believe they inflict on parents or other members of the environment through their speech. A very realistic problem faced by the male adolescent stutterer who is chronologically ready for military service is related to his speech. Many stutterers are deferred from service because of their speech. Some who are accepted are discharged, occasionally on the basis of a medical disability which is pensionable. This, many veterans have come to believe, may be a highly desirable status to achieve. Stutterers may use their speech to avoid social situations which they might find distasteful and so would like to avoid even if they were normal speakers. In brief, when a moderately intelligent human being has some form of disability, he usually puts it to some material use so that it is not always a disadvantage. He may not always be aware of the secondary gains that are associated with the disability. Stutterers are no exception in having a desire for such gains. Unless the stutterer can evaluate them, and after weighing both the possible advantages and disadvantages of his speech, decide to give up the advantages, therapy may be futile. Therapist and stutterer must work out this problem early in their program.[3]

Treating the Family

Occasionally, but probably not as often as some psychoanalytic therapists would have us think, the family of the stutterer is in greater need of psychotherapy than is the stutterer himself. If a study of the family picture shows this to be the case, appropriate treatment should be undertaken. Often the therapist will meet with resistance on the part of the family. In a clinic situation, such resistance may be overcome, or at least met, by a requirement that parents must participate in an educational and guidance program if their children are to be accepted for speech therapy. The educational program may include most of what was earlier discussed in our consideration of the primary stutterer. Beyond this, parents must be made to understand that secondary stuttering does not disappear all at once, even though symptoms may sometimes disappear for hours or days at a time.

The aim of psychotherapy for the parents is to reduce their anxiety and fears about their child's stuttering. Sometimes the parents entertain strong feelings of guilt, especially when stuttering is part of the background of the family. The stutterer as well as his parents can be helped if the parents can assume the attitude that stuttering symptoms are the result of some passing disturbance. Frequently, what they fear is stuttering may actually be only temporary non-fluency. Even when study of the child and his family suggests the possibility of predisposing factors to stuttering, there is no inevitability that stuttering must develop. If somehow the excessive "charge of anxiety" can be reduced, the parents will feel better, and the stutterers will be likely to improve because of it.

MAINTAINING PHYSICAL HEALTH

Whatever was said about the need to maintain the best possible physical health of the primary stutterer pertains to the secondary stutterer. The older stutterer should participate actively and with understanding in the maintenance of his health. Although a regimen of work, play, and rest should be established, it should not be so rigid as to cause the stutterer anxiety for any deviation. Instead, the stutterer should be helped to understand that the purpose of a schedule is to attain an objective—in this case, the objective of good health. If a modification of the routine is necessary, it should be taken in stride. Rigidity in attitude is conducive neither to good mental nor good

---

[3] The problem of dealing with the threatened loss of secondary gains and related psychological aspects of therapy for the stutterer are succinctly considered in an article by J. G. Sheehan, "An Integration of Psychotherapy and Speech Therapy Through a Conflict Theory of Stuttering," *Journal of Speech and Hearing Disorders,* Vol. 19, No. 3 (1954), pp. 474-482.

physical health. The stutterer and his family should both be helped to understand this.

APPROACHES AND TECHNIQUES BASED ON THE ASSUMPTION THAT STUTTERING IS A LEARNED FORM OF BEHAVIOR

Recently there has been a renewal of the point of view that essentially stuttering is a learned form of behavior not necessarily associated with basic neurotic personality or atypical neurology (see pp. 271-273).[4] We have found most of the techniques used by the therapists who hold this point of view to be decidedly effective in helping the stutterer to control his non-fluencies and the overt nonverbal behavior associated with them. Among the objectives of the techniques are the following:

1. To weaken the forces which tend to maintain and strengthen stuttering
2. To modify and decrease the severity of the stuttering blocks by eliminating the secondary symptoms of stuttering
3. To help the stutterer to speak, even though he stutters, in a relatively easy and effortless fashion rather than to avoid fears and blocks
4. To help the stutterer in an over-all adjustment to his environment.

Except for the therapists who are inclined to psychoanalytic approaches, and who would therefore minimize the need for any direct training to control or modify speech symptoms, the objectives listed above can be accepted by most therapists regardless of their theoretic inclination. We accept them, even though we are not always in agreement with the rationale or the assumed specific value of the given technique. Some of our reservations, and our alternative rationales, will be indicated later as the techniques are considered.

In our discussion of psychotherapy for stutterers, we emphasized the need for the stutterer to accept himself as a person who stutters. Through such acceptance, the tendency to conceal and avoid stuttering behavior will be reduced. The point was also made that the therapist must be able to accept his patient's stuttering, to listen patiently, and to look directly at the stutterer regardless of the severity of the speech blocks and evidences of struggle behavior. If the patient can feel assured that in his therapist at least he has a person who will not turn away from him because of his stuttering, he has the basis for beginning to feel accepted by others and eventually by himself.

The need for giving up avoidance (blocking on words, or substituting others for feared words, or postponing feared situations), which tends to strengthen stuttering (see p. 272), is discussed openly and directly with the stutterer. This may be done individually with the stutterer, or in a group

[4] Sheehan, "An Integration of Psychotherapy and Speech Therapy Through a Conflict Theory of Stuttering," *loc. cit.*

situation if more than one stutterer is available. The advantage of the group is that the stutterer is able to observe avoidance devices in others about which he is ready to be objective before he may be ready for objectivity about his own avoidance devices. He will be able to observe how stutterers back up on their words or phrases, or substitute words for those on which blocks occur. When a block occurs, the stutterer should be encouraged to "stay with it," until the blocked word is evoked, and to avoid backing up or substituting other words. Group approval and the approval of the therapist for the "avoidance of avoidance" constitute rewards which weaken the practice of the use of techniques of avoidance.

During this early stage of stuttering therapy, the patient should be encouraged to talk as much as possible, and not to evade any normal opportunity for talking. The goal to be achieved and rewarded is talking without resorting to avoidance devices. By talking more rather than less frequently than he might be inclined, the stutterer is helped to reduce the strength of the avoidance drive. While talking, the stutterer should be required to note the situations and the contents which are associated with his stuttering, as well as those which are associated with relatively fluent speech. These notes will provide the basis for an analysis of factors which are associated with the individual stutterer's varying degrees of difficulty in speaking.

There may be therapeutic value of a very different sort in urging the stutterer to talk more than is his custom. Some stutterers may have a strong need for the oral gratification which may be experienced in the various articulatory efforts associated with their stuttering. Ordinarily, these are produced with some feeling of impropriety. The desire for such oral activity, and the gratification to be desired, is given approval by the direction of the therapist to talk more even though stuttering may occur. In this "catharsis through stuttering," some stutterers may satisfy their needs for a long time and become ready for whatever therapy is necessary to give up stuttering for an indefinite time. Even if this is not so, the removal of the feeling that it is wrong to stutter may reduce the anxiety toward stuttering, and so serve to increase the fluency of speech.

Analysis of Stuttering Situations

In discussing therapy for primary stutterers, a series of questions were posed for the parents to help them to isolate and analyze the pressure situations which are conducive to the child's tendencies toward increased nonfluency. For the secondary stutterers, the job of analysis is done by the patients with the help of the therapists. The stutterers, encouraged to talk as much as they can, provide themselves with material for analysis. The individual stutterer is then able to observe with whom he stutters most and least. He may also be helped to discern whether the person or the subject matter most disturbs him. He may be surprised and pleased to learn that rather frequently he does not stutter, that with certain persons or on certain subjects he can talk with relative fluency and without apprehension or anxiety. The stutterer may take considerable comfort from this knowledge, and through it reduce the overgeneralized anxiety he has which makes him think of himself as a stutterer instead of a person who stutters in some situations and not in others. Most stutterers, we indicated earlier (see p. 269) are inclined to have increased difficulty in situations which require them to formulate the propositional unit, to evoke the proposition orally and individually, and to anticipate a response to which in turn they may have to continue to respond with further propositional evocations. They are likely to have reduced difficulty or no difficulty in situations which call for evocations which have lowered propositional value, or in which the responsibility for formulation is not theirs, as in reading or reciting from memory. Group speaking, in which there is usually no responsibility for the proposition and shared responsibility for the evocation, is almost always associated with fluent speaking. In general, whenever there is a reduction in the intellectual significance of what is uttered, there is likely to be an increase in fluency. Through analysis of his own speaking situations, the stutterer may be helped to know when he may expect himself to be fluent, and to accept his fluency situations just as he anticipates non-fluency situations. His need to exercise techniques for control may then be reserved for his own difficult situations. If the stutterer is intelligent and mature, the differences between propositional and non-propositional speech may be made clear to him. Through such understanding he may be able to feel relaxed and confident in his ability to talk freely where the situation does not call for propositional speaking. So, most "social-gesture" terms such as greetings and acknowledgments should become relatively easy for the stutterer who does not have a "bogey sound" in the term to disturb him.

"Bogey" words and "bogey" sounds, if they exist, call for individual analysis. In this analysis, the stutterer is frequently surprised to learn that the "bogey" is not present as frequently as he thinks. An evaluation of what the "bogey" words may symbolize, as well as a direct attack on evoking them, are recommended parts of therapy. Whenever possible, the stutterer's own evaluations should be used. His memory of the first time he blocked on a given sound or word as well as his free association to blocked words may provide useful material for the psychologically oriented speech therapist. After an analysis of the stutterer's reactions to a blocked word has been made, the stutterer should be encouraged to evoke this word as often as he can despite any blocking which may take place. In doing so, the apprehension the stutterer has for a word should be reduced and eventually eliminated.

Voluntary Stuttering

Voluntary or intentional stuttering is based upon the psychological principle of *negative practice*. The person must first do intentionally what he has been doing involuntarily and unintentionally, so that he may gain control over a habit which has been controlling him. The stutterer must learn to stutter intentionally, at first repeating his complete spasm with all the associated mannerisms. He should also be directed to try to feel as he does in his involuntary stuttering. He will, of course, not succeed in reproducing this feeling, as he is not likely to succeed in a complete reproduction of an involuntary spasm. But he must try! He may observe himself in a mirror, or imitate another patient who, by prior arrangement, has agreed to imitate him. The stutterer may also try to imitate how he sounds by listening to a tape recording of his speech. When he begins to become efficient at self-imitation, the stutterer is ready for his next step in voluntary stuttering. He must learn to repeat his evocation, but to modify it in one or more respects to be decided on in advance. Thus, the stutterer may decide that he will repeat the initial sound twice, or prolong the initial sound, or speak at a slower or faster rate. We should note that normally fluent speech is not the immediate goal. It is rather control of stuttering through modified stuttering. Even if the patient feels that he can speak without stuttering, he must pretend or fake stuttering—but to do so in a manner different from his usual way of stuttering. After he does it differently, the stutterer is further directed to stutter easily, without struggle behavior, without blocks, moving forward if possible, repeating if necessary, without tension if it can be done, and *without backing up.* The objective at this stage of therapy, which the stutterer must appreciate, is to modify and so weaken his own stuttering pattern and to substitute for it a more fluent form of stuttering. The patient must therefore be willing to stop on signal whenever he stutters, analyze what he has done, and then evoke the word or phrase again with voluntary and modified stuttering. Some of the techniques used by Van Riper, and which he terms cancellation techniques, include the following: [5]

1. The patient talks until he blocks. (The term "block" is used for any oral form of stuttering.) He is directed to pause and repeat the block openly, but without any effort at vocalizing. He is then told to try the word again, and to stutter on it in a different manner. He may prolong the sound, or repeat it with a "bouncy" effect. He is then asked to tell what he tried to do and to evaluate the success of his attempt.

2. The patient pauses after he has blocked. Then he duplicates his block silently. Following this, he says the word again, intentionally repeating the first sound slowly and easily.

Sometimes the stutterer has difficulty in the voluntary reproduction of his stuttering spasm. If this is so, the therapist should arrange a signal system by which the stutterer should fixate his articulatory act and any associated nonverbal behavior. Upon a second signal, the stutterer should try to exaggerate the spasm, or an aspect of it, until the impression is imbedded in his

[5] C. Van Riper, *Speech Correction,* 3rd ed. (New York, Prentice-Hall, 1954), pp. 421-423.

mind. Then the stutterer may be directed to relax slowly, or quickly, or moderately fast so that he can gain voluntary control over his spasm behavior as well as conscious awareness of formerly unconscious behavior.

3. After the patient blocks, he pauses and prolongs his pause until he observes that his listener becomes restless or tries to talk. At this point the stutterer resumes his talking, stuttering intentionally and calmly on the same word before he goes on to other words.

There are many forms of cancellation which the therapist and stutterer may devise. Whatever the device used, it is important that the stutterer be required to complete his blocked word before pausing and cancelling. This is important so that the stutterer will not experience a sense of relief from merely breaking through his block, and so reinforcing the breaking-through device. The voluntary stuttering techniques help the stutterer to realize that he can speak with some fluency even though he stutters. In addition, he is not trying to conceal his stuttering, and so is helped to confront the world as the person he is, without fear of discovery that he is what he is.

Establishing New Patterns of Stuttering

Up to this point, the therapeutic program has stressed self-acceptance by the stutterer, awareness of speech behavior, and voluntary control through the use of techniques of intentional stuttering. When this has been achieved, modified patterns of stuttering may be established through the use of specific techniques. These may include a bouncing or prolonging of initial sounds, or any other sounds on which the stutterer anticipates difficulty.

Bouncing is an easy, relaxed, controlled repetition of a sound as a way of moving on to the next part of a word. For example, the word *book* may be bounced as *b-b-b-book*. It is best to combine the last evoked "bounced" sound with the remainder of the word so that, if at all possible, a completely fluent word is evoked in its entirety.[6] The bounce-repeated sound should be initiated with the organs of articulation as relaxed as possible. There should be a bare minimum of articulatory contact. For a sound such as *p*, the lips should touch and be released with ease and without effort at strong implosion or release. Precision of articulation is not a goal; ease of articulation is!

Prolonging or lengthening of initial sounds of words is another recommended technique for voluntary stuttering. Vowel sounds and continuant consonants lend themselves to this technique more readily than plosive consonants. The latter can be lengthened only in the first phase of articulation when the speaker makes his articulatory contact slowly and easily. Many stutterers prefer to prolong sounds rather than to bounce, because prolongation sounds less like stuttering than does bounced repetition. If the stutterer has clearly faced up to his problem, and the therapist is convinced that prolongation is not being used as a concealment device, then there is no

[6] J. G. Sheehan, "The Modification of Stuttering Through Non-Reinforcement," *Journal of Abnormal and Social Psychology*, Vol. 46, No. 1 (1951), pp. 51-63.

distinct advantage of bounced repetition over prolongation of sounds. Both, of course, may be used as alternate devices. The advantage of alternating between the two, or of using both in voluntary stuttering, is that the speaker will not develop a dependence upon either one and so firmly establish a new pattern of stuttering. One of the purposes of controlled stuttering is to reduce apprehension and anxiety which breeds further stuttering. Little would be gained if the stutterer substituted a new habitual pattern for an old one.

When the bounce, or prolongation technique, or any variation of either is first used, the stutterer should be instructed to employ them in his utterance even though he feels no need to stutter. The stutterer, for example, might be directed to bounce on every initial sound at least twice, or to prolong each initial sound whether he needs to or not before continuing in his utterance. It may help if the stutterer uses visual cues by underlining the sounds in a passage he will read aloud. Later he may be directed to bounce only once out of choice. Always, however, he may continue to use the practiced technique as long as need be if he anticipates a spasm. At future practice periods the stutterer may underline the initial sound of every other word, or the first word of each new phrase, or every tenth word. A technique so practiced will not result in the formation of a new dependency habit. When the stutterer has gained some control in reading, he may begin to apply the same technique in a short prepared talk, and as soon as possible in a conversation. Small groups provide excellent opportunities for several stutterers to practice the same techniques with a feeling of security and approval.

Establishing New Patterns of Breathing

What needs to be taught in the way of breathing should be determined by an analysis of what the individual stutterer does which is a modification of normal breathing behavior during the act of stuttering. Modifications may include reversal tendencies (attempting vocalization on inhaled breath which is normally not done in speaking the language of most "civilized" countries), initiating speech after most of the breath has been exhaled, and holding the breath as part of the speech block. There are, of course, stutterers who emphasize thoracic rather than so-called diaphragmatic action in their over-all breathing and speaking pattern. This emphasis, however, is not peculiar to stutterers and would not in itself demand attention as an aspect of therapy for the stutterer. We are aware, of course, that many therapists have devoted considerable attention to establishing new patterns of breathing as basic therapy for the stutterer. We believe that whatever relief was obtained from stuttering through this approach was probably derived from (1) the value of the relationship with a therapist at a time when the stutterer was ready for some help, (2) temporary distraction from what the stutterer had to say to a new way of speaking, and (3) the direct help he might have obtained if he happened to have some incorrect breathing as part of his individual pattern of stuttering.

To overcome individual habits of incorrect breathing while stuttering, the stutterer must first be made to appreciate that the inhalation and exhalation are part of the synergy of acts involved in speaking. For the most part, during the considerable periods of fluency which most stutterers have, the synergy of their speech behavior incorporates adequate breathing for conversational speech. The stutterer should be made aware of this, so that he can have one of his own accomplishments become a basis for the correction of faulty breathing which may occur during stuttering. The stutterer will soon be able to appreciate that in our culture, speech is produced on expired breath, and that inhalation takes place quickly between phrases and exhalation slowly during the act of articulation. The stutterer should also become aware of precisely what he does wrong in breathing during stuttering, and to learn to reproduce the wrong act at will. The principle of negative practice should here be applied. When this is accomplished, the stutterer should then be given practice in correct breathing in those situations and on the selected words and phrases which are most disturbing to him.

One tendency common to many stutterers is a failure to synchronize exhalation with the start of their articulatory effort for speaking. Some stutterers will exhale a considerable amount of air before they begin to speak, and then find themselves without sufficient air to complete the first phrase of their utterance. In the use of any new technique for establishing controlled or voluntary stuttering, the stutterer must be helped to appreciate that the utterance of words requires a synergy of articulatory movements in association with respiration modified for speech. Each aspect of articulation must lead to the next so that a blended succession of sounds rather than a series of discrete sounds is produced. An essential aspect of articulation includes a flow of air which must be synchronized with the articulatory effort. So, the stutterer must realize that a sound such as p requires that lips be brought together and then quickly separated. For the sound to be transmitted so that another person may hear it, breath must flow as the lips are separated. On feared words, the stutterer will frequently fail to synchronize the aspects of articulation. He may hold his breath and keep his lips closed in making a p or expel his breath before he closes his lips, or inhale while doing so. Specific practice of what he is doing in order to make him aware of the abnormality of his articulation may precede the practice of the normal manner of articulation. In establishing voluntary production of normal articulation, emphasis should be placed on having a relaxed speech musculature. For this purpose, voluntary differential relaxation may be taught.

Differential Relaxation

Differential relaxation requires that the person be able to relax one set of muscles which are to be used in a voluntary act regardless of how tense other muscles may be. For the stutterer, the important set of muscles are those which involve the articulatory mechanism. We may begin teaching differential relaxation by asking the stutterer to exaggerate an unconsciously produced tense articulatory position. So, we may direct him to press hard, even harder than he does involuntarily, in the articulatory contact for a *t*. We then direct him to relax the contact while he exhales so that a *t* may be produced. Following this, the stutterer is told to make the slightest possible contact necessary to produce a *t*. When the stutterer can do this for one type of sound, he is given practice on others so that plosives, continuants, nasals, and affricates are all learned. Specific practice should be given on the stutterer's "bogey" words. The stutterer has achieved this goal when he can initiate an articulatory act with relative ease.

We have found no significant value in teaching the stutterer to articulate with his entire body relaxed. Normal persons do not speak while lying down except possibly while on the analyst's couch. Nor should they be taught to speak while in a state of slump. It takes some tension to hold the body moderately erect; to speak sitting up or standing up. The stutterer should be helped to speak with whatever tension is necessary for such a speaking position, but with the articulatory mechanism as relaxed as possible.

If the stutterer cannot directly get the sensation of a relaxed articulatory mechanism, if his lips continue to be abnormally tense or his throat too tight, he may be helped to gain the desired sensation through an associative process. The stutterer may be told to clench his fists while tightening his lips, and then to loosen his fists. His attention should at first be directed to how tight and loose fists feel. Then his attention is shifted to the change in lip tension which take place reflexively as his fists are tightened and loosened. Then the stutterer is directed first to tighten and then loosen his lips while clenching and relaxing his fists, and to concentrate on the sensation in his lips. The same approach should then be used with other organs of articulation. With a little practice, the stutterer should be able to appreciate relaxation where it is needed—in his articulatory mechanism. Once this is established, the stutterer must begin each speech attempt with a relaxed articulatory musculature, whether he is stuttering intentionally or speaking as fluently and as normally as possible. If, during the course of speaking, the therapist observes signs of tension, he should signal the stutterer to fixate at a point where there is overt evidence of tension. The stutterer must then pause and look at himself in a mirror to observe his tension manifestations, and then voluntarily relax. In this way, the stutterer is enabled to become aware of increasing tension before he engages in a full spasm. With practice, tension signs may become cues for relaxation rather than preliminaries to stuttering blocks.

Adaptation

Johnson and some of his associates employ the technique of repeated readings of the same material to demonstrate that the incidence of stuttering is reduced with successive readings.[7] The theoretic explanation for the reduction in stuttering with successive readings is that the occurrence of stuttering in the first reading dissipates sufficient anxiety so that there is less stuttering in the succeeding readings. We have found this to be true in practice, and use the technique of repeated readings to demonstrate to the stutterer that in some situations his severe non-fluencies can be quickly reduced and relative fluency of utterance attained. We have not, however, found a great deal of carry-over resulting from repeated readings to propositional evocation. In fact, our belief is that repeated iteration of any content, whether it is read aloud, or repeated from memory after an initial impromptu evocation, reduces the intellectual significance and propositional value of the utterance. In this way the speech situation is changed from one conducive to stuttering to one usually conducive to relatively fluent speech. We believe this to be the basic reason for the reduction in the severity of stuttering even when the stutterer repeats self-formulated speech.[8]

Rate Control has been suggested as one of the ways a stutterer can modify his stuttering behavior and so gain some voluntary control over his manner of speaking. Most stuttering is done rapidly. In contrast, fluent speech, except before the moment of a stuttering block, tends to be evoked more slowly. The stutterer may become aware of this by listening to a recording of his speech, or by observing other stutterers' speech. In modifying his rate, the stutterer should do so only when he finds himself stuttering. There is no need for him to do so during his fluent evocations. By slowing the rate of his stuttering, which may at first be practiced with intentional or pseudo-stuttering, the speaker is helped to direct attention to that part of his speech which needs attention. Stuttering slowly, repeating or prolonging slowly, can hardly be done without stuttering easily. The technique becomes still another way for the speaker to demonstrate that he is not trying to "get over with it quickly" in the hope that stuttering may be avoided. It becomes another way to reduce anxiety about stuttering, and so, ultimately, to reduce the incidence and severity of stuttering.

We strongly recommend that no attempt be made to slow down the stutterer's fluent evocations unless the therapist finds that the fluent speech is too rapid for easy listening. The practice of speaking at all times in an exaggerated slow manner has been used with stutterers for many, many years. Essentially, it is a distraction device, as is any which diverts the stutterer's attention from what he wishes to say to the mechanics of his speech. Distraction devices tend rather quickly to be outworn. The result is usually that the device is discarded, or else becomes incorporated into the total manner of speaking. The stutterer, instead of becoming free of his difficulty, may

[7] W. Johnson, F. L. Darley, and D. C. Spriestersbach, *Diagnostic Manual in Speech Correction* (New York, Harper, 1954), pp. 121-123.

[8] See P. Newman, "A Study of Adaptation and Recovery of the Stuttering Response in Self-formulated Speech," *Journal of Speech and Hearing Disorders,* Vol. 19, No. 4 (1954), pp. 450-458.

merely have something else on which he is dependent. In keeping with this point of view, the therapist must not permit rate control, or any other technique previously considered, to become part of the permanent pattern of the stutterer's speech. Each technique is to be used to help the stutterer to gain voluntary control of his way of stuttering, and is to be abandoned as soon as possible.

ULTIMATE OBJECTIVES

Through the use of the techniques and approaches discussed in the previous pages, some immediate objectives for the stutterer may be attained. Most stutterers should learn to be able to face their stuttering, to avoid concealment and with it to overcome the apprehensions and anxieties that have been associated with their unsuccessful attempts to keep others from recognizing them as stutterers. Ultimately, of course, the objective is for the stutterer to be a normal or relatively normal speaker. For some stutterers this may require considerably more psychotherapy than we have outlined in these pages. For the severely maladjusted person who happens to be a stutterer, there may be some danger in an approach which directly attacks stuttering symptomatology without first helping the stutterer to get over his need for stuttering. In such cases, the speech therapist who is not qualified by training and inclination to undertake psychotherapy with the stutterer has a duty to refer his patient to a qualified psychotherapist.

For the stutterer who is not much more maladjusted than the next person, a mental-hygiene approach should help to improve his adjustment. With such improvement, whatever the cause of his stuttering may be, the stutterer should be better able to accept his speech, and through such acceptance to reduce the severity of the stuttering. What may be left for some stutterers is a degree of non-fluency consistent with a somewhat different neurological mechanism. This non-fluency, if divorced from apprehension and anxiety, may be all some stutterers are able to achieve. The establishment of an attitude that sometimes, under situations which the speaker may recognize and anticipate, non-fluencies are likely to occur, may be of great help. It permits the speaker to accept his non-fluencies, and to employ techniques when necessary to reduce their severity. But more than this, the speaker no longer needs to feel that he is generally a stutterer, who must always exercise control for fear that severe non-fluencies may occur unless he does so.

14

Speech Habilitation in Cleft Palate

The great advances in knowledge and skill in the sciences in our time can undoubtedly be attributed, in large part, to the practice of specialization, to a minute and detailed concern for a small segment of knowledge. But specialization also has had its attendant evils, not the least of which has been a failure to see the many facets of a problem, a disinclination to cross the narrow boundaries of one's field of specialization and seek a larger synthesis of knowledge.

So until recently, the cleft-palate baby was a victim of this segmental approach to medicine. Very slowly has the surgeon, for example, come to the realization that he is looking not at a *hole* in the mouth of a child but at a *child* with a hole in his mouth. And as he looks at the child, he now is aware of the fact that others also have vested interests in the future of this youngster. The logical step is for all to look together, to think and discuss together, and by joining forces to settle upon a course which best promotes the welfare of the cleft-palate baby.

Who properly belongs in this circle? First of all, the parents are there, often overwhelmed by their misfortune, often attacked by guilt, shame, and the recurring questions: "Why did it happen to us?" and "Where do we go from here?" To the latter question the pediatrician makes a partial answer, for he is interested in the baby's nutrition and development and in protecting him from the respiratory infections to which these babies are especially susceptible. Fortunately for the parents' emotional and mental state, the medical social worker and the psychologist are present to answer their questions, allay their fears, and participate in the planning for the child and the home. Together, the maxillo-facial surgeon, prosthodontist, orthodontist, and speech clinician consider their mutual concerns: Is surgery the best habilitatory method for the palate? Or, in view of the extent of the cleft and tissue availability, is an oral prosthetic appliance or an artificial palate the better solution? Or should the hard palate only be closed by surgery, and a prosthesis be constructed to form the soft palate and velar-pharyngeal valve in due time? Which procedure will finally provide the more normal facial contour, safeguard growth potentials and dental conformations and development, and establish more normal muscle balances? In the end, which procedure will insure the best opportunity for an operable speech mechanism? What are the possibilities for the preservation of normal hearing? What time schedule should be set up either for surgery or prosthesis? As the program of habilitation proceeds, the orthodontist wishes to know what precautions will be taken to avoid the collapse of the maxillae following the loss of the deciduous incisor teeth. The educator joins others at the council table to explain the opportunities for special instruction in speech beginning even before the preschool age. He discusses the special services of psychologist, audiologist, and speech therapist, who by testing and laboratory-teaching assess the educability and potentialities for total habilitation of the child. And, in some instances, a representative of a parents' organization has been present to talk to the parents about the valuable assistance which their organization offers.

What we are emphasizing is that restoration of the child with a facial cleft cannot be achieved by one physician, one agency, or one division of our medical, educational, and social services. Our chances for final success are greater if from the beginning the problem is viewed as the mutual concern of a team of workers from several professional areas, and the course determined by decisions mutually arrived at and predicated upon a single assumption: This is the best of all possible courses for this child. This process is not a mere "additive function," as Dr. Koepp-Baker has said in his presidential address to the American Association for Cleft-Palate Rehabilitation (1952). Around the table interactions are felt and expressed, lines of thinking are developed, and emotional and intellectual factors are debated and determined as the cumulative result of group thinking. It is this "entity" consideration which goes far beyond the old order of consultations, interprofessional "courtesy-calls," and fleeting "look-see" trips into the minds of one's associates. By the same logic, the knowledge of the speech therapist— if he is to be an integral member of the team—must transcend the conventional boundaries of phonetic and phoniatric analyses of the speech of the child with a cleft palate. Unless the therapist understands the embryology, anatomy, and physiology underlying facial clefts, his value to the team will be lessened. Unless he knows what function can be expected of the structures and muscles following surgery or prosthetic habilitation, his speech training is incomplete. Unless he is aware of the psychological and social problems and knows how to approach them in relation to speech habilitation, the value of his teaching may be nullified.

TYPES OF FACIAL CLEFT

What Is a Facial Cleft?

A cleft is an opening which may extend through the uvula, soft palate, hard palate, premaxilla, upper lip, and superiorly into the nares or lateral-ward beyond the corner of the lip into the cheek. Figure 14-1 shows the four principal types of cleft: (A) cleft of the soft palate only; (B) cleft of the soft and hard palate; (C) cleft of the soft and hard palate and of one side of the premaxilla; and (D) cleft of the soft and hard palate and both sides of the premaxilla. Cleft lip is usually associated with the last two types.

Submucous Cleft

In some instances, the cleftness is not immediately apparent because the "primitive" palate (ectodermal covering) is present. The palate appears to be intact. In the classical view, the horizontal plates of the palatal bones and the maxillary shelves which form the bony vault have not joined. Another concept is that the deficiency resides in the muscles and tissues which normally penetrate and "fill out" the primitive palate. The result is an excessively nasal voice which "sounds like" a true cleft-palate voice.

Congenital Insufficiency of the Palate

Closely allied to a submucous cleft is the congenitally short palate which cannot effect a sufficient closure of the nasal port by its elevation and retraction. The result, again, is excessive nasal resonance. Both the push-back and pharyngeal-flap operations (to be described later) have been used to secure better palatal closure.

INCIDENCE OF CLEFT LIP AND PALATE

Formerly it was believed that one among 1000 live births would bear some type of facial cleft. Fogh-Andersen, a contemporary Danish investigator, finds a greater incidence in his country, setting the ratio at 1 to 665; he notes that 9 per cent of the stillborn possess facial clefts.[1] From a survey of 200,000 birth certificates filed with the Bureau of Vital Statistics in Pennsylvania in 1942, L. G. Grace finds a slightly lower incidence, 1 in 800.[2] Among the two and a half million men examined for compulsory military service, there were 1466 cases of cleft lip and palate. Vermont showed the highest percentage of cleft palate, one among 667 drafted men.

[1] P. Fogh-Andersen, *Inheritance of Harelip and Cleft Palate* (Nyt Nordisk Forlag; Arnold Busck, Copenhagen, 1952), p. 30.
[2] L. G. Grace, "Frequency of Occurrence of Cleft Palates and Harelips," *Journal of Dental Research*, Vol. 22 (1943), pp. 495-497.

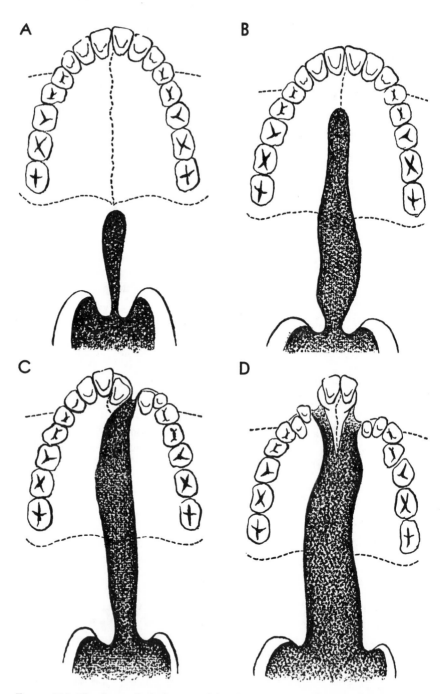

FIGURE 14-1. The four principal types of facial cleft: A. Cleft of the soft palate only. B. Cleft of the soft and hard palate. C. Cleft of the soft and hard palate and of one side of the premaxilla. D. Cleft of the soft and hard palate and of both sides of the premaxilla.

The figures pertain to men between 21 and 23 years.[3] Phair's statistical study of Wisconsin births results in an incidence ratio of 1 to 770.[4] Olin reported that in Iowa, cleft lip and/or palate occurred once among 699 live births.[5] Oldfield, writing in the *British Journal of Surgery* establishes a ratio of 1 to 600 for England.[6] From a survey of a school population of 64,000, Kessler established an incidence of one in 889.[7] One might safely say that the world over, one child in 750 will face the handicap.

The higher incidence of facial clefts in males is well known. The most widely accepted ratio, however, is about 1.5 to 1.[8] Fogh-Andersen presents two conclusions on sex ratios in his study of 703 cases of facial clefts. In the combined anomalies of cleft lip and palate, the proportion of males to females was about 2 to 1; in isolated cleft palate, however, the "sexual proportion of males to females is here about 1 to 2." [9] In a later publication, Fogh-Andersen reports a study of 1000 cases in which "girls constitute about twenty per cent only of the patients suffering from the severest of all the forms, i.e., double harelip associated with cleft palate, whereas they constitute nearly sixty-five per cent of the patients suffering from isolated cleft. . . ." [10] In a study of 724 cases, H. S. Vaughan agrees with Fogh-Andersen when he concludes that boys are less subject to minor palate clefts but far more subject to complete clefts of the lip and palate.[11]

The evidence on racial incidence is incomplete. Grace finds that of the total number born in 1942, 5.5 per cent were negroes but only 3.6 per cent of those born with cleft palate were negroes.[12] There is, then, a presump-

[3] N. A. Olinger, "Eugenic Aspects of Cleft Palate and Other Facial Deformities," *Journal of American Dental Association*, Vol. 31, No. 21 (1944), pp. 1431-1434.

[4] W. B. Slaughter and Gretchen Phair, "A Complete Cleft-Palate Program," *Journal of Speech and Hearing Disorders*, Vol. 17, No. 2 (June, 1952), pp. 123-129.

[5] W. H. Olin, "Statistics from the State University of Iowa Cleft-Palate Clinic," *News Letter*, American Association for Cleft-Palate Rehabilitation, Vol. 1, No. 4 (October, 1951).

[6] M. C. Oldfield, "Modern Trends in Harelip and Cleft-Palate Surgery," *British Journal of Surgery*, Vol. 37 (1949-50), pp. 178-194.

[7] H. Kessler, "A Study of Cleft-Palate and Harelip Cases in the Cleveland Public School System," *Oral Surgery, Oral Medicine, and Oral Pathology*, Vol. 4, No. 11 (1951), pp. 1381-1385.

[8] In the Speech Center at Rockford College where the summer resident program is limited entirely to cleft-palate children, 383 children have been registered. Of this number 235 were boys, 148 girls: a ratio of 1.6 to 1.

At the Institute of Logopedics, 235 persons with cleft-palate speech had been entered. The ratio of male to female was 1.45 to 1.—Reported by R. Schwartz, "Familial Incidence of Cleft Palate," *Journal of Speech and Hearing Disorders*, Vol. 19, No. 2 (1954), p. 234.

[9] P. Fogh-Andersen, *The Inheritance of Harelip and Cleft Palate* (Nyt Nordisk Forlag; Arnold Busck, Copenhagen, 1942), p. 35.

[10] P. Fogh-Andersen, "Harelip and Cleft Palate," *Acta Chirurgica Scandinavia*, Vol. 94 (1946), p. 217.

[11] H. S. Vaughan, *Congenital Cleft Lip, Cleft Palate, and Associated Nasal Deformities* (Philadelphia, Lea and Febiger, 1940).

[12] Grace, *op. cit.*

tion that the incidence of this defect is lower among negroes than among whites. Krantz and Henderson investigated racial strains in the maternal ancestry of those born with palatal clefts in Hawaii. They found the highest incidence of clefts in the Portuguese and Filipinos, "whose composition involves the widest differences in color fractions" and also the most immediate fusion in time. The incidence was lower among Hawaiians and Japanese "whose probable racial fractions do not differ markedly." [13]

EMBRYOLOGY OF THE FACE AND MOUTH

In order to understand why the processes, muscles, and tissue of the face and mouth do not unite according to schedule in the first trimester of embryonic life, one must review the normal development of these areas. The growth is complex because there are several interdependent parts, and each part must keep to a time schedule if the palate and lip are to be conjoined in the midline without mishap.

The oral cavity develops from the stomodeum, a depression on the ventral surface on the cephalad (head) section of the embryonic gut (see Fig. 14-2A). The deepening depression results in the union by apposition of the ectoderm and entoderm forming, in this way, the *stomodeal plate*. At four weeks the oral plate ruptures, forming an opening. The surrounding structures encircle it, producing the oral cavity. These surrounding processes, five in number, will unite finally to form the face. Projecting from beneath the forebrain is the *nasal* or *frontonasal process*. This process is median and the remaining processes are lateral, a right and left *maxillary process* and a right and left *mandibular process* (see Fig. 14-2B).

At the end of the fifth week the frontonasal process divides into a median and two lateral sections which will ultimately make up the nostrils (Fig. 14-2C). About the same time the two mandibular processes are fusing. From the dorsal ends of these mandibular processes, two extensions will develop and grow forward to separate the eyes from the buccal cavity: these are called the *maxillary processes*. As they approach the center (about the sixth week), they will fuse with the *lateral nasal processes* and then continue to grow until they meet the globular processes which are enlargements extending from the median nasal process. The globular processes will give rise to the primitive palate. The mesoderm of the maxillae also will make up the floor of the nose, the upper lip and philtrum, and the cheeks (Fig. 14-2D, E).

Now a second stage begins. About the eighth week two shelves emerge from the inner side of the maxillary processes. These shelves will form the main body of the palate and are called the *palatine processes*. (See Fig. 14-3.) At this stage of embryonic development, however, the tongue

[13] Henrietta Krantz and Florence Henderson, "Relationship Between Maternal Ancestry and Incidence of Cleft Palate," *Journal of Speech Disorders,* Vol. 12 (1947), pp. 267-278.

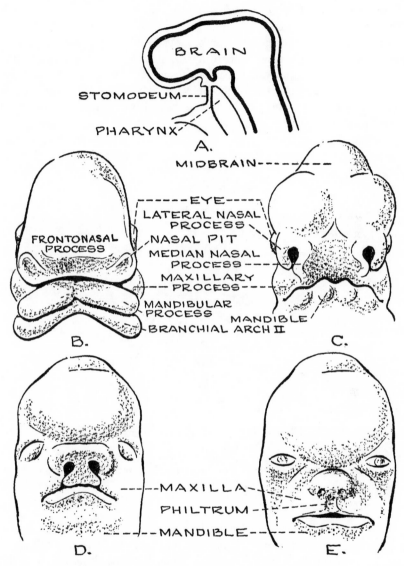

FIGURE 14-2. Palatal embryology: A. Development of the stomodeum. B., C. Development of the maxillary and nasal processes. D., E. Development of the maxilla, philtrum, and mandible.

is a relatively large organ, the mandible very small. The tongue is situated between the palatine processes almost in contact with the nasal septum which is developing from the frontonasal process and the mesoderm of the maxillary processes. With the growth of the lower jaw in a ventral direction, the tongue drops downward and so permits the palatine processes to meet in the midline at the free border of the nasal septum.[14]

The final stage now begins at about the ninth week. A triangular wedge in the primitive palate receives a membranous ossification and is known as the premaxilla. At the same time fusion of the palatine processes begins from the premaxilla and extends backward (see Fig. 14-3B). As the palatine processes continue their growth backward along the lateral walls of the pharynx they form the soft palate. By the twelfth week, union of the hard and soft palates should be complete.[15]

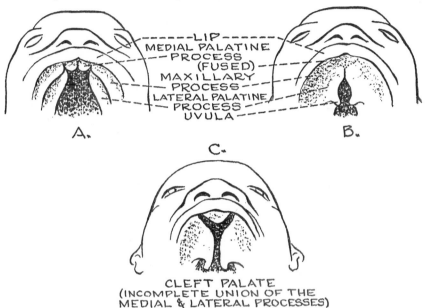

FIGURE 14-3. Palatal embryology: A. Stage in development of the palate (about 8 weeks). B. Final stage in development of the palate (9-11 weeks). C. Classical view of palatal cleft.

The Tongue

We include here also a brief exposition of lingual embryology, because many of the speech problems of this group are unrelated to the palatal or labial cleft per se, but are definitely associated with the dysfunction of the tongue.[16] The several parts of the tongue have diverse origins. The membranous sac which develops first originates in the internal lateral swellings on the mandibular arch in the fifth week. This ectodermal covering extends

[14] B. M. Patten, *Human Embryology* (Philadelphia, Blakiston, 1946), pp. 420-427.
[15] C. Kerr McNeil, *Oral and Facial Deformity* (New York, Pitman, 1954), pp. 14-17.
[16] Mildred F. Berry, "Lingual Anomalies in Facial Clefts," *Journal of Speech and Hearing Disorders,* Vol. 14, No. 4 (1949), pp. 359-362.

as far back as the foramen caecum. The covering for the root of the tongue is entodermal and once covered the ventral areas of the second, third, and fourth visceral arches. On the other hand, the muscles of the tongue originate much farther back in the mesoderm on the floor of the pharynx directly opposite the origin of the hypoglossal nerve; they migrate forward as paired muscles to fill the membranous sac. Whether the homologous muscles interdigitate is still debatable. Patten contends that they remain clear of the midline, because one can make a median incision of the tongue with little bleeding.[17] Arey and others believe that the fasciculi of the muscles are blended and that there is some interdigitation of the muscles.[18] Despite these areas of disagreement in the embryological development of the tongue, it seems reasonable to suggest that there may be clefts in the tongue as well as in the mandible, lips, or palate. The homologous members of the transverse lingualis muscle, for example, may fail to develop and thus will not meet at the median raphé, or they may not extend to their normal point of insertion in the fibrous tissue at the sides of the tongue. If either condition obtained, it could provide an area of asynergic function. Such a possibility might account for the bifed apex of the tongue. Similarly, the fibers of the genioglossus muscle, which has its origin in the genial spine of the mandible and insertion in the lingual fascia, may not be interdigitated or even united at the point of origin or insertion. Finally, if the tongue is mobile in embryo, is it not conceivable that the "cleftness" of the muscles may retard its flattening and lowering, thus producing or enlarging the palatal cleft?

Nature of the Developmental Failure Resulting in Clefts

We have presented this picture of embryonic development in detail so that the great variety in facial clefts may be understood more easily. The moment and duration of the period of interference will determine whether the failure is to be restricted to the muscle and tissue which comprise the lips, or whether it will extend to the union of the palatine processes with the premaxilla and with each other, or whether it will be limited to a cleft in the velum or soft palate. We shall discuss presently the possible sources of interference.

This concept of the failure in *union of the facial processes* is the classical view of the retardation in embryo (Fig. 14-3C). Recently Veau, Stark, and others have taken a "new look" at this problem and have questioned the earlier position that the fundamental defect lies in the failure in union of the facial processes. The critical developmental failure, they believe, is in the *mesoderm* from which the muscle and bone develop. Stark found in his study of nine cleft-palate human embryos that the mesoderm was deficient in the palate and absent on the affected side of the lip and premaxilla in a unilateral

[17] Patten, *op. cit.*, p. 437.
[18] L. B. Arey, *Developmental Anatomy* (Philadelphia, Saunders, 1942), pp. 203-205.

cleft and on both sides in a bilateral cleft.[19] In other words, the cleft occurred because the mesoderm did not penetrate the primitive palate, premaxilla, and prolabium. This interpretation accounts for several hitherto unexplained anomalies: namely, the submucous cleft in a palate that appears to be normal, the absence of a lateral incisor (the pulp of the tooth originates in the mesenchyme) in aborted clefts, and the rare midline cleft. In some people there is no outward cleft, but a developmental deficiency in meso-dermal volume can produce the same effects as a cleft. Such a defect also may be indicative of a fundamental failure in muscle development, not limited to the palate but extending to the tongue and facial muscles. In-vestigators have pointed out, for example, that the gag reflex of the cleft-palate child is noticeably weak.

ETIOLOGY OF CLEFT LIP AND CLEFT PALATE

No one has established the cause or causes of oral clefts. The theories at present emphasize the interruption of the nutritional or oxygen supply to the embryo. The interruption may be attributed to extreme malnutrition in the mother, vitamin A or B deficiency, the Rh factor, or to an atypical or insufficient circulation in the embryo. A defect in embryonic circulation could be responsible for the cleft, suggests Holdsworth, "since during the second month the cardiovascular system develops to replace simple fluid permeation as a form of circulation. Defective development at the periphery of adjoining processes at this time interfere with fusion, and once the ap-pointed time had passed growth would increase the gap." [20] Although Dr. I. Kaufman stresses the importance of heredity, he also believes that a defec-tive vascular supply, particularly at the terminal distribution, may be a probable cause of arrested development. He suggests that the vascular sup-ply to the right half of the head is greater than to the left and, therefore, it "probably accounts for the more frequent occurrence of the clefts of the lip and alveolar process on the left side." [21]

The experiment conducted by the Harvard School of Public Health in 1951 on the subjection of mice to intra-uterine anoxia suggests that anoxia may be the cause of many structural anomalies. "Cleft lip occasionally results from an insult (deprivation of oxygen) delivered on the 12th day; cleft palate in significant numbers (resulted) from anoxia on the 14th day." [22]

[19] R. B. Stark, "The Pathogenesis of Harelip and Cleft Palate," *Plastic and Re-constructive Surgery,* Vol. 13, No. 1 (January, 1954), pp. 20-39.

[20] W. G. Holdsworth, *Cleft Lip and Palate* (New York, Grune and Stratton, 1951), p. 17.

[21] I. Kaufman, "A Treatise on Harelip and Cleft Palate," *American Journal of Orthodontics and Oral Surgery* (Oral Surg. Sect.), Vol. 32 (1946), pp. 47-51.

[22] T. H. Ingalls, "Intra-uterine Causes of Cleft Palate, Mongolism, and Associated Defects of the Skull," Abstract in American Association for Cleft Palate Rehabilitation *News Letter,* Vol. 2; No. 1 (January, 1952).

Mechanical obstructions in utero are stressed frequently in medical literature as probable causes. Uterine tumors, cord interference, pressure of the lower jaw, and the interference of tongue and of hands and feet when the fetus is in a state of flexure may operate to retard or obstruct the normal union of the palate.

Among all the possible causes of oral clefts, hereditary factors have the greatest number of adherents at the present time. In a study of the families of 100 cleft-palate children, Simon reported that the defect had appeared either in one of the parents, in the brothers and sisters of the parents, or in the siblings of the propositus.[23] Kemper also supports the genic theory when he states that "in 20 per cent of the cases, the deformity is found in the immediate family or in one of its collateral branches." [24] Although Ritchie was able to find a familial incidence in only 9.7 per cent of his cases, he cites the survey of Davis who reported "one thousand cases of various deformities of the face and jaw, with hereditary tendencies in 54 per cent." [25] Coursin discusses a "constellation of genic factors" which may account for 50 per cent of the cases of cleft palate.[26]

Even if we grant that from 30 to 50 per cent of the cases can be traced to genic factors, we still have not defined *what* is inherited and *how* "it" is inherited. Does one inherit a low metabolic gradient reflected in a retardation of the development of skeletal structures such as the extremities, the spine, the mandible, and the maxilla? Or is the *x*-factor one which interrupts the normal *time sequence* in the embryonic development of the organs from the branchial arches? If, for example, the tongue is delayed at any stage of its development, or if the muscle pull of the tongue is insufficient at the critical period of palatal union, is it not conceivable that either defect may account for a cleft? Another theory is that one may inherit a constitutional predisposition to vitamin deficiency which, in turn, can produce cleftness. The study of the relation of hypothyroidism to cleft palate presents some evidence that the inheritable factor is a particular type of endocrine constitution which alone, or assisted by unfavorable environmental factors, produces the cleft.

The *manner* of inheritance has been studied exhaustively by Fogh-Andersen in Denmark. He concludes that in cases of *harelip combined with cleft palate,* "the manner of inheritance is presumably that of conditioned dominance (conditioned by the genetic milieu) with sex-limitation to males . . . the gene occurring generally as a recessive gene. . . . *Isolated*

[23] Joan E. Simon, *The Familial Incidence and Etiology of Facial Clefts.* Master's Thesis, Rockford College, 1950.

[24] J. W. Kemper, "Cleft Palate," *Journal of Oral Surgery,* Vol. 2 (1944), pp. 227-238.

[25] H. M. Ritchie, "Congenital Clefts of the Face and Jaws," *Practice of Surgery,* Vol. V; Ch. 9 (Baltimore, Lewis Publishing Co., 1955), pp. 20-25.

[26] D. B. Coursin, "Treatment of the Patient with Cleft Palate," *American Journal of Diseases of Children,* Vol. 80, No. 3 (September, 1950), pp. 442-453.

cleft palate is only hereditary in a rather small number of cases, and the manner of inheritance is here in all likelihood that of simple dominance with failing manifestation and sex limitation to females." [27] One concludes that the genetics of cleft palate are imperfectly understood.

REDUCTION OF THE CLEFT

Repair of Cleft Lip

The lip will be repaired by surgical intervention within the first year of a child's life. The time and method of closure will be a consideration for the team. The pediatrician wishes to be assured that the baby is in excellent physical condition, has achieved a weight of ten pounds at least, has adjusted well to his environment, and is able to withstand the shock of surgery.[28] As Koepp-Baker states, "Reasonably early restoration of the lip aids greatly in encouraging proper growth and conformation of the maxillary arch and approximation of the divided alveolar border." [29]

If the cleft of the lip is bilateral, the conservative surgeon may wish to perform the operation in two stages. If the premaxilla protrudes between the cleft lip, the method of repositioning it must be determined carefully. Because sutures through the alveolar border, formerly employed to hold the divided maxillae in position, interfere with the growth of the structure, the orthodontist has negated this practice. There are many minor modifications of the basic surgical method, but the objectives remain the same: to effect closure with a minimum of scarring, to preserve the vermilion border, to effect a normal tissue-mass, contour, and motility of the lip, and to adjust the nasal alae and floor. The goal, in summary, is to approach normality from the functional and cosmetological viewpoints. Often secondary cosmetic repair is delayed until later childhood and adolescence.

Surgery or Prosthesis for the Palate

The repair of the palate has two objectives: the restoration and preservation of a normal facial and palatal contour and the establishment of adequate velar-pharyngeal closure. The success of the latter objective will be judged largely by the degree to which the child attains normal voice and articulation. The determination of adequate velar-pharyngeal closure is complicated because it depends upon several factors, some of which are not completely understood. The result is achieved, in part, by a sphincteric

[27] P. Fogh-Andersen, *Inheritance of Harelip and Cleft Palate* (Nyt Nordisk Forlag; Arnold Busck, Copenhagen, 1942), p. 230.

[28] I. Kostrubala (College of Medicine, University of Illinois) finds that when surgical repair of palate is done at one year, the mortality rate is 9.5 per cent; at two years, rate is reduced to 5.7 per cent; at three years, it is 2.4 per cent.

[29] K. H. Baker, *The Rehabilitation of the Person with Cleft Palate and Cleft Lip* (Chicago, National Society for Crippled Children and Adults, 1949).

action in which the velum is elevated, the lateral walls of the pharynx move mesially, and the posterior wall may move forward. Another factor is the predetermined space relationship between the skull and the palate which is subject to wide individual differences. And finally, the degree of closure necessary to achieve a normal voice free from hypernasality varies from individual to individual.

If surgery is to be undertaken, the question of time must be answered by the team. Here the prosthodontist, orthodontist, pediatrician, surgeon, and psychologist raise some basic considerations. Coursin, Graber, Harkins, and Hixon independently have come to the conclusion that early surgery disturbs muscle balances and patterns of facial growth.[30] Coursin pointed out that the dimensional relationship of the face to skull at birth is as 1 to 9; at adolescence it is as 1 to 2.[31] The head develops rapidly during the first five years of life, gaining in that period five-sixths of its maximum growth. The mandible, a separate bone, continues to grow from six to nineteen years of age. Important, too, in the consideration of speech is the change in size and position of the maxilla and palate bones as growth proceeds. The anterior parts of the maxilla are shifted bodily as the cranium increases in size. As the pterygoid processes develop downward, the distance between their terminal positions increases, thus widening the palate by moving the maxillary shelves laterally.[32] A further argument for delay in palatal surgery is advanced by Kostrubala who has demonstrated that clefts are narrowed gradually by the pressure of the lip closure.[33] It is also claimed that roentgenographic studies of cases with early surgical repair show that the palate has grown more slowly than the surrounding soft tissue, the result of which is to increase structural inadequacy and malfunction.[34] In comparative measurements of the cleft palate, Buck reports that the average oral cavity in the cleft-palate person measured from front to back is shorter by 8.5 mm. than that of the non-cleft-palate person.[35] The sum total of this argument seems to be that surgical interference at a critical

[30] Snodgrass has suggested another reason for the retardation in cephalo-facial growth. In an exhaustive study of 23 cleft-palate children he found the group "characterized by generalized retardation and/or failure in growth." In other words, the slow growth may be attributed to a genic factor. (R. M. Snodgrass, *Heredity and Cephalo-Facial Growth in Cleft Lip and/or Cleft Palate Patients,* Monograph Supplement I, Bulletin, American Association for Cleft Palate Rehabilitation. [1954].)

[31] Coursin, *op. cit.*

[32] T. M. Graber, "The Significance of Growth Studies in Cleft-Palate Rehabilitation," *News Letter,* American Association for Cleft Palate Rehabilitation, Vol. II; No. 2 (April, 1952).

[33] I. Kostrubala, Symposium on Cleft Palate, Medical College, University of Illinois, 1951.

[34] T. M. Graber, "Changing Philosophies in Cleft-Palate Management," *Journal of Pediatrics,* Vol. 37, No. 3 (September, 1950), pp. 400-415.

[35] M. Buck, "Facial Skeletal Measurements and Tongue Carriage in Subjects with Repaired Cleft Palates," *Journal of Speech and Hearing Disorders,* Vol. 18, No. 2 (1953), pp. 121-132.

period may disturb permanently the growth and positional relations of the structures in the palatal area. In order to avoid such damage to the growth potentials, surgery may be delayed until the fifth or sixth year.

Another consideration in the decision for or against surgical intervention is the effect of the deformed maxillary arch on dental occlusion. Hixon, who cites studies by a Norwegian researcher, Egil Harvold, states that malposition of the permanent teeth will result in further medial movement of the maxillae and final collapse of the arch unless orthodontic treatment is introduced early to rotate the maxillary bones in the opposite direction.[36]

Having weighed all these arguments and perhaps after a period of waiting for the establishment of growth, the team may decide finally in favor of palatal surgery. In such an event, the maxillo-facial surgeon generally uses some modification of the Dieffenbach-Warren-von Langenbeck method (Fig. 14-4). The method involves a relaxation and mesial displacement of

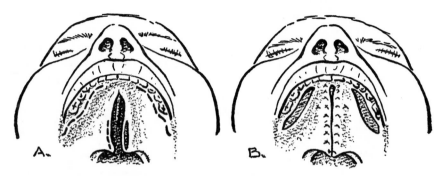

FIGURE 14-4. Langenbeck method of closure of cleft of the soft and hard palate.

the palatal tissue so that the flaps finally are approximated without undue tension and so that the granulations which develop on the raw surfaces of the flaps induce as little contraction as possible. In general, the aim of the surgeon is to meet these requisites:

1. The preservation of the contour of the dental arch to permit the eruption of teeth in normal position and to maintain the normal dimensions of the hard palate.

2. The pre-establishment of the unity of the palate in midline to provide a sufficient antero-posterior separation of the nasal and oral cavities.

3. The union of the soft-palate muscles, the levator palati, tensor palati, palatoglossus, palatopharyngeus, azygos uvulae at the palatal aponeurosis to assure the muscular movement necessary for speech and deglutition.

4. The re-establishment of the vascular supply and nervous innervation

[36] E. Harvold, "Observations in the Development of the Upper Jaw by Harelip and Cleft Palate," *Odontologisk Tidsskrift,* Vol. 3 (1947), p. 289.

to assure wholesome restoration and to prevent sloughing, cicatrizing, and paralysis of palatal tissue.[37]

Despite the care of those concerned with surgical repair, the results often fall short of the goal. When the tissues are stretched in a horizontal diameter, the anterior-posterior diameter may be shortened; the frequent result is a very short palate. Generally, oral resonance is reduced because the flaps which have been joined slant down, not up. Moreover, the mechanics of closure of the nasal port often are disturbed. The movement of the velum should be in a vertical direction and its function should be elevation; but instead of raising the palate, the muscles may act to pull the velum backward. (See Fig. 14-5.) Graber sums up the unsolved surgical problems when

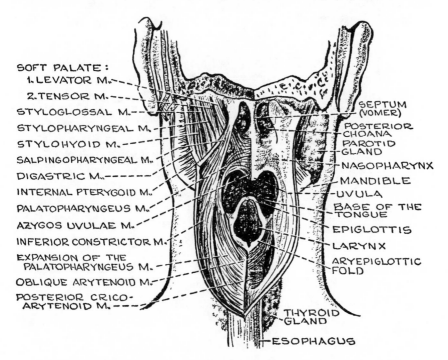

FIGURE 14-5. Muscles of the pharynx, larynx, and palate (posterior view).

he describes an operation for velar closure which resulted in an esthetic success but a functional failure: [38]

Both anterior and posterior pharyngeal pillars are taut; the musculus uvulae is functionless; the levator palati muscles show no contraction during any phase

[37] C. S. Harkins and R. H. Ivy, "Surgery and Prosthesis in the Rehabilitation of Cleft-Palate Patients," *Plastic and Reconstructive Surgery*, Vol. 7, No. 1 (1951), p. 3.
[38] T. M. Graber, "Changing Philosophies in Cleft Palate Management," *The Journal of Pediatrics*, Vol. 37, No. 3 (September, 1950), p. 400 ff.

of mastication and deglutition. The tensor palati muscles which normally elevate the soft palate ... contract but cannot overcome the downward pull of both pharyngopalatinus and glossopalatinus muscles. [See Fig. 14-6.] At four years of age, the closure of the cleft was a success; at 14 years the patient noticed difficulty of function; at 20 years the structure is completely inadequate for eating, swallowing and speech.

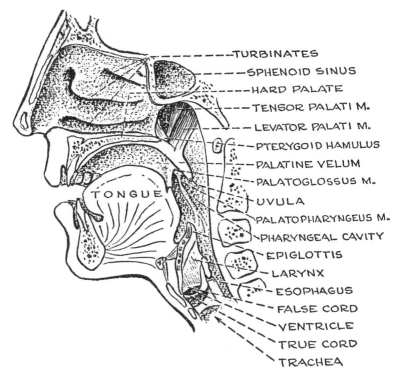

FIGURE 14-6. Median sagittal section through the head and neck.

Prosthetic Aid

If the team decides to delay palatal surgery, the prosthodontist may construct a temporary prosthetic appliance or obturator which may have three main sections: maxillary, palatal, and pharyngeal or "bulb." Such an appliance has been successful even with very young children, two and a half years old. Usually the appliance is worn until the child is seven or eight years old, when the team makes a final decision between surgery and a permanent prosthetic reconstruction of the palate.[39] (See Fig. 14-7.)

[39] C. S. Harkins and M. M. Nitsche, "The Cleft-Palate Child Is Crippled," *The Crippled Child*, Vol. 27 (1950), pp. 22-23, 29.

E. T. McDonald, "Speech Considerations in Cleft-Palate Prosthesis," *Journal of Prosthetic Dentistry*, Vol. 1 (1951), pp. 629-637.

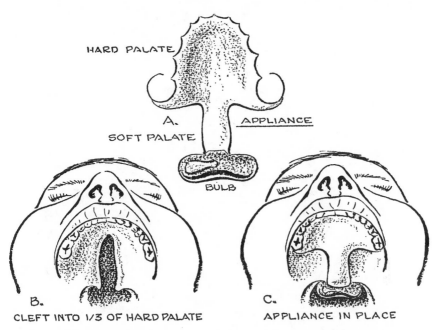

FIGURE 14-7. Non-surgical closure of palatal cleft by prosthesis (obturator).

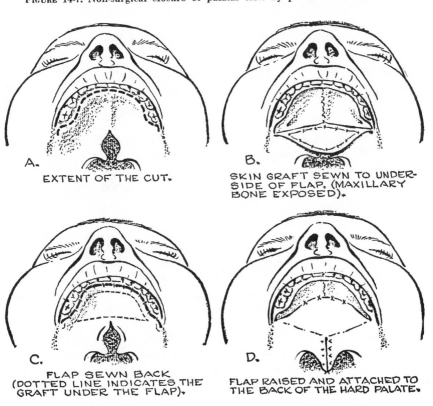

FIGURE 14-8. Lengthening of the palate by the push-back operation.

Congenital or Restorative Insufficiency of the Velum

For the congenitally insufficient or short palate, two operative techniques have been combined to produce a more effective closure of the nasal port. The Dorrance push-back operation in which the palate is retrodisplaced is sometimes performed. (See Fig. 14-8.) The more common practice is the

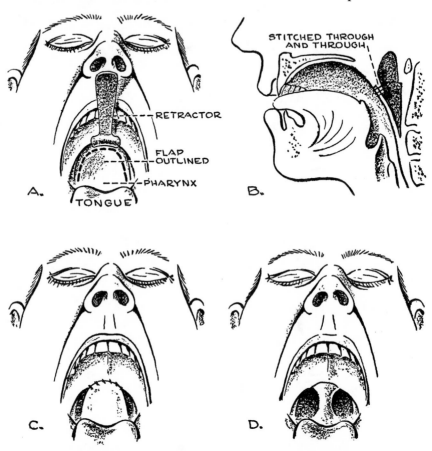

FIGURE 14-9. Pharyngeal flap operation to improve the velar-pharyngeal sphincter in palatal clefts. A. The soft palate retracted and the flap outlined on the pharyngeal wall. B. Side view of the flap of mucosa, pharyngeal fascia, and muscle which has been lifted and stitched to the soft palate. C. Front view of the flap attached to the soft palate. D. Front view of the flap which, having contracted, has formed a tube and has pulled the soft palate close to the pharyngeal wall.

pharyngeal flap operation in which the mucomuscular flaps are prepared from the walls of the pharynx and attached to the velum, thus assisting in maintaining its longitudinal dimension and also increasing the competence of the palatopharyngeal sphincter. (See Fig. 14-9.) The latter operation also is performed frequently when repaired clefts have not produced the desired results.[40]

ASSOCIATED PROBLEMS IN CLEFT PALATE

Dentition

As the teeth erupt, the pedodontist discusses his concern, the prevention of dental caries. Because of a prolonged soft diet and the tendency of parents to allow a high glucose and low protein intake, rampant caries is the typical picture. Here both the social worker and the psychologist must join with the pedodontist in parental and child-education programs designed to promote oral hygiene. The orthodontist also needs the help of the social worker and psychologist. Dental malformations and malocclusions are the rule rather than the exception in these children. In any traumatic zone, heightened sensitivity may result, but this is particularly true of an insult to the oral area since it possesses the most highly developed sensitivity at birth. The oral area of the cleft-palate child usually is subjected to more or less constant insult. One can understand why these children show great resentment toward any further tampering with the mouth. The family, the professional team, and the child must understand and learn how to cope with these normal reactions to injury. Once again, the psychologist and the social worker can render an indispensable service.

Respiration

The surgeon, pediatrician, otolaryngologist and speech clinician are all concerned with the common occurrence of respiratory difficulties of the cleft-palate subject. A deficiency or collapse of the nasal crura or deviation of the septum, common problems in cleft palate, may result in mouth breathing. The consequences of atypical respiration are not invariable, but frequently one sees cleft-palate children in whom the general physical potential is lowered because of the unwarmed, unmoistened air which enters the

[40] Moran states that the pharyngeal flap operation should not be combined with the push-back operation. He argues also that it is better to base the pedicle of the pharyngeal flap superiorly in the young "where there is a large amount of adenoid tissue. . . This is also the case where the distance from the free edge of the palate to the pharyngeal wall is over two centimeters. The pedicle of the pharyngeal flap can be based below if the distance is less than two centimeters and in the older group where the adenoid tissue is no problem." (R. E. Moran, "The Pharyngeal Flap Operation as a Speech Aid," *News Letter,* American Association for Cleft-Palate Rehabilitation, Vol. 1, No. 4 [1951].)

Herbert Conway, "Combined Use of the Push-back and Pharyngeal-flap Procedures in the Management of Complicated Cases of Cleft Palate," *Plastic and Reconstructive Surgery,* Vol. 7 (March, 1951), pp. 214-223.

Wilfred Hynes, "Pharyngoplasty by Muscle Transplantation," *British Journal of Plastic Surgery,* Vol. 3 (July, 1950), pp. 128-135.

Hector Marino and S. Renato, "Cleft Palate: Pharyngostaphylino Fixation," *British Journal of Plastic Surgery,* Vol. 3 (October, 1950), pp. 222-224.

lungs from the mouth. The health index may be subnormal because they suffer more or less constantly from upper respiratory infections. Because of the nasal obstructions, breathing for speech often is noisy, shallow, and irregular. The pediatrician will seek to reduce the frequency of respiratory infections, and the team may develop a plan for the restoration of nasal structure and function. Since the tonsillar and adenoidal tissue masses add bulk and thus assist in closing the nasal port, their removal is rarely if ever recommended.

Hearing

The lymphoid tissue (ring of Waldeyer) which surrounds the Eustachian tube is often infected, producing the sequelae of otitis media and reduced hearing (conduction losses) in many cases. Other cleft-palate children who have not suffered from otitis media also show hearing losses, probably because of the disparity in pressures between the outside and the middle ear and because the middle ear does not receive proper aeration through the Eustachian tube.[41] Although some investigators believe that nearly all cleft-palate children develop hearing losses of considerable degree, audiometric and other evaluations of the hearing of 383 cleft-palate children in the Rockford College Center (1946-1955) indicate that less than 60 per cent of the children suffer from a recognizable handicap in hearing.[42] It is possible that the difference in results may be attributed to the age differences in the groups which have been studied. In our Center, the age range is from three to nine years; the median age, five years. As these children grow, they who earlier had normal hearing may develop perceptible losses. Again, the team must be intent on the prevention of otitis media and provide for a periodic check on auditory acuity.

Intelligence

The question of the intellectual ability of cleft-palate subjects has been raised from time to time. There are scattered reports of low intelligence, but the most reliable and extensive investigations show their curve of learning potential to be comparable with that for the general school population.

[41] J. Sataloff and Margaret Fraser, "Hearing Loss in Children with Cleft Palates," *Archives of Otolaryngology,* Vol. 55, No. 1 (1952), p. 64.

[42] H. Westlake, Speech and Hearing Clinic, Northwestern University, correspondence with writer.

M. M. Halfond, "An Audiologic and Otorhinological Study of Cleft-lip and Cleft-palate Cases," School of Medicine, Duke University, *News Letter,* American Association for Cleft-Palate Rehabilitation, Vol. 2, No. 3 (1952).

Mildred F. Berry. Unpublished study, Speech Center, Rockford College, Rockford, Illinois.

PSYCHOLOGICAL AND EMOTIONAL RESTORATION

The psychologist, speech clinician, parents, and social worker already have entered the discussion at several points. They may expect to "do battle" with many environmental problems in the child's life. From the first, some members of the group will have to help the parents in their struggle against rejection and guilt. As the child grows, the counsellors and parents will encourage him in adjusting to his "different appearance" and in developing an emotional toughness and resiliency toward signs of rejection by the neighborhood, schoolmates, and the public. By degrees and often by indirect routes, they will try to bring him to a frank and honest recognition of his problem. All his counsellors will seek to develop in him adequate compensations, inner satisfactions, and a motivation for speech improvement and general learning reaching into adulthood. Anyone who has worked with these children appreciates the difficulties attendant upon the realization of these objectives. Our society has not yet recognized the universality of "differences." The premiums on physical perfection and normality, for example, are great despite the proof that nature rarely, if ever, provides perfection and "normality" is so rare as to be unmeasurable. It is time that we develop a tolerance toward the "different" person.

SPEECH HABILITATION

When the child comes for the first time to the speech clinic, how may his speech be described? What are the major differences between his speech and yours, assuming that yours approaches "normality"? What accounts for each difference? What differences can we expect to erase? In what order should they be attacked?

The speech of a few children in the group will be nearly standard. The sibilants may show some acoustic variant; there may be an occasional nasal overtone in such sounds as ē [i] or o͞o [u]; but, in general, the speech does not call attention to itself as being "different." Happily, we need not be concerned very long with this small segment.

More frequently, we must be concerned with children whose defect is apparent with the first vocalization, even to the most unperceptive among us. His speech may be described as (1) highly nasal, harsh or muffled in quality; (2) uncontrolled in loudness; (3) frequently shrill in pitch and sometimes changing with growth to an unnaturally low, "gravel" voice; (4) indistinct and inaccurate in articulation with frequent substitution of the glottal stop and with nasal "resurgence" in the sibilant sounds; (5) the whole often attended by such undesirable mannerisms as constriction of the nasal alae or aversion of the head in speaking. Speech habilitation for the post-cleft-palate patient, then, can no longer be thought as training only in velar closure. The problems arise in a chain-reflex fashion: the muscular deficiencies and imbalances in the mouth and throat provoke compensatory lingual and pharyngeal tensions which, in turn, may initiate undesirable patterns of phonation and respiration. And as these undesirable tensions and patterns have a common origin or focus, so must the therapy have a focal point of attack. The glottal-stop substitution for plosives illustrates the chain of response: the lips of the glottis are closed momentarily by great tension; the pharyngeal tissues, tensed in an attempt to close the nasal port, produce vibrations which increase the harshness of vocal quality; the jaw is tight and the tongue is buckled in the mouth as if to assist the elevation of the velum. The result is glottal articulation, a harsh quality, and uncontrolled loudness. If we recognize that we are dealing with a system of organs and muscles "out of balance," then is it not logical to predicate therapy upon a basic change in the whole pattern of speaking, treating intensively single parts of the pattern if necessary? The focal point of attack which we have found most advantageous in working with children is the development of a flexible articulatory mechanism, particularly of the front mouth. Following attainment of general flexibility, we move on to training in the (1) accurate production of speech sounds by direct phonetic education; (2) improved action of the velar-pharyngeal sphincter; (3) speech melody and rhythm; (4) removal of facial tics; and finally (5) controlled phonation.

The Development of a Flexible Articulatory Mechanism

The first objective in the speech habilitation of cleft-palate children is the development of a flexible articulatory mechanism, (a) with the focus of activity in the front mouth, and (b) with an adequate oral aperture as a general pattern of speaking.

Increase in the Flexibility and Precision of Muscular Action of Jaw, Lips, and Face. We shall begin with these muscles because their movements are visible and because we want to change the center of activity or tension from the pharynx and posterior mouth to the front mouth. Moreover, if we can make the jaw and lips flexible and precise in their action, we will also have taken the first step in establishing a larger mouth opening as a general speech pattern.

Changing the Position and Increasing the Flexibility of the Tongue. In the majority of these children we find that the tongue habitually is retracted in the mouth, producing a high-riding dorsum, and that the blade and tip are inflexible. Actually many of the faulty sounds characteristic of cleft-palate speech cannot be attributed directly to the structural anomaly and repair, but to the basic inflexibility of the tongue. These lingual problems may arise from basic defects in structure, from a neural deficiency, or from acquired compensatory patterns.[43] The child probably

---

[43] Mildred F. Berry, "Lingual Anomalies in Facial Clefts," *Journal of Speech and Hearing Disorders,* Vol. 14, No. 4 (1949), pp. 359-362.

learns very early, for example, that he needs to compensate for the defective velar sphincter. The bunching of the tongue, as in swallowing, is a natural although ineffectual "assistant" in closing the nasal port. The front tongue is immobilized; the pharyngeal muscles are tensed; the effect is adverse both upon articulation and vocal quality. The sounds *l, t, d, s,* and *sh* [ʃ] are most frequently distorted, and since these sounds depend upon delicate and fast movements of the front tongue, it is essential that he work to re-position the tongue in the mouth, change the focal point of tension from dorsum to tongue-tip, and increase its flexibility. The change in tensions will also relax the pharyngeal and laryngeal muscles, and if the front mouth opening also is larger, much of the muffled, harsh, or twangy quality will be eliminated.

Development of Intra-oral Pressure and Direction of the Breath Stream as Functions of Articulation. The lack of intra-oral pressure is particularly noticeable in the plosive and fricative consonants. The strength of the velar "seal" (i.e., the velar-pharyngeal sphincter) is one factor in the development of oral pressure, but it is not the only one. Equally important are the muscular activity of the cheeks, lips, jaw, and tongue and the timing of the articulatory apparatus with the chest pressure. Another requisite for oral pressure is evident in the articulation of the voiceless plosives *p, t,* and *k.* Many cleft-palate children can learn to make the voiced analogues *b, d,* and *g* quite easily but cannot produce *p, t,* and *k.* Why? One possible answer is that the timing and co-ordination of respiration, phonation, and articulation are faulty. For *p, t,* and *k,* the pressure in the buccal cavity must be equal to that of the chest so that there is no flow of air to activate the vocal folds. If the expiratory muscles increase the chest pressure, or if the buccal pressure is reduced so that there is an imbalance, the vocal folds will vibrate. Hence the child says "benny" for "penny," "baba" for "papa," "bob" for "pop," and so on. Another explanation is based on the observation that voiceless consonants require greater oral pressure than voiced consonants and, hence, the cleft-palate child finds it difficult to build up the pressure necessary for voiceless sounds.

Another problem is the nasal "resurgence" in the production of the fricative sounds: *s, z, sh* [ʃ], *zh* [ʒ], *f, v, th* [θ], and *th* [ð]. The breath stream is not completely impounded on these sounds, but they do demand considerable pressure and duration so that very often the initial acoustic effect is good, but as the sound is prolonged the breath stream recedes and nasal resonance becomes dominant. In alteration of the focus of tensions—or to put it in another way, in relaxing the laryngeal and pharyngeal muscles and increasing the front mouth flexibility—we also attempt to establish a "psychological focus" for the breath stream in the front mouth. Despite the current debate over the value of blowing exercises, we find that gentle blowing of candles, feathers, of paper butterflies against a mirror, or of ping-pong balls on an inclined plane increases the child's ability to direct the breath

stream. We would support Bloomer's study that the velar activity characteristic of blowing more closely approaches the action employed in speech
than does the velar action in swallowing and yawning.[44] We find, further,
that blowing exercises are helpful in relaxing the tension in the glottis and
moving the focus of tension to the front mouth. Children—even very small
children—find the harmonica an aid in sensing good palatal action and a
directed breath stream. They like also to use the megaphone in imper-
sonating such familiar characters as the circus caller, the parade major, the
radio announcer, or the square-dance caller.

Development of Accurate Production of Speech Sounds by Phonetic Training

There are numerous distortions, omissions, and substitutions in the
speech of the cleft-palate child. The clinician will choose to establish those
sounds which will make the greatest contribution to speech intelligibility
and which are appropriate for his age level. A four-year-old, for example,
may make a *w* substitution for the *r* sound with propriety. And we are not
greatly concerned over the *sh* [ʃ] substitution for a final *ch* [tʃ] in such
words as *catch, watch, touch,* if the child is under eight years old. Many
non-cleft-palate adults make the same substitution. A very common substitution for *t, d, k,* and *g* is the glottal stop; this is a cause for real concern
since it reduces markedly the general intelligibility. When the tension is removed from the larynx and pharynx and the front mouth opening is increased in area and flexibility, then the glottal stop, the bugbear of all
therapists, usually disappears. The steps in phonetic training which we have
found particularly suitable for the young cleft-palate child are: (1) sharpening auditory discrimination of sounds; (2) strengthening visual and
kinesthetic clues in establishing the position of the articulators for the new
sounds; (3) use of the new sounds in carefully structured speech situations;
(4) transfer of the new sounds to speech situations in other parts of the
program of the Center: preschool, crafts, finger-painting, organized games,
swimming, etc.; and (5) establishment of the "new speech" in unstructured,
free-speech situations: meals, free play, excursions to zoo, circus, or parks.
The case summaries at the end of this chapter will illustrate each of these
steps in detail.

Development of Velar Closure by Velar Exercises

In the older child with repaired cleft, direct training in velar closure may
be efficacious. As Kantner has pointed out, the benefit of such exercises
must be judged not only by the amount of air escaping from the nose but

---

[44] H. Bloomer, "Observations on Palatopharyngeal Action with Special Reference
to Speech, Swallowing and Blowing," *News Letter,* American Association for Cleft
Palate Rehabilitation, Vol. 2, No. 1 (1952).

by the *relative* amounts escaping from the nose and mouth.[45] If there is a general reduction at both points, the exercise obviously is not achieving its purpose. Such devices as the two-tiered feather stand, the nose cap, and the mirror held horizontally below the nose often are good checks on nasal emission. If the child learns to "sip" air over the tongue and expel it through the nose, and then reverse the process, he also may gain a kinesthetic appreciation of velar closure. Another kinesthetic aid is to increase the pressure of the velar sphincter muscles by prolonging the implosive phase of the consonants *p, b, t,* and *d.* Since *ē* [i] and *ōō* [u] require the greater closure *ä* [ɑ] and *ô* [ɔ] the least of the velar sphincter, it is wise to begin phonatory exercise with *ä* [ɑ] and then proceed slowly to *ē* [i] and *ōō* [u] sounds. The child may be helped in detecting the sounds which have excessive nasality by placing on the nares the end-plate of a stethoscope which will transmit the sound by rubber tubes leading from the end-plate to his own ears. He also can compare acoustic effects by intoning *ē* [i], alternating pinching and releasing the nares.

Development of Speech Melody and Rhythm

The broken staccato rhythm with its unfortunate effect upon melody will be noted particularly in the case summary of Steve (summary at the conclusion of chapter), who had had considerable training in articulation but was still using far too much tension in the larynx and pharynx. In small children, rhythmic pantomime accompanying speech and singing of tunes with a definite pattern are practical aids in the development of a sense of speech rhythm.

Development of Control of Facial Expression

A compensatory action which often is present even in very small children is the effort to close off nasal resonance by constricting the alae of the nose. Particularly is this true in the production of the plosive and fricative sounds. In bringing the tic under conscious control, the clinician may secure aid from the following practices: (1) holding the cheek muscles (with the fingers) so they cannot enter into the contraction; (2) voluntary constriction and relaxation of the ala; (3) slight eversion of the lips so that the upper lip cannot be pulled downward in order to assist alar contraction; and (4) mirror-checking. The child also may resort to blinking of the eyes and other facial grimaces which must be dealt with in the same general manner.

The Development of Controlled Phonation

Another problem which may be present is a hoarse, ventricular voice. We do not find this vocal characteristic in the very young cleft-palate child, but it is fairly common in the nine-to-twelve-year-old group. The causes

[45] C. E. Kantner, "The Rationale of Blowing Exercises for Patients with Repaired Cleft Palate," *Journal of Speech Disorders,* Vol. 12, No. 3 (1947), pp. 281-286.

may be several: (1) the chronic inflammation of the nasal and pharyngeal mucosa with the result that the secretion undoubtedly invades the larynx; [46] (2) the excessive tension in voice production which may result in hyperemia, nodules, etc.; and (3) the "rebound" of pharyngeal resonance upon the larynx vibration, thus producing injury to the folds.[47] Any one factor or a combination of these factors may produce the rough, jagged, and irregular folds which account for the peculiar pitch and quality. There are two obvious sources of correction: (1) changing the focus of tension and inducing complete relaxation of the larynx, and (2) raising the pitch and lowering the intensity of all speech.

PUTTING THE PRINCIPLES INTO PRACTICE: THE RECORD

There is no single tailor-made therapy suit which can be fitted to meet the needs of every cleft-palate child or adult. We have selected six cases which exemplify (1) different but representative speech problems, ones which a clinician will meet frequently in dealing with the cleft-palate child; (2) varying stages of habilitation; (3) surgical repair and closure by prosthesis; (4) different clinical techniques. Only one of the clinicians received her basic training in the department of the writer. No two clinicians came from the same college or university. A careful study of these case summaries will provide the student with detailed descriptions of the main goals, techniques, and materials employed in habilitating the speech of the cleft-palate child.

I. SURGICALLY REPAIRED CLEFT OF PALATE (COMPLETE)

The beginner: *Gary,* boy, 7 years of age, *surgical repair of the palate completed.* Entered 6/16/54; born 6/3/47. Well-nourished, blonde-complexioned boy, pleasant, assured; defective vision in one eye. Health excellent. One of four children; older and younger brothers both have cleft palates. No history of cleft palate on either side of the family. Gary is the only left-handed sibling; mother also is left-handed.

    I. DIAGNOSIS

        A. *General*

           1. Description of cleft and of palatal action

                a. Complete cleft from alveoli through uvula; pyriform shape.

                b. Surgical repair in 1953 and 1954; anterior portion closed in 1954. There is still a pinpoint opening at junction of hard palate and velum.

[46] E. T. McDonald and H. Koepp-Baker, "Cleft Palate Speech: An Integration of Research and Clinical Observation," *Journal of Speech and Hearing Disorders,* Vol. 16, No. 1 (1951), p. 15.

[47] R. Curry, *The Mechanism of the Human Voice* (New York, Longmans, 1940), p. 50.

    c. Structure and function of palate: anterior section of vault abnormally narrow. Sphincter ring action is prominent but velum is short, making an effective seal impossible.

    d. Anterior pillars of fauces far forward.

    e. Passavant's cushion somewhat hypertrophied. No observable assistance in closing the sphincter.

2. Lip mobility: good.

3. Tongue mobility: poor. Dorsum of tongue is retracted and raised; tongue-tip and blade are inactive.

4. Dental anomalies: none.

5. Nasal anomalies: none.

6. Audiometric evaluation

    a. 1/14/54 and 7/20/54: Pure-tone audiometer: left ear shows slight loss (25db.) at 500 and 1000 cps; right ear: 35 to 55 in the speech frequencies, 500 to 4000 cps. Greatest loss in high frequencies.

    b. Free-field testing for reception of speech indicates a moderate loss in right ear.

    c. Child's general auditory behavior supports loss: watches speaker's lips carefully; is unsure of response when testing for discrimination between sounds of high frequency.

    d. History of frequent attacks of otitis media.

7. Psychometric evaluation: Leiter International Performance Scale: 6/18/54: C.A. 7-0; M.A. 7-3; IQ 105.

8. Social maturity: Outgoing, independent, yet co-operative. Very helpful with other children. Most popular boy in the Center. Very talkative; probably is not very conscious of his speech problems because two sibs also have cleft palates. Results on Vineland Social Maturity Scale support these observations.

B. *Specific*

1. Articulation

    a. Substitutions: [ʔ]/k; d/g; b/v; m/f; h/t; h/d.

    b. Distortions: s; s-blends; z; th [ð]; r; l; sh [ʃ]; (medial) f.

    c. Omissions: final f; t; l; z.

    d. All vowels show nasal emission. Nasal emission on f, s particularly noticeable.

2. Voice

    a. Pitch: appropriate to his age.

    b. Quality: extreme nasality.

    c. Loudness: moderate.

II. Speech Therapy, Problems, and Progress

A. *Therapy*

1. Auditory training and discrimination

    a. Stimulation with sounds in isolation; select the two "sound alike" words; negative practice (the substituted sound; the "right" sound); when you hear "right" sound in accented word of sentence put red marble in box, green when the substituted sound appears.

b. Use of amplifier to distinguish between *h* and *t-d;* between [ʔ] and *k-g.*

c. Use of tape recorder for acoustic stimulation and self-criticism.

2. Development of intra-oral pressure
   a. Puff up cheeks, quickly release air.
   b. Blow tissue balls into checker-board squares.
   c. Close lips tightly, hold impounded air; then release, changing lip formation from [u] to [ɑ], and dropping the jaw slowly.
   d. Use of "bubble hat" for sustained pressure; slow release.
   e. Explode *p-p-p* against palm of hand; do the same with *t-t-t.*

3. Increasing tongue flexibility
   a. Front tongue:
      (1) hold mandible down; tap alveoli rapidly with tip; watch the position in mirror.
      (2) call on "kinfolk" teeth by touching with the tongue-tip the molar on each side, then pre-molar, canine teeth, etc.
      (3) work rapidly the see-saw movement of the tongue: *t-k-t-k,* etc.
      (4) lick honey from the upper lip, using a finely pointed tip.
      (5) sing "London Bridge Is Falling Down," using "la-la-la" instead of words. (Be sure mouth is wide open.)
   b. Back tongue:
      (1) pull the dorsum forward in [j] position; with tip behind lower teeth, raise and lower dorsum from [j] position.
      (2) put peanut butter on palate at [j] position. Use dorsum to remove peanut butter.
      (3) raise and lower the dorsum at will, watching the process in the mirror.
      (4) shift rapidly the position: tip-raised; lower dorsum to tip-down; raise dorsum.
   c. Rapid shift in tip-dorsum:
      (1) "This is the way Biddy calls her chicks, so early in the morning: "kluk-kluk-kluk," etc.
      (2) "Old Dobbin plods down the road,
          Drawing behind him the heavy load,
          Kloppety, kloppety, kloppety, klop.
          Kloppety, kloppety, klop!"
      (3) "Flippety flop, flippety flop.
          You April wind: Take care! Take care!
          Monday's wash, you'll rip and tear!
          Flip-flop; Flippety-flop!
          Flip, flip, flop."

4. Strengthening visual, kinesthetic and tactile clues in establishing specific sounds: *t, d, f, k, g, s*
   a. Demonstrate articulatory movements in sound alone, in syllables, words and sentences.
   b. Pictures accompanied by short stories calling for the new sound in initial, medial, and final positions placed in Speech Journal.
   c. Treasure hunt for pictures and printed words containing the new sound.
   d. Commissions to co-ordinator, director, recreational supervisor, etc., involving use of the new sound.
   e. House staff check: Carried card, "Can you guess my sound?" House staff paid "fine" if they could not guess the sound.
   f. Use of tape recorder: telling about trips to zoo, circus, Kiddie-land, etc. Self-criticism.

5. Co-ordination of learning: flexible articulators, wider mouth opening, "front" production, and acoustic check in connected speech
   a. Report on trips to zoo, circus, Kiddie-land, Sunday picnics, supermarket, etc.
   b. Speech "Leader" in dining room and in games on playground.
   c. Use of tape recorder for self-criticism.
   d. Report from group and indirect therapy: "Gary's cheerful and eager manner made him a true asset to group. His desire to communicate interfered somewhat with the development of a self-critical attitude toward his speech. He accepted any check, however, by the clinician without resentment. The transfer of speech patterns established in the clinic to free speech was very slow."

B. *Problems*
   1. Structurally inadequate velar-pharyngeal closure. Partial solution by emphasis on general resonance and increased flexibility of front mouth.
   2. General loss in acuity provides him with less ability to discriminate between sounds than average person.
   3. Narrow anterior palatal vault. This condition affects particularly the articulation of sibilants.
   4. Tongue has slow action. Until faster rate of "rocking" is established, words involving such a shift will be faulty. Examples: *tucker, cutter, gate.*

C. *Progress*
   1. Good production of *t, d* in the clinical situation in initial position, and of *f* in all positions.
   2. Good production of *g* has been obtained but *d/g* now is an occasional substitute instead of the glottal stop.
   3. The production of *s* and *z* now is as good as may be expected with the present oral structure.

4. Increased awareness of errors.
5. Acoustic discrimination has been developed, although it is not good.
6. Ability to correct himself in the clinical situation but he has not yet come to the stage of inclusion of corrected sounds *in free speech* in or outside of the clinic.

II. UNILATERAL CLEFT LIP; CLEFT OF PALATE; PROSTHESIS

The beginner: *Victor*, boy, 4½ years of age, palatal cleft; *prosthesis*. Entered 6/17/54; born 9/26/49.

I. DIAGNOSIS

  A. *General*

    1. Description of cleft: postoperative unilateral left cleft lip. The cleft of velum and hard palate, which does not extend through the alveolar process, is unrepaired; a prosthetic appliance is worn.
    2. Dental anomalies: none observed.
    3. Nasal anomalies: left ala wide and flattened.
    4. Lip mobility: good.
    5. Tongue mobility: good. Upward movements of tip are not as well co-ordinated or as rapid as others. Dorsum of tongue carried in elevated position.
    6. Velar-pharyngeal closure: velar tags make contact with the prosthesis. This lateral movement of the velar tags appears to be good.
    7. Audiometric evaluation: 6/19/54

a. Pure tone:	250	500	1000	2000	4000	8000
Right ear:	10	15	10	15	10	25
Left ear:	10	10	5	10	5	30

       b. Speech: General acuity good.
    8. Psychometric evaluation: Revised Stanford-Binet Intelligence Scale, Form L., 6/18/54
       C.A.   4-9
       M.A.   5-3
       IQ   111
    9. Laterality: left, but ambilateral tendencies were noted.

  B. *Specific*

    1. Rate: rapid.
    2. Articulation
      a. In contextual speech there is a fairly consistent glottalization of all but the labial consonants.
      b. Use of the nasals is frequent: *m/b, n/w, n/d,* and *n/g.*
      c. Omits *r* and all *r* and *l* blends.
      d. *t/th* [θ]; and *t* or *d/th* [ð].
      e. *t/sh* [ʃ]; *d/j* [dʒ].
      f. *t/k* and *k/g* are used inconsistently in the final position.
      g. *w/m.*

    h. *h/s* or the use of a glottal stop is relatively consistent.

    i. There are a few substitutions that could possibly be traced to the occasional use of Polish in the home.

3. Voice

    a. Nasal emission: There is slight nasal emission in all the consonants, which is especially noticeable in the fricatives and sibilants.

    b. Quality: slight nasality.

    c. Pitch: rather high for the age and sex.

    d. Loudness: adequate for projection.

4. Contextual speech is rapid and almost unintelligible. The content and sentence structure are good.

5. During the boy's illness he was taught without his prosthetic appliance. The therapist was surprised at how well many of the consonants were produced without the prosthesis. The vocal quality of the speech and the sibilants are improved by the prosthesis.

II. Speech Therapy, Problems, and Progress

A. *Report on individual speech therapy*

1. Therapy was directed toward the fulfillment of the following goals:

    a. To encourage tongue-tip activity and the lowering of the dorsum of the tongue.

    b. To aid in the development of intra-oral pressure.

    c. To develop better discrimination of sounds.

    d. To retard the rate of speech and lower the pitch.

    e. To develop articulation of the consonants *b, l, t, d, k, g.*

2. The above goals were approached by the following methods and techniques:

    a. Tongue-tip activity and the lowering of the dorsum of the tongue:

        (1) Sweeping the house.

        (2) Licking peanut butter and jelly from lips and alveolar process.

        (3) Licking candy stick held just outside the mouth.

        (4) Imitating the movements of the large red tongue of the clown.

        (5) Following the movements of a toy airplane.

        (6) Substituting "la", "ta", and "da", for the words of simple children's songs such as "Twinkle, Twinkle, Little Star," "Mary Had a Little Lamb," and "Lionel the Lion."

        (7) Kinesthetic approach to lowering the dorsum of the tongue by tapping that portion of the tongue with a tongue depressor or candy stick, and asking for voluntary raising and lowering of that portion of the tongue.

    b. Development of intra-oral pressure:

        (1) Blowing bubbles with soap and spool.

        (2) Blowing bubbles with Bubble Magic.

     (3) Bubble hat.

     (4) Races with balls of tissue.

     (5) Blowing candle flame with consonants.

     (6) Races with ping-pong balls using especially *p* and *b* to propel them.

     (7) Blowing colored confetti in a transparent box in articulating *s, f,* and *sh* [ʃ].

c. Better speech sound discrimination:

     (1) Tap Bang-A-Ball toy when sound is heard in isolation, syllable, word, or sentence.

     (2) Discrimination drill: Records, *Consonant Sound Discrimination* by Larsen.

     (3) Record, *Fun with Speech* (Van Riper), "Little Lamb's Story" (Britannica Films, Inc.).

     (4) Drop a marble in the red and blue box when the sound or word for which he is listening is heard.

     (5) Give the sides of the above box different names; a marble is dropped in the side when the child hears a certain name.

     (6) In picture album, child finds the picture (in group of 3 on page) representing word which does *not* contain "his" sound.

     (7) The child selects pictures containing a specific sound from a large group.

     (8) The therapist names picture cards or the pictures in the notebook, substituting other sounds for the one being studied. The child indicates right or wrong.

d. Retarding the rate and lowering the pitch:

     (1) The child re-told stories the therapist had read, using the illustrations of the books to help him remember. Attention to slow speech, careful articulation, and low pitch was maintained at all times, as in the following exercises. Books read were *Picnic at the Zoo, Millions of Cats, Copy-Kitten, Stories That Never Grow Old,* and *The Tall Book of Nursery Rhymes.*

     (2) The story of the *Three Bears* was re-told using the stage and the cut-out figures.

     (3) Recordings were made of his speech which were criticized both by the therapist and Victor.

     (4) Each day Victor told Bamse (large toy bear) something about his activities of the previous day.

     (5) Good speech was elicited from zoo, animal, family, and food pictures; the zoo visit provided an opportunity for much good speech.

e. Development of the articulation of specific consonants:

     (1) The consonants being studied were presented in isolation and in nonsense syllables while stringing beads, racing with cars, climbing a ladder and playing tic-tac-toe.

(2) The therapist's picture cards were utilized for drill on words and sentences with the consonants presented. In addition to drill, games such as the hiding game, the guessing game, the memory game, and the spinner game were played.

(3) *Baa Baa Black Sheep, The Three Little Kittens, The Three Billy Goats Gruff, Teeny-Tiny Woman, Make Way for Ducklings,* and *Mary Had a Little Lamb* were used for transfer of patterns.

(4) The notebook was filled with pictures of objects which illustrated the use of the consonants in all positions. Stories and sentences about the pictures were composed by Victor and written in the book by the therapist.

B. *Report on group therapy*

Victor has been a natural leader in the group. He enthusiastically responds to all activities and suggestions made. He has been very cooperative in tongue and lip exercises. He has attempted to speak more slowly with lower pitch and less volume. He is not consistent in his attempts, but responds well to reminders. When excited, his pitch and volume rise, but if reminded he can bring them both down. He has been using *s, f, k* in words and sentences, but he frequently needs reminders to articulate these sounds correctly.

C. *Problems in attaining goals*

Although an intelligent child and capable of very hard work, Victor would prefer to play games. For one week, therapy was conducted without the prosthesis because of illness. Although upon occasion the boy has produced excellent consonants, especially the plosives, the old habits are very firmly rooted and will require much time and patience to correct. Despite the boy's hard and energetic work, it frequently seemed that he could not articulate the consonants in question. The consistent glottalization of consonants produced many problems.

D. *Progress in therapy*

1. The attention span of the boy was lengthened considerably without much conscious effort in this direction.

2. Real progress was made in the consistent articulation of *b, k,* and *l* in isolation, nonsense syllables, words, structured sentences, and to some extent in general speech. No success with *g* was achieved; and *t* and *d,* although emerging, are not stable sounds in his speech.

3. Lip and tongue mobility was improved.

4. Speech sound discrimination has become excellent. High score on Larsen Consonant Sound Discrimination Test.

5. In the therapy situation Victor speaks slowly and uses a lower pitch which seems to improve articulation and intelligibility. Carry-over outside of the classroom was apparent except when he was excited or deeply absorbed in what he was doing.

III. SOCIAL ADJUSTMENT

Victor is an outgoing, mischievous child with an exceptional sense of humor for a youngster not yet five. He is happy and enjoys life, and his adjustment to the therapy situation was excellent. His initial misbehavior was really only an attempt to "try out" the therapist. He is intelligent enough to know when to settle down and work, and he is a serious, hard worker if the situation calls for such behavior.

III. *INCOMPLETE CLEFT OF PALATE WITH PROSTHESIS; BILATERAL HEARING LOSS*

The beginner (cleft palate and hearing loss). *Steven,* boy, 3 years, 10 months. Admitted for first summer, 6/13/55. Born: 9/20/51. *Incomplete cleft palate with prosthesis; bilateral hearing loss.* Description of child's appearance and speech at entrance to Summer Speech Center: Attractive, neatly dressed, alert, friendly boy, not yet four years of age. Speech is characterized by many omissions of consonants and by distortions and substitutions. His speech consists mainly of vowel sounds which have a nasal quality. Speech is not intelligible.

I. DIAGNOSIS

A. *General*

1. Description of cleft: complete cleft of soft palate and cleft of posterior third of hard palate. No surgical repair. Child has worn prosthesis for eight months.
2. Dental anomalies: none.
3. Nasal anomalies: none.
4. Lip mobility: good.
5. Tongue mobility: good.
6. Velar activity: could be achieved with aid of prosthesis, but is not consistently used.
7. Breath stream: occasionally controlled but more frequently uses nasal emission.
8. Audiometric evaluation: 7/23/55.

	250	500	1000	2000	4000
Right ear:	25	25	30	30	30
Left ear:	35	35	40	40	35

This is considered a valid evaluation;—Audiologist.
9. Psychometric evaluation: Stanford-Binet, Form L. 7/4/55.
   C.A. 3-10
   M.A. 4-6
   IQ 117
10. Laterality: right.

B. *Specific*

1. Rate: adequate for intelligibility and age.
2. Articulation
   a. Omissions: *t, l, s, k, g.*

   b. Complete omission of initial *p;* but consistent use of *p* in medial and final positions.
   c. Correct production with fair consistency of *b, m, w, n, r.*
   d. Substitutions in initial position: *v/f; b/v; d/th* [θ], *v/th* [ð], *j/z; j/sh* [ʃ]; *j/ch* [tʃ]; *d/j* [dʒ].
   e. Substitutions in medial position: *v/f; v/th* [ð]; *d/z.*
   f. Substitutions in final position: *b/f.*
   g. All medial and final consonants except those named in b, c, e, f, above are omitted.
3. Description of voice
   a. Pitch: good; normal for age and sex.
   b. Intensity: adequate for projection.
   c. Quality: hypernasal.
4. Contextual speech: reflects some immaturity in sentence use and connected phrases. In ideation, vocabulary, auditory memory and motivation for contextual speech, the child's abilities are average or above average for his age.

II. SIGNIFICANT DATA FROM CASE HISTORY

   A. *Presence of clefts in other members of family*
      1. Maternal great aunt: unilateral cleft lip.
      2. Maternal second cousin: unilateral cleft lip.
      3. The son of maternal second cousin: cleft lip and complete cleft of palate.

   B. *Number of siblings:* five.

   C. *Atypical behavior unrelated to cleft*
      1. Speech
         a. Speech inadequacies seem to be articulation problems rather than cleft-palate problems per se.
         b. Inadequacy of use of consonants might also have been affected by hearing loss depending upon length of time his hearing has been defective. (There is no record of defective hearing by earlier examining agencies.)
      2. Other: none.

   D. *Educational progress:* preschool.

   E. *Social development and progress:* Steven seemed to be a shy child, particularly so during the first several days in the Summer Center. After two days of class work, however, he entered into all tasks willingly and usually enthusiastically. He is friendly and gets along well with the other children but is a follower rather than a leader.

III. SPEECH THERAPY, PROBLEMS, AND PROGRESS

   A. *Report on individual therapy*
      1. Goals
         a. To develop motivation for good speech.

      b. To provide auditory stimulation and to develop auditory discrimination of sounds.

      c. To increase flexibility of the lips and the tongue.

      d. To develop an awareness of the function of the articulators in speech.

      e. To develop more adequate use of lips (particularly the upper) and of tongue-tip in articulation.

      f. To develop oral pressure and oral emission of breath stream during speech.

      g. To establish initial consonants in speech.

  2. Methods and techniques

      a. Direct therapy was given to develop *p, f, t, th* [θ], *l*. Work was concentrated on the development of these sounds in initial position because his articulatory problem was so largely one of omission of initial consonants.

      b. Auditory stimulation and discrimination:

          (1) Sounds presented in isolation through imitation of popping noises, the "angry kitty sound," the "clock sound," the "angry goose sound," and the "singing sound."

          (2) Direct stimulation from the therapist was used: as long as the therapist continued to make a certain sound, the child could walk about the room looking for hidden objects. When the therapist stopped making the sound, the child must stop walking.

          (3) Naming the objects and pictures, exaggerating the omitted sound.

          (4) Poems and stories for stimulation:

              (*a*) *The Three Little Pigs*

              (*b*) *The Angry Kitten*

              (*c*) *Tommy Tractor*

              (*d*) *Lady and the Tramp*

              (*e*) *Button Nose Book*

          (5) For practice in auditory discrimination the child puts marbles in a bottle, draws a line, raises his hand, or sticks out his tongue every time a specific sound is heard in combination with other sounds.

          (6) "Find the Sound" game: identification of the sound in different positions in words.

          (7) "Pick out the word" game: the child must identify the word containing the sound being worked on.

          (8) "Right-wrong" game: the child must tell if the sound is being used correctly by the therapist.

      c. Exercises to increase flexibility of the articulators:

          (1) Lips:

              (*a*) Imitation of pictures illustrating the various, exaggerated lip positions for the vowel sounds, [i, u, ɔ, ɑ].

              (*b*) Rapid protrusion and retraction of lip musculature.

(c) Raising the upper lip to display the gum ridge.

(d) Successive retraction of the right and the left sides of the mouth.

(e) Repetition of bilabial consonant sounds.

(f) Opening and closing lips in a protruded position.

(2) Tongue:

(a) Imitation of the therapist's tongue movements.

(b) Imaginative games in which the tongue performs some activity, such as "paint the fence," "clean the house," "jump out of the box."

(c) Rapid protrusion and retraction of the tongue.

(d) Tapping the tongue-tip against the upper lip.

(e) Stretching the tongue upward to touch the nose and downward to touch the chin.

(f) Pushing against a tongue depressor.

d. Exercises to build up oral pressure and direct the breath stream through the mouth: gentle blowing activities using tiny plastic boats, ping-pong balls, cotton balls suspended on strings, soap bubbles, tissue flags; the building up of pressure in the oral cavity until the cheeks are rounded outward, then without releasing the pressure, protruding the tongue outward; puffing out a candle flame.

e. Exercises to establish articulatory placement of sounds:

(1) Observation of his own use of articulators when talking before a mirror.

(2) Touching a tongue depressor to the alveolar ridge and the tongue-tip to help the child "feel" the placement of the sound.

(3) Naming p, f, th [θ] pictures from the child's notebook, the *Golden Dictionary* and *Sounds for Little Folks*.

(4) Put pennies in a piggy bank each time the sound is produced in isolation.

(5) Mail cards of animal, bird, fish; or choose a toy, as sound is produced in nonsense syllable.

(6) Make up sentences about the pictures in the child's speech notebook.

(7) "Go fish" for a word, using a magnetic fishing pole.

(8) Put pictures in a kangaroo's pouch when they are named correctly.

(9) Bounce word balls on a seal's nose.

(10) Climb the ladder by saying sentences correctly.

(11) Stock sentences employing words which contain the particular sound on which the child is working, such as: "I have a _____," or "This is a _____."

(12) Retelling of familiar stories using pictures as aids:

(a) *Lady and the Tramp*

(b) *The Three Little Pigs*

(c) *The Three Bears*

f. Because of the apparent hearing loss, direct therapy was conducted with the child near the therapist. An amplifier was used with the child. He was also given opportunity for direct visual stimulation either by being seated in front of the therapist or by both facing the mirror.

B. *Report on group therapy:* Steve works with great enthusiasm in the group activities. He attempts to produce the sounds on which he and the group are working. Sometimes his behavior seems immature, especially when he is seeking attention. Steve is very friendly toward the therapists and the other children.

C. *Problems in attaining goals*

1. There were no unusual problems for a child his age. The attention span is short, and he is inclined to be restless.
2. It has been difficult to develop oral pressure and to redirect the flow of the breath stream, but he has shown moderate progress.

D. *Progress*

1. Improved oral pressure on *p* and *f*.
2. He uses initial *p* in naming pictures in his book but not in spontaneous speech.
3. He is beginning to discriminate between initial *p* words correctly made and those with initial sound omitted.
4. He can produce *th* [θ] in initial position.
5. He can approximate correct *l* and *t* in certain words in therapy session and is beginning to use *l* in some spontaneous speech.
6. General understandability has improved because he uses articulators to better advantage. He also seems to have fewer omissions of medial and final consonants.

IV. SOCIAL ADJUSTMENT: He was very apprehensive of all new situations. Each time, however, he adjusted easily and quickly when he understood what he was to do in the new situation. Since then he has become the friendly, co-operative, smiling child who has won friends among his child and adult associates.

IV. SURGICALLY REPAIRED UNILATERAL CLEFT OF LIP; COMPLETE CLEFT OF PALATE (REPAIRED)

The advanced student: Linda, girl, 7 years of age. Admitted 6/17/54 for third summer to intensive training. Birth date: 8/3/47. A very attractive, well-groomed child; lip repair excellent, right ala slightly flattened. Parents are striving for perfection in the child; the goals are admittedly too high for Linda. Linda emulates parents perhaps too much.

I. DIAGNOSIS

A. *General*

1. Description of the cleft: *Postoperative unilateral right cleft lip and palate.* The velum is shortened. Lip repair in 1947. Palatal repair in

1948; surgical repair of a small opening just posterior to the alveolar ridge will be completed August 1954.

2. Dental anomalies: malocclusion; lower jaw protrudes.
3. Nasal anomalies: right ala flattened.
4. Lip mobility: adequate but the lower lip droops.
   Was muscle integrity disturbed in lip repair?
5. Tongue mobility: good movement, but tongue dorsum is high in rest position.
6. Velar-pharyngeal closure: adequate. There is diminished mobility of the velar musculature.
7. Breath stream: weak, but adequate.
8. Audiometric evaluation: hearing is normal for all speech frequencies.
9. Psychometric evaluation: Revised Stanford-Binet, Form L., 6/18/54, IQ 120; Children's Wechsler, 7/14/54, IQ 118.
10. Laterality: right.

B. *Specific*
   1. Rate: suitable for intelligibility and the situation.
   2. Articulation
      a. Articulation is excellent, both in the therapy situation and in general speech.
      b. All sounds are articulated correctly in single words. *d* and *b* and the sibilants are somewhat distorted by nasal emission in connected speech.
   3. Voice
      a. Quality: The voice quality is slightly nasal; nasal emission is present to a slight degree on all sounds, but it is particularly noticeable in *s, z, t, d, k, g,* and *b.*
      b. Pitch: The pitch is suited both to the child's age and sex.
      c. Loudness: adequate for projection.
   4. Contextual speech is in all respects excellent in content, and actually superior to the average for her age. General articulation, probably due to the extensive speech training, is also more careful than that of most children her age.

II. SPEECH THERAPY, PROBLEMS, AND PROGRESS

   A. *Report on individual speech therapy*
      1. Therapy was directed toward the fulfillment of the following goals:
         a. To increase tongue-tip activity and the lowering of the dorsum of the tongue.
         b. To develop better general speech, using careful articulation, more projection, and slower speech.
         c. To strengthen the lower lip muscles.
         d. To develop an awareness of the nasal emissions in her speech.
         e. To develop more oral emission of air during speech.
         f. To attempt to eliminate nasal emission from the articulation of the consonants: *t, d, k, g, s,* and *z.*

2. The above goals were approached by the following methods and techniques:

    a. Tongue-tip activity and the lowering of the dorsum of the tongue:

        (1) Sweeping the house.

        (2) Imitation of the movement of the clown's large red tongue.

        (3) Following the movements of a toy airplane.

        (4) Licking a candy stick held just outside the mouth.

        (5) Tapping the dorsum of the tongue with a candy stick to give the child an awareness of that area of her tongue. Drill in voluntary raising and lowering of the dorsum of the tongue was conducted before a mirror. Sketches on the blackboard helped to show the child what was desired and aided her in an awareness of what happens when she speaks, and what she must do if she is to improve her speech.

    b. Better general speech:

        (1) After the individual lesson the therapist and the child re-made the clothes of the large doll. This interested the child in the speech lesson and the sewing provided a means of eliciting much excellent speech.

        (2) Recordings were made of oral reading from books: *Picnic at the Zoo; Make Way for Ducks, Millions of Cats; The Little Island;* and *The Tall Book of Nursery Rhymes.* These were played back and criticized, and re-recorded in an effort to make better readings.

        (3) The story of the *Three Bears* was told and retold with the stage and cut-out figures. In this and all the above exercises, clear, well-articulated speech with good lip, tongue, and jaw movement was elicited. Projection, slow rate, and a pleasing pitch level were emphasized.

    c. Strengthening the lower lip:

        (1) Imitation of the therapist's lip movements was practiced before a mirror.

        (2) Exaggerated lip movement during the phonation of the vowels was practiced.

        (3) The better appearance that Linda presents when the lower lip is held in position was discussed. Attempts were made to approximate lips for longer and longer periods during the therapy session.

    d. Awareness of the nasal emission:

        (1) The therapist read nursery rhymes imitating various types of poor speech, including speech with nasal emissions. The child identified the type of speech being used.

        (2) Articulation of sounds with tissue or a feather held under the nose helped the child realize that air was emitted nasally

      (3) Recordings of word lists by both the therapist and the child helped the child hear the nasal emission.

  e. Direction of the breath stream orally:

      (1) Gentle blowing of bubbles with soap and a spool.

      (2) Blowing a candle flame with speech sounds.

      (3) Blowing a piece of tissue during articulation of the sounds of speech.

      (4) Races with balls of tissue.

      (5) Use of the box with tissue paper in illustrating the oral emission of air during the articulation of the consonants.

  f. Attempt to articulate specific consonants without nasal emission:

      (1) Drill before the mirror with tissue and feathers held alternately under mouth and nose helped the child emit the sounds orally.

      (2) Drill and speech games with the picture cards for the consonants presented. The child named and talked about the pictures. The spinner game, the hiding game, and a memory game were all played.

      (3) The game of tic-tac-toe elicited much good discrimination and articulation of the consonants presented both in isolation and nonsense syllables.

      (4) Much work with the notebook was utilized. Pictures of objects which illustrated the use of the consonants in all positions were placed in the book. Stories and sentences were written about them. The child found her own pictures in magazines and books to provide some additional training in discrimination.

B. *Report on group therapy*

    This child had the best speech in the group at the beginning of therapy, and still did, at the close. A quiet child, always well behaved, she became a member of the group quickly and always co-operated both with the therapist and the other members of the group. She made definite progress toward each of the goals listed above.

C. *Problems in attaining goals*

    There really are no problems in working with this child. Co-operative, intelligent, happy, she worked hard and had excellent speech at the beginning of therapy. However, the very excellence of her speech provided a difficulty in that there was little speech work that was needed. Her one remaining difficulty, the nasal emission, is a problem which may take years to correct, if indeed, considering the shortened palate and the diminished mobility of the palatal musculature, it may ever be corrected. Some improvement will undoubtedly be seen following the forthcoming surgery which will close the last opening in the palate.

D. *Progress*

    This child with her exceptionally good speech, her fine attitude, and her intelligent hard work, made the following observable progress:

1. She can now hear and recognize the nasal emissions in her speech and seems to understand why they are there and what she must do if she is to correct them.
2. Progress was made in the articulation of a less distorted *d* and *s*.
3. It is believed that the child is less worried about her speech, happier over the great progress she has made, and better able to accept the remaining defects which she may never be able to correct.
4. Very real progress was made in correcting the droop of the lower lip. She can approximate the lips for fairly long periods of time, and is eager to continue to work toward strengthening the lip muscles.
5. The child has better control of the breath stream, and can project it more consistently than at the start of the session.
6. The mother was counselled during the Mother's Workshop to modify some of her perfectionist goals for the child. Linda needs relaxation and fun.

III. SOCIAL ADJUSTMENT

As in all the other developmental aspects, Linda is socially mature for her age. However, this can be harmful, and the therapist was pleased to see the child assert herself more and become more lively and animated in both the group and individual therapy sessions.

V. SUBMUCOUS CLEFT OF VELUM

Christine: girl, 5 years of age, *submucous cleft of velum*. Entered 6/18/54; born 9/21/49. General description: tiny, beautiful girl; very regular features. Shy, but adjusted easily to the Center. Lives with grandmother and mother. No siblings and no playmates of her age in the neighborhood.

I. DIAGNOSIS

A. *General*

1. Submucous cleft of the soft palate. Uvula appears to be double. Velar tissue is thin; cross-striations are plainly visible.
2. Velar-pharyngeal closure: fair. There is considerable movement of the soft palate during vocalization.
3. Dental anomalies: dental caries.
4. Nasal anomalies: none.
5. Lip mobility: good.
6. Tongue mobility: only fair function, but potential is good.
7. Laterality: right.
8. Psychological evaluation: IQ 109 (Leiter International Performance Scale. Behavior is purposive; established rapport easily.)
9. Audiometric evaluation: Hearing is within normal range for all speech frequencies.

B. *Specific*
1. All consonants (with exception of those noted in (2) are distorted or omitted.
2. Sound substitutions: *w/th* [θ]; *p̃/f*; *sh* [ʃ]/ *ch* [tʃ].
3. Intra-oral pressure inadequate for all consonants.
4. Voice
    a. Quality: hypernasal
    b. Loudness: inadequate
    c. Pitch: fairly normal for age and sex

II. SPEECH THERAPY, PROBLEMS, AND PROGRESS

A. *The purposes of the therapy center in the development of greater oral resonance and in accurate articulation of the consonants. To this end, we attempted to:*
1. Develop intra-oral pressure.
2. Increase front mouth action: tongue-tip, lips, larger mouth opening.
3. Develop acoustic awareness and accurate sound discrimination.
4. Establish accurate articulation of *p, b, l.*

B. *Development of intra-oral pressure through:* (*a*) impounding the air, puffing up cheeks, sudden release; (*b*) forcible pressure of lips; hold impounded breath stream, then explode into *p*; (*c*) blowing: clown whizzer, wall fan, ping-pong ball over notched wood-bar; harmonica. Pressure-difference between *p* and *b* also established.

C. *Development of tongue-tip activity:* (*a*) follow movements of objects with tongue—airplanes, cars, flags, birds; (*b*) control of tongue while orange stick was held between the teeth (and over dorsum of tongue); (*c*) moving tongue around the "house" and into various "rooms;" (*d*) licking the lollipop.

D. *Stimulation and production of* p *and* b
1. Discrimination practice: (*a*) objects, names of which began either with same or different sound; (*b*) series of sounds presented during which she advanced a step on the speech-ladder when she heard *p* or *b;* (*c*) pictures in groups of three from which she selected the one that "did not belong," i.e., word represented did not begin with *p* or *b.*
2. Acoustic stimulation: (*a*) "Listen and say" stories: *The Pop-Corn Man, The Bunny Who Wanted a Motor, The Rabbit Hop.* (*b*) "Bozo, the Puppet says ⸺." (Hand puppet says the vowel merry-go-round [wheel with *p* at center].)
3. Pictures of objects and situations calling for *p-b* words and stories placed in her speech journal. Both instructor and child made up short stories about the picture.
4. Carry-over devices: "I'm going on a trip, and I'm going to take with me ⸺" (bag, bows, belts, beads, etc.); "I spy ⸺"; winning in farm lotto: pony, pig, barn, crib, porch, etc.
5. Telling the story: *The Plump Pig, The Three Bears, Peter Rabbit.*

E. *Stimulation and production of* 1.

1. The same procedure as for D (above) except in choice of illustrative materials: *The Lion Who Couldn't Talk; Little Lamb's Story* (recording, Encyclopedia Britannica Films); *Sing and Say* (Speech Development Records for Children by Elaine Mikelson); Fruit lotto (lemons, plums, melons, apples, etc.); singing: *Looby Lou, London Bridge.*

F. *Report of group therapy*

As "Chrissie" became more confident, the speech improved both in quality and quantity. She chose the part of the troll in *Three Billy Goats Gruff.* She obviously enjoyed being the leader. Although she was smaller than the others she made her way quite easily.

G. *Problems*

Cannot hope for better palatal action; palatal deficiency will always be present.

H. *Progress*

1. Definite improvement in intra-oral pressure.
2. Sound discrimination now is very good.
3. Tongue control also improved noticeably.
4. Accurate articulation of the consonants *p* and *b* was achieved in the initial position. This new pattern was carried over into spontaneous speech.
5. Accurate articulation for the consonant *l* was achieved in all three positions. This was carried over into free speech.

VI. *SUBMUCOUS CLEFT AND PALATAL INSUFFICIENCY; PROSTHESIS*

Donald, boy, 6½ years of age; *submucous cleft of velum; bifid uvula; congenital palatal insufficiency; frenulum of tongue very short; uses prosthetic aid.* Born: 1/21/49; entered Center 6/13/55. Description of child's appearance and speech at entrance: speech very nasal; talks easily; well-nourished child; pleasant.

I. DIAGNOSIS

A. *General*

1. Description of the cleft: submucous cleft of the velum, bifid uvula and congenital palatal insufficiency. Palate is inadequate for closure.
2. Foreshortened frenulum of tongue: surgical correction of foreshortened frenulum by Z-plasty which removed the web and mobilized the tongue. Surgery performed by plastic surgeon, Rockford, Illinois, July 14, 1955. The tongue-tip now moves easily to the alveolar ridge. When the tongue is relaxed, the dorsum still is elevated. Donald is able to produce all consonants requiring tongue action.

3. Ears: There is a healed central perforation of the right tympanic membrane and moderate retraction. The left tympanic membrane is normal.

4. Velar-pharyngeal closure: Speech is quite nasal unless adequate projection is used. He uses such compensatory movement as constriction of facial muscles, depression of the alae, etc. in order to effect velar-pharyngeal closure.

5. Lips: The use of the lips is poor. Retraction and protrusion are potentially good. He is capable of good lip movement; however, he does not use it in conversation.

6. Audiometric evaluation: 6/18/55

	250	500	1000	2000	4000	8000
Left ear:	15	20	30	15	15	30
Right ear:	5	5	10	5	0	5

Remarks: A valid test.

7. Psychometric evaluation: Stanford-Binet Scale.
   C.A. 6-5
   M.A. 6-8
   IQ   104

8. Laterality: left.

B. *Specific*

1. Articulation
   a. Substitutions are as follows:
      Initial position: *m/b, b/r, s/z.*
      Medial position: *m/p, s/z, sh [ʃ]/ ch [tʃ].*
      Final position: *sh [ʃ]/ ch [tʃ].*
   b. Omissions are as follows:
      Final position: *th [θ], l, z, k.*
   c. Distortions are as follows:
      Initial: *t, d, l, r, th [θ], j [dʒ].*
      Medial: *t, d, l, r, th [θ], zh [ʒ], g.*
      Final: *th [θ], t, d.*

2. There is considerable nasal emission of air on all plosives, sibilants, and fricatives. The intra-oral pressure is not sufficient to produce adequate speech. The structural apparatus for speech is not being used efficiently.

3. Voice: The pitch is normal for the child's age and sex. When Donald projects his voice, the amount of nasality is decreased; otherwise the voice quality tends to be excessively nasal. The intensity is characteristically weak.

II. Significant Data from the Case History

A. *Presence of:*

1. Clefts in other members of the family: Brother (No. 5) has a cleft palate; one-fourth of hard and all of soft palate.

2. Structural deviations in other members of the family: none.

B. *Number of siblings:* 6; propositus is first in family of six children, 3 boys, 3 girls.

C. *Atypical behavior unrelated to the cleft*
   1. Speech: none.
   2. Other: none.

D. *Educational progress:* will be enrolled in first grade in September 1955.

E. *Social development and progress:* finds it easy to make friends. Happy outgoing child with many friends.

III. SPEECH THERAPY, PROBLEMS, AND PROGRESS
   A. *Therapy*
      1. Lip exercises for flexibility of these musculatures. This was done in connection with the production of *p, b, m, f,* and *v.* Vowel exercises such as [u-i; u-i; u-i] were used. The exercises for the lip were co-ordinated with sounds so that the carry-over would be more beneficial and so that it would be easy to make and establish sounds in context.
      2. Intensive drill on tongue mobility followed surgical repair of the frenulum. Direct tongue exercises were done with the use of the mirror and also with motivational material such as lollipops and ice cream cones which necessitated lifting the tongue. After this type of therapy showed results, tongue exercises were combined with the following sounds: *l, t, d, th* [θ], *th* [ð]. This accomplished two purposes: moving the tongue and establishing the sounds in single words and in structured responses.
      3. Intensive drill on the consonant *k* proceeded after auditory stimulation and discrimination. He was able to produce the sound in single word and structured responses without resorting to compensatory movements of the musculature around the eyes and nose.
      4. Work on oral pressure was done in connection with the consonants *p, b, m.*
      5. Projection was stressed through use of poems, telling stories, "sharing times," etc.
      6. Some blowing exercises were used, but this seemed to produce more compensatory movements than did direct work on the sounds where pressure had to be adequate for accurate production.

   B. *Problems*
      1. There has been no real problem in working with Donald. He is interested in improving his speech, works hard and retains easily what he has learned.
      2. There is some evidence of a slight tic. He shakes his head slightly while speaking. This is not apparent all the time. He is aware of the tic.

C. *Progress in individual therapy*

1. The ability to move lips freely for sounds is established on the conscious level. Produces adequate *p, b, r, v.*
2. Don is capable of producing any sound requiring tongue-tip movement. He makes adequate *l, d, th* [θ], *th* [ð], and *t* sounds in single word responses and in structured responses. There is some transfer to conversational speech.
3. The consonant *k* can be produced with adequate pressure and good closure in single word responses and in structured responses.
4. Oral pressure appears good.
5. Don can project his voice when speaking; however, this is not his habitual pattern. When Don uses adequate projection and adequate oral pressure, the amount of nasality is definitely decreased.

D. *Report on progress in group therapy*

Donald participates in group activities with interest. He is always eager to try new things and lack of success does not seem to bother him. He is a quiet, diligent boy even in the group. Donald uses *p, b,* and *m* consistently and *k* less consistently in free speech. His speech is more intelligible since the release of a foreshortened frenulum by surgery in July 1955.

15

Speech Habilitation of the Cerebral-palsied

In 1862, in an obscure English medical journal, a young English physician, Dr. William John Little, summarized his discovery of a "new disease" in which he pictured the victim as feeble-minded, drooling, grimacing, cross-legged in gait, and without intelligible speech.[1]

Everyone who "walks or works" with the cerebral-palsied recognizes that Little's description fits some but not all cerebral-palsied individuals. And although we have come a long way in understanding many of their problems, we must go farther yet in our effort to select those children who have the potential for habilitation, and to provide a program of such comprehension and duration that the individual and society may realize maximum returns from their common investment.

CEREBRAL PALSY: DEFINITIONS

What is cerebral palsy? Even the term has been fraught with misapprehension. Apparently what Little tried to describe was one particular type of cerebral-palsied individual, the spastic, who had come by his disability through birth injury. We shall present two definitions of the term, "cerebral palsy." The first, formulated by Perlstein, has won general acceptance; it is "a condition characterized by paralysis, weakness, inco-ordination or other aberration of *motor function* due to pathology in the *motor control centers* of the brain." [2] This definition limits cerebral palsy to *motor dysfunction* produced by brain damage and eliminates those mentally defective children who also may suffer from motor disability but whose deficiency cannot be ascribed to *pathology* of the central nervous system.

[1] W. J. Little, "On the Influence of Abnormal Parturition, Difficult Labors, Premature Birth, Asphyxia Neonatorum, on the Mental and Physical Condition of the Child, Especially in Relation to Deformities," *Transactions of the Obstetrical Society,* London, Vol. 3 (1862).

[2] M. A. Perlstein, "Medical Aspects of Cerebral Palsy," *American Journal of Occupational Therapy* (April, 1950). Reprint, National Society for Crippled Children and Adults, Chicago.

The second definition more nearly fits our present understanding of the disorder, although it is less frequently defined in this way. Cruickshank and Raus regard cerebral palsy as "one component of a broader brain damage syndrome comprised of neuromotor dysfunction, psychological dysfunction, convulsions and behavior disorders of organic origin." [3] They recognize that in some cerebral-palsied individuals only a single factor may appear; in other individuals any combination of factors can be found. The impairment may be detected only in a mild deficiency in muscular control, so mild that only such fine muscular co-ordinations as those employed in speech betray the palsy; or it may be so severe that arms, legs, head, speech mechanism, hearing, and vision are markedly affected. Indeed, the neurological disability may affect the over-all behavior, including both receptive and expressive powers. The neuromuscular manifestations may be regarded as the most obvious symptoms of cerebral palsy, but other symptoms of mental retardation, atypical language development, disorders in sensory perception (audition, vision, etc.) and behavioral deviations must be taken into account by the speech therapist. The second definition, then, makes cerebral palsy *one of a complex of handicaps:* neuromuscular, emotional, psychological, and sensory; in this light it is not considered an entity. Anyone who has tried to habilitate the speech of the cerebral-palsied knows the complexities of the problem. Presently we shall discuss these several manifestations in great detail. We can best reconcile the two positions by regarding cerebral palsy as the neuromotor component of a brain-damage syndrome.

THE CEREBRAL-PALSIED POPULATION: INCIDENCE

There has been no complete survey of the number of people handicapped by cerebral palsy in the United States, but the estimate presented to the Midcentury White House Conference sets the figure at 300,000 for all ages; for the group, five to twenty-one years of age, at 80,000.[4] Pohl estimates that one cerebral-palsied child in 568 live births survives.[5] This figure agrees fairly closely with Wyllie's survey; he found two cerebral-palsied children among 1000 of school age in England and Wales.[6] Other American investigators who have made careful surveys of particular geographical areas find a greater incidence, varying from three to six cerebral-

[3] W. M. Cruickshank and G. M. Raus, eds., *Cerebral Palsy,* (Syracuse, New York, Syracuse University Press, 1955), p. 2.

[4] W. Johnson, chairman, American Speech and Hearing Association Committee on the Midcentury White House Conference, "Speech Disorders and Speech Correction," *Journal of Speech and Hearing Disorders,* Vol. 17, No. 2 (1952), p. 130.

[5] J. F. Pohl, *Cerebral Palsy* (St. Paul, Minnesota, Bruce Pub., 1950), p. 1.

[6] W. G. Wyllie, in A. Feiling, ed., *Modern Trends in Neurology* (London, Butterworth and Company, 1951), Ch. 4, p. 125.

palsied live births in 1000.[7] It is probably safe to conclude that at least three children in 1000 live births will be cerebral-palsied.

In view of these figures one might ask why this group has been so great a concern of the speech therapist. Three hundred thousand people represent a small percentage of the total population. It should be noted, however, that three-fourths of this group will have handicapping speech and hearing defects. And this handicap in communication becomes the individual's greatest deterrent to social acceptance, employability, and economic independence. Unless these individuals can develop intelligible speech, the doors of economic independence and self-realization on all levels are closed permanently to them. "If I only could tell you what I know!," wrote a ten-year-old athetoid to the author. What a world of frustration and agony is encompassed in this outburst, only those who have suffered alike or those who work closely with the cerebral-palsied can appreciate. The handicap in speech for these folk is far greater than the inability to walk or to write. Furthermore, speech calls upon a higher degree of accuracy in muscle movement than most of our motor activities. Precise movement has many components: direction, force, sequence, and duration; hence the way of re-education in speech is more difficult than in grosser motor activities. Even if there are only 60,000 cerebral-palsied young people (five to twenty-one years) with speech handicaps in the United States, the serious nature of the disability and the long road of habilitation make it one of prime importance to speech therapists.[8]

There are positive statements in the literature to the effect that incidence is higher in the first-born than in those born later, but very recent investigations do not confirm these statements. In an exhaustive study in New Jersey, more cerebral-palsied children were second in birth order than first.[9] More cerebral-palsied children are males than females, the ratio being about 1.3 to 1.

CAUSES OF CEREBRAL PALSY

The brain may be damaged by many agents—mechanical, infectious, metabolic, and genetic—but the common end result of most of these agents is interference with the oxygen supply to the central nervous system. The interference may take place before, during, or after birth.

[7] *Joint Committee to Study the Problem of Cerebral Palsy, Report to the Legislature of the State of New York,* Legislative Documents No. 55 (1949) and No. 61 (1953).

Connecticut State Department of Health, *The Study of Cerebral Palsy in Connecticut* (Hartford, Connecticut, State Department of Health, 1951).

[8] Snidecor estimates that 60 to 70 per cent of this group needs speech re-education. J. C. Snidecor, "The Speech Correctionist on the Cerebral Palsy Team," *Journal of Speech and Hearing Disorders,* Vol. 13, No. 1 (1948), pp. 67-70.

[9] T. Hopkins, H. V. Bice, and K. Colton, *Evaluation and Education of the Cerebral Palsied Child* (Washington, D.C., International Council for Exceptional Children, 1954).

Prenatal Causes

The brain is particularly susceptible to the loss of oxygen at any time and during the intensive period of its fetal development, six weeks to six months, it does not tolerate even a minimal oxygen deficit. One of the cerebral areas of richest blood supply and therefore most susceptible to anoxia (oxygen deficiency) is the premotor cortex. (See pp. 56-58.) Any infectious agent such as rubella (German measles) in the mother; or maternal diabetes, a metabolic agent; or a mechanical agent such as irradiation is known to produce irreparable brain damage of which cerebral palsy may be one manifestation.

Natal Causes

"The most difficult hurdle of life is birth." If the most recent surveys are correct, birth injury is still the most common cause of cerebral palsy. Pressures resulting from the use of forceps and from prolonged labor, breech delivery, or precipitate delivery can produce serious damage to neural tissue. Prematurity is a second major cause of brain damage at birth. The hazards of prematurity are several, namely, the small size and fragility of blood vessels which prevent the brain from receiving a normal supply of oxygen under normal tension; the inability of the premature to withstand changes in pressure without intracranial hemorrhage; and the delay in resuscitation following birth. Any one of these hazards may be sufficient to produce brain damage.

Paranatal Causes

The presence of an incompatible blood pattern between mother and child, the Rh factor, which is another established cause of cerebral palsy, is regarded by some leaders in the field as a paranatal (beyond birth) occurrence, by others as fetal or prenatal in origin. The Rh factor is thought to account only for approximately 3 per cent of the cerebral-palsied. As the infant develops, he also may suffer such infectious diseases as encephalitis and meningitis, of which cerebral palsy may be a sequela. Vascular disturbances and trauma to the skull after birth also have been known to produce cerebral palsy.

TYPES OF CEREBRAL PALSY

Five types or categories of neuromuscular involvement are commonly recognized: spasticity, athetosis, tension athetosis, ataxia, and rigidity; but these categories are not definitive either with respect to behavioral manifestations or the loci of neural damage. In this discussion, we shall be concerned with the three types occurring most frequently: spasticity, athetosis, and ataxia.

Spasticity

Forty to seventy per cent of the cerebral-palsied are said to be spastic.[10] This syndrome is characterized by exaggerated contractions of muscles when subjected to stretch (stretch reflex), clonic movements (alternating contractions and relaxations), and increased resistance to movement. In the classic picture of severe spasticity, the individual is described as one who walks with a jerky, unrhythmic gait, the legs rotated inward, the knees adducted, the heel lifted from the ground, the arm flexed against gravity, and the wrist and fingers flexed.[11] In some mild cases, the symptoms may be limited to strabismus, drooling, and hyperactive, distractible behavior. In very mild cases the only diagnostic sign may be the "extended" appearance of the fingers and rotation of the wrists in reaching for objects.

Formerly it was thought that spasticity resulted from damage to the primary motor area in the frontal lobe of the cerebral cortex (*Area 4:* see p. 47). This is the area in which the voluntary motor or pyramidal pathway originates. More recent research, however, has modified this concept and places the possible sites of damage at several points: the extrapyramidal zone (*Area 6,* p. 57), the premotor strip known as *4-S,* lying between *Areas 4* and *6* (p. 57), and other points on the extrapyramidal circuit such as the striate bodies basal nuclei, midbrain, and pons. (See Fig. 15-1.) [12] Grinker and Bucy conclude that "the old concept that spasticity and hyperactive tendon reflexes are a manifestation of damage to the pyramidal tract is erroneous. . . . A release of the postural reflexes from inhibition and the appearance of spasticity may result from destruction of the extrapyramidal system at several different points." [13] This release of the stretch reflexes from central inhibition and increased excitation from other neural areas result in exaggerated muscle tonicity and also interrupt the normal phasic responses of muscles.[14] The sequence of tensor and flexor action is disturbed resulting in alternating contraction and relaxation. When a motion is attempted, for example, the resistance to movement by the antagonists which normally would be inhibited increases markedly, and prolonged involuntary

[10] W. M. Phelps, "Recent Trends in Cerebral Palsy," Archives of Physical Therapy, Vol. 23 (June, 1942), p. 332.

Pohl, *op. cit.,* p. 13.

[11] Pohl, *op. cit.,* p. 7.

[12] J. F. Fulton, *Physiology of the Nervous System* (New York, Oxford Press, 1943), ix.

M. Hines, "Control of Movements by the Cerebral Cortex in Primates," *Biological Review,* Vol. 18, No. 1 (1943), pp. 1-31.

W. K. Welch and M. A. Kennard, "Relation of the Cerebral Cortex to Spasticity and Flaccidity," *Journal of Neurophysiology,* Vol. 7 (September, 1944), pp. 255-268.

[13] R. R. Grinker and P. C. Bucy: *Neurology,* 4th ed. (Springfield, Illinois, Charles C. Thomas, Publisher, 1949), pp. 275-276.

[14] Magoun and Rhines demonstrate that both central inhibition and central facilitation operate to produce the exaggerated stretch reflex. See H. W. Magoun and Ruth Rhines, *Spasticity* (Springfield, Illinois, Charles C. Thomas, Publisher, 1947).

muscular spasms follow. Whereas the "central governors" in the nervous system normally select, time, and grade muscle contraction, the spastic muscles, deprived of such governors, respond maximally to all stimuli.

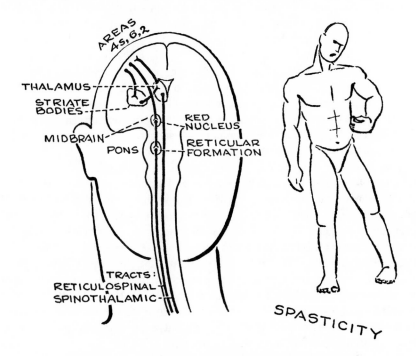

FIGURE 15-1. Possible sites of neural injury in spasticity.

Spastic speech is recognized by its slow, labored rate, lack of vocal inflection, guttural or breathy quality of voice, uncontrolled volume, and, most important, grave articulatory problems which reflect the inability to secure graded, synchronous movements of the tongue, lips, and jaw. Often the dysfunction in the laryngeal muscles produces sudden explosive increases in volume or abrupt changes in pitch, all without reference to the content of expression.

Athetosis

The athetoid group is somewhat smaller than the spastic. Estimates vary, but it is generally thought that from 20 to 30 per cent of the total number of cerebral-palsied individuals is athetoid. This syndrome, athetosis, is a form of involuntary, abnormal movement involving the skeletal musculature and characterized chiefly by its slow, writhing pattern. The muscle tone is usually increased, but it is not constant, so that sometimes the muscles may be normal in tone or even flaccid. When the effort to counteract this excess motion becomes habitual, the resulting counter-contraction of the muscles produces a different syndrome called tension-athetosis.

A single clinical picture of the athetoid is difficult to draw, but the following behavioral manifestations suggest the general outline: The posture changes almost constantly, but certain postures recur so frequently and regularly that they may be considered typical. The fingers, for example, are generally hyperextended and abducted, the wrists flexed, the forearm bent forward so that the palm of the hand is down, the plantar section of the sole of the foot flexed and inverted. The head often is retracted and rotated to one side. Facial grimaces may be constant. The mouth often is open and the tongue protruded. Slow, writhing movements are particularly noticeable in the hands and arms. These movements are accentuated by voluntary effort and emotional tension. They are absent during sleep.[15]

There is general agreement that athetosis is the result of lesion in the extrapyramidal system, but all the areas and tracts comprising this system still are undetermined. Some authorities would limit the lesion to the basal nuclei (striate bodies: see p. 51), and the pathways proceeding to and from these nuclei. Others extend the extrapyramidal system to include the nuclei in the cerebral cortex (notably *Area 6:* see p. 57), nuclei in the thalamus, midbrain, pons, and cerebellum, and the fiber tracts linking these areas and sending fibers to join the pyramidal tracts mediating voluntary responses. (See Fig. 15-2.) One may conclude that the site and degree of damage to the extrapyramidal system will determine the specific character of the motor behavior of the athetoid. The atypical manifestations may be limited and discrete or diverse and complex.

The speech of the athetoid, likewise, will not fit one stereotype. The individual who suffers from a constant, involuntary shift of tonus from one set of muscles to another, from an overflow of stimuli to muscles unrelated to the activity, and from a lack of direction and kinesthetic perception of movement, particularly noticeable in the tongue and jaw, may have completely unintelligible speech or no speech (mutism). On the other hand, the writer has met "medically-diagnosed athetoids" whose speech exhibits only a slight deviation in rhythm or articulation. In summary, the speech of the athetoid presents varying gradations of a pattern of irregular, shallow, and noisy breathing; whispered, hoarse, or ventricular phonation; and articulatory problems varying from the extremes of complete mutism or extreme dysarthria to a slight awkwardness in lingual movement. Since 85 per cent of the consonants used in continuous speech are made by the elevation of the sides and tip of the tongue [16] and since 75 per cent of the athetoids have great difficulty in elevating the tongue, it is apparent that distorted produc-

[15] F. R. Ford, *Diseases of the Nervous System in Infancy, Childhood, and Adolescence,* 3rd ed. (Springfield, Illinois, Charles C. Thomas, Publisher, 1952), p. 143.
[16] H. Westlake, *A System for Developing Speech with Cerebral Palsied Children* (Chicago, National Society for Crippled Children and Adults, 1951), p. 8.

tion of consonant sounds may be expected in the majority of cases. A more detailed analysis of muscular dysfunction will be considered in the testing and habilitation of the speech of the cerebral-palsied.

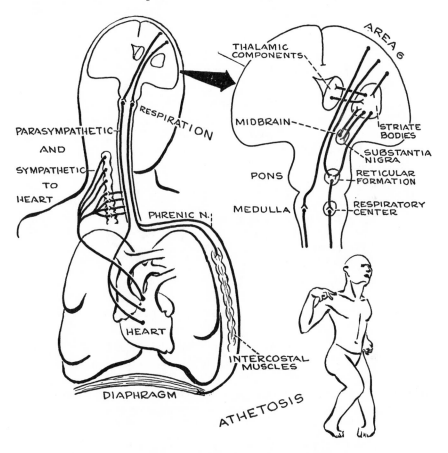

FIGURE 15-2. Possible sites of neural injury in athetosis.

Ataxia

A third group of cerebral-palsied individuals, comprising about 10 per cent of the total number, is known as ataxic. They exhibit a lack of balance and co-ordination in voluntary muscle activity. The non-co-ordination apparently results from an inability to integrate the components of direction, rate, and force in the muscular synergy.

Ataxia usually is ascribed to lesions in the cerebellum or to the pathways which connect it with the brain stem and cerebral cortex. Since athetoids also may be ataxic, it is difficult to prove that the ataxic component arises entirely from damage to one neurological area, the cerebellum and its associated pathways. Multiple pinpoint lesions scattered over the cortex and the brain stem may involve the extrapyramidal system, of which the cerebellum is a part, at various and widely separated points. (See Fig. 15-3.)

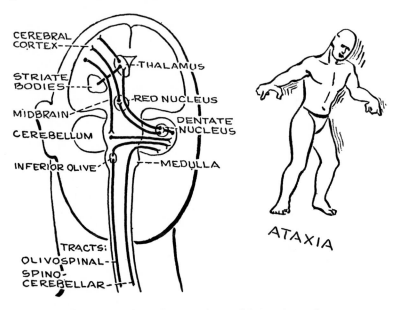

FIGURE 15-3. Possible sites of neural injury in ataxia.

The speech of the ataxic may be characterized by a slurring of articulation which lapses into unintelligibility if speech is continued beyond phrases or short sentences. Rhythm is disturbed and vocal pitch, loudness, and quality tend either to be monotonal or to vary spasmodically and without respect to meaning.

RELATED PROBLEMS IN SPEECH HABILITATION OF THE CEREBRAL-PALSIED

There are cerebral-palsied children, but there is also the individual cerebral-palsied child. So diverse are the problems that one cannot draw a single or a composite picture of cerebral-palsied children. Even within one group, the athetoid, for example, there are wide differences in muscular involvement, intellectual loss, sensory disability (peripheral and central), and emotional impairment. The neural damage may be limited to certain circumscribed areas or diffused over large, contiguous areas, or contained in small and widely separated areas in the cerebral cortex and subcortex. One would expect, therefore, to find a variety of associated neural problems which complicate habilitation of the speech of the cerebral-palsied. It is to these associated problems that we now give consideration.

Special Sensory Impairments

Audition. Palmer found in his study [17] that 25 per cent of the cerebral-palsied suffer from hearing losses of a receptive nature, but suggests that the incidence of loss among the athetoids is much greater. Others [18] report a definite loss (25db for three or more speech frequencies) in 13 to 15 per cent of the cerebral-palsied population. The loss attributable to the general syndrome of brain damage probably does not arise from cochlear dysfunction but rather from damage to the cochlear nerve as it enters the medulla or to the tracts and acoustic areas within the brain stem and temporal cortex.

If the loci of lesion in the cortex involve interpretive areas (Wernicke's, for example) or associated pathways, another type of central involvement, auditory aphasia, results. The individual hears and recognizes the sounds of the words, but he is not able to perceive their meaning. The general subject of aphasia will be discussed in greater detail in Chapter 16.

Vision. Spastic and ataxic children suffer more frequently from peripheral and central defects of vision,[19] although word blindness, for example, is not unknown among the athetoids. In this type of disorder known as dyslexia, the individual is not able to recognize the meaning of written or printed symbols. Recent investigations indicate that the loss may be in one or several areas associated with the organization of patterns of visual symbols: the midbrain, the lateral geniculate bodies, the thalamus, or the parieto-occipital cortex.

General Intellectual Deficits

The speech therapist must reckon with the possibility that the neural damage is so widespread as to result in generally enfeebled intelligence. The end of habilitation is to utilize undamaged areas, forcing upon these areas functions which "belong" normally to the damaged zones. There may not be, however, enough undamaged neural tissue to "pre-empt" for retraining. On the basis of test scores on the Stanford-Binet and Children's Wechsler intelligence scales administered to several thousand cerebral-palsied children, about one-half of the group earned intelligence quotients below 70; and approximately three-fourths had quotients below 90.[20] There was no material difference between the spastic and athetoid groups in intelligence.

[17] M. F. Palmer, "Speech Therapy in Cerebral Palsy," *The Journal of Pediatrics,* Vol. 40, No. 4 (1952), pp. 522-523.

[18] Hopkins, Bice, and Colton, *op. cit.,* p. 114.

B. R. Rutherford, "Hearing Loss in Cerebral-Palsied Children," *Journal of Speech Disorders,* Vol. 10, No. 3 (1945), pp. 237-240.

[19] Marion Cass, *Speech Habilitation in Cerebral Palsy* (New York, Columbia University Press, 1951), p. 18.

[20] H. V. Bice and W. M. Cruickshank, "The Evaluation of Intelligence," in W. M. Cruickshank and G. M. Raus, eds., *Cerebral Palsy* (Syracuse, New York, Syracuse University Press, 1955), p. 103.

Special Psychological Deviations

The atypical learning behavior of some cerebral-palsied children presents unusual problems in speech habilitation. We shall discuss three common behavior patterns which reflect psychological deficits of a specialized nature and which interfere with speech learning.

Distractibility. Learning involves the central power to inhibit responses to stimuli, both external and internal, and so to attend to the task at hand until the goal is achieved. The cerebral-palsied may over-react to all stimuli: changes in temperature, noises, pictures in the room, movement around him, and less evidently but nonetheless forcefully, to the sensory and associative impulses within the cortex and brain stem which overflow and which he has not learned to inhibit. Not only must the teacher of the cerebral-palsied reduce the number of stimuli present in the teaching situation; she also must teach the child to control voluntarily his own external, overstimulating environment and his internal nervous and emotional milieu so that he may realize a measure of stability and optimum integration for learning.

Defective Perception of Form and Space. Perception of form and space frequently is altered in the cerebral-palsied child. In attending to a puzzle, for example, he often pays more attention to the strange configuration of a piece than to its place in the puzzle. If it is a picture-puzzle he may interpret it in a bizarre manner, suggesting a possible but scarcely a logical concept. In a sorting test of edibles and nonedibles, nine of thirty-two spastic children grouped them according to color size, three grouped them according to familiar use, and one was unable to see any relationship.[21]

Perseveration. Goldstein, Eisenson, and other investigators of the brain-injured have called attention to the perseverative tendencies of these children. Their inability to shift quickly to new patterns of response is easily recognized in the speech clinic. Long after one speech situation has passed, the child often repeats the earlier response to a very different speech situation. This same inability to shift the response and to adapt to a new metier is apparent in his desire to stereotype all responses. On one occasion a cerebral-palsied boy, acting as announcer for a radio program had only to change one phrase, "this morning" to "this evening" in his introduction of the later program. Although the program was given on three successive days he was unable to modify his stereotyped response sufficiently to change the phrase from that which he had first learned. Is the clinician justified from a pedagogical point of view, then, in stressing repetition of the exercise, of the word, of the phrase? Is it possible that one thereby reduces further the already narrow margin of modifiability and lability of response of the cerebral-palsied? The clinician here, as elsewhere, steers a course between misgiving and uncertainty.

[21] A. A. Strauss and L. E. Lehtinen, *Psychopathology and Education of the Brain-Injured Child* (New York, Grune and Stratton, 1951), p. 57.

In moving from one level of thinking to another, the cerebral-palsied, likewise, finds it difficult to modify his neural behavior in order to achieve such a shift. So he prefers often to deal only in concrete verbalization rather than to venture into levels of abstraction calling upon a lability and ease of adjustment which he does not possess. But one is reminded, too, of a similar desire in college students; perhaps the shortcoming is not peculiar to the cerebral-palsied but to man.

Manifestations of Atypical Laterality. Many cerebral-palsied children are seriously retarded in developing unilaterality in motor response. Hand preference in the normal child, for example, is generally established by five years, whereas many cerebral-palsied children are still ambilateral at eight years. It has been suggested that the failure to establish unilaterality results either from damage to the originally "dominant" or lead hemisphere in the brain, or from a basic reduction in neural gradient affecting both hemispheres. The bearing of laterality upon speech development also is hypothetical. West is of the opinion that the chances of speech improvement are slight in cases of right hemiplegia of a normally right-handed child, whose parents and whose siblings are right-handed.[22] It has been the writer's observation that when unilaterality has been established, nervous tension is reduced and the problems in reading, writing, and speaking are fewer.

TESTING THE SPEECH POTENTIALITIES OF THE CEREBRAL-PALSIED

Motor Development

Since speech is essentially a motor activity and follows closely the order and form of general motor development, it is necessary to learn the schedule of motor growth in the cerebral-palsied child in the first conferences with his parents. When did he learn to hold up his head? to sit without support? to walk? to use the arms and hands in reaching and grasping? Since walking is dependent upon the controls learned in sitting and standing, he should not be urged to walk until he has realized the preceding goals. And if he is learning to walk, it probably is not wise to introduce speech learning; one complex motor activity is sufficient unto his day. Despite the wishes of parents, stages in motor development cannot be skipped; they are in a chain relationship which must be kept intact.

[22] R. West, "Rehabilitation of Speech," *Journal of Exceptional Children*, Vol. 16, No. 6 (1950), p. 169.
    Bauer and Wepman question the theory of "innate right cerebral dominance" and suggest that individuals commonly regarded as left-handed are more likely to be ambidextrous, and probably should be said to be people in whom lateralization has not fully developed. (R. W. Bauer and J. M. Wepman, "Lateralization of Cerebral Functions," *Journal of Speech and Hearing Disorders*, Vol. 20, No. 2 [1955], pp. 171-177.)

If his general motor development indicates a readiness for speech, the examiner turns to the observation of the motor proficiency of the organs directly concerned in speech. Most authorities believe that speech patterns emerge directly from the vegetative movements of chewing, sucking, and swallowing and hence, one should note such signs of "unreadiness for speech" as drooling, regurgitation of food and air, out-of-phase sucking reflexes during swallowing, and push-pull patterns of the tongue.[23] Although one recognizes these problems of the vegetative synergies, does it follow that their presence is a sign of "unreadiness for speech"? Much attention has been given, for example, to the integrity of the swallowing reflex as a precursor to speech. But, in reality, the laryngeal, velar-pharyngeal, and lingual patterns of swallowing must be altered considerably, if not reversed, in the production of speech. In the dominant oral action of swallowing, the posterior half and base of the tongue rise and move quickly backward, thus forcing the bolus of food into the pharynx. Simultaneously, the larynx rises forcibly.[24] It is these actions which the athetoid must *resist* in phonation and articulation. Is speech, then, actually built upon deglutitory patterns? Would it not be more accurate to say that speech interrupts the normal muscular synergy employed in swallowing? There may be other good reasons why these reflexes must be conditioned before direct speech training begins, but the premise of the evolutionary development of all parts of the speech synergy from vegetative reflexes is questionable.

Breathing

Observe closely the breathing of the athetoid cerebral-palsied child as he attempts to blow out the candles on a birthday cake or to produce a stream of bubbles in a flask by blowing through the tube extending into the water of the flask. His difficulties become apparent almost at once. At one time he may suck the candle flame toward him; or the water rises in the tube when he intended to force it in the opposite direction. One candle may be blown out or none; then, suddenly, in an explosive burst of effort, many candles are extinguished. His cycle of breathing often is distorted, too, when judged either by the time or amplitude of the inspiratory-expiratory movements. Exhalation may be very short and the inspiratory movement long. Or the breathing—as we have observed it particularly in the young spastic child— may be rapid and entirely shallow, providing little oxygenation to the system and insufficient strength in exhalation to produce a steady tone even for three or four seconds. Such breathing anomalies, as Palmer so aptly points out, result in hyperirritability in the respiratory centers which, in

---

[23] Palmer, "Speech Therapy in Cerebral Palsy," *loc. cit.*, Vol. 40, No. 4 (1952), pp. 521-522.
Westlake, *op. cit.*
[24] J. F. Fulton, *ed., Textbook of Physiology*, 16th ed. (Philadelphia, Saunders, 1949), pp. 946-947.

turn, produces even greater irregularities in the breathing cycle.[25] And, as we indicated in the examples above, there may be constant opposition in the thoracico-abdominal muscles so that the diaphragm is being forced up by the abdominal muscles, an act of exhalation, just as certain thoracic muscles which normally act in inhalation contract to enlarge the chest. The result is reversed breathing, which either may be constant or so irregular that it baffles the cerebral-palsied child when he attempts speech.

A further complicating factor which we have noted particularly in the athetoid is the obstruction of the breath stream either by partial adduction of the vocal folds, or by the elevation of the posterior tongue, or by extreme constriction of the oropharynx. The result is labored, stertorous, "noisy" breathing which appears as he gets ready to vocalize.

A study of the breathing pattern of the cerebral-palsied and a plan for re-education of the muscles involved are basic to the production of speech, and hence must be undertaken early in the program. If it is found, however, that the cerebral-palsied child of preschool age can maintain an even, steady exhalation for ten seconds, his breathing probably meets minimum physiological requirements for phonation.[26]

The Larynx

We come next to a consideration of the larynx, where there may be many or few involvements. An adult athetoid at present in the clinic of the writer affords a picture of the numerous phonatory problems which any athetoid may face. In an attempt to close the glottis, he depresses the mandible, buckles the radix of the tongue, pulls the larynx up toward the hyoid bone, and forces extreme contraction upon the constrictor muscles which "wrap" the pharynx with resulting alternating spasms of contraction and relaxation. The result is a tense, tremorous, guttural, breathy tone. Moreover, his attempts to co-ordinate phonation with articulation are entirely unpredictable. "Papa" very often becomes "baba" because phonation has not been synchronized with articulation.

The main questions to be answered in an analysis of laryngeal action are these:

1. What is the position of the larynx in the pharynx?
2. In phonation, is the larynx pulled up into the hyoid notch?
3. Is the larynx abnormal in shape and size? Is the thyroid angle obtuse?
4. Is there evidence of spasms of the vocal folds?
5. Do both vocal folds reach the midline on adduction?
6. Is there evidence of bowing of one or both vocal folds?
7. Is adduction wavering or sustained?
8. Are there extra-laryngeal vibrations produced by the ventricular folds or other tissues in the pharynx?

[25] Palmer, "Speech Therapy in Cerebral Palsy," *loc. cit.,* p. 518.
[26] H. Westlake, *op. cit.,* p. 5.

9. Is the radix of the tongue elevated greatly?
10. Can the person produce a tone without unusual depression of the mandible?
11. Are the thoracic-abdominal movements out of phase with phonation?
12. Are there attempts to phonate on inhalation?
13. Are the articulatory movements out of phase with phonation?

The Mouth

The inability of the young cerebral-palsied child to secure adequate breath pressure cannot be ascribed always or even entirely to asynchronous or shallow breathing. Particularly in the articulation of the plosives and fricatives, the breath pressure often is dissipated by nasal emission. Velar-pharyngeal closure during articulation for speech can be tested by these familiar methods: (1) placing a mirror below the nose in a horizontal position; (2) the "two-step box," on each step of which is a feather; in nasal emission the feather on the upper step is blown off; (3) the two-bottle series with tubes leading into the water in each bottle, one from the nose, one from the mouth; (4) directing the breath stream against ping-pong balls so that they are forced up an inclined plane; (5) blowing "tinsel balls" against a mirror. In the case of the athetoid, the tensor and levator palati muscles and the palatopharyngeus muscles which are concerned with closure of the nasal port may function properly in such reflex activities as yawning and swallowing, but in speech production they are out-of-phase with lingual, labial, and phonatory action. As a result, the closure either is not maintained or is effected too late in the production of the sound.

The Tongue

The most obvious and frequent disability in the cerebral-palsied's articulatory apparatus is the failure of the tongue-tip and blade to rise to the alveolar ridge without approximation of the mandible. Since 85 per cent of our consonants are formed by raising the sides or tip-blade of the tongue, it is apparent how markedly the disability in this single function affects speech. Because of the great number and the complexity of the muscles comprising the tongue, both the general contour of the muscle-mass and the function of the muscles may be bizarre and diverse. One sees most frequently large, amorphous, smooth tongues which fill the entire oral cavity; less frequently we have observed very small, inert tongues whose lateral borders do not reach the molar or incisor teeth. Earlier mention was made of a lingual position which reacts most unfavorably on phonation: the tip is retracted and the radix of the tongue is elevated, riding high against the wall of the pharynx. Another frequent anomaly is the lateral deviation of the tongue in all articulatory efforts. The principal problem of one athetoid now in our clinic is his inability to keep the tongue-tip within the dental ridge. The tongue constantly overshoots the mark when the jaws are approximated. Since the proprioceptive innervation of the tongue normally is rich, it would seem that in many athetoids, the impairment of their proprioceptive pathways must be a very great factor. They appear to have inadequate perception of the position and movement of the tongue. If the tongue-tip can be raised to the gum-line behind the upper front teeth seven or eight times in ten seconds without moving the lower jaw, its action may be considered to be adequate for developing speech.

In summary, the major questions of lingual movement which the examiner must answer are these:

1. When the tongue is resting, does the front tongue protrude beyond the teeth?
2. Does the tongue move in random manner when the subject is not attempting speech?
3. Is this patient able to raise the tip and blade of the tongue without raising the mandible?
4. In articulatory attempts, does the tongue deviate to left or right?
5. In articulatory movements, does the tongue-tip regularly protrude beyond the teeth ridge?
6. Are the general movements of the tongue random and undirected when the subject attempts speech?
7. Are the dorsum and radix of the tongue raised and impinging upon the pharyngeal walls even in the production of such open vowel sounds as "ah" and "eh"?
8. Is the mass of the tongue large, amorphic, filling the mouth cavity?
9. Is the mass of the tongue small, inert, showing no occlusion with the molars and incisors?

The Mandible

It is most unfortunate for the general appearance of the cerebral-palsied that the characteristic position of the mouth is open. Although in some cases its converse, a tightly approximated jaw, is seen, the more "typical" picture is that of a constantly depressed jaw. A further complication is the inability of the cerebral-palsied to make fine or speedy adjustments in oral opening. He can either open the mouth wide or close it entirely, but he cannot exercise the moderately fine gradations of opening and closing necessary for intelligible speech. Palmer describes another anomaly, the "mandibular facet slip," which occurs when "various muscular contractures of an aberrant sort" prevent the depression of the jaw "by a simple hinged movement." By a "compensating pull from the external pterygoids," the mandible is slipped from its sockets, thus depressing the jaw but resulting in slow, clumsy, ineffective movements.[27]

[27] M. F. Palmer, "Studies in Clinical Techniques: III. Mandibular Facet Slip in Cerebral Palsy," *Journal of Speech and Hearing Disorders,* Vol. 13. No. 1 (1948), p. 44.

Lips and Cheeks

In the athetoids, notably, and less frequently in the spastics, may be found eccentric movements of the lips varying from a "purse-string closure" to constant inversion of the lower lip so that it rides under the upper incisors. Associated with the writhing labial movements of the athetoid are involuntary contractions of other facial muscles, notably the zygomaticus, risorius, platysma, and buccinator muscles. Frequently when these contractions begin, there is a spreading wave to neighboring muscles of the neck: the sternocleidomastoid, thyrohyoid, genioglossus, and so on. As the athetoid attempts to counteract these contractures, he produces grimaces and gross eccentric movements which not only are unsightly but also are antagonistic to the purposive articulatory movements.

In assessing the skill of lips and cheeks, the therapist should consider these questions:

1. Do the lips close (a) with purse-string action? (b) with the lower lip under the upper incisors? (c) with lateral deviation of the lower lip?
2. Can he close the lips with little compression? with great compression?
3. What is the rate of closure of the lips in saying p (or b)? In 10 seconds: 5, 4. 3 or 2 times?
4. Can he evert the lips evenly? rapidly?
5. Can he protrude the lips evenly?
6. Are there extraneous movements of the facial muscles?
7. Can he control (inhibit) these grimaces? Under what circumstances? Is he free from grimaces when he is not speaking? Are there periods when he can talk freely without grimacing?

Phonetic Equipment

Some cerebral-palsied children, four or five years old, will have no speech. Others will have intelligible though distorted sound production. A few children will show such slight "clumsiness" of the articulatory organs as to require little or no training. The speech therapist needs a phonetic profile of the child. It may be argued that the phonetic equipment varies among the several types of cerebral-palsied children. Is the spastic's sound production, for example, so different from that of the athetoid that no basic profile can be outlined? Irwin reports that "as far as mastery of speech sound elements is concerned, there is no strong statistical evidence that differences exist among spastics, athetoids, and tension athetoids." [28]

The therapist must know the isolated vowels and consonants which the subject can produce with a recognizable though not necessarily acceptable result. He also must test the ability of the subject to link these sounds in syllables and words. In linkage does he prolong the consonants, or are they

[28] O. C. Irwin, "Phonetic Equipment of Spastic and Athetoid Children," *Journal of Speech and Hearing Disorders*, Vol. 20, No. 1 (1955), p. 56.

so weak as to be unrecognizable? Is the subject able to release medial and final consonants or does he prolong them unnecessarily? Can the subject release the voiceless consonant quickly and phonate the vowel on a single expiration? (At present, there are three cerebral-palsied children in the writer's clinic whose speech might be intelligible *if* we could accelerate release and linkage.) In syllable production is he able to observe time values resulting in an acceptable rhythm? These are some phonetic problems which the therapist must answer in determining the phonetic equipment of the cerebral-palsied.

TESTING IMPAIRMENT OF FUNCTIONS ASSOCIATED WITH CEREBRAL-PALSIED SPEECH

Intellectual Deficits

Extensive investigations have been carried on in the special area of the educability of the cerebral-palsied. In view of the vast amounts of energy and funds being expended on this handicapped population, it seems imperative that learning potentials and psychological profiles taking account of general and special intellectual deficits be determined. Most of the reports of investigations thus far raise more questions than they answer. Does the intelligence vary, for example, with the type of cerebral palsy? Hudson [29] was unable to find any differences between the spastic and athetoid groups, a conclusion that is confirmed by Bice and Cruickshank. [30] The spastics and athetoids, however, were found to be clearly superior to the group of ataxias and rigidities. Evans, on the other hand, reported on the basis of his survey in England that "over 60 per cent of the spastics as against 10 per cent of the athetoids were uneducable." [31]

In the total cerebral-palsied population, Phelps estimates that two-thirds is educable. [32] Stone and Deyton report that there now are 60,000 educable cerebral-palsied children of school age in the United States. [33] It would be interesting to learn their definition of "educability." Is a child with an intelligence quotient of 70 educable? As reported earlier in this section, the mean intelligence quotient for the cerebral-palsied has been reported to be below 70. [34] This mean quotient was derived, however, from the administration of the Stanford-Binet and Children's Wechsler tests. Did the administrators of these tests take account of the limited environment and, hence,

[29] A. Hudson, *Psychological Evaluation of Cerebral Palsied Children.* Doctoral dissertation, University of Wisconsin, 1952.

[30] *Op. cit.,* p. 93.

[31] E. S. Evans, in A. Feiling, ed., *Modern Trends in Neurology* (London, Butterworth and Company, 1951), Ch. 5, p. 143.

[32] W. M. Phelps, *The Farthest Corner,* 3rd ed. (Chicago, National Society for Crippled Children and Adults, 1947), p. 10.

[33] E. B. Stone and J. W. Deyton, *Corrective Therapy for the Handicapped Child* (New York, Prentice-Hall, 1951), p. 237.

[34] Bice and Cruickshank. *op. cit.,* p. 103.

restricted experiences of the cerebral-palsied? Did they take cognizance of the fact that tests based on speed, speech proficiency, integrity of hearing, motor proficiency, or a vocabulary based on school experience probably should be removed from the test battery for the severely handicapped in cerebral palsy? Hudson has modified the Arthur Adaptation of the Leiter International Intelligence Scale (which is nonverbal) so that the responses of the child may be detected by eye movement, facial movement, or movement of the head or hands.[35] Other measures of intellectual development which have been used with cerebral-palsied children are the Ammons Full Range Picture Vocabulary Test, Raven's Progressive Matrices, and the Columbia Test of Mental Maturity. The sampling, however, has not been sufficiently large to establish the reliability of the measures in testing the cerebral-palsied.

Despite all the reservations about mental tests and IQ scores which have been suggested here, we must conclude that mental tests, *properly adapted* to the cerebral-palsied child, are an index to his learning level and his adjustment, not to a cerebral-palsied society but to a physically normal, general society in which he must live.[36] The mean quotient for the cerebral-palsied population may not be as low as 70; certainly it is considerably below average. The therapist will be interested, not in one score but the results of tests and re-tests at intervals and under optimum conditions. The amount and rate of growth are more important considerations than a single score. The therapist must be prepared to answer the parents' recurring question, "But his mind is all right, isn't it?" In the overtone he will detect their inability to accept any finding of mental retardation in the child. They protest, in fact, against the possibility of such a finding by citing achievements which they have appraised without reckoning with the child's chronological age. The final answer to their question has been suggested earlier. One must take into account the specialized intellectual problems and unevenness in intellectual growth. One should not answer in terms of a numerical IQ; one may answer in terms of "the age of the child he is most like." [37]

Special psychological deficits, such as perceptual disturbances of form and space, which are associated with cerebral palsy interfere seriously with all learning including speech. Several sections of nonverbal tests of intelligence afford opportunity to observe the child's perception in the construction or completion of block designs. Does he perceive the design as a whole or only a segment of it? Other observations are suggested by these ques-

[35] Hudson, *op. cit*

[36] G. O. Johnson, "Mental Retardation and Cerebral Palsy," in W. M. Cruickshank and G. M. Raus, eds., *Cerebral Palsy* (Syracuse, N. Y., Syracuse University Press, 1955), p. 376.

[37] H. V. Bice, "Group Counselling with Parents of the Cerebral Palsied," *Psychological Problems of Cerebral Palsy* (Chicago, The National Society for Crippled Children and Adults, 1952).

tions: In drawings of figures on a ground, does he attend to the figure or only to some detail in the background? Does he make mistakes in identifying drawings of common animals or similar objects? Can he judge space and distances as evidenced by placing toys on a shelf, reaching for objects, etc.?

Appraisal of Emotional Stability

As cerebral inhibition over motor function is impaired in the cerebral-palsied, so one may expect to find a measure of diminished control over emotions. There are exceptions, to be sure, but the cerebral-palsied child generally laughs easily and long; he also cries easily and long. Because he has a low threshold for stimuli, he over-responds sometimes by such catastrophic reactions as rage, despair, anxiety, or extreme depression. As an adolescent, his emotional responses may be less overt; they often are impulsive, obsessive, and bizarre. If his training and environment are ideal, he may emerge as an emotionally stable adult despite his handicap. His more common lot is anxiety, withdrawal, frustration, and depression.

There are no adequate tests of emotional adjustment for the young palsied child, and as Bice has pointed out, it is most unfair to apply standard tests of emotion to the cerebral-palsied at any age when one realizes "that during genetic development the narcissistic period is seriously extended; that ego development which is dependent on kinesthetic exploration is markedly limited; that the body image is severely disorganized; that the process of introjection and identification is not smooth; and that birth trauma anxiety is a persistent variable." [38] The Vineland Social Maturity Scale administered to the parents offers some valuable clues to the emotional adjustment of child and family. The Goodenough Draw-A-Man and the Bender Visual Gestalt Tests also have been used in studying the child's behavior. However, day-by-day observation of the child is probably the most fruitful method of study. In co-operation with the parents, the clinician will study the child's relation to others, to himself, and to his physical environment. As the study continues, the clinician should be able to detect symptoms of such unhealthy emotional states as violent anger, anxiety, infantile autism, and obsessive and compulsive behavior.

Hearing Losses

We have referred earlier to the high incidence of hearing loss particularly in the athetoid group. The question again is not, "Does he hear?" but "What does he hear?" The therapist will need to determine a speech-hearing quotient, although this is not an easy task with the cerebral-palsied child. The quotient should be derived both from audiometer tests, if the child is able to co-operate in such tests, and from a study of the auditory behavior of the child. Many cerebral-palsied children cannot respond reliably to

---

[38] *Ibid.*

speech or pure-tone audiometry. Informal tests of speech hearing for the very young child which have been described elsewhere also may be tried. (See pp. 454-456). The psychogalvanic skin response test and electro-encephalography (see p. 455) are experimental procedures used with the young child—but they are still experimental. The most reliable data on the hearing of the cerebral-palsied probably will be derived from detailed observation of his auditory behavior over a fairly extensive period. In any case such data should supplement audiometer testing. In these observation periods the therapist will attempt to answer the questions:

1. Does hearing seem to be one source of contact with his environment? Or, does he behave as one unrelated to the environment?
2. Is he unduly apprehensive about movement? Does he watch others warily because he cannot hear, can only see their actions?
3. Are his expressive patterns (laughing, crying, etc.) those of a hearing child?
4. Does he respond to noisemakers (bells, clackers, chimes) when he cannot see them and is deeply absorbed in activity?
5. Does he enjoy sound toys (crying doll, squeaking mouse, sound fire engine) more than silent toys?
6. Is he arrested by your imitation of his vocalizations?
7. What is his response to musical recording?
8. What is his response to sudden amplification of sound against a background of silence? Against a background of music or noise?
9. Does he respond to voice and/or to speech?

By repeated observation of the child's behavioral manifestations of hearing, supplemented by speech and pure-tone audiometry if possible, the therapist should be able to estimate the child's speech-hearing quotient.

Kinesthetic Loss

No satisfactory test of kinesthesia (muscle sense) has been devised, yet it is desirable that the speech therapist evaluate the sensitivity to movement, resistance, and position of the cerebral-palsied. Generally this can best be done by securing the subject's response to pressure applied to the lips and tongue, and to directed movements of the articulatory organs. Through careful observation of the speech attempts, the therapist can determine whether the child actually has an understanding of their position, force and direction.

HABILITATION OF THE CEREBRAL-PALSIED

In the "team approach" to cerebral palsy which is currently employed in urban communities, the family of the cerebral-palsied has the advantage of expert counsel and service from people representing medicine, psychiatry, social work, physical and vocational therapy, special education, and parental organizations. These people act as a committee to formulate and assist in carrying out a comprehensive plan of habilitation of the handicapped child. As a special educator, the speech therapist is a member of this team. The vast majority of speech therapists, however, will work in small communities where they may have only the co-operation of a local physician and a physiotherapist. But whether the speech therapist operates as one of a team or alone, he will need to understand the child's environment, and in many instances, to assist in revamping this environment in the interests of the child.

Psychological Counselling

Counselling the Family. To establish a kind of environment—mental, emotional, and physical—in which the family and the child can live happily is the goal of counselling. The parents, first of all, must accept jointly the child and the problems which his life presents, as *their* problems. Doctors, psychologists, kinfolk, friends, and the neighborhood may have a share in his future, but the first responsibility is the parents'. They may never be able to realize their natural desire to see the child as a reflection of their profile, following their pattern, merging his identity with theirs, but they can, nonetheless, incorporate themselves into his "otherness" and so become a part of his world.

The parents also must seek an emotional security built upon the "three A's of affection, acceptance, and approval." The counsellor may be of great service in helping them to realize that it is natural for them to go through a valley of indecision, of positive rejection, of recurring dreams and wishes to be free of the burden; that it is normal to experience feelings of guilt, self-pity, tension, and depression. The confrontation of these attitudes and feelings through counselling and discussion will help them to accept a realistic view of their problems and to substitute the longer oar of reason for the short oar of emotion in guiding the fragile bark of their family life. If affection, acceptance, and approval yield a good return in emotional security, then the parents must teach the child that he also must trade in these coins. Recently we observed a demanding child of nine years whose street still was a one-way "give-me!" The parents had not denied, restricted, or disciplined the child. They were slaves to the tyranny of this handicapped child.

Acceptance of the child's mental status and progress in learning often is the most difficult of all tasks for the parents. Comparison is made, sometimes quite unconsciously, between sister Ann's school progress and Jimmie's, but Ann is not cerebral-palsied and Jimmie is. Jimmie also hears comments of "inattention" or "laziness" from the disappointed parents. Parents of Jimmie and of all cerebral-palsied children must be able to accept limited goals and to continue to encourage their children to realize their goals.

Parents frequently limit the physical environment of the child to the child's detriment. Recently each one in a class of cerebral-palsied children was asked to tell the group "three wishes" for experiences which he would like to have. These were their typical wishes: "go on a camping or fishing trip," "shop at the supermarket with Mother," "invite my friends to a picnic in the park," and "sing at a birthday party!" It is clear that these handicapped children did not wish to be passive observers of these experiences; they wished to participate actively in cooking hot dogs, pulling in the fish, finding the cans of soup at the market, and singing "Old MacDonald Had a Farm" at a birthday party! Parents of the cerebral-palsied should be on their guard against overprotection and should realize the value to the child of learning-experiences beyond the home.

Counselling the Child. Oftentimes the child cannot ask his own questions, but they are, nonetheless, real and worthy of consideration. How does the child himself regard his problem? Certainly the therapist is aware of the child's frustration resulting from inaccurate or unpredictable movements, or from poor results after great effort, or from constant restrictions of his achievements and his environment. She must understand his unhealthy responses of temper tantrums, negation, retreat from reality, or abnormal demand for attention, but she also must go farther than understanding: she must train him to adopt healthy, socially acceptable responses. She also must teach him to bear frustration without discontent, to cultivate a fearless and venturesome spirit, and to enjoy his life. She may even have to teach him to laugh at himself.

As the child grows out of babyhood into childhood, feelings of inadequacy and inferiority increase. The search for real compensations is a joint undertaking of therapist and child—and sometimes proves to be a difficult one. It may be that there is only a single ability which can be utilized, or one may have to capitalize on general qualities of character. If the child can recognize and admit freely that he is different from others and if he can appreciate why others regard his handicap as they do, he can find, at least, an inner compensation for his inadequacies. The therapist also must assist in developing the child's social responsibility. The fact that the stages of narcissism and egoism are quite naturally prolonged in these children should be understood, but it also should be the clinician's endeavor to shorten these periods and so accelerate the child's social growth. We have been encouraged with the response of cerebral-palsied children to parties which they have given for others and to social activities outside of the home in which they have had to meet with and adjust to other children. The fact that many cerebral-palsied children have learned to enjoy helping others has been most gratifying.

As the child "grows up," the therapist may point out to him particular psychological problems which he can understand even if he cannot solve them immediately. When he knows, for example, that such perceptual disturbances as a faulty conception of time or of direction with which he struggles are common problems of the cerebral-palsied, or that "sticking to a job *after* it is done"—that is, perseveration—also is not unusual, his attitude often changes from defeatism to optimism and courage. A twelve-year-old boy told his teacher recently, "I always seem to see what no one else sees in the picture." When he realized that "seeing by parts rather than wholes" was not unusual in the cerebral-palsied, he was reassured. Even projects to increase the attention span have been more successful when the child understood their purpose.

So the therapist's responsibility can never be limited to direct speech training. Speech embraces the total self and when the cerebral-palsied child or adult has learned through the therapist the proper concept of himself as a person of worth, it will be reflected in all his activities including speech.

Training the Speech of the Cerebral-palsied

Not all cerebral-palsied children need speech habilitation. In some cases the speech will be normal. In others their speech may be slightly arhythmic and monotonous; the tongue may strike the teeth rather than the alveolar ridge in such sounds as *t, d, n,* and *l;* or the quality of voice may be slightly breathy; yet judged by the average level of intelligibility, the speech "passes muster." From this point we find all gradations of speech deficiency, ending in the extremes of complete unintelligibility and mutism.

It is evident that one program or even four or five programs will not include therapy for every possible speech involvement of the cerebral-palsied. In presenting the management of two cases, the writer is attempting to suggest a rationale for habilitation rather than a list of principles and exercises. It is for the student or clinician to select those portions of the therapy which match most nearly the speech problems with which he has to deal.

John is an athetoid, four years old, who has no speech, although he makes "crowing sounds" or vocal attempts when stimulated strongly to do so. The results of the first period of examination and study extending over a three-weeks period (nine hours) may be summarized as follows: Chewing and swallowing reflexes are imperfect; he drools quite constantly. His intelligence is average, his hearing for speech is adequate. He has learned to stand but he is not walking. Sitting posture and head support are fairly good. Breathing is "reversed," shallow, acyclic. In phonation John over-adducts the vocal folds, producing a tense, tremulous, hoarse tone. His attempt to follow a tune learned in the nursery consists in spasmodic "ah-ahs;" he makes some gross pitch and volume changes which bear no resemblance to the melody of the song. If intent upon some object or activity, the vocal folds adduct slightly so that both inspiration and expiration are noisy. Involvement of the articulatory organs is severe: John cannot raise the tip or blade of the tongue; the dorsum can be raised part way but occlusion with the velum is not complete. Consequently, if he attempts the *k* sound he substitutes a weak fricative *h.* The habitual position of the mandible is depressed; if he closes the mouth, the upper teeth always are over the lower lip in the position for *v*. Nasality is relatively slight. A complicating factor is John's lack of motivation. He enjoys complete dependency; he is satisfied to sit in the nursery surrounded by blocks with which he plays in a half-hearted manner. Mention of his mother from whom he is separated brings tears. He likes to be carried and cuddled. In the speech clinic he hides his face when pressure to make speech attempts is applied. On the other hand, he laughs at the assistants engaged in some game of motivation, but he withdraws when attempts are made to make him a member of the group. Only at the last meeting did he attempt to say "Bounce the ball to me." No voice accompanied the attempt, however. He enjoyed the game and tried to participate in the "ring" playing ball by holding out his arms and making a speech attempt. Good!

Training in General and Special Motor Co-ordination for Speech. John was receiving training daily from a physiotherapist in posture and control of the gross muscles. The speech and physical therapists worked together on the control of salivation. An anti-drool mask was constructed which he wore each day for a half hour. Practice in sucking and swallowing, likewise, was a joint venture. The physiotherapist accompanied John to the speech clinic so the training in relaxation also was carried on in co-operation with her. In general we followed this routine:

1. *Passive relaxation of the muscles of the upper extremities with the lower extremities restrained by saddle sandbags.* This is the procedure: the therapist takes control of the arm and directs the child to let the therapist "use it." The child neither assists nor resists the action, but allows the movements; in other words, he inhibits any excitation to response on his own part. Passive relaxation of the extremities is followed by the same procedure with the head and neck muscles. The therapist rotates the head slowly from side to side, back and forward until complete rotation without resistance has been accomplished. When the child has succeeded in inhibiting his own responses, he is asked if he can sense the feeling of relaxation. Can he inhibit the excitatory impulses, and is he aware of the feeling of relaxation? When he achieves this goal with the extremities, relaxation of the muscles of breathing is initiated. Because of the extreme tension of the chest muscles in speech-breathing, restraint is placed on them while relaxation of the diaphragmatic muscles is encouraged. The therapist then "takes control" of the head and neck in order to secure passive relaxation of the supporting muscles in this area. Finally the child is ready for passive relaxation of the muscles most directly and visibly concerned with articulation: the jaw, lips, and tongue. John at present allows the jaw to drop wide open or to be closed by the guiding hand of the therapist but he resists *partial* closure, so important in articulation. Tapping the tongue or cheek with the tongue depressor sometimes is sufficient to induce passive relaxation of these muscles, although relaxation of the tongue still is difficult to achieve.

In the tongue we are dealing with a great group of interdigitating muscles; little wonder that John finds it difficult to "iron out the tongue" even when a small rubber roller is moved across it to aid him in the attempt. The roller, in fact, was a stimulus at first to aimless, writhing movements.

2. *Active relaxation.* The child now "takes over" and relaxes the muscles of the extremities, the chest-abdominal area, the head and neck, and the face and mouth consciously and without help from the therapist. He enjoys playing "Raggedy Ann," particularly when there is musical accompaniment to the verbal directions. That he has had only partial success in relaxing the facial muscles is evident from the fine twitching of the cheek muscles even when the lips apparently are relaxed. When the jaw is lowered, the tongue maintains a relaxed position only for a second, and then is retracted and the dorsum buckled. We have been using some assisting stimuli which, illogically perhaps, have helped him to keep the tongue in a relaxed, forward position. A small piece of gauze laid over the incisors apparently "locates" the tip of the tongue for him and increases his ability to gain control of the whole tongue. Other helpful reinforcers of relaxation are pieces of sponge rubber and corks of various sizes (both secured by strings) which when placed on the tongue encourage relaxation. He releases the tension in the chest muscles during quiet breathing, but he returns to the old pattern when phonation is suggested.

3. *Resisting movement with counter movement.* This step has been particularly helpful in facilitating action of the articulatory muscles. As the therapist moves the mouth into a position for *ōō* [u], John attempts to pull back the corners for *ē* [i]. As the therapist pushes the tongue back with a metal tongue strengthener, the child counteracts the push and often "in the contest" succeeds not only in pushing it forward but as the external pressure is released, often elevates the tip and blade. The therapist begins with considerable pressure and then gradually lessens it, thus preparing the child for "graded contractions."

4. *Active control of breathing muscles.* (It is unfortunate that we did not have the use of a respirator to assist in the establishment of rhythmic breathing. Reports of the use of this instrument are most encouraging.) In order to break a pattern of reversed breathing, we restrained the chest muscles and concentrated the child's attention on diaphragmatic-abdominal control. By gentle blowing of a candle flame, John is able to see the effect of controlled exhalation. He also demonstrates better control when he exhales in rhythm with some bodily activity: hand-clapping, head-nodding, "rocking chair" movement, swinging the arms, or beating a tom-tom.

5. *Active control of articulators.* John's problems now are two: (*a*) to contract and relax a group of muscles with a minimum of effort and (*b*) to grade the contraction and relaxation so that the action may be inhibited at any point before completion. The latter problem apparently is the most difficult of all. On command, John can open his mouth in "three steps"

but, as yet, he has not succeeded in grading the closure. Consequently when he tries to sing "la-la" and is told not to open the mouth quite so widely, he closes it entirely. He has learned inhibition and co-ordination of muscular activity in other larger synergies, however, especially in positions of head and neck and in slight or fine adjustments of the face and lips, so we may hope for success in control of the jaw. In the larger movements of the muscles of expression there are still some after-effects. When told to exaggerate smiling or frowning, for example, he is able to effect the smile or the frown quickly, but there is still evidence of fine twitching in the "relaxed" state.

The tongue remains the stumbling block and greatest deterrent to good speech. Here are some of the devices and exercises which have helped John to gain some measure of control over the tongue:

a. Elevation of the tip and blade
 (1) Suck air or liquid through slightly open lips and over the tongue.
 (2) Chew caramel candy, rolling the candy from side to side and slowly backward.
 (3) With jaw lowered, attempt to remove honey butter or peanut butter from alveoli of palate.
 (4) With tongue strengthener or blade under the tongue, raise the whole body of the tongue.

b. Pointing tongue-tip
 (1) With lollipop or honey on a tongue-blade, have him reach with his tongue for the sweet.
 (2) Dot the area around and beyond the lips with sugar or honey. Ask him to lick it off.
 (3) Suggest fine point by holding orange stick in front of mouth which he touches only with the very tip of the tongue.

c. Raising dorsum of tongue
 (1) Ask the child to yawn and to prolong or hold the yawn at mid-point. He should feel the elevation of the tongue against the palate.
 (2) Have the child "pretend" that he is sneezing. Halt the sneeze at mid-point. Again, does he feel the position of the elevated dorsum?
 (3) Hold the tongue-tip down and push the tongue backward. Is the "hump" of the tongue against the velum?

d. Grooving the tongue along the median raphé: (Since many alveolar sounds: s, z, sh [ʃ], zh [ʒ], and r require elevation of the sides of the tongue, thus producing a channel along which the breath stream slides, it is particularly important that John acquire this adjustment.)
 (1) Place the orange stick along the median groove, apply light pressure, and ask the child to curl the tongue around the stick.
 (2) With coted fingers, raise the sides of the tongue, "sticking" the tongue against the molars and bicuspids as far forward as the lateral incisors. The child then attempts to duplicate the adjustment without assistance.

> (3) Reinforce the "line" by tracing the median raphé with the
> the orange stick, first with heavy, then with light pressu
> tracing, ask him to feel the depression of the longitudinal gro

  e. Aid to the general perception and lability of lingual movement
> (1) Move the tongue-tip from side to side calling on each tooth and its homologue from molars to central incisors.
> (2) Move the tongue in and out of the mouth quickly in a repetitive movement to suggest the lapping of milk.
> (3) Suck liquid through a plastic or glass straw which is bent to lie over the tip and blade of the tongue. Sense the "curling" of sides and backward movement in swallowing.

6. *Auditory stimulation and discrimination of sound.* In stimulating the child to attend to sounds, we have resorted to many familiar devices: sounds of bells (ding, dong), whistles, toy cars, engines; sounds of animals: cat, dog, cow, lamb, etc.; and stimulation through pictures, the "peep-show" audiometer, etc. He also is able now to identify practically all the consonants in simple words said by the therapist.

Co-ordination of Respiration, Phonation, and Articulation in Speech. The therapist pauses at this point to review with John the state of relaxation and muscle control which will produce the right amount of strength and ease for his best voice and articulation. After being shown again how the therapist produces *ah* softly with a *slight* depression of the mandible, with the tongue forward in the mouth, and with a minimum of breath pressure, John tries the sound. From *ah* he proceeds to *ah—oh— ooh,* attempting to make the articulatory changes smooth and continuous. Various visual and auditory methods are employed to encourage length and steadiness of tone: pulling a string slowly from a clown's mouth or drawing a line on the board as long as the tone is continued; phonating into a candle flame with so little wasted breath that the flame is undisturbed; imitation by the clinician of good and poor production of the tone; or by making a tape recording by which the child may judge his own effort.

The next step was to learn the modes of production of speech sounds. We began with the plosives *p, b, t, d, k, g.* John can make satisfactorily the *p* and *b* sounds; *k* and *g* are weak. Although the tongue rises for the latter sounds, its elevation is insufficient to obstruct the breath stream. John is not able to obstruct the breath stream in the front mouth by occlusion of the tongue-tip and blade against the alveolar ridge and, hence, his *t* and *d* sounds do not approach intelligibility. The fricatives, *f* and *v,* have been easy to form, but as yet he does not have sufficient oral pressure to make a good *s* and *z.* Frequently there is nasal emission of the breath stream on these sounds, so that they possess little of the true quality of sibilants. Since he can make a good *th* [θ] and *th* [ð], we now are finding it easier to make the *s* by drawing the tongue back from the *th* [θ] position. The nasal sounds, *m* and *ng* [ŋ], he is able to make, but *n* still is not recognizable.

The mastery of timing of the muscles of breathing, the larynx, and the articulators remains a problem. John is able to say *ba-ba* clearly but he is not able to begin phonation after the *p* sound in *papa;* consequently he either unvoices the word completely or says *ba-ba.* He understands perfectly what he wishes to do but he cannot effect, as yet, the rapid shift in tension of the vocal folds. A second problem is his effort to continue articulation and speech after the expiration cycle has been completed; the result is that he attempts to speak on inhalation.

At the present time we are introducing speech units in order to set the few patterns which John has acquired. The speech units are those which he needs in his life at this point. So such expressions as "Hi"; "Bye"; "I want the ball"; "Milk, please"; "Comb my hair, please"; "Go to bed"; "My shoes off"; and so on are the focal units in our work with meaningful speech. Even these few expressions are not always intelligible to people outside the clinic, but at present we accept and praise every attempt at verbalization. Although this child often cannot respond or participate verbally in the conversation, some part of each clinic hour is devoted to talk about the events in his world: the trip to the park, the nursery school party, or his new suit. At the conclusion of each hour, he is told a portion of the serial story, "Erik of Norway." It promises to be the most protracted tale in all Norse folklore. It does increase, we believe, John's awareness of the world outside, trains him in listening and—we also hope—prompts him to identify John in some exploits with the venturesome Erik of Norway.

The second subject, *Karl,* has been selected not because phenomenal success has been achieved but, on the contrary, because he is representative of many young cerebral-palsied adults who have had years of training but who present, at eighteen or twenty years, physical, psychological, and speech problems, fixed and interrelated, which call for searching analysis and a diverse, labile program of habilitation.

Karl is an athetoid, tall, well-built, with a handsome face when it is in repose. He walks, rides horses, and drives a car, yet he must be considered a severe athetoid because of the serious involvement of speech and because of the extraneous athetoidal movements of head and face which are frequent and bizarre in form. He speaks and walks habitually with the head turned sharply to the left so that he appears to be looking over his shoulder. The motor impairment of limbs is relatively mild.

In analyzing Karl's major problems, we find that there is sufficient breath power but that he does not control its exit and attempts to continue speech after the air supply has been exhausted. Phonation is tense, harsh, guttural, and uncertain in the sense that in the production of a single tone he may begin with a tense but loud tone and end with a whisper. In phonation, the larynx is pulled forward and upward so that it seems to lie beneath the hyoid bone. The thyroid eminence is far too pronounced and the wings of this cartilage "fan out" so that the distance between the vocal folds is greater than in the normal larynx. The result is an increase in the problem of adduction. As Palmer has observed, "the problem of the obtuse angle of the junction of the thyroid cartilage actually lies in hypertonic anomalies of the extrinsic muscles of the larynx. The stretch on the lateral surfaces of the cartilage on each side widens the interarytenoid distance to such an extent that occlusion of the glottis can only be attained with great difficulty." [39] In Karl's case there is also evidence of spasms of the adductor muscles which close the glottis.

The problems of jaw and tongue movement are closely associated with phonation. Karl finds it very difficult to produce any tone unless the mandible is depressed and the tongue retracted. In an effort to control the aberrant, athetoid movements which interfere with depression of the mandible, he frequently slips the mandible from its sockets by contracting the external pterygoid muscles. Grading of the opening and closing of the mandible also presents a problem. The chief muscles producing closure, the masseter and temporalis, bring the jaw up very rapidly and almost at the same instant the muscles which lower the jaw, the geniohyoid, mylohyoid, and digastric, contract swiftly. The lingual difficulties are many. There is habitual retraction of the body of the tongue and elevation of the base. Karl is unable to raise or point the front tongue. The movements, which are clumsy and awkward, often are extraneous to the articulatory adjustments desired for speech. In themselves, the lips perform fairly well except for overcontraction and a tendency of the lower lip to form a closure with the upper teeth on such sounds as s, sh [ʃ], p, and b. The greatest problem is the extraneous muscle action of the face and neck: platysma, buccinators, sternocleidomastoid, etc. which distort facial expression. Accompanying the distortion is a spasmodic, torticollic movement of the head which persists as long as he attempts speech.

An associated factor in assessing the total problem of habilitation is word-blindness. Although he has learned to read simple sentences, he cannot read materials appropriate to his age. There are compensations, however, on which he is capitalizing. He has good hearing and a good mind. He enjoys learning "by ear." International problems, drama, and music are his special interests. He has a vocational and avocational outlet in a riding stable for which he alone is responsible. Karl feels great security in his home. He has found that "love is a coin in which all must trade." Beyond the family circle, however, he has few friends. He makes no effort to seek other cerebral-palsied boys of his age, although some motivation has been given him in this direction. Perhaps he is too sensitive to try his hand at meeting strangers and making friends. One is impressed by his character, by his

[39] M. F. Palmer, "Speech Therapy in Cerebral Palsy," *The Journal of Pediatrics,* Vol. 40, No. 4 (1952), p. 519.

desire to be of service to others, by his sense of worth, and by his good humor. In short, he has faced realistically his problem, but still does not have the "toughness" necessary to face the community. His world is small, too small; he wishes for wider boundaries but he feels that he himself cannot extend them. He has accepted the "lonely way."

Speech and Psychological Habilitation. Karl has learned well the lesson of relaxation and control of the large muscles of the body in his early training. Inhalation is adequate in the breathing cycle, but he has not learned to conserve the breath in exhalation.

Because the bizarre movements of the head and face attracted so much attention, it seemed wise to attack immediately the problem of conscious control of the muscles involved. From passive relaxation of the muscles of the neck, we proceeded to relaxation, to movement against resistance by forcing contrary movement, and finally to active movement under conscious control. Karl received help at this stage by the device of drawing a black line down the median raphé of the chin and then attempting to keep this line centered on a piece of tape pasted on the mirror. He also found helpful negative practice before the mirror of the aberrant contractions which have distorted speech and facial expression.

In direct practice in speech situations, he has learned to wait in greeting another person, for example, until he is sure of control of the head and facial muscles. He reports that he does best when he transfers the physical and mental set he has learned in riding in horse shows to the speech situation. He schools himself to look directly into the eyes of the auditor before he begins to talk. So far he has succeeded pretty well in reducing the aberrant movements in such simple situations as greetings, introductions, and short talks about his avocation—such as his first competition in riding.

Solution of his phonatory problems remains the riddle of the sphinx. If any single bit of advice has helped him, it has been our insistence on reduction of all tension and force in the chest and neck. The result is a voice of low intensity, but this is preferable, we believe, to the explosive, tense voice. Because the position of the larynx has been distorted he tries to keep the larynx in position by manual assistance. With the jaw only slightly depressed he attempts to phonate very softly, *oh* or *ah*. In order to keep the tongue forward in the mouth and so improve the quality of the tone, we have found that a piece of gauze over the lower teeth is a good tactile aid. Our first efforts have been directed toward gaining a steady tone with constant volume and pitch. He now is attempting to change

the volume in a crescendo-diminuendo production of

but the final *oh* generally ends in a whisper. Some improvement in pitch perception has come from his recent practice on a harmonica. At first it was impossible for him to play the scale because he took such "broad steps." He now can play the scale and tries to match his vocal tones with the low tones of the harmonica. He is able to make a few modulations in pitch when tension and pressure have been greatly reduced.

In working with articulation, we began with the jaw because it affected both lingual and laryngeal movement. To teach gradation of movement, the therapist assisted the movement; then Karl directed the jaw himself. Later he practiced before the mirror and recently has been able to lower or raise the jaw in five steps, holding each position for a few seconds. The tongue-tip moves for *la-la,* but he cannot consciously raise the tip-blade to the alveolar ridge with the jaw half depressed. A small rubber eraser or pencil between the teeth has helped him to find the desired jaw position. Other tongue positions which he now is able to assume are (*a*) predorsal section raised, tip down as for *j;* (*b*) sides of tongue against the molars and lateral incisors as for *s;* and (*c*) dorsum occluded against palate as for *k.* He has worked also to reduce the extraneous, writhing movements of the tongue. On command he can shift from *t* (tip down) to *k* without taking intermediate positions. Mirror practice has helped him to inhibit aberrant lingual movement. The lip action is strong although not always accurate. He has used negative practice to keep his lower lip from "folding" under the upper teeth. The chief problem here, however, is the elimination of the writhing movements of facial muscles which pull the lips down and to one side.

Here is a boy whose greatest ambition is to make his speech intelligible and to control hyperactivity and facial grimaces. We believe that he will be able to make himself understood and to reduce the extraneous movement. His speech will never be good; his voice will never be clear. He is, in every sense, a "marginal" person who will find it very difficult to make his way economically or socially in the world. In counselling him, we have attempted to develop in him a quality of "toughness" in facing reality, an interest in new avocations including making friends with other handicapped boys and girls, and a sense of worth of his own life. As yet he is reserved and finds it difficult to reveal his feelings. He has qualities which he should exploit. We have no predictable conclusion to this story. For him we hope for a useful and reasonably satisfying life.

Other Programs of Therapy

All therapists would not follow the regimen which we have just described. Evans,[40] for example, believes that action of the great muscles of the body should accompany vocalization. Specifically, he maintains that the cerebral-palsied individual "should walk or move his body, and while using the larger muscle groups which are usually under some degree of control, he should begin to talk." The basic theory is that if speech is a part of the totality of muscular response, then the improvement of gross muscle action should pre-

[40] M. F. Evans, "Children with Cerebral Palsy," in W. Johnson, *Speech Problems of Children* (New York, Grune and Stratton, 1950), p. 182.

cede and facilitate the improvement of fine muscle action employed in speech. In some cases we have known, attempts at gross bodily action are so absorbing that the subject finds it impossible to attend to the control of the speech mechanism; presumably this might not be the case if the control of the large muscles were mastered prior to speech training.

The Bobath Method. Another rationale of habilitation of the cerebral-palsied has been developed at The Cerebral Palsy Centre in London by Karl and Berta Bobath [41] and by Pauline M. Marland.[42] It is their belief that the lesions in the central nervous system (resulting in cerebral palsy) release the postural reflexes of the body mediated principally by the proprioceptive system. "These reflexes which cannot be observed in the intact human being because they have become modified and changed by the activity of higher centres into more complex and more differentiated motor patterns" [43] appear in exaggerated form in the cerebral-palsied. It is logical, then, to proceed on the basis that cerebral palsy should be treated by inhibiting reflexes, not by utilizing them. So long as exaggerated reflex activity remains unchecked and while there is spasticity, even an unimpaired proprioceptive system can only transmit messages of the abnormal state of tension in muscles and tendons. Movements initiated by response to stimulation of our exteroceptors, especially the eye and ear, are controlled and guided throughout their course by the proprioceptive system. Therefore, if the proprioceptive system cannot fulfill this important function, normal movements cannot take place, and normal patterns of movement cannot be laid down in treatment when muscle tone remains abnormal. If a patient is still under the influence of the primitive reflex patterns which alter his posture against his will, he can hardly be expected to be able to control the muscles of his tongue and lips for speech.

Therefore, the first step in treatment is normalizing the postural tone. In treatment, postures are reversed at the various joints: flexion is changed to extension, pronation to supination, adduction to abduction, and vice versa. These are called reversed postures or "reflex-inhibiting postures." The proximal joints, such as the neck, spine, shoulders, and hips are the most important for this "positioning." Some typical reflex-inhibiting postures are the following:

[41] Berta Bobath, "A Study of Abnormal Posture Reflex Activity in Patients with Lesions of the Central Nervous System," *Physiotherapy* (London), Vol. 40, Nos. 9, 10, 11, 12 (September, October, November, December, 1954), pp. 259-267; 295-300; 326-334; 368-373.

K. Bobath and Berta Bobath, "A Treatment for Cerebral Palsy," *The British Journal of Physical Medicine*, Vol. 15, No. 5 (May, 1952), p. 121.

[42] Pauline M. Marland, "A New Approach to Speech Therapy for Spastics," *International Association of Logopedics and Phoniatrics; VIII, Proceedings of the International Speech and Voice Therapy Conference, Amsterdam*, 1950. (Basel, S. Karger), pp. 14-21.

[43] Berta Bobath, *op. cit.*, No. 9, p. 259.

1. Supine, with flexed abducted knees, shoulders flexed and raised forward on the therapist's arm; head falling far back.
2. Kneel sitting with trunk forward on couch, head down between extended arms; dorsal spine extended.
3. Sitting with legs down over side of couch, hips well flexed, spine extended; extended arms raised to therapist's shoulders; head up (and central) but not back.

In these postures and others, when the initial struggle dies away, a remarkable change comes over the patient. He becomes quieter, and his limbs and body no longer resist the position because muscle tone has become temporarily normal. His facial expression becomes more natural, and breathing, swallowing, and control of salivation improve of their own accord.

The child is considered ready for speech when it is possible to put him into at least one or two reflex-inhibiting postures without difficulty.[44] Such a state indicates that reflex-inhibiting postures are being tolerated; proprioceptive sensations therefore can also be normal. Then the organs of speech not only look and feel different to the therapist, but also to the child. Both in children who have never spoken and those who have already spoken abnormally, the therapist facilitates sustained voicing and repetitive babbling with his hands so that they occur with no effort on the child's part. It helps most children if the therapist imitates the sound he expects him to make. A normal voice may be achieved by further adjustments of posture, especially of the neck and jaw. Breath control can also be steadily increased by this technique without any effort on the part of the child. The child must not only feel these changes in muscle tone, but he must also see and be conscious of what has happened.

After spontaneous voluntary babbling is achieved, the moto-kinesthetic method (with facilitation by the therapist) is used in teaching phonetic placement. Until the child acquires a full repertory of reflex-inhibiting postures, certain consonants are best learned in specific postures. Velar consonants, for example, are learned most easily "with the shoulders forward and head back, while alveolar consonants are easier with head forward and shoulders back."[45] Stimulation of language perception and auditory training may be needed, but they should be given only when the child is in a firmly established reflex-inhibiting posture. After spontaneous babbling and phonetic training have been achieved, the therapist introduces simple words and phrases, guarding always against a return to spasticity.

$$*\quad*\quad*\quad*\quad*$$

[44] Pauline M. Marland, "A New Approach to Speech Therapy for Spastics," *loc. cit.*, p. 19.

[45] Pauline M. Marland, "Speech Therapy for the Cerebral Palsied Based on Reflex-Inhibition," in C. Van Riper, ed., *Speech Therapy* (New York, Prentice-Hall, 1953), p. 237.

In presenting the "case" for the cerebral-palsied, we have assessed the importance of his problem, defined cerebral palsy and discussed the neurological damage involved in three major types: spasticity, athetosis, and ataxia. We have explored the problems both of speech and of the total behavior of the cerebral-palsied individual. Finally, we have outlined several programs of therapy which we defend only by saying, "in some cases they have been successful!"

16

Aphasia
(The Brain-damaged)

In our discussion of the language and speech of persons who have suffered from brain damage, we shall first consider the adult. The relationships of brain damage to linguistic impairment in the adult are relatively clear. The normal adult has usually learned to speak, read, write, and otherwise use language symbols. If he suffers from impairment in these functions following trauma or pathology involving the brain, it is reasonably safe to assume that the impairment resulted from the brain involvement. The young brain-damaged child who has not learned to speak and in general to use language symbols has not developed ways of behavior related to symbol usage. With the adult, we are dealing with modifications of behavior brought about by brain lesion. The problem is one of rehabilitation. With the child, we are dealing essentially with a developmental failure, and the problem is one of special training to compensate for the atypical development.

Aphasia will be used as a general term to indicate linguistic impairment associated with brain lesion. The terms *mild, moderate,* or *severe* will be used to indicate degree of impairment. The reader may also find the term *dysphasia* in the literature to indicate mild or moderate aphasic involvement.

THE NATURE OF APHASIA

The problem of aphasia brings us to a new aspect of our study of speech-defective persons. With the aphasic, our primary concern is no longer with the articulatory or vocal elements of speech but with the linguistic element and the problem of word meaning. An aphasic patient manifests an inability to deal with symbols; consequently all functions involving the use of language, a symbolic process, are disturbed. These functions include reading, writing, speaking, and the comprehension of speech. In most instances one of these functions will show a greater degree of disturbance than the others, but in almost all instances all these functions are disturbed to some degree.

387

Although an aphasic individual may have difficulty in uttering or writing a word because of motor inadequacies, the primary reason for his disturbance is in another field. Primarily, the aphasic individual has difficulty with language because he cannot associate experiences with representative symbols as normal persons do. Some aphasics cannot, for example, say or write *hat* in meaningful and appropriate context because the object *hat* and the sound or written representation of *hat* remain two different experiences. The reasons for this will appear in our later discussion.

Aphasia is in itself not a disease but rather a symptom complex related to a physiological disorder involving the brain mechanism. The disturbance in language is only one symptom of aphasia. Other symptoms include behavioral changes in the intellectual and emotional spheres and modifications in the attitudes and personality of the individual. Unless all of these elements in the symptom complex are considered, we shall be unable to get a true picture of the aphasic person.

THE ETIOLOGY OF APHASIA

Early students of aphasia generally held the point of view that the disorder was a result of a lesion in a localized area of the brain. Broca, in 1864, demonstrated that the speech of right-handed persons was affected by injuries to the left brain hemisphere, and that right-hemisphere lesions did not affect the speech of right-handed persons. Bastian, Kussmaul, Wernicke, and others who followed Broca, attempted to demonstrate that localized and specific brain areas were responsible for different aspects of speech, and that injuries to given brain areas resulted in different types of aphasia. For a while, the dividing up of the cerebral cortex and the discovery of new kinds of aphasic involvements became a popular undertaking among neurologists. More recent workers, including Weisenburg, Goldstein, Penfield, and Head,[1] are opposed to a strict localization theory, though they agree that the cerebral hemisphere on the side opposite the dominant hand is in control of speech functions. Head, the author of the monumental work on *Aphasia and Kindred Disorders of Speech,* believes that the capacity to use language in any form is the result of physiological activities of certain parts of the brain cortex. When these parts are disturbed, no matter what the cause, the result is a disorder of some degree in the individual's general capacity to use language rather than in any isolated manifestations in regard to language.

[1] T. Weisenburg and K. McBride, *Aphasia* (New York, Commonwealth Fund, 1935).

K. Goldstein, *Language and Language Disturbances* (New York, Grune and Stratton, 1942).

W. Penfield and T. Rasmussen, *The Cerebral Cortex of Man* (New York, Macmillan, 1950).

H. Head, *Aphasia and Kindred Disorders of Speech* (New York, Macmillan, 1926).

It may be of interest to note that even during the period of Broca's greatest influence, some of his contemporaries did not accept his views, or those of his followers, in regard to localization of brain function. Hughlings Jackson and later Sigmund Freud took the position that: "Different amounts of nervous arrangements in different positions are destroyed with different rapidity in different persons." [2] The effect of the destruction of cortical tissue may also produce different functional disturbances in different individuals.

The possible causes of cortical disturbance with which aphasic symptoms are associated are many and varied. They include tumors, brain-penetrating wounds, hemorrhages, embolisms, and thromboses of blood vessels supplying the cerebral cortex. Infectious diseases such as meningitis and encephalitis are frequent etiological associates. Degenerative diseases involving the brain, such as multiple sclerosis, are associated with aphasia in older persons. Epilepsies and allergies affecting the nervous system may also be associated with aphasia. Of the causes just enumerated, the vascular disturbances—embolisms, hemorrhages, and thromboses—are the most frequent.

In the adult, aphasic disturbances are frequently associated with "strokes," which are likely to be followed by paralysis or weakness on the right side of the patient's body. The vast majority of strokes are caused by hemorrhages of blood vessels of the brain, blocking of blood vessels of the brain, or hardening of the arteries. When hardening of the arteries is the cause of the stroke, the artery most commonly affected is the middle cerebral artery or one of its branches which supplies blood to the brain.

The longer life span of our population is increasing the number of patients who suffer from vascular diseases, strokes, and related disturbances in language and speech. Aphasia, a rare problem for the speech correctionist of a generation ago, is a comparatively common problem for the present-day speech correctionist.

Cerebral Localization and Aphasia

There is a growing belief among speech pathologists and neurologists that true aphasia results only from a lesion in the left cerebral hemisphere, regardless of the patient's preferred handedness.[3] This is in contradiction to the older point of view that the brain hemisphere controlling symbolic language function is the left hemisphere for right-handed persons and the right hemisphere for left-handed persons. This author agrees with Wepman in his observation that disturbances in motor speech (dysarthria) rather

[2] S. Freud, *On Aphasia* (International Universities Press, 1953), p. 99.

[3] See J. Wepman, *Recovery from Aphasia* (New York, Ronald Press, 1951), pp. 30-31, for a review of some of the recent literature on the subject of cortical dominance and linguistic disturbance.

than in symbol usage (aphasia) are likely to result if the right hemisphere is damaged in either a left- or right-handed person.

Somewhat more moderate positions are taken by Penfield and Rasmussen [4] and Grinker and Bucy.[5] These workers hold that speech may be represented in either the left or the right hemisphere in left-handed persons. Humphrey and Zangwill [6] studied a group of ten World War II cases with unilateral brain wounds who were "naturally left-handed patients of good intelligence." Five of the patients had lesions of the left and five of the right cerebral hemisphere. They found that aphasia was present in all cases of left-hemisphere lesion and in four of the five cases of right-hemisphere lesion. The left-brain-damaged cases had more severe involvements than did the right-brain-damaged ones. Arithmetic defects were more prominent among the patients with right-hemisphere wounds.

BEHAVIORAL AND INTELLECTUAL CHANGES ASSOCIATED WITH APHASIA

To understand the changes in behavior of the aphasic patient, we must constantly keep in mind that we are dealing with an individual who has suffered from damage involving the cerebral cortex and possible subcortical areas. As a group, though with considerable individual variation, brain-damaged persons present several types of behavioral tendencies. Over and above these tendencies for behavioral change, the aphasics have linguistic impairment. We will first review some of the most significant modifications which may take place as a direct consequence of the brain damage. These modifications are present in common with other brain-damaged persons who are not aphasic.

Increased Egocentricity

Brain-damaged persons tend to become ego-oriented. Where this tendency existed prior to the onset of the brain damage, it is likely to become aggravated. In some instances, the degree of egocentricity may be so great that the patient will find it extremely difficult to become concerned with or to attend to any situation which does not immediately touch upon his interests. He prefers, usually, to deal with concrete situations which are close at hand and which have some importance for him. An excessively ego-oriented patient may not be able to repeat a sentence such as "I drink coffee for breakfast" if he is in the habit of drinking another beverage such as cocoa, milk, or tea, for breakfast.

[4] Penfield and Rasmussen, *op. cit.,* p. 96.

[5] R. R. Grinker and P. C. Bucy, *Neurology,* 4th ed. (Springfield, Illinois, Thomas Publishing Company, 1951), p. 410.

[6] M. E. Humphrey and O. I. Zangwill, "Dysphasia in Left-Handed Patients with Unilateral Brain Lesions," *Journal of Neurology, Neurosurgery, and Psychiatry,* Vol. 15 (1952), pp. 184-193.

Motor and sensory disabilities may increase a patient's tendencies to egocentricity. If a patient cannot readily move about, or cannot easily reach out, he may become one who adjusts to living with things and in a world literally within his grasp. If a patient cannot easily hear, or is confused by noises he does hear, he may begin to shut out situations which he must strain to hear and comprehend. Tendencies to ego-orientation are not infrequently found among the physically handicapped who have no cerebrocortical damage. With such damage, the tendency may increase to a degree which constitutes a significant problem in rehabilitation.

Modification in Abstract Attitude

Patients with cerebrocortical damage frequently show increased difficulty in dealing with the abstract. In some instances, this difficulty may be permanent. In most instances, the authors believe, the actual difficulty is in an increased disinclination to be concerned with the abstract, rather than in an absolute loss for dealing with abstract situations. Where language disturbances are also present, as is the case with the aphasic patient, the tools (linguistic symbols) for dealing with abstractions are also impaired, so that difficulty added to disinclination presents a complicated problem.

Difficulty in dealing with the abstract becomes apparent when patients cannot readily pretend or project themselves into imagined situations. The patient who cannot say "I drink coffee for breakfast" because his habit is to drink milk, cocoa, or tea, manifests difficulty in pretending. The re-education of such a patient is difficult, because he cannot accept the point of view of his therapist. He becomes tied to his own past and immediate experiences, and cannot benefit from vicarious experiences.

Through motivation, disinclination to assume an abstract attitude may be overcome. For the few patients who actually suffer from an absolute loss of abstract attitude, motivation which includes planning for days ahead is of no avail. These patients must be dealt with concretely and specifically in terms of their immediate needs and surroundings. Their realities are the present and actual ones of their daily lives. They cannot accept points of view which are merely possible but not objectively true for them. The therapist must accept these patients on their terms, for they are not able to accept the terms and the abstract point of view of the therapist.

Another aspect of disturbance in abstract attitude is manifest in a patient's difficulty in grasping the essentials that belong to a given whole. An individual who cannot readily see that certain elements belong together and constitute a given configuration, continues to respond to the elements individually, and may never succeed in getting meaning out of them (responding meaningfully to them). Such a person may never see a forest, because he can see only separate trees.

A related impairment is the lack of ability to analyze a whole into its component parts, and then to synthesize the component parts into the essential whole. The tree is trunk, branches, and leaves; trunk, branches, and leaves constitute a tree. Component sounds constitute words, and sequences of words become related into phrases and sentences. These entities may not be apprehended as wholes by some brain-damaged persons. The child with brain lesion may therefore not comprehend what he hears. The adult may suffer from impairment of what he once understood.

Still another aspect of abstract behavior, of special significance for linguistic understanding and thinking, is the ability to see common factors or properties in somewhat different situations. Common properties make for the bases of generalizations, and make it possible for the same words to be applied to essentially similar but nonidentical situations. Some brain-damaged persons suffer from some degree of impairment in this ability. Others suffer from some anxiety in the use of this ability. The combination of impaired ability and anxiety make for a significant disability in generalizing behavior.

Experimental evidence tends to support our observation that impairment of abstract attitude in particular and intellectual deficit in general are temporary and tend to improve with training and language recovery. Wepman, for example, found that his group of 78 aphasic patients approximated their pretraumatic IQ's after a twelve-month period of training. His group showed an immediate deficit of 28.1 points in IQ directly after the onset of their aphasic involvements. After the period of training, the average deficit was reduced to 6.4 points.[7]

Perseveration

One of the most frequent behavioral modifications of brain-damaged persons is the phenomenon of perseveration. This is a tendency for a specific act of behavior, an attitude, or a "set" (mental or physical) to continue in operation when it is no longer appropriate to the situation at hand. This implies that usually the specific act, attitude, or "set" was appropriate to a previous situation. The patient who perseverates is not readily able to shift in behavioral attitude or inclination according to immediate situational requirements. He tends, instead, to persist in accordance with the demands of a previous situation to which he was required to respond.

The perseverating tendency is most likely to be present when a patient finds the situation too much for him to cope with either because of inherent difficulties in the situation itself or because of the quick succession of changing situations. Perseveration may be manifest either in a repetition of a previous response, or in a blocking and failure to make any response. Frequently, the patient is aware that his response is inappropriate, and yet is not able to change it for a more adequate one.

On a verbal level, a patient who may respond correctly to the question, "What do you wear on your feet?" may find it difficult immediately after

[7] Wepman, *op. cit.*, p. 72.

to answer the question, "What do you wear on your head?" A patient who is asked to recite the alphabet, and who readily succeeds in doing so, may find it difficult immediately after to count from 1 to 20, or to name the days of the week. He may, instead, persist in the recitation of the alphabet. Some patients, when asked to do a series of arithmetic additions, may find themselves unable to do subtraction, even though they may have previously demonstrated an ability to do subtraction.

The patient who manifests a perseverating tendency is almost literally in a mental groove or rut. Once in, he finds it difficult to extricate himself, and continues to move in a direction consistent neither with the needs of the situation nor with his own wishes. The patient's awareness of his own inadequate behavior produces feelings of frustration. Often, then, the patient will prefer not to do anything rather than to expose himself to embarrassment and frustration.

Affective Behavior

Brain-damaged persons frequently demonstrate a disturbance in emotional behavior. Such patients give way to impulse more readily than might otherwise be the case. Some patients, aware of this change, may withdraw from situations which they fear may disturb them. It is likely that these patients, previous to their brain damage, emphasized withdrawal as a mechanism for avoiding conflict or difficulty. Other patients, probably along lines consistent with premorbid inclinations, may become more overtly aggressive. In general, the author believes that modifications in affective behavior follow along lines which are exaggerations of previous inclinations. The cerebrocortically damaged person is not so much changed in inclination toward emotionality as he is in his reduced ability to control his inclinations.

Catastrophic Behavior

On occasion, brain-damaged persons, when confronted with a situation which calls for a response not immediately available to them, may react "catastrophically." A catastrophic response is one characterized by marked vascular changes, irritability, evasiveness, or aggressiveness. These changes may be interpreted as an attempt on the part of the brain-damaged person to escape from or to avoid the perplexing situation. If these behavioral manifestations do not help the person to avoid the situation—or exempt him from the need to make the response—he may exhibit sudden sensory or motor loss. In an extreme situation, loss of consciousness may take place.[8]

The significance of the catastrophic response may be understood if we compare the normal and the neurotic person's techniques for dealing with

[8] For a more detailed discussion of the catastrophic response, see K. Goldstein, *After-effects of Brain Injuries in War* (New York, Grune and Stratton, 1932), pp. 71-74.

an especially difficult situation. A normal person may resort to one of several devices. These devices may include making a decision, and possibly a verbalization, that the situation is too difficult and he need not be expected to cope with it. They may also include other devices such as becoming completely occupied with another task, or rationalizing the desirability of delaying the need for a response. In any event, some form of face-saving behavior may take place. A neurotic individual may resort to other devices to avoid a response to an excessively difficult situation. The neurotic may suddenly experience great fatigue, or entertain a severe headache, or in some other way suffer from some indisposition which makes it necessary for him to be excused from the perplexing situation. The choice of device for the brain-damaged person probably depends on what kind of a person he was before his brain involvement, and what, if any, sensory or motor losses he has or has had as a result of his involvement.

The aphasic patient, with reduced ability for verbalization, is more apt to be reduced to the employment of the catastrophic response than is the brain-damaged person without linguistic disturbance. The clinician, working with an aphasic, should interpret the patient's need for resorting to catastrophic behavior as a therapeutic error. It means that somehow the patient has been permitted to get involved in a situation beyond his immediate ability for an adequate response. This, if possible, should be avoided so that the patient may not learn to use catastrophic behavior as a habitual means of dealing with difficult situations.

Attention and Memory

Brain-damaged persons frequently suffer from disturbances of attention and memory. The basis for these disturbances in persons with cerebro-cortical involvement can be easily appreciated if we understand the psychological nature of attention, and the role of the cortex in the function of attention.

Attention is a state in which the individual becomes *set to select* and *respond* to a specific pattern of stimuli or to one situation to the exclusion of others. In order for an individual to be capable of selection, he must be able to inhibit potential responses to competing and at the moment extraneous (non-relevant) stimuli. In the human organism, the function of selection and inhibition of responses is assigned largely to the cerebral cortex. A damaged cortex cannot readily carry out this function. If the patient has impaired sensory reception and/or perception, the degree of impairment of function of attention is increased. With the aphasic patient, who may also suffer from disability in the evaluation of what he perceives, there is added difficulty in maintaining attention. Most brain-damaged persons become aware that they must increase their voluntary effort to attend. They must learn to use psychological blinders so that they may localize the situation to which attention is demanded. Frequently, even with the increase of effort, non-relevant stimuli may successfully compete with relevant ones. Responses may be made which, on an intellectual basis at least, the patient would prefer not to make.

Memory may become weakened for immediate situations because of a primary defect of attention. For the aphasic patient, memory may also be defective because of verbal difficulty. Without adequate verbalization, situations attended to cannot be properly recorded. Recall of remote events may seem to be impaired because of verbalization difficulty. That is, the patient may be able to remember events but lack the ability to make these memories known to others in a communicating situation.

Inconsistency of Response

Persons with brain damage are characteristically inconsistent in their abilities to respond appropriately to essentially identical or comparable situations. This is especially true of aphasic patients in early stages of their involvement. With recovery, whether spontaneous or associated with training, consistency improves. The lack of consistency may be a momentary affair. A patient may be able to respond appropriately at a given time when confronted with a situation such as the naming of an object and yet almost immediately after, be unable to evoke the name for the object. Similar defects may be found in all situations involving the interpretation or evocation of a symbol or a symbol situation. The difficulties of attention, and the ego-orientation of many brain-damaged patients, may in part explain the inconsistency of response.

Other Disturbances

No attempt has been made to discuss all the behavioral and intellectual modifications associated with brain damage. Those changes considered are among the most frequent to be found. Other modifications include reduced functional mental ability, anxiety, euphoria, and reduced initiative. Wepman [9] lists thirty-four non-language deviations found among aphasic patients. It should be pointed out, however, that few of the changes are nonreversible. Almost all have been found to be subject to improvement, either with spontaneous recovery or in association with directed, active language and speech therapy.

LINGUISTIC ASPECTS OF APHASIA

Propositional Speech

Purely from the linguistic standpoint, aphasia represents a disorder of symbolic formulation and expression. The aphasic's difficulty is not so much one of evoking words as it is a difficulty in the appropriate and necessary

[9] Wepman, *op. cit.,* p. 33.

use of language. That is, he can utter words (talk), and under emotional stimulation utter them vehemently and fluently, but he has difficulty in arranging and presenting words in meaningful units. The same man who has difficulty in evoking the words, "Give me my hat" when the situation calls for it may, in another situation, derisively utter "In your hat!" The first arrangement of words—"Give me my hat"—represents a unit of speech or, as Hughlings Jackson termed it, a *proposition*. Propositions are meaningful units of speech; when we comprehend a proposition we see relationships. Words which are uttered in isolation or in sequence are not propositions unless they have meanings. Most oaths, including the mild "In your hat!" are not propositions because they have no intellectual or propositional meanings, in the minds of either the listener or the speaker. The words *yes* and *no* may or may not be propositions, according to the situation in which they are pronounced. Most aphasic patients retain many words which may be uttered in automatic speech such as word counting, or in emotional speech, but the same words may not be evoked in propositional speech. Aphasics frequently "echo" words they hear spoken, much as infants in the echolalic developmental speech stage produce sound complexes which resemble words spoken by people around them. The echoed words, despite their resemblance to real words, have no communicative or propositional value. If we limit speech to the use of propositions, we would then be able to say that aphasics have more difficulty with intellectually significant speech than they do with evoking affect-laden words. Extreme cases of aphasia may be speechless, but even they are not likely to be entirely wordless.

Sub-propositional Speech

As has been suggested, most aphasic patients retain some ability to deal with linguistic symbols. Some of this may continue to be on a fairly high intellectual level. Under some circumstances, most aphasics can comprehend and use language in appropriate ways. Arithmetic ability, especially in simple computation, may also be fairly well retained. There are other forms of linguistic content which for many aphasics may be comparatively undisturbed. These contents are on a low or nonintellectual level and do not constitute true propositional speech. They do not have the specific appropriateness and intellectual significance of propositional speech. The sub-propositional or non-propositional linguistic forms include emotional evocations, automatic and rote content, serial language, and social gesture language.

Emotional evocations are the words uttered when an individual verbalizes under the influence of strong affect. Swear words and words of endearment are examples of frequently used emotional evocations. If we examine the verbal terms used when we are extremely angry or annoyed, we will find them without intellectual meaning. We say things which are literally not possible. Our terms of affection also, though not always as uncomplimentary, are frequently confused intellectually. Emotional language content, almost certainly because of its lack of true symbol significance, tends to be fairly well retained by most aphasics. This implies, of course, that the patient was familiar with and used such language before the onset of the linguistic disturbance.

Automatic content refers to any linguistic material which at one time was so thoroughly learned that it could readily be recited from memory. Many childhood songs, prayers, and some verse and poetry fall into this category. Such content has lost whatever intellectual significance it may have had to the individual when first learned and before it became committed to memory. When a given memorized context has been learned in association with a particular setting, such as words and music for a song, a modification of the pattern reduces the automaticity of the content. For example, if we attempt to recite rather than sing the words of a very familiar song, and inhibit the melody while reciting, we will find it surprisingly difficult to evoke the words.

Serial language refers to content which was originally learned in a given sequence. The alphabet, counting, and the days of the week and months of the year are examples of serial language content. Most aphasics are better able to evoke the days of the week in order than they are to answer the question, "What day comes after Tuesday?" The days of the week, beginning with whatever day the individual had learned to start the series, constitutes a sub-propositional speech utterance. Evoking the correct answer to a question such as "What day comes after Tuesday?" calls for a realization of a relationship. It constitutes a proposition, though not one of a particularly high order. Aphasics, it will be noted, are frequently able to evoke words when they are used in non-propositional utterances. The same word form may not be evoked in propositional situations.

Social gesture language includes phrases of salutation, greeting, or departures. They have approximate rather than specific appropriateness. A phrase of greeting such as "Hello" or "How do you do?" may be answered by the repetition of the same phrase, or another such as "Fine, how are you?" (regardless of whether these words are literally true), or a smile, or a handshake. It seldom is very important which phrase is used. In a true proposition, the choice of words is important and must be related specifically rather than approximately to the situation which calls them forth.

DEGREE AND TYPE OF LANGUAGE IMPAIRMENT IN APHASIA

The precise amount of language impairment in any given adult case of aphasia is difficult if not impossible to determine. Unless the clinician can obtain reliable information as to the patient's language ability prior to the onset of the disturbance, it is not possible to ascertain the extent to which the language function has been impaired. For an individual with an initially limited language ability, even a slight impairment may interfere markedly with his ability in oral expression. On the other hand, an aphasic patient who formerly had a very rich vocabulary may still find ways of expressing himself, though he may be suffering from a very great degree of language impairment.

The form of linguistic disability assumed in an aphasic disturbance depends not only upon the site, extent, and severity of the brain injury, but also upon the experiences, habits, education, and native intelligence of the individual patient. Of at least equal importance to any of the factors just cited is that of favored imagery. A person who habitually prefers the visual avenue for receiving stimulation, who "thinks" and recalls in visual images, is likely to suffer from more extreme impairment following damage to the visual (occipital lobe) area of the brain than would a person with dominant auditory imagery. Similarly, an individual with dominant auditory imagery is likely to show more impairment from a temporal lobe (auditory area) involvement than is a visual-minded person.

Because no two persons have identical speech characteristics, no two aphasic disturbances are ever alike. In a strict sense, there are as many kinds of aphasias as there are aphasic patients, and classification into discrete types is not possible. As a rule, however, one of the language functions in an aphasic patient shows greater impairment than the others, and on this basis, classifications may be attempted.

Although students of aphasia are not unanimous in their specialized classifications of the many types of aphasic disturbances, most contemporary workers recognize at least three broad types. These are: (1) *expressive aphasia,* in which the over-all ability to use spoken or written language is impaired; (2) *receptive aphasia,* in which the ability to understand spoken or written language is impaired; and (3) *nominal* or *amnesic aphasia,* in which the chief impairment is in the ability to recall and evoke the names of objects, persons, situations, and actions. The categories in this text follow these three classifications, with modifications which will be indicated.

Evaluative Disturbances

The patient suffering from *evaluative disturbances* has his greatest difficulty in the evaluation (interpretation) of language symbols received through the eye, ear, or some other sensory avenue or combination of avenues. Evaluative disturbances are those which the patient experiences in deriving meaning from linguistic symbols apart from any difficulty he may have in the sensory reception of the symbols. Auditory aphasia and alexia are two important subtypes of this disturbance.

Auditory verbal aphasia refers to disturbances in the comprehension of spoken language. Often, this type of impairment becomes apparent only when the speech content changes quickly, becomes complicated, or continues at length. Sometimes auditory aphasia is evident only when the patient feels tired, or is under some strain. We may examine a patient for auditory verbal aphasia by having him follow out simple oral directions such as "Show me your nose, mouth, etc." On a higher level, the examination items may include evoking responses to questions read aloud to the patient.[10]

Alexia is an impairment in the evaluation of recognized written symbols (silent reading). These disturbances, as in the case of auditory aphasia, sometimes become apparent only as the written content increases in quantity or complexity. Sometimes alexia is revealed chiefly in the evaluation of small words such as articles, prepositions, and conjunctions and other words which indicate relationships between phrases or serve as introductory words or as connectives.

Alexic disturbances may be tested by giving a patient some written material to read silently and then having him answer questions based on the reading. For severe disturbances in reading an arrangement may be employed which permits a patient to match a word, phrase, or sentence with an appropriate picture. Standardized reading tests for the primary grades employ such items.

Agnosias: Disturbances Related to Evaluation. For an individual to be able to evaluate symbols, he must first be able to receive and discern them. If sensory reception is reasonably good, recognition (discernment) of what is received must be determined. Agnosias are impairments in the ability of an individual to discern configurations of objects, pictures, or symbols. An *agnosia* is a loss of ability to recognize configurations normally received through a given sensory avenue when, on a purely physical basis, the sensory organ is not significantly defective.

An *auditory agnosia* is an impairment in an indvidual's ability to recognize sounds or combinations of sounds without regard to their evaluation. In some cases, auditory agnosias may exist for non-linguistic sounds such as mechanical noises or animal noises. Some patients are unable to comprehend what they are physically able to hear because of an agnosia for linguistic sounds. For practical considerations, this constitutes a *word deafness*.

Occasionally, we find a specialized agnosia for musical sounds. This form of disturbance, auditory musical agnosia or *amusia,* will disturb a patient's ability to appreciate music and, on the productive side, to reproduce a melody pattern. Amusia should not be confused with tone deafness or

---

[10] For an examination inventory which follows the classifications of this text, see J. Eisenson, *Examining for Aphasia,* rev. ed. (New York, Psychological Corporation, 1954).

inability to carry a tune. In speech, amusia may be associated with difficulty in the reception and therefore in the interpretation of inflectional changes and intonation patterns. In general, however, this form of auditory agnosia, which is usually a temporary aspect of the early stages of impairment, is not significant for speech comprehension. It may become significant in languages, such as Chinese, in which tonal changes are used for semantic distinctions.

Visual agnosia is an impairment in the recognition of configurations through sight. A person with visual agnosia is aware that he is seeing something, but he cannot recognize what he sees, or distinguish one visual configuration from another. Visual agnosia may be specific for objects, representations of objects (pictures), colors, geometric forms, letters, or words. It is unlikely, however, that an individual will have an agnosia for letters and not for words, or for single words and not for groups of words.

Before determining whether a person has alexia, it is important that he be tested for visual agnosias. A person who cannot discern patterns of letters in flat print will, of course, not be able to evaluate arrangements of letters as words and so will be unable to read. Alexia, however, frequently exists without associated visual agnosia.

Tactile agnosia is a disturbance in an individual's ability to recognize or identify objects or other configurations through the sense of touch. In deciding whether a person has tactile agnosia, it must first be determined that he has sufficiently acute tactile sense to make recognition possible. Except as possibly related to the reading of braille or other forms of raised print, tactile agnosia is not likely to be related to the evaluation of linguistic symbols.

The agnosias are, per se, sub-symbolic disturbances. They are significant because when they exist, they are primary disturbances which impair symbolic evaluation. If an agnosia exists, the patient must be trained to overcome this form of difficulty in order to be able to proceed to the comprehension of conventional language symbols.

Productive (Expressive) Disturbances

Productive (expressive) disturbances reveal the aphasic patient's disabilities in the use of symbols. These disturbances, it must be emphasized, refer to the formulation and evocation of the symbols, and not to the motor aspects of speaking or writing. In many cases, some degree of what appears to be a productive disturbance is essentially an evaluative difficulty. Actual impairment, or insecurity on the part of the patient about the accuracy of his comprehension, will manifest itself in communicative disability.

There are several subtypes of productive disturbances which may become apparent in the patient's efforts, in speaking or in writing, to deal with symbols and to communicate the results of his thinking. The subtypes which reflect the most common productive impairments include *nominal aphasia* or *anomia, agraphia* (writing disturbances), *acalculalia* (arithmetic disturbances), *paraphasia* (errors and distortions in symbol production), and *dysprosody* (melody disturbances).

Almost all aphasics manifest a greater amount of difficulty in one or more of the productive disturbances, and less difficulty in the others. It is rare for a patient to have an isolated difficulty for a single form of symbol disturbance. In general, disturbances in speaking and in writing parallel one another, though there may be considerably more difficulty in one form of productive function than in the other.

Nominal aphasia or *anomia* refers to a patient's difficulty in the evocation of an appropriate word called for by the situation. The difficulty is most likely to be reflected in nouns, because nouns constitute the major portion of most persons' vocabularies. Nominal difficulties are, however, not restricted to nouns. They may exist equally, and sometimes more severely, for adjectives, verbs, adverbs, or any other part of speech. Anomia is probably the most frequent and most persistent of the aphasic patient's difficulties. It is also the type which is most likely to remain as a residual disturbance when considerable improvement in general has taken place. Under conditions of fatigue, anxiety, or emotional disturbance, nominal difficulties are likely to reappear. Unless the patient has considerable evaluative difficulty, he is almost always able to recognize a word he cannot evoke.

A patient with nominal difficulty frequently learns to do what a normal person does when he has momentary difficulty in evoking an appropriate word. The aphasic may use a synonym as a substitute, use an equivalent phrase, employ a circumlocution, or use gesture as a verbal substitute. He may also resort to changing the subject so as to conceal his word-finding difficulty. If the nominal difficulty is not severe, the aphasic is much like the normal person who is not especially verbal and who is often on the hunt for the particularly "happy" word which eludes him. The normal pressures which make words elusive for non-brain-damaged persons exist as well for the brain-damaged. In addition, for the aphasic, there is difficulty in word finding which can be directly attributed to the cerebrocortical involvement.

In a test situation, nominal difficulties may be determined by asking a patient to name objects or pictures, to indicate their function, to complete incomplete sentences with words of various parts of speech, or to supply synonyms for words presented to him.

The following sample of conversation with a thirty-six-year-old male patient illustrates some characteristic nominal difficulties, both of omission and commission.

E. How are you today?
Pt. Fine, thank you, I guess fine.
E. What did you do this morning?
Pt. Reading.
E. Were you reading a book or newspaper?

PT. One of those.
E. Which one?
PT. The one everyday.
E. Do you mean a newspaper?
PT. Yes, newspaper.
E. Did you do anything else?
PT. Yes, pencil.
E. Were you writing a letter?
PT. Yes.
E. Do you like to write?
PT. Yes, but trouble pencil.
E. Is your pencil broken?
PT. No, but trouble.
E. Do you mean that you have trouble with writing?
PT. Yes, writing, spelling.

Agraphia (Writing Disturbances). In general, disturbances in writing ability, penmanship as such excluded, tend to parallel disturbances in speaking. The patient who is inclined to speak telegraphically is also likely to omit prepositions, conjunctions, and articles in writing. These omissions may not be as readily apparent in the final product of a patient as they are likely to be in the initial effort. A patient who is aware of his defect may go over his effort until a fairly satisfactory result is obtained. This, of course, is not possible in spoken evocations. The patient with a fairly good vocabulary may, when writing, choose synonymous terms for words he cannot readily evoke. If he writes slowly, only the patient will be aware of his difficulty. Severely involved patients, or patients with limited vocabularies, may produce writing as defective as the following sample:

> I patent at ————. Hurt Kor. Woundat top. Better.
> Hurt open made. Thand you.

After several trials, the patient corrected his effort to read:

> I am a patent at ————. I was hurt Korea. I was wounded
> my head. I am better now. Thank you.

Spelling. Disturbances in spelling constitute an aspect of agraphia. In general, written difficulties parallel but are less severe than oral spelling disturbances. The following indicate some oral and written efforts of a twenty-four-year-old patient who suffered a left temporal-parietal skull fracture.

Dictated Word	Oral Spelling	Written Spelling
Feeling	Felling	Feeling
Suppose	Suppoise	Supoise
Occur	Accour	Accur
Cabinet	Cabnet	Cabinet

Acalculia (Arithmetic Disturbances). These defects may be present because of essential difficulty in dealing with arithmetic processes or because of nominal or agraphic disturbances. If it is the latter, we actually have a word-finding impairment in an arithmetic situation. Fortunately for many aphasic patients, much of arithmetic becomes a matter of almost automatic computation by the time of adulthood. Even simple problems are solved according to rules and with little arithmetic reasoning. It is usual, therefore, to find arithmetic functions relatively well retained. True mathematical ability, which calls for the application of abstract concepts, may be more seriously impaired.

Dysprosody (Melody Disturbance). Disturbances in melody pattern are likely to be significant only in so far as speech melody (inflection and intonation) are concerned. This type of impairment explains why some aphasics continue to speak without the vocal variety and color which may previously have characterized their speech. In some instances, dysprosody continues as a residual after ability to deal with symbols in general has shown considerable improvement.

Disturbances for musical melody reproduction are less frequent and usually less severe than for speech. Usually the ability to reproduce well-known tunes is spontaneously recovered as general improvement takes place.

Paraphasia. Paraphasic defects are errors of commission or omission relative to grammar, word substitutions, sound substitutions, or sound or letter reversals. They constitute the large variety of faults which aphasics, to a greater or lesser degree, reveal in their speech or writing. Some of these may have been noted in the samples of speech and writing presented above.

The paraphasic errors of the aphasic are not unlike the slips of the tongue or pen which normal persons produce when they are under emotional strain or fatigue. They may be explained in a non-brain-damaged person as the unintentional products of a mind which is not able to maintain "intellectual vigilance" in a linguistic situation. The aphasic is not able to maintain such vigilance because of his brain damage. The possibility should not be overlooked, however, that the same forces which operate to cause a normal person to commit paraphasic errors also hold for the aphasic. The aphasic is not immune from normal linguistic psychodynamics.

In many instances, paraphasic defects have their origin in evaluative and receptive difficulties. The patient who is uncertain of his understanding is likely to manifest this uncertainty in his own speech. Frequently, paraphasic errors arise out of a failure to inhibit associated words. Some of our verbal associations occur in opposites, e.g., big-small; strong-weak; black-white; man-women. The verbal efforts of aphasics often contain uninhibited or partially inhibited associated words, so that "big-small" may be evoked as "ball," or "black-white" as "blite." When viewed in this light, some of the apparently meaningless word usage of the aphasic may assume more significance.

Perseverative tendencies are also reflected in the aphasic's language usage. Thus, words in full or in part may be repeated even though the patient is sometimes aware of the inappropriateness of his language production.

The following sample of conversation held with a 59-year-old male patient reveals some characteristic paraphasic errors of speech:

E. What is your name?
Pt. (*spelled*) C-O-H-E-M-P-B-E
E. What else are you called?
Pt. (*spelled*) C-O-M-P-D-A-E
E. You know that is not correct?
Pt. That is the truth; when is it going to be broken?
E. What do you mean by "when is it going to be broken"?
Pt. (*spelled*) S-C-I-I-H-E
E. Don't spell it, say it in words.
Pt. (*spelled*) C-O-H-M-M-E-E. When I first got it the whole time, education, millions of money, most time I think.
E. What kind of work did you do?
Pt. (*spelled*) L-L-O-H-V—none.
E. I'm not sure I know what it means.
Pt. I can't break anything I bust. I try it every day. Education stuff too. People have broken themselves of something broken. Won't stop.

Dysarthrias and Apraxias: Disturbances Related to Language Production

The production disturbances just considered involved symbolic associations and expression. They represented difficulties in linguistic symbol function. The dysarthric and apraxic disturbances, which we are about to discuss, are on a lower level. They are frequently present in aphasic patients, and constitute special types of motor dysfunctions associated with brain damage and language production.

Dysarthrias are defects of articulation which are caused by either central or peripheral nerve damage. Impaired nervous stimulation or control may result in misarticulations which, when severe, may make word recognition difficult. Frequently, but not always, dysarthric errors increase in severity as the patient has increased difficulty with the symbolic aspect of his speech. They tend to be aggravated also as word or sentence length increases. Tongue twisters, which are of some difficulty for most normal speakers, cause greater difficulty for patients with dysarthrias. Words such as *attentively* and *successively,* and phrases such as *Methodist Episcopal* are especially difficult. These may constitute test words for patients believed to be dysarthric. In some instances where there is relatively little difficulty, dysarthric errors may appear only when the patient tries to talk rapidly or talk under conditions of fatigue or strain.

Apraxias are disturbances characterized by disability in the voluntary and intended use of tools. When the tools are the organs of articulation, speech becomes directly affected and we have oral or verbal apraxia. When the tools are the arm and hand, writing becomes affected. A patient with apraxia may be able to formulate the language he wishes to evoke, but have his evocation impaired because of the motor involvement.

Some apraxias exist only for the use of tools extraneous to the body. Some patients are unable to use such necessary tools as brushes, hammers, and knives. When a patient is unable to use a pencil or a pen, writing obviously becomes disturbed.

Verbal apraxias are expressed in faulty attempts at speaking. If the involvement is severe the patient may be completely unable to speak. This state, fortunately, is rare except in very early stages of involvement. Oral apraxias, which may continue to some degree, constitute a special type of dysarthria.

THERAPY

General Principles

The limitations of this text do not permit of extensive discussion of therapeutic techniques and approaches. In general, the best techniques are those which are designed to meet the individual needs of the particular patient. Materials as well as approaches must be "tailor-made." Considerable help, however, may be obtained from the literature on remedial education.

No attempt shall be made to outline or condense the numerous specific therapeutic techniques which may be found in the periodical literature. Instead, we shall discuss general principles and problems of therapy and highlight a few specific techniques for the most frequent types of aphasic involvement.

Improvement in aphasic disturbance is, by and large, positively correlated with general physical recovery. Frequently, however, the patient reaches a plateau in physical improvement long before he has reached a plateau in linguistic recovery. Occasionally, however, a patient may make an almost full physical recovery with comparatively little linguistic improvement.

Although no hard and fast rules can be drawn, the following factors appear to be positively correlated with a good prognosis for linguistic recovery.

1. *Comparative youth.* The younger the patient, the better the outlook.
2. *Traumatic etiology.* Patients whose aphasic involvements are associated with head injury rather than cerebrovascular disturbances or

disease have, as a group, made more rapid progress in language improvement.

3. *Outgoing personality.* Patients who before the onset of their aphasic difficulties tended to be "easygoing" and sociable, improved more rapidly than patients whose personalities were on the reticent, withdrawn side.

4. *Flexibility.* An ability to be flexible and a willingness to assume an attitude or point of view of the therapist constitute traits which make for good learning and hence for linguistic improvement.

Because much of learning takes place through vicarious experiences, the patient who can place himself at the disposal of another's point of view is better able to learn, or relearn, than is the ego-oriented, rigid individual.[11]

Although the above factors have been found to be positively related to recovery, the absence of any one or more of them should not be interpreted pessimistically. Many well-motivated older patients have excellent records of improvement. Almost all patients, unless they are suffering from a disease which is progressive or which has caused widespread destruction of cortical tissue, are capable of some degree of improvement.

When to Begin Training. On the basis of recent observations, we recommend that language training be initiated as soon as the patient is physically able. This may be as early as a week or two after the onset of the patient's involvement. Early training need not be ambitious and should not tax the patient's energies. It may consist of brief periods of conversation with the therapist, or of listening to and discussing a radio or television program. One of the objectives of the early part of training is to have the patient understand that his linguistic as well as physical recovery is of interest and concern to others! Another is to prevent techniques of non-oral communication from becoming established. A third may be for pure morale purposes. Delay in training may cause the patient to feel that he is rejected, or permit him to become morbid about his social (communicative) ability.

Assessment of Abilities. The initiation of a training program should be accompanied by an assessment of the patient's assets and limitations. This should include an inventory of what the patient is able to do with ease, with relative ease, with difficulty, or not at all. The complete inventory should include an assaying of the patient's health history, his pre-aphasic manner of responding to illness, to frustration, and to the need for exercising "intellectual effort." Most of the information will be obtained from relatives of the patient rather than from the patient himself.

An evaluation of linguistic ability can be made through the use of an

---

[11] For further discussion of factors related to improvement, see J. Eisenson, "Prognostic Factors Related to Language Rehabilitation in Aphasic Patients," *Journal of Speech and Hearing Disorders,* Vol. 14, No. 2 (1949), pp. 262-264.

aphasia inventory [12] and educational achievement tests. These, if possible, should be administered by a *person other than the therapist* who will be handling the patient. The kinds and amount of testing should of course be determined by the patient's performance. No test should be administered if complete failure becomes apparent. With this information obtained, the therapist is in a position of knowing enough about his patient to undertake a training program.

Where to Begin Training. The immediate and most apparent needs of the patient should serve as a guide as to where to begin training. The hospital patient who has severe nominal difficulty should be helped to evoke terms which he immediately needs in order to make him a better and more comfortable patient. Words such as *doctor, nurse, water, towel, pillow,* and *blanket* should be incorporated into brief sentences which constitute polite requests. Acknowledgments of greetings are important to social living whether in the hospital or at home.

A patient with marked difficulty in speaking and writing should have speaking emphasized as a more immediate communicative need. Writing may wait until its importance is felt by the patient.

The pathway for stimulation should, in general, be the sensory avenue or avenues which are relatively unimpaired. The physician will provide information along this line to the therapist. Occasionally, despite some degree of impairment, a patient may prefer one sensory avenue to another which may be less impaired. This choice may be consistent with the patient's preferred imagery and should be respected.

The pathway for production should similarly be based on the patient's ability. If a patient can more readily respond orally than in writing, then oral responses should be emphasized. If the patient is more secure in his written responses, then these may be used, and oral responses built up in association with them.

Individual studies of patients will show that the complete reception-production circuit varies from patient to patient. For one it may be aural for reception and oral for production; for another it may be aural for reception and graphic (written) for production; for a third it may be visual for reception and oral for production. Ultimately, of course, the goal is to make reception and evaluation possible through any sensory avenue which is not seriously impaired, and production possible through any unimpaired motor avenue. As soon as possible, practice should be provided for multiple sense appeals, so that associations may be established.

Determining and Using the Original Approach. If it is possible to determine in what manner an aphasic originally learned a given content or process, or in what way the content was recorded, considerable time may

[12] See J. Eisenson, *Examining for Aphasia,* rev. ed. (New York, The Psychological Corporation, 1954).

be saved in the relearning process. If a patient learned ordinary cursive writing, and if a sample of his writing is available, this should provide the approach to the teaching of writing. If, on the other hand, the patient used manuscript writing, then this rather than cursive writing is recommended. In writing their arithmetic algorisms, it may make a difference if a computation is presented $4\overline{)80}$ or $4\underline{)80}$. If a patient learned to subtract by computing "Eight minus six is two" he may be confused by being taught "Six and what make eight? Six and two make eight." The approach of choice is one which the patient may indicate in his own attempts at computation. If he does not, a member of his family may provide the necessary information, or example, of what the approach should be.

Learning Principles. The basic principles which governed the original language learning of the patient pertain also to the relearning process. Associations are reinforced if they are rewarded. If insight and information can be added to or made to become an integral part of the reward, learning is likely to progress more smoothly than with non-informative rewards. For the aphasic, external and artificial rewards are seldom necessary. The verbal assurance that something is said "right" and is "good" supplies both natural reward and information.

Learning proceeds best when it involves situations which are meaningful and significant for the patient. If a patient's immediate needs can be satisfied through language which is learned, then an objective for the learning as well as a reward is provided. Wherever possible, therefore, real situations should be used to motivate learning and as a basis upon which a lesson or series of lessons may be structured. A letter which is actually to be written to a relative or friend is much better than a letter-exercise to an imaginary person about an imaginary situation.

Intensification of Stimulation. Many aphasic patients, and especially those with predominantly evaluative disturbances, require intensification of stimulation to overcome the apparent resistance they have to the reception of stimuli. Intensification of stimulation may be accomplished through an increase in the physical size or loudness of presented material, or through repetition of material, or through a combination of the two. If the material is audible, amplification of sound is recommended. If an amplifier is not available, speaking in a louder than normal voice may achieve the same purpose. Care should be exercised, however, that the loud voice does not suggest yelling. If visual material is used, the size of the print should be larger than the patient had been reading, but not so large as or of a kind to suggest the print of a child's book. Type of point size from 50 to 100 per cent larger than used in this text is recommended.

Repetition of stimulation is most likely to be successful when its use is not too apparent. Small children enjoy repetition, even though it is obvious. For the adult, it is usually preferable to incorporate a given word or phrase which is to be learned into several slightly different sentences. If it is desired, either for purposes of evaluation or evocation, to establish a new word or phrase, it should be brought up in several situations during the course of a therapeutic session rather than be successively repeated.

Negative Practice. By negative practice we mean the conscious and deliberate use of a response which was initially produced in error. A variation of this psychological technique may be used with aphasic patients. Aphasics, we have learned, frequently evoke inappropriate or wrong responses in their oral and written speech efforts. Such responses may be put to effective use by associating them with situations for which they may be appropriate. These are to be provided by the therapist. For example, if a patient responds with the word *soap* to the question, "What do you use for combing your hair?" the patient may be informed that "Soap is used for washing. A comb is used for combing your hair." This may be immediately followed by the therapist asking the patient, "What do you use for washing?" in order to elicit the word *soap*. Later, the therapist may return to the original question, "What do you use for combing your hair?" By taking advantage of what the patient is able to evoke even in error, appropriate associations may be formed.

Raising the Level of Response. In our discussion of the nature of aphasia it was pointed out that emotionally laden speech, automatic content, serial speech, and social gesture speech remain relatively intact for many aphasic patients. Considerable use may be made of these low-level linguistic speech contents by directing the patient's awareness to recall specific word forms and to use them as intellectually significant terms. For example, a patient who cannot readily evoke a particular day of the week so as to answer the question, "What day is today?" may be able to do so by going through the days of the week until he arrives at the correct day. In time, he may say the sequence of days quickly and silently, and evoke aloud only the appropriate day.

Familiar songs, verses, prayers, and such terms as "good morning" and "How are you?" may be used for the selection of words or phrases in appropriate situations. One patient who had considerable difficulty in spontaneously evoking the word *red,* learned to do so by thinking the sentence, "Three cheers for the red, white, and blue!"

Many patients who thought that they had outgrown nursery rhymes were able to make considerable use of them as aids to elicit terms which they could not otherwise evoke.

Group Training. The introduction of an aphasic patient to a group is recommended when feasible and practicable and when the patient is ready for it. Readiness is probably best determined by linguistic ability. The severely impaired patient should not be made a member of a group in which his limitations will make him self-conscious and conspicuous. It is best to wait until some degree of communicative ability is established so that some degree of participation becomes possible.

The feasibility and practicability of group training will depend upon the availability of patients to form a group. In private practice, or in small clinics, this may never be the case. In large hospitals or speech clinics, this may often be the case.

The values of group training include the following:

1. It provides the patient with an occasion for socialization. A sympathetic audience of persons "in the same boat" is assured.

2. Motivation from other patients, from peers rather than superiors, becomes possible.

3. The patient's own shortcomings may be seen in others. Their effects, and the need for overcoming them, become apparent to the individuals of the group. For example, telegraphic speech style and the difficulties it presents in communication may be impressed on one patient as he listens to it from another.

4. The patient may learn by observing others. The response the patient lacks the courage to make, may be made by another. Reinforcement may take place in much the same way as it does with normal persons who match their answers with the interviewee in a radio or television quiz program.

5. The group situation provides a patient with several listeners other than his therapist. He therefore is helped to adjust to others and to find out how others adjust to him. The tendency to speak or listen to only one person is avoided.

6. Group training also provides a patient with an opportunity to ventilate his feelings and to air his grievances before others who may share them. The unjustified feelings and grievances may be more adequately dealt with by persons like himself than by non-brain-damaged therapists.

The possible shortcomings of the group approach should be considered for a balanced evaluation of group therapy. Among the shortcomings are the following:

1. Withdrawn patients and reticent ones may find it difficult to attempt to respond in the presence of an audience. Some patients may be afraid to speak, or be content to have others carry their burden for them. Skilled direction on the part of the leader of the group should help to prevent these tendencies.

2. The rate of progress of a group as a whole may be too rapid for the slowest members and too slow for the most advanced. The slow members may feel overwhelmed, and the advanced ones may become impatient.

3. Group situations may become dominated by one or two aggressive members. Unless a skilled group leader prevents such domination, passive members may feel that they are being imposed upon or may become even more passive than their own inclinations would direct.

Motivation. Although most aphasics are desirous of entering into a training program, there are occasional exceptions. Some patients hope that complete recovery will take place spontaneously and effortlessly, and so put off direct participation. Others may be apprehensive about starting language training for fear of having to acknowledge the amount of their linguistic impairment. Occasionally a patient realizes that he is able to receive more attention and make more demands on his environment without words than he ever could with words. If this state of affairs has special values for him, he is likely to resist language retraining. Not infrequently, therefore, a considerable amount of persuasion is required to get some patients to agree to a program of language rehabilitation.

The direction and extent of motivation constitute problems in themselves. Although almost all patients improve to some degree, no reliable estimate can be made as to the amount of anticipated improvement for any patient. It is better to encourage the aphasic to work for the accomplishment of a series of short-term goals than to establish a long-term objective far removed from the patient's immediate abilities.

The goals and objective of the language programs should be correlated with the over-all training program planned for the individual patient. The question of whether a patient may be able to return to his former vocation, or needs to be directed and trained for a new one, must be considered. If a return to the former vocation is likely, then the terms, and in some instances the mathematics, of the vocation should be re-established. Appropriate reading and writing materials from the literature of the vocation may well be used. If, however, a return to the vocation is not possible because of motor or sensory involvements, it is probably best, at least at first, to avoid using the language of the vocation as teaching material.

Specific Techniques for Evaluative Disturbances

It is not possible, within the limits of this text, to present detailed specific techniques for the numerous forms of aphasic disturbances. In discussing specific techniques, it is important to remember that they are included as suggestions and not as prescriptions for dealing with the individual patient and his language problems. It cannot be overemphasized that the best approaches and the most effective techniques are those which are designed with reference to the needs, disabilities, and remaining abilities of the individual patient. The therapist should be prepared to find that an approach or procedure which was highly successful with one patient just does not seem to work with another. It may be possible to use some elements of the procedure for a third patient, or a fourth. In the long run, however, procedures, specific techniques, and materials must be "tailor-made" for each patient.

The literature on remedial education may well be used as source material and for suggested approaches. The aphasic, however, should not be treated as if he had an initial educational disability in one or more subject-matter areas. The problems of teaching a patient to read again or to spell again are only in some incidental ways the same as those of teaching either an average or a slow learner to read or spell in the first place. The essential problem with the learner without brain damage, whether he be apt or retarded, is to build up fresh associations in the hope that immediate learning of content and appropriate generalizations may take place. With the aphasic, it is not new learning but the reawakening and usability of what was once learned which the therapist is trying to bring about. Fortunately, the therapist does not have to reawaken all the old associations. In most instances, once some associations are re-established, others are spontaneously revived.

Improvement of Auditory Comprehension. If it is determined that a patient has difficulty in understanding audible speech (auditory aphasia), an approach which emphasizes association between visual and auditory stimulation is recommended. At first, pantomimic activity should be introduced in association with simple sentences appropriate to the action. Directions such as "Pick up the pencil," "Open the book," or "Close the door" and "Sit down, please" are examples. These directions should be spoken clearly, and somewhat more slowly and loudly than for ordinary conversation. They should, at the outset, be presented without variation until the patient is able to respond to them readily and consistently. Note that a short, complete sentence rather than a single word is used in each of the directions. Note also that, except for the article *the,* the remaining words are different for each of the directions. Distinctively different words which call for distinctively different actions will help to avoid confusion in establishing the first associations. If at all possible, the choice of the direction should be one which has some utility for the patient.

After total bodily activity is understood, emphasis should be placed on face and lip reading. In this phase of training, care must be exercised by the therapist that articulatory activity is not exaggerated or distorted. The therapist must try to speak as naturally as possible, even though the patient is observing his oral movements closely and intimately.

The principle of intensification of stimulation applies especially to patients with auditory aphasia. It should be borne in mind, however, that intensification should be reduced to approximate the normal as soon as possible.

Care should be exercised not to expose the severe auditory aphasic patient to quick-changing conversation or to rapid-fire speaking. Until the patient has evidenced ability to comprehend a considerable amount of what he hears, it is probably best not to include him in group situations with persons with little or no auditory comprehension difficulty. The patient should, however, be encouraged to listen to newscasts and especially to observe telecasts which enable him to make some associations between the words he hears and what he sees.

It is important that both the therapist and the patient make certain that the patient understands what he hears. The only way to be certain of understanding is to observe whether the response is appropriate to what is heard.

For formal teaching situations, Schuell [13] offers a number of suggestions along this line. These include:

1. Identifying objects in pictures named by the therapist.
2. Executing directions.
3. Answering questions.
4. Completing sentences intentionally left incomplete by the therapist.
5. Identifying specific words, phrases, or sentences spoken by the therapist. This may be done by pointing, underlining, or naming.
6. Paraphrasing by the patient of sentences spoken by the therapist.
7. Writing answers to questions presented by the therapist.

It should be noted that many types of response may be used for an auditory situation. The nature of the particular response which the patient can and should be encouraged to make should depend upon his abilities and the nature of the situation.

The patient whose auditory disturbances are on the level of *auditory agnosia,* who cannot recognize sound patterns, requires training to establish associations between sound and situation. If the auditory agnosia extends even to non-oral sounds, associations between objects and sounds must be formed. For example, a patient may be given a hammer to strike against a block of wood so that he becomes able to associate the sound of a hammer and the object *hammer.*

Occasionally it is necessary to establish recognition for articulate sound as a preliminary to establishing word recognition and understanding. This may be accomplished by having the patient and therapist sit in front of a large mirror, while the therapist produces simple vocal sounds and sound combinations with clear-cut visible movements. These are imitated by the patient. As soon as possible, the patient is encouraged to imitate the sounds through the sense of hearing alone.

It should be emphasized that auditory agnosia is a comparatively rare disturbance, except possibly in the early stages of involvement. Almost always, patients with auditory difficulty can recognize the symbols even though they may not be readily able to understand them.

Reading. A recommended first step is to determine whether a patient has better comprehension when he reads silently or when he reads aloud. This information should determine the basic approach to therapy. Some patients become confused by what they hear when they read aloud, and comprehend less than if permitted to read silently. Others, perhaps because they originally learned by reading aloud, require such reinforcement.

The patient who has both alexia and auditory aphasia will require a completely visual approach. Initially, simple sentences presented to him on a card or written on a blackboard may be acted out. For example, the sen-

[13] Hildred Schuell, "Auditory Impairment in Aphasia: Significance and Retraining Techniques," *Journal of Speech and Hearing Disorders,* Vol. 18, No. 1 (1953), pp. 14-21.

tence, "I smoke a cigarette" is one which most patients and therapists can enact as part of everyday experience. "I eat a piece of candy" is another. In a similar manner, a clearly defined action picture may be used with a simple sentence to accompany the action of the picture.

In the early stages of reading retraining, many patients are overwhelmed with large amounts of material. Others find it difficult to "keep their eyes on the place" when reading a paragraph. The use of a card with a slot which permits exposure of a few words at a time was found helpful for both of these difficulties. A slotted card slows down the rate of reading, which in itself may be of help to the aphasic patient. When the patient becomes secure in his ability to comprehend the written word, speed may be improved through the use of flash cards or by having material flashed on a screen. The alexic patient who has visual-field difficulty is also benefited by flash cards and screen exposures. These devices permit the use of large print at a sufficient distance not to be disturbed by visual-field limitation.

One of the early goals in reading therapy is to build up a readily functioning *sight vocabulary*. The contents of such a vocabulary should be determined in part by the patient's interests and needs and in part by the contextual material found in prepared literature. For the latter purpose, several lists may be used. Among these are the Buckingham and Dolch [14] list, the Gates list,[15] and the Durrell lists.[16] Also recommended are sight phrase cards which are based on reading lists. A valuable set of such cards was prepared by Dolch.[17] To supplement these cards, or sometimes in place of them, the therapist should prepare some of particular importance for his patient. These may be given to the patient as "homework" practice material.

The cards should be prepared in clear print of a size easy to read. In the early stages of training, it may be helpful to have realistic pictures to illustrate the words, phrases, or sentences. Magazines provide an excellent source for such illustrations.

Comprehension of written material should constantly be checked. Some of the suggestions made for checking comprehension of spoken material (p. 413) may be used directly or adapted for reading comprehension.

When the patient progresses to where he would like to read paragraphs or pages of material, a new problem must be met. The choice of material for the adult alexic patient must be relatively simple but not infantile. Probably the best early material is that which is prepared by the therapist for the patient. Rewritten news items are useful and have the advantage of being timely. Some of the authors' patients have enjoyed using special weekly

[14] B. R. Buckingham and E. W. Dolch, *A Combined Word List* (Boston, Ginn, 1936).

[15] A. I. Gates, *A Reading Vocabulary for Primary Grades* (New York, Bureau of Publications, Teachers College, Columbia University, 1935).

[16] D. D. Durrell, *Improvement of Basic Reading Abilities* (Yonkers, New York, World Book, 1940).

[17] E. W. Dolch, *Sight Phrase Cards* (Champaign, Illinois, Garrard Press).

newspapers prepared for grade-school pupils, such as *Young America* (Eton Publishing Company, Silver Springs, Maryland). More advanced readers have shown interest in the *Reading Skill Builder Series* published by the Readers' Digest Company.

The *development of comprehension* may be checked through the informal use of reading achievement tests. Such tests may also be used as practice reading material. Because most educational achievement tests have alternate forms, more formal testing, if desired, may still be carried out. In general, however, these authors recommend that as little formal testing as possible be done with aphasic patients. For most aphasics, the capacity to deal with material is more important than speed of performance. Formal tests frequently are interpreted by the patients as threats. They create anxieties which the therapist should try to avoid.

Visual Agnosias. If it is determined that a patient cannot discern visual configurations such as letters or words, training to improve this impairment should precede re-education for reading. Patients may be helped to recognize letters by finger-tracing, direct tracing with transparent paper, or copying on blackboards. It is frequently of great help to associate a letter with a common object beginning with that letter, and with the most usual pronunciation of the letter. Thus, a picture of a *book* may be used to illustrate the letter B. The letter B may be written directly on the picture or under it. If possible, an illustration may be made so that the shape of the figure suggests the letter. For example, the peaks of a mountain may be drawn to suggest the letter M; a snake may suggest the letter S; or a telegraph pole may suggest the letter T.

The patient with letter agnosia is encouraged to name the letters and to produce the most common sound for which the letter stands. Occasionally, patients may not be able to recognize letters and yet be able to recognize words. If this is found to be the case, there is no point in establishing letter recognition for purposes of reading. It is likely that patients who do not recognize individual letters learned to read through whole-word recognition, and feel no need to be concerned with letters as such.

Specific Techniques for Productive Disturbances

Word-finding. In terms of the patient's needs for productive language, the ability to find the appropriate word is the most vital. Much of the training to improve word-finding takes place informally, whenever a patient is spoken to about persons or things about him. In early formal training, it is best to begin with objects, and to use the same name for the given object until the term is firmly established. In establishing a name for an object, it is recommended that at first only those which have immediate utility for the patient be used. If the patient can have a need satisfied by calling for his *towel,* or *soap,* or *glass,* or for whatever else permits him to maintain dignity, these should be the terms introduced.

In establishing naming, the following procedure is recommended:

1. The function of the object is demonstrated, then the object is named.
2. The patient is asked to repeat the name after the therapist.
3. The name is incorporated into a short sentence, and spoken by the therapist with emphasis on the key word. The patient is encouraged to repeat the short sentence after the therapist.
4. If the patient is able to write, the sentence should be written with the key word underlined or capitalized.
5. At some later time in the therapeutic session, the patient should be given an opportunity to repeat the practice. Before the close of the session, the patient should be given a chance to evoke the name by himself.

This process, with whatever variations the resourceful therapist cares to introduce, may be applied to action words and descriptive terms as well as nominal words. As soon as possible it is urged that situations be created to give the patient an opportunity to use his naming ability in conversational occasions and in conversational sentence form.

Oral Apraxia. If it is determined that a patient's underlying difficulty is an impaired ability to control the movements of his articulatory mechanism, therapy must begin with this problem. The basic approach is for the patient to imitate the movements of the therapist, either in a face-to-face position or with both patient and therapist sitting before a large mirror. It is suggested that training begin with the production of such readily distinguishable sounds as the *ee, oo,* and *ah.* Visible consonants should then be combined with these vowels. The addition of the *p*-sound will result in combinations which have some expressive significance. Sounds only partially visible, such as *l* and *t,* may then be introduced; these may be followed by the non-visible sounds such as *k.* Wherever possible, combinations should be chosen which constitute words rather than nonsense syllables.

It is quite likely that once a few combinations are established the patient will make spontaneous progress with others. In severe cases, it may be necessary to manipulate the patient's articulatory mechanism to help him to move from sound to sound. This, however, is seldom necessary except in the initial stages of training.

Some patients fail to produce voiced sounds, or to distinguish between voiceless and voiced cognates. Awareness of the difference may be established by placing the patient's hand at the therapist's larynx while the therapist produces voiced sounds. Later, "the-hand-at-the-larynx" gesture may be all that is needed to remind the patient to produce a voiced sound.

Writing. Aphasic patients may have agraphia (writing impairment) for one of the following reasons: (1) There is a primary disturbance in the ability to use tools. This is an apraxia. (2) There is a paralysis of the hand and arm previously used for writing. This is a motor disability. Its solution may take the form of an immediate change of handedness for writing. (3) There is a disturbance in ability to recall the way a letter or combination of letters should be written. This may occur in addition to causes (1) and/or (2). (4) There is an impairment in the ability to spell. This is a higher form of aphasic writing involvement than the others.

If the patient's difficulty is on the basis of a primary apraxia for tools, a procedure along the following lines is recommended. Demonstrate the use of a piece of chalk as a writing instrument. Have the patient imitate the movement of chalk writing on a blackboard. If the patient's preferred hand is paralyzed, have the patient use the other hand. (It will usually be the left hand.) Make certain that the chalk is soft and that the blackboard is clean, so that an impression is readily seen. Begin with single lines and progress from horizontal to vertical to diagonal lines. As soon as possible, move on to printed letters and to printed words.

After the use of chalk as a writing instrument is established, a soft crayon should be introduced. The crayon should be relatively thick and easy to grasp. The paper should be large, and fixed so that it will not slide as it is used. When the patient has learned to use a crayon, he should then be given a large soft pencil. An ordinary pencil can be made easy to hold by winding a multiple-strand string around it about an inch from the point and about two inches up the length of the pencil.

If the problem is one of training the patient to use his left hand, the therapist will find Gardner's manual for left-handed writing [18] exceedingly helpful.

In the teaching of writing, whatever the cause, allowance must be made for visual disturbances. Material to be copied must be placed so that it can be seen. So also must the material on which the writing is to be done.

If the patient cannot recall letter formations, one approach is to present them to him for copying. The letters to be copied, which should be conventional and simple in outline, should be placed directly above his writing space. If this is too difficult, the patient may be helped by placing letters underneath thin, translucent paper for direct copying. As soon as possible, of course, the patient should be encouraged to write from dictation. If he has difficulty with some letters, these should be available for him to copy. As soon as the patient succeeds in writing with fair legibility, his own letters should become the basis for his copying. The therapist may find some useful suggestions for teaching writing in an article by Smith,[19] which was based upon experience with several rather resistant patients.

Words, phrases, and sentences as material for writing should be introduced at the earliest possible time. In his relearning process, the patient should not be required to struggle and experience unnecessary frustration

[18] W. Gardner, *Left-Handed Writing* (Danville, Illinois, Interstate Press, 1945).
[19] M. Smith, "Teaching an Aphasic How to Write Again," *Journal of Clinical Psychology*, Vol. 4 (1946), pp. 419-423.

for a letter or word he cannot recall. The elusive letter or word should be made available to him so that he may be encouraged to proceed with his writing effort.

Spelling. If the patient cannot recall the appropriate sequence of letters for the words he wishes to write, he has a true agraphia. For this type of difficulty, it is recommended that the patient's oral spelling efforts be compared with his written efforts. If his oral spelling is superior to his written results, then retraining should emphasize the oral approach. If, in addition, the patient seems to learn more readily by hearing how a word is spelled rather than by seeing it written, the auditory avenue for stimulation should be the one of choice.

Some of the approaches used for teaching spelling to non-brain-damaged persons are also applicable to the aphasic. Enlarged letters or letters written in a different color may be used to make the troublesome parts of words stand out if the visual approach is used. If the stimulation is auditory, then the troublesome parts of words can be enunciated more loudly and more slowly.

The selection of words for spelling should, of course, be based first on the patient's special needs. The patient should be encouraged to keep his own list of words which are difficult for him. These should be written both in conventional form and in a form best suited to help him to recall or recognize the correct spellings. In addition to these words, standardized spelling lists may be used as sources for spelling practice. The thousand most frequently used words of the Thorndike-Lorge word list [20] is also highly recommended. Additional specialized lists which may be of help were prepared by Gates [21] and Horn.[22]

Acalculia. The need for reteaching a process as close as possible to the way it was originally learned is especially applicable to difficulties in calculation. If this can be accomplished, the relearning of arithmetic will be accelerated. Another approach that will usually accelerate relearning is the tapping of automatic responses. Fortunately, much of arithmetic effort becomes almost completely automatic by the time most individuals become adults.

It is important not to confuse a patient's difficulty in evoking the appropriate nominal term for the result of an arithmetic process with an actual arithmetic disability. Inappropriate naming, or inability to name, constitutes word-finding difficulties in an arithmetic situation. It is more important that a patient know the correct price of what he buys, and makes the correct change, than it is for him to announce the results aloud.

[20] E. L. Thorndike and I. Lorge, *Teachers Word Book of 30,000 Words* (New York, Teachers College, Bureau of Publications, Columbia University, 1944).

[21] A. I. Gates, *A List of Spelling Difficulties in 3876 Words* (New York, Teachers College, Bureau of Publications, Columbia University, 1937).

[22] E. Horn, *Basic Writing Vocabulary,* University of Iowa Monographs in Education, No. 4 (Iowa City, University of Iowa Press, 1926).

The therapist will find many helpful approaches for patients with acalculalia in texts on arithmetic teaching, such as the one by Hildreth.[23]

Paraphasia. The correction of paraphasic errors frequently constitutes a continued therapeutic problem after appreciable recovery along other lines has taken place. Wrong words, transposed sounds, and ungrammatical sentences continue to be produced. Sometimes it helps to record the patient's speech and to have him listen as a critic. This technique enables the patient to hear himself as others hear him. The use of negative practice may bring some errors on a voluntary level. Written efforts may be improved by having the therapist note within a sentence where errors of commission or omission were made. The patient is then urged to correct his errors. It may be of some help to give the patient comparable material without errors to use as a model. With many patients who persist in paraphasic usage the problem is basically one of changing their attitude toward the need and wish for conventional speech. In some cases, however, some degree of paraphasia will remain as a residual of aphasia. It is probably best to accept the situation and to realize that even non-brain-damaged persons are occasionally paraphasic.

[23] G. Hildreth, *Learning the Three R's*, 2nd ed. (Minneapolis, Educational Test Bureau, Educational Publishers, 1947).

17

The Congenitally Aphasic Child

The term *congenitally aphasic* as used in this text refers to the individual who because of brain damage incurred before, during, or shortly after birth fails to develop language ability. In a broader sense, the term *congenitally aphasic* may also be used for individuals whose brain damage was incurred soon after they began to use language but before the habit of language usage had become firmly established.

It should be emphasized at the outset that all brain-damaged children are not congenitally aphasic. Some brain-damaged children may show no evidence of linguistic disability. Others may have only articulatory disturbances. Others may be mentally deficient, and so be unable to learn to use language. Still others may have severe hearing loss as well as mental deficiency. No child should be diagnosed as congenitally aphasic unless brain damage can be demonstrated directly or indirectly in either motor or perceptual involvement. The failure to develop speech, in and of itself, is not presumptive of congenital aphasia. Causes for failure to develop speech, other than on the basis of aphasia, have been considered in some detail in Chapter 5.

DIFFERENTIAL DIAGNOSIS

An essential problem of differential diagnosis for the nonspeaking child believed to be brain-damaged is (1) to determine whether the child is congenitally aphasic, and (2) to distinguish between the aphasia, if it is found, and the extent of other impairments which may be present. Hearing loss and intellectual deficiency are the two most likely associated impairments. Sensory loss other than hearing, perceptual disturbances, and motor involvements which may impair the co-ordinated activity of the speech mechanism need also to be determined. The last has been considered in the discussion of cerebral palsy, and so will not be taken up in our present discussion of differential diagnosis. Our emphasis will be to outline procedures to help the clinician to distinguish between congenital aphasia and

420

hearing loss, or congenital aphasia and mental deficiency, or congenital aphasia in addition to hearing loss and mental deficiency.[1]

Congenital Aphasia and Hearing Loss

A *physical examination* which includes a neurological and otological work-up should be given the child to determine whether there is any ear or nerve pathology which may be associated with hearing loss. Evidence of present or past pathology should be noted.

A *case history* should supplement the information derived from the physical examination. Parents may be able to furnish significant information about the child's early health history, especially as it may affect hearing. Any familial tendencies to hearing loss are noteworthy. The mother's illnesses during her period of pregnancy should be reviewed for any diseases such as rubella (German measles), which have been found to be associated with hearing loss in children. Any specific records about the child's early development, especially those which may include items about early vocalizations, sounds which resemble words, and early words, may be significant. If there are no written records or actual phonograph or tape recordings, the parent's memories should be of help. If possible, each parent should be consulted separately and their memories compared. A normal tendency for parents to overestimate the early abilities of their children should be taken into consideration in the evaluation of parental memories.

Among significant items to be looked for in the early sound-producing history of the child is a failure to do much babbling, or a failure of the child to have progressed from the babbling to the self-imitative lalling stage, or from the lalling to the echolalic stage. Any fixation at a stage in speech development (see pp. 18-21) may be suggestive of hearing loss. If, on the other hand, the history indicates that the child's preverbal sound-making history was normal, but that there was no progress beyond the echolalic stage, then aphasia rather than hearing loss may be suspected. Also, if the child's responses are consistent to mechanical noises of different pitches and intensities, but inconsistent to speech noises, then aphasic involvement rather than hearing loss may be suspected. This is especially so if the child responds to a new voice or an unusual human vocal sound, but fails to respond to the more familiar voices about him.

Through *observation of the child's behavior* in a play situation away from his parents, as well as in the presence of his parents, the clinician may be able to note much that is significant for a differential diagnosis. What kind of sounds does the child spontaneously produce while at play? Are the range and volume atypical for his age? (See pp. 37-39.) The aphasic child's voice is likely to be normal in pitch range and loudness. The child with a severe hearing loss may have a voice limited in pitch with marked and

[1] For a more detailed discussion of this topic, see J. Eisenson, *Examining for Aphasia*, rev. ed. (New York, Psychological Corporation, 1954), Ch. 4.

unexpected changes in volume. Does the child evoke sounds only when he thinks he is alone? Does he turn in the direction of mechanical sounds such as bells and switches? Does he ignore human sounds? The child with a hearing loss will respond more consistently to sounds, if they are loud enough to be heard, than will the congenitally aphasic child. The latter is likely to pay more attention to mechanical sounds that have direct meaning than to human word-symbol sounds.

Audiometric testing to determine possible hearing loss can best be accomplished through some technique employing conditioned responses. (See pp. 455-456.) Hardy and Bordley [2] believe that psychogalvanic skin-resistance audiometry can be used successfully as a technique for differential diagnosis in the young nonspeaking child.

Congenital Aphasia and Mental Deficiency

If loss of hearing has been ruled out as a likely cause for a child's failure to begin to use language, and the child is believed to have brain damage, it is important to determine whether the brain damage has resulted in mental deficiency and therefore in language failure. If there is no clear-cut evidence of brain damage, the possibility of mental deficiency must still be considered.

In taking the case history, note should be made as to whether the early sound-making stages were retarded in onset, and prolonged. Does the echolalic stage persist? Were there delays in onset of sitting and walking? Has the child learned to say a few words, but failed to add to his vocabulary for many months? Does the child have a poor attention span? Does he show little curiosity and little interest in his environment? Affirmative answers suggest that mental deficiency with or without associated brain damage is at least partly responsible for language delay.

Observations by the clinician of the child at play may provide some leads for a differential diagnosis. Is it difficult to obtain the child's attention? If obtained, is attention fleeting and likely to be easily distracted? Is there sometimes a morbidity of attention, so that the child becomes upset at any attempt to remove him from what he is doing? Is there marked perseveration which seems almost compulsive? Does the child enter a new situation with apparent enthusiasm which disappears suddenly and quickly? Does the child frustrate readily? Does the child, in general, show emotional lability? "Yes" answers to these questions would suggest aphasic involvement rather than mental deficiency.

[2] W. G. Hardy and J. E. Bordley, "Special Techniques in Testing the Hearing of Children," *Journal of Speech and Hearing Disorders*, Vol. 16, No. 1 (1951), pp. 122-131.

Perceptual Testing

Though a neurological examination should always be included as part of the physical work-up of the child suspected of being aphasic, the results are often not clear-cut. Correlative evidence of possible brain damage may be obtained through the use of tests for perceptual functioning. The ability to integrate and to interpret stimuli into organized and meaningful units or percepts is dependent upon the integrity of the nervous system as a whole. In once-normal adults who have incurred brain damage as a result of accident or disease, the perceptual process is known to be impaired. In brain-damaged children, the perceptual process is believed to be different than in normal children.[3] If we find a nonspeaking child who is not deaf performing perceptual tasks as in the manner of known brain-damaged children, we may suspect that the nonspeaking child is congenitally aphasic. Among the published tests which we have found to be useful in estimating perceptual ability in children are the Block Design subtests of the Wechsler Intelligence Scale for Children, the Bender Visual Motor Gestalt Test, and the Marble Board Test.

The Bender Visual Motor Gestalt Test[4] assesses visual perception through drawings as motor responses. The perceptual situations consist of a series of nine line drawings, each presented to the subject on a separate card. The examinee is asked to copy each figure as it is presented to him. Bender found that brain-damaged persons perform in characteristically different ways from those who are not brain-damaged in their drawing performances.

The Block Design Subtests of the Wechsler Intelligence Scale for Children[5] call for the construction of designs using colored blocks. The designs to be constructed are shown to the examinee on cards. Wechsler uses red and white blocks. Successful performances on block design tests require an ability to perceive patterns or forms, and to analyze and reproduce them.

The Marble Board Test is designed to measure visual perception through motor performance. The test is discussed in detail by Strauss and Lehtinen.[6] In the test, two identical cardboards are used. One board is used by the examiner for constructing patterns of red and black marbles. The examinee is directed to copy the completed patterns. As each pattern is copied, the moves are recorded on specially prepared record forms. When the examinee indicates that he is finished with his pattern-copying, his board is removed. He is then directed to make a pencil-line drawing of the pattern arranged on the examiner's board. Strauss and Lehtinen have found the marble

[3] A. A. Strauss and L. E. Lehtinen, *Psychopathology and Education of the Brain-injured Child* (New York, Grune and Stratton, 1947), p. 34.

[4] Loretta Bender, *A Visual Motor Gestalt Test and Its Clinical Use,* American Orthopsychiatric Association Research Monograph No. 3 (New York, 1938).

[5] D. Wechsler, *Wechsler Intelligence Scale for Children* (New York, Psychological Corporation, 1949).

[6] Strauss and Lehtinen, *op. cit.,* pp. 31-49.

board pattern-copying by brain-damaged children to be characteristically incoherent, disorganized, and disconnected.

Perceptual testing, or any other formal testing for the brain-damaged child, should not be administered unless the child is capable of understanding the task to be performed. If such understanding is not present, no valid conclusions should be drawn from the performance. If, however, the child seems to understand what he is to do, but performs poorly, the results may be significant. A word of caution is still in order. Mentally deficient children without brain damage frequently perform much like the brain-damaged. Expert clinical judgment is required to determine the differences. In fact, the entire matter of arriving at a differential diagnosis for the non-speaking child believed to be brain-damaged is one for the expert. The speech clinician who is aware of this and who reserves judgment until expert opinion is available will make a significant contribution to correct thinking about congenital aphasia.

Myklebust [7] who has made an intensive study of aphasic children, includes the following among their outstanding characteristics: The clinical histories of aphasic children reveal some retardation in development and confusion in regard to hearing. Observed behavior of aphasic children reveals hyperactivity and failure to use other sensory avenues to compensate for their confusion in hearing. Their auditory responses tend to be inconsistent. Often they seem unable to listen. The motor development of aphasic children appears to be generally retarded; motor in-co-ordination is evident in clumsiness in walking, throwing, and kicking. Motor activity lacks direction, and is often random. Socially, the aphasic children are deficient; often they make little distinction between friends and strangers. They do not show normal shyness to strangers or to new social situations. Emotional development is retarded; extremes of affect are often displayed in uncontrollable crying, screaming, or laughing. Disturbances of visual perception are often present in addition to disturbed auditory perception. Some aphasic children are echolalic and show perseverative tendencies. Attention is difficult to maintain, and they are impulsive and readily distractible.

THERAPEUTIC APPROACHES

Socialization

The first step in training, after it has been determined that the child is ready for direct speech therapy, is to make the child want to talk. Congenitally aphasic children frequently develop direct methods for satisfying their needs. When the direct method fails, crying, temper tantrums, and random motor behavior may be employed. When these emotional mani-

[7] H. Myklebust, *Auditory Disorders in Children* (New York, Grune and Stratton, 1954), pp. 178-180.

festations take place, one of several things may follow: (1) older persons in the child's environment may try to satisfy his needs; (2) the child may try to find a substitute satisfaction; or (3) the immediate need may lose its drive potency. As a result, the congenitally aphasic child is likely to play alone, or with indulgent and understanding older persons. Speech as a social tool and as a technique for socialization is therefore lacking. Wherever possible, early therapeutic efforts should be directed toward socialization. Such efforts, however, should not be accompanied by expectations which would be beyond the social abilities for a non-aphasic child of the same age. In this regard it should be remembered that small children play in the presence of one another before they play with one another, and that true co-operative playing frequently does not take place until the child is of kindergarten age or older.

The recommended social situation calls for a small group of children and the use of a few toys or games. Many children and many toys create distraction and confusion for most preschool children, and especially so for the brain-damaged. The group should, if possible, include normally speaking children so that most of the stimulation for speech comes from within the group itself rather than from the therapist. The essential role of the therapist in regard to the group as a whole, and particularly in regard to the aphasic child, is to create situations which naturally call for the use of speech. In such group situations, the aphasic child is given an opportunity to observe other children using speech, to see its values, and so to be motivated to imitate speech.

The group situation should be a permissive one in the light of the objectives of the therapist for the group. This means that only those toys and objects which the therapist wants used should be displayed. If the therapist does not want a phonograph or a set of blocks used, these objects should not be present either to distract the child, or to evoke a "No, we don't want to play the phonograph," or "No, we don't want to build a house," from the therapist.

Types of Activities

From the point of view of the aphasic child, the best activities are those which make any type of appropriate oral behavior a pleasure. Although ultimately true speech is the objective for the aphasic child, prelingual activities are strongly recommended in the early stages of therapy. Games which include the repetition of a syllable or a sound, or a short sequence of sounds in imitation of animal noises or mechanical noises, provide sound-making exercises on the level of the lalling and echolalic stages and afford the child considerable fun. Later, games calling for individualized responsive sound-making in which a "bow-wow" rather than a bark, or a "meow" rather than an inarticulate cry, might be introduced. The point to be stressed is that the child must like the game as well as his role in the game, so that the act of making an appropriate sound at an expected time is a pleasurable one. From here, the therapist must be vigilant and judge when the aphasic child seems to be ready for true speech. If the child has made one or more spontaneous attempts at speaking, even if these attempts or crude oral-vocalizations are accompanied by gesture, the time might be ripe for the introduction of a game in which a word, a phrase, or a short sentence is repeated several times. As soon as possible, the games should incorporate short social phrases such as "Hello" and "How do you do?" so that what the child learns can be put to use in real-life situations.

Recordings can be cut or put on tape which when played announce the child's name and direct him as to his expected response. If possible, the record should also include a pause during which the child may make his response. This highly personalized type of recording usually can be counted on to motivate a child to play his part. Small children, including aphasics, are likely to attend to stories if their own names are dubbed in, and are quite likely to respond to the "magic voice" of the playback if the voice directs them to make a roar like a lion, or to say "hello" to the dog, or to make a noise like a "choo-choo" train.

The Use of Rewards

Children who have passed the normal age for spontaneous speech-learning without beginning to speak, as is the case with the congenitally aphasic, need both special motivation to get them started and rewards to continue them on their way. The best possible reward is one inherent in the situation. If the child can get something through speech more quickly and more completely than he can without speech, the act of speaking becomes worthwhile in itself. The child who gets his drink of water, or his toy, or his parent by evoking the appropriate word has that word reinforced. If, however, nothing especially desirable happens at the evocation of a word appropriately used, not only is the particular word not reinforced, but there is a general devaluation of speaking as a way of life in which things can be made to happen without the need for direct action or emotional display on the part of the child. It becomes extremely important, therefore, especially in the early stages of training, for persons in the child's environment to co-operate by responding readily to the child's use of words. Occasionally, aphasic children who begin to speak do so selectively. They will speak for the persons who respond to them and make speech worthwhile. On the other hand, they may develop attitudes of apathy or of definite negativism toward both listening and speaking to persons or in situations where there is no quick responsiveness.

The specific use of rewards where rewards are not inherent in the speaking situation is strongly recommended. If the aphasic child, either in a small group or when working alone with a therapist, utters an appropriate word, a reward of significance to the child should be available. At our clinics, gumdrops are always at hand. (Gumdrops are used because they can be eaten quickly while work is continued.) If a child names something for the first time, if he identifies an object correctly or uses a word to indicate his wish or his need, he is given a piece of candy. In working experimentally with specific rewards with a severely aphasic five-year-old child, the author was able to note a definite increase in the use of immediately rewarded words and phrases over those which were permitted to be spoken without such reward. At the end of a two-week experimental period, the rewarded words continued to be evoked with greater consistency and readiness than those not rewarded. The look of pleasurable expectancy on the part of the child as she spoke her words served as reward to the author as well. The author recommends the use of rewards not only for appropriate responses but also for early attempts at oral communication. In a group play activity situation, it is necessary to have more than one clinician present to make certain that no aphasic child's efforts at communication go unnoticed.

Preferred Sensory Avenue

A major job of the speech therapist is to study the aphasic child to try to discover how the child seems best able to learn. Basically, this is a task of observing closely and keenly to see what sensory avenues the child prefers to use in exploring new situations. If the child prefers to look rather than to listen, if in conversation the child peers directly and closely at the speaker and seems to understand things better that way, it may be assumed that the visual approach is the one of choice. If, on the other hand, looking at things seems to confuse the child more than listening without looking, the auditory avenue may be assumed to be the one of choice. Occasionally, a child will learn best by direct tactual contact with a situation. A doll or some other toy may be manually explored for its size and shape and texture, and the same toy may hold little interest for the child for its noise-making possibilities. Such a child may prefer and learn best through the tactile sense. It is obvious, of course, that not many situations can be approached or appreciated through any one sensory avenue. Nor is it desirable to limit learning to a single sensory avenue even if it can be done. But it is possible, frequently, to emphasize one sensory avenue over another, and in such instances it should be the avenue of choice for the child. When the child shows definite ability in language learning, multiple sense appeal should be used. The basic appeal, however, should continue to be the one of the child's indicated preference.

Lip Reading

Where the child seems to learn best through the visual approach, speech (lip) reading may be taught successfully. In fact, some congenitally aphasic children are being taught to speak using the techniques employed for severely hard-of-hearing and deaf children. The writer considers this an excellent approach, but warns against teaching the congenitally aphasic child in a group with the congenitally deaf child, because the aphasic child is then likely to learn to speak with the voice and articulatory limitations of the deaf. This is both undesirable and unnecessary.

Intensity of Stimulation

It is a common experience of adults in speaking to small children to find that the child does not seem to hear until the adult has repeated his utterance two or three times or has raised his voice so that the child could not help but hear. The possible causes for the normal child's not seeming to hear need not be discussed. The congenitally aphasic child may not hear, or understand what he hears, because of a basic inability to respond to speech sounds unless the intensity is greater than normal. It is necessary, therefore, to determine experimentally at what level of intensity speech sounds need to be presented for a hearing reaction to take place. As responses to hearing become established, it usually becomes possible to reduce the intensity of auditory stimulation to one which ultimately is approximately or actually normal. New situations, however, may need to be presented with more than normal intensity.

The intensification of stimulation as a principle of training for the aphasic child is not to be limited to situations presented to the auditory sense. In the early stages of training, all materials, regardless of sensory appeal, should initially be presented with increased intensity. Visual material should be large—larger even than for the normal child. Large pictures, large blocks, large toys, should be the rule as training begins. Later, if it is possible, the same kind of material reduced in size should be substituted for the initial material. Ultimately, the materials should be of a size approximating the normal.

Repetition

The effect of intensity of stimulation can also be approached through repetition at about a normal level of intensity. The clinician should observe the amount of repetition necessary to bring about a response, and through experimentation, aim to reduce repetition to the minimum number necessary to assure the desired response. Ultimately the aim of the therapist for the child is to present the speech stimulus only once at normal intensity to obtain the appropriate response. The clinician must always be on the alert, however, to be certain that the child is attending before the stimulus-situation is presented. If this precaution is not observed, any apathy the child has for speech may become aggravated and become an added problem in training.

Slow Rate

In the early stages of training it is recommended that, whenever possible, the rate of presentation of material be slower than it is for the normal child. This pertains to the rate of speech as well as to the rate of material in general. The aphasic child seems to require a little more time to absorb what is presented. The rate of presentation, however, should not be so slow as to distort the sense of unity of material. For example, speech should not sound scanning, and the phrase as a unit should be clear. The therapist, at least in the early stages of training, might pretend that a wall of glass separates him from the child. The normal tendency would then be to speak both more slowly and more clearly. However, the psychological "wall of glass" should never prevent the therapist from direct and friendly contact with the child.

Small Units of Material

To the aphasic child with auditory disability, the world of sound may continue for an indefinite time to be one of buzzing confusion. The suggestions to intensify stimulation and to slow the rate of presentation help to make the selected unit of stimulation stand out from other environmental sounds. For the child with visual difficulty, the increased size of the material serves the same end. Another suggestion is to keep the unit of material short. A short unit, presented with increased intensity and at a determined slower than normal rate, helps the aphasic child to distinguish figure from background and so to make sensory discrimination and appropriate response more likely to occur.

It is not by chance alone that the small child who is just learning to talk uses either single words or very short (two- or three-word) phrases or sentences. These short units represent the child's own selection of what he is able to respond to out of all the stimuli with which he is directly or indirectly confronted. The aphasic child needs the help of the therapist and other adults in his environment to do for him what the normal child does for himself.

Symbol Association

Whatever the presented material may be, it should always be presented in association with either a *real situation* or an acceptable facsimile situation. *Water, egg, milk, spoon,* and so on, should first be taught with the actual material present. When the learning has been definitely established, pictures in association with the real material should be introduced. A later step is to substitute the picture for the real material. An ultimate step, if reading as an aspect of symbol association is the goal, is to present the printed word as a substitute for the picture. This, however, is not the concern of the clinician working with the young congenitally aphasic child in the early stages of training.

When it is certain that a child has formed an association between an object or picture and a word or phrase, several (three or four) objects or pictures may be presented and the child directed to select the appropriate item to the short oral request. If the material can be manipulated or otherwise employed, a second direction might give the child an opportunity to use the material appropriately. A bit of food may be eaten, a ball may be bounced, a drum beaten, or a horn blown. If the objects selected for naming and using are those which the child needs in his everyday experiences, the learning becomes functional and practice is assured.

Multiple Function of Objects to Establish Meaning

One of the dangers of training, and therefore one of the unfortunate limitations of learning, is that a situation is presented in a limited manner. A ball, for example, may be presented and only bounced. A ball, however, is more than for bouncing. It is for throwing and catching (or not catching), and squeezing and, for the small child, for tasting and biting. It is also for kicking and striking and for the many other uses a normal child can think of. All these uses to which a ball is put represent the *meaning of "ball."* In teaching the name of an object, it becomes necessary for the therapist to teach as many of the functions of the object as the training situation permits. These functions should, of course, not be taught all at once. Functional use should be taught as the child's abilities and experiences develop. The minimum objective should be to give the aphasic child at least the number of functional experiences as is normal for a child in his environment. If this is done, the child will not be inclined to accept only the first use of an object as the one to be associated with the name of the object.

The object itself should also be presented in the forms normal to a child. If *book* is being taught, books of different size and shape and color and texture should be used in progressive stages of training. If possible, only a single feature should be added at one time so that there is not too early a violation of the child's concept of the object. By gradually introducing the most usual features of an object in terms of a class of objects, the child's concept will not be too rigid or too concrete, and the tendencies towards rigidity and concretism may then be avoided.

Vocabulary Building

The first words a congenitally aphasic child is directly taught should be words he can use to indicate his needs or satisfy his wants. These will probably be related to food, to his own name, to the names of persons with whom he lives, and to the names of tools he must employ. Further vocabulary building should continue, at least in the early stages, along strictly functional lines in terms of the child's everyday life. In this respect, the words a congenitally aphasic child is taught differ from the vocabulary of the small child who attends school. The latter is introduced to a vocabulary which is basic to learning to read. He comes to school equipped with a functional vocabulary which the aphasic child usually does not have.

Pronunciation

In order to encourage all possible efforts at speech, a liberal attitude must be taken towards pronunciation. Any approximation of a verbal utterance should be accepted as correct. If the child hears other children and adults whose pronunciations are correct, in time more accurate pronunciation may be expected. In any event, correction of pronunciation or of articulation should not be attempted until the habit of oral speech is clearly established and the desire for accurate speech is motivated. Too early an effort at correction may discourage attempts to speak. This, by all means, is to be avoided.

18

The Young Aphasic Child

The young aphasic child—the child who develops speech normally and then, because of brain pathology, suffers an impairment in speech—presents special problems. The immediate effects of aphasic disturbance will vary considerably according to the age of the child at the onset of the disturbance and the degree to which speech and other symbol functions (such as reading, writing, and arithmetic abilities) had been developed. It should be borne in mind that among children under five of equal intelligence there is likely to be a much wider range of linguistic ability than among equally intelligent children over five.

The child of two or three who has not been an early talker, and who has not yet had the opportunity to learn to read or write, will not have developed symbol behavior to a stage where aphasic disturbance per se will cause marked behavior disturbance. Such a child may merely resort to a prelingual level of behavior, using crying and perhaps gesture to bring attention to and express his wants. If there is no spontaneous recovery, the training of the very young aphasic child should probably proceed along the same lines as that of the congenitally aphasic child. Fortunately, many young children recover spontaneously if the pathology is not too widespread and the pathological condition is not progressive.

For those brain-damaged children whose normal potential has been severely disturbed, so that they function as mentally retarded children with uneven development, special educational procedures must be used in terms of the specific problems and potentials of the individual child. Some of these problems, to be considered later, include ready distractibility and emotional lability.

OBJECTIVES OF TRAINING

The child of three or more, especially if his linguistic development has been precocious, may have severe psychological problems as a direct result of aphasic disturbance. This type of child suffers in a very real way from communicative disability. If there is little or no spontaneous recovery, the child must first be helped to accept his condition, and then retrained to improve it. If, as sometimes happens, the child withdraws into himself in order to reduce the likelihood of frustration because of his communicative disability, he should first be given immediate help through being taught a simple gesture language. Beyond this point, the child must be reoriented toward the understanding and use of conventional speech and other forms of symbol usage. The specific program of training will, of course, vary with the potentialities of the child and the knowledge of how much and what kind of symbol functions have been disturbed. Although the prognosis for young aphasic children is generally good, in some instances the brain damage may be so severe and extensive as to make only modest objectives possible. These objectives should be determined by the use of appropriate clinical psychological devices. Re-evaluation as training progresses is definitely recommended, so that the therapist may know whether the level of the objectives should be raised and their scope broadened.

For the child of five or six who has only limited linguistic ability, and who has not yet learned to read and to write, readiness for these accomplishments might well be included in the therapist's objectives. This is recommended because the aphasic child who is of an age when reading and writing are ordinarily expected may need special techniques or more highly individualized instruction than he is likely to get through nonspecialized instruction.

Similarly, the child who was able to read and/or write should, if at all possible, be brought back to his premorbid level of accomplishment before being considered for formal schooling.

REORIENTATION TO SPEECH

One of the problems frequently faced in the training of young aphasic children is that of reorientation to speech. This aspect of training is especially important in children whose speech development was slow and who therefore had not completely abandoned their prelingual techniques of crying, using gestures, or taking direct action to attract attention, to express themselves, and otherwise to reveal and seek to satisfy their needs. These children must be motivated to attempt conventional oral communication, and must be rewarded for their attempts. The approaches toward this end are essentially those which were considered for the congenitally aphasic child.

DIRECT TRAINING—EARLY STAGES

It is probably best to begin direct training with prelingual activities to give the child an opportunity to practice and to enjoy sound-making. This, as explained in the program for the congenitally aphasic child, can best be accomplished through games, songs, and play activities. If a group of small children is available, the young aphasic child should become a member of the group for play and games, especially for those which employ pantomime and are accompanied by simple repetitive sounds and sounds which resemble words. In general, the prelingual activities should recapitulate the stages of speech development through which the child progressed before the onset of his disturbance. He should practice sound-making, first for the pleasure of the act, then to build up an inventory of sounds and sound combinations produced as a voluntary act. Following this, the child should produce sounds which "echo" those of his environment. In the next stage, simple gestures accompanied by monosyllabic or disyllabic words should be established. In the first part of this stage, emphasis should be placed on the gesture, with the accompanying word an incidental aspect of the training objective. In the second part of the stage, the emphasis should be shifted to the conventional word.

CONTROLLING DISTRACTIBILITY

The ready distractibility and the increased and seemingly random motor activity of cerebral-palsied children is well recognized as a frequent characteristic of their behavior.[1] Sometimes these characteristics are present in brain-damaged children who show no other obvious evidence of cerebral palsy. Therapeutic approaches for this aspect of the behavior of the brain-damaged child have among their objectives: (a) helping the child to establish self-discipline and to exercise self-control, and (b) exercising control over the physical aspects of the environment so as to reduce stimulation of extraneous situations and thereby avoid the basis of distractibility. On this point, Strauss and Lehtinen hold that "the brain-injured child requires an environment especially suited to his particular needs."[2]

Strauss and Lehtinen, in keeping with their point of view which emphasizes environmental simplification, advocate a class size not exceeding twelve children, a classroom large enough to permit the children to be seated at a considerable distance from one another, and a minimum of decorative and illustrative material. The classroom should be as far from sources of noise as the building will permit, with windows facing a court rather than a street. Strauss and Lehtinen recommend that the teacher be dressed simply, without the decorative (and distracting) influences of ornamentation such as earrings, necklaces, or flowers.

The present author does not feel that most brain-damaged children, except perhaps in the earlier stages of training, require such extreme treat-

---

[1] See A. A. Strauss and L. E. Lehtinen, *Psychopathology and Education of the Brain-Injured Child*, (New York, Grune and Stratton, 1947), pp. 130-134.
[2] *Ibid.*, p. 131.

ment. Simplification of the physical environment is desirable, but not to the point where the classroom resembles a celibate's quarters. Furthermore, it is recommended that as soon as possible the brain-damaged child be given an opportunity to work in approximately normal contact with other children so that he can be prepared for everyday living outside of his school experience. An adequate degree of control from within must be established through directed interest. Although it is conceded that many and perhaps most children in their initial training may benefit from the use of physical "blinders," in the long run these must be replaced by psychological "blinders" if the child is to learn to live in a noninstitutional environment. It is the author's belief that many of the brain-damaged child's movements are more distracting to normal persons than they are to other brain-damaged children.[3]

CONTROLLING EMOTIONAL LABILITY

For the most part, emotional disturbances arise out of the brain-damaged child's inability to communicate his needs or to attain satisfaction through his own efforts when communication is not possible. Unless the tools of communication are provided through training, the child shows ready frustration. In addition, some of his ends are gained, or substitute satisfactions are found, through displays of emotionality. In part, also, the ready distractibility of the child becomes a basis for self-frustration. The brain-damaged child may initiate activity toward a given end and along an intended way. He may become distracted before achieving his objective, and then experience frustration because of his failure to complete what he set out to accomplish. A program of training to overcome distractibility, combined with tools for communication, provides the best safeguards for controlling emotional lability.

CASE REPORT—TRUE APHASIA IN A SIX-YEAR-OLD CHILD

ETIOLOGY AND FACTORS RELATED TO PATHOLOGY

A case of mixed aphasia, predominantly expressive, in a girl, beginning at age five. Etiology, probably cortical damage resulting from cerebral anoxemia (abnormally adverse reaction to anesthesia). History of measles one month prior to abdominal surgery complicates determination of etiology. Child's manifest left-handedness prior to pathology and ability to speak French as well as English are further complicating factors.

[3] In fairness to Strauss and Lehtinen, it should be pointed out that they too advocate that as soon as possible the brain-damaged child should be removed from a severely protected environment, with a regular class-group as the ultimate goal. "As the organic disturbances are lessened, the protections are gradually removed . . . and experiences in which a group participates become more numerous." (*Ibid.,* p. 135).

The child was first seen by a neurologist at age five and a half, at which time she was five days postoperative, having been operated on for an inflammation of a Meckel's diverticulum. She did not recover consciousness completely following the anesthesia, and at the time of the neurological examination she was still stuporous and out of contact with her environment. There were no localizing neurological signs.

Within two months the child learned to walk again and co-ordination improved to a point where there was no indication of any motor defect. There was no gross ataxia or any sign of sensory defect. She recognized neighbors and responded to her environment, but except for a few emotional evocations, she did not speak.

A month later, glutamic acid began to be administered with the hope that improvement might be accelerated and that seizures might be controlled.

EARLY HISTORY

The mother's report indicated that the child began to talk at nine months; was toilet-trained at ten months, and began to walk at twelve months. By the age of three she spoke French as well as English. By age four she was able to write her name and copy simple geometric figures.

LANGUAGE EXAMINATION

The child was referred to the Queens College Speech Clinic and first seen when she was five and a half years old. Except for echolalic repetition and a few emotional evocations, there was no speech, although the child was able to follow simple directions. Her general behavior was wild and uncontrolled. Toys were played with for short periods and then thrown away. Breakable toys were almost immediately destroyed.

PSYCHOMETRIC EXAMINATION

This was attempted, but because of the child's inattention and uncontrolled behavior, no scorable responses were elicited.

THERAPEUTIC PROGRAM

The child was introduced into the delayed-speech group for purposes of socialization. Individual therapy was initiated concurrently, directed at the establishment of object-symbol association.

At the end of a three-month period the child was withdrawn from the group because of her disruptive, destructive, and generally uncontrolled behavior. Individual work continued. There seemed to be an increase of emotionally evoked speech, but none in situations calling for identification or naming, or in response to verbal directions. There was no spontaneous conversation.

Therapy Notes. In an attempt to reduce inattention and distraction, the child was seen in a small room devoid of any materials except those to be used in therapy. The child was held in her mother's lap, seated to face the clinician. When presented with a toy she would hold it tightly and refuse to relinquish her grasp until she was ready to fling it away.

Nursery rhymes and songs which had been familiar to the child were recited by the clinician or mother. Occasionally the child would recite or sing the last line. The child continued to be distracted by outside noises.

During the period from February through May, the child began to evoke single words and a few phrases spontaneously. There was no assurance, however, that a word once evoked would be repeated as the situation was repeated. Some objects, were recognized and named. These included flowers, keys, doll, house, and ribbon. At one time the child complained, "This place is noisy."

The clinician's closing notes include: "Prognosis is poor. There are only three objects the child surely knows. These are a penny, a telephone, and a key. We have worked with simple toys. We have tried to place them in the proper spaces and to revive the memory of the colors. Since S. is unable to release any object she grasps, the insert toy has to be used in separate stages. Attention span is nil. Memory is equally poor. There has been no noticeable progress during the period of the child's attendance at the clinic."

During the summer months [of 1951], the child was trained by the Director of the Clinic, mostly because he was the only member of the staff who felt that the prognosis was not entirely hopeless. The training for the six-weeks' summer clinic term was directed initially at inhibiting random movement and establishing, on a voluntary basis, a repeated motor act. All appropriate responses were to be rewarded until their establishment could be taken for granted. Some of the daily lesson notes follow:

6/19: Session in play room. Random play with objects and materials including doll, doll house, teddy bear, pitcher, blocks, telephone.
Identification of some objects was spontaneous, including teddy bear, tub, "Hollis" for telephone (child's home exchange), baby, pencil. On two occasions the child asked, "What's that?"
There was little evidence of destructive behavior. Child put many toys into her mouth and chewed some crayon.

6/21: Marked reduction in random activity. Child was held firmly in her mother's lap, and objects were presented close to the child's eyes.
Child identified by naming pictures of a peach, an elephant, and a book of matches. A match was lighted and blown out by clinician. Then another was lighted and presented to child to be blown out. Child ignored lighted match.

6/25: Reward therapy begun. Child was given a gum drop to eat immediately after the correct identification of a picture-card. Pictures of *chair, fish, elephant* identified. *Candy* as an object identified.

6/27: Therapy as above continued. Spontaneous evocation of elephant. Child began to tear a sheet of paper on clinician's desk. Paper given to child, who was told, "Tear it up." S. tore paper and threw it into waste-paper basket and evoked "garbage can." S. given a second piece of paper and told to "Tear it up and throw it into the garbage can." S. did so and announced, "Garbage Can." In response to noise of a pneumatic drill outside of office, child spontaneously said, "Digging." Despite the appropriate identifications, and responses to directions, S. continued to look remote and her responses were usually delayed, in a fashion suggestive of the behavior of a child with primary autism.

6/28: S. attempted to take pencil from clinician's hand. Clinician said, "Say pencil and you may have it." After a pause, S. said "pencil." Pencil was given to S. who began to make random movements on paper with left hand. S.'s hand held in examiner's, and circular motion made. Clinician said, "Make an O." Hand was removed from paper after each circular motion accompanied by words, "Make an O." Twice in about 30 repetitions S. said, "Make an O."

Match lighted and child was directed, "Blow it out." There was evidence of inhibited lip movement as match burnt out. A second match was lighted and child again directed to blow it out. More vigorous blowing movement extinguished second and third lighted matches.

All pictures and objects correctly identified on previous day were again identified.

7/2: Continued drill to establish association between specific motor act of writing letter *O* and verbal direction of "make an O." Formation of association evident in child's evocation of "make an O" and spontaneous inhibition of writing movement after each circular movement in approximation of letter *O*.

S. shown cards with pictures including one of a birthday cake. Blew at pictures of candles and repeated "birthday cake" and "sing happy birthday." Perseverated on phrase "sing happy birthday."

Identified pictures of clock, book, boy, fish, candle, and said "lady" for picture of a nurse.

7/11: The mother reported that S. had a severe seizure in the early morning. Child showed unwillingness to name objects or pictures and indicated through pantomime her wish to write. Given pencil (left hand), and directed to "make an *O*," while her hand was held in E's. S. said "make a *W*" and proceeded to do so. She repeated, "make a *W*" and then asked for toy bird. Presented with bird, S. said, "Birdie says tweet." Later child threw toy bird away and repeated after E., "No birdie."

7/16: Mother reported that child had two severe seizures during week.

S. pointed to toy duck and asked "What's that?" When told it was a duck, S. said "Swimming in the water." S. shown picture of a bell and told "That's a bell." S. said, "Ding-a-ling."

QUESTION: "What does a birdie say?"——S. "Peep-peep."
  "   "What does a cow say?"——S. "Moo-moo."
  "   "What does a doggie say?"——S. "Moo-moo." Then spontaneously corrected to "bow-wow."
  "   "What does a pussy cat say?"——S. "Meow-meow." Then spontaneously, "It's hot in here."

Box of candy was taken out of drawer. S. tried but failed to snatch box.
E. "Do you want candy?"——S. No response.
E. "Do you want candy?"——S. (after long pause) "I want candy." S. was given a piece of candy.
S. pointed to toy telephone and identified it. Given another piece of candy. Then, spontaneously, "I want some more candy." Given candy.

The mother reports an increase in naming of objects about the house, and of calling persons by name. S. also announces some of the activities in which she is engaged. She responds directly to questions, but usually responds after a considerable pause, and sometimes by gesture alone. She does not, however, engage in conversational speech.

7/19: Today for the first time, the child was seated alone on a chair rather than held restrained in her mother's lap.

Child shown a picture of a farmer, a woman, and a birthday cake, and asked, "What is this?", said, "Cake."

E. "What else do you see?" said S., "O Boy."

E. "Tell me more."——S., "Puh," and blew at candle.

E. "What else?"——S. "A Lady."

E. "You may blow out a match." Lighted match held before child. S. "Puh," and then blew out the match. Given a piece of candy.

E. "Let's write." E. put pencil into child's left hand and placed his hand over child's. Said, "Make an *O*." Phrase repeated for line of *O*'s.

E. "Now, make a *W*." Line of *W*'s made.

S. was then given a paper and directed to "make an *O*." Child made a recognizable *O*.

At close of session S. was asked "Do you want to go home?" S., "No, I want paper." S. was given paper and said, "Make an *O*" as she wrote.

S. was given paper and pencil and told, "Good-bye."

7/26: (closing note): There is evidence of considerable progress in identification and appropriate evocation of single sentences. Rewarded identification (naming) seems better reinforced than items for which no rewards of candy were given. There is a marked reduction in uncontrolled motor activity and of destructive behavior. The language usage is about on a par with that of a two-year-old child.

19

The Handicapped in Hearing

REQUISITES FOR "NORMAL" HEARING

In one sense, the human ear is a poor specimen of evolutionary development. Both the dog and the cat have hearing ranges which exceed man's. The bat possesses an ultrasonic radar system, thus guiding its flight by the echo of its own sound vibrations reflected against its wings and equilibratory-sonic mechanism. The grasshopper has its "ears" in its knees, and even the lowly lizard can respond to sonic stimuli of 80,000 cycles per second. Then the physiologist reminds us that the organ of hearing in man is placed disadvantageously in a recess of the temporal bone where its cochlear section, the inner ear, is practically inaccessible, but where the middle ear has a direct connection with the respiratory system, via the Eustachian tube, and hence is subject to all the infectious diseases of respiration.

Despite these gloomy observations, it is clear that man's hearing generally is better than it need be. The cochlea is able to respond to vibrations as low as 20 per second and as high as 20,000 per second. For communication, we need a frequency range from 100 to 4500 vibrations or cycles per second. We are, moreover, vastly superior to other mammals in the higher neural functions relating to hearing, in our ability to synthesize, transmit, and interpret the sounds picked up by the receptors in the cochlea.

Normal hearing must be predicated upon our perceptive and interpretive powers in ordinary communication through speech. It must be judged not only or largely by our response to the intensity of a sound, but by our total auditory behavior.[1] It must be evaluated, for example, in relation to our language development; to our neural potential for reception and interpretation of sounds, and for integration and expression of ideas through language. Hearing should be measured, moreover, in relation to the maturation of other faculties and of patterns of general growth. The mentally retarded child has reduced sensitivity in receiving and interpreting auditory stimuli.

[1] H. Myklebust, *Auditory Disorders in Children* (New York, Grune and Stratton, 1954), p. 74.

The physically retarded are backward, too, in auditory maturation. Organic disturbances may affect the interpretation of speech sounds in the cerebral interpretive areas: the individual suffers from auditory aphasia. We may have poor auditory discrimination so that we cannot detect the speech sounds correctly, particularly in an environment of noises and tones; or we may be able to respond to many frequencies (pitch) but not to the pitch range of the voice. Hearing for speech is impaired, then, where there is a significant diminution in the powers of reception, interpretation, or integration of the sounds employed in oral communication.

THE DEVELOPMENT OF AUDITORY ACUITY

The infant normally responds to sound immediately after birth. A noise, for example, will set off the palpebral reflex (flutter of the eyelids). At four weeks he will turn his head toward the source of the sound. Between two and three months, he begins to relate hearing to vision. At first, noises are more attractive than the human voice, but at about five months he responds more readily to a quiet voice than to a noisemaker.[2] Between six months and one year, he not only recognizes the sound but also traces it to the source. At nine months he enjoys his mother's imitation of his own sounds more than he enjoys other sounds. Between one and a half and two years, he generally can respond to a voice of subdued loudness in speech; and at about three years he usually will respond both to speech and voice tests of his hearing.[3] During the first three years he has been learning both gross and fine discrimination of sound. In fact, this process of sound discrimination is practically complete by the end of his third year.[4] From the seventh month, the development of the baby's speech, thinking, and language has been proceeding slowly along with his hearing maturation. As auditory discrimination reaches its peak, however, his language as a tool of communication of his feelings, thoughts, and experiences pushes ahead very rapidly. So the child, endowed with a normal hearing mechanism and a normal body and mind in a normal environment, develops the requisite auditory skills.

[2] Jean Utley, "Suggestive Procedures for Determining Auditory Acuity in Very Young Acoustically Handicapped Children," *Eye, Ear, Nose, and Throat Monthly,* Vol. 28 (December, 1949), pp. 590-595.

[3] J. M. McLaurin, "The Inarticulate Child," *Laryngoscope,* Vol. 64, No. 6 (1954), pp. 454-466.

[4] H. Davis, *Hearing and Deafness* (New York, Murray Hill Books, Inc., 1947), p. 279.

THE HEARING MECHANISM

The Outer Ear

The visible part of the hearing apparatus, the outer ear, consisting of the pinna and the auditory canal, or meatus, may offer some assistance in locating the source of the sound and in collecting and focusing sound waves. Authorities are not agreed on the usefulness of the outer ear.[5] The pinna, immobilized in man through loss of its muscular action, leads directly into the auditory meatus. The meatus is funnel-shaped, about three centimeters in length, and ends in the tympanum or eardrum.

The Middle Ear

The middle ear, a narrow passageway one half inch in length, is practically filled by a chain of three small bones—the malleus, incus, and stapes—which transform the air waves of compression and rarefaction into mechanical vibrations. (See Fig. 19-1.) The tympanum which forms the diagonal partition between the outer and middle ear is a tough, flexible membrane, convex when viewed from the outside, with its fibers converging inward and upward to form a centrum, the umbo. To this point is attached the *manubrium,* or handle of the malleus (hammer) which, in turn, is connected by its head with the long process of the *incus* (anvil). The tip of the incus fits into the *stapes* (stirrup), the foot plate of which lies in the *oval window* opening on the labyrinth of the inner ear. As the drum vibrates, the ossicular chain goes through an imperceptible rocking motion, regulated in the main by the antagonistic action of two muscles, the stapedius, attached to the neck of the stapes, and the tensor tympani lying over the handle of the malleus. The motion of the last of the ossicular chain sets the fluid of the labyrinth in motion. The effect of the transmission of the air-borne sound by the ossicles is to reduce the extensity or amplitude and so increase the intensity or force of the vibrations. The tympanum's area is thirty times that of the oval window; the thirty-fold increase in pressure is needed when it strikes the highly compressed fluid that fills the inner ear. In other words, sound waves in one medium do not enter readily another medium of different acoustic resistance. The middle ear acts as the transformer. There are other doorways leading into the middle ear. The

---

[5] Davis (*op. cit.,* p. 20) ascribes little function to it in man. G. von Békésy and W. A. Rosenblith ("The Mechanical Properties of the Ear" in S. S. Stevens, ed., *Handbook of Experimental Psychology* [New York, Wiley, 1951], pp. 1078-1079) on the other hand, state (1) that the external ear and meatus (the auditory funnel) increase sound pressure level at the ear drum by as much as ten decibels over field pressure around the head, particularly at a frequency of 3000 cycles; (2) that the acoustical funnel assists in directional functioning; and (3) that it serves a protective function.

Eustachian tube opening into the anterior wall of the middle ear extends into the nasopharynx; it aerates the cavity of the middle ear and equalizes the pressure on the tympanum. The mastoid air cells lie above the middle ear and are connected with it. There is also a *round window,* lying below the oval window, which is covered by an elastic membrane and sometimes is called a secondary eardrum.

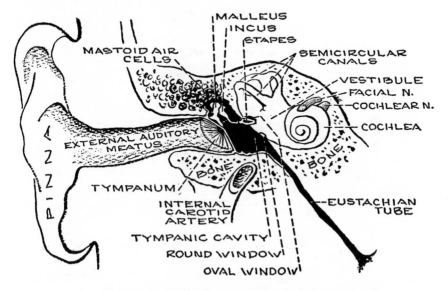

FIGURE 19-1. Semi-diagrammatic sketch of the ear.

The Inner Ear

The inner ear, lying in the recesses of the temporal bone, is composed of a bony labyrinth into which is fitted a series of membranous sacs and canals conforming to the outline of the bony labyrinth and bathed in its fluid, the perilymph. There are three principal parts of the labyrinth: the *semicircular canals,* which are not concerned with the hearing function but with balance; the *vestibule,* a chamber just behind the oval window; and the *cochlea,* a small shell-shaped concha, wound two and a half times around a central core, the modiolus. It is the cochlea, end-organ of hearing, in which we are most interested. If this spiral could be partially uncoiled and flattened, the structure would resemble the diagram, Figure 19-2. The tube, a little more than an inch in length, is completely divided into two passageways (except for a small opening at the apex), called the *scala vestibuli* and the *scala tympani.* The partition is the *basilar membrane* which stretches from a bony shelf attached to the modiolus to the outer wall of the cochlea and resembles a tapering carpet, relatively broad at the apex of the cochlea and very narrow at its base. Figure 19-2 makes it clear that the oval window opens into the vestibule near the end of the scala vestibuli, the round window into the scala tympani. The most important section of the cochlea is a small compartment, the cochlear duct or *scala media,* made

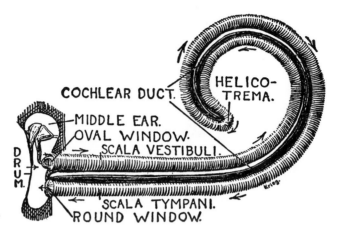

FIGURE 19-2. Diagram of the middle ear and cochlea.

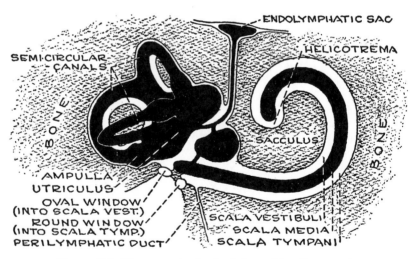

FIGURE 19-3. Diagrammatic sketch of the cochlea (inner ear).

by curtaining off a triangular wedge of the scala vestibuli by means of a very pliable, thin membrane, the membrane of Reissner or the *vestibular membrane* (Fig. 19-3). The floor of this compartment is the *basilar membrane* on which rests the *organ of Corti* containing the end-organs of the cochlear nerve in the form of hair cells which project their cilia into the cochlear fluid. Attached to the spiral lamina and lying over the hair cells is a gelatinous membrane called the *tectorial membrane* (Fig. 19-4). There are, in all, about 23,500 hair cells, from each of which project twelve to fifteen cilia into the liquid of the cochlear duct.

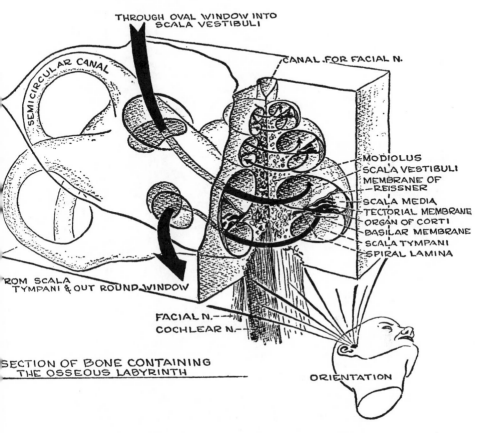

FIGURE 19-4. Section of bone containing the osseous labyrinth (middle ear; inner ear).

Transmission of the Sound Through the Cochlea

The excursion of the stapes in the oval window initiates a movement of the fluid in the cochlea which displaces the basilar membrane or tectorial membrane, or both, thus stimulating the hair cells and their nerve endings in the organ of Corti (Fig. 19-5). The rods, or supporting cells, of the organ of Corti are braced together at their tops to form a triangle with a part of the basilar membrane, and it is probable that the organ of Corti rocks as a unit when the basilar membrane bulges upward or downward. "The hair cells beside the pillar are squeezed, and the hairs themselves, loosely anchored in the gelatinous, cloud-like tectorial membrane above them, are bent from side to side." [6] In the transfer of the energy from the fluid to the hair cells, however, it is not a simple case of a transfer of mechanical energy, but of the creation of an electrochemical current set up by the difference in potential between the fluid and the hair cells.

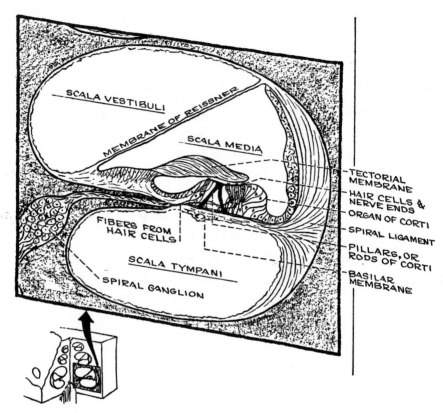

FIGURE 19-5. Cross-section of the organ of Corti (inner ear).

Theories of Hearing

Theories of hearing are numerous, but the one which has had the greatest attention is some form of the Place Theory. According to the adherents of this theory, the wave traveling up the cochlea impinges on the basilar membrane, the point of impingement depending entirely upon the frequency of the wave. Thus every discriminable tone is considered as having its own distinctive place of action in the cochlea, and hence in the fibers of the auditory nervous system.[7] Sounds of high pitch are assigned to a region of the membrane near the base of the cochlea (near the oval window),

[6] Davis, *op. cit.*, p. 62.

[7] E. G. Wever and M. Lawrence, *Physiological Acoustics* (Princeton, New Jersey, Princeton University Press, 1954), pp. 400-402.

low tones to the cochlear apex. The Place Theory is concerned almost entirely with the perception of pitch and provides little or no interpretation of other modalities of sound such as intensity, timbre, and phase. Some adherents of the theory have suggested that the intensity of the sound varies directly with the extent of the basilar membrane affected, or in other words, with the number of hair cells stimulated.

As a result of exhaustive investigations, Wever and Lawrence have combined the principle of place with frequency and have evolved the Volley Theory. Although they believe that every tone spreads its effect throughout the cochlea and is not limited to particular hair cells, they do ascribe peak regions for high tones to the basal end of the cochlea, regions of low tones to the apex. But *space* alone cannot determine tonal sensitivity. They find that the *frequency* or periodicity of the sound wave is reproduced in the frequency of the nerve impulses over the principal range of tones. The peculiar *form* of the movement patterns, then, is a determiner of pitch in that low tones will give broad and gently sloping curves, high tones sharp or peaked curves. In their view, intensity is not dependent upon the number of hair cells stimulated, but upon the voltage output of the individual hair cells. A potential is generated by each hair cell in proportion to the amplitude (or velocity) of the action at its location. At first, the intensity increases linearly, and then relatively, with an increase in the intensity of the stimulus until it reaches a certain maximum.[8]

Central Connections

The fibers from the hair cells have their first cells of origin in the spiral ganglion contained in the modiolus. Axons from these cell bodies run in the trunk of the auditory nerve through the internal auditory meatus to the ventral and dorsal cochlear nuclei in the medulla. From these nuclei the majority, but not all, of the fibers cross the midline to ascend in the brain stem in a bundle known as the lateral lemniscus. In their ascent they give off fibers to the acoustic reflex centers in the midbrain and thalamus, and end in the auditory area of the cerebral cortex situated in the temporal lobe. It is in the temporoparietal cortex that analysis, perception, and apperception of speech sounds probably take place, although recent neurological research would allocate some of these functions to subcortical areas, particularly to the thalamus. Any damage to, or absence of, any part of the hearing circuit results in an auditory disorder. We now turn our attention to the specific types of auditory disorders.

[8] *Ibid.,* pp. 409-410.

THE TYPES OF HEARING LOSS

Conductive Losses

Conductive losses are caused by a defect in some part of the sound-conducting apparatus, the outer ear and the middle ear. (Sound may be conducted by other bones of the skull to the cochlea, but that is distinctly a poorer route.) In this kind of loss, there may be a diminution in the intensity level of all sounds, or, more typically, of sounds in the low and middle frequencies. The deficit is the same, however, at all loudness levels. In other words, the reduction in decibels at every level will equal the decibel loss at the *threshold* for speech. As someone has said, the loss may be likened to the acoustic impression received by listening to a speech in the next room with intervening doors closed. "Please speak up!" is a plea for an increase in intensity.

Peripheral Perceptive Losses

Perceptive losses may be either peripheral or central. In a peripheral involvement, the sound-receiving apparatus, the cochlea, or the cochlear section of the acoustic nerve has been affected. The loss is rarely uniform throughout the cochlea. More common is a loss limited to the lower turns of the cochlea where the sounds of higher frequencies are localized. Such sounds as *f; v; s; z; sh* [ʃ]; *zh* [ʒ]; *th* [θ]; *th* [ð]; *t; d; p; b; k;* and *g* are in this group and they, unfortunately, are the critical determiners of intelligibility. A glance at Figure 19-6 will tell you, too, that *ô* [ɔ] as in *all,* is the most powerful sound and *th* [θ] as in *think* is the weakest. Imagine the auditory confusion which you would face if such words as *pin, tin, fin, thin, skin, shin, kin,* and *sin* sounded alike to you. Research reports of the Bell Telephone Laboratories show that suppression of sounds in the speech range above 1000 cycles leaves speech only 40 per cent intelligible to listeners with normal hearing. Below 1000 cycles, a suppression does minimal harm; the listener has an accuracy score of 85 per cent.[9] You can readily understand the magnitude of the problem of a person suffering from a perceptive loss in the high frequencies.

This type of loss, affecting a few or many frequency bands, is complicated, moreover, by the phenomenon of recruitment. Recruitment simply means that the loudness of tones appears to increase more rapidly than normal in a person with a receptive loss. The step-up in energy or loudness may be only a matter of five or ten decibels, but it produces a sensation of much greater loudness than it would in the normal ear. Yet in spite of the growth of loudness, the intelligibility of speech is no better. In fact,

[9] H. Fletcher, *Speech and Hearing in Communication* (New York, Van Nostrand, 1953), p. 86 f.

the intelligibility would improve if recruitment did not operate. Such an individual, suffering from a perceptive loss and recruitment, often finds the loudness-level baffling and is likely to say, "I can hear you, but I cannot understand you. Please speak more clearly."

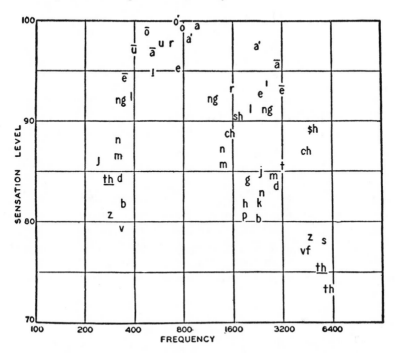

FIGURE 19-6. Position of consonants on frequency bands.

Central Perceptive Losses

A third kind of loss which affects the individual's ability to *recognize* the sounds of speech occurs because of a lesion or congenital defect in the *primary auditory areas* of the central nervous system. This loss is sometimes known as *cortical deafness,* although areas in the brain stem also may be instrumental in producing the impairment. Bilateral lesion of the medial geniculate bodies (thalamus), for example, produces total deafness.[10] Whether the lesion is in the cortex or the brain stem, the point to remember is that central perceptive deafness appears *only* if the lesion is bilateral. The perception of sounds at the cortical level has been ascribed to the second and third convolutions in the temporal lobe.

Perceptive recognition of sounds (central deafness) must be distinguished

[10] J. M. Nielsen, *A Textbook of Clinical Neurology* (New York, Paul B. Hoeber, 1942), p. 240.

from the *significant or meaningful interpretation and "re-auditorization" of speech sounds*. The resulting inability to understand speech is caused by a lesion in the *secondary acoustic areas* in the temporoparietal cortex, of which the best known is Wernicke's area. (See Fig. 4-11.) This impairment in recognition and interpretation of spoken language is called auditory aphasia and is discussed in Chapter 16.

CAUSES OF HEARING LOSS

Disturbances in hearing may have either a physiogenic or a psychogenic etiology. The roots may be in a defective hearing mechanism or in a psychic and emotional trauma which introduces "interference" in the hearing circuit. We must inquire further into the defective mechanism by determining whether the loss is the result of a familial, genic pattern, or whether it has occurred because of damage from a non-genic milieu either before, during, or after birth. Let us call hearing losses which are directly attributable to inheritance, *genic impairments*. Losses accruing from non-genic or environmental factors may be called *acquired impairments,* and are not transmissible to the next generation. In this connection, it should be remembered that environment may apply to prenatal as well as postnatal life. The deafness or hearing loss of a child resulting from rubella in the mother during the first trimester of pregnancy is an acquired deafness. Similarly, any damage to the hearing mechanism before or during delivery results in an acquired hearing loss.

Genic Impairments

Among the genic causes of auditory impairment are failures in the development of the ossicular chain, or of the auditory nerve or its end-organs in the cochlea. A more common genic antecedent is otosclerosis or chronic progressive deafness, the affliction of a million people in the United States. In otosclerosis, the ratio, female to male, is two to one. The formation of a bony, fibrous tissue which interferes with hearing sometimes occurs in the cochlea, but much more frequently it surrounds the oval window, and frequently immobilizes the stapes. As the disease progresses, there usually is some impairment of the auditory nerve. Specifically *what* the gene transmits which results in otosclerosis is not clear; recent evidence indicates that the individual may inherit an atypical blood chemistry which induces cellular, pathological changes in the otic capsule.[11] Not all cases of otosclerosis are genic in origin. Some may be caused by an interruption of the peripheral blood supply or infectious diseases, in which a familial pattern has played no part.[12] The first signs of the disorder may appear very early in life, but

[11] S. J. Kopetzky, "A Study of the Deafness Heritage in Otosclerosis," *Archives of Otolaryngology,* Vol. 52, No. 3 (1950), pp. 397-418.

[12] Dorothy Wolff, "Otosclerosis, Hypothesis of Its Origin and Progress," *Archives of Otolaryngology,* Vol. 52, No. 6 (1950), pp. 853-868.

generally it is an affliction of late adolescence and early adulthood. When the failure in maturation of auditory behavior is a direct consequent of inherited mental deficiency, it also must be considered a genic impairment.

Acquired Impairments

Hearing losses also may be acquired. Diseases which have been known to destroy or damage the hearing apparatus are meningitis, measles, mumps, scarlet fever, and whooping cough. If the mother suffers from any of these diseases in pregnancy, the damage to the fetus may be in several areas, including the cochlea. The loss in such cases is of a perceptive nature. If the child contracts these diseases after birth, and the virus invades the ear or the central nervous system subserving hearing, conductive and/or perceptive losses may follow. Anoxia when it is not produced by the Rh factor but by prematurity, or by injury before, during, or after delivery, can destroy or damage the hearing mechanism. Generally, the loss is perceptive, but conduction losses also have been recognized.

Although the use of antibiotics has reduced the number of children who suffer from acute or chronic suppurative otitis media, it is, nonetheless, the greatest single factor in the production of damage to the conductive mechanism of the middle ear.[13] Cleft-palate children, for example, are rarely free from otitis media, and hence frequently show significant conduction losses in hearing. Any respiratory infection which finds its way into the Eustachian tube can produce otitis media. Otosclerosis without a familial background also should be included among the acquired causes.

A smaller number of hearing losses can be traced to non-genic, psychological precursors. Transient or permanent reduction in auditory acuity, or in central perception, may accompany emotional disturbances such as hysteria and psychic depression. Several years ago, EZ, a junior in college, who had been in a speech clinic because she stuttered, complained of tinnitus and inability to hear her classroom instructors. She was a most attractive, well-groomed, but very tense girl who found the academic regimen increasingly rigorous. Her life was complicated by a love affair with a young man of whom her family did not approve. She decided also to change her academic major. When she first discussed her fear of deafness, she revealed that her mother wore a hearing aid and had "gone deaf" at about EZ's age, twenty years. She also remarked that she could hear better in a noisy social group than in a quiet classroom. Her voice seemed to be increasingly harsh and monotonous. All these observations tended to confirm her and our suspicions of otosclerosis. She said she heard some instructors and could not hear others at all. Otological examinations and laboratory tests were negative, but yet we were unconvinced. We decided to refer her to the college psychiatrist. Despite many signs to the contrary,

[13] E. P. Fowler and M. Basek, "Causes of Deafness in Young Children," *Archives of Otolaryngology*, Vol. 59, No. 4 (1954), pp. 476-484.

a diagnosis of hysterical deafness was confirmed. Time also has confirmed it. *EZ* is now happily married, and she is not deaf.[14]

DETECTION OF HEARING LOSS BY OBSERVATION OF BEHAVIOR

It is comparatively easy to diagnose a hearing loss in the child, sitting in the first or second grade of an elementary school, whose automatic response is "Huh?" He misunderstands directions. He may cock his head occasionally in favoring the better ear, or he may sit dreamily in the back of the room, shaking his head when called on. He may have poor marks in language arts. His speech articulation is poor. He may repeat the first or second grade. Anyone—even the most unseasoned "school-marm"—can locate the trouble in such a case. Waiting for these signs, however, is much too late. If confirmed hearing losses, with all their attendant educational and social problems, are to be prevented, they must be found in time to correct the conditions producing the loss. The only way to attack this problem is through the annual or biennial administration of hearing tests to all children of school age.

The detection of auditory loss in a baby of two years presents many more problems. The fact that he does not have any intelligible speech is indeed a sign, but it also may be a sign of many other things which may be wrong. Defective intelligence, damage to the central nervous system, lack of maturation, poor models, systemic illness of long duration, emotional disturbance, peripheral paralysis: the possibilities are numerous. The mother's report that the baby does not turn his head in response to her call *is* a symptom—but again it is quite inconclusive. We have known a good many children, both small and big, who are parent-deaf. One suspects them of developing very early in life a high resistance-threshold to vocal persuasions of parents. Some very young children will respond to soft but not to loud sounds. The journal of the behavior of *Ann,* who has been in a speech clinic for one year, includes a number of characteristic behavioral responses of the young deaf child as outlined by Myklebust.[15] Ann, two and a half years old, and entirely without speech, came to the speech clinic with her parents. Her father is a professional man, and the mother also is a college graduate. Ann refused to remove her hat or coat, of which she was very proud, or to remove herself from her father's lap during the first interview. She was extremely apprehensive, rejecting forcefully every toy presented to her. When the mother attempted to remove Ann's coat, she clutched wildly at the buttons, struck at the mother, and then screamed

[14] For histories of other cases, see R. Henner, "Psychosomatic Aspects of Surgical Treatment of Otosclerosis," *Archives of Otolaryngology,* Vol. 52, No. 6 (1950), pp. 177-187.

[15] Myklebust, *op. cit.,* pp. 111-141.

in a high-pitched, deafening squall. The medical history was not disturbing. The parents could think of no major illness; her only illness, in fact, had been a very short one, three days, at fifteen months when she ran a high temperature without apparent cause. The history of her prenatal life and infancy was uneventful. There was no report of auditory handicaps on either side of the family. The developmental record of sitting, walking, teething, toilet control, and so forth was not atypical. When the clinician asked how the baby "got along" in the family, the mother said, "She's driving us all crazy. She gets up at any hour of the night and wanders around. If she can't get the toy she wants she bites, kicks, and scratches her older brother or the new baby (nine months old). And, if I do not understand what she wants, or if I cross her, she sits by the hour screaming and bumping her head against the wall or the floor. Yet, she knows what the score is; nothing really passes her by." Apparently, Ann used no sound except screaming. Sometimes she mouthed a voiceless communication. She also was adept at gesture and mimicry. One time after she had found the clinician talking on the phone, she went to the phone, dialed, and then carried on a complete conversation in voiceless gesticulations, replaced the receiver, and nodded her head vigorously. Her visual and tactile senses were excellent. On her third visit to the speech clinic, she became interested in furnishing a doll-house. When the task had been completed—or so we thought—we removed the house and placed a set of miniature farm buildings and toy animals before her. She shook her head vehemently, quickly removed the farm, got up on a chair, and carried the doll-house back to the table. She knew what she wanted and she brooked no interference! In all her movements in reordering the room, she shuffled her feet noisily.

In the second month, the clinician gave her the Leiter International Intelligence Scale, a performance test. The results showed what we had anticipated—a truly accelerated child. She learned to identify each one of the noisemakers by the sound. She began to respond to the sounds which came from the auditory training unit.

During an intensive summer program in the clinic, her responses to free speech-reception tests indicated a very small residuum of hearing. Yet she enjoyed the preschool "rhythm band." She showed a remarkable rhythmic sense, particularly when she could have her favorite instrument, the sticks. Why were they her choice? You answer that one. The swimming pool was her delight. Each morning she raced in at eight o'clock, her "suit case" and speech notebook in hand, intent on being the first in line for the pool. She was equally absorbed in finger painting. Someone labeled her best one, "thunderstorm." The last day Ann was in her glory at the group demonstration. A great Humpty Dumpty sat on the wall and the five tiny youngsters were each to replace one piece, which would help to restore Humpty's facial facade, saying as he did so, "I put back his mouth, his nose, etc." Alas for Ann! She completed the first mission and then, wishing to show her parents how much she really knew, she attempted to snatch the remaining parts of Humpty from reluctant hands. Howls, yowls, and the stamping of feet ensued. The "police" broke up the demonstration. No bloodshed—or very little. To soften this bitter finale, let us repeat what her mother said, "She is now a different girl and we are different. Even her grandmother could not believe what she saw. Ann belongs to the family at last." We had eliminated by this plan of diagnostic study the possibilities of brain damage, auditory aphasia, and mental retardation. We arrived at a diagnosis of a very severe hearing loss caused by a febrile condition in infancy. A diagnosis based upon an hour's interview, no matter how expert the panel is, cannot be substituted, we believe, for a program of observation, study, and teaching.

In Ann's *Journal,* we have a profile of the auditory behavior of a very young child severely handicapped by perceptive deafness. The cause, type, extent, and duration of the loss have been spelled out. In an older child with a serious hearing loss, the picture is more complex. His communicative skills in language and vocabulary show a steady decrement when equated with his age. His speech is blurred and unintelligible. He speaks with too soft a voice, if his hearing loss is conductive, because he still receives the vibrations of his own voice through the skull bones, and it seems much louder than the voices of others. The perceptive-deaf individual, on the other hand, has a tendency to use overloud tones because he does not have the monitor of his own ear or of the secondary conductive mechanism through the skull to check him.

These are clues to the detection of hearing loss recognizable by a study of the child's overt behavior. No attempt has been made, however, to determine the amount or kind of impairment, or the adjustments which the individual has made to compensate for the loss. Such measures also must be made.

MEASUREMENT OF HEARING LOSS IN THE YOUNG CHILD

It must be understood that objective tests of hearing constitute but one part of the study of the total auditory behavior of the subject. In administering these tests, the student should keep in mind qualifications which we have discussed earlier, namely, that (1) pitch, loudness, and duration are not the sole criteria of hearing for speech; (2) acuity for the pure tones of an audiometer does not assure acuity for the complicated noises and tones of speech; (3) the child may respond to faint sounds or to speech, but not to loud sounds; [16] (4) he may feel the vibrations from a sounding body although he does not hear them; (5) his responses may be inconsistent

---

[16] I. R. Ewing and A. W. G. Ewing, "Ascertainment of Deafness in Infancy and Early Childhood," *Journal of Laryngology and Otology,* Vol. 59 (September, 1944), pp. 309-333.

from day to day; (6) he may hear speech sounds but be unable to interpret what he hears (receptive aphasia); and (7) he may hear but not respond because of an emotionally disturbed personality, or expressive aphasia, or mental deficiency.

The tests of hearing for the infant and the very young child are not standardized, so they offer, at best, only a crude evaluation. Infants a week old will respond by a flutter of the eyelids (palpebral reflex) to an Urbantschitsch whistle.[17] At five months, infants begin to localize sound by turning the head and eyes, and by reacting to voices of members of the family. Noisemakers ranging from 60 to 6200 cycles per second in frequency, and with an intensity spread from 50 to 105 decibels are frequently used as stimuli with the very young child whose typical response is to cease whatever he is doing.[18] A child twelve to eighteen months old has a tendency, however, to ignore loud sounds and respond more quickly to quiet speech. A child two to four years old can be taught to move a block when a bell is rung, for example, and then by this process of conditioning, to make the same response when the bell is sounded outside his visual range. By using noisemakers and musical toys of different frequencies, a rough measure of the child's perception of sounds in the speech-range can be obtained.

Some examiners have used the Maico Auditory Training Album, Record No. 1,[19] to establish the integrity of the child's hearing. A startle response from a very young child indicates that he hears the sound. Among the sounds contained in these recordings are a train whistle, vacuum cleaner, telephone, airplane, automobile horn, piano, and running water. Others have combined pictures,[20] a "peep-show," [21] or "jack-in-the-box" [22] with free-field pure-tone testing of very young children in order to interest the subject through these "rewards" which appear when he presses the button in response to a tone.

The psychogalvanic skin response test (PGSR) and the electroencephalo-

---

[17] E. Froeschels and H. Beebe, "Testing the Hearing of Newborn Infants," *Archives of Otolaryngology*, Vol. 44, No. 6 (1946), pp. 710-714.

[18] (a) Noisemakers standardized by Utley and by Ewing and Ewing include bells, whistles, horns, tom-tom, tambourine, triangle, and squeaking toys. Noisemakers can be checked as to frequency range with an octave analyzer on a sound level meter.

(b) Jean Utley, "Suggestive Procedures for Determining Auditory Acuity in Very Young Acoustically Handicapped Children," *Eye, Ear, Nose, and Throat Monthly*, Vol. 28 (December, 1949), pp. 590-595.

[19] Jean Utley, Auditory Training Album: *What's Its Name? A Guide to Speech and Hearing Development of Young Children* (Urbana, Ill., University of Illinois Press, 1950).

[20] J. Keaster, "A Quantitative Method of Testing the Hearing of Young Children," *Journal of Speech Disorders*, Vol. 12, No. 2 (1947), pp. 159-160.

[21] M. R. Dix and C. S. Hallpike, "The Peep-Show, A New Technique in Pure Tone Audiometry in Young Children," *British Medical Journal* (Feb. 2, 1952), pp. 235-244

[22] F. R. Guilford and G. Q. Haug, "Diagnosis of Deafness in the Very Young Child," *Archives of Otolaryngology*, Vol. 55, No. 2 (1952), pp. 101-107.

graph also are being used in testing for hearing loss in very young children, although at present the techniques seem difficult and the results inconclusive. In the psychogalvanic skin response (PGSR), the method is based on the establishment of a conditioned response to tone. The response is determined by measuring changes in the applied external current which are indicative of changes in resistance of the skin under electrodes.[23] The second method, electroencephalography, has been used by Marcus and Gibbs [24] also to detect loss in acuity in the very young child. Although a sufficiently large group has not been tested to insure validity, the "brain-wave picture" known as an electroencephalogram or EEG may prove to be an excellent method of determining acoustic impairment in children who cannot cooperate in other tests.

The Use of the Speech Audiometer to Measure Hearing of Young Children

For the child over three years old who understands language, speech and voice tests are valuable instruments. They represent an effort to evaluate the over-all hearing function, not simply the sensory capacity of the ear to perceive sounds of various frequencies and intensities. Such factors as discrimination, memory, fatigue, and language ability must be reckoned with in devising these tests of speech hearing. Although the test results correlate well with the pure-tone audiometric evaluations, they take account of such additional factors as analysis and synthesis of sound, memory, discrimination, and fatigue.

The speech audiometer presents a monitored, live voice delivered at known intensity levels through a high-fidelity amplification system. When the cue word, a monosyllabic noun, is presented, the child should respond by pointing to one of a series of pictures which the stimulus word suggested. Bangs has arranged such a group of 50 monosyllabic nouns in picture form which were recognized 100 per cent of the time by children three years old. The lowest level at which the child identifies 100 per cent of the words is established as his threshold for speech hearing.[25] The directors of the Cleveland Hearing and Speech Center devised a similar free-field speech test for hard-of-hearing children, three to six years old, in which 36 words and picture-cards in groups of six were presented, first without a hearing aid and then with amplification. The audiologist requested the name of the picture,

[23] W. G. Hardy and M. D. Pauls, "The Test Situation in PSGR Audiometry," *Journal of Speech and Hearing Disorders*, Vol. 17, No. 1 (1952), pp. 13-24.

Elizabeth R. Horton, *An Experimental Investigation into the Reliability of Psychogalvanic Skin Resistance Audiometry with Two, Three, and Four-year-old Children.* M.S. Thesis, University of Wisconsin, 1952.

[24] R. E. Marcus, E. L. Gibbs, and F. A. Gibbs, "Electroencephalography in the Diagnosis of Hearing Loss in the Very Young Child," *Diseases of the Nervous System,* Vol. 10, No. 2 (1949), pp. 170-173.

[25] J. L. Bangs and T. E. Bangs, "Hearing Aids for Young Children," *Archives of Otolaryngology*, Vol. 55, No. 5 (1952), pp. 528-535,

using the carrier phrase, "Can you find the ———?" The child was required to select correctly three of six cards at each level of intensity. His speech-reception threshold was established when he could no longer respond correctly to three of six cards.[26]

MEASUREMENT OF HEARING LOSS
IN OLDER CHILDREN AND ADULTS

The Pure-Tone Audiometer

When the individual is old enough to co-operate in testing procedures, the pure-tone audiometer is used routinely to determine the amount of impairment in the various frequencies of the speech range. The examiner can select the frequency by a turn of the dial on the audiometer, and the sound is received through headphones by the listener who signals when he hears the tone. The loss, computed in decibels [27] for each frequency level, is the ratio between the subject's hearing and "normal" hearing. (Sample audiograms are interpreted in Appendix 5.)

The severity of the loss must be judged not only in terms of a quantitative measure of decibels but also in terms of the age at which the individual incurred the loss and the rate of deterioration of hearing. Assuming that the impairment preceded the acquisition of language, we may say that a loss of 25 to 35 db. below normal threshold in the better ear for the speech frequencies (200 to 4000 cps.), is a mild handicap. A loss of 35 to 45 db. for speech reception in the better ear is moderate; from 45 to 70 db., the handicap is severe. A bilateral loss exceeding 70 db. in the better ear is indicative of a small residuum of hearing at best. With the totally deaf we shall not deal in this discussion.

The Speech Audiometer

The most satisfactory tests of speech hearing are of two kinds: (1) the threshold test of speech reception or intelligibility and (2) the articulation (or sound-discrimination) test. In the first type, the threshold for speech is obtained by measuring the difference in decibels between the intensity of speech required by a subject in order to hear 50 per cent of the words spoken and the intensity required by a normal listener to hear the same percentage. In this type of speech audiometer [28] the tape or phono-

[26] J. A. Irwin and Anne Shreve, "Hearing and Language Evaluation with Hard-of-hearing Children," *Archives of Otolaryngology,* Vol. 59, No. 2 (1954), pp. 186-191. For list of words used in testing procedure, see Appendix 5, p. 556.

[27] A decibel has only a *relative* value. It is an index of acoustic pressure based on the pressure level or power of the faintest sound that can be heard by the average ear. Zero decibels of hearing loss on an audiometer varies with each test frequency and is based on the normal (not best) adult hearing at each frequency.

[28] A speech audiometer is a modification of the pure-tone audiometer; it is provided with a turntable and electrical pick-up or a magnetic-type playback for use with recorded test material.

graphically recorded lists of words of the Psycho-Acoustic Laboratory, Harvard University,[29] or of the Central Institute for the Deaf [30] are used most frequently. The word lists are of two types: phonetically balanced one-syllable words and two-syllable spondee words. Each group of monosyllabic words in the phonetically balanced lists contains a distribution of speech sounds that approximates the distribution of the same sounds as they occur in conversational American English.[31] (See Appendix 5 for lists.) The spondee list also is made up of words, but they are two-syllable words with equal stress on each syllable.[32] (See Appendix 5 for list.)

In the articulation or sound-discrimination test, the ability of the subject to hear the speech sounds correctly is measured at an easily audible level. By such a test one can learn how fine a discrimination an individual can make among speech sounds when the intensity of the speech sounds no longer is an important factor. The discrimination loss is not measured in decibels, but by the difference between the percentage of words heard correctly and 100 per cent, a presumed maximum for normal listeners. If the subject gets 90 per cent or more correct, his discrimination is said to be normal. Although both phonetically balanced lists and the spondee words are used, it is believed that the intelligibility of speech, measured by *articulation gain,* is greater for spondee words than for phonetically balanced monosyllables.

For the young child, several picture-type discrimination tests have been constructed in which the child is asked to choose from among several similar pictures the one containing the two stimulus words. Word pairs representing objects which could be pictured easily were selected. Each word pair was phonetically balanced so that only one phoneme varied in each word of the pair. Pronovost and Dumbleton conclude that such a test "is valuable as an indicator of the adequacy of the child's speech sound discrimination" but that its validity would be increased under controlled acoustical conditions.[33]

Evaluation of Language

There are no standard brackets into which we can fit the language problems of the acoustically handicapped child. Variables of intellect, amount

[29] Auditory Tests Nos. 9, 12, 14 of Psycho-Acoustic Laboratory, Harvard University.

[30] Auditory Tests Nos. W-1, W-2, and W-22, Central Institute for the Deaf, Technisonic Laboratories, 1201 South Brentwood Blvd., Brentwood, Missouri.

[31] I. Hirsh, *The Measurement of Hearing* (New York, McGraw, 1952), p. 340.

[32] F. L. Weille, "Speech Audiometry in Practical Use," *Archives of Otolaryngology,* Vol. 55, No. 4 (1952), pp. 456-464.

L. A. Watson and T. Tolan, *Hearing Tests and Hearing Instruments* (Baltimore, Williams and Wilkins, 1949), pp. 438-463.

I. J. Hirsh, H. Davis, S. R. Silverman, E. G. Reynolds, E. Eldert, and R. W. Benson, "Development of Materials for Speech Audiometry," *Journal of Speech and Hearing Disorders,* Vol. 17, No. 3 (1952), pp. 321-337.

[33] W. Pronovost and C. Dumbleton, "A Picture-Type Speech Sound Discrimination Test," *Journal of Speech and Hearing Disorders,* Vol. 18, No. 3 (1953), pp. 258-266.

and type of loss, environment, and so on make it advisable only to describe the linguistic problems of some of these handicapped children. In a group of five-year-old children with a moderate loss, 35 to 50 db, in the better ear, sentences were short, adverbs and adjectives were absent, and there was confusion in pronouns, word order, and verb tenses. The responses to *why, when,* and *how* were frequently faulty. Their ability to follow simple verbal directions was a clue to their comprehension. If the hearing-handicapped child is able to respond verbally, a comparison of scores on the Leiter International Performance Test and the Stanford-Binet (verbal) test may be a rough index of the language impairment. It is always difficult, however, to measure the impairment of symbolization, not only of receptive language, but of expressive and inner language. For the acoustically handicapped preschool child, Gesell's detailed charts of language development for the normal child (see Appendix 3) form one basis for comparison. If the infant of six months is babbling, it is evident that language is developing and that there is a measure of hearing. The child who suffers from profound deafness may or may not babble. Children, profoundly or slightly deaf, use their voices, however, as a response of intervention. They may be speechless, but they are not voiceless.

HABILITATION OF THE HANDICAPPED IN HEARING

As is true in so many fields, we are long on theory and short on practice. When truth gets a hearing, the accolade should go to those unsung heroes, the teachers, who, day by day, train the hard-of-hearing in the ways of communication. Many can engage in research, testing, and diagnosis, and in publishing their results; few will accept the mental and physical rigors of putting into practice the theories they have evolved. There are five principal areas of aural habilitation: (1) auditory training, (2) speech reading, (3) phonetic practice, (4) training in language skills, and (5) psycho-emotional habilitation. The areas impinge, overlap, and vary in significance with the age of the subject and with the type, degree, and duration of impairment.

Auditory Training

For a child of two or three years, this is, perhaps, the most important area. He must be made aware of sound; he must learn to enjoy sound; he must be taught how to listen for sound. Both in gross and in fine discriminations, he must develop quickly his maximum skill. The writer observed Wedenberg's work with the very young, extremely hard-of-hearing children at Karolinska Sjukhuset in Stockholm, Sweden. Wedenberg has demonstrated dramatic results with the exclusive use of auditory training of the young child, first *ad concham* and then with a hearing aid. Speech reading (visual stimulation) should not be introduced "before the child has acquired the listening attitude, which he signifies by approaching and wanting to have words spoken into his ear." [34] It was found that even children who had been diagnosed as deaf had some residual hearing since they responded to intensive auditory training. Wedenberg was careful to point out, however, that the auditory approach alone did not produce similar results with older children. In fact, auditory training with the older group resulted in little improvement in speech intelligibility. Wedenberg concludes, therefore, that the results of auditory training depend chiefly upon the child's age when training begins, although he is cognizant of such other variables as the type and degree of hearing loss, the energy of the parents in motivating the training program, and the child's intelligence. The optimum time for the acoustically handicapped child to learn oral speech is in the first five years of life; after that time, the "teachable moment" has passed. Hudgins, who confirms Wedenberg's findings and reasoning, concludes that cues are important in the speech and language learning stages, in the early primary grades, but that when speech habits have been established auditory training per se, without the assistance of usual and tactile clues, makes a low return on the investment.[35]

As for the young child, whatever the degree of his loss, he should be trained to use the residuum of hearing he possesses, not only for improvement in intelligibility, voice quality, and language but also for the acquisition of a better understanding "of relationships between sounds and objects, sounds and actions, sounds and people." [36] Auditory training will serve different purposes in the different groups of the handicapped. Children with a 35 to 70 db. loss can learn to understand speech and language through the use of amplified sound. If the child has a loss exceeding 70 db., auditory training will benefit his voice quality, rhythm, and inflectional patterns, but he probably cannot learn language through hearing.[37]

Discrimination of Non-speech Sounds. Training usually begins with learning gross discriminations in sounds produced by horns, bells, whistles, pipes, cymbals, and drums. The child plays with them, hears them repeatedly, and then when one is sounded "out of sight," he attempts to identify the correct sound-maker.[38] Among the objectives of an auditory training

[34] E. Wedenberg, "Auditory Training of Severely Hard of Hearing Pre-School Children," *Acta Oto-Laryngologica,* Supplementum 110 (1954), p. 70.

[35] C. V. Hudgins, "The Response of Profoundly Deaf Children to Auditory Training," *Journal of Speech and Hearing Disorders,* Vol. 18, No. 3 (1953), pp. 273-288.

[36] Grace H. Lassman, *Language for the Pre-school Deaf Child* (New York, Grune and Stratton, 1950), p. 62.

[37] Alice Streng *et al, Hearing Therapy for Children,* (New York, Grune and Stratton, 1955), pp. 171-173.

[38] Other sources of gross sounds are: alarm clock, jungle sticks, metal crickets, baby cry, bicycle siren, boat whistle, typewriter, zylophone. (From the Illinois Plan for Special Education of Exceptional Children: *Those with Impaired Hearing,* Circular Series C, No. 12 [Springfield]), p. 27.

program, Bangs and Bangs stress the importance of skills in adjusting the child to the use of head phones: [39]

In order to make for a pleasant first experience in listening through the phones, it is important that the output signal be just sufficient to overcome the pathological threshold of each child as has been determined from audiometric tests. If the intensity level is set for each youngster before he dons the phones, then there will be less risk of his disliking the amplification as the result of a signal that is too loud.

Even though we have controlled the intensity level at which each child will be listening, there are always those children who are frightened by the sight of the headphones, or for one reason or another do not want to place them over their ears. To encourage each child to wear his phones, the following techniques have been successfully utilized.

1. There is on the market a toy which consists of a hurdy-gurdy man and an organ. When the handle is turned the music box plays a tune, and at specific time intervals the top of the box pops up and a monkey appears. A set of headphones was designed which fit over the head and ears of the organ grinder. At the beginning of the lesson the toy is put before the children, the headphones placed on the toy man's head and then the handle turned until the monkey appears. Each child who is willing to place his own phones over his ears is given an opportunity to play with the toy.

2. Another plaything is designed to represent a jet pilot in his plane. The aviator has headphones over his ears, and as the toy is pulled along the table the pilot's head revolves in a circular motion. Each child who is willing to use his phones is given the privilege of pulling the toy.

3. A large doll has been used in the same manner in that a pair of headphones was constructed to fit over its head. Each cooperative child is given an opportunity to hold the doll and perhaps remove and replace the phones.

Some techniques in gross sound discrimination which are employed generally are the following: [40]

1. Sound effects records utilizing the noises produced by a cow, dog, kitten and telephone bell are delivered to the phones by recording. The teacher has before her toy objects which represent the sound effects, and as the record plays she selects the appropriate object and pantomimes the activity. When the group demonstrates an interest in the procedure, each child is given an opportunity to perform alone. Notations should be made from day to day relative to the progress of each youngster.

2. Sound effects records utilizing the noises produced by a cow, dog, kitten and horse are delivered by recording. The teacher has before her pictures of the animals and a cardboard building with open windows. As the

[39] T. E. Bangs, "Methodology in Auditory Training," *Volta Review*, Vol. 56, No. 4 (1954), p. 160.

[40] *Ibid.*, pp. 161-162.

record plays she selects the appropriate animal and places it behind the window. The same procedure as described above is then followed until each child is able to select the correct animal by himself.

3. The teacher places on the table a drum, whistle, horn and cymbal, the sounds of which are presented via the hand mike and later the ceiling mike. Each child is given an opportunity to produce the sound effects, then one youngster is designated to hide his eyes while the teacher beats the drum. A response by pointing to the instrument which made the noise is given by the child, and the game proceeds. In like manner, each child is tested for gross sound discrimination.

These are steps in teaching a young child to enjoy sound. Even children who are severely handicapped will clap, keeping time with the chords played on a piano, or sing "high" and "low" with the high and low chords. Five-year-olds will keep their hands on the victrola feeling the rhythm of the "elephant walk," or "galloping horses," or "hopping rabbits." They like to develop their own interpretation of the victrola recording by marching, skipping, swaying, and so forth. They enjoy pantomiming "Looby Loo," "Here We Go Round the Mulberry Bush," "Bean Porridge Hot" or "The Farmer in the Dell."

Discrimination in Speech Sounds. Auditory training in fine discrimination for speech is the next step, but as Wedenberg suggests, it is probably the very young child who profits most by such a single sensory approach to speech sounds. Older children will have overlearned the speech patterns they possess and will hear what they expect to hear. Linguists have made the same observation about hearing adults who are learning a new language. They master the foreign speech much more slowly than children because they have overlearned the sounds of their native language and unconsciously fit the new phonemes into old patterns. For the older child certainly a combination of sensory approaches—"look, listen and feel"—is more profitable than any single approach.

In teaching discrimination between vowel sounds to young children, the difference between the vowels; ē [i] and ä [ɑ] may be presented alone, or in monosyllabic words, or in short phrases. Animal cries, such as *moo, baa,* and *wuff* are good beginners. The child imitates the articulatory movements and facial expression of the teacher. He may place his hand on the clinician's cheek to feel the difference in muscular adjustments between her production and his and to sense the vibration for voiced sounds. The child may identify a picture of the animal with the cry. The word may be printed below the picture. With older children the clinician often begins with the auditory recognition of entire phrases, learning to discriminate at first between words with very different phonetic patterns, and then to discriminate between similar phonetic patterns. From time to time single words which sound alike may be taken out of context for drill. *Boy-baby-ball; doll-daddy-door;* and *fish-foot-flower* are examples. Training in discriminating between similar speech sounds is the next step. Sounds such as *sh* [ʃ] and *s,* and *f* and *th* [θ] may be selected for drill. In this process of learning fine articulatory adjustments, the moto-kinesthetic method, developed by Edna Hill Young, has been employed with considerable success.[41]

All children will need to have auditory training in connected speech. Indeed it is possible that small units of connected speech should initiate auditory training since this is the way by which the hearing child normally develops language. The "piece" method and analysis of differences in individual sounds might well follow the "whole" method. Such training should include listening under poor acoustical conditions and against background noises. It involves acoustic discrimination through means other than loudness, through discrimination in pitch, quality, time, and melody. Since the hard-of-hearing individual has a false impression of the loudness of his own voice, he must practice several loudness levels, learning to talk against varying degrees of background noise. The natural inclination of both teacher and subject to use gesture instead of speech must be discouraged. Voice and hearing must be made correlates.

Speech Reading

Training in speech reading should proceed concurrently with auditory training in all except young children. As we have said earlier, the combination of auditory, visual, and moto-kinesthetic cues is more economical learning than the training of a single sense. *Speech reading* is the skill of understanding spoken language by watching the movements of the speaker's lips, face, and entire body. The definition makes clear why *lip reading* is an inaccurate term to apply to this skill. All of us, hearing or non-hearing individuals, employ speech reading to a considerable degree. The author, whose hearing is normal, found that she did not enjoy listening to a lecture from the back of a dimly lighted chapel although the voice of the speaker was entirely audible. When the lighting on the platform was changed so that she could see clearly the speaker's face, a seat in the rear of the chapel no longer posed any problem. When we are in doubt about our ability to grasp meaning, it is apparent that even hearing-folk depend more heavily upon seeing than upon hearing. During residence in a Scandinavian country, the author went frequently to a theatre where French sound-films were shown. Although she knew French better than Norwegian, in which the subtitles were written, she invariably chose to read the subtitles rather than to depend upon understanding the French speech—admittedly a "Hobson's choice" but illustrative of our greater reliance upon visual cues.

So the acoustically handicapped child must learn to understand not only the speech that he *hears,* but the speech that he *sees.* Speech reading is not sound-reading, although the early teachers of lip reading emphasized the

[41] Edna Hill Young and Sara Stinchfield Hawk, *Moto-Kinesthetic Speech Training* (Stanford, California, Stanford University Press, 1955).

reading of sounds. We do not learn speech normally by the analysis of phonetic components, and only about one-third of the speech sounds are visible. It is logical, therefore, for the child to learn to grasp whole meanings from segments of speech which afford him visual cues. He may catch only three or four words on the first presentation, but like the hearing child, he learns to fill in the gaps. And, like the hearing child, he does not analyze single sounds, or lip and visible tongue movements. The teacher has engaged him in a speech situation, in which he understands by grasping visual clues of lips, tongue, facial expression, bodily gestures, and situational props, combining these cues with the auditory stimuli.

These speech situations are drawn from his experiential milieu. With the young child it is made up of his family, his play, eating, and sleeping. Before he arrives at the speech clinic or special class, he undoubtedly has had informal speech-reading lessons, as for example: "Daddy is going in his *car*. He drives the *car,* too. Mother's *car* is blue. Mother goes to the store," and so on. With a group of toy car-models, varying in color and design, before the child, the teacher can continue the lesson of speech reading and at the same time develop his vocabulary of colors, shapes, and so forth. Soon the teacher will test the child's knowledge of "critical words and phrases" by such an exercise as this one: After placing toy airplanes, cars, balls, dolls, telephones, and other objects about the room, the teacher says: "Bring me the *blue airplane*. Who can find the *red ball?* Where is the Ford *car?* Please bring the *telephone;* say 'hello' in the *telephone,*" and so on. The use of lotto games (farm, fruit, animal), of large wood puzzles, of riddles, and of projects beyond the classroom: going to the supermarket, the zoo, or a parade are motivating materials for the preschool and first-grade youngster.

With the somewhat older child the teacher can explain that speech reading and "muscle-copying" of the speaker is a normal activity of many hearing-people who are intent upon getting the meaning. In fact we sometimes find ourselves saying what we *expected* the person approaching us to say, and we even "copy" the tone which we anticipated! So the hard-of-hearing can learn much by repeating the muscle action of the teacher. The teacher may begin speech reading with words and phrases employing mainly visible articulatory movements and a normal rate of speaking. The beginning sentences are simple in order, are of moderate length, and deal with highly concrete concepts. As the child progresses in speech reading, he learns to follow closely connected discourse and later to "read" conversation which typically is not entirely coherent or logical. Varying degrees of loudness of voice are used by the teacher, but at no time is lip movement exaggerated, even when the tone is inaudible. "See and Say" film-strips offer interesting exercises. The subject materials from the regular classroom— literature, geography, art—should be utilized at all times. As the student becomes more expert, he is given the opportunity to speech-read the rapidly changing dialogue of skits, to participate in choral verse where rhythm, stress, and accent are of great importance, and to watch films with, and then without, the addition of sound.

In the beginning, care must be taken to have the child face the speaker, to provide careful lighting, and to follow a daily routine in speech reading. As the child's skill grows, true speech situations should be tried in which he has only a side view of the speaker's face, in which many people are speaking, in which there is noise and confusion, in which he must comprehend the mumbler and the mouther. The instructor must take into account, here as in all learning, the range of individual differences in intellect, motivation, imagination, and sociability. Speech reading, finally, is not a substitute for a hearing aid. It is, however, a valuable addition to the armamentarium of the handicapped in hearing.

Phonetic Practice

The intelligibility of the speech of a person with a hearing loss will vary considerably according to the type, severity, and age of onset of the deficiency. The articulation of sounds of one who has always had a loss, or who suffered a loss in early infancy, will differ from that of a person who suffered a hearing loss at twenty. The last person is in need of "speech insurance," insurance against a deterioration of his speech because he no longer has normal hearing to monitor his expression. A good many individuals may have had a slight hearing loss from early infancy, yet their speech is sufficiently intelligible to pass muster. If the loss in the better ear is less than 40 db., it is possible that the defects in the articulatory patterns will be so slight as to escape attention.[42]

Articulatory Problems in Conductive Loss. Here is an illustrative case of the articulation resulting from a bilateral conduction loss (45 db. in the better ear). The boy was eight years old, and had worn a hearing aid for three months. All his speech was blurred and indistinct. As in so many deafened persons, his tongue was held in a retracted, bulging position, thus affecting both articulation and vocal resonance. The boy had a poor kinesthetic understanding of articulatory adjustment; the result was that the plosives, *p, b, t, d, k,* and *g* were weak. Voiced consonants were interchanged for voiceless. The fine co-ordination necessary for the sibilants *s* and *z* was lacking; *sh* [ʃ] was a common substitution for both sounds. The vowels *ŏŏ* [ʊ] and *ĭ* [ɪ] were missing. The fricatives *th* [θ] and *f* were interchanged; *r* was weak or absent. Such consonantal blends as *sl, fl,* and *sts* were slurred. For this boy intensive phonetic training was necessary. Drill

---

[42] In a study by Harriet Green (Master's thesis, Brooklyn College, 1940) diction was found to be intelligible for general educational purposes in a majority of cases where the loss was less than 40 db. in the better ear. When the loss in the better ear exceeded 40 db., diction was generally unintelligible. When the loss was as low as 20 db. in the better ear, the speech was found to be approximately normal.

on the defective sounds made correctly and incorrectly, and amplified with a portable aid, sharpened his acoustic awareness. He was taught the placement of the tongue, lips, and jaw for each sound. The moto-kinesthetic method was used to assist him in finding and maintaining the proper articulatory positions for some sounds. Intensive tongue and lip exercises before a mirror aided kinesthetic awareness and general flexibility. The steps in the production of the plosives were practiced, and the difference between the voiced and voiceless members of the pair explained. The boy learned quickly the final step in plosive formation, the explosion of the breath stream, by holding the back of his hand before the teacher's mouth as she articulated *p, t, k*. He was also able to feel the difference between these voiceless plosives and their voiced analogues, *b, d,* and *g*. The methods of correction of other sounds were essentially the same as for the normal-hearing person who has an articulatory defect. (See Chapter 7.)

The child who makes only a few, specific errors of substitution or omission of consonants will follow the same general procedure of sharpening auditory sensitivity for the right and the wrong way, seeing and feeling the proper articulatory position, drilling with the aid of amplified sound, and establishing the new sound pattern in conversational speech.

Articulatory Problems in Receptive Loss of High Frequencies. Some perceptive losses in hearing are restricted to the section of the cochlea near the oval window; thus the high frequencies will be lost. In such cases, the phonetic training will include the establishment of such high-frequency consonants as *s, z, sh* [ʃ], *zh* [ʒ], *f, v, th* [θ], *th* [ð], and *ch* [tʃ]. Here is a case history of a child who had such a loss. A boy five and a half years old was referred to the clinic by the school principal because the child's speech was unintelligible.

1. *Medical and developmental history:* The only childhood disease the boy had suffered was measles at two years. Teething was normal. Speech had been late in appearance and development. The mother could not remember if the child had begun to talk before the attack of measles. She had noted that walking had been retarded by the illness. Siblings, all older, had developed good speech at early ages. There was no history of familial mental deficiency.

2. *Speech, Psychological, Hearing Evaluations:* (*a*) Phonetic analysis of speech:

> Mary had a little lamb,
> meɪnɪ aə jɪˈl æm
> Its fleece was white as snow;
> ɪ wɪn ə wʌɪ ə noʊ
> And everywhere that Mary went,
> ɛn ɛnɪweɪ ə meɪnɪ ɛn
> The lamb was sure to go.
> ə jæm ə lu ə loʊ

Consonants missing: *f, v, s, k, g, t, d, sh* [ʃ], *zh* [ʒ], *th* [θ], *th* [ð]. (*b*) Psychometric evaluation: Score on Leiter International Performance test: 101. (*c*) Audiometric evaluation (speech and pure tone): Perceptive bilateral loss; 60-70 db. for frequencies above 2000 cps.

3. *Habilitation:* Following fitting of, and adjustment to, a hearing aid, he was given auditory training, speech reading, and intensive practice by visual motokinesthetic methods to establish the missing consonant sounds. At six and a half years, he was readmitted to the first grade in a small public school. Academic progress now is excellent. Speech is intelligible but not perfect.

Articulatory Problems of the Child with Severe Loss in Hearing for All Sounds. We have discussed the phonetic training of an individual with a moderately severe conduction-loss of hearing, of a child with a severe perceptive loss of the high frequencies, and of a child who has a mild loss and makes only a few sound substitutions. What about the phonetic re-education of the child, five years old, who has a very minute residuum of hearing, and, as a result, has no speech? The training for awareness of gross sounds and of speech sounds will be followed by elementary phonetic education. In speech reading he will attend to and duplicate, not single sounds, but phonetic units: words and phrases. Time will be devoted to the learning of differential values in particular sounds through the use of visual-moto-kinesthetic clues. In learning the difference between *p* and *b,* for example, he must have intense acoustic stimulation of the sound; he should learn to feel the appropriate muscular tensions in articulation and phonation by holding the hand along the jaw and pharynx, and by feeling the difference between *p* and *b* in the explosion of the breath stream against the palm of the hand. He will watch and copy the articulatory movements of the instructor. The goals of general speech development and intelligibility, however, remain uppermost. They take precedence over the perfect production of isolated sounds.

Voice Problems

Voice problems of the handicapped in hearing have been described in an earlier section. The individual with a perceptive loss must practice a variety of loudness levels until he has a feeling of the level suitable for most situations. The soft-voiced person with a conduction loss should practice increased volume, checking it over the amplifier until he has a subjective, kinesthetic monitor of his own voice. Some other voice problems which we meet frequently in the hard-of-hearing are sudden changes in pitch without respect to the meaning, peculiar intonation patterns, and monotonal voices. In addition to the methods suggested in the section on auditory training, the subject, with the aid of a portable amplifier, should tone-copy the instructor, sometimes reading and speaking with the instructor; at other times following, in tandem fashion, the instructor's expression. The reading and copying of the instructor's facial expression, raising the eyebrows for high tones, for example, should be encouraged. If the hard-of-hearing could learn to associate pitch changes with changes of facial expression, they should themselves be able to reproduce the visible inflectional changes which are so important to normal expression.[43]

Training in Language Skills

The total effect of auditory disorders upon verbal language development, and therefore upon thinking and behavior, is incalculable. We are interested here in a verbal language, which is only one of the languages by which we communicate ideas, feelings, and attitudes to others and to ourselves. A song from antediluvian college days had a grain of sense in it: "Every little movement has a meaning all its own." Gesture, bodily action, art, music, and oral articulation all are languages, symbolic systems of communication. Yet the profoundly deaf person, deprived of the last system, suffers deprivation in ideation, of which we hearing-folk can only guess. His first effort is to compensate by gesture. The three-year-old with a profound hearing loss, who came as a resident to the Rockford Summer Center, had a most complicated system of gestures. The gesture for "father" was unique: he placed an imaginary cigarette between his lips and blew nebulous smoke rings! We learned to understand much from his gesture language but not enough. What was he trying to tell us as he led us to the window and pointed to the west? What was he thinking about as he sat by the hour at that window, peering into the darkness? He could not use verbal language, and we were not sufficiently adept to interpret his gestures.

Carhart says on this topic of language skills: [44]

No phase of language acquisition is more important to personal development than the mastery of vocabulary and syntax. The years of childhood are filled with diverse experiences at home, in school, and on the playground. The speech of others is an integral part of these experiences. Hence, the experiences illustrate and define language for the child. He ceases to be baffled by idiomatic expressions like "He lost his head," or "She cried her eyes out." He builds a concept of the generic boundaries of words like "dog," "car," and "airplane." He defines the operational differences which distinguish the words, "walk," "run," and "skip." He codifies the qualitative differences symbolized by "good," by "black," by "quickly," and so on. However, the child cannot amass a satisfactory store of language symbols unless two conditions are met. First, he must have opportunity for diverse experience. Second, he must be able to perceive the auditory stimuli which are part of these experiences.

The summary by Gesell of the normal development of verbal language in children may be found in Appendix 3 of this book. The acoustically

[43] R. Paget, "Vocal Inflection," *Teacher of the Deaf,* Vol. 39, No. 230 (1941), pp. 31-34.

[44] R. Carhart, "Communications—Our Highway to Living," *The Crippled Child,* Vol. 27, No. 6 (1950), pp. 11-13.

handicapped child is retarded in his use of language because the concepts he gains through hearing are few. Even so simple a concept as the positions "over" and "under" are not easy to grasp with reduced hearing. Then, how does one explain the meaning of "forgiveness" or "freedom" or "generosity?" As the child learns to read or watches television, he makes some inferences about the abstract world, but he never truly catches up. Speech is a part of language, and insofar as he gains some facility in speech, his powers of ideation and expression are improved. The skills resulting from auditory and general sensory training, speech reading, and phonetic re-education promote language growth.

A language program for a small child must center in the child himself, his activities and interests. A basic vocabulary for language training of the young deaf child has been developed by the staff of the Central Institute for the Deaf. (See Appendix 5.) It is an excellent, orderly presentation of language growth, and could be modified to meet the needs of those with less severe handicaps in hearing. The more difficult time comes when the child goes beyond "what" to "why" and "how." There the second level of abstraction begins. In this process of language development the child's free use of finger painting, crayons, and pastels, of dancing and music, provides him with motivation and an opportunity to verbalize about the ideas and feelings which he has attempted to portray through another medium of expression.

Psycho-emotional Habilitation

The emotional problems found in the hard-of-hearing are not peculiar to that group; they probably could be observed in any group of "different children." If they are in any way peculiar to the group, it may arise from the fact that the full significance of the defect is not obvious immediately to others; they wear no crutches, braces, or bandages. They *appear* to be normal individuals. The problems are varied and the ways of meeting the problems also are highly individual. The person may retreat from his environment and live in an unreal world of his own design. He may "fight back," exhibiting over-aggressive, or antisocial behavior; or he may alternate between states of frustration and acceptance of his problem. The writer will never forget *Annie L.,* a university student with a very severe hearing loss. And particularly she cannot forget how Annie loped across the campus, shouting raucously in greeting. She was a student of agronomy (what a guttural *r!*), intelligent, outgoing, over-aggressive. She had problems, but she met them as she met life, "with a colossal welcome." *Jeff,* severely handicapped in hearing, also has problems. His school adjustment is very poor, despite his fine intelligence. He may throw a temper tantrum in the clinic, or he may be the soul of sweetness and light. He is presently trying to show his aggressiveness by antisocial behavior. He slips toys from the clinic into his pocket. He has "borrowed" two bicycles from the storage room and abandoned them before he reached home. Stealing for him is the halfway point between aggression and withdrawal. Jeff has problems, but unlike Annie L., he is unable to cope with them very successfully. Another hearing defective who fits neither of these groups is *Nancy,* who has almost completely withdrawn from life, although she is married and has a child. A very handsome girl, she professes no interest in people, in auditory training, or in herself. She entered the clinic at her husband's request but came very irregularly to her clinic appointments, evinced no interest in her speech progress, and dropped out after one year. She seemed unreal, and her responses to the world more unreal.

Some generalizations based upon investigation have been made about the personalities of the handicapped in hearing. Wells, Eisenson,[45] and others who have studied hard-of-hearing adults conclude that they are less stable, more introverted, and less dominant in their attitude toward life. Drennen claims that the deaf child feels isolated, depressed, and persecuted.[46] Recently Kessler made a study of children with moderate hearing loss and found that both groups, "treated and untreated," exhibit a significantly greater number of behavior problems than youngsters who have never had impaired hearing.[47]

The bewilderment, frustration, and resultant lack of security which all three cases cited here—Annie L., Jeff, and Nancy—reveal is understandable when one contemplates the unreality of a non-hearing world. A few years ago the writer was on a flight from London to Stockholm when the plane was "set down" without warning at Kaastrup Airport in Denmark, and we were surrounded by people of many lands, all very voluble, but no one speaking our language. Immediately we were wary, watching every visual clue in the behavior and speech of others, and, despite the good tea and smørbrød, experiencing a feeling of discomfort and of unreality about ourselves and the land of waving grass and the sea beyond. Yet we had retained possession of our distance receptors and they worked well for all auditory stimuli except speech. He who lives with blunted hearing for all sounds must compensate or retreat.

The small child, moreover, does not know why he is insecure. His symbol system for intervening in his environment is inadequate. His needs have increased, but his methods of satisfying them have not kept pace. He is alert to other sensory stimuli: smell, touch, sight. Unable to communicate, he resorts to emotional outbursts, loud crying, over-aggressive behavior, and temper tantrums. He indulges in compulsive, repetitive behavior, swaying with his whole body or banging his head against the wall. (It is thought that the head-banging and swaying may have a favorable effect upon the

[45] R. Pintner, J. Eisenson, and M. Stanton, *The Psychology of the Physically Handicapped* (New York, Crofts, 1941), p. 202.

[46] G. L. Drennen, "The Psychology of Deafness in Children," *Illinois Medical Journal,* Vol. 79 (1941), pp. 227-232.

[47] R. E. Kessler, *A Study of Children with Moderate Hearing Loss.* Ed. D. Thesis, Pennsylvania State University, 1953.

vestibular mechanism in the ear.) Young children with serious losses often present problems in eating and sleeping. They exhibit violent food dislikes and preferences. Failing to establish regular sleep habits, they upset the household by waking and walking when others are asleep. In normal emotional development there is a growing awareness of one's self and of others. The hearing-handicapped child often does not possess this awareness. He seems to have removed himself from his immediate environment, reacting neither to objects, people, or situations with a sense of reality. He may throw the toy or walk on the cat; they are insignificant to him. Likewise, there may be little evidence of contact with people. He may neither smile, laugh, nor display affection.

When the child with a hearing loss reaches school age, the evidences of social immaturity still may be present, but they have taken subtler forms of fear, shame, negation, or aggression. By the time he reaches school age, for example, he feels that there must be some stigma attached to his handicap. If this were not the case, why did the televised advertisement of hearing aids assure the listener that information is sent in a *plain* mailing wrapper and that this special hearing aid is so inconspicuous that "even your best friend won't know you are wearing one"? If the child did not have any unhealthy reactions before viewing the advertisement, he now suspects that he should have.

Tests of emotional stability cannot be given to the young child. The Vineland Social Maturity Scale, completed by the parents, offers clues to the emotional development of the child. Some assistance in finding emotional problems in teen-age or adult individuals is afforded by such tests as the Children's Apperception Test (CAT), the Thematic Apperception Test (for adults), The Bell Adjustment Inventory, and the California Personality Test, but they may be administered and interpreted only by clinicians trained in these testing methods.

Both direct and indirect counselling are employed in a program designed to serve one or more of these ends in emotional adjustment of the acoustically handicapped person: (1) to develop in him a realistic approach to himself, his environment, and his problem; (2) to build a stronger ego for protection against infantilism, suspicion, and regression; (3) to substitute awareness for anxiety, tolerance for frustration, understanding for suspicion; (4) to promote true compensations for the handicap; (5) to motivate participation in group activities and association with others; and (6) to promote a genuine interest both in a vocation and in avocations.

Parents must understand their own feelings in relation to the child handicapped by a hearing loss. Even the two-year-old baby reacts to their sighs and sorrow, to their apprehensions, to their feelings of guilt, rejection, and overprotection. Recognition of these feelings by the parents goes a long way toward their removal. Parents also must face the child's potentialities and future in a realistic fashion. Because the child has a hearing loss, *must* he be brighter than his classmates? The fallacy is patent, yet how many parents realize their mistake? It is the parents, too, who generally prepare the child for the fitting of a hearing aid. The child must know what to tell the curious, and—even more important—what to tell himself.

Living with hearing peers presents problems, but is good insurance against breaking with reality. His peers in hearing must understand the nature of the child's handicap. How great is his loss? What sounds will he be likely to misinterpret? If he has a receptive loss, his associates must realize that increasing the loudness of their voices only exaggerates the problem. If he is learning to speech-read, his friends should be sure that he can see their faces as they talk. The classroom teacher can do much to encourage him in all language activities. The speech teacher has a special responsibility, not only for his speech and language development, but also for his social adjustment. It is her job to gain the co-operation of the parents, teachers, and school leaders in encouraging this hearing-defective child to meet and conquer his little world.

Much attention has been given to the emotional education of the child handicapped by a hearing loss. More attention should be given to the adjustment problems of the individual who is faced with partial or complete loss of hearing in middle life. Such an individual is asked to adapt, often quite suddenly, to the loss of the sound-world. He must learn to accept a hearing aid. In order to conserve his speech, he must proceed immediately to learn speech reading, a totally unfamiliar task and one which he must take up after his days of language-learning are over. Frustrated by this strange, new, and very dead world, he often succumbs to deep emotional depression and insecurity. The task of the therapist with the acoustically handicapped has magnitude.

APPENDIX 1

Operating the Peripheral Speech Mechanism

Like all sound-producing instruments, the speech mechanism also must employ a motor, vibrator, and resonator; but unlike other instruments, the speech mechanism must share these organs with vegetative functions such as deglutition and passive respiration. Speech has been superimposed on these organs designed to support life; hence it must make profound alterations in these processes. In quiet breathing, for example, the nasopharynx, oropharynx, and laryngopharynx present a patent, tubelike cavity. The larynx, likewise, is open; the vocal folds are separated so that they do not obstruct the breath stream although they move in and out slightly with the respiratory cycle. The relaxed tongue fills the oral cavity so completely when the mouth is closed that there is no considerable resonating space. In speech many interruptions must be introduced into this "clear channel." First, the time-relations of quiet breathing are modified in order to secure a longer expiratory cycle and generally a shorter inspiratory cycle. (Although we normally speak on exhalation, every language apparently has some inspiratory "words" such as the Scandinavian "Ja-ha!" In such atypical conditions as cerebral palsy and stuttering, attempts to speak on inhalation are frequently observed.) Next, the vocal folds are adducted and tense so that their inner edges are taut and vibratile. Then the breath stream blows them open in a rapid, repetitive movement, 70 to 275 times a second, thus producing voice. The pharyngeal muscles act simultaneously with the levator and tensor muscles of the velum to produce a purse-string closure in the oral and nasal pharynx so that the breath stream enters the mouth. The back tongue is depressed; the tongue-tip may be raised; the oral cavity is modified in size and shape.

Precisely how are these adjustments accomplished for speech? In the production of articulate speech we require four components: (1) a steady stream of expired air (respiration); (2) progressive waves of vibration of the air molecules (phonation); (3) a reinforcement of some and attenuation of other vibrations in the resonating cavities; and (4) the alteration of the quality of the tone by the resonators and articulators so that distinctive phonetic or sound patterns result.

RESPIRATION: THE MOTIVE POWER

Contrary to popular belief, breathing is not the simple process of allowing the lungs to draw in the air. The lungs are not an active agent in the process. They may be drawn out with the expansion of the thoracic cage and their natural elasticity will act as a passive force in expelling the air, but in no sense should the lungs be regarded as a true motive force. And we cannot say that the synergistic action of muscles in breathing for speech always proceeds in the same way.

Breathing is the algebraic sum of muscular forces, main and accessory, which in a given situation respond in a particular way to the stimuli. In some cases, for example, the action of the diaphragm is dominant; in others, attention to the expansion of the costal cage in a lateral direction may be most effective in controlling the breath stream. Frequently cerebral-palsied children whose diaphragmatic action is poor and uncontrolled are able to develop the costal muscles sufficiently to produce a good motive power for speech.

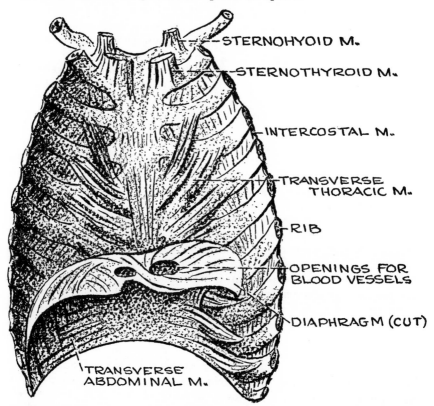

FIGURE I-1. Muscles of the anterior thoracic cage, chest muscles, and diaphragm (viewed from behind). (Adapted from W. Spalteholz, *Hand Atlas and Textbook of Human Anatomy*, Vol. I [Boston, Little, 1953], Fig. 162, "Paries Anterior Thoracis Cum Musculis."

Normally inhalation results from a three-way expansion: (1) By the descent of the double-domed diaphragm, the thoracic space is enlarged in a vertical direction. If the ribs to which the diaphragm is attached have been fixed, the double domes which are slightly irregular in shape will be somewhat flattened and the central, tendinous portion of the diaphragm pulled downward (Fig. I-1). (2) By the action of the external intercostal muscles, assisted by the scaleni and pectoralis muscles, the ribs and the sternum are raised upward and outward, thus increasing the thoracic space in an antero-posterior direction. (3) By the torquing of the ribs, chiefly the fifth and seventh, space is increased laterally. This last action is effected chiefly by the intercostal and the serratus muscles (Fig. I-2). The reduced pressure created in the thoracic cavity results in an inrush of the air in order to equalize the pressure. The air distends the lungs, filling the thorax completely. Inhalation has been accomplished.

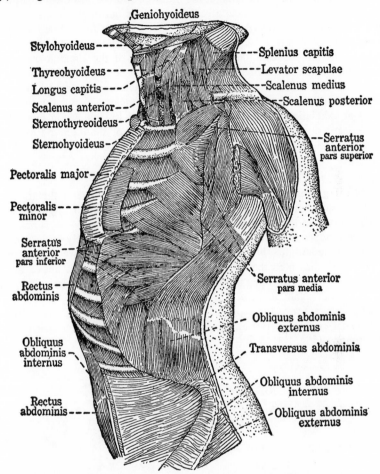

Geniohyoideus

Stylohyoideus

Thyreohyoideus

Longus capitis

Scalenus anterior

Sternothyreoideus

Sternohyoideus

Pectoralis major

Pectoralis minor

Serratus anterior pars inferior

Rectus abdominis

Obliquus abdominis internus

Rectus abdominis

Splenius capitis

Levator scapulae

Scalenus medius

Scalenus posterior

Serratus anterior pars superior

Serratus anterior pars media

Obliquus abdominis externus

Transversus abdominis

Obliquus abdominis internus

Obliquus abdominis externus

FIGURE I-2. Muscles of the thorax and abdomen.

Contrary to the practice of many voice and speech teachers, great amounts of air need not be inhaled for good tonal production. In an attempt to secure greater intake, students very often attempt to raise the upper ribs and the clavicle, producing unusual tensions with little effect on thoracic expansion. Curry reports that "many individuals make use of much less than two liters of air during phonation. The volume of air does not bear a close relationship to the intensity of the voice." [1] The important factor is the efficient utilization of

[1] R. Curry, *The Mechanism of the Human Voice* (New York, Longmans, 1944), p. 14.

the breath in phonation. This efficiency depends, in large part, on the co-ordination and "staying power" of the muscles of inhalation and exhalation.

In quiet exhalation, the diaphragm relaxes and thus moves upward, the internal costals counteract the external costal muscles, and the ribs drop to a position of rest. The decrease in thoracic area forces the air out of the lungs. In exhalation for speech, the lower ribs are fixed in the raised position while the abdominal muscles which are attached to these ribs apparently act to compress the abdomen. In the process, the maintained tension of the thoracic muscles increases the tension in the diaphragm so that it may counteract the movement of the abdominal muscles. The maintenance of thoracic expansion and the antagonistic action of the diaphragm and abdominal muscles account for the precise control of exhalation of the breath stream for speech. Changes in intensity, for example, are much more dependent on this control than on the volume or pressure of the breath stream.

PHONATION: THE VIBRATING AGENT

The exiting breath stream courses through the bronchi and the trachea, at the upper end of which is the so-called "voice box." But it really does not resemble a box, and there are no strings resembling the name *vocal cords*. As the air column moves into the larynx, it is obstructed incompletely by a protruding shelf of muscle and membrane on each side. The opening between these muscular wedges is known as the *rima glottidis*. The laryngeal walls above the *rima glottidis* then recede forming a pocket on each side, the ventricles of Morgagni, only to jut out again to form the false vocal bands. The epiglottis, a saddle-shaped cartilage, forms the superior boundary of the larynx; it projects from the inner border or the superior anterior wall of the larynx to reach nearly the root of the tongue (Fig. I-3).

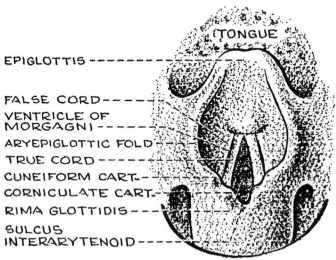

FIGURE I-3. Superior view of the larynx.

The membranous tube of the larynx is enclosed in a cartilaginous framework, a modification and continuation of the tracheal rings. The ring resting upon the trachea is a signet-ring-shaped cartilage, the cricoid; the signet, however, is not in the front but occupies the posterior one-third of the larynx (Fig. I-4). The next ring, the thyroid cartilage, is much wider in the front and flares incom-

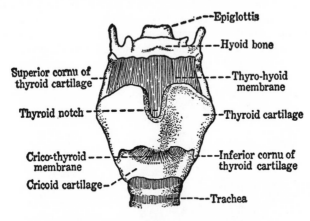

FIGURE I-4. Anterior view of the skeletonized larynx.

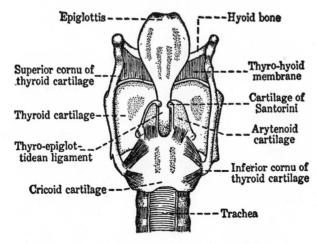

FIGURE I-5. Posterior view of the skeletonized larynx.

pletely into cornua or horns two-thirds of the way around to the back. In this opening between the horns at the back appear two pyramidal-shaped cartilages, the arytenoids, resting upon the signet of the cricoid (Fig. I-5). Capping the arytenoid cartilages are two pairs of smaller cartilages, the corniculate and cuneiform, which form tubercles to assist the epiglottis in closing the larynx when the aryepiglottic sphincter is in action. This entire cartilaginous framework is suspended from the hyoid, or tongue bone, by the thyrohyoid membrane and muscle.

How do the muscles and the larynx act together to close the glottis, thus producing tone? The mechanism is a two-fold one of adduction and tension, and, in the process, both extrinsic and intrinsic muscles are operating.

Extrinsic muscular action (Fig. I-6). The superior, middle, and inferior constrictor muscles, great paired muscle sheets which "wrap" the entire posterior pharynx, contract simultaneously with the general sphincteric action of the larynx. Together with the palatopharyngeus muscles (some fibers of which insert

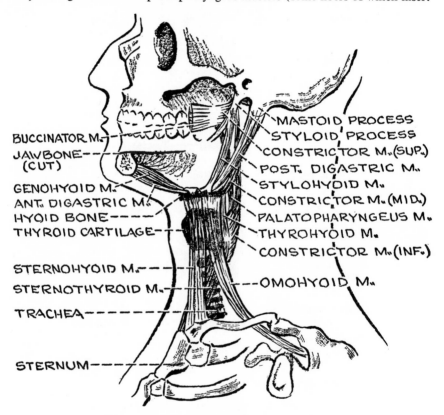

FIGURE I-6. Extrinsic muscles of the pharynx and mouth.

into the upper thyroid), they act to fix the larynx in position. The cricopharyngeus muscle holds the cricoid cartilage in place, bracing it back against the vertebral column while the cricothyroid and the sternothyroid muscles act to approximate the thyroid and the cricoid cartilages so that the anterior notch of the thyroid moves downward and a little forward.[2] In this action two extrinsic muscles, the sternohyoid and the omohyoid, assist in lengthening the vocal folds in phonation by drawing the hyoid bone slightly downward. There are other

[2] *Ibid.*, p. 64.

extrinsic muscles which oppose, in general, the infralaryngeal muscular action which we have just described. These muscles, geniohyoid, digastric, and stylohyoid, contract to raise the hyoid bone, thus elevating the radix of the tongue. The fixation of the hyoid and the thyroid which, in turn, fixes the position of the larynx depends upon the relative strength of these opposing sets of supra- and infrahyoid muscles.

The intrinsic laryngeal muscles (Fig. I-7). There are, also, internal muscles which act to bring the vocal folds to the midline of the larynx and to tense them. In this action the arytenoid cartilages are drawn in an arc inward and posteriorly so that the folds are brought together. To accomplish this end, the horizontal section of the interarytenoid muscle approximates the cartilages as the oblique fibers of the same muscle swivel the arytenoids so that their attachments, the vocal folds, meet. At the same time, the lateral cricoarytenoid muscles also contract to approximate the arytenoids. The action of the third muscle, the thyroarytenoid, cannot be described exactly. There are those who hold that as the thyroid cartilage moves downward the thyroarytenoid muscle contracts,

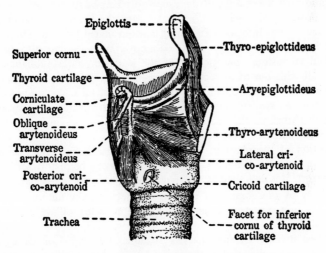

FIGURE I-7. Intrinsic muscles of the larynx.

thus tensing its membranous edge, the vocal fold, and at the same time pulling the arytenoid cartilage forward. Others argue that contraction of the thyroarytenoid muscle actually relaxes the membranous edge of the vocal fold much as the wrinkling of the base of a paper fan will ripple the periphery. In either case, the action is balanced by the opposing tension of the interarytenoid muscle, and the total result must be the algebraic sum of the opposing forces at any moment. In adduction the final goal, both of external and internal muscular action, is to increase the "stiffness constant" of the vocal fold.

How the action of the laryngeal muscles is modified to secure pitch change is a debatable question. One possible view of the change for higher pitches, those above 1000 cycles for example, is as follows: A separational pull on both ends of the vocal folds (arytenoids and anterior thyroid) resists the shortening of the folds; the thyroarytenoids are less tense but other muscles, especially the crico-thyroid, are more tense, thus increasing stiffness and thinning the membranous edge of the fold until it appears translucent. For high pitches it is possible that the mode of vibration may be changed in yet another way. At ordinary pitch levels the vocal folds come into direct contact at the beginning and end of each vibration cycle and the membranous edges are displaced mainly horizontally for a maximum of 4 mm., but also slightly upward in the ventricle (about ½ mm.), thus producing an elliptical configuration. In higher pitches, however, the vertical displacement becomes greater, the horizontal less, and the folds may touch only on one to two millimeters of their depth.

RESONATION: THE MODIFYING AGENT

The sound wave produced at the larynx now enters the resonating cavities: the pharynx, mouth, and nose. The largest though not the most mobile of the resonators is the pharynx, a tubular passage extending from the base of the cranium above to the margin of the esophagus below. As is apparent in Figure 14-6, the posterior surface is closely related to the cervical vertebrae; the anterior surface opens into the nasal, oral, and laryngeal cavities. The uppermost one-third is known as the epi- or nasopharynx. With the aid of a rhinoscopic mirror held in position, one notes first the posterior nares (choanae) on the anterior wall with the nasal septum between them. On the lateral wall of the epipharynx is the medial opening of the Eustachian tube. As the posterior wall of the epipharynx sweeps upward, its mucosa is thrown into folds by lymphoid tissue which makes up the adenoids (pharyngeal tonsil). The epipharynx ends with the upper surface of the velum.

The portion of the pharynx which opens anteriorly into the oral cavity is known as the meso- or oropharynx. Its boundaries can be plainly seen in Figure 14-6; superiorly it is delimited by the uvula, laterally by the glossopalatine arches, and inferiorly by the dorsum of the tongue. Between the anterior (glossopalatine muscle) and posterior (pharyngopalatine muscle) pillars are lodged the palatine tonsils.

The lowest division of the pharynx is called the hypo- or laryngopharynx which extends from the level of the hyoid bone to the opening into the esophagus at the level of the sixth cervical vertebra. Its anterior border above is marked by the epiglottis; the aperture of the larynx is the lower boundary line. Laterally the hypopharynx is bounded above by the medial surfaces of the thyroid cartilage.

Changes in pharyngeal resonance can be produced largely through increased tension of the walls by the contraction of the constrictor muscles which encircle the pharynx and by the elevation or depression of the larynx by supra- and infralaryngeal muscles (described in an earlier section).

The nose. Unfortunately for vocal quality, the size and shape of the nose vary greatly. The nose resembles roughly a three-sided bony pyramid. The nasal septum, rarely straight, separates the two cavities. Its structure is not simple, however, for one large cartilaginous plate and four bony plates unite to make the septal partition (Fig. I-8). The medial edges of the palate process of the maxilla and the horizontal process of the palate bone contribute to the "floor," but the great bony framework is formed by the ethmoid plate and the vomer (ploughshare in shape) which join to make up the posterior and superior septum. The cartilaginous portion is quadrangular and forms the anterior and inferior section of the nose. From the lateral walls of the nose project three shelf-like processes, the turbinates, which increase vastly the area for filtering, warming and moistening the air. (See Fig. I-8.) Opening into the nose are the paranasal sinuses: frontal, ethmoid, sphenoid, and maxillary.

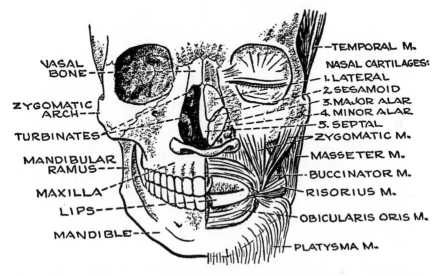

FIGURE I-8. Anterior view of muscles, cartilages, and bones of the face. (Adapted from F. L. Lederer, *Diseases of the Ear, Nose, and Throat* [Philadelphia, F. A. Davis, 1953].)

Although the concept prevails that the velum and pharynx close the entrance into the nose for all sounds except [m], [n], and [ŋ], the degree of closure is variable. Russell, Curry, and others believe that "in certain resonant bass voices the nasopharynx is open most of the time in speech, yet the open nasopharynx does not necessarily produce nasality of voice." [3] Certainly in all good voices a measure of nasal resonance enhances the timbre or richness of quality. The maximum velar-pharyngeal closure is found in the production of the plosive consonants: [p], [b], [t], [d], [k], and [g]. The mechanism of the sphincteric closure involves many muscles including the levator and tensor palati muscles which raise, tense, and retract the velum (Fig. 14-8). The palatopharyngeus muscles also contribute to the closure by contraction of their salpingopharyngeal portions which narrow the lumen of the pharynx. Two very small muscles, the azygos uvulae, raise, shorten, and broaden the uvula, assisting velar-pharyngeal closure. Further assistance to the closure of the nasal port may be given by Passavant's cushion, a pad of muscle fibers from the superior constrictors and from the salpingopharyngeal fasciculi of the palatopharyngeus muscles.

[3] G. O. Russell, *Speech and Voice* (New York, Macmillan, 1931), p. 18.

The mouth. The most mobile and the most controllable of the resonators is the mouth. So labile are its muscles that it may assume a variety of shapes to modify the tonal complex. The palatoglossus muscles may constrict the posterior aperture. The great buccinator muscles of the cheeks, and to a less degree the risorius, zygomaticus, and platysma muscles, may constrict or enlarge the lateral boundaries. The lips also have great freedom of movement, and by retraction and pursing, they may alter greatly the resonating oral cavity. In this action the sphincter muscle called the orbicularis oris, which encircles the lips, assumes a dominant role, although the cheek muscles assist the action. (See Fig. I-8.)

The structural conformation of the roof of the mouth, the palate, also is a determinant of oral resonance. The hard palate is formed by the premaxillary bone and by the horizontal processes of the superior maxillary and palate bones; the free posterior border terminates in the soft palate, at the end of which is the grape-shaped pendant, the uvula. (See Fig. 14-6.) The brilliance of oral resonance will depend, in part, on the density, rigidity, and tension of these tissues. The general shape of the roof also bears directly upon resonance. For example, a low vault, or again a high, narrow vault, will have a selective effect on the frequencies to be reinforced or modified.

Although the tongue and mandible are primary organs of articulation, they also modify the shape of the oral cavity and so affect resonance. The tongue, a highly mobile muscular organ, may assume a variety of positions involving the tip, the blade, the dorsum, or the sides. The frenum linguae, a membranous strip on the under surface, determines the mobility of the tip. The base of the tongue is attached to the lower jaw by the genioglossus muscle which spreads out fanwise to be inserted into the whole tongue from tip to root (Fig. I-9). The action of this muscle is complex: some fibers retract the tongue; others act in protrusion; others depress the dorsum, thus increasing concavity. The styloglossus muscle which inserts in the outer sides of the tongue retracts and elevates the sides; the hyoglossus which runs from the hyoid bone to the sides also retracts the tongue but depresses the sides. And still another muscle, the palatoglossus which makes up the anterior faucial pillar, contributes to lingual movement by elevating the dorsum at the same time that it depresses the soft palate. Then the tongue is capable of altering its form quickly by its intrinsic muscles: the lingualis complex of longitudinal, transverse, and vertical fibers. The apex may be broad or pointed; the body of the tongue may assume a concave or convex shape; or the whole tongue may be broad or narrow. It is apparent that lingual position and movement will alter the resonating potential of the mouth.

Finally the mandible operates to change the shape and size of the oral resonator. In the fact that the mechanism of closure is stronger than the mechanism of opening we may have an explanation of the tendency to speak with closed mouth and, therefore, muffled resonance. In closure, the major muscles are the masseter, which originates in the zygomatic arch and inserts into the lateral surface of the mandibular ramus (posterior articulation of jaw with skull), and the temporalis, which is attached to the temporal bone and the medial surface of the mandibular ramus (Fig. I-8). The internal pterygoid also assists in closure. The muscles acting to depress the lower jaw and open the mouth are the geniohyoid, the mylohyoid, and the digastric muscles, all of which emerge from the body of the mandible to form the floor beneath the tongue and link the jaw with the hyoid bone. The distortion of oral resonance by the ungraded and unpredictable action of the mandible in cerebral-palsied speech is a frequent observation in the clinic.

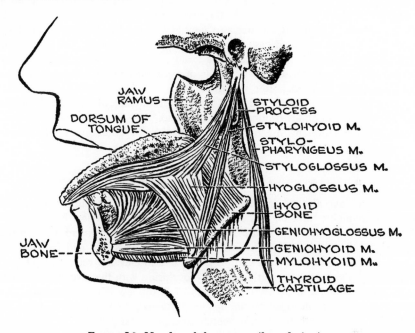

FIGURE I-9. Muscles of the tongue (lateral view).

One must not think of resonance, however, as resulting in an increased vocal intensity. Husson estimates that the actual intensity of the sound at the oral aperture is only about 20 per cent of the total energy produced at the larynx. 80 per cent has been dissipated in "parasitic vibrations and in the sound pulse in the trachea and bronchi." [4] The resonating cavities act "to increase the flow of energy from the source in the larynx" by reducing the resistance of the surrounding medium. Quality, that component which some people believe gives individual distinction to their voices, will depend in some part upon the size, shape, and "texture" of the walls of the resonators. And none of these factors is fixed within one resonating system. The rigidity, the smoothness of the surface, the density of the tissue: these textural factors, for example, vary from cavity to cavity and also are subject to diurnal variation. Illnesses, emotional changes, and mental activity may be reflected quite clearly in the voice quality. In order to produce maximum resonance, the natural frequencies of these cavities must be coupled with the laryngeal vibrations. When this coupling is perfect it is as-

[4] R. Husson, "La Phonation; quelques aspects énergétiques des principaux Phénoménes Acoustiques ep. diffipatiss," *Revue de Française Phoniatrie,* Vol. 4 (1936), p. 20.

sumed that the "lowest natural resonating frequency of the cavities is the same as the fundamental of the larynx." [5] If good coupling cannot be achieved, some voice scientists believe that the resonating pressures may react upon the vocal folds, causing them to vibrate with great amplitude. The result is a hoarse, discordant quality of weak intensity. Is it possible that this failure in synchronization is a partial cause of the harsh, throaty voice heard so frequently in cleft-palate speech? Resonating cavities also may add discordant partials to the tone through vibration of tensed tissues in the throat, mouth, or nose. The squawking voice of the vendor, the nasal twang of a radio crooner, the tense rasping quality of the political huckster, often are results of the imposition of these supralaryngeal vibrations upon vocal-fold vibration.

So, in sum, voice quality will have three determinants: (1) the fundamental and harmonic vibrations produced by the larynx; (2) their selective reinforcement or attenuation by the resonators; and (3) the addition of inharmonic components produced within the resonating cavities.

ARTICULATION: THE PHONETIC AGENT

Since we have already described the basic adjustments of the articulators—the lips, mandible, tongue, and soft palate—a few illustrations will show how they assume a dominant role in carving all consonantal sounds and assist in the formation of some vowel phonemes. The plosive sounds, [p] and [b], for example, require bilabial closure and pressure, and an elevated velum. In [t], [d], [n], and [l], the tongue-tip and blade make occlusion with the alveolar or dental ridges of the palate. In the sibilants, [s] and [z], the jaw is raised, bringing the upper and lower teeth together; the lips are retracted, the tongue-tip is free, but the sides occlude with the lateral dental surfaces as far forward as the lateral incisors, thus permitting emission of the breath stream in a narrow groove over the tip and through the narrow orifice between the central incisors. (See Fig. 7-1.) In the plosives, [k] and [g], the jaw is depressed and the dorsum of the tongue rises occluding with the anterior section of the velum. The occlusion of dorsum and soft palate in producing the nasal continuant, [ŋ], is slightly posterior to that for [k] and [g]. In all sounds except the nasals, [m], [n], and [ŋ], the velum rises to approximate closure of the nasal port.

The articulatory adjustments for the vowel phonemes are much less precise and definite. For the front vowels, [i], [ɪ], [e], [ɛ], [æ], and [a], the general action is to narrow the front of the mouth between the blade of the tongue and hard palate and to widen the pharynx. In the back vowels, [u], [ʊ], [o], [ɔ], [ɒ], and [ɑ], the lips are constricted, the dorsum of the tongue is elevated toward the soft palate, and the pharyngeal cavity becomes progressively larger. The neutral vowels require no definitive position of the tongue; it is generally in a resting position. These adjustments admit of wide variability; lip-rounding or retraction, for example, will alter the quality of a vowel, [e] or [ɛ], although it still may belong to its phoneme or "vowel family."

It could be argued, likewise, that consonantal adjustments vary from person to person. Certainly wide variation should be expected when one considers the

[5] Curry, *op. cit.,* p. 55.

number of the muscles of tongue, lips, cheeks, and palate and the great number of intricate adjustments of which they are capable. Many people make the *s*-sound, for example, with the tongue-tip raised; others make an equally satisfactory sibilant with the tip lowered. If the sound [k] is preceded or followed by a front vowel, the occlusion of the lingual dorsum with the velum is farther forward than when it is preceded or followed by a back vowel.

Similarly there is wide variation in speed of articulatory adjustment, a human and familial variable dependent upon nervous potential. And within the articulatory organs themselves, there is a rate differential in movement of from five to nine repetitions per second. As might be expected, the tongue-tip is the fastest articulatory organ, the soft palate the slowest.

APPENDIX 2

Supplementary Materials: Pathways to Speech

SUMMARY OF THE CRANIAL NERVES

Many of the twelve cranial nerves exiting from the brain stem have more than one component: in other words, they carry both sensory and motor impulses. Although we present here a summary of all cranial nerves, the speech student will be interested primarily in the italicized portions describing those functions of cranial nerves V and VII through XII which are most directly related to the speech processes. Their specific functions are discussed in greater detail in Chapter 4, pages 63-65.

I. OLFACTORY NERVE: Special visceral afferent fibers with cells of origin in the olfactory epithelium; termination in olfactory bulb.

II. OPTIC NERVE: Special somatic afferent fibers with cells of origin in the retina; terminations in thalamus, midbrain, and occipital cortex.

III. OCULOMOTOR NERVE: (a) Somatic efferent fibers with cells of origin in midbrain; termination in extrinsic muscles of the eye. (b) General visceral efferent fibers (autonomic) with cells of origin in the midbrain; termination in intrinsic muscles of the eye. (c) General somatic afferent fibers; proprioceptive fibers for the eye muscles.

IV. TROCHLEAR NERVE: (a) Somatic efferent fibers with cells of origin in the midbrain; termination in the superior oblique muscle of the eye. (b) General somatic afferent fibers; proprioceptive fibers for the superior oblique muscle.

V. TRIGEMINAL NERVE: (a) General somatic afferent fibers, exteroceptive with cells of origin along nerve trunk outside of brain stem; supplies sensibility to skin and mucous membrane of the head. (b) General somatic afferent fibers, proprioceptive with cells of origin in the pons; sensory terminations in the muscles of mastication. (c) *Special visceral efferent fibers with cells of origin in the pons; termination in the muscles of mastication.*

VI. ABDUCENS NERVE: (a) Somatic efferent fibers with cells of origin in the pons; termination in the lateral rectus muscle of the eye. (b) General somatic afferent fibers; proprioceptive fibers for the same muscle.

VII. FACIAL NERVE: (a) General visceral afferent fibers with cells of origin on the nerve trunk outside the brain stem; supply deep sensibility to face. (b) Special visceral afferent fibers with cells of origin on nerve trunk outside of brain stem; termination in the taste buds of anterior two-thirds of tongue. (c) *General visceral efferent fibers (autonomic) with cells of origin in area between pons and medulla; termination in submaxillary and sublingual salivary glands.* (d) *Special visceral efferent fibers with cells of origin in lower pons and medulla;*

486

termination in superficial muscles of the face, in platysma, posterior belly of the digastric and stylohyoid muscles.

VIII. ACOUSTIC NERVE: A. *Cochlear nerve: Special somatic afferent fibers with cells of origin in the cochlea (inner ear); central fibers end in ventral and dorsal cochlear nuclei of medulla, in midbrain, thalamus, and temporal lobe of cerebral cortex. Reception and perception of sound.*

B. Vestibular nerve: Special somatic afferent fibers with cells of origin on nerve trunk outside of brain stem; terminations in the medulla, pons, cerebellum, and parietal cortex. Perception of equilibrium.

IX. GLOSSOPHARYNGEAL NERVE. (*a*) *General visceral afferent fibers with cells of origin on nerve trunk outside of brain stem; termination in sensory end-organs of pharynx and posterior third of the tongue.* (*b*) Special visceral afferent fibers with cells of origin on nerve trunk outside of brain stem; end-organs in taste buds of posterior third of tongue. (*c*) General visceral efferent fibers (autonomic) with cells of origin in the medulla; termination in the parotid gland. (*d*) *Special visceral efferent fibers with cells of origin in the medulla; termination in the stylopharyngeus muscle.*

X. VAGUS NERVE: (*a*) General somatic afferent fibers with cells of origin on nerve trunk outside the brain stem; provides sensibility to skin of external ear and joins with the trigeminal nerve (V) in providing sensibility to skin of face. (*b*) *General visceral afferent fibers with cells of origin on nerve trunk outside of brain stem; sensory fibers to the pharynx, larynx, trachea, esophagus, and thoracic and abdominal viscera.* (*c*) Special visceral afferent fibers with cells of origin on nerve trunk outside of brain stem; end-organs in the taste buds of the epiglottis. (*d*) *General visceral efferent fibers (autonomic) with cells of origin in the medulla. Autonomic innervation of the thoracic and abdominal viscera.* (*e*) *Special visceral efferent fibers with cells of origin in the medulla and termination in the striated musculature of the pharynx and larynx.*

XI. ACCESSORY NERVE: (*a*) *General visceral efferent fibers (autonomic) with same cells of origin and termination as the vagus nerve (X).* (*b*) *Special visceral efferent fibers in two groups: (1) those with same cells of origin and termination as in the vagus nerve (X), and (2) those with cells of origin in the cervical cord and termination in the trapezius and sternocleidomastoid muscles.*

XII. HYPOGLOSSAL NERVE: (*a*) *Special somatic efferent fibers with cells of origin in the medulla and termination in the musculature of the tongue.* (*b*) *General somatic afferent fibers; proprioceptive fibers for the tongue.*

Although the fundamental behavioral responses of the individual must be effected finally through the cranial and spinal nerves which have their origin or initial termini in the brain stem and spinal cord, man is not, cannot be, a spinal or decerebrate organism. Even the major reflexes involving movement, such as walking or grasping, which are integrated in the spinal cord, cannot be effected without the aid of higher centers. Speech, like other complex processes, goes through a multiplicity of operations: (1) transmitting impulses from the sense organs of hearing, touch, pressure, sight, and movement; (2) connecting and relating these impulses at brain stem and cortical levels; (3) relating and integrating further the functions of sensory, motor, memory, and ideational areas in the cerebral cortex; and (4) exciting the muscles of breathing, phonation, and articulation through the great efferent tracts which terminate in the cranial and spinal nerves, and, through their autonomic components, providing the "feeling components" of speech.

OUTLINE OF AUTONOMIC INNERVATION OF SEPARATE VISCERA [1]

LACRIMAL GLANDS

PARASYMPATHETIC: *Preganglionic neurons:* Leave the brain in the facial nerve; but from the geniculate ganglion on, travel as part of the great superficial petrosal and vidian nerves to the sphenopalatine ganglion. *Postganglionic neurons:* Fibers arising in the sphenopalatine ganglion run in a branch of the maxillary division of the trigeminal nerve to the lacrimal gland. Some fibers also run to the gland in the ophthalmic division of V.

Function: Vasodilation and stimulation of secretion.

SYMPATHETIC: *Preganglionic neurons:* From intermedio-lateral cell column of the spinal cord ascend the sympathetic chain to the superior cervical ganglion. *Postganglionic neurons:* Fibers arising in the superior cervical ganglion ascend through the carotid plexus and run the terminal part of their path with the parasympathetic fibers in the deep petrosal and vidian nerves.

Function: Vasoconstriction.

SALIVARY GLANDS

PARASYMPATHETIC: *Preganglionic neurons:* Cells of origin in the superior salivatory and inferior salivatory nuclei. Fibers from the superior nucleus run in the nervus intermedius of VII to submaxillary and sublingual ganglia. Fibers from the inferior nucleus run in the glossopharyngeal nerve (IX) to otic ganglion. *Postganglionic neurons:* Run to the submaxillary and sublingual glands, and to the parotid gland.

Function: Vasodilation and salivary secretion.

SYMPATHETIC: *Preganglionic neurons:* Same as for the lacrimal gland. *Postganglionic neurons:* Fibers from the superior cervical ganglion ascend along plexuses on the external carotid and maxillary arteries to the glands.

Function: Vasoconstrictor and secretory.

HEART

PARASYMPATHETIC: *Preganglionic neurons:* Arise in the dorsal motor nucleus of the vagus (X) nerve and terminate in ganglia of the cardiac plexus or in the auricular walls. *Postganglionic neurons:* Run along the coronary arteries from the intrinsic ganglia to auricular muscle, to the sinoauricular node (chiefly right ventricle) and to the auriculo-ventricular bundle (chiefly left ventricle).

Function: Cardiac inhibition and probable coronary artery constriction.

SYMPATHETIC: *Preganglionic neurons:* Fibers arise from the intermedio-lateral cell column of the spinal cord and form two groups, one terminating in upper thoracic chain ganglia, the other ascending to synapse in the cervical ganglia.

[1] Adapted from J. F. Fulton, *Textbook of Physiology,* 17th ed. (Philadelphia, Saunders, 1949), pp. 236-237.

Postganglionic neurons: One group arises in the thoracic ganglia; a second group in the cervical ganglia. Both run as superior, middle, inferior and thoracic cardiac nerves, to form the superficial and deep cardiac plexuses. Afferent, sensory fibers run in the middle, inferior and thoracic cardiac nerves. Their cardiac terminations are found in the pericardium, heart wall, and walls of the aorta and coronary vessels. The afferent fibers of the ventricles are primarily concerned with cardiac and vascular reflexes.

Function: Cardiac acceleration, coronary artery dilation, and conduction of cardiac pain.

LUNGS

PARASYMPATHETIC: *Preganglionic neurons:* From the vagi and run to the hilus of the lung. *Postganglionic neurons:* In the anterior and posterior pulmonary plexuses.

SYMPATHETIC: *Preganglionic neurons:* From the intermedio-lateral cell column of the spinal cord—upper 3 or 4 thoracic segments to thoracic and inferior cervical chain ganglia. *Postganglionic neurons:* From thoracic ganglia and inferior cervical ganglion to the pulmonary plexuses.

Function: Stimulation of the thoracic sympathetic chain produces bronchodilation as does section of the vagi, which demonstrates the parasympathetic tonic constrictor action on the bronchi. This constriction may be brought on by vagal stimulation or reflexly from irritation of the mucous membrane of the upper respiratory tract.

ESOPHAGUS

PARASYMPATHETIC: Supplied by the vagus nerves.

Function: Stimulation of contraction of the muscular wall.

SYMPATHETIC: Supplied with motor and sensory nerves by thoracic fibers primarily from the fifth and sixth segments. The lower portion and the cardiac sphincter of the stomach are supplied by branches from the aortic plexus and the splanchnic nerves, which run through the celiac plexus and along the arterial branches.

Function: Stimulation of cardiac sphincter. Conduction of pain in sudden distention.

ABDOMINAL VISCERA

PARASYMPATHETIC: Fibers of the vagus nerves course through the preaortic plexuses without synaptic connections, to terminate in the intrinsic visceral plexuses, i.e., phrenic, adrenal, renal, spermatic or ovarian, gastric, hepatic, splenic and superior mesenteric. In the intestinal wall they end around ganglion cells in the plexuses of Auerbach and Meissner. From the splenic flexure to the rectum the wall is supplied by the sacral parasympathetics.

Function: Stimulation of peristalsis, secretion and vasodilation of the digestive glands. The vagi also carry afferent fibers.

SYMPATHETIC: Fibers from the lower 7 or 8 and upper lumbar segments pass through the chain ganglia and along the splanchnic nerves to terminate in cells of the preaortic ganglia. Postganglionic fibers from these ganglia accompany the blood vessels to the various viscera. In the case of the adrenal glands, the preganglionic axons terminate directly around the medullary cells. Afferent fibers follow courses similar to the above. Their cell bodies are in the lower 6 thoracic dorsal root ganglia.

Function: Inhibition of peristalsis, secretion, and vasoconstriction. The afferent fibers transmit reflex stimuli, sensation of nausea and pain of distention.

PELVIC VISCERA

Fibers reach the viscera from the inferior mesenteric ganglia (fibers to the sigmoid colon and rectum) via the plexus; via the hypogastric plexuses; and via the pelvic splanchnics or nervi erigentes. These nerves all contain sensory fibers.

THE ENDOCRINE SYSTEM IN VERTEBRATES [2]

ENDOCRINE GLAND AND HORMONE	PRINCIPAL SITE OF ACTION	PRINCIPAL PROCESSES AFFECTED
Adenohypophysis (*anterior pituitary*)		
Gonadotrophins Follicle-stimulating hormone (FSH)	Ovary	Development of follicles; with LH, secretion of estrogen and ovulation
	Testis	Development of seminiferous tubules, spermatogenesis
Luteinizing or interstitial cell-stimulating hormone (LH or ICSH)	Ovary	Luteinization, secretion of progestin (see FSH)
	Testis	Development of interstitial tissue, secretion of androgen
Adrenotrophin (ACTH)	Adrenal cortex	Secretion of cortical steroids
Thyrotrophin (TTH)	Thyroid	Formation and secretion of thyroxin
Growth hormone	General	Growth of bone and muscle, protein retention
Neurohypophysis (*posterior pituitary*)		
Oxytocin	Smooth muscle, particularly uterine	Contraction, parturition
Vasopressin	Arterioles	Blood pressure

[2] Adapted from C. D. Turner, *General Endocrinology* (Philadelphia, Saunders, 1949), p. 13.

ENDOCRINE GLAND AND HORMONE	PRINCIPAL SITE OF ACTION	PRINCIPAL PROCESSES AFFECTED
Ovary		
Estrogen (estradiol)	Accessory sex organs	Maturation and normal cyclic function
	Mammary glands	Development of duct system
	General	Development of secondary sex characteristics
Progesterone	Uterus	Preparation for implantation, maintenance of pregnancy
Testis		
Testosterone	Accessory sex organs	Maturation and normal function
	General	Development of secondary sex characteristics
Adrenal cortex	General	Metabolism of electrolytes, water, carbohydrates
Cortical steroids		Involution of lymphoid tissue
		Resistance to stress
Adrenal medulla	Heart muscle; smooth muscle, particularly arterioles	Pulse rate and blood pressure, contraction of most smooth muscle
Epinephrine (adrenalin)		
	Liver and muscle	Glycogenolysis
Thyroid		Metabolic rate, calcification of bones, nervous activity, metamorphosis
Thyroxin	General	
Pancreas (*islets*)		
Insulin	General	Utilization of carbohydrate
Parathyroid		
Parathormone	General	Metabolism of phosphate and calcium
Alimentary tract		
Secretin	Pancreas	Secretion of alkali and fluid
Pancreozymin	Pancreas	Secretion of digestive enzymes
Cholecystokinin	Gall bladder	Contraction and emptying
Enterogastrone	Stomach	Inhibition of motility and secretion

APPENDIX 3

Clinical Materials: Retarded Onset and Development
of Speech

A CHART OF DEVELOPMENTAL SEQUENCES [1]

A summary chart of the critical items in the computation of the developmental quotient is presented here. However, it is suggested that the examiner have a thorough understanding of Gesell's philosophy of infant and child development. Among the books on the subject with which he should be familiar are: *Developmental Diagnosis; The First Five Years of Life;* and *Infant Development.*[2]

AGE	MOTOR BEHAVIOR	LANGUAGE BEHAVIOR	PERSONAL-SOCIAL BEHAVIOR
4 weeks	head sags; hands fisted	throaty sounds; heeds bell	regards faces
16 weeks	head steady; postures symmetrical; hands open	coos; laughs; vocalizes socially	plays with hands and dress; recognizes bottle; poises mouth for food
28 weeks	sits, leaning forward; grasps cube; rakes at pellet	crows; vocalizes eagerness; listens to own vocalizations	plays with feet and toys; expectant in feeding situations
40 weeks	sits alone; creeps; pulls to feet; crude prehensory release	says one word; responds to his name	plays simple nursery games; feeds self cracker
12 months	walks with help; cruises; prehends pellet with precision	says 2 or more words	co-operates in dressing; gives toy; finger feeds
18 months	walks without falling; seats self; tower of 3 cubes	jargon; names pictures	uses spoon clumsily; toilet regulated

[1] Adapted from A. Gesell and Catherine S. Amatruda, *Developmental Diagnosis,* 2nd ed. (New York, Paul B. Hoeber, 1947), pp. 11-14. Clinical materials and procedures are described in the basic volume.

[2] A. Gesell and Catherine S. Amatruda, *Developmental Diagnosis* (New York, Paul B. Hoeber, 1941).

A. Gesell, *The First Five Years of Life* (New York, Harper, 1940).

A. Gesell, *Infant Development: The Embryology of Early Human Behavior* (New York, Harper, 1952).

AGE	MOTOR BEHAVIOR	LANGUAGE BEHAVIOR	PERSONAL-SOCIAL BEHAVIOR
2 years	runs; builds tower of 6 cubes	uses phrases; understands simple directions	verbalizes toilet needs; plays with dolls
3 years	stands on one foot; builds tower of 10 cubes	talks in sentences; answers simple questions	uses spoon well; puts on shoes; takes turns
4 years	skips on one foot	uses conjunctions; understands prepositions	can wash and dry face; goes on errands; plays co-operatively
5 years	skips on alternate feet	articulation is intelligible; asks "why?"	dresses without assistance; asks meanings of words

CHART OF THE APPEARANCE OF VOWEL AND CONSONANT SOUNDS IN PRELINGUISTIC VOCALIZATIONS DURING THE FIRST TWELVE MONTHS OF LIFE [3]

	VOWELS	CONSONANTS
Birth—1 month	i, ɪ, ɛ, u, ʊ	h, k, ʔ
1-3 months	e, æ, oʊ	g
3-6 months	ɑ, ɔ, ʌ, ə	j, m, p, b, w
6-8 months		t, d, n, l
8-12 months		ʃ, s, z, tʃ

COMPOSITE TABLE OF MEAN LENGTH OF SENTENCE IN SPOKEN LANGUAGE [4]

	AGE IN YEARS								
	1½	2	2½	3	3½	4	4½	5	5½
Sentence Length in Words	1.2	1.8	3.1	3.4	4.3	4.4	4.6	4.6	5.1

[3] Based upon studies made by Lewis, Irwin and Chen, Shohara, and McCarthy as reported in Dorothea A. McCarthy's, "Language Development in Children," in L. Carmichael, ed., *Manual of Child Psychology* (New York, Wiley, 1954), pp. 492-631.

[4] Adapted from tables prepared by Dorothea A. McCarthy in "Language Development in Children," L. Carmichael, ed., *Manual of Child Psychology* (New York, Wiley, 1954), pp. 492-631.

CLARK PICTURE PHONETIC INVENTORY [5]

RECORD BLANK

Name _____ Age _____ Grade _____
Address _____ Phone _____
Test Score _____ Date _____ Examiner _____
    Remarks_____

Retest Score_____ Date _____ Examiner _____
    Remarks_____

Retest Score_____ Date _____ Examiner _____
    Remarks_____

Retest Score_____ Date _____ Examiner _____
    Remarks_____

Voice:

    Pitch _____Flexibility of Articulators_____
    Rate _____Tongue _____
    Loudness _____Lips _____
    Quality _____

KEY

Red—first test	No mark—satisfactory 1 p (p)
Brown—second test	Check—wrong 1ᵛ p (p)
Black—third test	Number crossed—stimulated $\cancel{1}$ p (p)
Blue—fourth test	Number underlined—
	doubtful 1̲ p (p)
	Omitted— (—) (—)

No.	Sound	Key	No.	Sound	Key	No.	Sound	Key
	INITIAL			*MEDIAL*			*FINAL*	

CONSONANTS:

No.	Sound	Key	No.	Sound	Key	No.	Sound	Key
1	p [p]	pencil ( )	2	p [p]	puppy ( )	3	p [p]	pipe ( )
4	b [b]	bell ( )	5	b [b]	baby ( )	6	b [b]	bath tub ( )
7	m [m]	mouse ( )	8	m [m]	mamma ( )	9	m [m]	drum ( )
10	wh [hw]	whistle ( )	11	wh [hw]	steering wheel ( )			. . . .

[5] *Clark Picture Phonetic Inventory,* Communication Foundation, Ltd., Box 8865. University Park Station, Denver.

CLARK PICTURE PHONETIC INVENTORY (*cont.*)

No.	SOUND KEY INITIAL		No.	SOUND KEY MEDIAL		No.	SOUND KEY FINAL	
12	w [w]	window ( )	13	w [w]	wigwam ( )	. . . .		
14	f [f]	foot ( )	15	f [f]	telephone ( )	16	f [f]	knife ( )
17	v [v]	violin ( )	18	v [v]	overalls ( )	19	v [v]	stove ( )
20	th [θ]	thumb ( )	21	th [θ]	birthday cake ( )	22	th [θ]	month ( )
. . . . .	. . . . . .		23	th [ḍ]	feather ( )	. . . .		
24	t [t]	tie ( )	25	t [t]	potato ( )	26	t [t]	kite ( )
27	d [d]	duck ( )	28	d [d]	indian ( )	29	d [d]	bed ( )
30	n [n]	nail ( )	31	n [n]	penny ( )	32	n [n]	sun ( )
33	l [l]	leaf ( )	34	l [l]	balloons ( )	35	l [l]	ball ( )
36	r [r]	rake ( )	37	r [r]	carrot ( )	38	r [r]	ear ( )
39	s [s]	santa claus ( )	40	s [s]	bicycle ( )	41	s [s]	glass ( )
42	z [z]	zipper ( )	43	z [z]	scissors ( )	44	z [z]	nose ( )
45	sh [ʃ]	sheep ( )	46	sh [ʃ]	washing machine ( )	47	sh [ʃ]	fish ( )
. . . . .	. . . . . .		48	zh [ʒ]	treasure chest ( )	. . . .		
49	ch [tʃ]	chicken ( )	50	ch [tʃ]	matches ( )	51	ch [tʃ]	watch ( )
52	j [dʒ]	jumping ( )	53	j [dʒ]	soldier ( )	54	j [dʒ]	cage ( )
55	k [k]	cat ( )	56	k [k]	monkey ( )	57	k [k]	book ( )
58	g [g]	goat ( )	59	g [g]	wagon ( )	60	g [g]	pig ( )
. . . . .	. . . . . .		61	ng [ŋ]	ink ( )	62	ng [ŋ]	king ( )
63	h [h]	horse ( )	. . . .					
64	y [j]	yo-yo ( )	65	y [j]	onion ( )	. . . .		

CLARK PICTURE PHONETIC INVENTORY (cont.)

No.	Sound	Key		No.	Sound	Key		No.	Sound	Key	
	INITIAL				MEDIAL				FINAL		

VOWELS:

No.	Sound	Key		No.	Sound	Key		No.	Sound	Key	
66	e [i]	tree ( )		67	i [ɪ]	pumpkin ( )		68	e [ɛ]	tent ( )	
69	a [ɛ:]	chair ( )		70	a [æ]	hand ( )		71	u [ʌ]	cup ( )	
72	u [ɝ]	girl ( )		73	a [ə]	banana ( )		74	oo [u]	broom ( )	
75	oo [ʊ]	football ( )		76	o [ɔ]	corn ( )		77	a [ɑ]	arm ( )	

DIPHTHONGS:

No.	Sound	Key		No.	Sound	Key		No.	Sound	Key	
78	a [eɪ]	gate ( )		79	i [aɪ]	pie ( )		80	o [oʊ]	coat ( )	
81	ou [aʊ]	house ( )		82	oi [ɔɪ]	boy ( )		83	u [ju]	music ( )	

L CONSONANT COMBINATIONS:

No.	Sound	Key		No.	Sound	Key		No.	Sound	Key	
84	bl [bl]	black bird ( )		85	cl [kl]	clown ( )		86	fl [fl]	flag ( )	
87	gl [gl]	glove ( )		88	pl [pl]	plate ( )		89	sl [sl]	sled ( )	

R CONSONANT COMBINATIONS:

No.	Sound	Key		No.	Sound	Key		No.	Sound	Key	
90	br [br]	tooth brush ( )		91	cr [kr]	crown ( )		92	dr [dr]	dress ( )	
93	fr [fr]	frog ( )		94	gr [gr]	grapes ( )		95	pr [pr]	apron ( )	
96	tr [tr]	train ( )		97	thr [θr]	thread ( )		. . . .			

S CONSONANT COMBINATIONS:

No.	Sound	Key		No.	Sound	Key		No.	Sound	Key	
98	sk [sk]	skate ( )		99	scr [skr]	scrub ( )		100	sm [sm]	smoke ( )	
101	sn [sn]	snowman ( )		102	sp [sp]	spoon ( )		103	spl [spl]	splash ( )	
104	spr [spr]	sprinkle ( )		105	st [st]	star ( )		106	str [str]	streetcar ( )	
107	sw [sw]	swing ( )		108	squ [skw]	squirrel ( )		. . . . . .			
109	qu [kw]	queen ( )									
110	x [ks]	books ( )									

FULL-RANGE PICTURE VOCABULARY TEST [6]

ANSWER SHEET—FORM A

R. B. Ammons and H. S. Ammons

NAME_____ AGE_____ SCORE_____ MA_____

EXAMINER_____

PLATE 1

pie (1.7)
window (1.7)
seed (6.5)
sill (6.7)
transparent (13.3)
rectangular (14.7)
sector (16.0)
illumination (16.0)
culinary (17.2)
egress (A6.3)

PLATE 2

athletes (8.6)
competition (15.0)
revelry (A4.0)
ebullience (A6.4)

PLATE 3

counter (4.0)
pump (4.4)
clerk (6.4)
sport (7.6)
recreation (10.8)
pugnacity (16.9)
replenishment (A3.1)
retaliation (A4.1)

PLATE 4

shrubbery (9.8)
dwelling (11.7)

PLATE 5

surf (12.5)
isolation (12.9)

PLATE 6

horse (1.5)
wagon (2.3)
insect (6.7)
transportation (8.6)
antiquated (A3.8)

PLATE 7

discussion (7.7)
skill (10.9)
amour (13.8)

PLATE 8

firecracker (2.7)
clothes (3.0)
explosion (4.9)
clean (5.5)
dehydration (A4.3)

PLATE 9

farm (4.1)
currency (12.2)
tranquillity (16.5)
agrarian (A6.2)

PLATE 10

furniture (4.4)
steel (6.0)
refreshment (6.2)
liquid (7.3)
container (9.5)
centigrade (14.5)

PLATE 11

clock (1.6)
locket (3.0)
numbers (3.4)
engraving (9.8)

PLATE 12

hot (5.2)
fear (7.4)
nutrition (10.4)
gorging (12.8)
poverty (13.9)
mastication (A2.6)
itinerant (A4.5)
coercion (A4.6)
corpulence (A5.5)
insatiable (A5.6)

PLATE 13

telephone (2.1)
crying (2.9)
accident (3.0)
vehicles (9.5)
destruction (10.0)
portrait (10.2)

PLATE 13—CONT.

communication (10.6)
consolation (13.4)
negligence (14.3)
bereaved (15.4)
deleterious (A6.2)

PLATE 14

danger (5.6)

PLATE 15

bed (1.6)
newspaper (2.5)
anaesthesia (11.7)
immersion (14.6)
displacement (A5.0)
perusing (A5.0)

PLATE 16

propellers (3.7)
harbor (8.1)
locomotive (8.2)
nautical (16.5)

SCORES

Plate 1_____
       2_____
       3_____
       4_____
       5_____
       6_____
       7_____
       8_____
       9_____
      10_____
      11_____
      12_____
      13_____
      14_____
      15_____
      16_____

TOTAL
_____

[6] R. B. Ammons and Helen S. Ammons, *The Full-Range Picture Vocabulary Test* (New Orleans, R. B. Ammons, 1948).

FULL-RANGE PICTURE VOCABULARY TEST (*cont.*)

NORMS BY FORMS

FORM A		FORM B	
SCORE	MENTAL AGE (YEARS)	SCORE	MENTAL AGE (YEARS)
6	2.5	6	2.5
12	3.5	12	3.5
17	4.5	17	4.5
21	5.5	20	5.5
25	6.5	25	6.5
29	7.5	29	7.5
33	8.5	32	8.5
37	9.5	37	9.5
42	10.5	41	10.5
46	11.5	45	11.5
50	12.5	49	12.5
54	13.5	53	13.5
58	14.5	57	14.5
62	15.5	62	15.5
69	16.5	69	16.5

ADULT PERCENTILES

SCORE	PERCENTILE	SCORE	PERCENTILE
84	99	84	99
82	95	82	95
80	90	81	90
78	80	78	80
75	70	75	70
73	60	73	60
70	50	71	50
67	40	68	40
65	30	65	30
60	20	62	20
57	10	58	10
55	5	55	5
52	1	52	1

THE BOSTON UNIVERSITY SPEECH SOUND DISCRIMINATION PICTURE TEST [7]

I. INSTRUCTIONS FOR ADMINISTERING AND SCORING THE TEST

1. The examiner is seated beside the child.

2. Place the picture sheets in numbered sequence, face up in a pile in front of the child.

3. Go through all the sheets and name the pictured objects which the child does not recognize.

4. Use picture No. 1 (cat-bat) for familiarization instruction as follows: "We are going to play a game with these pictures. Each page has three pictures on it like this. On this one there is a picture of a cat and a bat, a bat and a bat, and a cat and a cat. When I say two words, you point to the right picture. If I should say *cat-bat,* you would point to this one. Which one would you point to if I said *bat-bat?* Now listen carefully, because I am only going to say it once. Point to *cat-cat.*"

5. If the correct responses are made, and you are sure the child understands the procedure, proceed with the test. For each sheet, say, "Point to ————————." Read the pairs as listed on the score sheet. Go through the series of picture sheets twice, the first time using the pairs listed in column 1, and the second time using the pairs listed in column 2.

6. Beside each pair on the score sheet are two of the numbers, 1, 2, 3, and the letter R. These correspond to the position of the pictures from left to right on the picture sheets. The position of the correct picture is designated by R. To score, check the symbol in the same relative position as the picture to which the child points. Thus if the child points to the correct picture, you will check the letter R. If he points to the wrong picture, you will check the number which indicates its position on the picture sheet.

7. There is no time limit on the test.[8]

SCORING: The number of correct responses is taken as the test score.

The mean score for 434 children tested was 65.5 and the standard deviation was 6.55. Measures indicated that the distribution was strongly skewed negatively. "In view of the skewedness of the distribution of the results of this test, one would be justified in assuming that any score one or more standard deviations below the mean would indicate poor ability in speech sound discrimination." [9]

[7] Boston, Boston University, 1955.
[8] W. Pronovost and C. Dumbleton, "A Picture-Type Speech Sound Discrimination Test," *Journal of Speech and Hearing Disorders,* Vol. 18, No. 3 (1953), p. 266.
[9] *Ibid.,* p. 261.

SCORE SHEET FOR THE BOSTON UNIVERSITY SPEECH SOUND DISCRIMINATION PICTURE TEST [10]

*Name*_____   *School*_____

#	Word				#	Word			
1.	cat-cat	R	2	3	1.	cat-bat	1	R	3
2.	fish-fist	1	R	3	2.	fist-fist	1	2	R
3.	ship-ship	1	R	3	3.	chip-ship	R	2	3
4.	pole-pole	1	2	R	4.	pole-bowl	R	2	3
5.	cows-couch	R	2	3	5.	cows-cows	1	R	3
6.	cap-cup	1	2	R	6.	cap-cap	R	2	3
7.	pin-pin	1	2	R	7.	pen-pin	R	2	3
8.	bone-bone	R	2	3	8.	bowl-bone	1	2	R
9.	bed-bread	R	2	3	9.	bread-bread	1	R	3
10.	zoo-shoe	1	2	R	10.	zoo-zoo	R	2	3
11.	block-block	1	2	R	11.	clock-block	1	R	3
12.	coat-coat	1	R	3	12.	coat-goat	1	2	R
13.	cone-comb	1	2	R	13.	cone-cone	1	R	3
14.	chain-chain	1	R	3	14.	chain-train	R	2	3
15.	can-pan	1	R	3	15.	can-can	R	2	3
16.	clown-crown	1	2	R	16.	crown-crown	R	2	3
17.	pen-pen	1	R	3	17.	pan-pen	R	2	3
18.	boat-boot	R	2	3	18.	boat-boat	1	2	R
19.	pan-fan	1	R	3	19.	fan-fan	1	2	R
20.	lock-lock	1	R	3	20.	log-lock	R	2	3
21.	fox-socks	1	R	3	21.	fox-fox	1	2	R
22.	coat-coat	1	R	3	22.	coat-cat	R	2	3
23.	rock-lock	1	2	R	23.	rock-rock	R	2	3
24.	toes-toes	R	2	3	24.	ties-toes	1	R	3
25.	wash-wash	R	2	3	25.	wash-watch	1	2	R
26.	tie-pie	1	R	3	26.	tie-tie	R	2	3
27.	stairs-chairs	R	2	3	27.	stairs-stairs	1	R	3
28.	face-face	1	R	3	28.	vase-face	1	2	R
29.	mouse-mouth	1	R	3	29.	mouth-mouth	R	2	3
30.	knot-nut	1	R	3	30.	knot-knot	1	2	R
31.	boat-boat	1	R	3	31.	goat-boat	R	2	3
32.	ring-ring	1	R	3	32.	ring-wing	1	2	R
33.	grass-glass	1	2	R	33.	glass-glass	R	2	3
34.	cat-cat	R	2	3	34.	cap-cat	1	2	R
35.	ice-eyes	R	2	3	35.	eyes-eyes	1	R	3
36.	pan-pan	R	2	3	36.	pan-pin	1	R	3

[10] *Ibid.*, p. 260.

SHORT TEST OF SOUND DISCRIMINATION [11]

Mildred C. Templin

EXAMPLES:	KEY: All D Except:
te-de	A. 1, 8
ere-ere	B. 1, 6, 8, 10
os-og	C. 3, 6, 8, 9
	D. 4, 9, 10
	E. 3, 9
	F. 3, 7
	G. 3, 6

A.	B.	C.	D.
1. te-te	1. ne-ne	1. fo-θo	1. pe-ke
2. hwe-we	2. dʒe-tʃe	2. vo-ðo	2. tʃo-ʃo
3. ne-me	3. ʃe-tʃe	3. zo-zo	3. ki-ti
4. ðe-de	4. im-iŋ	4. ʃe-ʒe	4. eb-eb
5. fi-vi	5. hwi-wi	5. fi-θi	5. ehwe-ewe
6. he-pe	6. ge-ge	6. ze-ze	6. en-em
7. se-ze	7. dʒi-tʃi	7. mai-nai	7. eð-ed
8. θe-θe	8. fai-fai	8. θe-θe	8. ehe-epe
9. ʒe-dʒe	9. ðe-ve	9. he-he	9. ov-ov
10. vo-bo	10. pe-pe	10. dʒi-ʒi	10. eθ-eθ

E.	F.	G.
1. eʒ-edʒ	1. eð-ev	1. if-iθ
2. ov-ob	2. et-ep	2. aim-ain
3. ed-ed	3. ep-ep	3. eθ-eθ
4. en-en	4. of-oθ	4. ini-iŋi
5. edʒ-etʃ	5. ov-oð	5. ef-ep
6. eʃ-etʃ	6. ed-eg	6. eð-eð
7. imi-iŋi	7. em-em	7. idʒ-iʒ
8. ihwi-iwi	8. eð-ez	8. ep-ek
9. eg-eg	9. airai-aiwai	9. otʃ-oʃ
10. is-iz	10. eʃ-eʒ	10. ez-eð

[11] Mildred C. Templin, "Study of Sound Discrimination Ability of Elementary School Pupils," *Journal of Speech Disorders,* Vol. 8, No. 2 (1943), p. 132.

ADMINISTRATION AND SCORING OF THE TEMPLIN SHORT TEST OF SOUND DISCRIMINATION

Administration: The examiner sits so that the child cannot see his lips. Practice items are given so that the test is clearly understood. The child is given a form marked off in squares and, depending upon whether the syllables are heard as the same or different, the child places an *S* or a *D* in the proper square in response to each stimulus pair.

Scoring: The examiner counts the number of errors made on the test. The average number of errors made on the *Short Test of Sound Discrimination* is 18.29. *More errors than 18.29 would indicate that the child is below average in his ability to discriminate between sounds.*

TEST FOR AUDITORY MEMORY SPAN

The following test for auditory memory span is a modification of Virgil Anderson's test for auditory memory span by Ruth Metraux.

The vowel and diphthong test consists of three parts, each containing a series of sounds, beginning with one sound and continuing to ten sounds, one sound being added each time. The consonant test is constructed in the same manner, with series from one to nine. The test is devised, as the original structure of the test for adults indicates, so that the sounds are evenly distributed throughout the entire test, and in various positions. None of the units forms meaningful associations, and there are no units or combinations of sounds in adjacent series. There is a period of silence between adjacent sounds. The sounds are delivered at the rate of one per second (metronome: 60) for the vowels, and slightly under one per second for the consonants (metronome: 56).[12]

For temporary standardization, a series of three tests was tape recorded. Practice trials were given to make sure the child could say every sound. By screening the mouth, the stimulus remained auditory.

Instructions were given as follows, "We are going to play a game. You listen to the sounds you hear me say to you, and then you tell the sounds back to me. Let's practice first to be sure you can make the sounds." After the practice trials: "As long as I am talking, you keep your lips and tongue quiet, but when I finish, tell me as many sounds as you remember, even when you don't remember all of them." Depending on the age, the child is turned so he does not face the examiner. Each series is played only once for the child. When the test changes from vowels to consonants, the examiner says, "Now we are going to hear some different sounds, but we will practice again just to be sure we can make the sounds."

Separate scores are taken for the vowel and consonant tests. A basal score for one test is the number in that series which the child reproduces immediately before the lowest level failure in the group. He receives an added ⅓ of a point to the basal score for every series correctly reproduced regardless of intervening failures. The child is given credit only when the complete series is reproduced and in the correct order.

---

[12] Ruth Metraux, "Auditory Memory Span for Speech Sounds: Norms for Children," *Journal of Speech and Hearing Disorders,* Vol. 9, No. 1 (1944), pp. 31-38.

RECORDING

Vowels

Group A

These are practice sounds. Ready? (2 sec. pause)

   ɑ oʊ   (3 sec. pause)
   eɪ ɔ   (3 sec. pause)
   u æ   (3 sec. pause)
   i aɪ   (3 sec. pause)
      (Break)

First you will hear one sound. Ready? (2 sec. pause)

   ɑ
      (Break)

Now you will hear two sounds. Ready? (2 sec. pause)

   aɪ, i
      (Break)

Now you will hear three sounds. Ready? (2 sec. pause)

   ɔ, u, æ
      (Break)

Now you will hear four sounds. Ready? (2 sec. pause)

   u, i, ɔ, oʊ
   æ, aɪ, u, eɪ, ɑ   (5 sounds)
   oʊ, ə, i, æ, eɪ, aɪ   (6 sounds)
   ɑ, oʊ, u, aɪ, eɪ, ɔ, i   (7 sounds)
   eɪ, æ, i, ɑ, aɪ, u, oʊ, ɔ   (8 sounds)

Group B

   eɪ
   æ i
   oʊ ɔ ʊ
   ɔ aɪ ɑ æ
   oʊ ɑ eɪ u i
   u oʊ ɔ i æ aɪ
   ɔ oʊ ɑ i aɪ æ eɪ
   oʊ u eɪ æ aɪ ɔ i ɑ

Group C

   æ
   aɪ ɔ
   ɑ u oʊ
   i ɑ eɪ u
   aɪ æ i ɔ oʊ
   ɑ u eɪ æ oʊ ɔ
   eɪ ɔ i aɪ u oʊ æ
   ɔ oʊ ɑ i æ eɪ u aɪ

Consonants

These are practice sounds. Ready? (pause 2 sec.)

kʌ fʌ   (pause 3 seconds)
pʌ tʌ   (pause 3 seconds)
sʌ ʃʌ   (pause 3 seconds)

Group A. First you will hear one sound. Ready? (pause 2 sec.)

pʌ
fʌ kʌ
ʃʌ fʌ pʌ
kʌ sʌ ʃʌ tʌ
fʌ pʌ sʌ kʌ pʌ
tʌ fʌ sʌ pʌ kʌ ʃʌ
kʌ tʌ fʌ tʌ ʃʌ sʌ pʌ
tʌ kʌ ʃʌ kʌ pʌ ʃʌ tʌ
sʌ ʃʌ kʌ fʌ pʌ ʃʌ sʌ tʌ kʌ

Group B.

kʌ
fʌ pʌ
tʌ ʃʌ sʌ
sʌ tʌ kʌ tʌ
fʌ kʌ ʃʌ tʌ pʌ
tʌ ʃʌ pʌ sʌ kʌ fʌ
sʌ pʌ tʌ kʌ tʌ ʃʌ fʌ
pʌ kʌ fʌ tʌ pʌ sʌ ʃʌ pʌ
kʌ ʃʌ tʌ ʃʌ kʌ sʌ pʌ fʌ sʌ

Group C.

fʌ
pʌ sʌ
tʌ pʌ fʌ
sʌ fʌ ʃʌ kʌ
ʃʌ sʌ tʌ pʌ kʌ
kʌ ʃʌ fʌ pʌ sʌ tʌ
pʌ tʌ sʌ tʌ kʌ ʃʌ fʌ
tʌ fʌ pʌ kʌ sʌ pʌ kʌ ʃʌ
sʌ tʌ fʌ kʌ ʃʌ sʌ ʃʌ tʌ
kʌ fʌ pʌ ʃʌ tʌ pʌ sʌ tʌ kʌ

RANGE AND MEANS OF SCORES OF EACH AGE GROUP [a]

AGE	NO.	WEIGHTED VOWEL		WEIGHTED CONSONANT	
		RANGE	MEAN	RANGE	MEAN
5	21	1.67-4.33	2.68	1.00-3.00	2.0
6	37	1.67-4.67	3.07	1.33-3.33	2.35
7	60	2.00-6.00	3.39	1.33-4.00	2.63
8	50	2.33-5.33	3.45	1.33-4.67	2.65
9	56	2.00-5.33	3.70	1.33-4.33	2.86
10	75	2.33-5.67	3.78	2.00-4.33	3.09
11	72	2.33-6.00	3.47	1.33-4.67	2.93
12	43	2.67-5.00	3.49	2.00-5.00	3.12

[a] For purposes of reporting, the age groups are designated with a single digit, such as age 5, age 6, etc. However, age 5 includes all children between 4 years, 6 months and 5 years, 5 months; age 6 includes all children between 5 years, 6 months and 6 years, 5 months, etc.

OSERETSKY SCALE (*MOTOR PROFICIENCY*) [13]

RECORD BLANK

*Score-Sheet No._____

Date_____.

Name _____   Motor Level _____

Date of Birth _____   Mental Level (I.Q.) _____

Age_____   Motor Retardation_____

School Attending _____   Motor Acceleration _____

Class _____

AGE	GENERAL STATIC		DYNAMIC MANUAL		GENERAL DYNAMIC		SPEED		SIMUL. MOVEM'T.		SYNKIN-ESIA	
	R	L	R	L	R	L	R	L	R	L	R	L
15-16												
13-14												
11-12												
10												
9												
8												
7												
6												
5												
4												

Motor
Level

---

* Score-Sheet used at the Antonio Aurelio da Costa Ferriera Institute. (The categories from left to right correspond to tests 1-6 at each year. Note that "right limb" may be interpreted as "preferred" and "left" as "alternate," and that in the use of alternative limbs the time, trials permitted, and other conditions of success are not always identical nor always unequivocally stated.—EAD.)

[13] E. A. Doll, ed., *The Oseretsky Test of Motor Proficiency* (Minneapolis, Educational Publishers, 1947), p. 1.

	TRIALS PERMITTED	TIME PERMITTED RIGHT LIMB	TIME OBSERVED RIGHT LIMB	TIME OBSERVED LEFT LIMB	TIME PERMITTED LEFT LIMB	OBSERVATIONS

FOUR YEARS

1. To remain standing; one foot advanced; eyes closed ⎯⎯⎯

2. To touch the point of the nose, eyes closed ⎯⎯⎯

3. To hop in the same place, feet together 7 times ⎯⎯⎯

4. To put 20 coins in a box ⎯⎯⎯

5. To describe circles with index fingers, arms extended at sides ⎯⎯⎯

6. To clasp the hand; right, left, both ⎯⎯⎯

FIVE YEARS

1. To balance on tiptoe ⎯⎯⎯

2. To make a ball with silk thin paper ⎯⎯⎯

3. To hop on one foot 5 meters ⎯⎯⎯

4. To roll 2 meters of thread on a spool ⎯⎯⎯

5. To put 20 matches in a box, one by one, 10 with each hand ⎯⎯⎯

6. To clench and bare the teeth ⎯⎯⎯

SIX YEARS

1. To balance standing on one leg ⎯⎯⎯

2. To throw a ball at a target (1.5M. distant) ⎯⎯⎯

3. To jump over a rope (20 cm. high) ⎯⎯⎯

	TRIALS PERMITTED	TIME PERMITTED RIGHT LIMB	TIME OBSERVED RIGHT LIMB	TIME OBSERVED LEFT LIMB	TIME PERMITTED LEFT LIMB	OBSERVATIONS
4. To draw 20 r.h. and 12 l.h. perpendicular lines _____						
5. To roll a thread from a spool to the index finger, while walking _____						
6. To strike a table with a mallet _____						
SEVEN YEARS						
1. To balance on tip-toe bending forward from the hip _____						
2. To trace through 2 mazes _____						
3. To walk a line for 2 meters placing one foot following (*a seguir*) the other _____						
4. To distribute 36 cards in 4 piles _____						
5. To tap floor alternately with the feet _____						
6. To knit the eye-brows _____						
EIGHT YEARS						
1. To crouch on tip-toes _____						
2. To touch the thumb to all the fingers of the same hand _____						
3. To kick a box a distance of 5 meters hopping on one foot _____						
4. To run 5 meters, pick up a match box, make a square, etc. _____						
5. To tap the floor rhythmically with the feet alternately, tapping the table with the corresponding index fingers in the same rhythm_____						
6. To wrinkle the forehead _____						

IOWA PERFORMANCE TEST OF SELECTED MANUAL ACTIVITIES [14]

SCORE SHEET

Name_____ Age_____ Sex_____

Examiner_____ Dextrality Quotient_____ Date_____

Place a check mark in appropriate spaces below to indicate whether activities listed were performed by the right hand (R), the left hand (L), or both hands (B), neither hand predominating.

	R L B		R L B
1. Pull down curtain.	— — —	33. Pick up card.	— — —
2. Pull down curtain.	— — —	34. Pick up card.	— — —
3. Take article from desk.	— — —	35. Lay down card.	— — —
4. Take article from desk.	— — —	36. Lay down card.	— — —
5. Tear paper from tablet.	— — —	37. Tear paper from tablet.	— — —
6. Turn over paper.	— — —	38. Turn over paper.	— — —
7. Sharpen pencil.	— — —	39. Fold paper.	— — —
8. Write with pencil.	— — —	40. Sharpen pencil.	— — —
9. Erase with pencil-tip eraser.	— — —	41. Turn page of book.	— — —
10. Write with pencil.	— — —	42. Turn page of book.	— — —
11. Draw a picture.	— — —	43. Draw a picture.	— — —
12. Put pencil in desk.	— — —	44. Put pencil in desk.	— — —
13. Take crayon from box.	— — —	45. Pick up scissors.	— — —
14. Take crayon from box.	— — —	46. Put scissors in desk.	— — —
15. Color with crayon.	— — —	47. Pick up pen.	— — —
16. Color with crayon.	— — —	48. Take top off pen.	— — —
17. Put crayon in box.	— — —	49. Take top off ink bottle.	— — —
18. Put crayon in box.	— — —	50. Fill pen.	— — —
19. Close crayon box.	— — —	51. Write with pen.	— — —
20. Close crayon box.	— — —	52. Put top on pen.	— — —
21. Pick up scissors.	— — —	53. Erase with pencil-tip eraser.	— — —
22. Put scissors in desk.	— — —	54. Fold paper.	— — —
23. Point to block.	— — —	55. Pick up pen.	— — —
24. Point to block.	— — —	56. Take top off pen.	— — —
25. Pick up block to pile.	— — —	57. Take top off ink bottle.	— — —
26. Place block on pile.	— — —	58. Fill pen.	— — —
27. Pick up block to pile.	— — —	59. Write with pen.	— — —
28. Place block on pile.	— — —	60. Put top on pen.	— — —
29. Pick up block to carry.	— — —	61. Pick up chalk.	— — —
30. Pick up block to carry.	— — —	62. Write with chalk.	— — —
31. Point to card.	— — —	63. Pick up chalk.	— — —
32. Point to card.	— — —	64. Write with chalk.	— — —

[14] W. Johnson and D. Duke, "Revised Iowa Hand Usage Dextrality Quotients of Six-Year-Olds," *Journal of Educational Psychology*, Vol. 31, No. 1 (1940), pp. 45-52.

SCORING, MATERIALS, AND PROCEDURE AND NORMS FOR THE IOWA PERFORMANCE TEST OF SELECTED MANUAL ACTIVITIES

Scoring: The purpose of this test is to determine a person's dextrality quotient (percentage of right-handedness) on the basis of observation of 64 operations in the performance of 32 activities. The dextrality quotient for each subject can be found by means of the formula

$$DQ = \frac{R - (B/2)}{N} \text{ , in which R and B represent}$$

the number of operations performed by the right hand and by both hands (neither hand predominating), respectively, and N represents the total number of operations performed.

Materials: The materials needed for the test are: A room with a window having a shade which can be easily manipulated by a seven-year-old child; a desk of the type from which articles are taken with equal ease from both sides, i.e., the open shelf type, and in which the articles to be removed are not observed; a pencil; a small pencil sharpener of the type held in one hand; a tablet of paper of customary school size; a pencil with eraser attached; a box of crayons; scissors in which the finger holes are the same on both sides; five regular flash cards; a blackboard; a piece of chalk; eight 1¼ " cubes; a fountain pen with regulation screw top and side lever for filling; a bottle of ink; and a large picture book with pages which can be readily handled.

Procedure: Before calling the child, the tablet, pencil, pencil sharpener, and crayons are placed in the desk. As soon as the child enters the room the following directions are given:

"Will you please *pull down the curtain* a little? That is fine, but will you please *pull it down* a trifle more?" See that the child has taken his hand from the curtain before being instructed to make the second adjustment. Also, be sure that he approaches the shade so that it can be as readily pulled with one hand as with the other.

"Now will you please *take the articles out of the desk* one at a time and place them on the top of the desk?" The first two responses are recorded for this item. The tester picks up the articles and places only the tablet in front of the child, and says, "Please *tear out* one sheet of paper and *turn over* the paper."

The tester then puts the pencil and pencil sharpener in front of the child, and says, "Please *sharpen the pencil.*" The activity is scored by recording the hand that does the actual turning.

The tester next places the pencil directly in front of the child and continues, "*Write* your name at the top of the paper. No, please *erase it,* and *write it* at the bottom of the sheet. Now will you please *draw* a picture; and when you are finished, *put the pencil in the desk.*"

Then a box of crayons is placed directly in front of the child by the tester who says, "Now *color* the picture." Note which hand is used in *taking out each crayon* (score the first two), in *coloring,* in *placing each crayon* in the box (score the first two), and in *closing the box.* In case the child does not voluntarily use more than one color, the tester may say, "Let's use another color for this part of the picture." As soon as the child is through and no longer has his hands on the box, say: "Let's look in the box to see if we have all the crayons in it." This gives a second score for *closing the box*.

Next the scissors are placed directly in front of the child. "Cut off the bottom line, please." Note the hand used in *picking up the scissors*. "Now *put the scissors in the desk.*"

The tester next arranges the blocks in a straight line from one side of the table to the other, the middle block being directly before the child, and says, *"Point to A; point to G,"* etc. Be sure to see that the child is relaxed and ready to start with neither hand favored before the second letter is named. The first two letters, the only ones scored, are called off in a definite order, the sixth from the left being called first and the third from the left next. "Now pile the blocks one on top of the other to make a pile eight blocks high, being sure to *pick up* only one block at a time." Note the hand used in *picking up*, as well as in *placing*, the second and fourth blocks. The blocks are again put on the desk, and the tester instructs the child by saying, "Please carry these over to that desk one at a time." If there is not a second desk handy, some other surface may be substituted. Record the hand used in *picking up* first and third blocks. Do not record the hand used in carrying the blocks.

Next the tester places five flash cards on the top of the desk and says, "Please *point* to the cards as I name them." Call first for the second from the left and then for the fourth from the left. "Now please *pick them up* one at a time and now *lay them down* one at a time." (For these last two items, record the first two responses in each case.)

Now a tablet is placed directly in front of the child, and the tester says, "Please *tear out* another sheet of paper; *turn over the sheet of paper;* and *fold it* in the middle." The hand which actually creases the folded edge is the one recorded.

Next the pencil sharpener and pencil are again presented in the midline, and the child is instructed to *sharpen the pencil.*

Following this activity, the picture book is presented in the middle of the desk, and the tester says, "Please *turn* to the picture of Casper Carrot." Any picture will do so long as two or more pages are turned. Record the hand used in turning each of the first two pages. Then after the pencil is again presented directly in front of the child, the examiner says, "Now *draw* the picture, and when you are through *put the pencil in the desk.*"

Next the book is removed and the scissors are placed directly in front of the child, and the tester says, "Please cut out your picture, and then *put the scissors in the desk.*" Also, the hand used in *picking up* the scissors is recorded.

The bottle of ink and the pen are next presented directly in front of the child, care being taken to see that the pen is placed on neither side of the ink bottle. The tester says, "Please *pick up the pen, take off the top,* (record the hand doing the actual turning) put them both down, *take the top off the ink bottle, fill the pen,* and *write your name.* Then *put the top back on the pen.*" While the child is doing these things, the tester should put the top back on the ink bottle. The tester next says, "Please *erase* your name. Now *fold* the paper so that the ink spot will not show. *Pick up* the pen, *take off the top,* put down the pen, *take the top off the ink bottle, fill the pen, write* your name, and *put the top on the pen.*"

The last two activities are concerned with the blackboard. The child is directed to stand squarely in front of it where the chalk can be as easily reached with one hand as with the other. The tester says, "Please write your name." Score the hand used in *picking up the chalk,* as well as in *writing.* Lastly, the tester asks the child, "Will you please *print* your name?" This also gives the second score for *picking up the chalk.* This concludes the test.

Any remarks by the child or further directions by the tester, in case there is difficulty in grasping the directions, need not be curtailed, provided they do not influence hand preference. Total test time: 20-25 minutes.

NORMS: In the following table, the lowest and highest percentiles, respectively, represent the lowest and highest D.Q. in each group. Suppose a six-year-old child scores a D.Q. of .86. By referring to this table it is to be found that he falls at the 70th percentile for his age group. This means that he is more right-handed than 70 per cent and less right-handed than 30 per cent of the six-year-olds tested by Johnson and Duke. In such terms any child's score may be evaluated. It must be kept in mind, of course, that these norms are only for the age levels indicated in the table. The score of a child at some other age level is to be evaluated by reference to the table only by taking into account the difference in age. This can be done only with a limited degree of accuracy, of course, and evaluations should be tempered accordingly. However, it will be noted that differences between high-school-age subjects and the two groups of younger subjects are not great. Since the activities involved in this test were originally selected by observing actual school-room activities of six-year-old children, it would seem reasonable to conclude that the hand which an individual has come to use consistently for a given activity at the age of seven years or so is the hand he will use for the same activity eight to ten years later.[15]

TABLE

Scores on the Iowa Performance Test of Selected Manual Activities, by Percentiles, for Six-Year-Old, Seven-Year-Old, and High-School-Age Subjects.

PERCENTILE	SIX-YEAR-OLDS [a] N = 50	SEVEN-YEAR-OLDS [b] N = 100	HIGH-SCHOOL-AGE [c] (13-19 yrs.) N = 100
0	.07	.12	.01
10	.52	.63	.43
20	.65	.71	.64
30	.74	.78	.69
40	.80	.81	.74
50	.82	.83	.79
60	.84	.85	.84
70	.86	.88	.87
80	.90	.92	.91
90	.94	.95	.95
100	1.00	1.00	.97

[a] W. Johnson and D. Duke, "Revised Iowa Hand Usage Dextrality Quotients of Six-Year-Olds," *Journal of Educational Psychology,* Vol. 31, No. 1 (1940), 45-52.

[b] W. Johnson and D. Davis, "Dextrality Quotients of Seven-Year-Olds in Terms of Hand Usage," *Journal of Educational Psychology,* Vol. 28, No. 5 (1937), pp. 346-354.

[c] W. Johnson and V. L. Bissell, "Iowa Hand Usage Dextrality Quotients of One Hundred High-School Students," *Journal of Educational Psychology,* Vol. 31, No. 2 (1940), pp. 148-152.

[15] *Ibid.*

MODIFICATIONS OF THE OBJECTIVE TEST OF LATERALITY BY ABRAM BLAU [16]

1. *Cutting Test.* This requires a single type of scissors with fingerhold, made so as not to discriminate against the use of the left hand. The child is asked to cut out circles drawn on a piece of paper, first with one hand and then the other. In all probability, the child will not be able to manipulate the scissors with each hand. If he does, the relative dexterity of each hand can be seen. Record the more expert hand.

2. *Batting Test.* Require the child to hold a bat as if ready to strike a ball to be pitched by the examiner. Record the upper hand which is nearer the batting end.

3. *Crossing Thumb Test.* Ask the child to clasp his hands in front of his body. The examiner may demonstrate what is wanted. Record the hand with the thumb on top. Folding the arms may also be tried.

4. *Sighting Eye Test.* Ask the child to sight a distant object through a small hole in a large piece of paper or cardboard held at arm's length in front of the face. Without moving the paper, the left eye is closed while the right is open; if the object is still visible, the child is right-eyed, if not, he is left-eyed. The observer can usually check this by observing which eye is being used.

5. *Nose and Finger Near-Seeing Test.* Have the child hold his finger in a vertical position about a foot in front of the nose. With both eyes looking at the finger, have the child bring the finger toward his face. Observe to see if the finger moves toward the right or left eye. The eye toward which the finger moves is the dominant eye for near seeing.

6. *Kicking Test.* Ask the child to kick, as if at a football. Record the kicking leg.

7. *Crossing Legs Test.* Ask the child to cross his legs while seated. Record the upper leg.

8. *Hopping Test.* Ask the child to hop on one leg. Record the leg used.

SELECTED ITEMS FROM THE HARRIS TESTS OF LATERAL DOMINANCE [17]

Simultaneous Writing. Using a printed record blank and two pencils of equal length, the subject is asked to write the numbers 1 to 12 in vertical column with both hands at the same time, as fast as he can. Vision of what he is doing is blocked with a cardboard shield. Any full or partial reversal with either hand is noted, relative co-ordination of the two hands is noted, and the result is rated on a five-point scale: strong right, moderate right, mixed, moderate left, and

[16] Abram Blau, as reprinted in Harry Bakwin and Ruth Bakwin, *Clinical Management of Behavior Disorders in Children* (Philadelphia, Saunders, 1953), p. 297.

[17] A. J. Harris, *Harris Tests of Lateral Dominance* (New York, The Psychological Corporation, 1955), pp. 12-13.

strong left. Exact directions for administering and scoring are given in the Manual.

"This test is based upon the principle that when both hands attempt to perform the same movement simultaneously, the non-dominant hand tends to do it mirrorwise, reversing the left-right directions.

In this test, the strongly right-handed person makes no reversals with his right hand; he may make as many as ten reversals with his left hand, or none at all. The tendency to mirror with the left hand is felt by many who consciously resist it and succeed in making the left hand follow the right without reversing. The strongly left-handed makes no reversals with the left hand and may or may not reverse with the right hand. The median number of reversals in the non-dominant hand is three. The digits written with the dominant hand are much better formed than those written with the non-dominant hand.

When an individual makes a reversal with his dominant hand, or reverses with both hands, one can be fairly certain that a real directional confusion exists. Most of the cases who have reversed with both hands or with the dominant hand only have shown marked reversal errors in their reading and writing. Evidence of conversion has been obtained in fewer than half of these cases, but conversion may have occurred in some of the others. Within two years after conversion a child will usually reverse with both hands on this test; after two or more years, he sometimes will produce a clear right-handed record."

SPEECH STIMULATION MATERIALS

BOOKS

1. *The Indoor Noisy Book,* by Margaret Wise Brown (New York, William K. Scott, Inc., 1942).
   The story of Muffin, the little dog who had a cold. All about him he could hear noises in the house: a broom sweeping, the clinking of silver, the telephone bell, vacuum cleaner, cook in the kitchen beating eggs, etc.

2. *The Country Noisy Book,* by Margaret Wise Brown (New York, William K. Scott, Inc., 1940).
   The story of Muffin when he goes to the country on the train; he hears all the sounds of a train: *ding-dong, choo-choo-chook, chookachooka; toot;* sounds of the farm: rooster, lamb, cow, dog, duck, etc.

3. *Listening for Speech Sounds,* by E. Y. Zedler (New York, Harper, 1956).

4. *Noises and Mr. Fliberty Jib,* by Gertrude Crampton (New York, Simon & Schuster, 1947).
   The story of Mr. Fliberty Jib, a man who has a headache, and all the sounds and noises that aggravate him and make his headache worse.

5. *Picture Sounding Rhymes,* by Mary Alice Stoddard (Racine, Wisconsin, Whitman Publishing Company, 1943).
   This is a book of brightly colored pictures of animals with rhymes about what they say.

6. *See It, Say It, Do It,* by Gladys M. Horn (Racine, Wisconsin, Whitman Publishing Company, 1951).
   This book contains pictures beginning with the same sound to identify and reproduce, and arrange on a page. Examples: Find the snowman, the soup, slippers, swing, etc. Find the flag, fire, fan, fish, four, etc.

7. *See It,* by F. S. Winship (Racine, Wisconsin, Whitman Publishing Company, 1952).
   This book contains brightly colored action pictures involving objects and situations within a young child's experience.

8. *What We Do Day by Day* (Chicago 6, National Dairy Council, 1950).
   There are pictures of the things children do day by day, such as eating, washing, sleeping, playing, etc.

PHONOGRAPH RECORDS

1. *Genie, The Magic Record* (Decca Records, Inc., 1946).
   This is a recording of a story featuring Genie, the Magic Record, as the main character. During the episodes, Genie meets many things which make

515

well-known environmental sounds, such as a fire engine, a door opening, footsteps, etc. He names each one and then the sound it makes is heard. The descriptions and sounds are employed very cleverly in the story.

2. *What's Its Name?* This is an Auditory Training Album by Jean Utley (Minneapolis, The Maico Company, Inc.) and (Urbana, University of Illinois Press). This album contains two records. Both sides of the first record contain well-known environmental sounds such as a telephone ringing, a car starting, a dog barking, etc. The second record contains three familiar nursery rhymes: *Little Boy Blue, Jack and Jill,* and *Little Jack Horner;* and a story, *The Three Bears.*

3. *I'm Dressing Myself,* by Gene Lowell and Philip List (Young People's Records, Inc., 100 Sixth Ave., New York).
   This record contains the voices of a mother and her son. They name the articles of clothing as he puts them on.

4. *The Little Fireman* (from a story by Margaret Wise Brown, Young People's Records, Inc.).
   This record contains a story about firemen, describing them with accompanying story and sounds.

5. *The Circus Comes to Town* (Young People's Records, Inc.).
   This record contains a story about a circus employing a different voice and sounds for the fat man, tumblers, bicycle rider, the clown, juggler, etc.

6. *I Wish I Were*——— (The Children's Record Guild, 27 Thompson Street, New York).
   This record contains a song about wishing to be different things, such as a grasshopper, a giant, etc. and the sounds that these things make when they walk, go swimming, etc.

7. *The Chugging Freight Engine* (Young People's Records, Inc.).
   This record contains a story about the train and the sounds it makes.

8. *Let's Help Mommy* (Children's Record Guild).
   This record contains a story about two little children who decide to help their mother on the day of their father's birthday. It includes the sounds of the things they help to do, such as vacuum the rug, sweep the floor, etc.

9. *Old MacDonald Had a Farm* (A Little Golden Record. Rockefeller Center, New York, Simon & Schuster).
   This record contains the song, and all the sounds that the animals on the farm make.

10. *The Choo Choo Train* (A Little Golden Record).
    This record contains a story about a train and the sounds that it makes.

11. *Tootle* (A Little Golden Record).
    This record contains a story about Tootle, the train, and the sounds that he makes.

Commercial Games

1. *Fruit Lotto* (New York, Ed-u-Cards Company).

2. *Farm Lotto* (New York, Ed-u-Cards Company).

3. *Zoo Lotto* (New York, Ed-u-Cards Company).

4. *Object Lotto* (New York, Saml. Gabriel Sons and Company).

5. *Timmy Time—The Color Wheel Clock* (St. Paul, Minnesota, Sifo Company).

6. *Kentucky Derby Racing Game* (Racine, Wisconsin, Whitman Publishing Company).

7. *Fun Cards* (New York, Parker Brothers, Inc.).

8. *Picture Dominoes* (New York, Ed-u-Cards Company).

9. *Peanut, the Elephant* (New York, Parker Brothers, Inc.).

10. *Playskool Postal Station* (Chicago, Playskool Manufacturing Company).

These games may be used as motivators for speech. Every time the child discriminates or says a sound or a word correctly, he may place or move a card, a block, etc.

SOUND DISCRIMINATION GAME

Strings are attached to the pictures on the left side of the page. The child places the string on the matching picture at the right when the teacher says: "Find the ———."

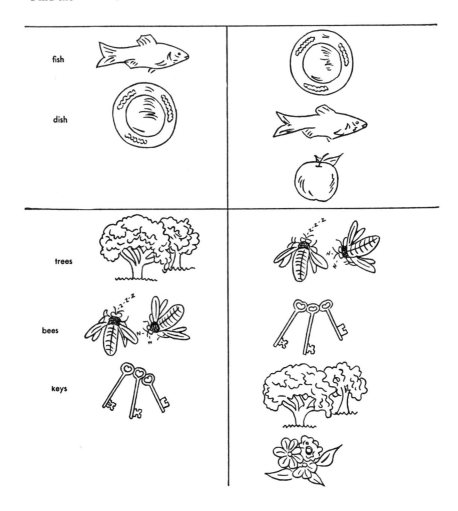

SOUND DISCRIMINATION GAME (cont.)

cat

bat

rat

rose

nose

bows

SOUND DISCRIMINATION GAME (cont.)

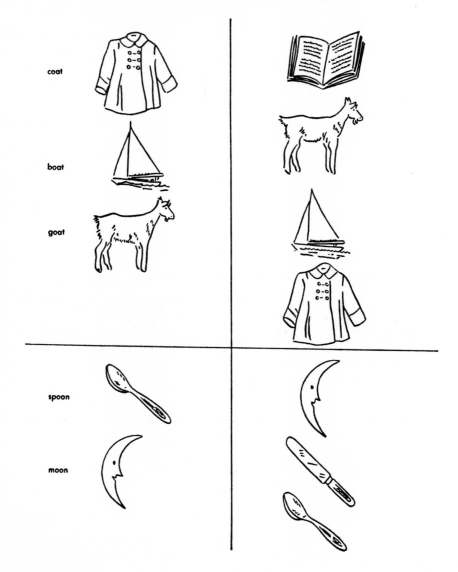

coat

boat

goat

spoon

moon

SOUND DISCRIMINATION GAME (cont.)

can

man

fan

pie

fly

tie

SOUND DISCRIMINATION GAME (cont.)

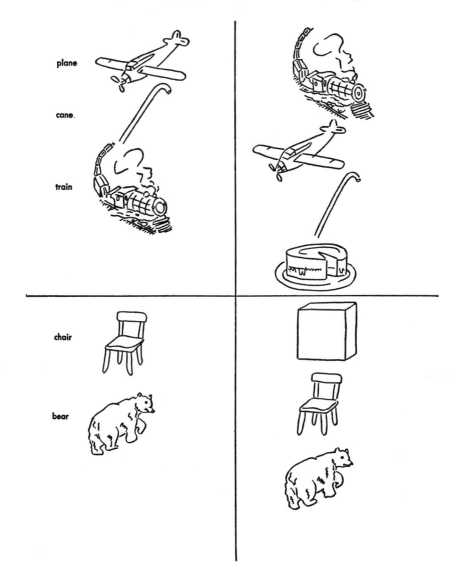

plane

cane.

train

chair

bear

THE PHONETIC ALPHABET AND KEY

TABLE OF VOWELS

I. *Front Vowels*

[i]:	keep	[kip]	
[ɪ]:	it	[ɪt]	
[e]:	chaotic	[ke-ɑtɪk]	(a pure vowel only in unstressed syllables in American English)
[ɛ]:	met	[mɛt]	
[æ]:	that	[ðæt]	
[a]:	laugh	[laf]	(not found in General American pronunciation; midway between [æ] and [ɑ])

II. *Back Vowels*

[u]:	who	[hu]	
[ʊ]:	could	[kʊd]	
[o]:	obey	[obeɪ]	(a pure vowel only in unstressed syllables in American English)
[ɔ]:	all	[ɔl]	
[ɒ]:	odd	[ɒd]	

III. *Central Vowels*

[ɝ]:	bird	[bɝd]	(General American pronunciation; appears in stressed syllables only)
[ɚ]:	murmur	[mɝ·mɚ]	(General American pronunciation; appears in unstressed syllables only)
[ɜ]:	bird	[bɜd]	(Southern and Eastern pronunciation)
[ʌ]:	cup	[kʌp]	(appears only in stressed syllables)
[ə]:	sofa	[soʊfə]	(appears only in unstressed syllables or as a substitute for [ɝ] in Southern pronunciation, as in *there* [ðɛə]
[ɑ]:	calm	[kam].[18]	

TABLE OF DIPHTHONGS

[eɪ]:	day	[deɪ]
[aɪ]:	die	[daɪ]
[oʊ]:	low	[loʊ]
[aʊ]:	now	[naʊ]
[ɔɪ]:	boy	[bɔɪ]
[ju]:	cute	[kjut]

[18] Sometimes called a back vowel.

523

TABLE OF SEMI-VOWELS

[hw]:	why	[hwaɪ]
[w]:	well	[wɛl]
[j]:	yes	[jɛs]
[r]:	red	[rɛd]

TABLE OF CONSONANTS

I. *Stop Plosives*

[p]:	pack	[pæk]
[b]:	back	[bæk]
[t]:	tip	[tɪp]
[d]:	dip	[dɪp]
[k]:	come	[kʌm]
[g]:	gum	[gʌm]
[tʃ]:	witch	[wɪtʃ]
[dʒ]:	judge	[dʒʌdʒ]

II. *Continuant Fricatives*

[f]:	life	[laɪf]
[v]:	live	[lɪv]
[θ]:	cloth	[klɔθ]
[ð]:	mother	[mʌðɚ]
[s]:	sink	[sɪŋk]
[z]:	zinc	[zɪŋk]
[ʃ]:	ash	[æʃ]
[ʒ]:	azure	[æʒɚ]

III. *Nasals*

[m]:	more	[mɔr]
[n]:	none	[nʌn]
[ŋ]:	long	[lɔŋ]

IV. *Lateral*

[l]:	light	[laɪt]

APPENDIX 4

Historical and Diagnostic Journals

RETARDED SPEECH

I. IDENTIFICATION

1. Name of subject:
2. Birth date:
3. Sex:
4. Race:
5. Nationality:
6. Address:
7. Telephone:
8. Name of father:
9. Referred to Clinic by:

II. FAMILY

A. *Father*

1. Name:
2. Birth date:
3. Living_____ deceased_____ divorced_____ not living in the home _____
4. Education: grade_____; high school_____; college_____
5. Occupation:
6. Date of marriage:
7. Church affiliation:
8. Presence in him or his familial line of the following: (Note exact relationship to father and describe manifestation carefully.)
   a. sinistrality_____
   b. ambilaterality_____
   c. strabismus_____
   d. motor non-co-ordination

   _____
   e. hearing loss_____
   f. speech defects_____
      (1) delayed speech _____
      (2) defective articulation

      _____
      (3) infantile perseveration_____
      (4) stuttering_____
      (5) cleft-palate speech

      _____

(6) cerebral-palsied speech_____
(7) aphasia_____
(8) voice problems_____
(9) other speech defects

_____

g. reading problems_____
h. mental deficiencies_____

9. Health status:
   a. General index: good_____ fair_____ poor_____
   b. Major illnesses:
   c. Structural defects:
   d. Rh negative blood:

B. *Mother*

1. Name:
2. Birth date:
3. Living_____ deceased_____ divorced_____ not living in the home_____
4. Education: grade_____; high school_____; college_____
5. Employment outside of home: full-time_____ part-time_____
6. Church affiliation:
7. Presence in her or her familial line of the following: (Note exact relationship to mother and describe manifestation carefully.)
   a. sinistrality_____
   b. ambilaterality_____
   c. strabismus_____
   d. motor non-co-ordination

   _____
   e. hearing loss_____
   f. speech defects
      (1) delayed speech_____
      (2) defective articulation

      _____
      (3) infantile perseveration_____
      (4) stuttering_____

525

II. FAMILY (*cont.*)

B. *Mother* (*cont.*)

    (5) cleft-palate speech _____

    (6) cerebral-palsied speech_____

    (7) aphasia_____

    (8) voice problems_____

    (9) other speech defects

g. reading problems_____

h. mental deficiencies_____

8. Health status:

    a. General index: good____ fair_____ poor_____

    b. Major illnesses:

    c. Structural defects:

    d. Rh negative blood:

C. *Siblings*

1. Record in order of age; note birth date, sex; indicate premature births, multiple births, stillbirths, abortions, deaths; star propositus. (Example: 1) Phyllis; F; 3/12/36; 2) s.b. M; full term, 6/11/38; 3) Henry; M; 5/9/42, 7½ months; 4) ab., 3 mos., 1944; 5) ab., 4½ mos., 1945; 6) James; M; 10/22/49; 7) John; M; 2/3/52 (Dec. 1/6/53, pneumonia).

2. Note presence of

    a. delayed development of speech_____

    b. defects of speech

        (1) defective articulation _____

        (2) infantile perseveration____

        (3) stuttering

        (4) cleft-palate speech _____

        (5) cerebral-palsied speech_____

        (6) aphasia____

        (7) voice problems_____

        (8) other speech defects _____

    c. reading problems_____

    d. sinistrality_____

    e. strabismus_____

    f. motor non-co-ordination _____

    g. hearing loss_____

    h. cleft palate_____

    i. cerebral palsy_____

    j. other developmental or structural defects_____

3. Education

    a. Note atypical school progress (identify sibling):

    b. Basic interests:

4. Health

    a. General health and nutritional index of each sib.:

    b. Frequent illnesses:

    c. Chronic disorders: (bronchitis, sinusitis, etc.)

    d. Record occurrence, date, duration, severity of:

        (1) specific infectious diseases: upper respiratory infections, measles, pertussis, pneumonia, scarlet fever, rheumatic fever

        (2) disorders of the nervous system: convulsions, chorea, epilepsy, nervous breakdowns, psychoneuroses

        (3) endocrine disorders: hypothyroidism, delayed thymic involution, pituitary imbalance, diabetes

        (4) diseases of mouth and pharynx: hypertrophied tonsils, adenoids, etc.

        (5) allergic disorders: eczema, asthma, hayfever, migraine, etc.

        (6) circulatory disorders: blood, lymph

        (7) Rh negative blood:

5. Social adjustment

    a. Number of individuals living in home: (Note relatives, domestic servants, etc.)

    b. Housing: apartment____; house____; sharing home with relatives____; adequate____; crowded____

    c. Communication:

        (1) Languages spoken in home:

        (2) Standard of speech proficiency: in home: low____;

average____; high____
in community:
low____; average____;
high____

(3) Amount of speech in
home: much____;
average____; little____

(4) Motivation to com-
municate in home:

d Social interests: clubs,
church, sports, music, art,
recreation, etc.:

e. Intra-family problems of
adjustment:

f. Is the atmosphere of home
characterized by:
(1) happiness
(2) unhappiness
(3) security
(4) love
(5) excess of affection
(6) overprotection
(7) sternness
(8) rigidity
(9) sociability
(10) silence
(11) interest in life and
events beyond home

III. THE CHILD (PROPOSITUS)

A. Prenatal history

1. Age of father
____; of mother____.
2. Health of mother during
pregnancy:
(Note all untoward condi-
tions and diseases: hemorrhage, uremia, rubella, etc.)

B. Natal history

1. Premature____; postmature
____; at term____
2. Delivery
a. Head____; breech____;
Caesarean____
b. Length of hard labor____
c. Use of: anesthesia____;
instruments____
d. Atypical behavior of infant: anoxia____; cya-
nosis____; kernicterus
____; convulsions____;
difficult to resuscitate____;
feeding problems____;
respiration problems____
e. Physician's name and address:

3. Birth weight:
4. General health index, as indicated by:
a. Feeding (regaining of
birth weight):
b. Crying:
c. Reaction to stimuli:

C. Developmental history

1. Nutrition
a. Feeding: breast____;
bottle____
b. Gained weight steadily
c. Sensitivity to foods____
2. Responses to stimuli: light____;
sound____; moving objects
____; people____
3. Give the age in months when
the following took place:
a. raising head____
b. rolling over____
c. first tooth____; 8 teeth
____
d. sat alone____
e. crept____
f. took first steps: with sup-
port____; alone____
g. balanced walking____
h. running____
i. established laterality
(holding spoon, crayon,
etc.)
j. gained voluntary control
of bladder____; bowels
____

D. Health

1. General health index: high
____; average____; low
____
2. The following is a list of diseases. Note the age when the
disease occurred, severity (1,
2, 3); degree and duration of
fever; sequelae.
a. Specific infectious
diseases:
(1) upper respiratory in-
fections (cold, bron-
chitis)____
(2) influenza____
(3) pneumonia____
(4) mumps____
(5) measles____
(6) scarlet fever____
(7) chicken pox____
(8) small pox____
(9) whooping cough____

D. *Health* (*cont.*)

    b. Disorders of the nervous system: tics, convulsions, chorea, epilepsy

    c. Medical treatment:
        age   description
      (1) ears
      (2) nose
      (3) eyes
      (4) teeth
      (5) surgical operations

    d. Structural anomalies:

    e. Severe shock or injury _____ what _____ age of injury_____

E. *Speech and language* (Record all sounds phonetically)

  1. Date in months:
    a. Random vocalization____
    b. Imitation of sounds____
    c. Meaningful sounds____

  2. First words: (Date in months; also note words)

  3. Intelligible phrases: (Date in months; also note phrases)

  4. Rate of development of sounds: normal_____; retarded_____; accelerated _____

  5. Factors motivating or retarding normal development
    a. Need for speech
    b. Presence of speech models
      (1) Reading and speaking to child by others
      (2) Imitation of baby talk by elders
    c. Bilingualism in home
    d. Emotional problems: negativism, etc.

  6. Description of vocabulary of child

  7. Problems in reading: substitutions, mirrored reversals, etc.

  8. Recording (if possible) of child's speech

F. *Mental and physical maturation, as evidenced by*

  1. Developmental quotient (DQ):_____

  2. Psychological quotient (IQ):_____
    (Indicate tests used)

3. School progress
    a. Present grade
    b. Aptitudes
    c. Extracurricular interests
    d. Factors retarding progress
    e. Factors accelerating progress

G. *Physical examination*

  1. Organs of speech
    a. Head and face
      (1) Scars, evidences of surgery or injury about head or face _____

      (2) Symmetry of face during smile: symmetrical_____; lax left_____; lax right_____

      (3) Lips: upper: large_____; normal_____; small_____ lower: large_____; normal_____; small_____

      (4) Mobility: (pucker and retraction) poor on right____; poor on left____; normal____ Number of times subject can say *pah* in 5 seconds_____

      (5) Mouth breather: yes _____; no_____

    b. Mouth
      (1) Teeth: type of closure____ structure of teeth _____

      (2) Tongue
        (*a*) size: normal ____; large____; small____
        (*b*) blade: normal ____; short____
        (*c*) position on protrusion: normal____; deviation to right____; to left____
        (*d*) control of tip: lifts easily____; with difficulty

_____; unable to lift _____; swings to left easily_____; swings to right easily____; unable to effect lateral movement____

(e) mobility: number of times subject can say *tah* in 5 seconds____

c. Hard palate
   (1) High_____; medium _____; low_____
   (2) Peaked_____; narrow_____; broad _____
   (3) If there are scars of cleft, describe site and extent:_____.

d. Soft palate
   (1) Length: adequate _____; short_____
   (2) Mobility: number of times subject can say *kah* in 5 seconds _____
   (3) Ability to drink through straw_____
   (4) Color: light_____; medium_____; dark _____
   (5) If there are scars or cleft, describe site and extent:_____

e. Uvula
   (1) Length: long_____; short_____; normal _____; absent_____
   (2) Condition: edematous_____; congested _____

f. Tonsils
   Present_____; large_____; medium_____; small_____

g. Pharynx
   (1) Color: light_____; medium_____; dark _____
   (2) Condition: edematous_____; congested _____
   (3) Size: small_____; medium_____; large_____

h. Nose
   (1) Structural deviations: deviated septum_____; polypi_____; others_____
   (2) Columella: adequate _____; inadequate_____

2. Hearing (peripheral and central)
   a. Loss in general acuity: (attach audiogram)
   b. Loss of certain frequencies: (attach audiogram)
   c. Sound discrimination test score:_____
   d. Auditory memory span _____
   e. Evidences of auditory aphasia_____

3. Motor proficiency
   a. Static motor tests: score _____
   b. Dynamic motor tests: score_____
   c. Motor skills tests: score _____

4. Laterality
   a. Dominance: strongly right _____; moderately right _____; about equal_____; strongly left_____; moderately left_____
   b. Ratio: R:L on tests of:
      (1) Hand dominance_____
      (2) Eye dominance_____
      (3) Foot dominance_____
      (4) Knowledge of directions_____

H. *Social history*
   1. Attitude of parents toward child:
   2. Discipline of child: administered by_____; usual form _____; most effective form _____; least effective_____
   3. Behavior problems:
      Age began   Description
      a. Nervousness_____
      b. Shyness_____
      c. Showing off_____
      d. Negation_____
      e. Rejection_____
      f. Aggression_____
      g. Prevarication_____
      h. Temper tantrums_____
      i. Excessive jealousy_____
      j. Extreme possessiveness_____ (objects, people, etc.)_____

H. *Social history (cont.)*

3. Behavior problems (*cont.*)

   k. Enuresis_____
   l. Sleeplessness_____
   m. Nightmares_____
   n. Strange and persistent fears_____
   o. Talking, crying in sleep _____
   p. Thumb sucking_____
   q. Food idiosyncrasies_____

4. Child reflects
   a. Stable adjustment_____
   b. Excessive tensions_____
   c. Great insecurity_____
   d. Overprotection_____
   e. General maladjustment _____

I. *The speech problem*

1. Full description of speech at present:
   a. Detailed list of symptoms:
   b. Present status: improved _____; stationary_____; retrogressing_____.

2. Etiology:

3. Articulation tests:
   a. Isolated sounds:
   b. Sounds in position: initial _____; medial _____; final_____
   c. Consonant sounds in blends:
   d. Copying connected speech of therapist:
   e. Free conversational speech:

Sounds: omitted_____; distorted_____; substituted_____; inserted _____

4. Voice tests
   a. Pitch: high_____; low_____; normal_____
   b. Loudness: strong_____; weak_____; normal_____
   c. Quality: nasal_____; guttural_____; aspirate_____; oral_____; denasal_____; harsh_____; normal_____

5. Speech rhythm
   a. Scanning_____
   b. Monotonous_____
   c. Irregular_____
   d. Normal_____

6. Speech rate
   a. Slow_____
   b. Fast_____
   c. Normal_____

7. If problem is late appearance of speech:
   a. What attempts to communicate with: eyes_____; hand gestures_____; jargon _____; babbling_____
   b. Does child observe immediate environment?
   c. Does child attempt to imitate sounds made by therapist?

IV. SUMMARY

A. *Diagnosis* (write paragraph)
B. *Prognosis* (write paragraph)
C. *Therapy* (write paragraph embracing general principles)

VOICE DISORDERS

Name: Case Number:

Address: Telephone:

Birth date: Sex:

Referred by:

Therapist or Diagnostician:

I. DESCRIPTION OF PROBLEM BY REFERRAL AGENT:

II. DIAGNOSTICIAN'S FIRST IMPRESSION OF VOICE PROBLEM:

III. SUMMARY OF DIAGNOSIS:

IV. DETAILED ANALYSIS

    A. *Medico-physical background of subject*

        1. General systemic disorders:

            a. Chronic colds

            b. Chronic sinusitis (accompanied by postnasal drip)

            c. Severe illnesses involving the respiratory organs:

                Whooping cough _____

                Scarlet fever _____

                Virus infections _____

                    pneumonia _____; influenza _____; diphtheria _____

                    rheumatic fever _____

            d. Hyperthyroidism _____

            e. Hypothyroidism _____

            f. Retarded sexual development:

                (1) Primary sex organs _____

                (2) Secondary sex organs _____

            g. Allergies: (producing prolonged inflammation of mucosa of respiratory organs)

                (1) Hayfever _____

                (2) Asthma _____

        2. Disorders and structural anomalies involving speech organs:

            a. Breathing mechanism

                (1) Conformation of costal cage:

                    pigeon-shaped _____

                    inverted _____

                    collapsed _____

                    normal _____

    (2) Breath escaping without vocalization _____

    (3) Normal exhalation for speech (in c.c.) _____

b. Laryngeal pharynx

    (1) Laryngitis: (evidence of chronic irritation, necessity for clearing throat; chronic, unproductive cough) _____

    (2) Laryngeal growths: nodules on vocal folds, ulcers, etc.

---

c. Oral and nasal pharynx

    (1) Lingual tonsils: hypertrophied _____; atrophied _____; diseased _____; removed (date) _____

    (2) Adenoids: hypertrophied _____; atrophied _____; diseased _____; occluded posterior opening into nares _____; removed (date) _____

    (3) Pillars of the fauces: torn _____; scarred _____; inflamed _____

    (4) Nose: deviated septum R _____ L _____; corrected _____
growth on turbinates _____; removed _____;
collapsed crura R _____; L _____; corrected _____;
normal _____; partial obstruction _____
        anterior _____
        posterior _____
      complete obstruction _____
        anterior _____
        posterior _____

    (5) Mouth:

        (*a*) Palate: velum length: short_____; normal_____; asymmetry _____; condition of the uvula _____; distance from the posterior wall of the pharynx in rest position _____

                Palatal arch: very high _____; low _____; normal _____

                Cuspid width: wide_____; narrow _____; normal _____

                Molar width: wide _____; narrow _____; normal _____

                Palatal clefts: hard _____; velum _____; complete palate _____; alveolar _____; submucous _____

        (*b*) Tongue: microglossia _____
                  macroglossia _____

                Frenulum: short _____; normal _____; very thick _____; abnormal attachment _____

Position in mouth: retracted _____ ;

　　　　　　　　humped _____ ; flaccid _____ ;

Size in relation to mouth and dental arch:

　　　　　　　　large _____ ; small _____ ;

　　　　　　　　normal _____

(c) Maxilla: protruding _____

　　　　　receding _____

　　　　　normal _____

(d) Mandible: prognathic _____

　　　　　receding _____

　　　　　normal _____

(e) Teeth: condition of anterior teeth _____

　　　　　missing teeth; describe position _____

3. Voice hygiene

   a. Are subject's vocal organs subjected habitually to: heavy smoke _____ ; sudden changes in humidity and temperature (air conditioning) _____

   b. Does subject smoke excessively _____

   c. Does subject indulge in excessive and loud speaking _____

   d. Does subject work where he must talk above the noise of machinery, etc. _____

4. Impaired sensitivity to sound

   a. Hearing: below normal at following frequencies:
      　　　　　(attach audiometric chart)
      normal _____

   b. Pitch discrimination
      (1) Percentile score on test of pitch discrimination _____
      (2) Sound 15 pairs of notes, each pair differing by 2 semitones at 400, 1200, 3000, d.v. and see if subject can tell whether first note is higher or lower than second.

   c. Tonal memory
      (1) Can subject carry a tune?
      (2) Percentile score on test of tonal memory _____

II. Psycho-emotional Factors

   A. Intellectual evaluation

   1. IQ: _____

   2. Educational achievement: grade _____ ; retarded _____ ; advanced _____ ; normal _____

B. *Emotional profile*

1. Does voice reflect state of frustration _____; defeat _____; negation _____; lack of interest in life _____

2. Does subject speak with:
   a. excessive tension of laryngeal muscles _____
   b. excessive tension of lingual, velar, buccal, and labial muscles and
      _____
   c. general lack of tension _____

3. Is there evidence of social maladjustment:
   at home _____; at school _____
   Describe in terms of withdrawal, negation, temper tantrums, regression to infantilism, etc.

4. Attitude toward voice problem:
   a. does not recognize it _____
   b. minimizes difficulty _____
   c. talks freely about problem _____
   d. is objective _____; highly subjective _____

5. Tests of social adjustment and emotional stability
   a. Vineland Social Maturity Scale   Score _____
   b. Thematic Apperception Test   Score _____
   c. Bell Social Adjustment Scale   Score _____

6. Familial and environmental factors
   a. Is there anyone in immediate family or among close associates with similar voice problem? Describe:
   b. Is there a familial history of:
      emotional instability _____; hypertension _____; sluggishness _____; describe:
   c. How does family regard subject's problem:
      resents discussion by others of problem _____
      never discusses it _____; talks freely about it _____;
      refuses to recognize problem _____

III. DIRECT OBSERVATION OF THE VOICE IN OPERATION

   A. *Acoustic impression of voice characteristics of subject*

   1. Pitch
      a. too high _____; too low _____; monotone _____;
         repeated pitch pattern _____; peculiar pitch pattern _____;
         narrow pitch range _____; pitch level appropriate to age _____; to sex _____; normal _____
      b. Is habitual pitch level also the optimum pitch level for this person?
      c. fundamental in d.v. on frequency analyzer _____

2. Loudness:

    a. over strong _____; weak _____; lacking in variety _____; uncontrolled _____; inappropriate to meaning _____; normal _____

    b. Is weak intensity coupled with
      (1) oral, thin quality _____
      (2) breathy, hoarse-husky quality _____

3. Quality:

    excessively nasal _____; nasal twang _____; denasal _____; harsh guttural _____; breathy, hoarse-husky _____; oral, thin _____; orotund _____; hollow-pectoral _____; normal _____

4. Rate and rhythm: staccato _____; mono-rate _____; normal _____

B. *Study of vowel phonemes which reflect most markedly voice deviations:* peculiar regional inflectional patterns _____

over-strong intensity	weak intensity	high pitch	low pitch	nasal quality	denasal quality	hoarse quality	breathy quality

C. *Study of the operation of the voice mechanism*

    1. Breathing

      a. Is the muscular action predominantly: thoracico-abdominal _____; clavicular _____; frequently reversed _____?

      b. Is breathing controlled _____; spasmodic _____; weak _____; strong _____?

      c. Can subject intone *ah* for 15 seconds on a single exhalation?

      d. Note the number of exhalations per minute during oral reading of a descriptive passage: _____.

      e. Does the subject frequently exhale breath before vocalization? Yes _____; No _____.

f. Is there evidence of disruption of the synergy of breathing (collapse of chest; spasmodic stroking of diaphragm, etc.)? Yes _____; No _____.

g. Are there excessive tensions of muscles of chest and neck during phonation?

2. Phonation

  a. Are there evidences of excessive tensions:
   (1) elevated thyroid cartilage _____
   (2) hypertension of the extrinsic neck musculature _____
   (3) constriction at the faucial opening _____
   (4) pinching of the tone at the glottis _____

  b. Does the pitch range appear to be normal for the size of the larynx?

  c. Are there non-harmonic vibrations which may be initiated by the ventricular folds, supraglottic structures, etc.?

  d. Does breath escape unvocalized?

3. Resonation-articulation

  a. Is the faucial isthmus: narrow _____; normal (equals size of bucco-pharyngeal orifice) _____; very wide _____?

  b. Is the oral aperture in intoning *ah* about one and one-half times the size of the faucial isthmus? Yes _____; No _____.

  c. Is the velar-pharyngeal closure of the nasal port effective?
   (1) Is action of levator and tensor palatini muscles speedy _____; slow _____; partial _____; complete _____?
   (2) Is there a noticeable movement of Passavant's cushion in closure? Yes _____; No _____.
   (3) Test of effectiveness of closure in non-speech activities:
      (*a*) swallowing water _____
      (*b*) playing harmonica _____
      (*c*) whistling _____
      (*d*) inflating balloons _____
      (*e*) blowing bits of paper against mirror _____
      (*f*) gag reflex _____
      (*g*) number of times he can say *kah* _____
   (4) Test of effectiveness in speech sounds in connected speech
      (*a*) Note:

	nasal full resonance	nasal partial resonance	absence of nasal resonance
m			
n			

(*b*) Note nasal resonance of vowels and diphthongs when uttered:

alone with non-nasal sounds (preceding or following)	with nasal sound (preceding or following)

i

ɪ

e

ɛ

æ

a

ɑ

ɒ

ɔ

ʌ

ɜ

ʊ

u

aɪ

ɑu

ɔɪ

ju

oʊ

(*c*) Test nasal emission of breath stream by presence of mirror placed horizontally beneath nose for:
 (i) vowels clear _____clouded _____
 (ii) nasals clear _____clouded _____

(*d*) Flexibility of oral resonator
 (i) Tongue: retracted _____; humped _____; crowded within dental arch _____; immobile _____; non-co-ordinated _____; co-ordinated _____; flexible _____; ability to point tongue _____; maximum protrusion _____; no. of times he can say *tah* _____; direction of air stream in production of [s] ____; no. of times he can touch the corners of the mouth alternately with the tongue _____

 (ii) Jaw and lips: hypertense _____; stiff and inflexible _____; mobile _____; opening, very narrow _____; moderately wide_____; wide and flexible _____

 (iii) Lips: protrusion _____; retraction-unilateral _____; retraction-bilateral _____; no. of times he can say *pah* in 5 sec. _____; adequacy of labial tissue _____.

IV. Summary: Description of Voice

CLEFT PALATE

GENERAL INFORMATION

Name of child _____

Age _____ Birth date _____ Sex _____ Race _____

Address _____

Telephone _____

Description of child's appearance and speech _____

_____

_____

Name of parents or guardian _____

Source of referral _____

Diagnosis, description of cleft:

I. FAMILY HISTORY

Father: Name _____ Address _____

Age _____ Height _____ Weight _____ Birthplace _____

Is he living with family_____dead_____divorced_____remarried_____

Present occupation _____ Previous occupation _____

State of health now _____ How far did he go in school _____

Which hand does he prefer _____ Was he ever changed _____

Abnormalities of palate, tongue, jaw _____

_____

Church attended: _____ National descent _____

Mother: Name _____ Address _____

Age _____ Height _____ Weight _____ Birthplace _____

Is she living with family_____dead_____divorced_____remarried_____

Present occupation _____ Previous occupation _____

State of health now _____ How far did she go in school _____

Which hand does she prefer _____ Was she ever changed _____

Abnormalities of palate, tongue, jaw _____

_____

Church attended: _____ National descent _____

Siblings

Name	Age	Hand Pre-ferred	Age Started to Speak	Health	School Progress	Abnormalities: Palate, Tongue Jaw

II. SPEECH PROBLEMS IN IMMEDIATE FAMILY

Stuttering _____

Delayed Speech _____

Hearing Loss _____

Defective Articulation _____

Voice Problems _____

Cleft-Palate Speech _____

Reading Problems _____

Brain-Injured _____

III. MEDICAL HISTORY OF THE IMMEDIATE FAMILY

Is there or has there been in the immediate family any of the following:
(If so, state who, when, severity, medication, etc.)
Anemia
Diabetes
Congenital heart, lung, eye, ear
Cerebral palsy
Epilepsy
Convulsions
Migraine headaches
Asthma
Hayfever
Sinus
Mongols
Physical deformities
Any Rh negative blood: Fa _____; Mo _____; Sibs _____
Excessive nervous tension

IV. PARENTS' FAMILY

Siblings of Parents:

	SEX	AGE	ALIVE	DEAD	ABNORMALITIES OF PALATE AND/OR TONGUE	CAUSE OF AND AGE AT DEATH
Mother's	___	___	___	___	_____	_____
	___	___	___	___	_____	_____
	___	___	___	___	_____	_____
Father's	___	___	___	___	_____	_____
	___	___	___	___	_____	_____
	___	___	___	___	_____	_____
	___	___	___	___	_____	_____

V. SPEECH HISTORY

Is there in the family history any of the speech problems listed under II above; if so, discuss.

_____

_____

_____

_____

VI. IS THERE IN THE FAMILY HISTORY ANY OF THE FOLLOWING:

Anemia
Diabetes
Congenital heart, lung, eye, ear
Cerebral palsy
Epilepsy
Convulsions
Migraine headaches
Asthma
Hayfever
Sinus
Mongols
Physical deformities
Any Rh negative blood
Left handers
Multiple births
Miscarriages, still births
Premature births

VII. PRENATAL HISTORY

How many pregnancies has mother had_____ Which was this child_____
Any miscarriages _____ How many _____ Which pregnancy _____
Any babies born dead _____ How many _____ Which pregnancy _____
Any premature babies _____ How many _____ Which pregnancy _____
State of mother's health before this pregnancy _____
_____ during _____
_____ after _____
At what month did she first consult physician during this pregnancy _____

_____

Did mother have any radiation during or shortly before this pregnancy_____
Did mother have German measles, scarlet fever, anemia, kidney infection, or other infections during first trimester of pregnancy _____

_____

When _____
Did mother take any medication during pregnancy _____ What_____

_____

Hormonal, vitamin, mineral, nutritional deficiencies during first trimester of pregnancy _____

VIII. NATAL HISTORY

Was child full term _____ Premature _____ How much _____
How long was hard labor _____ How long before birth did the
amniotic sac rupture _____
Presentation _____
Was delivery normal _____ Instrumental _____

Was delivery in home _____ Hospital _____ Name and address
of hospital _____
Physician's name and address _____
Was anesthetic used _____ What _____ At what stage _____
Medication during labor _____ What _____

IX. BIRTH CONDITION OF CHILD—DISCUSS IN DETAIL

X. POST-NATAL HISTORY

Did child cry, breathe, nurse like a normal baby _____

How was child's health the first 2 weeks of life _____

How was the child fed _____
Did the child leave the hospital with the mother _____

XI. DEVELOPMENTAL HISTORY

Weight at birth _____ 6 months _____ 1 year _____
at present _____
Give age at which the following first occurred: held head up _____
tooth erupted _____ sat alone _____ walked _____
gained voluntary control of bladder _____ bowels _____
Did child suck fingers _____ which hand _____ for how long _____
Was child hard to break of this habit _____
From what age did child show preference for one hand _____
does he now _____ which one _____ has anything been done to
influence handedness _____

XII. HEALTH-MEDICAL HISTORY OF THE CHILD

Description of Cleft Palate

Group I—Pre-Alveolar Cleft (Lip)

1. Unilateral—Right—Complete _____
                          Incomplete _____
               Left — Complete _____
                          Incomplete _____
2. Median—Complete _____
               Incomplete _____
3. Bilateral—Right—Complete _____
                          Incomplete _____
               Left —Complete _____
                          Incomplete _____
4. Description of nostrils:

Group II—Post-Alveolar Cleft (Palate)

1. Soft Palate _____ Extent in 1/3's _____
2. Hard Palate _____ Extent in 1/3's _____
Approximate measurement of widest portion of cleft:

_____

Palatine Arch—High _____ Low _____

Sketch outline of cleft:

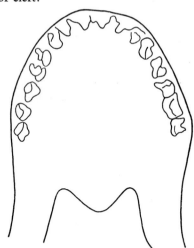

Group III—Alveolar Cleft

1. Unilateral
   Process—Right—Complete _____ (extends thru Alveolar
                                                              Process)
                  Incomplete _____
          Left—Complete _____
                  Incomplete _____

Palate—Complete _____ Incomplete _____
Palatine Arch—High _____ Low _____
Lip—Unilateral _____ Bilateral _____ Median _____
Complete _____ Incomplete _____

2. Median—Complete _____ Incomplete _____
3. Bilateral
Process—Right—Complete _____
Incomplete _____
Left—Complete _____
Incomplete _____
Palate—Complete _____
Incomplete _____
Lip—Right—Complete _____ Incomplete _____
Left — Complete _____ Incomplete _____

Operations

A. Primary Closure ⎰1. Lip
                     ⎱2. Hard palate
                     ⎰3. Soft palate

B. Lengthening of the velum
C. Velar-pharyngeal flap operation

Year   Nature of Operations   Hospital   Surgeon & Address   Results

D. Teeth
1. Description of teeth _____
2. Orthodontia
    a. Name and address of orthodontist _____
    b. Present status _____

E. Fauces
1. Area of faucial isthmus _____
2. Condition of faucial tonsils _____
3. Condition of faucial pillars _____

F. Tongue
1. Size (in relation to dental arch) _____
2. Characteristic position of tongue during rest _____
3. Frenulum _____; short _____

G. Motility of peripheral speech structures
1. Lips
    a. Protrusion _____
    b. Retraction: Unilateral _____ bilateral _____
    c. Number of times subject can say *pah* in 5 sec. _____

2. Tongue
   a. Maximum protrusion _____
   b. Ability to point tongue _____
   c. Direction of air stream when making a prolonged [s] _____
   d. Number of times subject can touch corners of mouth alternately in 10 sec. _____
   e. Number of times subject can say *tah* in 5 sec. _____

3. Velar-pharyngeal sphincter
   a. Gag reflex _____
   b. Can he drink through straw _____
   c. Number of times subject can say *kah* in 5 sec. _____

Prosthesis

A. When was prosthesis made _____
B. Name and address of prosthodontist _____

C. Has it been adjusted _____; When _____
   What adjustments _____

Other Structural Defects

A. Eyes _____
B. Ears _____
C. Syndactylism _____; Supernumerary toes _____
   Supernumerary fingers _____; Club foot _____

Medical treatment unrelated to cleft

A. Is he under medical treatment now _____ Give name and address of clinic or physician treating child _____
   For what is child being treated _____
B. Has the child ever had any operations other than for cleft _____
C. Ear infections (otitis media)
   1. Date of first infection _____; was drum ruptured _____
      spontaneous rupture _____; surgical incision _____
   2. Dates of recurring infections: _____

   3. Present state of middle ear: Suppurative otitis media R___; L___
      No evidence of infection at present _____
      Drum scarred: R _____; L _____

D. Check diseases child has had:

	Age		Age
Measles	____	Chronic cough	____
Mumps	____	Eczema	____
Chicken pox	____	Hay fever	____
Whooping cough	____	Hives	____
Scarlet fever	____	Chronic indigestion	____
Diphtheria	____	Ear aches	____
Frequent colds	____	Suppurative otitis media	____
Convulsions	____	Others	____

E. Has the child ever had a prolonged high fever _____

F. Has the child ever had any severe shock or injury _____
What _____; when _____

G. Immunizations: smallpox _____; diphtheria _____
tetanus _____; whooping cough _____; poliomyelitis _____
others _____

H. Health status
1. Is the child in good health now _____; has he always been
well _____
2. Is appetite good _____; Does child eat regularly _____
Does he eat between meals _____
3. Does the child chew normally _____swallow normally_____
Has he always done so _____
4. Does child sleep regular hours _____ time of retiring _____
arising _____ restless sleep _____
5. Is child a mouth breather now _____ has he always been _____

XIII. SOCIAL DEVELOPMENT

1. What are child's chief amusements _____
2. What games and toys does he like best _____
3. Does he play with children outside family ____younger ___older ___
4. How does he get along with other members of family _____
5. Does child often become angry _____ how does he show it _____
6. Does child avoid social situations _____
7. Who administers the discipline _____ What method _____
8. Is child willing to try new things _____
9. Score on Vineland Social Maturity Scale _____
10. Does child share a bedroom _____ with whom _____
11. Does child share a bed _____
12. Did any adults besides mother and father ever live in home
_____
_____

XIV. SPEECH AND LANGUAGE DEVELOPMENT

Did child babble like a normal baby _____
_____
At what age did child say words _____ What words did he say
first _____
When did he first use speech purposefully _____
How is speech now _____
When is the speech defect most noticeable _____
What other means of communication has the child used _____
_____ does he use them now _____
Does he use consistently specific sounds to designate certain objects or
people _____

Speech Evaluation

A. Verbal Comprehension
1. Points or looks at objects named
2. Opens mouth at request
3. Closes eyes at request
4. Indicate *yes* or *no:*   *a.* Do you like candy?
                              b. Is this a chair?
                              c. Am I your mother?

B. Phonation
1. Duration (in seconds)
2. Quality

C. Hearing
1. Non-verbal
   a. Audiometer
   b. Noisemakers
   c. Psycho-galvanic skin response
   d. EEG
2. Verbal
   a. Following commands
   b. Repeating words with examiner's face hidden.

D. Breath control
1. Blow feathers
2. Extinguish a match
3. Extinguish a lighted candle
4. Adequate for sustained phonation

E. Articulation: sounds omitted _____; distorted _____; substituted _____
Can imitate speech sounds _____

F. Jaw
1. Open
2. Close
3. Open and close rhythmically

G. Recording of Speech

XV. Educational History

Does child attend pre-school _____ kindergarten _____ school _____
Does child follow his age group in school _____ Are there any
special difficulties _____
IQ Tests _____ Date _____ Score _____

XVI. EXAMINATIONS

List the names and addresses of any physicians and clinics that have examined the child _____

_____

Has an electroencephalogram ever been taken _____ when _____
_____ given by whom _____ where _____
_____ results _____
Neurologist's report (attach here)
Physician's report (attach here)

XVII. THERAPY

Speech
Psychotherapy

XVIII. PROGNOSIS AND RECOMMENDATIONS

CEREBRAL PALSY

I. GENERAL INFORMATION

  A. Name of child:
  B. Age:
  C. Birth date:
  D. Sex:
  E. Race:
  F. Address:
  G. Telephone:
  H. City-State:
  I. Name of parents or guardian:
  J. Source of referral:
  K. Description of child's appearance (ambulatory? drools?, etc.):
  L. Diagnosis: Athetoid _____; Spastic _____; Ataxic _____;
     Tension Athetoid _____; Rigidity _____.

II. FAMILY HISTORY

  A. Father:
    1. Name _____
    2. Address _____
    3. Age_____ Height _____ Weight _____ Birthplace_____
    4. Is he living with family _____ dead _____ divorced _____
      remarried _____
    5. Occupation _____
    6. State of health now _____ How far did he go in school _____
    7. Which hand does he prefer _____ Was he ever changed _____
    8. Church attended _____ National descent _____

B. Mother:
1. Name _____.
2. Address _____
3. Age_____ Height _____ Weight _____ Birthplace_____
4. Is she living with family _____ dead _____ divorced _____
   remarried _____
5. Occupation _____ Previous occupation _____
6. State of health now _____ How far did she go in school _____
7. Which hand does she prefer _____ Was she ever changed _____
8. Church attended _____ National descent _____

C. Siblings:
(List sex, age, hand preferred, age started to speak, health, and school progress (normal or retarded) of each sibling):

III. SPEECH PROBLEM IN IMMEDIATE FAMILY
A. Stuttering:
B. Delayed Speech:
C. Defective Articulation:
D. Voice Problems:
E. Cleft-Palate Speech:
F. Brain-Injured (cerebral-palsied speech, etc.)

IV. MEDICAL HISTORY OF THE IMMEDIATE FAMILY
Is there or has there been in the immediate family any of the following:
(If so, state who, when, severity, medication, etc.)

A. Anemia:
B. Congenital heart, lung, eye, ear:
C. Cerebral palsy:
D. Epilepsy:
E. Convulsions:
F. Migraine headaches:
G. Asthma:
H. Hayfever:
I. Sinus:
J. Mongols:
K. Physical deformities:
L. Any Rh negative blood: Fa _____; Mo _____; Sibs _____.
M. Excessive nervous tension:
N. Diabetes:

V. PARENTS' FAMILY
Siblings of Parents:
(List mother's siblings, sex, age, alive or dead, cause of and age at death, and status of their children):
(List father's siblings, sex, age, alive or dead, cause of and age at death, and status of their children):

VI. Speech History

(Is there in the family history any of the speech problems listed under III above; if so, discuss.)

VII. Medical History

(Is there in the family history any of the conditions listed under IV above; if so, discuss.)

VIII. Prenatal History

A. How many pregnancies has mother had _____ Which was this child _____

B. Any miscarriages _____ How many _____ Which pregnancy _____

C. Any babies born dead _____ How many _____ Which pregnancy _____.

D. Any premature babies _____ How many _____ Which pregnancy _____

E. State of mother's health before this pregnancy (discuss): _____ _____ during _____ after _____

F. At what month did she first consult physician during this pregnancy _____

G. Did mother have any radiation during or shortly before this pregnancy _____

H. Did mother have German measles, scarlet fever, low blood pressure, anemia, kidney infection or other infections, or hormonal deficiencies or excesses during pregnancy _____ when _____

I. Did mother take any medication during pregnancy _____ what _____

IX. Natal History

A. Was child full term _____ premature _____ how much _____

B. How long was hard labor _____ How long before birth did the amniotic sac rupture _____

C. Presentation _____

D. Was delivery normal _____ Instrumental (Discuss):

E. Was delivery in home _____ Hospital _____ Name and address of hospital _____

F. Physician's name and address _____

G. Was anesthetic used _____ What _____ At what stage _____

H. Medication during labor _____ What _____

X. Birth Condition of Child

A. Was the child jaundiced _____

B. Was resuscitation difficult _____

C. Did the child have any blood transfusions _____ how many _____ when _____

D. Did he receive any medication _____ what _____

E. Was there evidence of hyper-irritability (manifested as seizures, twitching, marked positive Moro or startle reflex) _____

F. Was there evidence of listlessness (the child who is hypotonic, difficult to feed or to awaken, who chokes readily with feedings, or who does not demonstrate a Moro reflex) _____

G. Was there at birth any of the following conditions:

    1. Cyanosis:
    2. Pallor:
    3. Stiffening:
    4. Arching:
    5. Strabismus:
    6. Nystagmus:
    7. Bruises:
    8. Cephalhematoma:
    9. Structural abnormalities:

H. Did the child cry and breathe like a normal child _____

XI. POST-NATAL HISTORY

A. Feeding difficulties:

    1. Refusal to nurse:
    2. Difficulty in sucking:
    3. Difficulty in swallowing:
    4. Vomiting frequently:
    5. Crying excessively during feeding:
    6. Hyper-irritability during feeding:
    7. Feeble cry during feeding:
    8. Drowsiness and listlessness during feeding:
    9. Excessive grunting during feeding:

B. Status of child's health during the first two weeks of life:

C. Did the child leave the hospital with the mother:_____

XII. DEVELOPMENTAL HISTORY

A. Weight at birth_____6 months_____1 year_____at present_____

B. Give age at which the following first occurred: held head up_____ tooth erupted _____ sat alone _____ first steps _____ crawled _____ gained voluntary control of bladder _____ of bowels _____

C. Did child suck fingers_____which hand_____for how long_____ was child hard to break of this habit _____

D. From what age did child show preference for one hand _____ does he now _____ which one _____ has anything been done to influence handedness _____

XIII. HEALTH-MEDICAL HISTORY OF THE CHLID

    A. Is the child in good health now_____ Has he always been well_____

    B. Is he under medical treatment now _____ Give name and address of clinic or physician treating child _____

    C. For what is child being treated _____

    D. Has child ever had an operation _____ for what _____ when _____

    E. Has child been immunized for small pox_____diphtheria_____ tetanus_____whooping cough _____poliomyelitis _____ others _____

    F. Is appetite good _____ Does child eat regularly _____ between meals _____

    G. Does the child chew normally _____ swallow normally _____ has he always _____

    H. Does child sleep regular hours _____ time of retiring _____ arising _____

    I. Has child had any severe shock or injury _____ what _____ age of injury _____

    J. Has child ever had a prolonged high fever? Discuss:

    K. Check in the list below diseases child has had:

	Age		Age
Measles	____	Chronic cough	____
Mumps	____	Eczema	____
Chicken pox	____	Hayfever	____
Whooping cough	____	Asthma	____
Scarlet fever	____	Hives	____
Diphtheria	____	Chronic indigestion	____
Frequent colds	____	Constipation	____
Convulsions	____	Ear aches	____
		Draining ears	____

    L. Is child a mouth breather now _____has he always been_____

    M. Other symptoms of brain injury:
        1. Special sensory defects: vision _____ hearing _____
        2. Psychological defects:
          a. Intellectual deficiencies: IQ score _____
            (1) Is there difficulty in perception of form and space _____
            (2) Is there an inability to abstract _____
            (3) Is there an inability to generalize _____
          b. Linguistic defects:
            (1) Does the child understand spoken language _____
            (2) Is there any special problem in reading _____
            (3) Speech defects not related to cerebral palsy directly_____
            (4) Does the child perseverate in speech and in actions_____

    c. Behavioral deviations:
        (1) Lack of emotional control _____
        (2) Hyperactivity _____
        (3) Impulsiveness _____
        (4) Poor attention span _____
        (5) Distractibility _____
        (6) Listlessness _____
        (7) Irritability _____

N. Neurological examination:
    1. Has an electroencephalogram ever been taken_____when_____
       given by whom _____where_____results _____
    2. Convulsive disorders:
       a. Major seizures _____ when _____
       b. Minor seizures _____ when _____

XIV. Evaluation of Speech Mechanisms

    A. Breathing:
       1. Is the child's breathing shallow _____
         reversed (opposition in thoracico-abdominal muscles) _____
         distorted (exhalation period very short while inspiratory move-
         ment long) _____ stertorous and labored _____
       2. Length of time (in sec.) the child can maintain a steady exhala-
         tion _____

    B. Larynx:
       1. What is the position of the larynx in the pharynx _____
       2. In phonation, is it pulled up into the hyoid notch _____
       3. Is the larynx abnormal in shape and size _____
       4. Is the angle obtuse _____ Are the "wings" widespread _____
       5. Is there evidence of spasms of the vocal folds _____
       6. Are there extra-laryngeal vibrations produced by the ventricular
         folds or other tissues in the pharynx _____
       7. Is there opposition of the thoracico-abdominal muscles in phona-
         tion _____
       8. Does the child attempt to phonate on the inspiratory movement
         _____
       9. Is the radix of the tongue elevated greatly _____
     10. Can the child produce a tone without unusual depression of the
        mandible _____
     11. Are the articulatory organs out of phase with phonation _____

    C. Breath control (test for velar-pharyngeal closure):
       1. Place a mirror below the nose in a horizontal position: Does the
         mirror become clouded _____
       2. The "two-step box," on each step of which is a feather: Is the
         feather on the upper step (under the nose) blown off _____
       3. Can the child blow a ping-pong ball up an inclined plane _____

4. Can the child extinguish a lighted candle _____

5. Can the child keep little pieces of paper against a mirror by blowing them _____

D. Tongue:

1. Can the child raise the tongue-tip to the alveolar ridges with the mandible depressed _____

2. Number of times the child can touch the tongue-tip to the alveolar ridges in ten seconds _____

3. In articulatory attempts does the tongue deviate to left or right_____

4. In articulatory movements does the tongue-tip regularly protrude beyond the teeth ridge _____

5. Are the dorsum and radix of the tongue raised and impinging upon the pharyngeal walls even in the production of such open vowel sounds as [ɑ] and [e]? _____

6. Is the mass of the tongue large, amorphic, filling the mouth cavity _____

7. Is the mass of the tongue small, inert, showing no occlusion with the molars or incisors _____

8. In rest position, does the tongue-tip protrude beyond the teeth ridge _____

E. Mandible:

1. Is the mandible constantly depressed _____

2. Is the mandible tightly approximated _____

3. Can the child open and close the mandible rhythmically _____

4. Can the child make finer gradations of opening and closing _____

F. Lips and cheeks:

1. Can the child protrude the lips _____

2. Can the child retract the lips: unilaterally _____
bilaterally _____ the lower lip to one side _____

3. Number of times the child can say *pah* in 10 seconds _____

4. Does the child constantly keep the lips in a "purse-string" closure position _____

5. Does the child constantly keep the lower lip inverted (under the upper incisors) _____

6. Does the child involuntarily produce grimaces _____

7. Can he retract the lips evenly _____ rapidly _____

XV. SPEECH AND LANGUAGE DEVELOPMENT

A. Did child babble like a normal baby _____

B. At what age did child say words_____ What words did he say first_____
_____

C. When did he first use speech purposefully _____

D. How is speech now _____

E. When is the speech defect most noticeable _____

F. What other means of communication has the child used _____
    Does he use them now _____

G. Does he use consistently specific sounds to designate certain objects
    or people _____

H. Speech evaluation:

   1. Verbal comprehension:
       a. Points or looks at objects named _____
       b. Opens mouth at request _____
       c. Closes eyes at request _____
       d. Indicates *yes* or *no:* (1) Do you like candy? _____
                                     (2) Is this a chair? _____
                                     (3) Am I your mother? _____

   2. Phonation:
       a. Duration (in seconds) _____
       b. Quality _____

   3. Hearing:
       a. Non-verbal
           (1) Audiometer _____
           (2) Noisemakers _____
       b. Verbal
           (1) Following commands _____
           (2) Repeating words with examiner's face hidden _____

   4. Co-operation:

   5. Can imitate speech sounds:

   6. Phonetic profile:
       a. What sounds in the child's speech are recognizable:
           consonants _____; vowels _____
       b. Can he build up enough intra-oral pressure to produce plosives
           (especially the voiceless plosives) _____
       c. Are the medial and final consonants very weak or are they
           prolonged so that they are not recognizable _____
       d. Can the child link consonants, especially voiceless plosives,
           with vowels so that the syllable or word is recognizable _____
       e. Are there long periods of waiting as the child goes from a
           consonant to a vowel (evidencing the lack of ability to make
           swift changes in the articulatory mechanism) _____
       f. In linkage, does he prolong the consonants or are they so weak
           as to be unrecognizable _____

XVI. Social Development

   A. Score on Vineland Social Maturity Scale _____
   B. What are child's chief amusements _____
   C. What games and toys does he like best _____
   D. Does he play with children outside family____younger____older____
   E. How does he get along with other members of family _____
   F. Is the child willing to try new things _____

G. Does child often become angry_____ how does he show it_____
H. Does child avoid social situations _____
I. Who administers the discipline _____ What method _____
J. Does child share a bedroom _____ with whom _____ Does child share a bed _____
K. Did any adults besides mother and father ever live in home _____

XVII. Educational History

A. Does child attend pre-school _____kindergarten _____school_____
B. Does child follow his age group in school _____

XVIII. Examinations

A. List the names and addresses of physicians (and clinics) that have examined the child:
B. Neurologist's report (attach here):
C. Physician's report (attach here):

XIX. Therapy:

A. Physical:
B. Speech:
C. Psychotherapy:
D. Vocational:

XX. Prognosis and Recommendations

APPENDIX 5

Clinical Materials: The Handicapped in Hearing

AUDIOMETRIC RECORDING: THE AUDIOGRAM

Audiogram I is a typical case of a person with nerve impairment of hearing. The thresholds for air and bone conduction do not differ significantly. Hearing is not improved to a great extent, as compared with air conduction, when the stimulus is carried to the nerve endings by bone conduction. The auditory nerve, therefore, is impaired.

Audiogram II is a typical case of a person with a conductive loss. The bone-conduction threshold for both ears is approximately normal, but the air-conduction threshold is raised considerably. This difference between the bone-conduction threshold and the air-conduction threshold indicates that there is a defect in the conduction mechanisms in the outer or middle ear. The auditory nerve is functioning normally.

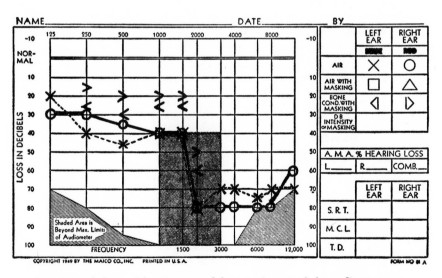

AUDIOGRAM I. Loss of hearing caused by impairment of the auditory nerve.

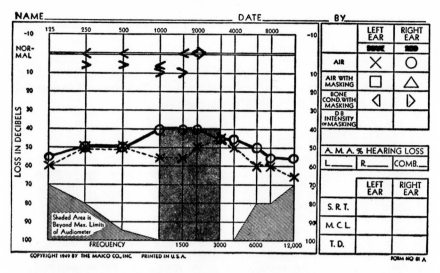

AUDIOGRAM II. Loss of hearing caused by impairment of the conductive mechanisms.

THE IRWIN AND SHREVE TEST OF SPEECH HEARING [1]

In this free-field speech-reception test, a list of 36 familiar words is given to the child. The words are presented in groups of six on picture cards. The audiologist requests the name of the picture, using the carrier phrase, "Can you find the ————?" The cards are presented at different levels of intensity, and the child is required to select correctly three out of six cards at each level of intensity. This testing procedure is continued with the audiologist decreasing the intensity until the child can no longer respond correctly to three of six cards. This level is scored as the speech-reception threshold. The same procedure is used for both tests aided and unaided by a hearing instrument. The unaided score is obtained first and then compared with the aided score to compute the gain with the hearing instrument.

Following is the list of the 36 words used in the above test procedure:

1. eggs	13. eye	25. horse
2. iron	14. apple	26. cake
3. boat	15. stove	27. thumb
4. girl	16. chair	28. ice cream
5. candle	17. cookies	29. pie
6. rabbit	18. top	30. soup
7. coat	19. boots	31. car
8. orange juice	20. chickie	32. kitty cat
9. spoon	21. tie	33. house
10. dog	22. lady	34. table
11. baby	23. airplane	35. arm
12. mouth	24. milk	36. cup

[1] J. A. Irwin and Anne Shreve, "Hearing and Language Evaluation with Hard-of-hearing Children," *Archives of Otolaryngology*, Vol. 59, No. 2 (1954), p. 187.

ARTICULATION AND SPEECH INTELLIGIBILITY TESTS

I. PHONETICALLY BALANCED WORDS

Lists of Words used in Auditory Test No. W-22, Central Institute for the Deaf. Phonographically recorded sets obtainable from the Technisonic Laboratories, 1201 South Brentwood Blvd., Brentwood, Missouri.

List 1

1. ace	14. east	27. mew	39. there
2. ache	15. felt	28. none	40. thing
3. an	16. give	29. not	41. toe
4. as	17. high	30. or	42. true
5. bathe	18. him	31. owl	43. twins
6. bells	19. hunt	32. poor	44. up
7. carve	20. isle	33. ran	45. us
8. chew	21. it	34. see	46. wet
9. could	22. jam	35. she	47. what
10. dad	23. knees	36. skin	48. wire
11. day	24. law	37. stove	49. yard
12. deaf	25. low	38. them	50. you
13. earn (urn)	26. me		

List 2

1. ail	14. else	27. new	39. star
2. air	15. flat	28. now	40. tare (tear)
3. and	16. gave	29. oak	41. that
4. bin	17. ham	30. odd	42. then
5. by	18. hit	31. off	43. tin
6. cap	19. hurt	32. one	44. too
7. cars	20. ice	33. own	45. tree
8. chest	21. ill	34. pew	46. way
9. die	22. jaw	35. rooms	47. well
10. does	23. key	36. send	48. with
11. dumb	24. knee	37. show	49. young
12. ease	25. live [lɪv]	38. smart	50. yore (your)
13. eat	26. move		

List 3

1. add	14. end	27. nest	39. tan
2. aim	15. farm	28. no	40. ten
3. are	16. glove	29. oil	41. this
4. ate	17. hand	30. on	42. three
5. bill	18. have	31. out	43. though
6. book	19. he	32. owes	44. tie
7. camp	20. if	33. pie	45. use
8. chair	21. is	34. raw	46. we
9. cute	22. jar	35. say	47. west
10. do	23. king	36. shove	48. when
11. done	24. knit	37. smooth	49. wool
12. dull	25. lie	38. start	50. year
13. ears	26. may		

List 4

1. aid	14. dolls	27. near	39. tin
2. all	15. dust	28. net	40. than
3. am	16. ear	29. nuts	41. they
4. arm	17. eyes	30. of	42. through
5. art	18. few	31. ought	43. toy
6. at	19. go	32. our	44. where
7. bee	20. hang	33. pale	45. who
8. bread	21. his	34. save	46. why
9. can	22. in	35. shoe	47. will
10. chin	23. jump	36. so	48. wood
11. clothes	24. leave	37. stiff	49. yes
12. cook	25. men	38. tea	50. yet
13. darn	26. my		

II. TWO-SYLLABLE SPONDEE WORDS

Words used in *Auditory Test No. 9*, Psycho-Acoustic Laboratory, Harvard University.

List 1

1. airplane	15. doorstep	29. oatmeal
2. armchair	16. dovetail	30. outlaw
3. backbone	17. drawbridge	31. playground
4. bagpipe	18. earthquake	32. railroad
5. baseball	19. eggplant	33. shipwreck
6. birthday	20. eyebrow	34. shotgun
7. blackboard	21. firefly	35. sidewalk
8. bloodhound	22. hardware	36. stairway
9. bobwhite	23. headlight	37. sunset
10. bonbon	24. hedgehog	38. watchword
11. buckwheat	25. hothouse	39. whitewash
12. coughdrop	26. inkwell	40. wigwam
13. cowboy	27. mousetrap	41. wildcat
14. cupcake	28. northwest	42. woodwork

List 2

1. although	15. hotdog	29. playmate
2. beehive	16. housework	30. scarecrow
3. blackout	17. iceberg	31. schoolboy
4. cargo	18. jackknife	32. soybean
5. cookbook	19. lifeboat	33. starlight
6. daybreak	20. midway	34. sundown
7. doormat	21. mishap	35. therefore
8. duckpond	22. mushroom	36. toothbrush
9. eardrum	23. nutmeg	37. vampire
10. farewell	24. outside	38. washboard
11. footstool	25. padlock	39. whizzbang
12. grandson	26. pancake	40. woodchuck
13. greyhound	27. pinball	41. workshop
14. horseshoe	28. platform	42. yardstick

ARTICULATION AND SPEECH INTELLIGIBILITY TESTS (*cont.*)

II. TWO-SYLLABLE SPONDEE WORDS (continued)

Words used for *Auditory Tests Nos. W-1* and *W-2,* Central Institute for the Deaf, St. Louis, Missouri. (Available on phonograph records from Technisonic Laboratories, 1201 South Brentwood Blvd., Brentwood, Mo.)

1. airplane	13. greyhound	25. padlock
2. armchair	14. hardware	26. pancake
3. baseball	15. headlight	27. playground
4. birthday	16. horseshoe	28. railroad
5. cowboy	17. hotdog	29. schoolboy
6. daybreak	18. hothouse	30. sidewalk
7. doormat	19. iceberg	31. stairway
8. drawbridge	20. inkwell	32. sunset
9. duckpond	21. mousetrap	33. toothbrush
10. eardrum	22. mushroom	34. whitewash
11. farewell	23. northwest	35. woodwork
12. grandson	24. oatmeal	36. workshop

LANGUAGE OUTLINE: FIRST LEVEL: TEACHING OF THE ACOUSTICALLY HANDICAPPED [2]

VOCABULARY

I. NOUNS

    A. *People*

1. family		2. Other associates	
mother		baby	man
father		boy	woman
daddy		girl	nurse
			clown

    B. *Toys*

ball	gun	marble	wagon
doll	horn	pail	
drum	kite	top	

    C. *Animals, birds, etc.*

bear	dog	horse	tree
bee	duck	lamb	turkey
bird	fish	leaf	turtle
calf	flower	mouse	worm
cat	frog	puppy	
chicken	goat	rabbit	
cow	goose	sheep	

    D. *Food*

beans	coffee	peas	sugar
bread	corn	pepper	tea
butter	cracker	pie	tomato
cake	gum	potato	water
candy	ice cream	salt	
cookie	meat	soda	
cocoa	milk	soup	

[2] Committee of Teachers of the Central Institute for the Deaf, "Language Outline," *American Annals of the Deaf,* Vol. 95, No. 4 (1950), pp. 357-359.

E. *Parts of the Body*

arm	feet	nose	tooth
ear	hair	teeth	
eye	knee	thumb	
face	mouth	toe	

F. *Objects in the environment*

barn	crayon	knife	soap
basket	cup	letter	spoon
bed	door	light	star
boat	fan	moon	sofa
book	feather	mop	sun
box	farm	movie	table
bus	flag	paper	towel
car	fork	pencil	window
chair	house	pipe	window-sill
comb	key	shelf	

G. *Clothing*

boot	coat	purse	tie
bow	dress	sock	shoe
cap			

H. *Places*

home	park	school	store

II. VERBS

be	dance	like	see
blow	drop	laugh	skip
bow	eat	make	spin
bounce	fall	march	tear
break	go	open	throw
buy	have	pull	walk
carry	hit	push	want
catch	hurt	put	wash
come	hop	roll	wave
cough	jump	run	write
cry	kiss	shut	yawn

A. *Special verbs*

give to	run after
put on	take off

III. ADJECTIVES

numbers 1-5	big	good	sick
red	clean	happy	sleepy
yellow	cold	hungry	slow
green	cross	little	smooth
blue	dirty	naughty	sorry
purple	fast	new	tall
brown	fat	old	thirsty
black	fine	rough	warm
white	funny	sharp	well

IV. PRONOUNS

I   you   he   she   it   we   they
me   it
my

V. PREPOSITIONS

in   on   under   to   with   for

VI. ADVERBS

fast   slowly

VII. CONJUNCTION

and

VIII. TIME WORDS (associated with happenings and not days of the week)

after a while   today   tomorrow   yesterday

IX. CONNECTED LANGUAGE

A. *Language constructions to be used by the child:*
   1. Simple subject
   2. Simple predicate
   3. Compound subject—noun and pronoun
   4. Compound predicate
   5. Simple direct object

B. *Two or three connected sentences used by the child by the end of the level.*

C. *News—ideas from the children.*

D. *Calendar and weather* (present progressive and past tenses.)

The sun is shining.	It is raining.
The sun shone yesterday.	It is snowing.
It is windy.	The wind is blowing.
It is cold.	It is cloudy.
It is warm.	It is smoky.
It is hot.	It is rainy.
It is foggy.	It is sunny.

E. *Group letters*

F. *Games* (a suggested list. Teach the names and appropriate expressions.)

Tag	It is __ turn.
Hide and Seek	__ are out.
Drop the Handkerchief	(is out.)
Ring Toss	__ is "it."
Cat and Mouse	__ are "it."
Pin the Tail on the Donkey	__ am "it."

G. *Nursery rhymes and fairy stories to be told by the teacher.*

Jack and Jill	The Three Bears
Jack Horner	Little Red Riding Hood
Little Bo-Peep	Peter Rabbit
Rock-a-bye Baby	etc.
Little Boy Blue	

INDEX